Blind
passion

Blind
passion

A True Story of
Magnificent Love

VINCENT I. PERRY

To order additional copies of this book, contact:
Xlibris
844-714-8691
www.Xlibris.com
Orders@Xlibris.com
815434

Preface

The following narrative is a true story, an autobiographical love memoir. Vincent I. Perry is the pen name of one of the two lovers. The story is documented from Dorothy's journal and as remembered in minute detail by Grant Duncan, supplemented by the memories of other persons who figure in this narrative. Virtually all calendrical dates are accurate. Only a small fraction of them are estimates. Almost all the personal names used throughout the narrative, including Grant Duncan, are pseudonyms, designed to protect the identities of the persons involved.

This wonderful love story is published to honor the sacred memory of Grant's blessed and most beloved Dorothy, his one great love and the one true "divine gift" to his life in accordance with the meaning of her name. It pays tribute to Dorothy's extraordinary character as a human being, her nearly saintly goodness, and her incomparable loving nature. The story constitutes a most beautiful testimony to the power and majesty of true love between a man and a woman.

VIP

Thank you, my dearest Dorothy Alice, for blessing my life with thirty years of loving perfection! You were my first and only girlfriend and my one and only lover! This book declares our magnificent true love to the entire world!

Grant Duncan

#

Introduction

The following narrative is not a romance novel of fiction, but a personal love history, a love memoir. It is therefore a work of nonfiction. The distinction is crucial in understanding the nature of the book's content. A work of nonfiction is firmly grounded in facts and events that actually took place. Accordingly, a work of nonfiction does not lend itself to having the facts and actual events being distorted, falsified, or ignored in order to conform to the conventions of a fictional literary genre.

The following narrative is a true story that traces the origin and development of a love affair between a young blind college student and a much older married woman and mother of three children, and how their love for each other became complete and total, thereby transforming their lives and eventually culminating in their lovely marriage. The events described occurred between 1965 and 1976 in a college community in the state of Illinois, a place termed University City for the purposes of this narrative.

As with all historical accounts, this story is based upon factual sources of information; and in this case there are two sources: Dorothy's journal entries and Grant's phenomenal memory to recall personal experiences. One major advantage that fiction has over nonfiction is that the author of fiction can compose a full narration of events by inventing them, whereas the author of nonfiction must be bound by the facts; and if his sources of information are not complete, the author is not allowed to fill the gaps with his own fabrications. Consequently, the following narrative does contain gaps, and these gaps result from the basic nature of human memory. With very few exceptions, all of us cannot remember large amounts of routine activities in our lives: such as what we ate for breakfast one week ago. Rather, our memories tend to recall events that are of an unusual or extraordinary nature, such as a car accident, the breaking of a leg, the birth of a child, a particularly memorable party, etc. Therefore, since much of the following narrative is based upon Grant's memory, the events described tend to be rather extraordinary ones that made a very deep impression upon Grant, so much so that he had no difficulty many years later, following the death of his darling Dorothy, in recalling the actual dates on which these events occurred; and although his memory could not recall numerous routine happenings, his recollection of extraordinary events is so abundant that the mere narration of them in sequence constitutes a reasonably full account of the history of Grant's and Dorothy's love-life. Moreover, as the result of the thirty years of their love-life and marriage, Grant could also easily recall and reproduce here the exact speech patterns and idioms commonly used by his beloved, as well as portions of their more memorable conversations and Dorothy's own recalled memories of past events.

To those readers who might object that the narrative contains too many detailed descriptions of sexual activity, Grant replies that to him, none of them is the least bit pornographic, because these incidents were the natural physical manifestations of the complete and total love that Grant had for his darling Dorothy, and that Dorothy had for her beloved Grant. Thus, in Grant's opinion, these explicit descriptions of sexual activity are neither gratuitous nor pornographic. They are certainly erotic, but they are also necessary in offering powerful testimonies to the complete and total love between these two people.

The principal theme of the narrative is charting the course of Dorothy's life from a middle-aged unhappily married woman to one who discovered true love with a much younger man, and how the life of these two lovers was totally transformed and perfected by their love.

In many ways Dorothy's personal odyssey from unhappy wife to a very happy remarried woman was typical of those times. Before 1970 or so divorce in our society was not very socially acceptable. Consequently, many young women who, like Dorothy, graduated from high school shortly after World War II quickly married and began having children, as the conventions of the day largely dictated. But after ten years or so many of these women found themselves to be unhappy in their marriages, but social conventions required them to endure their unhappiness until finally divorce began to be socially acceptable. The consequence was that many longstanding marriages began to break up, and many divorcees rediscovered happiness in newly formed marriages.

The events of Dorothy's life as described in this narrative conform to this general pattern. But this story is quite unusual in that Dorothy's new husband was half her age and was also blind. Both these circumstances prompted some of Dorothy's immediate family members to be strongly opposed to the love affair and marriage, whereas their loving union was admired and fully embraced by the couple's university friends.

Her journal entries vividly reveal the picture of a woman, trapped in an unhappy marriage, who was often confused about her own feelings because her own living reality was at variance to social conventions and expectations, who was belittled and criticized by her mother and sisters, frequently worn down and overwhelmed by her domestic duties (which were compounded by a chronically absent husband), and, despite all her best efforts as a devoted, thoroughly capable, and loving mother, was often thwarted by the uncooperative human failings of her children. The narrative documents how this talented and intelligent woman, possessing a remarkable personality and extraordinary goodness, slowly found a path out of her perplexing wilderness of unhappiness, first by achieving success in the singing organization, the Sweet Adelines, then by becoming an accomplished swimmer, and next by finding an important escape out of her unhappy home life by involving herself in volunteer work for blind students at the university, and finally realizing full redemption and total transformation as the result of one of her blind students falling totally in love with her, and she with him.

Chapter 1

The Disillusioned Mother and Wife

University City, Illinois: October 27, 1965, Wednesday

Dorothy stepped out of the front door and walked down to the edge of the yard to collect the mail from the mailbox. The catch for the day consisted of a few bills and a single personal letter from Lester Klingner, her father's oldest brother. When she returned to the house, she laid the bills aside to be taken care of at another time. But she immediately opened the letter from her Uncle Les to find out what news he had to report. It brought her up to date as to his precarious health. His only real problem seemed to be high blood pressure and a somewhat rapid heart rate, not too bad for someone nearly seventy years old. Besides Uncle Les' usual humorous remarks on his current situation in life, including his acquisition of a German Shepherd puppy, the letter contained a very important item of news. Uncle Les, whose wife Diana had died fourteen years ago without them having any children, was now designating his niece Dorothy as his sole heir and executor of his will. He therefore asked that she henceforth keep him informed of her telephone number and mailing address; and although he did not have very much in the way of valuable possessions or savings, he nevertheless insisted that Dorothy not tell anyone at all of his decision, because it could generate minor resentments among other family members. This would therefore be their own little secret.

Dorothy's father, born in 1905, had died of cancer almost two years ago. During the funeral proceedings in Homewood, Illinois, a southern suburb of Chicago, where Dorothy and her siblings had grown up together, Uncle Les had cried and grieved so profoundly for his brother, who, unlike himself, had a sizable family of children and grandchildren. Uncle Les was heard to lament amid his weeping, "Why wasn't it me who became sick and died? Oh Babe, you had so much to live for! Why wasn't it me!"

For the past few decades Uncle Les had lived in Chicago itself. Consequently, when Dorothy and her family came to visit her parents in Homewood, they had never seen very much of her Uncle Les. But Babe's death had brought Dorothy and Uncle Les together through their common grief to form a very close relationship that they had continued to foster by exchanging letters since the time of the funeral.

Dorothy's father, who always went by the name Babe during his adulthood because of his fondness for Babe Ruth, had been such a kind and loving man. Unlike most marriages in which the husband-father assumes the role of the disciplinarian while the wife-mother is the dispenser of tender loving care, Dorothy's parents had played somewhat opposite roles. Her mother Gloria had a somewhat stern demeanor, was rather sharp-tongued, and sometimes exhibited an explosive temper. Babe, on the other hand, possessed such sweetness and goodness of character that it endeared him to virtually everyone. While Dorothy and her sisters were growing up, children in the neighborhood often came to their door to ask if Mr. Klingner could come out to play with them. He always went the extra mile to please people; and if he was at all able to render a kindness to someone, he invariably did. For example, when his only son Timothy (born many years after his sisters) was playing football in high school, he showed up for every game with a video camera to tape it for everyone; and this was in the day when video cameras were a rarity. No wonder then that Babe was much loved, and his death was greatly mourned by many. He had died not long before the assassination of President Kennedy. While the nation was plunged into a collective grief, Dorothy's family was struggling with their own terrible tragedy. Indeed, their loss had rendered them all so emotionally vulnerable that the president's death seemed to affect them more grievously than it otherwise would have. Dorothy had loved her father so dearly, and she still missed him so very much and thought of his loving nature constantly.

Babe and Gloria were married in 1924; and their daughters were born in 1925 (Ginger), 1928 (Dorothy), and 1930 (Bethany). Their third daughter had arrived not long after the stock market crash that ushered in The Great

Depression. Since Babe and Gloria were ordinary people of very slim means with three little girls to care for, they had come close to giving Dorothy to Gloria's brother and sister-in-law to raise, but in the end they decided to keep all three children together and to do their best in providing for them.

Since the two younger sisters were only a year and a half apart in age, Dorothy and Bethany were inseparable during their youth, but they were about as different as they could be. Bethany was a real tomboy and ready to do or try anything. Dorothy, on the other hand, was much more the proper little lady whom Bethany was always dragging into her latest cooked-up mischief. Dorothy inherited from her father his characteristic qualities of goodness and sweetness, the likes of which were so rare and fine. As Dorothy grew up, these traits became increasingly evident and were combined with intelligence and strength of character to make her a truly extraordinary young woman. Because of the similarities in their overall personality Dorothy had always been her father's favorite daughter, so much so that he was unable to conceal his favoritism. Uncle Les shared much of Babe's youthful and playful spirit, and he recognized the same in his niece Dorothy. Consequently, his decision to designate her as his sole heir and executor of his will was a resounding testimony to how very special and truly magnificent she was.

Perhaps the greatest joy of Dorothy's youth had been music. Her family was too poor to afford musical instruments or music lessons of any sort, but they did have a radio that served as Dorothy's teacher of the popular music of the day. She possessed a real knack for learning melodies and the words of songs and was constantly singing songs that she learned from the radio. As she grew up, she acquired a nearly encyclopedic knowledge of contemporary music. Singing seemed to be not only a natural gift, but also an expression of her innate inner joy and beautiful personality. As she began to physically mature during her teen years, her singing ability became quite considerable, and her voice was feminine, rich, and so perfectly expressive of her charm and grace.

Throughout her years in elementary, junior high, and high school Dorothy exhibited a keen intellect and an eagerness to learn and excel, especially in literature and history. But when she approached her parents with the idea of her going to college, for about the first time in her life she found herself disappointed with her loving and beloved mother and father. Despite her obvious academic proclivities, they countered her desire to attend college on three grounds: first of all, it would be rather expensive;

secondly, since neither Ginger nor Bethany were the least bit interested in going to college, funding Dorothy alone for higher education would be seen by her sisters as gross favoritism; and thirdly, even if she were to attend college, chances were that she would soon meet some nice young man and would wind up marrying him before ever earning a degree. So, like most other young females of her day, Dorothy found her future prospects to consist of working small jobs, such as an usherette in a theater and a bookkeeper at a small business, as well as dating, so as to find the right guy to marry.

By the time that Dorothy graduated from high school in 1946, she had already had her share of eager suitors. Not only did she possess such a charming and gracious personality and disposition, but she was also quite a beautiful young woman: five feet three and a half inches tall, weighing just under one hundred pounds, slim and curvaceous, long lovely brown hair, beautiful green eyes, and a flawless complexion so fair that she sunburned easily. She eventually met George Patterson, who was four years older, had served in the US military during World War II, and had grown up in nearby Deerfield. After a courtship of several months, they were married in the spring of 1947, on the silver anniversary of George's parents. Dorothy's younger sister Bethany married Richard Decker six months later. Their oldest sister Ginger had married Jim Lawson two years earlier. Their first child, James Junior, became the first of Babe and Gloria's several grandchildren.

All three of these young couples, the Pattersons, Deckers, and Lawsons, continued to live in and around Homewood and formed a slowly growing circle of the Klingners, brothers-in-law, and grandchildren. In his usual open-hearted manner, Babe insisted that all three of his married daughters and their husbands spend every Sunday afternoon at their house. The event began with Gloria, assisted by her daughters, setting out a magnificent Sunday dinner around noon, followed by relaxation, much talking, and various forms of amusement, such as playing pinochle. These Sunday afternoon get-togethers pleased Babe to no end and forged strong and loving bonds among them all.

Dorothy kept her job as a bookkeeper for a small manufacturer of auto parts until she gave birth to her first child Sally in 1951. Wesley was born two years later in 1953. After earning his architecture degree, George was hired by Glenn L. Martin Aircraft in Baltimore, Maryland, which obliged them to move away from their families. This was the first of what turned out to be many moves throughout Dorothy's life.

While in Baltimore, Dorothy's family lived in a brand-new residential area full of young families like themselves with many small children, an ideal environment for Sally and Wesley. As happened throughout her entire life, no matter where she lived, Dorothy's personality succeeded in attracting lasting friends to herself like a magnet attracts iron filings. Her disposition was so vibrant, charming, and gracious. In whatever situation she found herself, her natural inclination was always to go above and beyond the normal call of duty to put people at ease and to do them a kindness. She was rarely heard to complain, but always stressed and sought out the positive, and never gossiped. Added to her sunny disposition was an endearingly whimsical and humorous nature that usually succeeded in turning every ordinary daily activity or situation into a joyous and enjoyable occasion. In short, one would have been hard-pressed to discover a person more selfless, loving, and lovable than Dorothy. Like her father, she opened her home and heart to any and all; and the neighborhood children became so accustomed to her kindness and generosity that they would come into the Pattersons' yard and ask, "Miss Dorothy, have you made any cookies for us today?" She often had, and the children were always welcome to them.

Since the Pattersons had now left the loving circle of relatives and in-laws that they had formed in Homewood, Dorothy began a practice that continued throughout the rest of her life: writing long informative letters to her parents and other close friends. Dorothy now set aside a portion of every Sunday afternoon to write her letters, at least one a week to her parents to keep them abreast of how and what they were all doing. Dorothy found letter writing to be not the least bit difficult or irksome. Rather, it was a real joy and served as an important means of self-expression, allowing her to utilize her knack for language and permitting her with a cathartic medium for venting her thoughts and feelings. Babe and Gloria came to look forward to the arrival of Dorothy's long weekly letter; and oftentimes Babe came into the house from the mailbox announcing, "We have another book from Dorothy!"

Dorothy developed another Sunday tradition during these Baltimore years that she also continued for the rest of her life. After coming home from services at their church, Dorothy prepared a very nice noontime dinner at which both the parents and children ate properly with good manners and behaved themselves. The tone and mood of this occasion were what George introduced from his own family tradition, whereas the splendid meal always represented to Dorothy those early years of her marriage when she and George enjoyed the hospitality of her parents. Dorothy balanced the formality of the noontime dinner with the other half of the family's weekly Sunday tradition. Sunday supper henceforth became a time of special treats that the children enjoyed so much. Dorothy popped corn for everyone and often made a batch of fudge to go along with the popcorn, and everyone had soda as their beverage.

Dorothy's third and last child, Carol, was born in 1957. Her birth came ten years after her parents' marriage, and it was at this time that Dorothy began to realize that she no longer loved George, but like so many other women of the day, who were living at a time when divorce was largely socially unacceptable, her only really viable option was to remained married and to lavish her affection and attention upon her three children to ensure that they would have a stable and loving home environment in which to develop.

George remained with Glenn L. Martin for just four years before making the first of his many changes in employment. While he proceeded to Seattle, Washington, to receive clearance and training for government work through Boeing, Dorothy and the three children returned to Homewood. This period of separation from George confirmed Dorothy's realization that she was no longer attracted at all to George and did not miss him in the least. She further came to understand that the children also seemed to be happier in his absence.

George's and Dorothy's parents had raised them very differently. George's folks had been very authoritarian, expecting their children to obey their parents unquestioningly. It was not that Dorothy's parents had reared her and her siblings without discipline, but Babe and Gloria had tempered it with love and kindness and had always given their children considerable leeway; and of course, Babe had actually been rather indulgent, especially when the children were quite young. These two differing parenting styles were clearly reflected in Dorothy's and George's personalities and led to constant friction as the children grew up, and as their parents needed to makes all sorts of decisions about what they could and could not do, and how they should do it. Dorothy had very definite standards of behavior and responsibility that she expected of her children, but given her intelligence and unerring judgment in virtually everything involving human interaction, she was also very understanding, reasonable, and flexible. George, on the other hand, tended to view things in rather simple terms and expected his judgment and decisions to be accepted without question. As a result, rearing their three children had gradually developed into a contest of parental wills;

and since George became very disagreeable toward everyone whenever he did not get his way, Dorothy had slowly learned that in order to keep peace in the family and to prevent George from taking his aggravation out on the children, she usually had to let him have his way, but because he was often not at home, Dorothy was largely able to handle things as she saw fit. Living back in Homewood, therefore, near her parents and two sisters and their families, while George was away in Seattle, proved to be a welcome extended vacation of sorts.

But in the spring of 1961 Dorothy and the children rejoined George for about four months in Seattle. In later years Dorothy's most vivid memory of this segment of her life was the majestic beauty of Mount Rainier that she could see from her kitchen window, and upon whose majesty she gazed every day as she stood at the sink doing the dishes. But they were soon relocated to Great Falls, Montana, from which George went out as a field engineer for the building of Minuteman Missile silos. There they lived in a trailer court provided by Boeing, and Dorothy and the other wives became fond friends, helped one another with their children, and did some of their daily chores together, such as washing and drying their family's clothes in a trailer set up to serve as their laundromat. While living here, Dorothy and George became good friends with their church minister and wife, Roger and Olive Robinson, who were so kind and open-hearted. The wife was the daughter of the prominent Church historian, Roland Bainton. The friendship between the two couples was responsible for both George and Dorothy becoming very active participants in church affairs. Dorothy now began to teach Sunday school for the younger children, for which her grace and charm, intelligence, and beautiful appearance and smile were so well suited. Then in late 1962 Boeing relocated the Patterson family to Kimball, Nebraska, where George continued his work as a field engineer for the Minuteman Missile silos. During these years in Montana and Nebraska George and Dorothy took the kids on various outings to explore the wonders of this region of the country. They visited Yellowstone Park, Mount Rushmore in the Black Hills of South Dakota, and other places. But Dorothy daily found beauty in her surroundings, especially while living in Montana, as she carried out her routine chores of ironing clothes, preparing meals, and looking after the children: for so many of her days began and ended with the dazzling beauty of a Big Sky Country sunrise and sunset.

While living in another Boeing trailer court, George and Dorothy became fond friends of John and Doris Thompson. The two men took the first step toward forming a business partnership by building and selling a house while they were still employed by Boeing. They both, however, eventually quit their jobs with Boeing and went into fulltime business for themselves by forming a construction company in Kimball. TP Construction, taking its name from Thompson and Patterson, soon failed and went bankrupt, leaving both families financially high and dry. In the aftermath of this disaster Dorothy's parents regularly sent them money as they could afford, but the Pattersons' situation remained precarious and very stressful for all until George was able to find a new job. This one brought them back to Illinois and not too far south from Dorothy's relatives and friends in Homewood, as well as not too far away from Newton, where George's parents were now living. Consequently, in the spring of 1965 the Patterson family left Kimball and arrived in University City, Illinois, where they hoped to do well in making a fresh start with George being employed by the Curtis Construction Corporation (CCC).

University City is located in central Illinois, south of Chicago, surrounded by the flat prairie whose rich black soil produced corn and soy beans in great abundance. At this time University City boasted a population of several tens of thousands. As indicated by its name, the city was the home of one of the state's major universities. The whole community therefore had the character of a college town; and when classes were in session during the fall and spring semesters, the community received a sizable infusion of students.

For the next two and a half years, until they succeeded in having their own new home built, the Pattersons lived at 1712 Yale Drive in southwest University City. Although living in Baltimore and the western states had been quite an adventure, Dorothy was so glad to be once again within relatively easy driving distance of Homewood, so that she could visit relatives and old friends frequently, and they could visit her. But she also often thought of the many good friends whom she had made in different places over the past ten years. Not being able to see them again saddened her, and she vowed to stay in touch with them by exchanging letters. George was employed by CCC to build and sell churches; and his work regularly took him out onto the road for the entire week, traveling throughout his designated region of Illinois, Indiana, and Ohio, but occasionally he had to travel as far east as West Virginia and western Pennsylvania. As a result, Dorothy was often the only parent at home to watch over and care for the three children, whose different ages, interests, and needs kept her fully occupied.

Although Sally, Wesley, and Carol had the same parents, they had very different personalities and inclinations, and rearing all three under the same roof was both daunting and educational. Why wasn't part of the pregnancy deal to have the parents-to-be to come before an all-knowing panel of experts whose duty was to inform them of what was going to be in store for them, not only for the next eighteen years, but probably for the rest of their lives? The child would be amenable to their guidance and upbringing in some things, but in other things the parents would be fighting an on-going and, likely to be, largely futile battle to reshape certain unpleasant innate traits into something that they were not. Instead, having and raising children basically involved on-the-job training for the parents. As Dorothy's three children matured and began to exhibit fundamental personality traits that were either positive and thus perfectly acceptable or somehow negative and requiring varying degrees of parental strategizing and accommodation, Dorothy gradually learned the true wisdom encapsulated in the serenity prayer: "God grant me the serenity to accept what I cannot change, the courage to change what I can, and the wisdom to know the difference between the two." Dorothy wrote these words in one of her favorite books of sayings, so that it could remind her periodically of its sound advice. Unfortunately, the prayer was also all too apt for her unhappy marriage, but by now Dorothy's own innate traits of goodness, sweetness, intelligence, and consummate grace and charm had produced in her an incomparable diplomatic talent to bring serenity and calm out of chaos and turbulence and to top it off with the most beautiful and engaging smile, even when she was often hurting or seething inside.

Since the family had moved from Kimball to University City during the course of the children's school year, the kids had to be taken out of their familiar school environment and inserted into a new one. Sally and Wesley had succeeded in making the transition without too much trouble. They had finished out respectively their eighth and sixth grades after coming to University City, and they were now in their freshman and seventh-grade years. Sally was an average student and possessed personality traits quite the opposite of those of her mother. She was very self-centered and often fractious; and it was often difficult to get her to cooperate in doing things around the house. When confronted with things that she did not wish or had no interest in doing, her normal response was to do things half-heartedly (and usually slovenly), to sulk, and quite often to become argumentative and disagreeable.

Wesley seemed to be quite gifted intellectually, was not the least bit athletic, but rather adept at and interested in music. While they were living in Great Falls, they had purchased a piano; and Dorothy, Sally, and Wesley had begun to take lessons. Sally had also learned to play the violin for the school's orchestra, but she was not all that enthusiastic about it. Wesley had taken up the saxophone for his school band, and he seemed to be genuinely interested in developing his musical talent. His actual performance in school, however, left much to be desired. Although he possessed his mother's innate sweetness of character and had acquired from her very early a real love of reading, he hated homework, and Dorothy and George struggled mightily with him to try to have him develop the necessary self-discipline and motivation to do his work diligently, well, and in a timely fashion. Unfortunately for Wesley, he took after his father in chaffing at rules and authority, wanted to be his own boss, consistently procrastinated, and always seemed to leave everything in a disorderly mess. Trying to keep Sally and Wesley on the straight and narrow against their natural inclinations tested Dorothy's maternal love and ingenuity on a daily basis.

Carol, her youngest, however, posed an entirely different kind of challenge. She possessed her mother's natural goodness and sweetness and was so eager to please. She was never happier than when helping her mother around the house, so much so that Dorothy had to place limits on what she should do, because otherwise, Carol would want to do all the work. It was just the opposite with Sally. Carol was perfectly content to be a homebody, to have her mother teach her how to do various domestic things (such as sewing and ironing), and to be under Dorothy's loving, patient, and instructive guidance, but per progress through the early grades of her formal education became problematic and was never fully resolved; and this on-going problem was the source of tremendous heartache for Dorothy and frustration for Carol. During their last autumn in Kimball Carol had entered the second grade, but she had to have her tonsils removed; and as the result of a precarious convalescence, she had missed quite a bit of school and failed to develop her ability to read as well as she needed to. The situation became much worse when she tried to finish out second grade in University City. The school system in Kimball taught children to read by the whole-word method, whereas grade schools in University City taught reading by phonics. Carol had not sufficiently caught on to the former before being subjected to the latter. The result was a very confused child, who, the school experts insisted, must repeat second grade.

Years earlier, Dorothy's parents had faced a similar situation with their youngest child Timothy; and the clash then between parents and school personnel now prompted Gloria to advise Dorothy and George not to accept the school's diagnosis, but to urge that Carol be allowed to enter the third grade with her classmates. In the end, however, the school experts insisted that they knew what was best, and Carol was now repeating second grade and receiving special instruction outside her regular classroom.

All this occurred in the days before much was done to diagnose learning difficulties and to integrate solutions into the normal school environment. By now, because of the conspicuousness of her special treatment, Carol's classmates were beginning to call her unkind names, and she was becoming increasingly discouraged and traumatized by school, so much so that this sweet little girl often woke up in the morning with a stomachache from the stress of having to face another unhappy and frustrating day at school. Dorothy spent considerable time with Carol in trying to help her learn how to read by the phonics method, but her effort and patience largely went for naught. Consequently, Carol was always lagging behind in her formal education, and this produced so much anguish for both Carol and her loving mother, who cherished the child's genuine good-heartedness and quickness in learning domestic things.

February 14, 1966, Monday

Dorothy sat alone at the kitchen table, clad in her pajamas and robe and slowly working her way through a second cup of coffee. It was 10:00 A.M. The kids were all in school, and George had also left early this morning and would be gone all week traveling about to various work sites in Indiana. True to her most loving nature and constant concern for her children, Dorothy needed to get herself going, to get out of the house to buy some nice little Valentine's Day gifts for Sally, Wesley, and Carol to surprise them when they arrived home later in the afternoon.

Dorothy had arrived home last evening, after spending the weekend at Mercy Hospital. She had admitted herself Friday late afternoon into the mental ward for consultation and observation, but by late Sunday afternoon she had become so uneasy about her surroundings that she had discharged herself and driven back to the house. Given the popular stigma attached to mental illness, no one except George knew of Dorothy's admittance into the mental ward. They had decided to tell the children that their mother had gone to Homewood for a while to help her mother.

Dorothy's inner crisis had been brought on by a combination of things. The first severe hammer blow had been her father's death, and a second one soon followed with the ignominious collapse of TP Construction in Kimball. Though severe and traumatic, Dorothy had weathered the chaos and upheaval caused by these disasters quite well until they had arrived in University City. The third gigantic hammer blow to her psyche was Carol's difficulty in school that had gradually worsened during the past few months. But even that too Dorothy had been able to endure, although it rent her maternal heart so much. The final hammer blow that had finally done her in had been a steady barrage of telephone calls from creditors in Kimball. Since George was usually gone during the work week, Dorothy was the one who was left at home to receive these calls. TP Construction's bankruptcy had left many people holding the bag; and when creditors called the Patterson residence in University City, they were invariably rude, crude, nasty, threatening, and insulting. Even before their hounding had begun, Dorothy had long felt tremendous guilt and shame over the financial collapse of George's and John Thompson's partnership. In her worldview in which decency reigned supreme, people did not back out of their obligations. Gloria had tried to assuage her daughter's guilt and shame by pointing out that the bankers had no one but themselves to blame. They were in the business of estimating and taking calculated risks. They had decided to loan George and John Thompson the necessary seed money to get them started in their small construction business, while knowing full well that the two men did not have any sizable savings upon which they could rely if things began to get tough.

This argument had been some solace to Dorothy until recent months when the nasty and threatening telephone calls had begun. It became so bad that she had begun to cringe every time the phone rang, and she had to answer it alone there in the house. Usually, by the time the creditor had finished with her, she was in tears and felt so miserable. This relentless campaign of telephone calls had been the last hard hammer blow responsible for her seeking refuge this past weekend in the mental ward. There were, of course, other smaller hammer blows that had made their own contributions as well. Rather than providing her with a source of emotional and mental comfort, her marriage to George added to her unhappiness and frustration. They disagreed on so many things, especially concerning the kids; and although she was relieved to have him out of the house and on the road, where he could not pester her (sex had long been nothing more than another one of her necessary and most disagreeable chores), his chronic absence foisted upon her virtually all responsibilities for maintaining a nice house, watching after three very active kids, and constantly being on the run to get them to and from their various activities. It was really quite a bit for one person to handle under normal circumstances.

Dorothy had felt badly about abandoning her children while seeking refuge in the hospital, but she had reached a point at which she had realized that if she wanted to continue caring for them, she needed to reach out for help before totally breaking down and then being of use to no one. She had explained her troubles to a psychiatrist, who had prescribed tranquilizers to help her relax; and the medication had made her feel better there in the hospital, but as she moved about the floor on Saturday and Sunday, she had encountered patients who were truly mentally disturbed, and this had really frightened her. She worried that if she hung around here very long, she might begin to be like them. Accordingly, by Sunday afternoon she had resolved to herself that no matter how bad things became in her domestic situation, she would never allow herself to sink so low that she would need to return to a place like this again. Her children needed their mother, and henceforth she would persevere to be there, no matter what!

Chapter 2

Dorothy's Diary

August 9, 1966, Tuesday

Dorothy stood at the kitchen sink washing the supper dishes and placing them in the dish drainer. She was also singing along with one of her numerous albums that was playing on the phonograph. Right now it happened to be Sons of the Pioneers, one of her father's favorite groups; and they were singing "Ghost Riders in the Sky." As usual, singing lifted her spirits; and for the past several weeks she had been playing her records a few hours almost every day, even some of her Christmas music. In her view it was never too early or too late to play those cheerful uplifting songs. Although the kids teased her about her choice of music (which included the Andrews Sisters, the Mills Brothers, Mitch Miller, Tennessee Ernie Ford, Burl Ives, and the sound tracks of various musicals, such as *Oklahoma, Music Man, Flower Drum Song, The Sound of Music*, etc.), they enjoyed it too, and Dorothy often heard them singing and moving in time to the music. It made the whole house somewhat brighter.

They had now been living in University City for about a year and a half, and everyone in the family was fairly well adjusted into their new situation. George's job was going along well. The worst days of the recent past appeared to be behind them, and a new brighter future seemed to be on their horizon.

George and Dorothy were once again fully involved in the affairs of their new church. George was always serving on some committee or board, whereas Dorothy was teaching second grade Sunday school, was a member of the Women's Social Concerns Society (including its executive committee), participated in a Wednesday reading and discussion group, and was always willing to pitch in to organize different social activities. The children too were active in their own church functions and groups that were appropriate for their ages.

Both George and Dorothy had been raised in a church environment, but as with so many other things, their experiences and views with respect to Christianity were quite different. George and his parents had a rather fundamentalist view of everything biblical. whereas Dorothy and her family had always taken a non-literal view of such things. In fact, Dorothy could never become interested in the whole concept of a Last Judgment and a heaven and hell. She could not even bring herself to embrace the idea of Jesus as the Son of God. The notion really took a leap of faith, one that she simply could not bring herself to perform. Thus, Jesus' divinity was something about which she did not trouble herself. She did, however, greatly respect Jesus as a teacher of ethics, morality, and especially love and common decency in dealing with one's fellow human beings. To her, those things formed the real value and meaning of Christianity; and she attempted to conduct her life in accordance with what Jesus had called the greatest commandment, to love God with all one's heart and to love one's neighbor as oneself. Indeed, one would have been hard-pressed to find anyone who better embodied and lived according to this principle, but telling Dorothy this to her face would have surprised and embarrassed her greatly.

During the previous spring, as Wesley was finishing the eighth grade, he had run afoul of his father's fundamentalist beliefs when he let it be known that he was being taught biological evolution in his science class. George had hit the roof, and he and his son had engaged in some very heated arguments. Dorothy had simply stood aside from the confrontation, figuratively shaking her head in disgust at her husband's blockheadedness. To his credit, Wesley had stood his ground and had not allowed his father to browbeat him into accepting his fundamentalist views. Dorothy inwardly beamed with pride to see her son hold his own in the verbal combat.

The family's involvement in their church had had other interesting ramifications. The Pattersons had agreed to serve regularly as a host family for a foreign student who was sponsored by their Church to study in the U.S., and who was enrolled in classes right there in University City at the university. The idea was to provide the person with various kinds of help in running errands and to give them a kind of home away from home by having them over to their house on a fairly regular basis to have a home-cooked meal, to chat about things, and simply to relax in a genuine family setting. The program was tailor-made for Dorothy's open-hearted nature and willingness to assist anyone in need.

As if all her church related activities were not enough, Dorothy had also been doing some community-based volunteer work for senior citizens. When their church had been asked to call for helpers, Dorothy had stepped forward and had her name placed on the list of volunteers. The service involved placing telephone calls to senior citizens to remind them of appointments or to check on them to make sure that they were doing ok. Her name as a prospective volunteer had then found its way to the Rehabilitation Center at the university. Someone there had recently called to see if she would also be interested in becoming a volunteer reader for one of their many blind students. She readily agreed; and after answering questions as to what subjects she thought herself well suited to read, she was informed that when the fall semester began in about a month, she would be hearing from a student interested in having her as his or her reader, probably for one two-hour session every week.

When Dorothy placed the last clean dish in the drainer, she dried her hands and went into the master bedroom. All the kids had scattered in different directions after eating supper; and as usual, George was out of town in connection with his job. She was therefore all alone in the house except for the company of her beloved German Shepherd Fraulein that had been her constant companion since her puppyhood two years before in Kimball, Nebraska. Dorothy opened up her drawer of lingerie and pulled out from the very bottom a spiral notebook. She then propped herself up on the bed in a comfortable sitting position, opened the notebook to the page with the last bit of writing on it, paused to compose her thoughts, and then began to write. In the meantime Fraulein had settled herself down on the floor beside the bed.

About five years ago when they were living in Montana, Dorothy had begun to keep a journal in which she recorded her daily activities, those of other family members, and her own thoughts and feelings. The journal provided her with a valuable outlet for self-expression. As a wife and mother of three very active children, she was constantly giving and providing for others, even more so than the average housewife, in part because George was gone so much and was not available to share the domestic burdens, and in part because Dorothy's basic nature impelled her to see to other people's needs. But few people ever worried much about her needs.

She had already filled three good-size spiral notebooks with her writing and was now working on a fourth one. Since she had never had a place in which she could keep these writings locked securely away from other members of the family, especially George, she had always been rather circumspect about fully expressing her thoughts. Consequently, her innermost feelings concerning her marriage were always expressed in very cryptic and guarded language, a kind of personal code to herself; and there was much that she dared not even write down at all from fear of detection. Thus far, however, as best as she could tell, George still did not know that she had been writing in a journal, because she did so when she was all alone, and she kept the books hidden away in a place where George was unlikely to be looking around for something.

Although there had necessarily been occasional short gaps in her journal because of her very busy domestic life, her troubled state of mind during the previous winter had obliged her to leave off writing altogether for a period of about ten months. There had simply been too many other more pressing matters that had demanded all her energy and attention. But she had finally emerged from that awful time and was largely her old wonderful self again. Everything was now pretty much under control, and she was beginning to have odds and ends of free time for herself. It was only natural then that she now resume writing in her journal. As in the past, the effort would be both cathartic and would allow her to give some kind of meaning and purpose to her life, which so often to her seemed nothing more than a chaotic and endless succession of daily chores and duties in the service of others.

Her handwriting was clear with an obvious feminine grace, enhanced by the fact that she used pens of different colored ink as her mood and whimsy prompted her. Even though she wrote everything down spontaneously, the pages were free of cross-outs, false starts, marginal insertions, or attempted erasures. There was nothing there except her neat flowing script, word after word, composed in a simple and often telegraphic style, resulting from the fact that the entries were usually rapid jottings made during bits and pieces of her scarce free time. Even misspellings were non-existent. In short, the journal entries were manifestations of the intelligence and flare for language that she had exhibited since high school.

The overwhelming bulk of the journal was a record of daily routine events and activities that comprise the largest part of everyone's life. But this somewhat monotonous record of routine things was a striking testimony to Dorothy's exemplary parenting of her children. Her level of energy and caring was colossal and so rarely encountered; and what she did not expend on her children was lavished upon other relatives, friends, and acquaintances. The journal also charted the children's slow progress toward adulthood (such as Sally obtaining her driver's permit and Wesley attending his first party of both girls and boys), the family's interaction with their Patterson and Klingner relatives, and so many other large and small happenings, such as the building of their new house at 1801 Rachel Drive, just a few blocks away from where they were currently living. It would take nearly a year for the house to be built, and then it would be more than another year before all the minor details were finally completed.

Perhaps most important of all, however, the journal was the regular venue for Dorothy to express her innermost feelings and frustrations. Despite her most valiant efforts to guide the kids in proper directions, things so often never worked out as she hoped. The kids were regularly bearing out the truth of that old adage about bringing a horse to water but not being able to make it drink. Consequently, Dorothy often felt defeated and succumbed to self-doubt in thinking that she must be a failure as a parent. But by all objective standards she was an ideal parent, as the record of the journal so fully documented. She had no definite goals or ambitions for any of her three children. She simply wanted them to become interested in worthwhile pursuits, to reach their full potential, and to be happy, well-adjusted people. She exerted so much of her daily thoughts and energy in supporting them in whatever way they needed. Although they often fell short of her optimistic expectations, all three children were perfectly aware of their mother's magnificent love for them, and they all usually reciprocated in kind.

Her biggest source of inner misery, of course, was her unhappy marriage with George. But she was really not sure what had caused their marriage to founder, and what, if anything, could be done to improve it. She often sought refuge and solace in prayer and religious meditation, but they never brought her genuine happiness. About all that they could do was to urge her to accept her unhappy lot and to hope that God might someday deign to bless her personal life unexpectedly. Eventually, however, her learning to swim and her singing in Sweet Adelines provided her with new valuable outlets for her talent and energy, and her own personal success in these pursuits began to form within her a totally new sense of self-worth that had nothing to do with her children and husband.

Author's Note: Here follows a series of verbatim extracts from Dorothy's hand-written journal in which she describes her life, thoughts, and feelings in her own words, covering the four-year period August of 1966 to August of 1970. Brackets are used to enclose explanatory phrases or comments inserted by the author.

Journal Entries

Aug. 9, 1966 (Tuesday): Have been feeling lately that I want to write things down in a book, like I used to. The last time that I wrote was on October 1, 1965, almost a year ago. It has been a terrible year, and I hope that things are on their way up. Many things have happened this past year. I will try to remember as much as I can to write it down, but the events will not be in order. My memory jumps around too much. We're still in the house on Yale Drive. I hate this house, and I don't really know why. I don't even think that I like University City, which is silly, because it is a nice town. Mom, Ginger, and Bethany all feel that we should move back to where they live, but I am not sure that that would be the best thing either. Tim is in Pearl Harbor, has been since Jan. or February, I guess. On December 6 mom, Bethany, and I flew to Charleston, South Carolina for the commissioning of his ship, the USS Davidson. The ceremony was on December 7 and was very nice, also very cold, damp, and windy. Had cake and coffee and a tour of the ship. We flew back home about 7:00 A.M. on December 8. Ellen, Stanley, Lawrence, and David [George's sister-in-law and her sons, fathered by George's sole sibling Fred, who had died suddenly of a heart attack in 1962] came [from Sout Carolina] to University City for Christmas (should say, before Christmas), and we all drove down to Newton [Illinois, home of George's parents] for a week. It was a wonderful week. We all enjoyed being together. George's company closes during Christmas week. The boys [Ellen's sons] were disappointed that we didn't have any snow while they were here. New Year's weekend we went to Homewood, because Tim was home on leave. In the spring I taught Georgia Samson how to drive. Should say that we taught her, because about twenty years ago she had a license. She got her license at the end of April. I didn't do much with the piano, made a stab at it, playing and practicing it. Quit completely in March. Wesley joined the YMCA in October or November and started judo lessons. In January or February started Carol with a tutor, hoping that it would help her learn to read. She went three afternoons a week after school for 45 minutes. We stopped the lessons at the end of May, because the school psychologist said that she was under too much strain.

Aug. 10, 1966 (Wednesday): Rained most all day today. It was most welcome, because this has been a very dry summer. Most crops have not grown because of the dryness. Carol had to miss her swimming lesson today. She has two weeks of lessons at the high school Pool, 45 minutes lessons for $2.50. Took Carol to the orthodontist today. In May I took her to Dr. Lord, and he started treatment in on her. She has several things wrong with her mouth, mostly upper teeth. Today was Wesley's last day at summer school: band. They had their concert at 6:00 P.M. at the junior high. It was very good. We were home by 8:00 P.M. George is out of town. He left Monday and will return Saturday. Wesley stayed up to watch *The Late Show.* I slept on the couch until he went to bed.

Aug. 11, 1966 (Thursday): George called at 7:15 A.M. He was supposed to call last night, but his meeting lasted too long. Wesley mowed the back yard, Sally vacuumed the rugs, Carol took swimming lessons. The expansion band on Carol's appliance wouldn't stay in, so I had to take Carol to Dr. Lord. Then took Sally to Dr. Hanson for her regular appointment. Stopped at Smith's and picked up $8.75, which the WSCS [Women's Social Concerns Society for the Church] contributed for each child going to camp. Had Wesley change clothes, and we all went to the shopping center. Wesley and Carol got new shoes. Sally got a new dress. We ate supper at the drug store. Wesley went to a Boy Scout meeting at our church. He thinks he will join the troop. To bed at 10:00 P.M.

Aug. 12, 1966 (Friday): Forgot to mention that yesterday about noon one of our mamma guppies had babies while we watched. She had about twenty. Once two came out and looked like they were Siamese twins. We watched them quite a while, and then they disappeared. Mamma must have eaten them as she did several others. They were in a guppy breeder, but the babies didn't stay below as they are supposed to. This morning they were all dead except for one guppy baby. About ten babies were missing. So, the mother must have eaten them. Wesley went on a Boy Scout hike this morning, ate lunch at Steve Glaser's house, played tennis at Herb McCoy's, and came home about 5:00 P.M. Carol had last swimming lesson. Ricardo Flores, our Filipino student [foreign college student for whom Dorothy's family was serving as a host through their church] came over about 4:00 P.M. with some place mats that his wife had sent us. He left when I took Sally to Mercy

Hospital for Candy Striping. She goes at 5:00 P.M. and is through between 6:30 and 7:00 P.M. Watched TV and went to bed about 10:00 P.M.

Aug. 13, 1966 (Saturday): Gloomy and rain and cool all morning. Ironed. Carol and Sally ironed too. Carol would iron everything if I'd let her. George got home about 1:00 P.M. I Went to the grocery store. Kids watched TV all morning.

Aug. 14, 1966 (Sunday): Went to 9:00 A.M. church. There is no church school during August [Dorothy normally had a Sunday school class that she taught]. Ricardo Flores brought his roommate to church today. We pick Rick up every Sunday for church. George and Wesley pulled weeds in the back all afternoon. I finished packing Wesley's suitcase. Sally and George packed too. They left about 6:30 P.M. for Homewood. Sally is going to Patti's [Bethany' daughter], and George to Ginger's. George will be back on Wednesday, and he will probably bring Patti and Sally with him. If not, then Bethany will bring them on Friday. George has several meetings in Indiana and an interview in Evanston.

Aug. 15, 1966 (Monday): Up at 5:00 A.M. Left here at 6:30 A.M. to take Wesley to camp near Lewistown, Illinois. It was foggy almost all the way there. Arrived there at 9:00 A.M. Got Wesley registered and settled in his cabin. Met his counselor, etc. Carol and I left at about 10:00 and got back to University City at about 12:00. We ate lunch at the dime store. Bought Carol a bride, groom, and baby (shower decorations) to play with. Laid and sat around all the rest of the day. Carol said that it was lonely and too quiet. I wrote and mailed a letter to Wesley. To bed about 9:45 P.M.

Aug. 16, 1966 (Tuesday): Was awake several times during the night. Carol and I got up at 7:00 A.M. and washed two loads, mostly sheets. Carol watched TV a little, also played with my salt and pepper shakers [Dorothy had a large collection of differently shaped shakers]. She didn't know what to do with herself half the time. She does not like to play alone. At about 11:00 A.M. she and I made a cake, and she insisted upon blue icing. Susan [Rostow, Carol's friend next door] came home about 12:30 and came over to invite Carol to the cottage [a vacation retreat of the Rostows in the nearby small community of Pleasantville]. Carol was real pleased. They left about 3:30 P.M. So I was all alone with Fraulein and the fish. I made up the beds, watched TV, ate, and wrote letters to Wesley and Marianne Buckland [one of Dorothy's mother's sisters]. Earlier in the morning I had written to Tim too. To bed about 10:15 P.M....

Aug. 20, 1966 (Saturday): Up and left at 7:30 A.M. to pick up Wesley from Epworth-Spring Camp. Got there at 9:50 A.M. Stayed there about a half hour or so. Wesley wanted to go back to Dickson Mounds. They visited there during the week. It is an Indian burial ground, dates back to 900-1300 A.D. There are traces of three buildings in addition to the burial area. Must be 200 skeletons there in their original positions. It was most interesting. Ate dinner there. Then went to New Salem and Springfield. Couldn't find any motel vacancies anywhere. Decided to skip the Illinois State Fair, because it was so crowded. Went to Lincoln's home. Had to wait about a half an hour in line. Kids were impressed. Drove back to New Salem. Kids weren't too impressed. They were disappointed to miss the fair. It was hot at New Salem, but it was nice. Ate at the New Salem Lodge, cost $14.50 including tip. Wesley and Carol each bought a toy. Drove on home. Got here at 9:30 P.M....

Aug. 28, 1966 (Sunday): Church at 9:00 A.M. Ricardo went with us as usual. Today was dedication of our new hymnal. We sang, sang, sang. Forgot to put pork roast in oven before we left, so our dinner was a little late. Rick stayed all day. Wesley got home [from a Boy Scout overnight campout] about 3:30 P.M., tired, dirty, and happy. George made him work in the yard, because he hadn't done a good job. After supper at 4:00 P.M. Sally and I went to Rick's apartment to drive him to his new apartment. What a mint someone makes off of these college kids! Rick and his friend Vic pay $70 for a room. It is a very run-down place. There are four or more rooms rented in a house. We brought Rick here for supper, took him home about 7:00 P.M. Mrs. Shelton borrowed our card table. Her daughter gets married this Saturday. Wesley stayed up late to watch *The Late Show*. I slept on the couch. He woke me up at 1:00 A.M., and I went to bed....

Sept. 10, 1966 (Saturday): Vacuumed, washed, made a banana cake and three loaves of banana bread. George went to the store for me. He also went to Thompson Lumber and told them to start on house [the house at 1801 Rachel Drive]. George will do much of the work himself for the down payment. Sally didn't feel good today....

Sept. 17, 1966 (Saturday): Went to the shopping center twice, also grocery store. Sally had cramps today. Did two loads of wash. John Daniels, my blind student [at the university], called today. I will meet him at the Rehabilitation Center at 12:45 P.M. Tuesday [every week] to begin reading for him. Each blind college student needs ten readers to read to him each week....

Sept. 21, 1966 (Wednesday): ... George went to see the company (CCC) lawyer, because we have received two personal property tax bills for TP

Construction from Kimball, and also because we received a letter from a lawyer here in University City that Mac the plumber from Scott's Bluff [Nebraska] hired. As of now, everything is still ok.

Sept. 22, 1966 (Thursday): Had a nice lunch and shopping spree with Barbara Samson and Gladys Hartman [old friends visiting for a day from Homewood]....

Sept. 26, 1966 (Monday): ... Wesley is not allowed to watch TV tonight, because his room was not clean when he left for school. That is a new rule. Am trying to find a way to help him keep his room picked up....

Oct. 3, 1966 (Monday): Did laundry, cleaned stove and all waste baskets, mended. Rick called. His wife had a sixth girl on September 21. He was so tickled. Later he called to ask if he could come over and tape some of our records. He just bought a new recorder. Invited him for supper....

Oct. 5, 1966 (Wednesday): Carol spent half the night with me [in bed]. Lovely cool sunny day. Took Carol and Wesley to choir. Sally stayed late at school, so skipped Candy Stripers. Sally went to a program planning meeting at 7:00 P.M. No TV for Wesley all this week so far because of messy room. Received letter from mom....

Oct. 9, 1966 (Sunday): Went to early church. Rick went with us. Wesley's choir sang. Wesley and two girls sang a part while the rest of the choir made background noises. Wesley is the only boy. I'm real proud of him. Rick stayed here until about 6:00 P.M.... I made taffy apples....

Oct. 11, 1966 (Tuesday): Visited [Carol's] school. Beth Hudson had lunch here. Read to John Daniels. He fell asleep. Came home and took a nap. Picked Sally up from school and took her to the orthodontist. Took Wesley to judo and picked him up. Supper, made pecan rolls, to bed about 11:30 P.M. Today was Circle [Church activity], but I had to miss because of John. Will try to change time with him....

Nov. 18, 1966 (Friday): Haven't written since my return from lovely Hawaii [Dorothy went there between Oct. 16 and 31 with her mother and sister Bethany to visit her brother Tim while he was on leave]. Much has happened. Took me quite a while to get down to earth after our trip. Our foreign student [Ricardo Flores] left on November 1. We saw him off at the airport. Met David Williams there also. He's a missionary to Rick's town and is here for a year to study. Work is progressing on our house. The Folks [Dorothy's collective term for George's parents] came one Saturday,... and dad helped George put partitions up in the house.... Wesley did the sound for a play at school. We went to see it. Had school conferences for Carol. Miss

Adison is an excellent teacher. She really makes school fun. Miss Harper is also excellent. She is the special teacher. She had tears in her eyes as she talked to us. Wesley did better on his report card this time. Sally is having difficulty in chemistry....

Nov. 24, 1966 (Thursday, Thanksgiving): Today we had pancakes for breakfast. Then dad [Patterson] and George went to work on the house. Put the turkey on at 7:00 A.M. Ate dinner at 12:30 P.M. Mom and Bethany called. Dad and George went back and worked until 7:00 P.M. Sally, mom [Patterson], and I began working on booklets that mom needs done. The kids were nasty to each other all day, and so was George. To Bed about 11:00 P.M.

Dec. 1, 1966 (Thursday): Ironed. Invited Jane Collingwood [a neighbor] over for a coffee, but she was going out. Wrote to Ellen Patterson. Carol came home with about 6 or 8 papers, all with D's and F's, which really upset me. No judo tonight. Mr. Castle has left the Y. Will probably teach at one of the junior high schools. It snowed almost all day. Roads were bad when I took Wesley to the Y....

Jan. 24, 1967 (Tuesday): Back again after a lapse [in writing since early January, following another lapse covering almost all of December]. Not very dependable lately. Guess I'm getting old or something. It is 6:45 P.M. Just finished dishes. Sally is on the couch. She has to rest [before drying the dishes]. She thinks of a million excuses to let the dishes drain as long as possible. Wesley is on the bed reading, and Carol is in the tub. Tonight when Wesley cleared off the table, he gave the left-over meat (about one half pound of steak) to the dog. I was going to use it for our supper tomorrow. I told him to put his scraps in the dog's dish, and he didn't listen closely. When he grows up, we will have a lot of laughs together. George left today for Michigan City (northwestern Indiana], then Cincinnati, etc. He will return Saturday morning.... I have joined The Book of the Month Club again. Ordered *Doctor Zhivago*, *Everything But Money*, and *The Source*. Seems like they will never get here....

Jan. 26, 1967 (Thursday): ... Grade school closed at noon [because of bad weather]. I picked up Carol. It was raining, almost sleet, and was windy and icy. Junior and high schools closed at 2:00 P.M. Got Sally but not Wesley until 3:00. He stayed in Industrial Arts. I was so mad at him. Spanked him, and he must be home by 3:45 or telephone from now on, or he'll be spanked hard. All electricity went off at 2:00 P.M. Went out to Burger King for hamburgers. Wind was up and very icy. Couldn't walk on the street. Sally studied by candle light. Electricity came back at about 7:00 P.M. and stayed on until about 10:15. and then out again. Put extra blankets on the kids' beds. George called from Marion, Indiana while the lights were on.

Jan. 27, 1967 (Friday): Woke up off and on all night. I got so cold. Our room is the coldest in the house. Finally I put my wool hat and my robe on. Later I got up and put more covers on Wesley, and then Frau and I moved into the girls' room. It was 3:30 A.M., and a little snow was on the ground. Got up at 6:30. It was almost 55 degrees in the house. Made a cup of instant coffee from the hot water tap. When kids got up, we had coffee and cocoa and beef bouillon all from the hot water tap. We dressed in as many socks, tight slacks, shirts, sweaters, bath robes, and hats as we could get on. Wore gloves except when we were doing something where we couldn't. Busied ourselves picking up the house, making beds, etc. Hendrsons [neighbors] called. No power either. At least half of University City had no power. Hudsons called, invited us over. Their fireplace and kitchen stove, just to cook, kept their house's front end in the seventies. Mom called. Chicago is snowbound. Had 21 inches of snow. Drifted five to six and even twelve feet in height. Took mom three hours to get home from Chicago on the IC [Illinois Central railroad]. Lots of kids are isolated in their schools. Took blankets and food and went to Hudsons about 10:30 A.M. Hated to leave Frau. Fixed blankets and rugs on the couch for her, and curled up. Could hardly get the ice off the car windows. Snow had drifted in our front yard. Mr. and Mrs. Anderson were at Hudsons also. Had a warm dinner. Sally, Dorothy, and Fred [Hudson] napped a little. I played a game of Aggravation with Mr. Anderson. Then Carol played a game with us, then Chris [Hudson], then Wesley, then Fred. Then ended up playing two games with Fred, Mr. and Mrs. Anderson, and me. Kids all played and argued. Dorothy did dishes. Sally and I went home to check on Frau, to feed her, to let her out, etc. Just at suppertime George came. He had called mom from Indiana, and she told him not to try to come there. So he just came straight on home. Electric came on at 7:00 P.M. Andersons went home about 8:00 P.M. We left at 9:00 P.M. Kids didn't want us to leave. Three astronauts were killed in their rocket at the launch pad in Florida: Grissom, White, and rookie (his first flight) [the Apollo I fire during a simulation and involving Gus Grissom, Edwin White, and Roger Chaffee]. I don't know the details. Got things in order at home, and I went to bed. Lost one fish only, the red tail sharp. Was glad for our transistors [battery powered radios] all day. Loaned Carol's radio to Collingwoods across the street....

Feb. 16, 1967 (Thursday): Scrubbed and waxed floors. Dorothy Hudson and I shopped at grocery store after lunch and then discussed, among other things, other church school lessons. Sally and I tangled after supper. I ended up spanking her, and she refused to eat. So I said that she leave the table and not eat at all. She told me that I couldn't make her do anything: sit, eat, etc. Don't know who was most upset. Started *Doctor Zhivago*....

Feb. 20, 1967 (Monday): ... George left for Indiana at 9:00 A.M. He had planned to leave at 8:00 A.M. No wonder Wesley is a pokey messer.... At 6:45 P.M. I picked up Dorothy Hudson, and we went to school board meeting. There was much discussion about this bussing of the school kids. The newspapers and news were biased toward the negro in their reports, I think. I am against bussing the kids, but I don't feel that I am prejudiced. This could be an explosive situation.... [Dorothy in fact harbored no prejudice against people because of the color of their skin, but she opposed bussing, because she wanted her children to have what she regarded as a normal childhood experience in being able to walk to and from school]

Feb. 28, 1967 (Tuesday): ... In the evening I made umpteen phone calls to Miss Adison's third grade mothers to get pioneer foods for a program Miss A. wants to have on Friday....

March 3, 1967 (Friday): I fixed Carol's pioneer dress, cleaned house, got dressed, and went to school 1:00 P.M. Must have had 75 or 80 mothers, visitors, friends; and Miss A's third grade kids were there. Mothers made, and we served Johnny cakes, succotash, spoon bread, squash, and Indiana pudding, and also great apple cider. The kids all looked so cute. Even Miss Adison was dressed as a pioneer. Mom and Patti [Bethany' daughter] came on the 9:55 P.M. train. George got home about 2:00 A.M. or so, I guess.

March 4, 1967 (Saturday): Had fried mush for breakfast this morning, went shopping. Mom got three dresses at department store. She bought Carol new white dress shoes, gave Patti money for a purse, Sally for a girdle, and Wesley new shoes and a model car. Patti fell on the way to the car and split her slacks real bad, a new outfit Bethany just bought her. We laughed so hard that mom wet her pants, and we laughed all the harder....

March 6, 1967 (Monday): Up at 5:00. Woke up at about 4:15 because of Frau and couldn't go back to sleep. Got snow now. Wrote letters to Mom Patterson, Mom Klingner, and Ming. She is our new foreign student. She is twenty-four, is Chinese, and is from Formosa. Full name is Ming Yang Su....

March 26, 1967 (Sunday): Up at 4:45 A.M. to go to Sunrise Service. Wesley had a part in it. He did very well, so did Chris Hudson and Peggie N., the girlfriend of Sally's that we take with us to church most every Sunday. The service was composed entirely of Junior and Senior Youth Fellowship members except for organists. Very impressive! After the service Sally and the young church kids went out to breakfast. Wesley's choir (they sang in the 6:30 and 8:45 services) had a breakfast at the church. I ate with them. Went home, put ham on [for Sunday dinner], etc., and then Carol and I went to church school. Wesley and Sally attended both 6:30 and 8:45 services. George and The Folks attended 11:00 service. George went to 6:30 A.M. service, picked up Ming Yang at 12:30. Today she had a small replica of a Chinese instrument similar to our violin, a record for us, and a Chinese book for Carol. George's folks are nice to her, but they don't like it when we invite her here. They don't understand and like the host family idea. They don't like the kids to have friends over. They never liked it when George and I had friends when we lived in Deerfield [at the beginning of their marriage]. With their attitude I can understand why George never had any friends. We had a small Easter basket for Ming Yang....

March 28, 1967 (Tuesday): At 9:45 I took Ming Yang to the shopping center. Her tape recorder from Goldblatts wasn't working. They fixed it. I helped her choose two dresses. She got a garment bag with S&H green stamps, and I took her grocery shopping.... Ming Yang gave me four brass coasters from Taiwan. I hung them on the wall....

Apr. 4, 1967 (Tuesday): ... I am reading *The Source*....

Apr. 6, 1967 (Thursday): ... Made six loaves of bread, four banana and two apricot. Took Eddie and Kitty Collingwood to lunch with Carol and me. Mark got hurt, and Jane had to take him for x-rays. Carol and I were going to go out to eat once a week as long as she does good schoolwork. Dr. Miller [a psychologist] suggested doing something. Carol's report card was a pleasure. Went up in four subjects from D to C, down in one....

Apr. 8, 1967 (Saturday): Up early. Wesley went to church at 6:30 A.M. to work at pancake breakfast. He came home about 1:30 P.M. and then slept all afternoon. Sally slept late. Grandma and Grandpa [Patterson] refused to go. So George, Carol, and I went to eat pancakes at 7:00 A.M.... Grandma had her usual enthusiasms for things when I brought them [Carol and her friend Susan Rostow] home.... Then took Sally over to Dickersons to see their three little kittens. George said that we should get two of them. Sally was so surprised and pleased. I think that we will take the gray and black ones. They are four weeks.... He [Wesley] was also tickled [about the kittens]. When we got home, he told Carol too. Then Sally told grandma and grandpa. They had their usual enthusiasms....

Apr. 9, 1967 (Sunday): Today George was lay participant at both services. Wesley's choir sang at the early service. Was surprised that George's folks wouldn't get up and get ready to go to the early service. They did get ready and drove to Homewood to see Leanna Kelly. She is not well. Carol told Grandma, she was glad that they were leaving. The Folks are so nasty to the kids that the kids don't even enjoy them, and they certainly don't enjoy the kids....

Apr. 18, 1967 (Tuesday): ... Mom called last Thursday night. Tim had called her from Hawaii to tell her that he made second class. He also said that he will leave for Vietnam on Tuesday Apr. 18, which means today. He is on his way.... The Folks left at 7:00 A.M. George left for Goshen, Indiana at noon. He will be gone a lot in the next three weeks. So I suppose that The Folks won't be back for a while. I am glad: for I can get a rest. I can't keep going under such stress as they create by always looking on the negative side of things....

Apr. 23, 1967 (Sunday): ... Starting today Sally is the official dishwasher. She'll get one dollar per week. Wesley gets his $1.25 for mowing the lawn....

Apr. 25, 1967 (Tuesday): ... Supper. ... Carol did her report on machines [a written book report]. Sally did dishes and homework. I helped Carol, then sewed, then set my hair, and read. Am still plugging my way through *The Source*. It is good but very slow going. Letters today from mom and Uncle Les. Les sounded so good this letter. The last letter, just before Christmas, was so different, and I had worried. To bed about 10:00 P.M.

Apr. 27, 1967 (Thursday): ... Started Carol on drying the dishes. Will pay her 75 cents per week for her job....

May 2, 1967 (Tuesday): ... Went to see Miss Adison at 8:00 A.M. She says Carol is doing so much better. Carol passed into the Fish group at the swimming class. She was so proud....

May 3, 1967 (Wednesday): ... Took Wesley to choir. Next week he starts private voice lessons with Anita Montgomery.... Carol is doing well with her piano lessons.

May 17, 1967 (Wednesday): ... Got a letter last Friday from Tim. He was off the coast of Russia. Said he had spent $400 in Japan....

May 25, 1967 (Thursday): ... At 6:00 A.M. George, Wesley, Carol, and I left for Vienna, West Virginia, where George had to present the key to a church group at their dedication service. It was Christ Lutheran Church. It was a lovely service. George sold the church two years ago and was project engineer for them. We stopped in Dayton and visited with Arthurs [Montana friends]. Laurie has grown so.... Not much sleep. Two letters from Tim in past two weeks. Am anxious to see the dishes he bought us in Japan.

May 30, 1967 (Tuesday): Another Memorial Day is here. Kids have had four days off school. They have only eight days of school left. Mom and Pat are here. They came by the train on Saturday. They will leave this afternoon for home. Mom is talking very strongly of coming here when she retires next December. I got a new dress for Ron Thompson's wedding [son of George's former business partner]. I don't like Sally's new bathing suit. It shows too much of her tummy. Took mom shopping yesterday. She got two dresses, and I got three inexpensive cottons. I have gained so much weight that very few of my clothes still fit me. Last spring I weighed 105 pounds. Now I'm 130....

June 3, 1967 (Saturday): ... Got my set of China that Tim sent from Japan. It is lovely. Has a single rose on most pieces, service for twelve, made by Noritake China. According to value on package, Tim must have paid about $45 per set [others sets were purchased for his mother and other two sisters]. Also, he paid about $15 to mail each set. I unpacked it all and made sure that it was all ok. I would love to use it now, but I suppose that it is wisest until we move.... Won't let Sally with Rick anymore. He was in the jail for a fight last Saturday, and we know nothing about it. Told Sally, if he would come and talk to us, then we'd let her go. Now she has a date with a Dwain Smith....

June 9, 1967 (Friday): ... Priced Noritake China at Marshall Fields [in Chicago]. A 92 piece set sells for $119.99. Tim sent us a 96 piece set....

[Entries in the journal for June 16-18, Friday through Sunday, describe the family's trip to Cincinnati to attend Ron Thompson's wedding.]...

June 30, 1967 (Friday): Up at 6:00 A.M. At the house to paint by 7:00 A.M. Left at 9:00 to take Sally to work [baby-sitting during the week]. Left at 11:30 and returned at 1:30 P.M. and painted until 5:00 P.M. Got the kitchen and main bath done, and almost all the living, dining, and hall done. Sally worked, had a date with Dale, but he didn't show up. Carol and Susan played at Kathy Collingwood's new house all morning. Carol helped me in the afternoon and at 4:00 P.M. went swimming with Sally. Ate at Steak and Shake. I'm exhausted. Painted almost the whole house this week. Am reading *The Death of a President*. Good, but dull in places.... To bed at 11:45 P.M.

July 2, 1967 (Sunday): Cooled off today. It was pretty hot yesterday. I am tired. I am also discouraged. Why do I so often feel like I have two left feet after and when Bethany and mom have been here?... Mom and Bethany wanted to leave at 10:00 A.M. Guess it was 10:30 or so when they did. Then went to the store. Got chicken to bake for our dinner. I picked up Ming Yang at 1:00 P.M. Ate dinner amid much noise from Sally. She wanted us to hurry, so she and Patti could go swimming. Ended up making them stay home for quite a few reasons. Took Ming Yan home at 4:00 P.M. Now it is almost 8:00 P.M., and I am tired....

July 12, 1967 (Wednesday): ... After supper we went to Pekin, Illinois to look at carpets there [for the new house] that George can get through CCC. It was 1:00 A.M. by the time we got home, and I was pretty short tempered. Found a pink for the girls, a green for Wesley, and two different golds for us....

July 15, 1967 (Saturday): Got stones delivered for driveway. Kids had to move and shift the stones around. George worked on the wall tile in the bathroom. Girls and I went to bank and lumber yard, where we chose Formica tops for kitchen cupboards and bathroom vanity....

July 16, 1967 (Sunday): Carol, Wesley, and I went to Sunday school. Dorothy Hudson did not come [because she was away on vacation], so I was alone again [to teach both first and second grades]. The rest of the family met us for church. Ming Yang Su came for dinner. Sally and Patti went to Alice's after much crying and pouting by Sally, which made Ming Yang uncomfortable.... Carol is doing good on her piano lessons. George and I had another old famous argument. He wants to quit CCC and to go into business for himself: some company gets together men with money with other men who want to be their own boss, and puts them in business. I told him, as before, that I wish he'd grow up and quit dashing from one green field to another, etc; and he says it's all my and the kids' fault, because we spend too much money, etc. As usual, we end up at the same dead end street. I get so confused trying to sort out my feelings and stuff....

July 18, 1967 (Tuesday): George left this morning, making executive calls in Indiana. Feeling very low lately. Am not sure if it is because of unrest with job, or because I haven't taken yeast lately. So I'll take yeast and hope.... Was really looking forward to a letter from mom as usual on Tuesdays, because I was so low in spirits, but the mail came early, and so there was no letter....

July 22, 1967 (Saturday): ... The Folks came about 8:30 A.M. Asked Mom Patterson to go look at carpets that I liked. She wasn't interested.... Later, as I hung my wash, I was thinking how glad I am for the kind of parents I had. Must remember to tell mom in letter tomorrow.... I weigh 130 pounds now. That's too much....

July 23, 1967 (Sunday): ... I read the paper, especially the want ads [probably thinking about going to work], then made lemonade and took it to George [at the new house]. Stayed about an hour. Wrote to mom. Popped corn, ate....

July 29, 1967 (Saturday): Beautiful morning at 6:00 A.M. Yesterday got cards from Barbara Samson, Uncle Willie [Patterson] and his new wife Abigale, and Grandma Patterson. Mom came on the train today. It was late, and we had to wait about 45 minutes. George started putting up the kitchen cabinets. Picked up the rose bathroom rug today. Mom liked my choice of gold rugs at Sears. Mom had her hair done at Goldblatts....

Aug. 7, 1967 (Monday): ... [concerning bringing Wesley back from summer camp with some other friends of Dorothy's] We sang both ways. Sang so hard, we drove right past our turn. Fifteen miles before we discovered I missed it.... Also stopped at Dickson Mounds.... Ate dinner at A and W in Havana.... Sure was tired when we returned. George was a little angry. Jealous, I guess, because we were gone so long. Sometimes I wonder.... Went to Sunday school. George met us for church. Later he was moping around feeling sorry for himself, because he had to work on the house....

Aug. 16, 1967 (Wednesday): Haven't written in my journal lately. Don't have much free time when George's folks are here. They left yesterday afternoon. They helped a lot, and I am glad for it, but I sure wish their attitudes were better. I'm getting fed up and am about ready to explode. Last week on Saturday morning I took Ming Yang to the post office to mail stuff to herself in New York. Had about 15 or 20 packages. Went to the bank for her, to bus station for her ticket. Had her for dinner on Sunday and then took her to the bus station (Wesley and I) at 5:00 P.M., and waited until the bus left. I went to house and watched George and dad work. I wrote a letter to my mom on a paper sack, no stationery with me. Sure got irritated at The Folks. They are so bossy, and mom is afraid she's going to do some work and I won't. She always says, "Are you going to work over at the house?" Blah!...

Sept. 4, 1967 (Monday, Labor Day): 1801 Rachel Drive, have been in our new house for a week plus two days. Moved on Aug. 26. Ray Butler and Chuck Everitt helped us. The Folks were here. They came on 8,22 and stayed until 8,28. Had a pouring-down rain five minutes after the men were all through. Sears installed our carpet on 8,24, plus installed the old carpet in our bedroom. Dad got all our fixtures up. They are all early American and look so nice. There is still a lot to do on the house. Had a bedspread for a bathroom door until last night when George got the real door up... Phones were installed on 8,24. Have yellow one in kitchen on long cord and have jacks in all bedrooms and back bath with turquoise phone for those....

Sept. 9, 1967 (Saturday): ... Am "regusted" [Dorothy's own funny word] with George. He isn't a very good businessman. He flubs so much. He doesn't check things or follows through at all. The wallboard man overcharged us a hundred dollars, and we can't get it back. Then he didn't get a definite price from Pioneer on the floor, and now he's sent his bill, and it is way too high, and I think that Pioneer charged us way too much for the house in the first place. Things like this happened with the business in Nebraska all the time....

Sept. 11, 1967 (Monday): ... My stomach is upset. Must go get milk, iron, bathe Frau, hang wash, cook supper....

Sept. 13, 1967 (Wednesday): ... Ironed. Still no postcards from Canada from mom. Very "regusted" with Wesley tonight: late from school, 4:45, watered the street and driveway instead of grass, left without shutting off hose and saying he was leaving. Took Sally driving [she now had her driver's permit]. She had five phone calls this evening. I am tired, screamed too much at Wesley....

Sept. 21, (Thursday): ... Deckers are going to have a new addition to their family [Bethany, wrongly, thought that she was pregnant]. I wonder if we are. I am two weeks late, which seldom happens. Today I was busy all day making goodies for Tim....

Sept. 24, 1967 (Sunday): What a beautiful sunrise this morning [probably viewed by Dorothy alone as she sat in the living room looking out the picture window and writing in her journal].... Got an extra long letter from Tim yesterday. He is well in Vietnam.

Sept. 25, 1967 (Monday): ... Started my period. I was two weeks late. Thought surely I was pregnant. Little disappointed that I wasn't, What a relief!

Oct. 3, 1967 (Tuesday): Felt lousy yesterday. Painted but didn't move very fast. George worked on CCC stuff. Folks came about 4:00 P.M. or so. They are their usual selves: nasty to the kids, etc. It's too bad that the kids have to dislike their visits so much. Me too! I get so mad at George when they are here. He is so much like them that it hurts. Today the social worker from Carol's school comes. Tomorrow, the final inspection of our house. Thursday and Friday we sign papers, and then the house plus all the payments will be ours. Sears and Penney's have both called about late payments. Each week we get further behind. We owe so much money, it scares me. I think perhaps I will have to go back to work.

Oct. 6, 1967 (Friday): ... John Daniels called. This year I'll read to him at 9:00 A.M. on Tuesday. Start next Tuesday....

Oct. 7, 1967 (Saturday): ... Wish that Sally would become friends with Debbie [next door neighbor]. She needs more friends than just Alice. I have so many wishes. If God has as much trouble with all the others as with me, then He really has His hands full....

Oct. 12, 1967 (Thursday): ... Am in the midst of taking care of Mark and Nancy Morgan [two small children]. I sure haven't got much done this week, but it's not all due to them. Tuesday morning was mostly spent in reading to John Daniels at the Rehab Center. Nancy was very good. Sat on my lap all the while I read....

Oct. 22, 1967 (Sunday): ... George had an interview at university for job. He asked for 12,000. They only offered 11,4, and now they are checking to see if they can go that high. Had a lovely visit with the family [Deckers and Lawsons to see the new house].... I went to church with Dorothy Hudson. Enjoyed it but too fundamentalist for me. Wish she wouldn't leave our church....

Oct. 28, 1967 (Saturday): Slept late this A.M., about 7:15. Carol brought us breakfast on a tray: toast and honey butter, cupcakes, nuts, milk, and juice. Last year when she did this, she would always bring Seven Up to drink. It pleases her so much to do something for others. Then she went out to shake the rugs, swept the porch and scrubbed it. Now she is cleaning her room, so that she can go to the movies....

Nov. 4, 1967 (Saturday): ... The plays [at Wesley's junior high school] were both good. The last one was the best. Kids began to arrive here [at Dorothy's house] about 9:45 P.M. [after the plays]. I was really surprised when later I counted 54 kids. They were really well behaved. Stayed in family room and kitchen, and bathroom, all evening. Didn't leave a mess or anything. They were all quite cute. At 12:05 A.M. I told them that they had to go home. Many had already left. Jean Adams helped with the party. We served popcorn, pop, and sloppy joes. Wesley was so pleased, because the party was such a success....

Nov. 10, 1967 (Friday): Visited school [Carol's, on Tuesday]. Nancy [Renehan, a pre-school girl whom Dorothy was baby-sitting for a neighbor] was good. Ironed in afternoon. Folks pulled in at 5:00 P.M. No warning, just expected we'd have food for them, I guess. Left again about 9:30 Wednesday. Evelyn came over, very upset. Seems a colored couple moved next door to Renehan's, and they are all upset. Afraid I didn't give her much comfort.

Ironed more, am getting caught up. I've ironed only the necessary items since we moved in August. So I really have a pile. George has decided not to take the university job. He likes his freedom and says that he can make more money at CCC, and he doesn't want to waste all the work he has already done on his territory. I hope that I can accept his decision with good grace forever. I don't think he knows or cares how much of his fatherly responsibility he is shirking by being away so much. I wonder if he has noticed that all the other CCC wives are all skin and bones and nervous looking. I have, and I have wondered.

Nov. 12, 1967 (Sunday): Mom is here for a few days. Tim will come tomorrow. We went up to Homewood Friday night and returned last night. Brought a U-Haul full of boxes, clothes, a chair, Patti's (used to be Sally's) chest of drawers, and night stand, a chest of Tim's etc. We will bring the rest of mom's stuff on December 1st weekend. Tim looks good, is losing his hair. Mom is so proud of him. He brought us some kimonos. Last Friday I went to visit Wesley's life science class (National Education Week). He wanted me to come. Sally laughed and said that everyone would laugh at him. But he was a little embarrassed when I first got there, and wouldn't look up. After a while he brought some stuff over to show me....

Nov. 15, 1967 (Wednesday): ... Been busy going through mom's boxes and stuff and putting them in attic. Wesley has had a good time with grandpa's [Dorothy's Grandfather Klingner, who was a very good musician] banjo, accordion, and mandolin....

Nov. 21, 1967 (Tuesday): George's been home since last Wednesday night, and I wake up every morning between 4:00 and 5:00 A.M. [from not being so worn out and exhausted]. I sure do like having him home. How I wish he would be home every day [to help out with all the work]. Yesterday he took hair drier and mixer to be repaired and took Sally's electric blanket to Penney's. They tested it. It was bad. So they gave us a new blanket. Sally was so pleased. Let's see. I Started a sweater for Carol for Christmas. Yarn was on sale at Goldblatts. [long list of things done] Made a chocolate pie for George, my first. He liked it.... Sally drove herself to Doctor Hanson this afternoon. She is growing up. I vacuumed whole house and dusted living and dining rooms. Vacuuming is a big job in this house. Also did four loads of washing, washed hair, made banana bread and cranberry relish. Carol helped me. She is so sweet and always so willing to help. She read tonight at bedtime almost as if she enjoyed it. George put the tiles on the walls in the bathroom. Sally took the red car to Georgia's for a while after supper. I knitted on Carol's sweater. Am on my last cup of coffee for tonight. Good night!

Nov. 28, 1967 (Tuesday): Had a good enjoyable time in Homewood over Thanksgiving. I made six pies and cranberry relish.... There were twenty at Lawsons for Thanksgiving dinner. ... Bethany and Richard are pretty much at odds. She says that he has been terrible since she thought she was pregnant. She says she doesn't care either. ... Visited with Virginia on Friday afternoon. She seemed pretty good. Didn't get to stay as long as I wanted. George and I went to Rosy and Bud's Saturday night. Got back to Deckers at 3:00 A.M. Had such a good visit....

Dec. 4, 1967 (Monday): Well, December is here and so is mom [moving in from Chicago to stay]. We (Carol, George, and I) went up to Homewood to get her Saturday morning and came back in late afternoon....

Dec. 14, 1967 (Thursday): I sewed [nightgowns for Christmas presents]. Mom made candles, got six made. Mom and I kept bothering each other, so neither of us gets a lot done, but I am sure enjoying having her here, and I hope she feels the same....

Jan. 1, 1968 (Monday): Watching Cotton Bowl Parade on TV. Mom's color set is sure nice.... Now it is noon. Rose Bowl Parade is on.... I am doing laundry, made hot mush for breakfast, will have fried mush for supper....

Jan. 11, 1968 (Thursday): Still cold and snowy. Been taking the kids to school every morning.... Blue car wouldn't start at all [because of the cold] on Sunday or Monday till garage man came out and started it at 11:30 A.M.... On Monday 1,8 I was involved in first [auto] accident. A man slid into me as I waited at stop sign on Boardman on Center Street. So I spent the whole afternoon in going to Allstate to get an estimate, stopping at police station to get report paper, etc....

Jan. 23, 1968 (Tuesday): It is 11:10 P.M., and I am wide awake. Had a program discussion at church tonight on Vietnam. Vi Gibson and I did refreshments. Our committee on social concerns sponsored. Very interesting. Only eighteen there. Felt very tired and worn out today. Didn't do much. Made three batches of Russian tea cookies. Last night I made three batches of oatmeal cookies.... George called last night. He was on TV. The presentation at Eaton [Ohio] was televised. He was so tickled....

Jan. 27, 1968 (Saturday): ... In afternoon I grocery shopped and took nap and then read *Confessions of Nat Turner*....

Feb. 1, 1968 (Thursday): Wesley is so hard to handle lately. He must be upset about something, or perhaps it is just age fourteen. This week I have sewed. Made up my nightgown and lined Wesley's drapes (mom did most of the sewing) after I made them over the way he wanted them. Carol got her report card. Went up in four and down in two subjects. Reading was D last grade period, now C. Spelling went from C to B. English from C to B. Arithmetic from D to C. Social studies and health sciences from C to D. She got excellent in music. She is still reading below level, though. Somehow we've got to help her overcome her reading handicap. It is almost 11:15, and I am tired.

Feb. 10, 1968 (Saturday): ... Bethany and Patti were here last weekend.... Bethany is down in the dumps. She and Richard are heading for a divorce.... Bethany will have a hysterectomy on Tuesday February 20. I plan to go up.... Sally and Wesley got their report cards. Sally got an F or incomplete in home economics, D in physical education, C in history, B in secretary prob, and A in secretary English. Wesley got a C in math, band, civics, and English, B in PE and science, and A in drama. Wesley has a new girlfriend, Ellen from our church. Life is funny. I sure wish I understood it all....

Feb. 14, 1968 (Wednesday): Today is Valentine's Day. 21 Valentine's Days spent with George. Where have all the years gone?... [list of Valentine gifts that Dorothy gave members of her family]... Went to Sweet Adelines again last night. I think I will like it....

Feb. 15, 1968 (Thursday): ... Soaked my poor corns [on her two baby toes] in Johnson's foot soap. This morning we cleaned as usual. Don't take long with mom here. At 2:00 P.M. Evelyn came over with *Rose Mary's Baby*. Read it after supper. Kooky book! Wonder what the author was trying to prove.... Carol sleeps with me when George is gone lately. I don't sleep good with her, and I am not sure whether I should let her do it, but I do.

Feb. 18, 1968 (Sunday): Yesterday was such a busy day. I didn't even remember who I was. I don't like that kind of day.... George got home from Ohio about 2:00 A.M. Saturday. He is not happy with things at work. He sits around and does nothing and feels sorry for himself, but this too will pass, I suppose. Life is not a test of faith. It is one of endurance, I sometimes think....

Feb. 22, 1968 (Thursday): [detailed description of Dorothy's busy time in Homewood when Bethany had her hysterectomy].... Went to bed [after returning to University City] at 7:45 just to get some peace and quiet.... Sometimes I am so concerned about her [Sally]. Sometimes she has a lousy personality. She is so hateful....

Feb. 25, 1968 (Sunday): On Friday Sally ... dropped me off at Rehab Center, where I read to John Daniels.... Gee, she [Sally] is so hateful. It makes me sick.

She has so much to learn before she can be happy. Will she ever learn? How much will she hurt and be hurt before then?...

Feb. 27, 1968 (Tuesday): It is 11:30 P.M. I am tired. Got home from Sweet Adelines about 11:00 P.M.... Yesterday did four loads of wash.... Today I made Rice Krispie candy and some Special K candy. Also ironed.

March 2, 1968 (Saturday): ... George came home 1:00 A.M. Thursday morning. He is not very happy with things at CCC. I don't know what to do with that guy!... [George] fixed our bed, bolted a support spot under the bed, so that it doesn't sink in the middle anymore. I had told him that I was going to move into Wesley's extra bed until he fixed it.

March 5, 1968 (Tuesday): ... I went to Sweet Adelines. Tonight Mr. Archer [their instructor or director] listened to my range. Said something about "must have sung before." I said, "No, but I sing at home." Said I had a wonderful range, almost two octaves, from F to F sharp two octaves up. I felt very good. He would like me to try tenor later on if I would like. I paid my dues and joined the Sweet Adelines....

March 12, 1968 (Tuesday): A full week has passed again. I am not really much interested in carrying on this writing, but still I continue. The joy I felt last Tuesday night seems so silly now. Maybe it is because I don't feel good. Have had very bad cold. Feel bad inside, outside, upside, downside. Wonder why my family makes me feel this way. I think I came to a conclusion this weekend though. No matter what I do or say or think, Mom will think I should do something different. It is the same for Ginger and Bethany too, I think. I wonder why. I hope when she makes me feel badly because I don't do something her way, I can remember this conclusion. Now back to this past week. Bethany and Patti came this Friday about 8:00 P.M. Patti had no school on Monday. So they stayed till yesterday. Left about 3:00 P.M. Enjoyed her visit till Monday morning when she and Mom started in on me about going to work. It hurt me deeply when Bethany said I yell too much at the kids, and I'm wrong and down in a rut. Then mom started in on my church friends and stuff. I'm a terrible flop in everything I do according to them. Bethany is a lot like mom.... I am reading *Gone with the Wind*....

March 15, 1968 (Friday): Mended on Wednesday. Was down in the dumps by Wednesday night and worse Thursday morning. Had several phone calls, and then I perked up. Thank you, God, for people.... Finished *Gone with the Wind*. Sally still feels lousy [from some illness]. Cleaned house today. Baked German chocolate cake, because Adams [husband and wife] came over. Went to grocery store. Mom had hair done. Took Carol to Y for swimming lesson. Rained all afternoon. Showed Adams our [home] movies. Hope they weren't bored. They stayed till 1:30 A.M. Enjoyed watching them and remembering, but it hurts knowing that these are all friends that we'll never see again. Plaices are in Maine, Shirleys in Alabama, Williams in Florida, Robinsons in Montana, and here we are in Illinois.

March 16, 1968 (Saturday): George, Carol, and I walked to Adams to see their camper. It is lovely. In evening we went to meeting at church, where the board voted to give one thousand dollars to the OIC program. I was proud of our people. This is a program to help the colored people mostly, have their confidence in themselves, so they want to and can get a job and stay with it. Trying to raise $25,000 to start the program. I still have a head cold and can't reach the darn high notes in the tenor part in our two songs, and I want to! And even without a cold I don't think I can. Oh me!...

March 18, 1968 (Monday): ... Nobody was here at suppertime, and I was so mad. Must learn to control myself. I tried to sing the tenor part in our Sweet Adelines songs, but I can't do it, and I'm sad. Things and ideas are getting confused in my head. Joan said Mr. Archer has asked D. Shelly not to sing in competition. I would die if he told me that. I want to be a success at something. It seems that I am a failure as wife, mother, and daughter. So I would like to succeed at something.

March 19, 1968 (Wednesday): Beautiful sunny morn. I am tired and not nearly as keyed up as I have been on other mornings after Sweet Adelines. Guess I did ok. I guess. But not real good. Must really learn to breathe right if I am to sing tenor. We went out after practice. Got home about 12:15....

March 25, 1968 (Monday): ... Friday was our 21st anniversary, but it was no different than any other day. I gave George a card, and he said "happy anniversary." A small gift from him would have meant a lot, but there was nothing. I made us a cake. Got cards from a couple of people. Marianne Griffin and Laurie Larson came over in P.M., and we distributed the Girl Scout cookies. There was lots of activity at our house once the girls got out of school. By 6:00 P.M. $48.50 had been turned over to me....

March 29, 1968 (Friday): George was gone all weekend, home yesterday about noon. He has the new-car fever again.... I think she [Dorothy's mom] enjoyed herself [at an all-day seniors outing]. She doesn't do much but sit around most days. I hope she is not unhappy. I think I annoy her. Guess I always have. Tuesday night was Sweet Adelines, and I was pretty happy along with two other girls. We were honored by being told by Mr. Archer that we were the only three who sang with showmanship, like we really enjoyed it. So then the other girls teased us a lot. We do have a good time. Didn't stop [at the Jolly Rogers restaurant] afterwards. I would have liked to... Felt awful all day today. Didn't even enjoy Sweet Adelines... Very very low at bedtime, cried a little....

March 31, 1968 (Sunday): ... Mom was feeling pretty silly today.... Sally went to see *Bonnie and Clyde* with Kathy.... Felt better about singing tenor today.... Cut out a dress for me. Our usual supper of popcorn....

Apr. 11, 1968 (Thursday): Many moons have passed since my last note. Today I got up at 5:15 A.M. Had time to think and put first things first, etc. I feel much better. Continued reading in *Prayer Changes Things* by C. A. Allen. It is a very good book. I wish I could remember to practice all that I believe and know to be right. I have no follow-through, I guess [nothing else could be farther from the truth!].... Sally has a thing going with Dale.... Grandma got Carol new shoes yesterday. She is at the point where her feet are lady's but her age is still child's. She didn't like the shoes we chose for her and wouldn't even wear them home. She was spitting mad, but she got over it. Now she likes them.... I think I am doing better in singing tenor, I hope. I am enjoying it more. Only five more practices till contest, about two and a half weeks. My costume is almost done [which Dorothy, of course, was making for herself].

Apr. 19, 1968 (Friday): ... Had second [singing] lesson from Anita Montgomery yesterday. Boy! I do everything wrong. I hope I don't get discouraged and quit trying.

Apr. 24, 1968 (Wednesday): Say! Only got five hours sleep last night. Wonder how soon I'll collapse? Boy, will I be glad when this contest is over. I'm getting sick to my stomach. We practiced extra Sunday. Some last night. We will practice on Thursday and again Saturday at contest. Plan to leave about 9:00 A.M. on Friday. The Barbershoppers [men's singing organization parallel to the Sweet Adelines] will have a party for us after Thursday practice; and oh I pray that I'll concentrate enough to do everything right and good!... Hideo [foreign exchange student from Japan] came over Sunday afternoon, and he is coming today for dinner.... Supposed to get new car today if the loan goes through.

Apr. 29, 1968 (Monday): Well, here we are fifth-place winners at Rockford. Oh, how glad and excited we were when they called out our name. Last year nineteenth, this year fifth. There were 21 contestants at competition.... We left here Friday morning about 9:30 A.M.... Arrived at Rockford about 2:30 P.M. We shared a double room with [names listed]. Just had a grand time the whole time. We sang about 4:15 P.M. on Saturday. Judy Michaels' husband told us we weren't very good and not to expect to be even in tenth place, and we were disappointed. But about 10:00 P.M. or so, it was all over with. They called our names as fifth-place winners. Oh joy! Oh rapture! We partied until the wee hours that night. Kathy and I left about 4:00 A.M. We had to be up at 7:30 to get ready to leave and also to go to our critique. The four judges had pretty much good things to say about us, and we were real glad....

May 2, 1968 (Thursday): ... Richard has told Bethany that he will help with the bills, etc. if she and the kids want to move out. So Bethany plans to move out in early June when Rick [her son in college] is there to help. I have hit a new low also. I think nothing seems to be right with or for me.... I got mad at Wesley, then later, because he had left a mess and destruction in his wake all over the house. Oh I wish I wouldn't get mad like that!...

May 12, 1968 (Sunday, Mother's Day): ... Never know what to give George's mom. She never likes anything we give her anyway. Am feeling defeated and deflated, etc. George came home Friday night. CCC wants him to open up a new office in Columbus, Ohio in June. So here we go again! All I can think of is why why why! And a million and a million more why's!

July 26, 1968 (Friday): Haven't taken the time to write lately. Guess I haven't cared. George hasn't opened the Ohio office yet, though he is looking for a place, I guess. We have more or less decided not to move to Ohio when they ask us to. Don't really know when it will come to that, though. Mom is no longer with us. She's been at Bethany' since June 5 when we went on vacation. She decided to go see if her presence will help the situation there. Bethany and Richard are heading for a divorce.... Mom was here for a few days, from Sunday to Wednesday of this week. She showed me how to crochet, and I have started an afghan by using all my old extra balls of yarn.... We went to South Carolina to visit Ellen and the boys. Took George's folks along. I was so sick of The Folks by the time we got home that I don't care whether I ever see them again. And I was sick of George too, because whatever nasty thing Grandma says about the kids or me, he agrees with. I've had it up to here with those guys. So I haven't been too happy with George lately either. I've almost had it up to here with him also. We also went to Baltimore for our first visit there since we moved away in 1959. We stayed at Dwight and Ruth Dever's. Had such a nice time. We went during July Fourth weekend.... Sally was a lousy stinker all the time because she didn't want to go [because she wanted to stay home to be with Dale]. She had the car privilege taken away for a month because of her actions.

July 27, 1968 (Saturday): ... Wesley, Carol, and I went to see *Gone with the Wind*.... I crocheted a little. I'm starting to teach Carol to knit also.

Aug. 8, 1968 (Thursday): ... Tuesday night was Sweet Adelines. Last week I started singing lead rather than tenor. Archer isn't happy about it, but I can't sing tenor. Now Jean Miller is going to try to sing tenor. Suppose he asked her to do so, and I suppose Midge will have something to say about me leaving tenor section when she gets back from her vacation....

Aug. 17, (Saturday): ... Of course, Tuesday night was Sweet Adelines. I love singing lead. Went to Jolly Roger's afterwards as usual. The pizza's so good there....

Aug. 25, 1968 (Sunday): Yesterday I didn't feel very good. He got home about 11:30 p.m. on Thursday. I always hate it when he comes home late in the night. I wish I knew what is going to happen in the next few years. Maybe I'm glad I don't know. I sometimes feel as though I can't go on feeling as I do for much longer, and I don't know if it's George's job or me or what. Have I failed George? Has he failed me? Or have we failed each other? Mrs. Ulansey has called from the Rehab Center and wants me to read Spanish to Julie, my summer blind student, this next year. So I am going to read to her. Maybe something other than Spanish, maybe Spanish. I hope to bring her home at times, so that she can goof off and stuff. She plays the piano and likes to mess in the kitchen, etc.... George worked on reports and stuff all weekend. I wonder how he thinks he will ever finish this house at that rate.... Today Wesley got sassy and spent the day in his room....

Aug. 27, 1968 (Tuesday): It is very late, 1:05 A.M Wednesday. Got home from Sweet Adelines tonight about midnight. Read, set hair, had a cup of coffee, ready for bed now.... [list of activities earlier in the day]. At 3:40 P.M. Vi and I had to go to school meeting [at Carol's elementary school] to learn to register the kids tomorrow. Had to leave at 5:30 for Sweet Adelines sing-out at nursing home, then on to Howard Johnson's for regular practice. Tonight Midge and Mary Murray asked Joan and me to join once a month potluck (husbands and wives). I am pleased [because it was a clear acknowledgement of the respect that Dorothy's singing had earned among her fellow Sweet Adelines]. Had pizza at Jolly Roger's after practice as usual.

Aug. 28, 1968 (Wednesday): I am so tired tonight. Biked farther than usual. I feel that it is that time [period]. I was thinking today that I'm looking for a miracle. There are many kinds, and I'll let the good Lord decide what is best for me....

Sept. 8, 1968 (Sunday): Bedtime. Sally and Dale are in living room. They are arguing. I have the feeling that they will break their engagement one day. I don't think either of them is mature enough for marriage, not even in one year....

Sept. 12, 1968 (Thursday): It is 9:30. I am ready for bed. I feel miserable, dejected. I am tired of being a mother and wife. Seems as though it would be nice to be an unmarried career girl. Wonder if everyone's kids are as miserable as mine. Even Carol is getting miserable, sloppy, etc.... Tuesday I joined the YMCA for three months. So did Jean Archer. She's almost as backward about swimming as I am. Bonnie Mason (Sweet Adelines) got us to join. Neither of us could put our face in the water or anything else.... Gladys [Hartman] and Barbara [Samson] were here [from Homewood]. Wednesday night was also another sing-out at a local high school. Thursday morning was my second swim lesson. I was so pleased when it was over. Both Jean and I learned to keep our faces in the water and hold our eyes open and to do the jelly roll float. And we are practicing a few other things too. I am just tickled pink!...

Sept. 19, 1968 (Thursday): ... Had sing-out at Rebecca Lounge. They were good audience, and it was a good singing room. Home by 8:45. Carol read another two pages to me. I told her I'd give her a penny for each page she read, two pennies if she'd read it perfectly. She still confuses *when then, where there, a an*, etc....

Oct. 1, 1968 (Tuesday): Well, here it is October already. Before I know, Christmas will be here again, and I won't be ready for it as usual. Last week was the usual run run run week; and yet I accomplished nothing. I should slow down, but I don't know what to cut out.... Wesley got his first paycheck on Wednesday, $9.81 after taxes.... I finished Tim's slippers for his birthday....

Oct. 7, 1968 (Monday): ... Had to be ready by 12:15 to go to Evelyn's house to pick up stuff for Halloween hootenanny at Carol's school. Came home and counted out 558 pieces of candy for the guessing game our fifth grade room is in charge of. Read while Carol was at first Girl Scouts meeting this year....

Oct. 8, 1968 (Tuesday): Today is Tuesday. How nice! I do enjoy Sweet Adelines, and I did do well in swimming class today. I can go across the pool now on my face, because I can get to my feet that way. I still can't get to my feet from my back. Read to Julie in the afternoon. George left at 4:00 P.M. for the week. Wesley rode his bike to work. I drove to Sweet Adelines, did not go out afterwards, because our car wanted to go home....

Oct. 10, 1968 (Thursday): ... Am so disgusted with Sally. She lied to me again. Insisted that Dale's folks invited her to spend the night there, and then Dale's mom told me she didn't. I wish I knew what to do for Sally. Why does she lie? And I think that Dale is as bad as she is. What a lovely marriage they'll have!...

Oct. 13, 1968 (Sunday): Up at 5:30. Left here at 7:15 A.M. George left in such a hurry, trying to prove that we never wait for him, that he forgot his wallet.... About noon mom, Tim, George, Carol, and I ate at an Oriental place near Uncle Les'. Got to his house about 2:30 P.M. and left about 4:45 P.M. He looks well and seems well. Boy, those dogs of his are really something! They piddle everywhere, anytime. So consequently, Uncle Les' place smells something fierce!...

Oct. 22, 1968 (Tuesday): Home from Sweet Adelines. Feel real good. Feel like I sang well tonight. Also sang in a quartet tonight for quartet promotion. Someone different sings each week. Afterwards I got lots of compliments. Of course, it was an easy song. Had our usual pizza at Jolly Roger. There were six of us girls there. Did pretty good at swimming this A.M. too. Thank you. Read today to Julie after lunch from 1:00 P.M. to 4:00 P.M.... At 7:30 P.M. we sang at department Store. Carol came along....

Oct. 29, 1968 (Tuesday): ... My period hasn't started yet. I am a week late. Am I pregnant, or is it my change beginning?... Went to church at 7:15 to start coffee and to get things going. I was in charge of coffee to be served at 9:00 A.M. Things went well for coffee and for luncheon. It was very elegant, and there were many compliments. I left at noon to go to TV station studios for our Sweet Adelines tape for The Sun Up TV show. That was fun. Then went back to church to help clean up....

Oct. 31, 1968 (Thursday): Swimming in A.M. Picked up refreshments for Carol's class Halloween party and then took them to school at 2:00 P.M. No bicycle riding all week so far. Joan and I went to shopping center and picked out earrings for Sweet Adelines and silver sparkles for our hats. After supper we put the sparkles on the hat bands. Carol went trick or treating with Pam, then by herself, then with David Gilbert. Wesley and Glenn fixed up a loud speaker outside, hid it in the flowers, and put a pumpkin beside it; and Wesley talked as Mr. Pumpkin to all the kids. They had fun....

Nov. 1, 1968 (Friday): [various errands described] George got home about 5:00 P.M., very tired, very crabby. I was flowing pretty hard. I finally started, thank goodness! So we didn't go swimming....

Nov. 5, 1968 (Tuesday): Voted today, crowded. Swim lesson in A.M. I jumped off deep end today, and wow me! I did it! I really didn't want to. Did it three times. Got my kickboard today. Read to Julie all afternoon. Had to go early to Sweet Adelines practice. It went better tonight. George is so disgusted lately. He sure is egocentric and egotistical and a bunch of other things. I don't even like him. Chorus [in their church] will be better off without him when he quits this summer, as I understand he intends to do.

Nov. 6, 1968 (Wednesday): Sally and Carol and I were up early to listen to election returns. Glad to see Sally take an interest in something. It is 11:00 A.M. and still nothing definite on the election. Looks as if Nixon will get it. He did.

Nov. 8, 1968 (Friday): Finished cleaning and then made two Jell-O salads for the [Sweet Adelines concert] afterglow. Made a cake, made lasagna, made six batches of mush. Bethany called to remind me that they were coming to supper, then lo and behold, who should drive up at 4:30 P.M. without letting me know that they were coming a day early? That's right! Grandma and Gramp Patterson. They do it every time, and it makes me so darn mad!... I went to dress rehearsal at 6:30 P.M. All went pretty well....

Nov. 9, 1968 (Saturday): We barely made it [all the necessary preparations for the Sweet Adelines concert]. It was a good show, one of our best, they all said. After the show Bethany, George, and I went to the afterglow at Howard Johnson's. That was over at 1:00 A.M. Took Bethany home, and then George and I went to after-afterglow at Paul Sawyer's. I was disappointed that there weren't more groups singing. We came home at 4:30 A.M....

Nov. 30, 1968 (Saturday): [long entry describing busy Thanksgiving visit in Homewood]

Dec. 3, 1968 (Monday): ... Today I did a mess of skip-over things in the A.M. Went at 11:15 A.M. to pick Julie [Nelson, blind student returning to the university after Thanksgiving break] from airport. Waited an hour for plane. She and I ate lunch at Steak and Shake. Took Carol to orthodontist. Picked Sally up at 4:30, George at 4:45. After supper did spelling with Carol, went over Sally's book report, did four loads of laundry, picked up in bedroom, wrote checks, paid bills. George is still home. Guess he'll leave Wednesday morning. Weather is cloudy and damp.

Dec. 6, 1968 (Friday): Tuesday morning I swam. Golliosky zero! I even turned my head and took several breaths. Little ole me did!... Thursday night went to sing-out over at our church for WSCS. My goodness, did we ever get the compliments! I was so elated when I got home. Today it is cold and clear.

I must clean the house. I really hate to clean. I did get it all cleaned except the dining room by noon. Have a bad cold, feel terrible.

Author's Note: At this point Dorothy stopped writing in her journal and did not resume again until June 29, 1970, thus leaving a gap of slightly more than a year and a half. When the entries resume, it seems that she was writing with greater assurance and far less emotional turmoil and confusion, probably resulting from her gaining of self-confidence from her success at swimming and in the Sweet Adelines.

During the chronological gap in Dorothy's journal the political climate in the United States, which had already become highly polarized in recent years over the issue of civil rights for blacks, became even more exacerbated over the war in Vietnam, finally reaching a crescendo in early May of 1970 when National Guard troops shot and killed four college students at Kent State University in Ohio. As usual, Dorothy took rather little interest in major political issues unless they impinged directly upon her family. She simply devoted her energies to raising her three children to the best of her ability. Also, as she had always done throughout her adult life and had taught her children, she treated everyone whom she encountered with respect and dignity and greeted them with an open heart and her most radiant smile. She always judged people by the content of their characters and never by the color of their skin. Consequently, Martin Luther King's pleas for social justice, which were in part based firmly upon the highest ethical standards in the Bible, always struck a responsive chord in Dorothy's mind. In fact, during this period, whenever Dorothy happened to be in the presence of her sister Bethany, the two of them often argued about the civil rights movement, because Dorothy sympathized with those who appeared to be the victims of discrimination, whereas Bethany harbored negative views of blacks that were quite common among white Chicago suburbanites at the time.

Wesley was Dorothy's child who was most affected by the radical political and social climate of this period, which was spilling over from the university into his high school. In fact, Wesley was responsible for making his parents stop using the word "colored" and instead to employ the term "black," which was now becoming current as the only polite way to refer to people of African descent. Whenever Dorothy or George would say "colored" in Wesley's presence, he immediately interrupted them and asked, "What color were they? Green? Blue? Orange?" Pretty soon his parents got the message and altered their vocabulary accordingly.

A far more contentious issue arose between Wesley and George when the former decided to paint his bedroom red, white, and blue. Protesters against the war in Vietnam had been desecrating the American flag by burning it in public, and the colors were to be seen regularly as forming the pattern to shirts, pants, and dresses. These three colors therefore became a battle ground between critics of American foreign and domestic policies and defenders of Uncle Sam. When Wesley asked his mother if it was ok for him to paint his room in these colors, she consented, viewing it as a rather harmless form of youthful rebellion. After obtaining Dorothy's sole permission, Wesley bought the paint and repainted the walls of his bedroom in alternating wavy diagonal stripes of red, white, and blue; and Wesley's current girlfriend helped out by painting white stars in the blue stripes to resemble the American flag. When George returned home from his week of travel related to his job and encountered Wesley's repainted bedroom, he was extremely annoyed and unhappy with his son's choice of self-expression, but Wesley had gotten his way, and the bedroom remained as Wesley wanted it.

Another contentious issue between father and son arose over the length of the latter's hair. Wesley wanted to be "with it" by imitating the hippies of the day in having his hair grow long, but this too won George's severe disapproval as a sign that his son had little respect for his parents. The issue finally came to a head one day when George decided to give his son a haircut and thereby reassert parental authority. He physically grabbed Wesley, forced him down into a chair, and proceeded to trim his hair with a pair of scissors, but the haircut abruptly ended amid an angry uproar when George carelessly clipped Wesley's ear, badly enough that it bled.

Despite his adoption of certain aspects of the current counterculture, Wesley maintained his loving relationship with his mother. From his earliest years she had fostered in him the love of reading and of music. Dorothy now enticed Wesley to read more by having the two of them read murder mysteries together. They swapped the same paperback between themselves and carried on a guessing game as to who had done it. It was really fun to read this way to see which of them could figure it out first before reaching the end of the story.

Wesley now acquired his first guitar, purchased with his own money from working odd jobs. It was a wide-neck classical-style guitar fitted with nylon strings, a good choice for beginners with untrained fingers. He began to take lessons to learn the basics of chording and eventually became a fairly good guitar player. Of course, his taste in music took in the rock and roll of the day and especially the folk music of the counter culture.

As always, music continued to be one of Dorothy's greatest joys. She kept up her piano playing and kept adding to her growing collection of record albums. One of her favorites was the sound track to the movie Camelot, whose songs she memorized, loved, and sang frequently. Another record album that now joined her collection was Carol's sixth grade class singing a variety of American traditional songs: Consider Yourself, The Sound of Music, The Impossible Dream, A New Mind, The Good Old Days, Take, Five, Windy, Stout Hearted Men, Sixteen Tons, What the World Needs Now, Johnny has gone for a Soldier.

By now Carol had become good friends with a neighbor and classmate, Pam Gibson. They did so many things together, and it was an extra bonus to their friendship that their mothers, Dorothy and Vivian (Vi), were also good friends and participated in the same activities. The two girls were therefore in and out of both houses constantly; and Pam became so familiar with Frau that she even let the dog take turns in licking her ice cream cone.

Carol now became an avid fan of the TV series *Dark Shadows*. It was a soap opera whose theme was not steamy romance, but the occult, just the sort of thing to attract the attention of someone Carol's age. Her favorite character in the series was a vampire named Barnabas. Since the show was televised in the middle of the afternoon, Carol often ran home from school as soon as classes were out, so that she and her mother could sit down to watch the program. As usual, Dorothy was happy to spend this time with her youngest child. Sharing the show's creepiness and spooky surprises was yet another way in which mother and daughter deepened their love for one another.

Sally graduated from high school in June of 1969, and in the following August she and Dale were married. It was a rather large formal wedding, well attended by relatives and friends of both families. Dorothy made the dresses for herself (burnished gold), Carol (pink), and Patti, Bethany' daughter and hence Sally's cousin, who was Sally's age and served as the maid of honor. Although Dorothy had also hoped to have the honor of making Sally's wedding gown, Sally snubbed her offer, indicating that a mere home-made dress would not be good enough for such an important event. She had to have a real, store-bought dress. True to Dorothy's misgivings, the marriage proved to be a disaster and lasted exactly one year. About the only lasting consequence of the marriage for the Patterson family turned out to be a dog. Sally and Dale purchased a German Shepherd; and as their marriage was falling apart, this animal, named Gretchen, joined Dorothy's home permanently and became dog number two.

Dorothy remained fully involved in the two activities that had recently been giving her a real sense of true accomplishment and validated her self-worth: singing in Sweet Adelines and swimming. She steadily progressed through all the Red Cross swimming lessons offered by her local YMCA, passing one test after another until she had completed the entire regimen. She had begun in total fear of water and had ended as a very able and accomplished swimmer. It marked a major turning point in her view of herself; and she treasured the Red Cross paper awards, which certified her successful completion of each stage, as documents formally attesting to her genuine worth.

Into both these beloved activities Dorothy now introduced Jeanne Douglas. The two women had met at their church and became instant fondest friends. Their personalities, attitudes, and life experiences seemed to mesh perfectly. Jeanne had been born in Oklahoma and had lived part of her life in Kansas and Colorado, but now she and her husband Jack had been obliged to move to University City because of Jack's line of work. Jeanne's western roots and Dorothy's own experience in Montana and Nebraska initially gave them an obvious common topic for conversation. But what really brought the two women together into a perfectly harmonious friendship were their down-to-earth characters, their open-heartedness toward all, and an almost invisible inner strength and courage that resulted from persevering through life's hardships.

Like George and Dorothy, Jack and Jeanne had three children, but all of them were boys; and since the Douglas couple was about ten years older than the Pattersons, all three of their sons were adults by the time that they arrived in University City. One of their sons, John, however, was mentally retarded and was still living with Jack and Jeanne, who lovingly cared for him. Fortunately, their other two sons had turned out well and were leading productive and responsible lives. John alone was such a heavy cross for caring parents to be forced to bear. This no doubt greatly affected Jeanne's outlook toward life: to empathize with other people and their misfortunes; and in view of life's basic unfairness, to be thankful for and accepting of all little blessings that happen to come one's way.

Dorothy's sympathy naturally drew her into an acquaintance with Jeanne. She was glad to run small errands for her and succeeded in involving her in church bake sales and other special events. They began to do many small things together, and Carol was often available and willing to baby-sit with John while Jeanne was away from the house. The two women were soon completely comfortable with each other and could talk about anything, from the most serious issues of life (such as the trials and tribulations of raising children) to the most frivolous, about which they could easily make one another laugh. Jeanne eventually asked Dorothy to read two books: *Flowers for Algernon* and *I Never Promised You A Rose Garden*. Both were works of fiction that dealt with the nightmare of mental illness and retardation. Dorothy found them both to be profoundly moving and helpful in understanding much better the Douglas's situation.

At first Jack was uneasy about his wife running around with her new friend from church, but he gradually came to understand that Dorothy was not just any ordinary person. She could be funny and silly and made his wife laugh, but she was also a person of extraordinary love and compassion; and his wife both needed and deserved to have such a special friend, capable of easing her burden through both serious talking and laughter.

Since Dorothy had learned how greatly therapeutic swimming and singing in Sweet Adelines had become for her own life, she eventually persuaded Jeanne to join her in both activities. They frequently attended swimming and singing together, traveling back and forth in one of their cars; and Jeanne also discovered that they did much to help her maintain a calmer outlook on life.

Excerpts from the Journal

June 29, 1970 (Monday): Been a long time since I wrote. Maybe I'll start up again. It is a good way to let off steam. George is in Newton. Went Saturday, will return today. He helped his dad put in a shower. We had all planned to go, then Carol got a baby-sitting job for Saturday night. So she talked her dad into letting us stay home. George wasn't very happy about it. He did his usual "I'm sorry for myself" routine. "You don't really want to go anyway." Then I tried to talk to him about it, why I feel the way I do about his folks, and he got mad and said forget it. I don't see how we can solve any problems if he won't discuss them.... In the evening [Saturday] he [Wesley] went to Mr. Carlson's [his last year's chemistry teacher) house.

Then they played Putt-Putt Golf. Sunday morning Wesley and Carol went to Sunday school, and I joined them for church. In the afternoon Wesley and Mary Peterson (his latest) went collecting for HEED School, new project for emotionally upset children. Then they picked Mr. Carlson up and played Putt-Putt Golf again. Then Wesley brought Mr. C over, so I could meet him. He is different or something.... Had popcorn for supper when we [Dorothy and Carol] came home from swimming. Carol and I were in bed by 9:30. Wesley was lying in bed reading.

July 1, 1970 (Wednesday): On Monday morning I picked up around the house. In afternoon swam with Jeanne, her grandson Mark, Carol, and Evelyn. Came home early, after one and a half hours, because I was getting sunburned. Took care of Pam. Back was pretty hot by evening. Tuesday morning swam at the YMCA 7:30 to 9:30. I am very proud of my advancement in swimming. Can do almost anything now within reason. Beginners look at me, they think I'm a pro. It is so funny. Did not go to pool in afternoon [with Carol, Jeanne, and others]. Went to Sweet Adelines in evening. Went to Jolly Roger's afterwards. Don't enjoy that as much as I used to. Wednesday ... in afternoon Carol and I went to the pool with Jeanne Douglas and her grandson. Wesley goofed around with Bill until time to go to work. George worked late. So we didn't get to go to the first Wednesday evening church service.

July 3, 1970 (Friday): ... Spencer, Carol's little charge [for baby-sitting], arrived today. He is a darling, just nine months old, loves everybody.... George and I quarreled again last night. He was angry because he suggested going to Newton this weekend, and Wesley doesn't want to go. He has a date, and "none of us love his folks, and no one wants to do what he wants to do." And in a way, he is right, and yet he is so wrong. I have become so disillusioned with George over the years that I don't even care anymore. If the kids didn't need a father, I don't think I'd care if he went away and never returned. I'm not sure.

July 10, 1970 (Friday): ... George's mom was her usual, disgusting to me, self [during a recent visit of George's folks]. Spencer is still with us. He is so cute and acts as if he belongs here. He goes home Sunday.... Mom and Bethany came at noon Monday. What chaos! Mom and Bethany acted like fish wives, yelling how what a doodoo head I was to keep Spencer. I knew what their reaction would be. I just wasn't prepared for it so soon.... Last Sunday I cooked Sally and Dale's Christmas turkey from the grocery store. They came for dinner. We made home-made ice cream. Mary [Wesley's current girlfriend] came over. She and Wesley played tennis later. Sally and Dale left. Sally came back alone. She and Carol played tennis. Sally was here again on Monday. She and Dale haven't gotten along since Dale came back from National Guard. On Wednesday she left him again for the fifth time. The other times he has beaten her in one way or another. This time she says it is for good. Yesterday she went to assistant D.A. and filled out a complaint against him. Now Assistant D.A. will send a letter telling Dale to leave her alone. He (Dale) has been here twice and has called about ten times. She has also called a lawyer. Last night she went to Georgia's, I hope, and didn't get home until 12:45 A.M. I must talk to her today.

July 12, 1970 (Sunday): Am not sure of the date. I know it is Sunday though. Ha! Today Spencer will leave us. He has been fun and not too much work. Carol has already decided what to do with the thirty dollars.... Sally and I went to the lawyer's office. She has to return on Monday to sign the papers and bring $75, and then Sally's lawyer will file suit. Dale called umpteen times. He also got the letter from the Assistant D.A. and was angry about that. Last night was potluck at Douglas's.

July 23, 1970 (Thursday): ... Tonight Carol's softball league played another game. They lost, but Carol made a catch from center field that was a wow! Bases were loaded, two outs, and she caught a long fly. She was so tickled, she cried while everyone congratulated her. Each week her team gets better.... Sally is staying with a friend, Janet and Bill Simpson. She has met a fellow who is running around with him [Bill Patton]; and we told her what we thought. So she left. It makes me sick to think of it. She is so childish and selfish and foolish. Today I swam another quarter mile. That's 22 lengths of the pool. George is at Barbershoppers. He joined several months ago. Carol stayed all night last night with Claudia Evans.

Aug. 4, 1970 (Tuesday): Today is Tuesday, swimming day. Since I wrote last, I've had a birthday and so has Sally. It was my forty-second and Sally's nineteenth. She is working at the Food processing plant in the lab as a tester. She likes it. It is part-time, four days per week, six and a half hours per day, $2.30 per hour. She wears a white uniform furnished by the plant. Last Sunday Wesley did the sermon in church. Minister on vacation. He did a pretty good job for a young kid. The whole service was done by the youth. We've got pretty good youth in our church. I worked Saturday and Sunday at the Book Emporium. I worked there all last winter too. I started out liking it, ended up hating it.... Made myself two dresses last week and got material to make Carol and me each a winter dress.... These new invisible zippers are really nice. Now it is evening. Just got home from Sweet Adelines. Met at Barb Sawyer's. Swam several hours this morning. Worked three hours in the afternoon.... She [Carol] had a game tonight. It was a good game, though they lost. Carol is getting to be a pretty good little ball player. I went to her game at her School and then went to Sweet Adelines a little late. Wesley caught a cold, almost stayed home from work.

Aug. 14, 1970 (Friday): Dogs woke me up at 5:30. There was a cat fight nearby. Dogs wanted out. Decided to stay up. Today will be a big day for Sally, I hope. We are due in court for the divorce. Unless Dale contests it, it will be all over by 1:00 A.M. He called the other night. He wants back everything he paid for. [items listed] Sally's lawyer called him a few choice words when he talked to George and Sally yesterday morning. A week ago on Friday or Friday night Sally left her car on the street all night. Somebody loosened lug nuts (that hold the tires on) on three tires of her car. Who else? Accidentally discovered it Saturday while she was driving. There was a funny noise. Sally's back home. Been here a week. She still likes her job. I made myself another dress. Want to make a bathing suit. Bought a big pattern book from the sewing shop for fifty cents. Took a lady yesterday for Telecare to the doctor, drugstore, dentist, and grocery store. Our Sweet Adelines are participating in Telecare now. It is a project to help older folks remain in their own home under their own steam.... George is in Cincinnati today. Left yesterday afternoon and will return late tonight or tomorrow. We've had words lately. He's approached me, and I've refused. He says I'm holding back to try to prove a point, and I said it is the way I honestly feel. Very blah as far as he's concerned. So then he cries he is a good father. Just ask the kids if they love him or not, or is too strict. He thinks that is our only problem. I don't have words to tell him. I am reading *Friendly Persuasion*, borrowed from Book Emporium. I sure read a lot this past year. We can borrow any book we want from the store. I am going to work three days next week.

Aug. 15, 1970 (Saturday): Stayed in bed till after 7:00 A.M. today. Was up from 1:30 till 3:00 A.M. during the night, because Sally wasn't home yet. I laid in bed and imagined all sorts of horrible things. So I got up and dusted and picked up the living and dining rooms. Got letters from Carol [who was visiting her Patterson grandparents in Newton] and Doris Thompson yesterday. At 9:25 A.M. we met Sally's lawyer at courthouse. Then we went into the hearing. Dale did not come. Sally's lawyer questioned her. Then Dale's did. Then Sally's lawyer questioned me, and then it was all over. Sally will get the decree in the mail next week. In the afternoon Dale and his mom came over to get the Tupperware that Dale insisted he had to have before he would ok the divorce. Had to put it out in the yard, because he would not come in to get it.... Had a few loud words with Wesley. Guess it started out because I said he stayed up too late and goofed around on the weekend and then didn't feel like working during the week. He gets his feelings hurt so easily, and he gets simply furious with me, but he never stays mad....

Aug. 20, 1970 (Thursday): ... Decided I could cut out something and sew all day. Instead, I lay in bed all day. I felt lousy, weak and shaky. Even canceled our going to Sharon's shower, a girl from work. It stormed from about 5:30 to 9:00 P.M. Quite badly at times. Frau is frightened of storms. Gretchen doesn't pay any attention. Went to bed about 9:30. Sally went to Georgia's, as she does every evening. Wesley worked.

Aug. 21, 1970 (Friday): Yesterday Sally slept all day, Wesley worked, I wrote a letter to Carol [who was now visiting her Grandma Klingner in Homewood for the rest of the month[. Took a lady to Prairie Shopping Center, then home, then downtown where I waited for her for a few hours, and then picked her up and took her home. Named Mrs. Clark, for Telecare. She used a walker. In the afternoon I cut out a skirt (long) for Carol and a bathing suit for me. Got Carol's skirt all done. George and I went to eat at the Ponderosa. He went to the Barbershoppers, and I cut out a yellow plaid I just bought. Felt lousy, had the cramps. Sally went to work at midnight as usual.

Chapter 3

Dorothy and her University Kids

August 24, 1970, Monday

It was the middle of the morning. George had left for the week at the crack of dawn; Sally was still in bed sleeping after working the night shift at the Food processing plant; Carol was still with Grandma Klingner in Homewood; and Wesley was ..., who knows where, off goofing around with a friend or something. The two dogs were lying down on the carpet in the family room, and Dorothy was busy in the kitchen several feet away, unloading the dishwasher.

The telephone on the wall next to the doorway leading into her laundry room rang. "Hello," she said in her lovely feminine voice. "Hello, could I speak with Mrs. Dorothy Patterson please." "This is she." "Hello, Mrs. Patterson, this is Ron Woodward from the university Rehabilitation Center. I think that we have met briefly while you were here sometime reading for one of our blind students." "Oh yes, I remember you." "As you may or may not know or remember, among other things, I'm the orientation and mobility instructor for the blind and visually impaired students that we have on campus. I'm trying to round up volunteers to help us out next week in teaching our new freshman students their way around on campus. I know that you have been a volunteer reader for the past few years, and I was wondering if you would be interested in being one of our volunteer mobility instructors for next week?"

Dorothy was slightly surprised but pleased by this request. "That would be fine, I guess," she replied cautiously, "but I've never done anything like that before. What all would I have to know and do?" "Oh I'm sure that you would do fine. It really isn't all that hard apart from all the walking that you'd have to do. We have seven new blind students arriving next Monday morning, and we'll be assigning a volunteer to each one to work with them all five days next week, morning and afternoon, to teach them their way around their dorm, to and from all their classes, and anything else that can be worked in. I'm asking all the volunteers to show up here at the Rehab Center this coming Friday morning at 10:00, so that I can tell and show you everything that you will need to know in advance. If you're interested, I'm sure that you'd do a good job."

There was a short period of silence on the line as Dorothy quickly thought about the offer. It sounded interesting. She would have to miss swimming next week, and Carol would be starting school, but what the heck! "Yeah, I could do that." "That's great. I'll see you then this Friday at my office in the Rehab Center. Thanks so very much for your help. We really appreciate it."

August 28, 1970, Friday

Dorothy parked her blue Falcon in the parking lot next to the Rehab Center and walked around to the front entrance. She paused at the information window just inside the door to find out where Ron Woodward's office was located. As she turned down the hall to go there, she saw a cluster of people standing together outside his office doorway. She joined them and wound up being the only middle-aged person among them. Four were young women about her Sally's age, probably college students themselves. A fifth female seemed to be a few years older. The sixth person was a male, also appearing to be a few years older than the four girls. When introductions were made a few minutes later, the two slightly older ones turned out to be graduate students, Faith Martin and Ed Jackson. The former was a nun working toward her Ph.D. in clinical psychology, and the latter was studying physical therapy for people with major disabilities.

The group of seven stood together somewhat shyly, waiting for Ron Woodward to join them. His office door was wide open, but he was seated behind his desk talking on the telephone. As he hung up and stepped out to greet them, another man came out of another office several doors down the hall and joined them too. "Hello," he said, "I'm Doctor Dan Potter." I'm in charge of testing and counseling our students. I'll be drifting about in the background this coming week to help out with the mobility instruction. I wish to thank all of you for giving us your time in assisting our students, and I look forward to seeing more of you next week." Having said this, Dr. Potter turned about and went back into his office.

Ron Woodward now took over. He was a pleasant looking man, probably about thirty years old. He spoke with a quiet voice that gave the impression of one possessing a calm and unruffled demeanor. "Ok, three of you I already know, Faith Martin, Ed Jackson, and Dorothy Patterson." He smiled and nodded toward the three as he mentioned their names. "But I don't know you others." He then proceeded to read the names of the other four from a list in his hand, and they responded in turn. Woodward continued. "Our new group of seven blind students are all very capable young people. Otherwise, they wouldn't be coming here. I've already met them all, and they all seem to be good cane travelers. You therefore shouldn't have much trouble at all in giving them the mobility instruction that they'll need to get started as college students here, but you will need to know something about cane technique and how blind people find their way about. So, first, we're going to step outside here, and I'll give you a quick little lesson on some of the things you'll need to know."

As Woodward spoke these last words, he stepped a few paces down the hall and pushed his way through a side door of the building. The little group followed and was soon standing on the sidewalk that ran along Spurlock Street next to the Rehab Center. As the group formed a semicircular halo around Woodward, he pulled from his pocket a folding cane. It was a bundle of six metal tubes covered with white or red paint, held together by an elastic band fitted to the rubber grip that formed the top end of the cane. Woodward slid the elastic band off and let the other segments fall down while he held the rubber grip. As the other five segments, each measuring about eight inches in length, fell toward the ground, they were all snapped into the form of a rigid cane by an elastic cord that ran the length of the apparatus. He now held upright in his hand a cane measuring about four feet in length.

"All these students will be using a cane like this. Let me first show you the standard technique used in walking down a sidewalk." Woodward stepped back about ten feet from the group and lowered the top of the cane to his waistline and pointed it outward in front of him with its bottom tip touching the ground. "You're supposed to hold the cane by its grip in your right hand, to lock your right elbow against your side, and then extend your right forearm out in front of your body. Then as you step forward, you move the cane from left to right and right to left, far enough to be the width of your body. This checks to see if there is any object or step a few feet ahead. The sideways movement of the cane is supposed to be synchronized with each step. As the person steps forward with the right foot, the cane should be swung to the left and vice versa."

Woodward now turned around and walked away from them about fifty feet. He then turned to face them, adjusted the cane into its proper position, and then started to walk toward them, so that they could see how he was using the cane. It swung side to side with each step, the cane's nylon tip making a small tapping sound as it was touched down to the left and right. When he came back up to the group, he halted and said, "Well, that's how it's done. It's pretty simple. Any questions?"

When no one responded, he continued, "Ok, now I'll show you about the only other important thing that you'll need to know about cane travel outdoors." He now stepped from the middle of the sidewalk to its edge, so that one of his shoes was brushing against the grass. "We call this the shoreline," he said, as he moved the cane back and forth so that it struck the edge of the grass. "when a blind person is looking for a sidewalk leading into a building or something similar, they will move over to the edge of the sidewalk and use their cane to feel for the entry way." Woodward demonstrated this by stepping down the sidewalk, moving the cane's tip back and forth and stopping when it touched the hard concrete entrance leading into the side door, instead of the grass. "You'll need to show your blind student differences in the shoreline to help them find entrances or other intersecting sidewalks. Do you have any questions now?"

After a short pause, the questions started coming. "Do blind people count steps to know how far to go before turning?" asked one of the young females. "Usually blind people who travel with a cane don't count steps, because they are having the cane look for changes in the shoreline and check for things in front of them. But there are exceptions. If they need to walk across a large open paved area where there isn't any shoreline, they may need to count steps to know about where they need to turn or whatever."

"Exactly how are we to walk with them when we are instructing them?" Dorothy asked. "Excellent question," Woodward responded, "I needed to be getting to that next. You should first explain things to your student; and if it is a bit tricky, you may first want to walk them through the route by having them take your arm and walking with you as you describe the route. But after you think they understand where they are going, you need to turn them loose on their own. You should walk behind them several steps and intervene only when they seem confused or have clearly done something wrong. Remember, after the week that they have with you, they will be entirely on their own. Nobody is going to be walking with them to make sure that they are going in the right direction. You therefore need to perform a kind of balancing act, giving them the help that they need, but also letting them travel largely on their own. Some routes will obviously be easier to learn than others; and most of what you will be doing is simply walking the same routes over and over again until the two of you are sure that your student has it down pat."

They now reentered the Rehab Center, and Woodward taught them a few other things that they would need to know about how a blind person traveled with a cane inside a building, because the volunteers would need to teach them the way into their actual classrooms. After they had been oriented to all the basics of cane travel that they needed to know, they moved from the hallway into a large library-like room across the hall from Woodward's office. They all sat around a large conference table, and Woodward handed out copies of maps of the university campus.

"Between now and Monday morning when all the fun begins, you'll each need to become acquainted with the college campus. Be sure to know your directions: north, south, east, west; because a blind person uses these directions as vital information in traveling about. Learn the layout and names of the streets, and also learn as much as you can about the buildings and sidewalk patterns." Woodward now took them through a brief orientation of the campus area, pointing out the streets and then giving them a quick overview of the Quad, the large main area about which many of the class buildings were located. After this general orientation, he gave each of them the schedule of their own student with another map on which he had drawn what he thought to be the best routes to be taken to their various classes.

Just as they were finishing the entire orientation session, one of the young females asked, "what will be our actual work schedule next week?" "Oh, I forgot to mention that. We'll be starting at 9:00 and working until 4:00. We'll all meet here at the Rehab Center, and the day is pretty much yours in terms of where you think you need to go and do with your student. Doctor Potter and I will be around to give you support and advice if and when you need it. You shouldn't be nervous. We're not here to criticize the job you'll be doing. We'll be here to help you and your student. Lunch will be your own responsibility. You can take your lunchtime with your student whenever you both decide. Unfortunately, the whole university is basically shut down this week and next week too. The week after that will be orientation week for the regular incoming freshmen, and then things will start to be crowded and lively. But right now, about the only place open that serves lunch is the cafeteria in the basement of the Student Union. You'll probably have to eat there. But that's actually a good thing, because there are all sorts of services offered in the Student Union, and you can use the occasion to teach your student how to get there, and what else is there that might be of use to them. One other thing. In case you like to swim, the Olympic-size pool at Franklin Gym will be open between 4 and 5 and available for any of our blind students or you volunteers who are interested in ending the day with a relaxing swim. So, if you are so inclined, bring your swim suit along."

When Dorothy returned home, she sat down at the kitchen table and spread out all the material that Ron Woodward had given her. Her student was going to be Dennis MacDonald. He would be living in a dormitory called Holmes; and his four classes for the fall semester would require him to travel to buildings scattered about, two of them on the Quad, but the other two a good distance away from it. Wow, it was going to be a week of lots of walking. She had better give her corns on her two baby toes a good soaking over the weekend. But it would also be nice to end each day with a refreshing dip in the pool at Franklin Gym. She would certainly bring her swimming bag of necessary things along with her each day. After heating up some left-over macaroni and cheese for her lunch, Dorothy continued to study the maps and designated routes. She wanted to be well prepared for her student, come Monday morning. Tomorrow would be largely taken up with driving up to and back from Homewood to fetch Carol from her mother's, but she should be able to squeeze in more study time on Sunday, after attending church, teaching Sunday school, fixing dinner and cleaning up, and her weekly letter writing.

September 1, 1970, Tuesday

When Dorothy had tried to set out again for the Rehab Center Monday morning shortly before 9:00, the little blue Falcon refused to start. George had already left for the week and had taken the other car, of course. Consequently, Dorothy had been grounded for the day. A mechanic had come over from an auto repair garage to haul the car away and had returned it later in the day.

The problem had been some wiring in the ignition system either shorting or burning out. In any case, she had had to call Ron Woodward at the last minute to tell him that she could not make it that day, and she was so very disappointed for herself and sorry to have let them down.

But today was a new day, and everything would work out well, she hoped. Dorothy was slightly nervous and excited, because she had never done anything quite like this before. She had really been looking forward to this new experience, but she was also a bit worried that she might not do as well as she should. After parking in the parking lot and walking around to the front of the building, she saw that Ron Woodward and Doctor Potter were standing with the blind students, easily identifiable from their white canes. A few of the other volunteers were already there as well. When Dorothy joined the group, Ron Woodward introduced her to a short young man. He was her student, Dennis. As soon as the other volunteers arrived, they all stepped aboard a Rehab bus that then pulled away from the curb to take them to their first destination of the day.

Like most other buses, the Rehab bus could be boarded at either a front or rear door, but each door had a wheelchair lift along with a regular set of steps and hand rail for the able-bodied. The interior of the bus was almost entirely empty to accommodate students in wheelchairs. There were padded benches along the sides and at the rear for those not in wheelchairs, and the group of sixteen sat in these places as the bus moved along. The seven blind students consisted of two females of Japanese descent, two black males, and three Caucasian males, all of them apparently right out of high school. Dennis was one of the three Caucasian males. He seemed to be slightly shorter than Dorothy, just barely over five feet, but he was extremely muscular.

After traveling for only a block down Spurlock, the bus turned onto Walnut Street and halted. They were now on the western side of the Men's Dormitory Area, and Woodward addressed all three of the Caucasian males and one of the blacks, "Ok, Dennis, Bob, Grant, and Larry, we're near or at your dorm. So let's get out, and you and your volunteer can spend some additional time remembering what you learned yesterday and can then work your way over to campus in learning or repeating a route to one of your classes."

The four pairs and Woodward stepped off of the bus and began to move off in two different directions. Two pairs proceeded farther down the sidewalk to the entrance into Forester Hall, while Dorothy, Dennis,

Larry, and his volunteer walked straight ahead into Holmes. Dorothy and Dennis spent the next hour in going over the ground floor of the building: its hallways, entrances, stairways, and lounge area. Virtually all rooms were doubles, but Dennis happened to be assigned to a room that was at the end of a hallway on the first floor, and it accommodated three, not two students. They then found the entry into the cafeteria, and then they went down into the basement and explored a tunnel system that joined three of the dorms and contained a room of vending machines and another with washers and dryers.

By midmorning Dennis seemed fully familiar with everything that he needed to know about Holmes itself. Now their real work began. Dennis again repeated what he had learned the day before: walking out of Holmes' east end and along a wide diagonal sidewalk that eventually took them to a small building containing the Snack Bar and Post Office. They entered the building from the rear; and after quickly reviewing its interior, they went out the front door and onto the sidewalk running along the south side of Jordan Street. They now began walking toward the Quad that was still several blocks away. They advanced in stages with Dorothy explaining the next bit of unfamiliar terrain before letting Dennis move ahead.

Their first main stop was at the Armory, a huge edifice with an indoor running track on the ground level and apparently used (at least at one time) for ROTC or military training drills. Dennis would have his speech class in a classroom on the second floor, which they now located. They next began their slow but steady progress toward the Quad itself. where Dennis would have his algebra class in Arnold Hall. As they were walking along the eastern side of Wagoner Street that formed the western side of the Quad, Dennis suddenly stopped for no apparent reason. When Dorothy caught up with him, he asked, "What is that building over there to the right?" Dorothy was surprised by the question. "How do you know that there is a building over there?" she asked. "I can hear it." Dorothy stood motionless for a few seconds and strained to hear what Dennis was apparently hearing. When she heard nothing except the traffic moving along Wagoner Street to their left, she asked, "What do you mean? I can't hear anything. There's no noise coming from the building." "I know," Dennis replied, "but I still can hear it. It's like sonar. I can hear sound bouncing off of it, or sound shaping itself around it." Dorothy was dumbfounded. "Really," was all that she could manage to say. She then consulted her map of the university and announced that this building was Lincoln Hall.

Shortly before noon they had succeeded in finding their way to Arnold and to Dennis' classroom; and luckily for them, it turned out to be a rather easy walk from there to the Student Union, where they had lunch in its cafeteria in the basement. As they sat and ate, they exchanged bits of personal and family information. They actually wound up having a number of things in common, because Dennis had grown up on the southern edges of Chicago and had been blind since birth. When asked about his well-muscled physique, Dennis laughed quite loudly, which he seemed to do a lot, and explained that he had wrestled during all four years in high school.

In the afternoon they first retraced their steps to Arnold Hall. Then they walked back to the Armory and his classroom there, then back to Holmes, and finally over to the Rehab Center, where Dennis would be going for his PE class. Ironically, the entrance into the Rehab Center posed a slight problem for cane travelers. The building was set back away from the sidewalk, but a roofed porch ran out to the street's edge, so that students could be sheltered from rain and snow while waiting to board a Rehab bus. The problem was with the pillars that supported this roof, because they were rather narrow for about two feet above the ground, and then they broadened out and became much thicker. The blind students had already discovered this oddity, a few having done so at the expense of a bent cane that had been caught beneath the thicker part of a pillar. This had led them to joke that the architect for the building must have had it in for blind people. But the design had actually been intended to give students in wheelchairs slightly more room in which to maneuver.

Dorothy's and Dennis' interaction throughout the day had been filled with good humored kidding of all sorts. Dennis quickly realized that this lady really had a delightful personality. Dorothy in turn had learned that Dennis was very extroverted, had a really friendly and winning way with people, and laughed easily and loudly. They had had a really good time together. In fact, at times during their day together, as she walked behind Dennis, she merrily sang from The Wizard of Oz, "Follow the Yellow Brick Road! Follow the Yellow Brick Road!" Dorothy had wanted to take in the swimming hour at Franklin Gym, but Carol was just beginning seventh grade at her junior high school, and she needed to get back home to help her with things.

September 2, 1970, Wednesday

Dorothy and Dennis spent the entire morning in retracing three of his four routes that they had covered the day before: from the Rehab Center to Holmes, and then from Holmes to the Armory, and finally to Arnold Hall. After another lunch in the Student Union cafeteria and some mobility instruction there, they were ready to take on the challenge of finding their way to Dennis' German classroom in Morton Lab. It had been easy enough to teach Dennis his way to these first three places, because they could be approached and entered along regular sidewalks that ran along the streets. But in order to go to his German class, Dennis needed to know how to travel across to the other side of the Quad, which was crisscrossed with a complex network of sidewalks. It took quite a bit of explaining on Dorothy's part, but by now she had learned that Dennis was an exceptionally fine traveler with his cane and picked up things very quickly. Thus, by the end of their second day they had succeeded in introducing Dennis to all four of the routes that he needed for his classes. They both felt rather jubilant, because they now had two more days in which they could go over the routes again and again and could also work on learning their way to other useful places, such as the library. Like yesterday, Dorothy reluctantly had to skip the swim hour at Franklin Gym, because she had to get back home to be there with Carol.

September 3, 1970, Thursday

Dorothy and Dennis again spent the morning in walking through all four routes to his classes. All went well until they set off across the Quad to Morton Lab. As Dennis approached the large paved area between Morton Lab and the Chemistry Building, Dorothy suddenly realized that Dennis was heading toward a large post that stood in the middle of an area formed by the intersection of several main sidewalks. It was a steel reinforced concrete vertical shaft, octagonal in shape and about ten inches thick, surmounted by a light to provide illumination at night. Dorothy had not thought to show this obstacle to Dennis, but now he seemed to be drawn to it like iron to a magnet. Dorothy was so taken by surprise that for a few seconds she was torn with indecision as to what to do, and those seconds were just long enough to cause disaster.

Since Dennis assumed that he was traveling along a completely open sidewalk, his guard was somewhat down, and he was also moving along quite briskly. As a result, his cane did not give him quite enough warning. As soon as its nylon tip struck the base of the concrete shaft, Dennis began to react, but his momentum was too much for him to stop completely in time. He therefore slammed into the shaft with considerable force, and the impact opened up a deep gash on his forehead. As Dennis cried out in surprise and pain, Dorothy's heart sank. She rushed up to Dennis and apologized effusively while examining the gash on his head. It was quite gruesome looking: swollen, cut, and bleeding. But after the worst of the pain had subsided, Dennis insisted that it was all right. He didn't need to go to the infirmary for stitches or medication. The cut would soon stop bleeding on its own, and it would heal itself up over the next week or so. Dorothy was somewhat surprised by his nonchalance, but Dennis patiently explained that he and other blind people were more or less accustomed to such bang-ups. Despite his reassurances, Dorothy felt tremendous guilt and realized that she would henceforth have to be far more observant in describing the landscape to her blind student.

While they were eating lunch in the Student Union, Ron Woodward approached and explained that there was going to be a reshuffling of volunteers for the afternoon. Grant's volunteer had to take some placement tests, and so Dorothy would work with him while Ron took charge of Dennis. As he spoke, Dorothy could see him eyeing Dennis' head wound; and when he finished his explanation of the changes for the afternoon, he asked, "how'd you get that bump on your noggin?" "Oh," Dennis replied with a dismissive laugh, "I had a disagreement with a post." "Looks like the post won the argument." "Ah man, you know how it goes." To Dorothy's relief Ron simply chuckled, patted Dennis on the shoulder, and walked off to let them finish their lunch.

Grant Duncan, Dorothy's blind student for the afternoon, must have been about six feet tall, had flaming bright red hair, and was also quite muscular, but not nearly as much as Dennis. As it turned out, he had also wrestled in high school. Also like Dennis, he seemed to be a very good cane traveler and usually required only one explanation to pick things up. He and his regular volunteer had already taken care of the routes to his classes for calculus and German, and they had been working on the final two, rhetoric and anthropology, when Dorothy took over. Both these classes were going to meet on the eastern side of the Quad, one in Morton Lab and the other a bit farther south in Davidson Hall. Thus, Dorothy and Grant spent the afternoon working on the complex maze of sidewalks that went from the western to the eastern side of the Quad. But Dorothy was careful to show Grant the concrete post that Dennis had so dramatically discovered on his own that morning. She had learned her lesson and was going to make sure that the mistake didn't happen again.

As they sat down to rest briefly on one of the stone benches that flanked the entry into an open courtyard between Morton Lab and the Chemistry Building, Dorothy exclaimed, "Oh my, my dogs are sure barkin'!" "What's that mean?" Grant asked. "You've never heard that expression before?" "No, afraid not." "It means that my feet are very tired and are letting me know it," Dorothy explain. Grant smiled in response. As they took a break from the constant walking and standing on concrete, they chatted about themselves and their families. Grant was about to turn eighteen and had lost his vision during the sixth grade from a detached retina. He came from a small town called Fairmont, located on the opposite side of the Illinois River from Peoria in central Illinois. Dorothy remembered being in that area briefly three years ago to look at carpets for their new house.

When Grant indicated that his major was going to be physics, and that he hoped to become employed someday by NASA, because celestial mechanics was his main interest, Dorothy was pleasantly surprised and responded by mentioning that her brother Timothy, who happened to be quite a bit younger than her, had been working off and on recently for NASA. His main job was to maintain the TV monitors used by the medical center of the University of Illinois in Chicago, but since they were the same as the ones employed by NASA in Mission Control in Houston for the Apollo space flights, he had been hired as an independent contractor to come there periodically to keep their system fully functional. This greatly impressed Grant. During his last three years in high school he had been utterly fascinated with all the Apollo missions. He and two other friends had spent much of their time in making small rockets propelled by solid fuel engines, and Grant had a full collection of plastic models of the U.S. rockets, including a gigantic one of the Saturn 5A that sent the Apollo Command, Service, and Lunar Modules on their way to the moon. Since taking physics during his junior year, he had been teaching himself calculus and astronomy.

By the time that their afternoon of mobility instruction had ended, Grant seemed to know and understand the pattern of sidewalks that dominated the central area of the Quad. For today and tomorrow Dorothy had arranged that Carol stay at Pam Gibson's house, so that she could be looked after by Vivian until Dorothy came home. She was therefore free to go swimming at Franklin Gym, and by now she was looking forward to a relaxing swim. Grant, however, did not have a swimming suit, and so he returned to his dorm room while Dorothy joined Dennis and four others in the pool: Faith Martin and one other female volunteer and the two blind females of Japanese descent. Dorothy leisurely swam laps and stopped to chat with the other five in the pool, especially the two blind girls whom she had thus far not had a chance to meet. Both were also from Chicago, and both seemed to be very pleasant and intelligent. Their names were Debbie Ito and Nisa Shoto. Debbie was totally blind, but Nisa had a little bit of sight. As it turned out, Nisa was actually not a freshman, but a junior. She had already completed two years of college work in Chicago and was now transferring to the University here. She would therefore be a the university for no more than two years.

September 4, 1970, Friday

Dorothy's week of volunteer mobility work was now over, and she was enjoying her last hour on campus by swimming in the pool at Franklin Gym. It had been such a stupendous week. Today there had been another reshuffling of volunteers, and Dorothy had spent the morning with the other Caucasian male blind student. She had therefore come to know, at least to some degree, three of the seven new freshman students. He was Bob Snider. Like Dennis, he had been blind since birth. His family lived in Aurora, a sizable community not too far from Chicago. He was very polite but also seemed to possess a great sense of humor that Dorothy found endearing.

As she leisurely swam her lengths of the pool, her mind was full of so many things. She had been serving as a volunteer reader for a few blind students over the past few years, but this week of activity had really drawn her much further into things. She had covered so much of the campus on foot, gone into many of its buildings, and had become so impressed with the students with whom she had worked. They all seemed so well adjusted, very intelligent, and highly motivated young people, full of energy and ready to take on college life and the world with such youthful enthusiasm. Their zest for life was infectious and resonated with her own inner youthful spirit. In addition, her loving and caring nature caused her to worry a bit about these kids. They would certainly soon be encountering various problems, both big and small; and were there other things that she could do to help them?

It seemed as if a new door had been pushed slightly open along her path of life. Should she walk on past, or should she open the door and step through?

As their hour of swimming was coming to an end, Dorothy swam over to Dennis. She simply could not bring herself to tell him goodbye. How could she simply walk away from all this and pick up her life where she had left it a week ago? So, after telling Dennis how much fun she had had this week in working with him and the other two blind students, she asked, "How can I tell you goodbye and never know how well my mobility instruction has helped you?" To this question that tinged Dorothy with both worry and sadness, Dennis' boisterous nature prompted him to respond smoothly: "That's easy, Mrs. Patterson! Have us all over to your house for a party!" "That sounds like a great idea," Dorothy replied, "we'll do that." She then recited her telephone number to Dennis for him to memorize, and she said that he should call her Sunday afternoon for the details, but since this coming Monday would be Labor Day holiday, why didn't they plan to have their party sometime that day? They parted company with this agreement firmly in place, and Dorothy was genuinely pleased and thrilled with the prospect of inviting these seven blind students into her home.

September 7, 1970, Monday

It was 12:45 P.M. and time for George and her to leave in both cars to pick up the blind students. Dennis had spread the word about the party, and all seven were excited to come. In fact, they were going to be joined by an eighth person, Tom Foster, who was somewhat visually impaired but had good enough vision that he had not needed to have a volunteer mobility instructor like the rest. He had been able to learn the campus on his own. Also, one of the female mobility volunteers, Faith Martin, who had been swimming at Franklin Gym last week, had expressed interest in coming and had offered to help Dorothy in organizing the party.

Dorothy had spent much of her weekend in cleaning the house and putting everything in order, as well as shopping for things at the grocery store: paper plates, cups, hamburger, hot dogs, buns, potato chips, and the like. Plus, she had made two large trays of Jell-O and a huge bowl of banana pudding. They would be cooking the burgers and weenies outside on a charcoal grill, but it was going to be too hot for them to sit out in the yard to eat. They would therefore sit indoors and be comfortable in the new house's air conditioning.

Of course, ever since they had been living in University City, Dorothy's home had always been open to the occasional foreign exchange student for whom the Pattersons served as host family; and Dorothy had brought Julie Nelson, to whom she had been reading, over to the house several times to relax and enjoy herself. But today was going to be something entirely different: a cross between a formal potluck dinner and evening for Sweet Adelines couples and a party staged for Wesley or Carol.

As usual, George was perfectly happy to go along with whatever his wife had devised to form part of their social life. He had never been very good at making friends, and virtually no one else was in Dorothy's league in that particular department. He therefore usually followed the line of least resistance and let her take the lead in such matters; and things almost always turned out well and were interesting. There were far worse ways of filling one's free time, sitting mindlessly in front of the boob tube being one.

George drove the newer and more capacious Ford LTD to pick up six of the students who lived close together in the Men's Dormitory Area: Dennis, Grant, Bob, Tom Foster, Larry Barton, and Moses Truman. Since he had never met them before, he stepped out of the car, introduced himself, and received introductions from them in turn. In the meantime Dorothy drove the blue Falcon to pick up the other three: Debbie Ito at Miller, and then all the way over to Nash Hall to pick up Nisa and Faith.

When the two cars arrived at the house, Dorothy began to organize a group mobility session by describing how they were going to move from the driveway to the back porch and into the family room. As they entered the house, Dorothy introduced them all to her younger daughter Carol, who was now thirteen and had just started seventh grade.

As they all stood huddled together in the family room near the back door, the two dogs cautiously approached and began to sniff Grant's and Dennis' legs. "Hey, you have a dog!" Grant and Dennis exclaimed simultaneously. "No," Dorothy replied, "We have two." "What kind," Grant asked. "Both German shepherds, one named Fraulein or Frau, and the other named Gretchen." While she was still speaking, Grant and Dennis had both dropped to their knees and were petting and stroking the two dogs and talking to them. "Good German names for German Shepherds," Dennis commented. "Yep," Dorothy responded with pleasure, "and my maiden name is Klingner, and my two Klingner grandparents immigrated to this country from Germany."

Dorothy again gave the group a brief mobility lesson by explaining the basic layout of the family room, adjoining kitchen, and dining and living rooms, where she planned for them to be during their stay here. She ended her verbal tour of the rooms with the exhortation that they all make themselves comfortable. It was interesting to watch them slowly moving about the family room and kitchen, cautiously using their hands to examine everything they encountered. A few sat down on the couch and stuffed chairs in the family room, while the others continued to move about.

George had already gone outside to tend the grill. Dorothy and Faith began to set things out on the kitchen and dining tables. Carol, of course, was at hand and eager to help her mother. Nisa asked to be shown the piano; and when Dorothy guided her to it in the living room, she sat down on the bench and began to play. She was actually quite good, better than Dorothy and any of her kids, who had been taking piano lessons for many years. Consequently, while the other students accommodated themselves to this unfamiliar house, and while things were being made ready for their meal, the house resounded with pleasant piano music.

As the hot dogs and burgers started coming in from outside, Dorothy sat the students at the kitchen and dining tables and had them begin to eat. Pretty soon everyone was more or less seated and eating. Since the students had by now spent an entire week with one another, they knew each other fairly well, and the kitchen and dining rooms were filled with their good natured joshing of one another. When Dorothy asked Dennis how his head was feeling from the collision with the concrete post, he blithely replied, "Oh it's doing fine." Larry then added, "It probably knocked some sense into his silly ass. Pardon my French." Several, including Dennis, laughed. It was clear that the incident had already become the first of what would be many humorous stories shared by this group.

Dorothy could hardly believe how fast the food disappeared, and she began to worry that they might not have enough, but they did. The students accompanied their eating with continuous praise of how good everything tasted. Dorothy had never received so much praise in so short a time, and it made all her work to prepare everything totally worthwhile. But the real shower of praise came when the students began to take their first bites of the banana pudding dessert. Dennis and Larry virtually howled with delight.

After they had all eaten and things were cleared away, they all began to relax and talk. Dorothy moved about and visited with each of them, jotting down their telephone numbers on a notepad along with their birthdays, and urging each one to be sure to call her if she could ever help them run errands or other things.

Dennis had brought along his guitar but had left it in the car. Carol now fetched it for him, and Dennis sat on the living room couch and began to chord and sing songs. Others, including Dorothy, joined in, whenever they knew the words. It was settling down to be a really enjoyable afternoon with these kids.

When Dennis seemed to run out of songs, Grant asked him for the guitar, and then he began to play. Dennis' playing had been fine, but Grant's was on an entirely different level. He started off by playing several instrumentals in which his right thumb picked out a rhythmic bass line of quarter notes while his index and other fingers played the melody. It sounded so very nice. When he started in on one song (it turned out to be entitled Nine Pound Hammer), the rhythm and melody were so neat that Larry began to clap in time to the music and exclaimed, "Now that boy's gittin down!"

Dorothy was now surprised to notice that Wesley had cautiously joined the group. During the past year he and his father had had one fight after another, and Wesley had become increasingly withdrawn. Thus far today while the students had been here, he had stayed in his room and had avoided everyone. But Grant's guitar music had fascinated him, and he stood next to the piano near the hallway and closely watched Grant's fingers. After Dorothy introduced Wesley to everyone, he began to ask Grant questions about his playing. He then fetched his own guitar, and the two began to try to find common songs to play together. Grant eventually asked to see Wesley's guitar, because its sound was rather different from what he was accustomed to. It was because of its nylon strings, which were much easier on the fingers and allowed someone to play and practice much longer than with steel or bronze strings. When Wesley finally absented himself and went back to his room, Grant continued to play Wesley's guitar and was now sufficiently uninhibited to sing. He therefore led them in a long series of songs. Dorothy knew the words to most of them and thoroughly enjoyed singing along.

When the music finally came to an end, the easy socializing resumed; and Dorothy was able to learn more about several of them. She was thoroughly in her own element: putting everyone at ease with her incomparable grace and charm, and contributing much to the relaxed atmosphere by her lovely singing. Tom Foster and a few others were now in the family room and had the TV going. Bob Snider was plunking out simple melodies on the piano, and Dorothy had her Camelot album playing on the phonograph in the dining room. Everyone was doing something and seemed to be having a grand old time at it.

Amid these varied activities Grant slowly moved his way down the long hallway from which Wesley had emerged some time before; and eventually he found Wesley's room. He was stretched out on his bed reading. As Grant knelt in the doorway, the two of them carried on a conversation about music. Grant's family, both mother's and father's sides, came from Kentucky, coal mining country and the home of so much that had shaped country music. In fact, the area was the home of Merle Travis, who had pioneered the finger style of guitar playing that Chet Atkins had perfected and made famous, and which Grant loved so much and tried to imitate; and Grant's mother (who was herself quite a good guitar player) had actually known the two men who had influenced Merle Travis the most, but who had never become famous for their playing. Wesley, on the other hand, had encountered variations of finger style through its use by the contemporary folk musicians of the counter culture.

When it came to be the middle of the evening, Dorothy popped corn to serve as an easy supper for all to eat. The merriment continued on for a few more hours till bedtime. They then piled themselves back into the two cars, and Dorothy and George dropped them off and came home. The students had obviously thoroughly enjoyed themselves. Dorothy had too.

September 20, 1970, Sunday

Since the party on Labor Day Dorothy had had no direct dealings with the blind students. All the kids had been busy getting themselves ready for their first semester of college. But this afternoon their church was going to have a hiking event at Lincoln Park, a very large area with trails and grounds for picnicking. Dorothy had therefore called the seven students to invite them to come, but only four of them were willing to get away from their studies: Dennis, Bob, Grant, and Nisa.

One reason why Dorothy had wanted to organize this event today was that it would soon be Dennis' seventeenth birthday, and she wanted to surprise him with a little party. Accordingly, instead of driving out directly to Lincoln Park, they came to the lovely big house at 1801 Rachel Drive, and the students were treated to pieces of a sheet cake that Dorothy had just made. The four were pleasantly surprised; and even though the cake was nothing really special, the students made Dorothy feel as if she had served up something truly elegant and wonderful. Dennis was genuinely touched when they all sang Happy Birthday, and Dorothy presented him with a simple but clearly heart-felt birthday gift of oranges and All liquid detergent for washing his clothes.

They then got back into the Pattersons' two cars, joined by Carol and Wesley and a friend each. When they arrived at Lincoln Park, they joined the Pattersons' church group and went for a brisk hike and then simply lounged around talking. The four blind students had just completed their very first week of college classes and had fun in sharing their first impressions and experiences. Dorothy was delighted to be included within their circle. Her repayment for organizing and orchestrating this event was simply her pleasure in seeing the four students enjoying themselves on this sunny autumnal afternoon.

September 26, 1970, Saturday

Dorothy had been spending much of her day in doing several loads of laundry, folding up the clothes, and putting them away. She now glanced out the laundry room window for the umpteenth time that afternoon, and this time she saw a car coming around the house to the garage along their curving driveway. Dennis and his parents had finally arrived.

Tom and Helen MacDonald had driven down to University City earlier in the day to visit Dennis and to attend a banquet at the Rehabilitation Center that evening. This banquet was held every autumn, shortly after classes started up, to greet new incoming disabled students and their parents, to invite alumni back to campus, and to honor both disabled students and staff with awards for their exceptional achievements and service. Along with prepared speeches and the announcements of these awards, there was always a kind of talent show in which students were encouraged to perform, thereby providing both entertainment for everyone and displaying their talents. Dennis would be playing the guitar and singing tonight at this banquet that he and his parents would be attending together.

After Dennis' parents had decided to come to the banquet, Dennis had called Dorothy to see if they could come over to her house, so that Dennis' parents could meet this wonderful woman, who had been so helpful to him and the other blind students.

The two dogs were now barking and standing at the back door in the family room. Dorothy stepped between them and opened the door as Dennis and his parents stepped up onto the porch. "Hello," Dorothy said in her most pleasant voice, "I'm Dorothy Patterson." As she spoke these words of greeting, she held out her hand to shake those of Dennis' parents and accompanied her words and gesture with her radiant smile. "My name is Helen," replied Dennis' mother." "And I'm Tom," said Dennis' father.

As the trio stepped into the family room, Dennis knelt down on the floor while exclaiming in his usual boisterous manner, "Hey, you dogs, how are you doing!" Both animals came to Dennis and received his enthusiastic pats, petting, and silly dog talk while the other three looked on with amused expressions. George and Carol now entered the kitchen, and further introductions were made. They all then went into the living room and sat down in chairs and on the couch to begin their formal visit.

Dennis' parents began by saying how much Dennis had already told them about Dorothy and her family, and they were so pleased and grateful that she had been willing and able to help their son so very much. After Dorothy received their thanks with a smiling laugh and some self-deprecating words, the two couples began exchanging information about themselves. As soon as Tom and George learned of one another's occupations (Ken being a carpenter and George a building engineer), the two men spiraled off into their own conversation of shop talk, while the two mothers talked about their families and children, including humorously critical remarks about Dennis, to which he responded with either peals of laughter or with protests of mock outrage. The formal visit ended after about a half an hour with Dorothy genuinely pleased to have met Dennis' parents and vice versa.

Now that classes were fully underway, Dorothy received a telephone call from Julie Nelson, for whom she had been reading for the past two years; and they agreed upon a time when they could meet once a week. A few days later, however, Debbie Ito, one of the new blind students also called to see if Dorothy could serve as one of her regular volunteer readers as well. Despite her already full schedule of things and a household to look after, Dorothy nevertheless agreed without hesitation. She certainly could not abandon Julie. Besides, this was going to be her last semester anyway; and after all, she had also urged all the new blind students not to hesitate to call upon her if she could be of help. She therefore decided, she could and should read to both of them every week for the fall semester.

Dorothy thus began to make weekly visits to Debbie in her dorm room in Miller; and she read whatever Debbie needed to have read except for her calculus. Higher mathematics had never been Dorothy's strong suit. But they always had both a good and productive time, and the two quickly became well acquainted with one another. They preceded and ended each reading session with informative chitchat; and since they shared a good sense of humor, they enjoyed interspersing their serious reading with puns and other humorous interjections. Sometimes Debbie's roommate, Kathy Grant, who was a very nice and pleasant young lady, happened to be in the room, but she did not mind at all having the two there, and vice versa. On the contrary, all three enjoyed being in the same dorm room with Dorothy's reading being the centerpiece for a few hours. It was a striking testimony to Dorothy's grace and charm.

Given her seemingly boundless generosity, Dorothy's weekly reading sessions with Debbie soon came to include occasional short shopping trips for various necessities. When Nisa also called one day to see if Dorothy could take her shopping too, Dorothy gladly agreed, and soon these two women had also developed a solid friendship based upon mutual admiration and respect for one another's intelligence, charm, and goodness. Consequently, Dorothy was beginning to create her own niche in the university environment through her association with these blind students; and she found her involvement in their lives to be emotionally rewarding, intellectually fulfilling, and offering her a much needed and salutary escape out of her conventional, rather troubled and unhappy life as wife and mother.

From talking with all the new blind students Dorothy had learned that none of their parents knew braille. Her immediate reaction to this was "well, how then does your mom or dad leave you a written message or note?" The answer was "They didn't." This really surprised her. She was sure that if she had a blind child, she would learn braille, so that they could leave notes or messages to each other. When Dorothy began to express curiosity about braille during her reading sessions with Debbie, the latter began to show her some basics about it.

Throughout their lives blind people occasionally encounter sighted individuals who are curious about braille, and who after being shown a few basic things, such as the alphabet, tinker with it for a week or so and then abandon it altogether. When it became clear to Debbie that Dorothy's interest went beyond idle curiosity, she began to show Dorothy more and more things; and soon Nisa was teaching her things as well. As a result, during the fall and spring semesters of this academic year Dorothy devoted a considerable amount of time and effort to learning this complex writing system; and Debbie and Nisa served as her teachers.

October 8, 1970, Thursday

Grant was stretched out on his bed in his dorm room on the first floor of Forester. It had been a long day of classes, and now he was just resting and waiting for the dining hall to open up. Then after being joined by Bob Snider, whose room was at the other end of the hall, the two of them would walk over to Holmes to pick up Larry and Dennis, and the four would eat supper together at their usual table.

Grant's rest, however, was interrupted by the telephone ringing on the edge of his desk near his feet at the end of the bed. He sat up quickly and grabbed the receiver. "Hello," "Hello, Grant?" the voice on the other end of the line questioned. "Yeah," he replied. "This is Dorothy Patterson. I'm calling about your trip back home to visit your family. You mentioned it to me a few weeks ago when we were at Lincoln Park. When did you say you'd be going home?" "This coming weekend." "Oh good, that's what I was hoping, because I'm going to be attending a Barbershop contest this Sunday with George and a few other fellas in Peoria, and I thought that we could maybe save your parents a trip to and from University City if we could pick you up Sunday and bring you back with us." "Yeah, that would really be nice, and I'm sure my parents would really appreciate that." "Ok, give me your home telephone number, and we'll give you a call from the Holiday Inn probably around 7:00 or so Sunday evening, and we can then figure out where to meet to bring you back with us." "That sounds really neat. I'll be looking forward to that."

October 11, 1970, Sunday

Grant had had a really nice visit home this weekend. He had not been here since early Monday morning August 31 when his parents had driven him to University City to begin his week of mobility instruction; and he would not be coming back again until Thanksgiving break.

Last night his parents had had friends over to the house for an evening and late night of card playing. While they sat around the kitchen table playing and talking, Grant had been listening to records on his mother's cabinet stereo. He had just bought an Arlo Guthrie album called *Alice's Restaurant*, and he had played it several times. Since his brief encounter with Wesley Patterson a month ago, Grant had purchased two Arlo Guthrie albums and had learned a few of the songs on them. He had also bought a set of nylon strings like those on Wesley's guitar, because even though the sound was not quite as resonant as that produced by steel or bronze strings, they were so much gentler to the fingers and allowed him to play and practice for a much longer time.

Like Dennis' parents, Grant's mom and dad were both happy to learn that he had been befriended by Dorothy. It was nice to know that their son could call upon a responsible and caring adult if he needed to. When the telephone call finally came, Grant's mother answered it, and Dorothy was on the other end. After exchanging greetings, Grant's mom thanked Dorothy for this really nice act of kindness; and as usual, Dorothy dismissed it laughingly as the most natural and normal thing in the world. They then handed the telephone receivers to their husbands and let them figure out where they should rendezvous. They eventually decided upon an easy-to-find gas station in East Peoria that would be on the Patterson's route back to University City.

The Duncans arrived first; and when the Pattersons drove up, all got out of the cars and spent a few minutes in greeting and chitchat. Grant had just two things to take back with him: a large duffel bag stuffed full with all sorts of things, and his guitar. George dropped the duffel bag in the trunk, and Grant kept the guitar to hold in the car. After saying their farewells, everyone got back into the two cars and went their own ways.

George and Dorothy had driven up to Peoria with two other Barbershoppers. These two men sat in the back seat while George in the driver's seat, Grant in front next to the passenger door, and Dorothy sitting between them. They spent virtually the entire time of the trip in singing songs that Grant chorded on his guitar.

Grant had a really nice electrical guitar at home that his parents had bought him several years ago, but once he began playing finger style, he preferred to play an acoustical guitar. About two years ago he had bought a very basic hollow body guitar from a friend for $25. It sounded good enough and was so inexpensive an instrument that Grant used it all the time for most of his playing, because it could be carried around without a case and without fear of doing it any real damage. If it were to be broken beyond repair, so what! It wasn't worth much money-wise anyway. The neck had already fallen off once before, and Grant and a friend had put it back on by drilling a big hole and bolting the neck back into place with an enormous screw and bolt. Also, in order to make the strings resound somewhat better, Grant had small pieces of aluminum foil underneath the strings at the bridge. In short, the instrument was certainly nothing at all to look at, and Grant even reveled in its simplicity and rather junky appearance. That night, However, in the darkness of the car all that mattered was the pleasant sounds that came forth from that instrument; and it was accompanied consistently not only by Grant's voice, but Dorothy's most lovely voice as well.

Journal Entry
Resumed from August 21

Oct. 19, 1970 (Monday): Have wanted to write many times lately, but I keep running out of time. There is so much that I want to put down on paper. After Wesley's birthday one evening he brought Reverend Perkins over to talk to us about leaving home. Guess he feels like he can't grow up at home. We set too many rules and regulations. I wish I had written this down sooner. I could have remembered more things in detail. He asked the minister to come along and to help us all hold our tempers. We usually end up yelling at each other. After several hours of talk he decided he'd stay home a while anyway. I think his friend Kurt was influencing him. About this same time I spent a five-day week helping the new blind university students find their ways to their classrooms and around the university. Wow! What a workout! Walk, walk, walk, and then more walking. I worked with Dennis MacDonald two days, Bob Snider and Grant Duncan each one day. Monday I didn't go because my car was in the garage being worked on. On Thursday and Friday I also got to go swimming in Franklin Gym with the kids. Really had fun then. So, on Friday at 5 P.M. when I had to tell the kids all goodbye, I felt very sad. We had talked (mostly Dennis) about having a party at my house sometime. As I left, Dennis said we should have a cookout, and I said ok. So on Labor Day we took two cars over to get the kids plus one of the volunteers that I had gotten to know. She is a grad student, also at the university. There were eight kids plus Faith Martin: Nisa Shoto, Debbie Ito, Dennis, Bob, Grant, Moses Truman, Larry Barton, and Tom somebody [Foster], who has a little sight. He wasn't in our group but got included in the fun, because he knew the kids and was with them when we discussed the fun. Cooked hamburgers outside but ate inside, because it was so hot. We listened to records, TV. Dennis brought his guitar. Nisa and Bob both played the piano. Took them home about 10:30 P.M. They ate like it was going out of style. At the end of September our church had a hike and a picnic at Lincoln Park. Took Dennis, Bob, Grant, Nisa along. None of the others could go. Carol brought her new friend Sarah Dunaway, and Wesley brought a friend (Marilyn) along. We stopped at home for a small surprise birthday party (17 years old) for Dennis. Gave him box with a half-cup measurer and bottle of All and 14 oranges. Several weeks ago Dennis' folks were here for the weekend, and he brought them over to meet us. Last weekend we picked Grant up in Peoria as we came through and brought him back to campus and met his folks.

Late October 1970

It was about 7:00 P.M., and Grant was alone in his dorm room. His roommate Rick Willis was off somewhere. Grant was seated at his desk listening to a reel of tape on his reel-to-reel tape recorder. It was one of the books for his anthropology course. When someone unexpectedly knocked on his door, he stopped the machine, walked over to the door, opened it, and simply said, "Yeah?"

"Hi, Grant. It's Dorothy Patterson. Carol and I came over to wish you a happy birthday and to give you a few little treats." Grant was totally surprised. He stepped back from the doorway and invited them in. Carol walked over and sat down in his chair at the desk while Dorothy and Grant sat side by side on the edge of his bed. Carol remained silent throughout their brief visit. Paper rustled and plastic crackled as Dorothy removed several items from a bag and placed them in Grant's lap. It was an assortment of cookies and a bag of marshmallows. Dorothy described the items as she laid them out.

Grant was almost speechless with astonishment. He felt like such an utter fool in not knowing what to say, but he did his best to stammer out his thanks and appreciation for their thoughtfulness. "Well," Dorothy said, "we didn't plan to take up much of your time and keep you away from your studies. We just wanted to stop by to let you know that we were thinking of you." Grant repeated his thanks as best he could in his surprised state of mind. Then Dorothy and Carol were up on their feet and moving back out into the hall.

The visit had lasted just a few minutes, and Grant hoped that he had been sufficiently gracious and polite. He always felt like such an uncouth oaf about such things. He was truly awestruck by this gratuitous act of hit-and-run kindness. How extraordinary it was for this woman, married with three kids of her own, to trouble herself at all with the birthday of someone whom she hardly knew. This sort of sweet solicitude, concern, and generosity was encountered so very rarely, but as Grant and the other blind students were now beginning to learn, it was so typical and characteristic of this amazing woman.

November 3, 1970, Tuesday

As Dorothy came driving up Walnut Street, she saw all three of them, Bob, Grant, and Larry, standing near the street at the western entrance into Forester Hall. She slowed down and had the car come to a full stop right beside them. She then leaned across the front seat and shouted out the window, "Hey, you guys, are you waiting for a taxi?" "Yeah!" they all shouted laughingly in unison. "Well, get in, and let's go!" Dorothy continued north on Walnut Street for more than a mile until they finally reached their destination, an electronics supply store. Bob had called yesterday afternoon to see if she could take him there, because he needed various things; and when he had mentioned it to Dennis, Larry, and Grant at the supper table, the latter two had decided to come along too.

After parking the car in front of the store, Dorothy shepherded her three blind guys into the store and up to the counter. Luckily on this Tuesday afternoon business was non-existent, and they were the only customers there. A woman about Dorothy's age stood behind the counter. It turned out that she and her husband owned and operated the store. What now ensued was not your regular retail transaction. It began as one, but it soon developed into a kind of sidewalk carnival that decided to wander inside and belly up to the counter.

Bob went first, soberly informing the owner what all he needed: various batteries, cassettes, and patch cords. As he was placing his order, Grant and Larry started their exchange of wise cracks with Dorothy adopting the role of amused referee and sometimes joking participant. By the time that Bob's needs had been met, and it was someone else's turn to make his requests, the lady behind the counter had also been drawn into their circle of fun. She abandoned her formal impersonal demeanor and began interacting much more naturally with this older lady and her three blind charges. The relaxed and friendly atmosphere, which Dorothy's presence did much to create, actually stimulated more commerce across the counter, as the three students were emboldened to ask about more products, and the store owner was eager to serve them. The end result was a smashing success for all concerned: the owner had just sold quite a quantity of assorted items, and the three young men departed stocked up with about everything that they would need for quite some time. Once again Dorothy Patterson had been the orchestrator of a deed both wonderful and beneficial to everyone involved, including Dorothy herself, who derived immense satisfaction from it all. Shopping expeditions like this quickly taught the blind students that shopping with Dorothy was not only practical and enjoyable for the obvious reasons, but was also extremely advantageous, because she possessed such perfect diplomatic skills that she always seemed to know instinctively what to say or how to act in order to break the ice with even the most frigid persons and to induce them to treat her blind companions with the same dignity accorded sighted customers.

By the beginning of October Dennis had met Kitty Carpenter, and the two were soon inseparable. She came from Ohio and was in her junior year at the university. She was attending college from out of state, because she was confined to a wheelchair, and the university was about the most wheelchair-accessible campus in the country at the time.

During her childhood Kitty had suffered from rheumatoid arthritis, and the disease had severely affected her joints and had also stunted her growth. She was quite diminutive and petite: only about four feet ten inches tall and weighing 80 pounds. Dennis could easily lift her in and out of her wheelchair and took great pleasure in doing so. It gave him the perfect reason for having his hands on her body. She had long, flowing, blond hair, a very pleasant voice, a cheerful and witty disposition, and was quite intelligent with a broad knowledge of English and American literature.

Since her dorm room was in Nash Hall, situated several blocks east of the Men's Dormitory Area on Jordan Street, she and Dennis were constantly going back and forth between Holmes and Nash. Luckily for Kitty, Dennis was a superb traveler and had rather little difficulty in pushing her wheelchair safely along the sidewalk. Kitty, of course, served as navigator, informing Dennis of upcoming curbs, telephone poles, and other obstacles. As a result of them constantly being together, Kitty became a member of the freshman group of blind students whom Dorothy was now regularly assisting in various ways.

Despite his athleticism and virtuosity as a traveler, Dennis was always somewhat backward when it came to mundane things such as fixing food or looking after his clothes. Even though Forester, Holmes, and Garfield Halls had a laundry room of washers and dryers in their shared basement for students to use, Dennis still balked at the whole business of having to do his own laundry. When Dorothy heard him grumbling about this, she offered to become his laundry service by picking up his bag of dirty clothes, taking them back to her house, washing, drying, and folding them, and then returning them to Holmes. After a few weeks Dorothy went a step further in inviting Dennis to come on over to the house and relax there while she did his laundry; and since Kitty was often with him, Kitty came along too. Her wheelchair folded up and was easily loaded into the trunk of the car. As a result, by the middle of the fall semester Dennis and Kitty were paying regular afternoon visits to Dorothy's house.

Journal Entries
Resumed from October 19

Dec. 29, 1970 (Tuesday): Almost the end of another year, another Christmas past. Grandma Patterson came here for Christmas. She's done pretty good, all things considered. Grandpa died just before Halloween. They moved into their new house in town [in Newton] on Friday; and he went to the hospital on Sunday and died on Tuesday. George was there in Newton on Friday, Saturday, and Sunday. He came home, and then he went back on Monday. Ellen and David Patterson flew to University City and went to Newton with me and the kids. They drove back to Columbia [South Carolina] in grandpa's car. Mom P gave it to them. In November, the night before our Sweet Adelines show, Wesley left home. The last straw was when George made some threat, "You get your hair cut, or else I'll..." Then Wesley went over to the school. He was working the lights for the Sweet Adelines show and then called later to tell me that he wasn't coming home. For about a month he was with some kids on campus, but then he moved in with Mr. Carlson, a science teacher at the High school. Guess he's having a ball. He comes home now and then, very friendly. Goes to church with us sometimes and even sits with us. We all went to church together on Christmas Eve, then drove to Candlestick Lane to look at the decorations and lights. Just beautiful! Wesley stayed overnight and spent all day Christmas here. He is truly a young radical, has all kinds of extreme ideas on pollution, war, life in general, etc. He is having growing pains. To a remark of Carol's he said, "If there is a world, then...!" So pessimistic. Enough said. [long list of Christmas presents that members of the family gave and received] George didn't have anything to do with Christmas this year.... I got a can opener from Sally, earrings and pin from Carol, bath brush, soap, and cologne from Jim

Junior [Lawson, Ginger and Jim's oldest son] (he had my name [in family gift exchange]), Light for above sink from Grandma P, money from Gram K, beautiful silver chip dish with blue color in center dish from Debbie Ito, and a lovely card and headscarf from Nisa Shoto, both blind girls at the university, and gloves and a lovely blue pants suit from George. Just before Christmas my mom came to University City. Sally and I went to get her to visit and to have me make her a pants suit top to go with some blue slacks she had. Bethany and I picked out some blue and white flowered material. There were enough scraps left to make me a top too. She liked the top so well that she decided to stay a second week, so I could make her a full pants suit or pants dress, slacks, and top and dress. Made a deep gold double knit suit and deep blue double knit dress. Mom did all the work [housework] for two weeks. Not quite. I worked several days at Book Emporium. Took Debbie Ito and roommate and Sally another day shopping several times, and sewed and sewed and sewed. In that time I made for mom pants top, pants suit and dress, velveteen dress for Carol to wear Dress Up Day (last day before Christmas at school), pants top for me, a pale blue double knit pants suit (just like the one I made myself at showtime) for Bethany. Wow! I was real pleased that mom liked what I made, and that it fit well. Just yesterday (12,28,70) we drove to Homewood, so Mom P and George could visit in Deerfield, and Carol and I in Homewood. Bought some red wool material and some brown Milium lining to make Carol a maxi coat. Also bought three yards (60 inches wide) light double knit to make me something, pants suit maybe, sometimes called pant dress. They are all the rage now. Very comfortable and practical. Made one for Carol from pink corduroy and one for Sally in orange material. Pat and Barb and Marilyn all want me to make some for them too. I did not send any Christmas cards this year. Too busy sewing. Also, not much in the mood for it. George and I are not getting along lately. Or else maybe I should say that I have just had about all that I can take of him. He belittles the kids, never likes their friends, can't see any of his own faults. If ever I say anything to him, he whines that I don't love him, I spoil the kids, it's my fault that they don't respect him, I've never stood behind him in his jobs. Things can't go on like this much longer. Haven't been to the YMCA much at all in December. I will be behind. Don't know if I mentioned it before that Sally has been transferred to the second shift, 3:30 to midnight, and is on fulltime five days per week at the food processing plant. She also bought herself a car, a gold Chevrolet Nova, I think, four speed, big motor and tires.

Still has her black Chevy 1963 Impala. I had a wreck in it last September or early October.

Jan. 1, 1971 (Friday): Sally went to Homewood yesterday. Patti is coming back with her today. Patti got mad several months ago and quit her office job. Then she got a Christmas job at Marshall Fields, but it is all over now. So I asked her to come and visit. Last night George and I went to New Year's Eve party at Evans's. It was a Barbershoppers' party. Came home about 1:30 A.M. Played charades. Grandma and Carol stayed home. Was surprised that Carol didn't have a baby-sitting call. Wesley came over yesterday with two hand-dipped candles he made. He took the red car, so he could go call on a girl. He's coming back for dinner today. Sally took out some Allstate insurance, hospital and health, yesterday. $35 for three months. She hasn't had any insurance since she's been back home, and I got worried with car trips back and forth to Homewood, icy roads, etc. She can't get insurance from her job for another month. George got Sally's color TV working again. So we are a two TV family again.

Jan. 2, 1971 (Saturday): [written early in the morning and describing events of the day before] Today when I got up, I discovered snow on the ground. We might get some winter yet. New Year's Day Wesley came home. Said he had run out of clean clothes. Patti and Sally came home about 5:00 P.M. Had pizza from Village Inn for supper. Carol stayed overnight with Claudia Evans. Earlier in the day they went to see the movie *Love Story*. In late P.M. I started cutting out Carol's coat and slacks only to discover that I was missing the side front piece from the pattern. Got the slacks all cut out and also the lining. George worked all day on the shower stall, and it is all done now except for the door. He redid some of the grouting in the bathroom by the tub.

Jan. 2, 1971 (Saturday): George and Gram drove to Decatur to visit a cousin of Gram's. The rest of us did odd jobs around here. I called Penney's and told them about my pattern purchased at Penney's in Dixie Square, Homewood; and they said to come in and pick up the piece I was missing. Wesley had two pairs of jeans I had to repair. Got most of Carol's slacks made today.

Jan. 3, 1971 (Sunday): And now it is Sunday January 3. No one is up yet. I like it quiet like this in the early morning. Today we will take down the tree. Gretchen and Frau and Missy [the cat] are all wandering around the kitchen. I sure enjoy those dogs. Don't feel much for the cat, but I love to watch the dogs outside [in the fenced-in yard and walking them in the open field behind the house] and to play with them etc. They are magnificent! Went to late church. Carol went to Sunday school and helped in church nursery. Had sauerkraut and pork roast for dinner. Patti and Sally went to see *Love Story*. Bethany called to talk to Pat while they were gone. Took down the tree today. George told Carol "She **HAD** to take the tree down." Nobody else was going to, all were busy, because she had put it up. He made it a punishment instead of fun or a job or anything. So Wesley and Grandma helped her. She was upset, said next year she wasn't going to help put it up. I finished her slacks, and she wore them to church confirmation class. Julie [Nelson] called, and I called Nisa. The university is filling up again. School starts tomorrow [for last classes and then finals]. Repaired Wesley's jeans again today. Didn't do a good job yesterday. Wrote some answers to Christmas cards received. Wesley went to church too. Mom and George are watching TV now. It is 9:50 P.M., and I am ready for bed.

Jan. 5, 1971 (Tuesday): Yesterday George worked in A.M. and took Gram P home about 3:30 P.M. He had a meeting to attend in Newton. I worked on Carol's coat. Wesley and Carol returned to school. It is very windy, so I took them to school. Patti and Sally goofed, took showers, washed hair, watched TV. Patti painted and colored after Sally left. Wesley and I had quite a discussion when he came home. He sure is mixed up in his ideas. Guess this is part of growing. I hope I can keep that in mind. Today it is two degrees above. Will take the kids to school on the way to swim.

Jan. 12, 1971 (Tuesday): Today mom leaves for California [to visit sisters and families]. She called last night to say goodbye. Worked three days last week [at the Book Emporium]. Wasn't supposed to work at all. Worked most of my spare time on Carol's maxi coat. Finally finished it on Sunday morning. It looks beautiful. Carol is so tickled with it, said people would think she was the Queen of Sheba. Vi said she looked like a princess. The coat is red trimmed with fur from an old coat of Ginger's. Read to Julie last week. Read to Debbie yesterday. No more reading to Julie. She'll be through this Friday, ready for graduation. Patti went home on Friday on the train. Sally started going over to her supervisor's apartment after work. Stays there too long. It was my turn on Sunday evening to feed the church confirmation class. Made Jell-O Marsettie, cupcakes and Koolaid. About twenty kids. Swam last Tuesday and Thursday mornings. I am very pleased with my swimming. Think I am over the hump. Am scheduled to work Thursday and Friday this week and also will work today, because Vi called and asked me. Suspect I will wear my wig {Dorothy's joke about her hair].

When classes resumed at the university in late January of 1971 for the spring semester, Dorothy's interaction with the blind students soon took a new and important turn. One Friday evening, when Dennis, Kitty, Bob, Nisa, and Debbie were enjoying themselves at Dorothy's house, she hated to end their evening of fun by calling things to a close and taking them back to their dorm rooms. She therefore suggested that they simply stay the night, and they would worry about things in the morning. Thus began the custom of student sleep-overs. They slept wherever they could without complaint: any bed that happened to be unoccupied for the night by Wesley, Sally, or Carol, the living room couch, the family room couch, or simply a sleeping bag spread out on the lush thick gold carpet of the living room. Of course, given Dorothy's generosity and perfect hospitality, she would not let the students return to their dorms on the morning after with empty stomachs. As a result, the students were not only usually treated to a supper when they came over during the evening, but they were also fed breakfast.

The students never ceased to be amazed as to Dorothy's open-hearted behavior. They often shook their heads figuratively in wonder. How many people were there who would befriend a group of blind college students? How many would go so far as to have them over to their house for a meal and simply to relax and have fun, not once or twice, but regularly, and how many would even be genuinely pleased to have them spend the night? They knew for a fact that none of their own parents would ever do this; and the realization convinced them that Dorothy Patterson was a truly unique human being. They now displayed their gratitude, respect, and affection for her by bestowing upon her the honorific name "Ma." To them she was no longer Dorothy or Mrs. Patterson, but Ma, their loving mother away from home, whom they in turn loved and adored. Dorothy was immensely pleased by being called by this name. It was a signal proof of her worth to these students and of the real love that they had for her; and these wonderfully gifted students, though physically disabled, began to serve the important role of a surrogate family in place of her own that at times seemed to her to be so dysfunctional.

After years and years of being consistently belittled by George's mother, her own mother, and her sister Bethany, Dorothy had finally stumbled upon a group of people who saw in her the most remarkable qualities. To them, all her actions and behavior exhibited such extraordinary class and poise. Although they could not see her radiant smile, they could certainly hear it in her voice that was so beautiful and able to express so accurately all the wonderful personality traits that she possessed. She often engaged in funny word plays that added to her captivating charm. Although she was a very proper woman in the sense that she did not use profanity, her playful and mischievous nature was clearly exhibited by a phrase that she often uttered at this stage in her life: "As they say in south Russia, tough shitsky, you all!" The only other slightly profane utterance that she allowed herself was, "damnation, hell, shit, and poop," which she always uttered in a rush as if to mitigate the naughtiness of this phrase. In addition, her voice conveyed to the blind students her energy, vivacity, intelligence, and her great joy and love of life. Despite her age and her status as a wife and mother of three children, she was nevertheless not at all set in her ways, but had more the demeanor and world view of a young, enthusiastic, and intellectually curious college student. She greeted new opportunities and experiences with open-armed gaiety, zest, gusto, and playfulness, characteristics that her young blind college students shared and greatly admired in her. She was not the least bit conceited or wrapped up in herself, but as the students had already learned at first hand over and over again, she always exhibited consummate grace and the sweetest concern and solicitude toward others; she greatly enjoyed being with people and doing things with them; and she always made these activities so much fun by her dazzling charm and wit.

Besides these wonderful personal traits, Dorothy possessed two other things that further engendered fascination and admiration among the blind students: her domestic skills and her experiences in having lived in several different places throughout the country. She was a consummate cook, who by her knowing touch made everything turn out to taste so delicious. She was also such a talented seamstress, knitter, and crocheter. So many of her clothes were things that she had made, and she was eager to teach Nisa and Debbie how to crochet and knit. At this early stage in their lives, the blind students had done relatively little traveling. Consequently, Dorothy's occasional anecdotes about Baltimore or Montana made her even more intriguing.

Dennis and Kitty's relationship continued to go great guns on into the spring semester, but with an interesting twist. Bob Snider had by now also come under Kitty's spell; and even though she and Dennis were fully devoted to each other, Kitty was not averse to receiving the cautious romantic attentions of another. A kind of love triangle therefore arose among the three friends, and Dorothy's house was one place in which the various scenes and acts of this drama were slowly played out.

Kitty Carpenter was also responsible for another blind college student being absorbed into the group. His name was Rick Janson; and like Kitty, he was a junior. In fact, they had first met two and a half years before during their own freshman orientation week conducted by the Rehab Center. Consequently, just as Kitty had been drawn into the group through her association with Dennis, so Rick was now brought in through his friendship with Kitty. Rick was a perfectly pleasant young man, but unlike the other blind freshmen, his mobility skills left much to be desired. He often had difficulty in finding and keeping his bearings and was easily confused as to where he was, and which direction was which. As a result, the other male blind students enjoyed teasing Rick relentlessly about this and occasionally played a prank on him in which knowing (or not knowing) where to go was the key element; and when Rick, as usual, walked right into the carefully laid trap, he was showered in laughter, but he fortunately always bore the ignominy with good grace.

The layout of Dorothy's house was quickly becoming very familiar to the blind students. Of course, the Pattersons had been living in this large new beautiful house for only three and a half years. It was therefore situated on the extreme edge of an expanding residential area in southwestern University City, so that right behind the house lay a huge open field that stretched to the west for about a half a mile, where it was finally bordered by a north-south highway. Dorothy enjoyed taking the two dogs for long walks over to and back from this highway. As she walked through the overgrown grass and weeds and up and down the gullies, the dogs scampered about and smelled everything to their hearts' content. They occasionally came upon a rabbit and chased it for a short distance.

The front of the house faced east on the west side of Rachel Drive right where it joined Boardman. Along the front of the house, arranged north to south, were the living room and three bedrooms. The bedroom next to the living room (the front bedroom) contained a set of very elegant twin beds with four high posts that could hold a canopy. The room also served as Dorothy's sewing room, because she kept her sewing machine here along with a phonograph for playing records to keep her company as she sewed. The center of the three bedrooms was Wesley's room and had its walls still painted with alternating diagonal wavy stripes of red, white, and blue.

A north-south hallway separated the front from the middle part of the house. in this middle section, arranged from north to south, were the dining room (an open area just behind the living room), the kitchen, laundry room, two back-to-back bathrooms, and the master bedroom. Behind the dining room and kitchen lay the large rear part of the house, consisting of a good-size family room and a one-car garage.

The way in which Dorothy furnished this house and maintained it further reinforced the students' impression that Dorothy possessed impeccable taste and was a person of consummate elegance. She had personally chosen the lovely gold carpet that covered the living room, dining room, and main hallway. Her living room couch, piano, dining table and chairs, and china hutch were really beautiful pieces of furniture. So many things in the house, both large and small, including the plates from which the blind students ate, contributed to this impression of elegance and taste.

Perhaps the one object that best epitomized the house and Dorothy herself was a large metal milk can used on dairy farms. It measured twenty-five inches high and was thirteen inches in diameter with two big metal handles on opposite sides of the vessel's shoulder. Over its mouth had been fitted a circular metal seat, so that the object could actually serve as a peculiar kind of stool. It had been painted a mustard yellow and bore on its body an American eagle in green. Dorothy had received it as a gift from a friend and kept it in the living room standing at the right end of the piano, where the rustic object seemed right at home and exuded a simple down-to-earth elegance and charm.

Although by now the blind students were fully familiar with the interior of Dorothy's house, at least one of them, Bob Snider, was still not entirely clear on the configuration of the surrounding yard; and his topographical ignorance had one lasting consequence. Right after the students had returned to campus in late March after their spring break, Dorothy had some of them over to the house to spend the evening and night. Gretchen was in heat at the time; and when she continued to behave anxiously after Dorothy had gone to bed, Bob decided that she must need to go outside to relieve herself. But rather than letting her out into the fenced-in side yard through the one door of the family room that led outside through the garage, Bob instead let her out the other door at the back porch where there was no fencing at all. Gretchen was therefore able to run free around the neighborhood and, as they eventually learned, returned home after being impregnated. After the puppies were born, all were given away except one. This one they kept and named Erica, who thus became dog number three.

Journal Entries
Resumed from January 12

May 26, 1971 (Wednesday): One week ago today our puppies were born. On May 19 Gretchen had five pups, two male and three female, father unknown. First born about 4:00 P.M. Carol and three friends were in the family room. Gretchen was in her favorite spot, gray chair. Carol called me from another room to say there was a pup in the chair too. We didn't expect them for another week. After Gretchen was through with the first one, carried it to the spot in the garage that I had ready for her. Just fixed it that morning. And Gretchen followed me. Then she had two more puppies in the garage, and I took them from her, broke the sack, and cleaned them, rubbed, tied and cut cords. Wow! Those were the vet's instructions. An hour and a half passed and no more puppies, though she kept acting like she was going to have another. So I called the vet. Took her there. Pups too. He gave her a shot and told George to hurry home. Just after they got home, Gretch had two more pups. Last one was breach, no problem. George took care of these two pups, because I had to get ready to go to a sing-out. I sang in an octet too. First night the pups stayed in the garage, but then the next day we brought them into the house, because it's been getting so cold at night. We'll put them out as soon as they start walking. They are so cute! Two are black with white, and one is brown with spots. One is all brown-black, and the other is tan.

May 28, 1971 (Friday): Had our carpet cleaned last Friday. Looks real nice except for where Gretchen two nights later made a mess. What a mess it was too! Sally and Bob are still going strong. Bob is moving into town next week. He works here and goes to school here. So this is more practical for him. I only hope Sally doesn't spend too much time there. She probably will though, because he comes here after work (midnight) and stays until 5:00 A.M. or so. So now Sally will probably be over there instead. She is having a recurring bladder infection and also has a vaginal fungus infection. So she's got her problems. Read to Deb twice this week. It is almost time for finals. Two weeks ago we had a party for all our University kids. Only six [Dennis, Bob, Kitty, Nisa, Debbie, and either Rick or Faith] of the nine [minus Grant, Larry, and Moses] could come, and just three of the six could stay overnight. They brought a corsage for Carol because she was being confirmed at church the next day, and they brought a dozen roses in a vase to me plus a card in braille which I had to read.

July 1, 1971 (Thursday): This year, 1971, is about half over. Just finished a hot spell, I hope. Today it will only get into the middle 80s. Wesley is in Canada. He and Curt Frank are on a bike hike. They started out being very angry with me, because I wouldn't drive them to downtown Chicago to take the train to Wisconsin. I was up in Homewood visiting and sewing for mom, and I picked them up (Bob and Sally in Bob's car picked them up also) in Homewood, but refused to take them the next morning to Chicago. Had various reasons such as too far, too dangerous to have bikes hanging out of car. I was invited to lunch at Barbara Samson's. So they found someone else to take them, I guess. We've had two phone calls and two postcards, one to Carol from him. Last night he said they would start home soon. He says he's having a ball. Sally is living with Bob now. Neither one wants to get married yet. They went up to Homewood when I did and stayed for about five days. They think they have an easy answer to life, but I think that they are not being very mature or smart. They won't listen. University kids!

July 21, 1971 (Wednesday): Well, Wesley is home now except not staying at our house. He got mad at me when I told him he had to tow his own if he stayed here. And he won't take any orders or discipline from us. So he went to Mr. Carlson's. Now he has decided to join the navy. He goes to Chicago for physical etc. on Thursday. He thinks he is underweight though. Sally and Bob are having occasional spats now. Timothy H. Klingner and Marilyn are now residents of Houston, Texas, where Tim has a job with NASA's space program. He is maintaining the TVs that monitor the space flights. He and Marilyn were both tickled with the new job. Still have four puppies. Grandma P is here for a visit. She came up for a cousin's wake. We got her Sunday morning. Left here 6:00 A.M. Got back at 11:00 A.M. Took Faith out to dinner on Sunday. She's our friend who helps us with our blind kids. She's a nun and is here getting her Ph.D. in clinical psychology, I think. Faith Martin is her full name.

July 27, 1971 (Tuesday): Well, Grandma P has gone back home again. Took her home Sunday. She insisted on going home, and then after she got there, she said, "The rest of today and tonight will be so long and lonely." Boo hoo, poor me, etc.! Why does she act like that? She and my mom were talking about photo albums when we were in Homewood on Saturday. Mom said how much she enjoyed looking at the pictures. George's mom said that she doesn't like to look at them, because they make her feel too badly. In other words, she feels sorry for herself. Why can't she be positive rather than negative? George is often this way too. Well, I really wanted to write today about Wesley. Last week (Tuesday) he decided he wanted to join the navy. So we signed a permit for his physical, which he got in Chicago on Thursday. He passed. So he came back to get another permit signed by us, so he could join, which we did. So now he goes into the navy this Thursday. He is really excited about going. Maybe he knows he needs the discipline and knows he can accept it from the navy when he can't accept it from us. Who knows? He says he decided to go, because he doesn't know what else he wants to do, and he can't find a job he likes. He was a little underweight, but they took him anyway. So now he is gathering up the things he'll need to take with him. Saturday mom gave him Tim's old sea bag. So now he is carrying a navy wallet, and he and Carol are wearing old navy work clothes. He is also eating lots of bananas and other things to give him weight. So our house is emptying gradually. Last night Carol and I went shopping. I bought a desk at Lane Furniture, solid maple, early American style. It was $159. Hope I won't be sorry I spent the last of my mad money.

July 28, 1971 (Wednesday): Mom is in Houston with Tim and Marilyn. She went yesterday. She'll probably stay a month. Tim is busy with this July 26 space flight to the moon. It should last nine days with a ride on the moon too. Yesterday I brought Jeanne's glass tea tray home. She doesn't use it or want it. The glass in the bottom is broken. I put my plants on it, and they complement each other [a gold metal two-level cart on wheels to hold Dorothy's houseplants in the living room by the picture window to receive the morning sun]. Mr. Carlson and the kids there had a party for Wesley last night. I was very glad, but yet I am unhappy this morning, because Wesley didn't bother to come home all night. I will not be sorry to have Wesley away from Mr. Carlson. I still don't like him. He is a blowhard among other things. Wesley leaves tonight at 1:00 A.M., which is really tomorrow, July 29, 1971. 1975 he'll come home. He is in four years of active and one year of inactive service. Sally was here last night. She didn't go to work again. I'm sure she misses too much work for her own good. I think I wish she'd forget about Bob. He enjoys going out with the boys to have a drink too much. Perhaps it wouldn't cause trouble, but I think it will.

July 29, 1971 (Thursday): Well, Wesley left at 1:00 A.M. today. Carol, George, and I took him to the bus station. He is very pleased with himself. He went yesterday and had his hair cut. Said he wanted to make a good first impression. How different he looked! He had me take pictures of him with his long hair and his guitar, and later I took a picture of him in his sailor's suit. He took a box of chocolate chip cookies with him to eat on the way. Carol and I made them. We had to be very careful. She and I are both on a low carbohydrate diet. Carol started the diet at 150 pounds, and I am 132 pounds. Grandma P was here when we started. I weigh four pounds more than she does now. She was on a low carbohydrate diet too because of her diabetes. Sally came over yesterday to say good luck to Wesley. She had just come from Doctor Miller's office (clinical psychologist at Mental Health Clinic). She said that he said she is headed for a nervous breakdown. I wonder if that is exactly what he said. Oh well! Anyway, he is referring her to a psychiatrist, because she wants something to settle her down. I think she is letting her relationship with Bob bother her. She wants this to be the real thing, and she's afraid it isn't, etc.; and she doesn't want him to go with the fellows for a drink etc. Sally can twist things up in her own mind. It is lunchtime now. Carol is baby-sitting with Spencer Adkins, our little summer-last baby.

July 31, 1971 (Saturday): My desk came on the 29th, but the top is warped and is also broken in one spot. So they are ordering me a new one. Wonder how Wesley is doing. It ought to be about 5:00 A.M. in San Diego. Am working on a Peanuts puzzle. Deb gave it to Carol for her birthday. Also am trying to finish *Bury My Heart at Wounded Knee* before I must return it to the Book Emporium. Carol decided that she wanted to clean up Wesley's room last night. So she did. She did it in less time than I could have.

Aug. 1, 1971 (Sunday): Got our first letter from Wesley last Wednesday. He said they were being worked so hard he was almost sorry he had enlisted. First time he got to sit down for an hour was when he went to church. He isn't known for his diligence and concentration on long hard projects. About ten minutes is his length of interest span. Carol and I are putting some antique paint on Sally's old bedroom set. Spanish gold. Will also do my sewing machine, and an old TV cabinet made into a desk, and our old sewing center that I keep vegetables in. We like it. Nobody else likes the color. Carol cut out a jumper the other night, and I cut out a dress. Carol made her jumper, all except the facings; and it didn't fit right, so I am fixing it. Am having Sweet Adelines here Tuesday night, a farewell party for Jeanne Douglas.

Aug. 21, 1971 (Saturday): I wonder what Wesley will be doing today. Work as usual, I suppose. Sent him a box of cupcakes last Saturday. Mom, Ginger, and Bethany sent him a $20 money order. Got our third letter from him yesterday. He is in a special company. They started out with 75 men, down to 62 men now. Thirteen had to get out., too much stress. Wesley said for a while he was wondering if he'd make it also, but it is better now. He says, "I guess I'm beginning my first steps to becoming a man." The company has won special honors and now gets to carry the flag (company). They have $104 for the goal of $500 for an orphanage. So he wants us to send some money. He said he's made good scores on his test and will be able to go to whatever school he'd like. This letter was written 8,17. Sally goes to the hospital on Monday for minor surgery, meatotomy. They will cut and fold back an extra piece of something in her urethra. She'll come back home on Thursday. Carol and I spent Monday through Thursday in Homewood this week. Came home yesterday morning. Bethany was on vacation. Patti, Garry [Ginger and Jim's younger son], and Carol went to the Sand Dunes on Thursday [located at the very southern end of Lake Michigan in Chesterton, Indiana].

Chapter 4

Their Second Academic Year

September 4, 1971, Saturday

It was about 5:00 A.M., and Dorothy was the only one up in the house and was likely to be for quite some time. That was how she wanted it. She was sitting at her lovely new desk with her first cup of coffee for the morning. By looking through the window to her immediate left she could keep an eye on the dogs as they browsed and scampered about the fenced-in side yard.

Dorothy's best friend, Jeanne Douglas, had just moved away; and the loss made Dorothy view the arrival of the university's fall semester with great anticipation and eagerness. The university kids had come to mean so much to her in providing her with a sense of true worth and an important emotional and practical means of escaping from her unhappy home life. The latter, of course, neither the blind students nor her closest friends seemed to suspect, because Dorothy kept her innermost feelings and unhappiness tightly locked up inside her; for experience over the years had taught her that whenever she voiced her dissatisfaction to George, he was never the least bit sympathetic, but regarded it all as a personal attack and was soon directing his anger with her against Sally, Wesley, and Carol. But occasionally the pressure inside Dorothy became too great for her to contain entirely, and this created a recurring pattern of periodic outbursts from her, followed by really bad times with George until things gradually settled back down again into their usual state of quiet unhappiness.

Although she had initially had doubts about purchasing the desk as a birthday present to herself, all those doubts had now been completely removed. It was a beautiful piece of furniture whose presence between the living and dining rooms contributed so nicely to Dorothy's elegant and tasteful arrangement of these two rooms. She was already beginning to collect small objects, such as a letter opener whose handle was shaped like a rose, to add to the desk's decor. These items were both utilitarian and aesthetically pleasing.

More importantly, the desk had quickly come to represent to Dorothy her own private haven and refuge. This is where she now always sat by herself to write her letters to family and friends and to write in her journal. Since the large file drawer could be locked, she kept it so, and she now had a reasonably secure place for her journals.

The desk now stood figuratively at the eye of a storm. The storm, of course, was all the daily chaos and unhappiness that swirled around her, but the desk was the place of relative calm to which she could retreat and, at least for a time, enjoy a small amount of inner contentment. This was especially so, like now, when she arose from bed long before anyone else in the house was up. She could sit quietly at her desk with a cup of coffee and write letters. As she did, her spirit was soothed by the scene before her: beautiful morning sunlight spilling into the living room onto the gold carpet with the greenery of her houseplants, now sitting on Jeanne's two-level tea tray, forming a verdant backdrop to Dorothy's view out the picture window. After taking another sip from the cup, she removed the pen from the elegant little stand that Wesley had made for her a few years ago in one of his shop classes, and she began to write.

Journal Entry
Resumed from August 21

Sept. 4, 1971 (Saturday): Another school year has begun. Carol started school last Tuesday. A grown-up eighth grader now. She has English, math, PE, home economics, industrial arts, maybe more. I can't remember. So far all is well. She also has science. Just remembered, she has same teacher as Wesley had when he was in junior high. She meets Jim across the bridge, and they ride their bikes together to school. Got a letter from Wesley on Tuesday. Three pages this time. He is a squirrel now. First he was a worm. Seems to be doing ok in the letter writing department. He's written to quite a few people. Sally got a letter on Tuesday also. Sally got a new car on Thursday, a Buick Skylark, green, power steering, tape player, air conditioning, etc, a new 1971. Sally also had minor surgery the week before, meatotomy. There was a growth or something on her urethra, which was cut and stitched down or something. [a diagram illustrating the procedure] She was in on Monday and home Wednesday. I spent most of Tuesday at the hospital. After she came home, she stayed here during the day and went to the apartment at night. She went back to work on Wednesday of this week, and I just completed another orientation week at the university. This year there were only three blind kids, a boy and two girls. There were several partially sighted kids, but I didn't work with them. This year Nisa also worked and helped train the new kids. She's such a nice girl. The new kids are Sarah Lundy who has a dog named Hunter, Susan Williams who is from University City, and Renny Fulton from Chicago. Renny and Dennis are pals. I worked all week with Susan. She is a transfer student, junior from Augustana [College]. We had a grand time, a very tiring time, a very glorious time! Hard to say in less than 80 pages what goes on in this one week. We walk, we laugh, we walk. Susan's dorm is Nash. So we walked from Nash to the Quad to each of her classes and back to Nash. We do that six or eight times during the week. At the end the student does it all alone. We also walk to any place else that the student might need to learn or will want to go alone at a later date, like the post office, the library, snack bar, etc. Then we swim for about an hour in the afternoon. Last night we took Renny Fulton bowling at the Union. Then we ate pizza at the dorm. Got home about midnight. Today Renny is coming over to help George to get Wesley's car working. Thursday night James Jr. [Jim Lawson] was here for his once the month overnight [resulting from his travels associated with his job].

When the fall semester at the university began in September of 1971, there were some changes that occurred in the membership of Dorothy's group of blind students. There were four deletions and one and a half additions. Faith Martin and Rick Janson became too busy with their own personal concerns and participated in the group's activities only very rarely. Moses Truman and Larry Barton now dropped out altogether, as they were increasingly absorbed into the black student culture of the university. The half membership addition involved Grant. He had been very much a part of the group during the fall of 1970, but as he became more absorbed in his studies, he did not have sufficient time to participate in the weekend sleep-overs that had begun during the following spring semester. But when the new academic year began, he did his very best to maintain full participation in the group.

The one truly new addition to Dorothy's group of blind students was Renny Fulton, and what an addition he was! He and Dennis had known one another for about twelve years, since early grade school; and their shared experiences over the years had made them as close as two friends could be. He was black, indeed, as black as the ace of spades, as he himself liked to joke. He was about five years older than Dennis. He had been born in a log cabin in a very poor community in rural Mississippi; and when he was about five or six years old, his father abandoned Renny's mother, which, along with other unsavory deeds, forever damned Renny's recollection of him. One year later Renny's mom, Rose, moved to the south side of Chicago. She had long known that Renny's eyesight was extremely poor, but because she did not know that visually impaired children could receive a normal education, she kept her son out of school until he was about nine years old. Consequently, throughout his years of formal education Renny was always about four years older than everyone else in his class.

Dennis and Renny attended school together until their junior year in high school. During their freshman and sophomore years they wrestled on the same team, but Dennis' parents then withdrew him from the school and enrolled him in a Catholic school, because his original high school by then was almost entirely black and had become extremely dangerous; and Dennis' parents were afraid that serious harm might come to Dennis if he continued there. Renny graduated from high school at the same time as Dennis. He therefore should have been among the group of blind students who entered the university in the previous fall, but Renny had not bothered to get all of his paperwork done in time and had thus missed the deadline for admission into the university. Like his belated start on his formal education, this snafu perfectly epitomized one of Renny's very few faults: his habitual and excessive procrastination.

Renny was about six feet tall and possessed a very muscular build. His eyes were afflicted with retinitis pigmentosa (RP), a condition that covers the retina with pigmented spots and thereby reduces one's vision, varying with the degree of pigmentation. Renny was not entirely blind, but had some light perception and under certain conditions could actually make out shadows. Unlike most sightless people, whose eyes appear strange to the sighted, because they remain unfocused, Renny's eyes had the appearance of someone with normal vision. In addition, Renny walked and moved with the same bodily assurance of a sighted person, so that if he happened to have his cane folded up and tucked out of sight, many people often were unaware that he was actually blind.

These unusual physical traits were at least matched, if not exceeded, by Renny's extraordinary personality. He possessed a magnetism and charm that were irresistible. Everyone whom he encountered instantly became his friend. He was a great jokester and could find humor in about anything and usually did. He had a deep resonant voice that could be modulated into a rasp or squeak; and his laugh, when unrestrained, was a kind of raucous horselike whinny, which in itself often prompted people to laugh along with him.

By the time that Renny arrived on the university campus he had somehow acquired an uncanny knack for fixing about anything involving an internal combustion engine and the related workings of an automobile. When combined with his generous and friendly nature, he was always eager to help anyone in fixing his or her car and always did so without charging a dime. His payment lay in the mere enjoyment of tinkering with an automobile and in rendering someone a real kindness.

Nisa and Kitty Carpenter were still living in Nash Hall, and Debbie was also still in Miller, but there had been some minor reshuffling of dorm rooms for the guys in the group. Dennis was still in his triple in Holmes, and Bob was still in the same room in nearby Forester, but Grant had now moved over into Holmes and was just several doors down from Dennis. Renny, on the other hand, was now rooming in Grant's old room in Forester with a rather nice guy named John Rogers. As a result, Dennis, Renny, Bob, and Grant became a very close-knit quartet and spent most of their free time together.

September 17, 1971, Friday

Dorothy and George parked their two cars in the parking lot next to the university library and then stepped out into the cool evening air. Carol was with them, and Dorothy took the lead in walking over to the Quad and up to the main entrance of the Auditorium. By now, of course, Dorothy knew her way around the university extremely well; and her familiarity with the campus gave her a true sense of comfort, pride, and belonging. Yep, there they were, standing on the sidewalk waiting for them: Dennis, Renny, Bob, Grant, Kitty, Nisa, and Debbie. After joyous greetings were exchanged, the group of ten joined others in entering the Auditorium, but they walked down the center aisle all the way to the front row of seats before sitting down, because that way Kitty could stay in her wheelchair and not have to worry about being in someone's way.

The first week of classes had just ended, and this was the first major event for this group so far in the new academic year. During her week of volunteer mobility instruction Dorothy had happened to see an advertisement of the movie *Camelot* to be shown tonight here at the Auditorium; and she had wanted everyone in her group of blind students to experience this movie and its beautiful music, which Dorothy already knew by heart from playing the record countless times. The action that unfolded on the screen required no explanation for the blind students, in part because they were already familiar with the outline of the Arthurian legend that formed the basis of the story, and in part because the music and staging were self-explanatory. When the movie finally ended, it was clear that it had gone over very well with all members of the group.

After they had successfully exited the Auditorium, wheelchair, canes, and all, the group made their way to the parking lot, piled into the two cars, and soon arrived at 1801 Rachel Drive, where they sat together in the adjoining family room and kitchen, talking and eating snacks, while Dorothy's Camelot album provided the appropriate background music.

"Hey, Renny," asked Debbie, "do you know who Lancelot in the first part of the movie reminds me of?" "No, who?" "You, because you both have such inflated egos." As Debbie and others chuckled at Renny's expense, he reached over and pinched Debbie's left breast. "Ou, Renny, stop that!" Debbie protested as she slapped as his hand. Renny exploded in laughter that sounded much like the braying of a donkey. Bob instantly gave his excellent imitation of Renny's laugh, at which everyone laughed uproariously. "Hey, Debs," Renny boastfully teased, "you'd do really well if you hung around me!" "Get lost, Renny," Debbie answered back with mock disdain. "You tell him, Deb," interjected Dorothy, always on the ready to defend feminine independence against Renny's self-centered male chauvinism. She now sang, "I got along without ya before I met ya, gonna get along without ya now." "Hey, Ma," Renny asked, "who's side are you on?" "What's wrong?" Dorothy asked, "Can't you take a little teasing too? I thought you were a big boy. That's what you want everyone to believe, isn't it?"

The giddiness of the party soon settled down into a pleasant jocularity; and after the Camelot record had played itself through twice, Dorothy turned off the machine. Carol now headed off for bed, and Grant took Wesley's guitar from its case next to the piano and began playing. He began with a series of finger style songs; and even though they were played as instrumentals, Dorothy knew words to several of them and sang along with them so cheerfully and sweetly: Camptown Races, Maggie, The Bells of Saint Mary's, Red Wing, Freight Train. He then switched to chording and singing songs: Jimmy Crack Corn, Mountain Dew, Just Because, Your Cheating Heart, Folsom Prison Blues, etc. Dorothy and others joined in when they knew the words. George yawned, stood up, bid everyone good night, and walked off to bed. He had hoped to be joined by his wife, but he well knew from long experience that she would stay up for at least as long as the music lasted, and probably even longer. For Dorothy, when given the choice of going off to the bedroom to join her husband in bed or to stay up with her university kids, there simply was no contest. She always avoided or at least postponed the former as much as possible. Besides, given her love of music and the pleasure that it always gave her, she wanted to stay here to join in the singing with her lovely voice.

Grant's repertoire of songs largely consisted of traditional American melodies, such as Jimmy Crack Corn, or were hillbilly or country and western songs. So many of them reminded Dorothy of the music that she remembered as a child being performed on WLS radio's Barn Dance Show. She really loved this music, and she could even feel it affecting her deep down inside. As she watched Grant's mouth forming the words, a strange thought drifted through her mind: what would it be like to kiss those lips?

October 16, 1971, Saturday

Camelot had been such a success a month ago that a few of the group had already purchased their own copies of the album and were learning the words to the songs, but tonight George and Dorothy had collected them from their dorms and had brought them out for a totally different kind of musical experience. They were all seated in the high school auditorium, and for about an hour and 45 minutes they were entertained by half a dozen Barbershop quartets. The blind students knew very few of the songs that were sung, because they were ones chosen not because of their popularity, but how well they lent themselves to being sung in four-part harmony.

As soon as the show had ended, and the applause ceased, Dennis arose from his seat, worked his way out to the aisle, unfolded his cane, and slowly worked his way through the exiting people until he reached the bottom of the auditorium. "Hey man, that was really great!" he exclaimed to no one in particular. But soon he was engaged in conversation with one participant after the other, congratulating each and trying to engage them in a discussion of their singing.

Like Dennis, George had come down to the front and was talking with several Barbershoppers whom he personally knew from his own participation in the local chapter. When he saw that Dennis was doing his best to schmooze with the performers, he stepped over to him and said, "Hey, Dennis, let me introduce you to our friend and one of the Barbershop music directors." "Hey that would be great, man!" Dennis enthused. George guided Dennis over to two men engaged in conversation, and they stood back until the two parted. George now stepped forward with Dennis, "Chuck Evans, let me introduce you to one of our university friends, Dennis MacDonald." Then turning to Dennis, "Dennis, this is Chuck Evans, who knows about all there is to know about Barbershop singing." While shaking hands with Dennis, Chuck smiled in response to George's compliment and said, "Well, I know some things, but I don't know nearly that much."

Dennis now began to ask the questions whose answers he really wanted to know. "How long does it take to put together a Barbershop quartet?" "Well, that all depends upon the skill of the members, and how much time they invest in it." "But the harmony sounds so intricate. How hard is that to achieve?" "That again, depends in part upon the skill of the members, but you'd be surprised. It isn't quite as hard as you might think, because we have a large standard repertoire of songs with the four parts already mapped out, and about all it takes is for the members to learn their different parts and then practice together." "Wow, that really sounds neat!" "Why? Are you interested in becoming a Barbershopper?" "Well, actually, I think I'd like to form my own group." "Well now, if that's the case, tell you what. If you want to start up your own quartet, tell George here, and he can tell me, and I'll see if I can spare some time to help you out." "Really? That's really cool, man! Thanks a lot! I'll sure do that."

As Dennis and George walked up the aisle to join the other members of the group to leave, Dennis was thrilled with the idea that Renny, Bob, Grant, and he might be able to form a Barbershop quartet.

As might be expected, by now the different courses and activities pursued by the blind students were leading them off into many divergent directions, and trying to keep track of it all was a bit like attempting to discern the patterns in the colors of an ever-shifting kaleidoscope. But some obvious patterns did emerge and formed the subplots to the on-going drama being acted out by the entire group. For one thing, Grant and Dennis had not only become very close friends, but their personal friendship was now strongly reinforced by shared academic interests. They were at the same level in their study of German; and although they were in two different sections of fourth semester German, their reading material and exercises were identical. They therefore frequently pooled their resources by swapping braille and cassette recordings, by sitting in on one another's sessions with a German reader, and simply by trying to converse with each other in German. Whenever they attempted the latter in Dorothy's presence, she was always so pleased and once exclaimed, "Oh wow, guys, that sounds so neat! It reminds me of my two Klingner grandparents who often spoke to one another in German, and we kids always thought that it was so funny. I can still remember one telling the other, 'daus die Glimmer' when they wanted the lights turned out."

Throughout his high school years Grant had avidly studied science and mathematics in the hope of someday becoming an engineer or physicist. He had not been much interested in the humanities or social sciences until his senior year when his class in English literature and third year Latin class, in which they read large portions of Vergil's epic poem *The Aeneid*, finally fired his imagination. Vergil had led him to Homer's *Iliad* and *Odyssey* in translation; and when he had arrived last year as a freshman on the university campus, he could recite from memory the first half of Book I of *the Iliad* and many other long passages, as well as many short poems in their entirety. By spewing out bits of this memorized material at odd moments, Grant had by now earned the reputation of being an overly studious nerd, whom the other members of the group tolerated with polite amusement. During the previous summer break, however, Grant had begun to read some of Plato's philosophical dialogues, and he therefore returned to University City with his newest obsession, Socrates. This took the concrete form of Grant fulfilling his history requirement by signing up for a two-semester sequence of the ancient world, which covered the ancient Near Eastern civilizations, Greece, and Rome. He was also enrolled in a course on Classical Civilization that treated Greek thought and literature in translation. Since some of Grant's enthusiasm for these subjects had been rubbing off onto Dennis, the two were now classmates in this Classical Civ course.

Besides their shared experience in formal studies, Dennis and Grant had common interests in reading major works of literature that they obtained as recorded books (termed talking books) from the Hild Library for the Blind in Chicago. As one of them read and finished one book and raved about it to the other, the other borrowed the book and got himself up to speed; or sometimes they would actually listen to the same book together, discussing it as they went along. They now drew Dorothy into their reading and literary discussions by loaning her the records, which she then listened to on her phonograph as she sat at her sewing machine in the front bedroom. This interaction drew them into a shared intellectual experience that all three thoroughly enjoyed and greatly cherished. It was yet another way in which the college students acknowledged Dorothy as their peer, and she was genuinely flattered and pleased to be embraced as one of them. She had long ago missed her opportunity to attend college, which she still regretted; but her interaction with her university kids was now allowing her to associate herself with a college environment, and it appealed to her greatly. None of her three children would ever attend college; and unlike herself, George possessed no intellectual curiosity or open-mindedness, but Dorothy was clearly gifted intellectually and had long been a very avid reader. She therefore felt proud and privileged to become a third participant in Dennis' and Grant's literary discussions.

Another subplot within the group involved Debbie. Like last year, Dorothy served as one of Debbie's readers, but as the semester progressed, she found herself serving less as a reader and more as an amateur therapist. Debbie was quite intelligent, possessed a fine sense of humor, and was usually a very pleasant person, but she sometimes became poutish and whiny. This latter trait was apparently a manifestation of something much deeper, recurring bouts of depression, probably resulting from some chemical imbalance in her brain. In fact, even before coming to University City, Debbie had received quite a bit of psychological counseling from a woman named Mrs. Putnam in Chicago. Debbie had done very well during her freshman year, but she was now struggling to keep herself on an even keel. Debbie now began to talk to Dorothy about her innermost feelings (largely involving her parents, her sister, her brother-in-law, and her childhood experiences) in an attempt to purge herself of anxiety and to try to gain new and more healthy perspectives by having Dorothy offer Debbie her own views on things. Unfortunately, talking out her perceived problems only provided temporary relief and never penetrated to the real root causes. But what it meant for Dorothy was that Debbie gradually became more dependent upon their conversations, spent more and more time at the house, and required Dorothy to invest an increasing amount of her time and energy into trying to keep Debbie mentally well.

The other major subplot centered upon Nisa. While she had been serving as a student intern at the Rehab Center just before the beginning of the fall semester, she had encounter Sora Takahashi, a graduate student from Japan who was earning his Ph.D. in rehabilitation services. Sora quickly became romantically interested in Nisa, and a relationship between them began to slowly develop during the academic year. But at the same time Renny also became increasingly interested in Nisa, and she did not totally discourage Renny, but their interaction always took place within the rather restricted confines of the group, so that Renny was usually frustrated in not being able to pursue Nisa as fully and as ardently as he wished.

Renny always considered himself to be an irresistible lady's man, and so Nisa's reserve toward him upset him greatly. But what really outraged him was that Nisa seemed to be more romantically inclined toward Sora. Since Renny was about eight inches taller than Sora and probably outweighed his slightly built rival by about forty pounds, Nisa's apparent preference was especially galling to Renny. He therefore often vented his frustration and rage in private conversations with his best friend Dennis. "How can she be attracted to him?" Renny would bellow, "I don't get it!" "Yeah man, I know," Dennis would calmly reply, "but there's a lot of things going on here. Nisa is American, but she's been raised in a strong Japanese background of her parents, and what they think or would say must count a great deal with her, and Sora is native Japanese. So it's just not a matter between you and him." Dennis' analysis was accurate, but it did little to lessen Renny's annoyance and frustration.

November 7, 1971, Sunday

The only two sounds that disturbed the silence of their dorm room in Holmes were someone's stereo system being played too loud several doors down the hall and a continuous series of soft popping sounds made by Grant as he used his slate and stylus to write braille. It was a rather typical Sunday afternoon for the two young college students. Grant's roommate, an agronomy major from a large farm in western Illinois, was stretched out on his bed reading a textbook for one of his courses, while Grant was seated at his desk. He had spent all morning in getting completely caught up in the reading for all his courses and in doing other work for the week of upcoming classes. He was now using some of his precious spare time to record a few recent dreams in what he called his Dream Book. It was a kind of journal, but it only recorded dreams that Grant could remember.

He had been keeping this dream journal for nearly a year, and it had been the outgrowth of another peculiar project that he had begun on January 1 of 1970, just as he was finishing his senior year in high school. The ending of one year and the beginning of another had somehow prompted him to consider how much of his life was being spent asleep. If a person actually slept the recommended eight hours a day, that constituted an entire third of one's life. What a shocking realization! But if one could get by perfectly well with slightly less sleep, one could in effect lengthen one's conscious life by a decent margin, during which he might be able to accomplish important or interesting things. Consequently, Grant began to keep a simple log, a mere list of how much he had slept the night before, estimated to the nearest fifteen minutes. Then at the end of each month he averaged out how much he had slept. This sort of accounting had revealed that on average he slept six hours and twenty to thirty minutes. Grant had found this to be reassuring. At least it was better than eight hours! During the winter of his freshman year he had begun to keep his Dream Journal. All of the new experiences and things learned had caused him to have some really wild and interesting dreams, and he had decided to record them as a possible means of introspection and self-analysis. Of course, he realized that dreams quite often meant nothing at all, but were simply the product of the rational part of the brain trying to make sense out of a chaotic kaleidoscope of images and experiences, both old and recent, dredged up by the mind. Nevertheless, they were often interesting and could sometimes offer insights into his aspirations or things that were causing him anxiety.

As he finished recording his most recent dream from the night before, he opened the rings of the notebook and placed the pages in it. He now reflected upon some of his more recent dreams. They usually involved things related to his studies, such as a nightmare in which he was forced to stare at a complex of numbers, lines, and arcs and was expected to decipher what they meant; but of course, he couldn't. Or the dream might simply be a wild curiosity, such as one that he had during the past summer in which he met and talked with King Mithridates of Pontus, who had long posed a serious challenge to the ancient Romans' rule over the eastern Mediterranean. Grant occasionally mentioned some of these goofy dreams to other members of the group, and they usually laughed about them. This simply reinforced their view of him as an overly studious nerd. In fact, recently Dennis and Kitty had come up with a nickname for him: Marcus Unrealius Britannicus, the Britannicus referring to his extraordinary memory, like the *Encyclopedia Britannica.*

But now as he looked over his notes and pondered some of his more recent dreams, something very different emerged, several dreams involving himself and Ma or Nisa. They were perfectly innocent dreams in terms of their actions, but they clearly demonstrated that he was harboring very strong affections for them both. The realization was very unsettling. He knew, of course, that Nisa was already dating Sora, and that Renny was also constantly paying court to her quite openly, which she did not totally discourage. Since he liked Renny so much and knew how upset Renny already was about having Sora as a serious rival, Grant decided to do nothing at all in regard to Nisa. Why bother? Things were already complicated enough with her being pursued simultaneously by Renny and Sora. Besides, Grant had never been at all successful in having a girlfriend. Why start now when he had plenty enough to do and worry about with all his studies?

The same rationale, of course, also applied to his attraction to Ma. But wow! Was that ever a lulu! After all, she was his parents' age, not to mention the fact that she was already married! Yet, in strict objective terms, putting age and marital status aside, his strong affection for her was perfectly reasonable, logical, rational, and understandable, because he had never encountered anyone who possessed such goodness, kindness, charm, grace, sweetness, and caring to the extraordinary degree that she did. In addition, despite her age and status as a wife and mother of three, she was vivacious, dazzling, and witty, and always exhibited such class, poise, elegance, and unerring taste and judgment in about everything. How could he not come under the spell of someone like that? He had recently read a translation of Sophocles' *Antigone* and was struck by one passage sung by the chorus that began: "Wonders are many, but none is more wondrous than man himself." That could be easily rewritten as: "Wonders are many, but none is more wondrous than Dorothy Alice Patterson." But Ma was even more unobtainable than Nisa. The only sensible thing to do was to keep his feelings and thoughts entirely to himself while enjoying their company and admiring them both from afar.

November 19, 1971, Friday

The blind students were having another really nice evening at Ma's house. They would soon be going home briefly for Thanksgiving break. George, Renny, Nisa, and Debbie were sitting around the table in the kitchen playing cards. George and Renny got along so well, but of course, Renny got along splendidly with everyone; and besides, it made sense to be on friendly terms with a highly skilled, and expense free auto mechanic who was at one's beck and call. As expected, their card game was accompanied by all sorts of banter between Renny and the two females. Dennis and Kitty were at the table in the dining room, just enjoying being together while listening to music on the phonograph. Bob was also nearby to form a kind of trio with them, but right now he was sitting at a small organ that Jeanne Douglas had given to Dorothy when she moved away a few months ago. Always the tinkerer, Bob with his perfect pitch was messing around with the instrument and creating soft sounds.

Grant was sitting alone on the couch with a notebook of braille notes in his lap. He was studying his physics for an upcoming hourly exam. Of the entire group, he alone was studying. In fact, he rarely came to the house without a braille book or notebook, so that if things were quiet enough, he could squeeze in valuable study time. But the schoolwork to him most of the time did not represent laborious, unpleasant mental effort. Rather, he found it to be truly thrilling to see how a differential equation could express and encapsulate the description of a natural phenomenon. When his mind finally succeeded in grasping these things, he was invariably rewarded with a real thrill. It was like Archimedes stepping down into the public bath and suddenly understanding the principle of what we now term specific gravity. The thrill that he had experienced had led him, so the story goes, to run naked through the streets of Syracuse in Sicily while excitedly shouting, "Eureka! Eureka! = I have found it! I have found it!"

Dorothy was simply drifting about, overseeing everyone in the group, straightening things up, sitting down a popcorn bowl here, refilling a drink there. As she moved about, she interacted graciously and wittily with whoever was close at hand; and she was usually humming or singing along with the record playing on the phonograph.

She was now in the dining room, talking with Dennis, Kitty, and Bob, and was standing just behind the couch on which Grant sat. "Now that's a real jaunty tune," she cheerfully observed, "it puts a spring in one's step and makes you want to dance the two step." Ma's comment caught Grant's attention, and for a few minutes all he did was to enjoy the thought of this wonderful woman moving in time to the music. As she stepped around the couch and into the living room to survey things, Grant plucked up his courage and asked, "Mrs. Patterson?" Dorothy stopped and replied "Yeeees, Mr. Duncan." She had drawn out the "yes" very humorously with that beautiful and marvelously expressive voice of hers in response to Grant's unaccustomed formality in addressing her as Mrs. Patterson rather than the usual appellation of Ma. Grant had spoken spontaneously without any real forethought. His unusual choice of address had stemmed from his strong attraction to her, which seemed so inconsistent with the obviously maternal Ma. But he had also been too shy to address her as Dorothy. So his brain had apparently opted for Mrs. Patterson. All this became clear to Grant as soon as he had uttered those two words, but Dorothy, of course, had not understood why Grant had addressed her so, although she had construed it to mean that he was somehow being too formal or serious; and by addressing him humorously as Mr. Duncan, she was attempting to tease him back into thinking of her as Ma.

Dennis, Kitty, and Bob could not help but hear this interchange, and they all chuckled at Dorothy's humorous retort to Grant's formal address. But now Grant plunged ahead. "How would that two step that you mention go? Can you show me?" "Sure!" she replied brightly. "You can put your hands on my shoes, and I'll show you how the steps would go." She now stood a few feet in front of the couch and waited for Grant to kneel on the carpet. He reached out and found her feet and placed his hands on the tops of her shoes. She now began to move side to side and slightly about, taking two steps one way and then one step back. As she did, she hummed a tune, and Grant's hands followed her movements. The cuffs of her slacks gently swayed and brushed the backs of Grant's hands. When the brief tutorial was over, Grant simply said, "Thanks, that was neat." He resumed his position on the couch, and Dorothy continued her rounds to see that everyone was well tended to.

Dorothy had just fulfilled her on-going role of the perfectly gracious hostess that she always was, as well as helping her blind kids understand so many things. But to Grant the simple demonstration had meant much more. Touching her shoes and feeling the cuffs of her slacks had been quite thrilling. Her shoes clearly indicated that she must have petite and dainty feet. How fitting for such a wonderful woman! Unlike Dennis and Renny, whose extremely extroverted natures led them to punching and poking and grabbing people by the arm or shoulder, including Debbie, Nisa, and Dorothy, both Grant and Bob were much more reserved and restrained, so that touching someone would have been viewed as out of place. So, Grant's brief physical encounter with Dorothy's feet had been rare and wonderful for him.

At 10:00 the group began to separate into two parts: those who wanted to go back to the dorms, and the others who planned to spend the night. The former comprised Grant, Bob, and Nisa, all of whom wanted to be sure to have a good start on tomorrow's studies. As these three made their way to the back door in the family room to go out to the car on the driveway, Renny, especially unhappy at Nisa's departure, plaintively asked, "Why do you guys have to be such party poopers?" Nisa mildly answered, "Renny, I've got lots of work to do and a reader to meet at the library tomorrow morning." When both Bob and Grant underscored Nisa's remark with similar ones of their own, Dennis responded, "Gee whiz, guys, we all need to take time off to rest and relax!" At this remark Grant launched into a brief diatribe, "Yeah, well, that's what we've been doing all evening. Now we need to get back to business. You know, you and Renny have been skipping a lot of classes this semester, and maybe you should be worrying about that!"

There was a stunned silence for several seconds, because there had been some real steel in those words, but then Renny and Dennis passed off the criticism with humorous rejoinders. But Dorothy had been impressed by Grant's words, and she would forever remember the image of him standing at that back door, reading Renny and Dennis the riot act.

December 17, 1971, Friday

Tonight was going to be their last group get-together before they scattered off to their families for Christmas break. Bob, Kitty, and Debbie were at the house with George and Carol, but Dorothy and the other four (Dennis, Renny, Nisa, and Grant) were driving around University City with two other car-loads of people from their church to spread the season's cheer by singing Christmas carols.

After finding parking places, all climbed out and assembled before the nearest house. They then began to sing God Rest Ye Merry Gentlemen. The sun had gone down hours ago. It was a cold winter night with about two inches of snow on the ground. It crunched as they walked along from house to house, but despite the darkness and cold, they were all genuinely warmed by their collective presence and the joyfulness embodied in the songs they sang.

Even though it involved so much hurly-burly with all the shopping and gift-wrapping, Christmas was still Dorothy's favorite times of year. It had been that way ever since she had been a child, because her father had enjoyed it so much. They always had a Christmas tree that her father loved to decorate, and he placed beneath the tree a set of toy train tracks and train cars with a landscape of small carved figures made by her Grandfather Klingner, who had been so skillful with his hands; and her father also laid down small mirrors to imitate the surfaces of ponds. The other part of the Christmas season that really pleased Dorothy was, of course, the music. In fact, she enjoyed it for its own sake and often played her Christmas records during other seasons of the year. As a result, this evening of Christmas carols with her church friends and university kids pleased her to no end.

All four of the blind students were thoroughly enjoying themselves too. Dennis, the perennial ham, always on the lookout for a stage on which to perform, was having a ball, not just with the singing, but also talking with other members of the group and shouting season greetings to people who opened their doors to them. Nisa had never done anything like this before and wanted to enjoy this experience, especially in the company of this wonderful woman whom she had come to respect and admire so much, and like whom she so aspired to be. Renny was there in part because his best friend Dennis was there, in part because Nisa was there, and largely just because Renny was Renny, and he loved being out doing things with people. Grant was there in part simply as a member of their little group, but primarily because he could be in the presence of Dorothy and Nisa. It proved to be especially gratifying, because as they moved along from house to house, he took Dorothy's arm as they walked together. He had never been one for buying Christmas gifts, but before they left the house tonight, he had presented Nisa with an album of lovely piano music played by Floyd Cramer. The gift had surprised everyone, and they had listened to the record before they departed. Grant had also asked his mother, who headed the dairy and produce department of a supermarket, to have one of her sales representatives mail to Dorothy a basket of assorted fruit. Despite his resolution to keep his feelings about Dorothy and Nisa to himself, giving them these gifts seemed natural to him, but his feelings had obviously obscured his rational judgment, because although a gift to Dorothy could have been and was easily construed as thanks for all that she did for the blind students, the same was not true for the gift to Nisa. But since it was not followed by any other overt gestures, it was soon forgotten.

Journal Entry
Resumed from September 4

Dec. 26, 1971 (Sunday): Christmas is over. Seems like I've been preparing for it for so long. Really got myself into a tizzy. I think I must not let that happen. My stomach was really bothering me, and this is a lousy pen. Maybe not. That's better. It keeps skipping. Also, hurts my hand to hold it. [Now Dorothy switches pens, this one with a different color ink] Everyone is still asleep. Doesn't seem like Sunday should be today. Wesley was out late. George and Carol sat up and watched Jerry Lewis movies. I slept on the couch. Got phone calls from both grandma [Dorothy's mother] and Bethany. Bethany wasn't sure what it was that I had made her. She thought it was a hostess gown. Patti thought it was a robe. It was a robe, made like a monk's habit with straight sleeves and a hood. Made Carol one also. Made Sally and Patti long light blue nightgowns trimmed with black lace. They all turned out beautifully. Made mittens for Donny and Davie [children of Garry, Ginger and Jim's younger son] and Rickie [son of Bethany' son Rich[. Many things have happened since I last wrote. Most important for Sally. She and Bob are engaged now. Gave her a ring several weeks ago. It is lovely. They set date for May 20. It will be small, only relatives. Wesley is home on leave now. Been home eight days, will return on Tuesday. He's at Port Hueneme, California. He is in the Seabees. He's going to builder's school. The CBs are part of the marines, and the marines are part of the navy. So he can wear either uniform. This time he wears the Marine uniform, not dress, most of the time. Last leave he only had the navy one. So he wore that. He likes the navy, or he seems to. As I sit here writing, I have three dogs fighting and playing at my feet: Brownie [Grandma P's dog] (we're baby-sitting), Gretchen, and Erica. Wesley's gained weight, though he still eats rather little. School'll be over in February. Then it looks like he'll be off to Greece. In September (about the 26th) George, Carol, and I flew to California, so that we could see Wesley's boot camp graduation. My mom loaned us the money. CCC owes George $10,000, but they can't pay it, at least at present. Wesley went to San Diego for boot camp. We flew to LA, had rented car, hotel room, plane fare at a bargain rate, a "See California" trip plan. Spent time with George's Aunt

Ethel and Uncle Shirley, and Uncle Walter and Cora. Saw a lot of Aunt Lucille [Dorothy's aunt], Lois [her daughter] and her girls, Kathy and especially Marianne. Marianne went with us to Disneyland and to the Wax Museum; and she and Carol and Kathy went to Knott's Berry Farm, while George and I went to see the parade that Wesley marched in and played in. He played the bells in the Drum and Bugle Corps. Spent Tuesday Wednesday Thursday in LA, then on Friday we drove down to San Diego for the graduation. It was very impressive. Wesley played his bells with the Drum and Bugle Corps, and the Blue Jacket Choir sang, and the band played. Then the men all marched to the field, and we were all bussed there for the graduation. Afterwards we just sat around and talked till 6:00 P.M. or 8:00 P.M. (Can't remember which). Around 4:30 P.M. we had dinner in the mess hall. Visited with my cousin Sharon in San Diego also. Carol swam in the hotel pool several times, me once. George left San Diego on Monday at noon. Carol and I stayed a day longer and flew home with Wesley. Bethany picked us up at the airport, and we stayed in Homewood Tuesday night. Wesley drove us home on Wednesday. He had leave until almost the end of October. While home, he told the reason he joined the navy was to get away from the drugs that are around here. I hope he exaggerated a lot. He usually does, but he claims to have been on drugs almost constantly at times. He's such a nutty kid. I wonder why he turned out like he did. George and Carol are up now, and I can't concentrate. So I'll quit for now. Forgot to mention that Sally and Bob moved into a new apartment on south Walnut Street a month ago.

Following a Christmas break of about ten days, classes formally resumed at the university on Monday January 3, 1972. Two days earlier on New Year's Day the Pattersons picked up Dennis and Renny and brought them back to University City with them as they were returning from a brief trip to Homewood. Classes for the fall semester went on for another two weeks (ending on Friday Jan. 14) and were then followed by another week of final exams (Monday Jan. 17 to Tuesday Jan 25). Once the blind students were no longer attending their regularly scheduled classes but were preparing for and taking their exams, Dorothy's life and household were frantically busy, as her journal entries for this period reveal.

Journal Entries
Resumed from December 26, 1971

Jan. 5, 1972 (Wednesday): Wesley called Saturday, no, Sunday night. He may get discharged from the navy because of his drug use. How sad! Don't know any details. We went to Homewood last week: Thursday, Friday, and Saturday. Dennis and Renny came back with us. They stayed here Saturday and Sunday nights. Bob, Grant, Kitty, and Nisa came for supper Sunday night. Monday night Debbie came here to study. I popped corn around 10:00 P.M. George took her home about 11:30 P.M. She'll be leaving at the end of the month [when the fall semester ended[. She's going to take a semester off from school. Nisa will graduate at the end of the month. Went to Sweet Adelines last night. Did I say before that Gram K, Ginger, Jim, and Garry went to Houston, Texas for Christmas? Tim and Marilyn moved there in August. Tim works at NASA for Philco Ford. Gram P went to Columbia [South Carolina] to be with Ellen and her family. Both Lawrence and Stan [sons of George's deceased brother Fred] are married, and each has a son now. One named Fred Mayland (Stan's), and Lawrence Earl (Lawrence's). She's coming home this weekend. There are four kids in our third generation. Jim and Pat Lawson have two boys: Donald, born several weeks after dad died; Davie, who is six; and Rich and Barb have two boys: Richard Earl III, who is three; and John Eric, one month. Pat Lawson [Ginger and Jim's daughter-in-law] had a tumor or cyst removed from each breast last week. They were benign. Mom gave me her wedding band to be given to Carol at a later date. I am wearing it.

Jan. 15, 1972 (Saturday): Wesley called yesterday. He sounds good. Said he asked for a Captain's Mast, and the discharge from the drug threat is no longer a threat. He's been tried on that count and was okayed. So now they can't try him again. He sounded relieved, and we certainly are too. I called George right away to let him know. Wesley also said he would get Carol a Pea coat and mail it this weekend along with clothes he no longer needed and some presents he bought. He got his dad an engraved desk set (pen and pencil), Carol a Carpenter record, and a book of poetry for me. I felt ten years younger after he called. Bob Snider called about 5:15 P.M. He couldn't hear. So he called the student health center, and they said to come right over. So I took him. We were there about an hour. They cleaned out his ears and put medicine in one. It was sure cold out, 3 above zero, I think. I knitted on Carol's mittens while I waited. Sally came over to do her laundry yesterday. Gram came home last weekend. We drove to Chicago to get her. Nisa stayed here with Carol. We left here at 6:00 A.M. and got back about 1:30 P.M. Stopped for a few minutes in Homewood. About 4:00 P.M. that afternoon (Saturday) Renny, Carol, and I went shopping for Carol's skates (iceskates), which are a birthday present from Renny and Dennis. The day before we shopped for skates for Renny, Dennis, and Debbie. That day Debbie, Bob, and Kitty had supper here (Friday). Then Renny came home with us for supper. Nisa was still here. After supper I took the kids to the new Physical Education Building to iceskate. Nisa and I were going to watch for a few minutes but ended up staying the whole time. Everyone was having such a good time. Renny skates like you wouldn't believe. Carol has only been on skates a couple of times. Dennis never before. Debbie was pretty good. She took lessons. On Sunday afternoon Carol, Renny, Dennis, and Bob went skating. Bob used an old pair of skates we had here. They were two sizes too small, but he used them anyway. Gram P and I played cards that same afternoon from 4:30 to 9:00 P.M. with time out to pop corn and eat it. Things are bad at CCC. No paychecks for five weeks. We borrowed money from Newton Bank. Guess George did get some money from CCC yesterday, but I don't know how much, because I was at the hospital with Bob when he got home; and he went back to work last night before I got back. They are all bunching up into a few offices and will rent the rest of the building.

Jan. 16, 1972 (Sunday): Soon will be time for early church. We've missed so much lately that I think the building will collapse when we go today. Yesterday morning Carol and I went swimming with Nisa and Renny at new Physical Education Building. We were the only ones there besides Ron and Bob [probably life guards], who had to be there. Came here for lunch. Nisa had to be at the library by 2:00 P.M. Renny stayed here, and he and George worked on the car (LTD). I proofread a paper for Renny. Also set hair and took five minute nap. Betty [Washington, Carol's friend] came to stay with Carol while George and I went to Barbershop installation banquet. We dropped Renny off at dorm on our way to the banquet. Midge and Chuck [Evans] invited everyone over afterwards, but we didn't go. Very cold today, never got above zero.

Jan. 17, 1972 (Monday): Wow! Eighteen above zero at 5:30 A.M. We're having a heat wave! Very windy. Yesterday morning [Sunday] I got up at 5:00 A.M., because Widdle [= "Little," Dorothy's cute affectionate name for Missy the cat] wanted to go out. We don't usually keep her in at night, but it was so cold, we did. As usual, she made a mess in the bedroom. So I stayed up.

Got ready for early church, but the cars wouldn't start. Called Shackmans, but they were gone already. Called Adams and Dickersons, but they weren't going. So I stayed home. So I went back to bed at 9:00 A.M. and slept till 12:30. I knitted most all day, popped corn. Betty and Carol went to the shopping center and then changed bedrooms for Carol. She wanted the little room, Wesley's old one. George worked on cars and also worked on income tax junk. He can't find our 68 return, and he needs it. Bethany called last night. She has a week off starting February 3. She needs a traveling companion on a trip to Houston to see Tim and Marilyn; and of course, I said yes. We'll fly. Leave on Thursday, return the next Thursday. Wow! Sure is nice to have relatives with money. Talked to Renny, Dennis, and Debbie, Bob, and Grant on the phone. Dennis and Kitty are coming to dinner tonight, and I'll read to Dennis while Kitty does laundry and homework. We're going to have sauerkraut. George and Carol took two loaves of bread over to Renny. Got a paperback copy of *Everything But Money* for Wesley today, Monday. Scrubbed and waxed the kitchen floor, took all morning. Earlier I finished letters to both moms and Wesley. Mailed letters and book to Wesley, grocery shopped, took Bob to the health center on campus again. His ears are fine now. Came home, put sauerkraut on to cook, and took nap. Got a letter from Jeanne. Also a piece of material from Socorro Carino in the Philippines. It is a pretty green piece with embroidery. Carol went to Betty Washington's house after school. George picked up Kitty, Dennis, Debbie, and then Carol on his way home from work. Guess it was 6:30 P.M. before they got here. Had chicken (Carol can't eat pork [because of her diet]), Jell-O, rolls, and tapioca pudding. Kids watched TV and studied. I read to Deb from 10:00 P.M. to midnight. Deb and I talked till 12:30. Then she said she wished there was some way to pay me back for all I've done for her. The house is a haven, etc. All the kids stayed here overnight.

Jan. 18, 1972 (Tuesday): Up at 5:15. Awake since 5:00 A.M. Missy got left in the house running loose (we generally put her in the shower stall) and woke me. Bethany called last night. We are going to leave a day early. Made bacon and scrambled eggs. All four kids left with George. I went swimming. Left here a little late, about 8:25. Swam my quarter mile, kicked a quarter mile, had lesson. On my way home I went past the post office to mail some letters, past bank to deposit money for Renny, over to Arnold Hall for Deb, over to Nash for Dennis, dropped Dennis off at Holmes, picked up Deb's things at Garfield [dormitory], stopped at jewelry store with charm and bracelet to be soldered for graduation present for Nisa, stopped at grocery store. Just got home when the phone rang. It was Dr. Potter. He wanted Deb to go see a Dr. Young at the Mental Health Clinic. Mrs. Putnam had called from Chicago, because she was worried after her talk with Deb the night before. Mrs. Putnam is a psychologist in Chicago who knows and has helped Deb. So I had to present it to Deb in such a way that she would accept it. Wow! What an assignment! We talked at least a half an hour or more. Couldn't let Deb know that Mrs. C had anything to do with all this. So now Deb is going at 9:00 A.M. tomorrow. Set my hair, dried it, helped Deb make salmon casserole for supper. Also made hot fudge sauce for ice cream. Deb paid for dessert ingredients. Nisa called. We talked and invited her to come to eat. So George picked her up on the way home. I went to Sweet Adelines. Deb really wanted me to stay home.

Jan. 22, 1972 (Saturday): On Wednesday I took Deb to see Doctor Young. He gave her two kinds of tranquilizers (to me, I should say). Also, he asked her to give me her sleeping pills. She didn't talk too long to him, because she could come back next week if she'd like. Then we shopped for yarn for Deb to make her hot pads. At 5:00 P.M. I went to pick up Nisa and Renny and also ran into Dennis, Kitty, Bob, Grant, and so brought them all home for supper. Had to scrounge around to find more food. Grant said the nicest thing that evening. He said, "The food tastes so good here, and it's so good to get away from the dorm food. Heck! Even the ice cubes taste good here." These kids are easily satisfied. They eat anything and are happy. Deb had a reader coming at 7:00 P.M. So we shut the doors to the living room area and tried to keep quiet. Dennis studied several hours in the red-white-and-blue room. Grant worked on a paper using our typewriter. He sat on the couch. Kitty and Bob worked on the extra table with one on her typewriter, the other on a braille machine. Renny, Nisa, George, and I played yahtzee and Hearts. Carol had to baby-sit. Kitty, Dennis, and Nisa stayed overnight. Renny, Bob, and Grant went home. Thursday I swam. Debbie, Dennis, Kitty stayed here. Nisa went to her dorm as George went to work. At 2:00 P.M. I took Dennis and Kitty to their dorms and picked up Grant, Bob, and Renny for shopping. Went to record store and radio shop, Sears and Penney's, and made a quick stop at doughnut shop. Got back at 5:30. Deb had a reader at 2:00 P.M. and also at 7:00 P.M. Carol watched TV. George went to Barbershoppers, and I slept from 7:00 to 9:00 P.M. Then I did two loads of laundry. George picked up Nisa on his way home. On Friday I did laundry all day: ours, Nisa's, Debbie's, Dennis', and Kitty's. George took Nisa several places and ended up being treated to lunch at Uncle Joe's by Renny, Dennis, Kitty, and Nisa. I tried to clean house, but it wasn't easy, because Deb followed me, and we talked. She made another appointment to see Doctor Young. She and I both talked to Doctor Potter. Carol read several short stories to Deb. Deb was tricked into it very slyly, and Carol was so pleased to read to Deb. The first pill Deb took was too weak. The second we tried was too strong. So Doctor Young said to take two of the weaker ones, and that seemed to do the trick. She was better yesterday afternoon than she's been all along. She talks to Mrs. Putnam almost every day. She suggested that Deb see Doctor Young once more.... Knitted in the evening and went to bed early. This morning (Saturday) it is foggy. I slept till 6:30 for a change. This afternoon at 2:30 we are going to a Barbershop show in Chicago. Will ride with the Meyers. A bunch are going. We'll caravan down, eat supper at the Barn, and then on to McCormack Place for the show. Carol is going to help Kitty pack up and move and then will stay overnight there; and Deb is going to stay at her dorm and pack up etc. Wesley telephoned yesterday, collect this time. Just wanted to talk. George was fired from CCC on Thursday morning. They owe us $10,000, and he has a piece of property that Roy owns. Roy wanted George to give it back, and we said no. So Roy fired him. The evening in Chicago was fun, but we spent $38. It wasn't that much fun.

Jan. 26, 1972 (Wednesday): Slept till 6:30 A.M. Of course, I didn't get to bed till 1:00 A.M. Grant and Bob were still at the kitchen table talking when I went to bed. Invited them over special for dinner, because all the other kids come over more often. So that was just to make up. Deb was here, of course, because she's still staying here. Deb went with me to visit Sweet Adelines last night. It was visitor's night. Must have had twenty guests. Last Sunday was a lost day, more or less. Got to bed about 2:30 A.M. and was up at 6:30 A.M. Went to early church and Sunday school. Came home and took a nap till noon. Had hot dogs from Der Wienerschnitzel for dinner. Went back to bed and slept till 4:00 P.M. Picked Carol and Deb up at 6:30 P.M. Went to bed about 9:00 P.M. On Monday morning I took Sally wedding dress shopping and also visited The House of Flowers. Sally got a lovely long plum colored dress with white lace trimming, with full sleeves. Cost her $48. Her first one cost us $160. I wanted to make one this time and last time also, but she still doesn't think much of my sewing, I guess. In the afternoon Deb and I took a French test at the Rehab Center. Yesterday morning I skipped swimming and did things around the house. Took Deb over to the university in afternoon to do some odd jobs. Then she helped me get supper for Bob and Grant. While we were at Sweet Adelines, George helped Bob mount something or other on his phonograph. When we got home, Grant was asleep on the couch [in the living room]; George was dozing in front of the TV [in the family room]; and Bob was goofing with the phonograph. Carol was asleep. We sat in the kitchen a while, and the kids ate an unbelievable amount of food: sandwiches and cookies I brought home from Sweet Adelines, and banana pudding I had here. This morning Deb had another appointment with Doctor Young at the student mental health center. Also, today George will take Sora to the bus station to go visit Nisa in Chicago. Sora is a Japanese fellow who is a student here. Then Kitty, Bob, Renny, and Dennis will move in for a few days.

Jan. 29, 1972 (Saturday): Got up at 5:05 A.M. Below zero. These past few days have been busy ones with the family increased. Skipped swimming both days this week. Wesley called at noon on Tuesday, mostly to talk. He will be home on the eleventh or twelfth of February. I will return from Houston on the tenth. So I'll stay in Homewood till we hear from him. He sounds good. Yesterday I took Carol and a school friend to Sewfro to buy supplies. They begin sewing instruction next week. Carol was sick Monday Tuesday Wednesday and went back Thursday and Friday. She baby-sat Thursday and Friday also. Got a letter from Nisa the other day. Renny and Dennis left yesterday [for the end of the semester]. They'll be back Sunday [for the beginning of the next semester]. I'm not sure if they'll come here or to the dorms. Deb had decided on Wednesday to return home. She doesn't like the confusion, etc. with "our additions." But now I think she has decided to stay. She is a very fussy child. I think her folks have let her have her own way way too much. Tonight Bob has a date with a girl on campus. On Thursday night George took Bob, Renny, and Dennis to Barbershoppers. Guess they had a ball. They even got a tenor and sang in a quartet. I collected ten dollars each from Kitty and Bob, and five dollars from Renny and Dennis toward groceries. Norm's Repairs put a new motor in our dishwasher yesterday. We've had trouble with it since July. They've been lousy about their repair service.

Jan. 31, 1972 (Monday): Sally, Bob, and I went to Marge Malaise's house, and Sally picked out her cake. Carol went to 4H. Bob had a date with a girl on campus. George and Deb drove him over there about 7:15 P.M. and went back after midnight. Then he and Deb sat up and talked till about 2:00 A.M. Went to early church and Sunday school. George just stayed for church. Kitty and Carol fixed dinner on Saturday and again on Sunday. They even cleaned up the kitchen afterwards. At 6:00 P.M. we moved Kitty from Nash dorm to

Miller. Dropped Carol, Kitty, and Betty off at Physical Education Building to ice skate and dropped Bob off at church. Picked them up again at 8:00 P.M. (church) and 9:00 P.M. (ice skating). I've been taping records, using Bob's phono and Debbie's recorder. Deb was all wound up by bedtime. We had just started to talk when everyone got home.

The spring semester for the university formally began on Monday, February 7. Since Dorothy was away from University City visiting her brother Tim in Houston for a week (Feb. 2-9), the blind students simply returned to their dorm rooms on Sunday, the day before classes began. There were, however, several important changes. Debbie was no longer on campus, because she was taking the semester off to become fully mentally well. Nisa had finished her work at the university but continued to stay in University City as a Patterson house guest until she finally left on Sunday March 26, but even after that she frequently visited University City and stayed at the Patterson's house. Kitty was now living in Miller, which was much closer to Dennis and Bob in the Men's Dormitory Area than her previous dorm room in Nash Hall. Dennis had finally left his triple room in Holmes and was now rooming with Renny in his room in Forester. Bob remained in his dorm room just down the hall from Dennis and Renny, and Grant was still in his Holmes dorm room, a short walk from Forester.

Another important change involved Dennis and Grant. They were now enrolled in two classes together. One was an intermediate level German class in which they were reading German literature and discussing the material in class in German, taught by a truly charismatic teacher Herr Bauer (Mr. Farmer). It turned out to be a wonderful experience for both Dennis and Grant. They also signed up for the same physical education course in wrestling. The class was taught by a young black man named Dell Emerson, who had been on the U.S. Olympic wrestling team. But besides being an absolutely fantastic wrestler, he was also a genuinely nice guy with a tremendous sense of humor; and Dennis and Grant liked and greatly admired him. Not only did they attend this class together, but they usually walked to and from the gym together as well. All these shared experiences succeeded in making Dennis and Grant even closer friends, so that Grant soon confided in Dennis his strong feelings of affection for Dorothy and Nisa; and thereafter Dennis served as Grant's trusted confidante in these matters.

Journal Entry
Resumed from January 31

Feb. 13, 1972 (Sunday): So I am back from Texas now. Had a good time. Did a lot of good eating at German restaurants and Mexican ones. All our meals were eaten out except for the pizza, sauerkraut, and western steak Bethany and I prepared. Went to Galveston and San Jacinto to sightsee and, of course, to NASA. That was most interesting. Saw Mission Control and some huge vacuum chambers where all the space things are checked; and saw where the moon rocks are taken and kept germ-free. Spent at least thirty dollars on souvenirs. Flew Branif there and Delta back. Also flew on a small plane from Houston into the suburbs where Tim lives. Buddy [Bethany' new husband-to-be] drove us to the airport and picked us up again. We got to Homewood around 4:00 P.M. Then at 10:00 P.M. Bethany and I drove back down to the airport to get Wesley, who is now home on leave before he goes to Adak Island in the Aleutians. Patti Decker wrecked her car the day we got to Houston, about 11:30 P.M. She swerved to miss a car, hit some ice, and ran into a telephone pole and fence. Police said they don't see how the girls got out alive. Janet was not injured at all, and Patti had her nose broken, plus bruised everywhere: her face, her legs, her arms, her eyes swollen shut almost. Stitches in her ear, mouth, and nose. Was in the hospital for three days. She looked bad when we saw her, but she looked good compared to how she had looked the week before. Wesley and I got home about 4:00 P.M. on Friday. He visited around with mom, Bethany, and Ginger during the day. He wanted to see Garry [his cousin], but he didn't get home from school. I must write to Rich and Barb. I left my car with them to use [during the trip to Houston] with half a tank of gas. When I picked it up, it was full. Nisa is here now. Don't know for sure how long she'll stay. She's got the blue room [end bedroom]. Carol's room is right by the blue room. It's the red white and blue room [middle bedroom]. But Wesley is in there, and so Carol is in the pink room [front bedroom]. Don't know what George has been doing all day since I've been gone except being a housefrau. he's very good at piddling around and getting not much done. He and Wesley are so much alike, it scares me. When I finally realized this a few years back, it was almost more than I could take. Yesterday (2,12,72) I worked from 8:00 A.M. to 5:00 P.M. at The House of Flowers [because of extra help needed for the Valentine's Day crush]. Today I am dead. Partly I am tired from being on my feet all day, and partly it is from roller skating we did the night before with the Rehab kids at Church. It was fun. Bill said not to come to work today till 10:00 A.M.

The one really big change that affected Dorothy's group of blind students at this time was Bob, Dennis, Grant, and Renny forming themselves into a Barbershop quartet that they eventually named The Out of Sighters. The dream that Dennis had first conceived last fall was now being realized. As Dorothy noted in her journal, George had taken Bob, Dennis, and Renny as visitors to a Barbershop meeting in late January as the semester was ending; and the experience had persuaded Bob and Renny to embrace Dennis' dream. As soon as classes resumed in February, the three talked Grant into completing the quartet.

The spring Barbershop concert in University City was scheduled for Saturday April 8; and it was customary that after all such formal events, there was an informal afterglow in which other, not nearly so polished groups performed. Accordingly, as soon as The Out of Sighters came into being, it was their goal to become good enough so as not to embarrass themselves too greatly by singing a few songs during the afterglow. Consequently, the lives of these four blind guys for the first half of this spring semester were dominated by meeting and practicing their singing.

True to his word given to Dennis last fall, Chuck Evans gladly agreed to be the group's instructor. All five first met on Sunday afternoon February 13 in Dorothy's living room. Chuck had the four young men stand in a line in front of the couch and first asked each of them to sing something, so that he could decide who was going to sing what part. After only a short time taken up with this testing, which was, of course, accompanied by all sorts of humorous remarks and wise cracks, Chuck determined that Grant would sing bass, Dennis baritone, Renny lead, and Bob (who happened to have perfect pitch) tenor. Chuck filled out this first session by quickly teaching each one his part for a simple and short song, Bill Grogan's Goat. Chuck used Dorothy's piano to play each part that the person then had to imitate and follow, accompanied by critiques, and then more repetition until Chuck was relatively satisfied. After about 45 minutes they were finally ready to put it all together for the first time as a group; and then they sang it over and over again while Chuck carefully listened and offered comments and advice. He then dismissed his pupils with instructions to learn this simple song as well as possible before their next lesson on the following Sunday.

In the meantime Dorothy had, of course, done her part in helping the fledgling little group along. Chuck had indicated that they would next learn to sing The Old Songs. Dorothy therefore obtained the quartet sheet music for this song and used a cassette machine to record all four parts on a tape that the guys then used to learn their parts. When they reassembled on the following Sunday February 20, The Out of Sighters had not only done a pretty good job in mastering Bill Grogan's Goat, but they also already had a good start on The Old Songs. Chuck was impressed, at least by their diligence, if not by their talent.

Obviously, the four could not spend all their waking hours in practicing. They were college students and had their courses to worry about. The tension between these two commitments caused almost constant friction, because Bob and Grant were much more conscientious about their studies and were more reluctant than Dennis and Renny to devote more and more time to their singing. Dennis and Renny further aggravated this problem by their overall lack of self-discipline and procrastination. Their normal meeting place was Dennis and Renny's dorm room, but so often when Bob and Grant arrived, they discovered that Dennis or Renny was in the middle of something else, and they had to sit around until all four were finally ready. As a result, virtually every practice session began with volleys of verbal abuse, usually, but not always, hurled at one another good-naturedly; and of course, at least forty percent of the words that were shot back and forth were profane or obscene. Despite these frictions, the four thoroughly enjoyed themselves in their common enterprise, and the sophomoric hilarity that characterized their interaction soon manifested itself in their collaborating in rewriting the words to Bill Grogan's Goat. Its original words were as follows:

Bill Grogan's goat was doing fine, ate six red shirts right off the line. Bill took a stick, gave him a whack, and tied him to the railroad track, the railroad track. The whistle blew. The train drew nigh. Bill Grogan's goat was doomed to die. He gave a heave of awful pain, coughed up the shirts, and flagged the train, and flagged the train.

The Out of Sighters changed these words to go like this:

Bill Grogan's balls were doing fine till they were hung right on the line. Bill's wife came out, gave them a whack, and tied them to the mother fucking track, the mother fucking track. The whistle blew. The train drew nigh. Bill Grogan's balls were doomed to die. He gave a heave of awful force, tore off his balls, and died of course, and died of course.

The four greatly enjoyed singing this emended version of the song, but they always did when it was just the four of them singing together in Dennis and Renny's room. Often they were unable to sing it to its end, because one of them would lose his composure and burst into laughter, at which he was joined in his uncontrollable mirth and also roundly abused for disrupting the singing. After keeping this song a secret among themselves for several weeks, they finally disclosed its existence to Dorothy; and after quite a bit of encouragement from her, they somewhat reluctantly sang it for her, and she received it graciously with condescending amusement.

Since Wesley's leave was scheduled to end on Thursday February 24, Dorothy decided to combine his need to fly out of Chicago with her desire to visit her relatives once again in Homewood. She and Wesley drove to Chicago; and after seeing him off, Dorothy visited her mother and sisters in Homewood over the following weekend and then returned to University City Sunday morning in time to be there for the Out of Sighters' next singing lesson with Chuck Evans. But the quartet had had an impromptu lesson the day before. Since George was by himself, he offered to bring the Out of Sighters over to the house for an extra practice session that he would conduct. Although none of the four blind students let on, the rehearsal was really hilarious, because George never could carry a tune, and here he was attempting to help these four blind guys, one of whom had perfect pitch, with their various parts. He would tunelessly sing a section and then ask one of them to imitate him. Well, they certainly were not going to imitate him exactly. As far as the members of the quartet could judge, he never suspected how outrageously funny he was to them that Saturday afternoon. When they were all safely back on campus, they were finally able to let out the merriment that they had been struggling to contain.

Another humorous incident occurred during one of the formal Sunday afternoon lessons conducted by Chuck Evans. It resulted from Renny's inability not to say something off-color in formal company. At the very beginning of the practice session the four blind guys were, as usual, assembled in Dorothy's living room together with George and Chuck. Dorothy was working nearby in the kitchen and was well positioned to monitor the session from that vantage point. Chuck wanted to take Renny through his part of the group's newest song, This is My Country. After being asked to sing his part alone, Renny began by singing "This is my cunt ree." He stopped at the end of this phrase, apparently expecting everyone to laugh uproariously at his obscene play on words. But since Chuck was their parents' age and not well known to them, Bob, Dennis, and Grant all maintained a stony silence. Both George and Chuck also said nothing. No one was prepared to respond, either humorously or disapprovingly, to Renny's obscene rendition. Everyone was clearly doing his best to ignore it and to pretend that Renny had not just sung those words in that way. But Renny was not to be deterred from having his little joke. He therefore repeated the same line, just as ostentatiously as before: "This is my cunt ree!" Again, there was no response from any of the other five males in the room, but another tense silence stretched on for several seconds. At this point Dorothy walked from the kitchen into the living room and defused the tense silence simply by saying with a sweet little laugh in her voice, "All right, Renny, let's knock it off." After the rest now joined in with a few chuckles, the lesson proceeded smoothly.

Journal Entry
Resumed from February 13

March 14, 1972 (Tuesday): Today is swimming. Nisa has been coming with me. Days are getting longer. It's real light by 6:00 A.M. now. Been busy since I last wrote. Wesley was home till Thursday February 23 or 26 or something. When he left, he was feeling very uneasy about his coming experience. He now has decided that he does not like being in the navy, but he hasn't decided what to do about it. We have not heard from him yet. It will be three weeks Thursday since he left. I finally sent a letter to his old address in California with "Please Forward" on it. Hope he can hang on a while longer. Sally had a wedding planned for March 4. Everything was ready except the groom. The night before, he said no. I think he's been saying no in his own way all along, but Sally just won't listen. They're seeing Doctor Miller now, and they'll decide by the middle of April whether it will be go or abort. I think for Sally's sake that abort would be the best answer, but who am I to judge? Julie Nelson was here for six days during the wedding week. She came with some people from her town who have a married daughter here. She was to go back with them on Sunday, but she stayed until Monday and flew home. She had such a good time, she just couldn't leave. We enjoyed her, but I had forgotten how slow moving she was. The kids have been coming over every

Sunday, because Renny, Bob, Dennis, and Grant are singing in a Barbershop quartet and are trying to get to be good enough to sing at the afterglow for the men's show on April 8. The state of things between George and me has been very bad since I came back from Houston. I think it is because Nisa is here. It seems that whenever anyone is around, George has to show off and act worse than usual. It has taken me a long time to realize this. That is why he has always acted so lousy to me when his folks are around. It helps his self-esteem. I'm sorry I don't. If I didn't have to sleep with him, perhaps I could feel differently and react differently toward him. He has been terrible lately. He hangs on me all night long and acts like a spoiled two-year-old would toward the mother. I don't want to be his mother. I wish he would grow up and act like an adult rather than a child all the time. I don't know how much more my nerves can take. Thank you, God, for introducing me to swimming and to the kids at the U of I. Both things are so good for me. I can get rid of pent-up emotions and also relax and forget everything. Jeanne is coming this Thursday. Oh wow! Will I be glad to see her!

March 18, 1972, Saturday

Three weeks from tonight would be the big night for the Out of Sighters. They had been taught four songs, of which they were planning to sing two at the afterglow: This is My Country, and My Wild Irish Rose. They had therefore agreed at the table in the dorm cafeteria that as soon as they had all finished eating supper, they would rendezvous at Dennis and Renny's room and would have a really serious practice session.

Unlike so many times when they had agreed to meet to work on their songs, Renny and Dennis were ready to go. All were in agreement that time was running short, and they should start being really serious and keep their horsing around to a minimum. After running through all four songs and being rather pleased with how they had performed, Dennis suggested, "Hey, guys, we need to sing somewhere else instead of this damn little dorm room. We should start singing in a place much bigger that's something like the big room we'll be singing in three weeks from tonight." When all agreed, they began trying to figure out where a place like that might be. Several ideas were tossed out and rejected for various reasons until Bob suggested, "Hey, how about the big open area on the other side of the dorm outside the lounge and dining hall entrance? If we stood and sang there, we wouldn't be disturbing the people inside the lounge or anyone else except those happening to be walking by."

They then walked over to the agreed upon place, stood together side by side, and began their singing. The cavernous space and smooth floor and wall surfaces formed a kind of echo chamber that made their singing really resound. As they finished This is My Country, Renny remarked with pleasure, "That sounded pretty damn cool!" "Yeah man, it sure did!" affirmed Dennis. "Yeah, it did sound pretty good," agreed Bob in his rather reserved way. As they continued singing, students were constantly walking past them on their way to Saturday night dates and other things. Since all members of the quartet were blind, none of them could tell from people's expressions what impact their singing might be having upon them, but they had long grown accustomed to that, and all but Bob generally took the attitude, "Hey, fuck them!" But as they were singing My Wild Irish Rose for the third time, they were aware that several people had walked up to them and had stopped. As soon as the song ended, the Out of Sighters were greeted by these passers-by with their own song in four part harmony: The Whiffinpoof Song. It really sounded good!

They were four college students visiting from another college. They happened to drive up to University City for the weekend to visit some friends and just happened to be walking by. They had been singing together since high school and had even performed once on their local radio station. By now all eight had moved into the lounge and were sitting around a big table, just talking and finding things out about one another. The way in which they had met lent a special excitement and pleasure to their conversing; and as they spoke, one of the four from the other college went over to the piano that stood ten feet away and began playing; and man, could he play! His repertoire contained many jaunty tunes from ragtime and blues. His rendition of St. Louis Blues was magnificent and added further enjoyment to their chance encounter. But since the four strangers were on their way to a party, they eventually excused themselves and left. Nevertheless, their meeting served to boost the confidence of the Out of Sighters.

March 22, 1972, Wednesday

Dennis and Renny were lounging on their beds in Forester, just killing time before heading off to eat supper in the cafeteria with Bob and Grant. "Hey, Renny," Dennis said, "I need to talk to you about something serious."

"All right, Dennis. What is it?" "Well, Carol called Kitty today and said that she wanted to organize a surprise wedding anniversary party for Ma and George, and she wanted to make sure that we could and would like to come. But she also wanted to know if we had any ideas about the party itself." "Fuckin' A, man. We'll go. But do you think Ma will really want a party?" "Why shouldn't she?" "Well," Renny cautiously began, "I'm not really sure how she feels about George, and whether she would like to have an anniversary party." "You don't think they're happy together?" Dennis asked with obvious surprise in his voice. "Well, Dennis, I really don't know," Renny replied, now talking with obvious seriousness, "I really don't know. But it's funny. I've never noticed them calling each other by any kind of endearment like honey, or sweetheart; and I've never been aware of one ever kissing the other, even as a casual standard greeting. Don't you think that's a little odd for a supposedly happily married couple?" "I had never realized that before," Dennis said in genuine amazement, "I guess you could be right about them. You know, we all just assume that everything is fine between them, because Ma is so cool in dealing with everything. But maybe things really aren't right in their marriage. But anyway, Carol, I guess, is going to have this surprise party, and we certainly should be there."

March 24, 1972, Friday

It was just a few minutes after 7:00 in the evening, and the surprise anniversary party was about to begin. Nisa, of course, was already there in the house as a house guest. Dennis and Kitty had come over earlier in the day ostensibly to do their laundry; and Renny had also just come along for the ride. Nothing odd about that. Then after they had been at the house for a while, Kitty casually suggested to Dorothy that since they would all be going off for a week, starting tomorrow, for spring break, why didn't they see if Bob and Grant were interested and able to come over, and they could have a nice little get together. As expected, Dorothy readily agreed, called both of them, and had George collect them when he had to go out to run some errands. Thus, everyone had been craftily assembled at the house.

At 5:30 Dorothy and George left the house and joined another couple to dine out in commemoration of their twenty-fifth wedding anniversary. When they had been married in 1947, that day had also been the twenty-fifth wedding anniversary of George's parents, a synchronism which Dorothy had come to despise over the years.

As soon as Dorothy and George had left the house, Carol and Nisa had taken over the kitchen and had made a cake that Carol had then iced and decorated with "Happy Anniversary 25." Carol placed the cake on the dining table, so that it could not be seen by her parents when they first came home and entered the house through the back door in the family room. She and Kitty then took up posts in the living room to watch for their return. Carol wanted everyone to be in the living and dining rooms when her parents arrived, and then they could spring into the kitchen through two different doors (one leading into the hallway and the other going into the dining room) and yell, "Surprise! Happy Silver Anniversary!"

The critical moment finally arrived. Kitty spotted the Patterson car and that of the other couple coming down Boardman and turning onto Rachel Drive. Carol quickly got everyone into position, but where was Grant? Perhaps he was in the bathroom right now. When Dorothy and George entered the kitchen area, the surprise was joyfully sprung, and Carol proudly carried the cake from the dining room and placed it on the kitchen table for her parents to see. The reactions from both Dorothy and George were totally devoid of emotion. It was as if they were greeting someone about whom they really didn't care. As the next few hours passed by, Dorothy did not enliven this get together with her usual vivacity and dazzling charm. She was rather quiet and subdued.

Grant's reaction to the silver anniversary party was highly personal and emotional. Actually, he was not in the bathroom when Dorothy and George arrived, as Carol had thought. He had been sitting for quite some time by himself in the family room, keeping the dogs company, since they were not allowed to come into the nicely carpeted living and dining rooms. Or were they keeping him company? In any case, when the dogs alerted him as to the arrival of the cars, he stood up from the couch and had proceeded as far as the kitchen when the door opened, and the four adults stepped inside. Grant then halted and stood motionless near the kitchen table about twelve feet away from them as they politely said their good-evenings to one another. He felt a mixture of feelings: wondering at them as a married couple for 25 years, and wishing that somehow he could be Dorothy's husband in place of George. Indeed, his physical nearness to and distance from Dorothy right then seemed to mirror perfectly how he wanted to be so close to her spiritually and emotionally, and yet they were so distant from one another. That particular moment had such a profound impact upon Grant's mind that for the rest of the party he was in a kind of mental fog.

March 26, 1972, Sunday

Dorothy, George, and Carol would be arriving soon to pick up Renny and Dennis to give them a ride back to Chicago, as they took Nisa home and also paid another visit to relatives in Homewood. The university would be closed this coming week for spring break. Renny and Dennis were therefore throwing together whatever they would need for their brief vacation. As usual, they talked incessantly as they moved about the room and gathered up things, but ever since the party the other night the really big topic that had been on their minds had been Ma's and George's reactions. Since they had stayed at the house until just a short time ago, they had not had an opportunity to discuss the matter openly.

"Well, Renny," Dennis began, "looks like you might be right about Ma and George. Man! that was a real dud of a party; and she didn't seem to be the least bit pleased by it." "Boy! You got that right!" Renny rejoined, "They've always seemed to me to be rather distant toward one another." "Yeah well, I guess I never really paid it much attention, but I will now. That's really something, because I think everyone else in the group has assumed that they have had a happy marriage, because Ma is always so cheerful." "That might be how she behaves toward everyone else, but it's not how she acts toward George," observed Renny.

Journal Entries
Resumed from March 14

March 29, 1972 (Wednesday): Jeanne came and left again. She was only here from 2:00 P.M. Thursday till 9:00 A.M. the next day. Enjoyed the visit though. I am working this week at The House of Flowers. It is Easter or spring vacation for school kids. Sally came home tonight for good this time, I think. She didn't want to talk. Nisa is gone. She left Sunday. We took her, Renny, and Dennis home. Dropped the boys off, and then we had dinner at Nisa's. Her mom and dad are swell. Brought home three African violets [as gifts from Nisa's parents]. They are lovely. Got two letters from Wesley now. He is very cold in Adak, and windy; Not much to do. But Wesley seems in good spirits. Had our 25th anniversary. We went up to Homewood; and Lawsons, mom, Bethany, and Buddy took us out to dinner to the Sportsmen's Club. Got a money tree with 25 one-dollar bills on it, and then 25 dollars from Buddy. On the anniversary itself Nisa made dinner; and she and Carol cleaned up. Then on Friday Carol had the University kids come over for a party for us. She planned it well. I hated it because of how I feel about George, but I had to pretend I was pleased.

March 31, 1972 (Friday): Worked eight hours every day this week so far. Today will be a twelve hour or more day. I get tired, but we have fun. Mostly I've wrapped plants, I've also answered the phone, waited on customers, folded boxes for roses, fixed bows, etc. We've had a short note from Nisa, and Carol got a letter also. None from Wesley yet this week. George took his mom home on Tuesday afternoon. She was here since the Wednesday before, our joint anniversary. Carol worked most of yesterday on a culotte dress for herself. She did a good job. She did it all herself. Cut it out also. I gave a little assistance with the zipper, because she never put an invisible one in before. Carol's report card this time was about her best: 4 B's, 2 C's, and 1 D in math. Almost at a standstill with my grade 2 braille. Have some of it learned. [Dorothy's journal abruptly ends here]

April 8, 1972, Saturday

After attending the Barbershop concert, the party of nine climbed back into the two cars and traveled to the Howard Johnson's Hotel to the afterglow. Nisa had returned to University City on the bus in the early afternoon, and she had brought with her a blind friend named Judy Carson. Besides Dorothy, George, and the four Out of Sighters themselves, the only other person in their group was Kitty. Carol had preferred to spend the night with a friend. The afterglow was held in a very large banquet hall decked out with long tables. It began with four Barbershop quartets singing two songs each. The groups stood near the wall at one of the room's narrower sides, so that they could be heard fairly well by everyone. The first group interspersed their singing with corny humor derived from the popular TV show, *Hogan's Heroes*.

When it came time for the Out of Sighters, they took up their position, unfolded their canes for everyone to see, and then Dennis formally announced, "We're a quartet known as the Out of Sighters." After a burst of laughter, he continued, "And we're going to sing two songs: first, This is My Country; and then, My Wild Irish Rose." Bob with his perfect pitch served as their pitch pipe to get them started. After polite applause following the first song, they enlivened the beginning of My Wild Irish Rose with a silly gag. Renny, who sang the lead, began with a pitiful sort of note. Grant reached across and gave Renny a hard thump on his chest with his fist. "All right now, sing it right," Grant ordered. After some laughter, they started up and performed it quite well. Following the final applause, the Out of Sighters stepped away to make room for the fourth and last group. Chuck Evans approached and congratulated them, and they in turn thanked him for his invaluable help. So began and ended in one brief performance the public career of the Out of Sighters.

The four blind guys sat back down at their table, and everyone there was in a jubilant mood. When the fourth quartet had finished their singing, the designated master of ceremonies led the entire gathering, largely consisting of Barbershoppers and Sweet Adelines, in a series of sing-alongs. He would call out the title of a well-known song and start it off, and everyone in the banquet hall joined in. The volume of the singing was quite high, and the mixture of male and female voices was very beautiful. When they sang Let Me Call You Sweetheart, Grant was deeply moved, because the song's lovely words together with the haunting music seemed to express so exactly how he felt toward Dorothy and Nisa, who were both seated across from him.

April 9, 1972, Sunday

When the afterglow began to break up around midnight, the party of nine climbed back into the two cars. Grant was very careful to follow Nisa, so that he could sit beside her as they all went back to 1801 Rachel Drive. He had recently decided that he needed to inform Nisa of his strong feelings of affection toward her. He was sure that such a profession would lead nowhere, because Nisa and Sora were becoming increasingly serious, and even Renny was now out of the picture. But Grant was hoping that the confession would prove to be purgative and would mitigate his inner anxiety. Thus, after he and Nisa were sitting side by side in the back seat, he whispered to her, "Nisa, if you wouldn't mind, I would like to talk with you alone for a few minutes when we get to the house." She agreed, and they sat in silence for the remainder of the journey.

While other members of the party were using the bathroom or simply moving about the house, trying to decide what to do now, Grant and Nisa went into the front bedroom and shut the door behind them. Nisa sat down on the edge of the twin bed nearest the door, and Grant began to pace back and forth in front of her. After thanking her for allowing him to speak to her privately, Grant spent several minutes trying to express himself and finally succeeded rather haltingly in telling her that for some time now he had been attracted to her very strongly. Nisa thanked him and advised that henceforth he not keep his feelings concealed but let the other person know how he felt. They then joined the others in the living and dining rooms, and Grant felt both relieved and elated.

At this point Dorothy, Nisa, Judy, Dennis, and Grant all decided to stay up a while longer, but everyone else soon went off to bed. All five were feeling joyous from the evening of singing and being with other people. They simply sprawled on the carpeted floor of the dining room and talked. Initially, Dennis and Grant conversed in German, because Dennis had known that Grant intended to speak with Nisa; and since Dennis wanted to know what had transpired, and how it had gone, Grant did his best to explain it all in German, so that Dennis alone would understand what he was saying. They even used code words to refer to Dorothy and Nisa, so that their names could not be picked up from their conversation. During their earlier heart-to-heart discussions Grant had already coined the phrase *die genadstige Dame* to refer to Dorothy. It translated literally as "the most merciful" or "most gracious lady" and was a superlative form of an Austrian courtly way of addressing a woman as *genadige Frau*, gracious or merciful woman.

They were having so much fun (and Grant was especially pleased to have both Dorothy and Nisa included in this exclusive group) that they soon agreed that they would all try to stay up till morning. Since Nisa's friend Judy was new to Dennis, Dorothy, and Grant, the trio had many questions for her and vice versa. At one point when the conversation seemed to flag, Dorothy happened to remember that a recent Time Magazine she had contained an article that might interest Grant. She fetched it, and the article turned out to be a very interesting treatment of archaeological excavations of ancient royal Scythian tombs in Ukraine that confirmed the Greek historian Herodotus' description of Scythian burial customs (Time Magazine, Jan. 17, Tracking the Scythians). Dorothy read the article aloud, and Grant commented on it as she did. All five succeeded in staying up past dawn, and Grant in fact did not go to bed until he returned to his dorm room late on Sunday afternoon. The past eighteen hours or so had been truly exhilarating for him.

Nisa and Judy returned to Chicago by bus that same afternoon; and on the next day Nisa wrote two letters (one in print and the other in braille) and mailed them in the same envelope to George and Dorothy Patterson. The text of the braille letter, which Dorothy carefully preserved inside the final volume of her journal, and which Grant unexpectedly found 31 years later after his beloved Dorothy's death, was as follows:

April 10, 1972

Dear Mom,

I'm writing this letter today, so that the experience will still be fresh in my mind. First of all, thanks so much for having us at your home. I think Judy really enjoyed herself, and on the way home on the bus, that was all she could talk about. She said that she's never had this kind of experience before--true blue American style home like you see in the movies. I'm really glad for her, too. I only hope that she'll do this more often. I guess George's already told you, but we couldn't get on the first bus that left at 3:00. So they had to make a special bus for us. It didn't leave until 4:00. So we got in Chicago at 7:30. I guess by that time my dad had called your home already. I only regret that by calling the Carsons my dad worried them. I don't think Carsons had any idea we were coming at a specific time. Judy was just supposed to call when we got to the station. I worried a little about getting around in the station since it's so big, but as soon as we went upstairs and parked our luggage, a security man came and helped us find the telephone and our seats. He was really nice. I wonder what he thought of us--two blind girls traveling, especially since I was leading Judy. At any rate, we got home safely. I enjoyed myself, but I don't want to go through the confusion very soon again. I wish I could have stayed longer and got to see Sora alone.

I'm writing a written letter to George, so he shouldn't ask you to translate this braille one, but nevertheless the first part will be about the same.

I didn't get a chance to tell you what Grant and I had talked about, and I don't know if he wants me to tell anyone, but I'll tell you anyway. Just in case something like this occurs again, I want you to see if you could help him. Apparently Dennis knows something about this.

At first Grant was really not saying anything. If you remember, he has told us that he keeps a record of his dreams. Well, after the first week of school, I guess he had some kind of dream about me. You know for Grant to have a dream about anyone, it must be something significant. He said that he really didn't think about that for a long while, and by the time he recognized the fact that he was attracted to me, Renny and I were seeing each other, and Grant wanted to maintain Renny's friendship. He told me that by telling me how he felt that had helped him to think things through. I told him that I did like him very much and that I respected and admired him still more. I suggested in the future he'd go ahead and tell people (girls in this case) how he felt or at least give some kind of hint. I knew Grant liked me very much, because he gave me the piano music record for Christmas, and he's been participating in activities much more. I remember one time he came to see us bowl when we were in the league. He was really interested in how I bowled. I guess those were his subtle hints. I hope he finds someone, because he's really a great guy. From talking to him Sunday about his past, it struck me that he's really a nice guy and above all very human. I think I could have liked him even more than Renny if I had had a chance. But as you see, it's too late. I hope Grant finds a girl who could really help him to become more open and free. I told him that it's a shame he doesn't communicate more, because he's got so much to share.

Well, that's the extent of our conversation and my impressions. While I was writing this letter, Judy called me during her break at work, and she sounds terrible. She says she could hardly think straight, she's so tired. That nut got a tape from England yesterday and stayed up until 11:30 listening to it. I had hard enough time getting up at 6:30 to have breakfast with my father. But I took an hour nap from 8 to 9. I'm going to write George now. Thanks again for everything.

Love,
Nisa

Author's Note: Following Dorothy's death 31 years later, Grant, her deeply grieving husband, conducted a thorough search and examination of all of her files and papers in order to systematize all possible information about his darling for permanent safe-keeping and to form a fitting and lasting memorial to his most blessed beloved. Despite all the braille letters that Dorothy had written and received during her years of association with her blind university kids, This braille letter from Nisa was the only one among Dorothy's effects; and as already stated, it was preserved inside the fourth and final volume of Dorothy's journal, which ended at this point. These facts have led Grant to speculate that Nisa's letter may have tipped Dorothy off to how Grant was feeling about her, so that when he confessed his strong attraction to her three months later on the evening of July 10, it may not have come as a total surprise to Dorothy, who may have been suspecting his attraction to her for some time. Furthermore, needless to say, the abrupt ending of Dorothy's journal around this time would have become necessary, because once the two lovers were embarked upon their magical summer described in Chapter 5, there was no way that Dorothy took risk entrusting her thoughts and feelings to a continuation of her journal.

Grant's serious conversation with Nisa had one important consequence for the two of them. It formed the basis of a very nice friendship. Before that they had been together as participants within the same group, but they had not conversed much. Although Nisa had now graduated and was living with her parents in Chicago, she did visit University City fairly regularly over the next several months, primarily to see Sora. Whenever she came, she was welcome to stay as a guest at the Patterson house; and on a few occasions she and Grant encountered one another there and had very nice and friendly talks.

But for the remainder of the spring semester Grant continued to harbor and conceal his very strong feelings of affection toward Dorothy. Since he realized that this was a rather hopeless quest, he began to punish himself physically as if he were some kind of medieval monk who used mortification of the flesh to subdue his unwanted cravings. This mortification took the form of sleeping on his dorm room floor in his sleeping bag. Since he happened not to have a roommate for that semester, this odd practice did not attract unwanted scrutiny. His idea to do this had stemmed in part from the fact that several of the blind students occasionally slept on the nicely carpeted floor of Dorothy's beautiful house when they stayed there overnight, but sleeping on the hard tiled concrete floor of the dorm was a very different matter. Grant often awoke with aches in his body, especially his arms and legs.

April 27, 1972, Thursday

As Grant turned off of the main sidewalk and onto the wide entryway into the Rehab Center, he was careful to try to walk straight up the middle and to avoid those damnable pillars along the two edges. When he advanced to the doorway itself, his foot stepped on the mat that triggered the electrically powered door to swing open, like the ones in groceries stores, but this one was not there for people with shopping carts or their arms full of grocery bags. This door was designed to give easy access into the building for those in wheelchairs who had limited use of their hands.

Grant had an appointment at 11:00 with Evan Collins, the man who administered the state's DVR program (Division of Vocational Rehabilitation) that funded much of the college education for university students with disabilities. Grant was going to ask Mr. Collins to allow him to attend summer school. When he entered the outer office, the secretary there asked him to have a seat. Grant located a chair with the end of his cane and eased down into it. Several minutes later Mr. Collins' voice boomed forth through the doorway that led into his inner office, "Ok Grant, I'm free to see you now." Grant arose, stepped through the doorway, and found the empty chair that sat directly in front of Mr. Collins' desk.

After he had seated himself, Mr. Collins asked, "Ok, what can I help you with?" His voice was really something to listen to, and his enunciation and diction were so elegantly precise. Bob and Grant had speculated that he was the product of some drama program or an acting school of some sort. His voice and diction alone gave them the impression that he was the most cultured and cultivated man in the entire Rehab Center. His voice was so deep and resonant, a real joy to the ear. Grant had once told Bob that it was a stereo voice, because it possessed all the fullness and richness of a really good stereo system.

"Well," Grant began, "I've been thinking about going to summer school this summer." "And why is that?" "Well, I came here to college with the idea of majoring in physics or becoming some kind of engineer, but I have also become very interested this year in ancient history and classical studies. I took Latin in high school and have continued to read Latin on my own, because I enjoy it so much, but to fulfill my history requirement, I took a two-semester sequence this year covering the ancient world; and I've really become fascinated with ancient history. I'm therefore thinking about having two majors, one in physics and another in history."

"A degree in physics or engineering makes really good vocational sense, as I'm sure you know, but I never discourage anyone from obtaining as broad an education as possible. I myself really love literature and history. In fact, this past Sunday I was asked to take over a Sunday school class of youngsters, and I mostly talked about major ancient historical events, because the kids usually don't know anything about the historical setting of the Bible." "That's neat," Grant simply responded. After a short pause Mr. Collins continued. "I've been looking over your grade transcripts. You're doing exceptionally well: all A's last semester and all of them not easy courses. How are you doing this semester?" "I'm basically just continuing on with the logical sequence of math and physics courses plus my sequences in ancient history, classical civilization, and German; and I'm doing as well as last semester. I should get all A's again, I think."

"What would you be taking in summer school?" "There's an advanced history course on Alexander the Great and the Hellenistic world that I would like to take and is not offered very often. It would be my first really serious history course and would count toward my major in history. Plus, I could take a second advanced history course. There's one on fascism between the two world wars that would really be interesting."

"Everything you've said makes sense and is backed up by your record, but just let me say one important thing based upon my experience with other students. You really need to be careful about going to summer school. Unless you really need to have a course, it's usually better to have the summer off to rest and relax. You don't want to burn yourself out, and that can happen. I would hate to see you upset your splendid record by having that happen." "I understand." Then after another longer pause, Mr. Collins said, "Ok, if you're sure that you really want to attend summer school, I'll approve your summer school courses." The meeting was over. Grant thanked him and left the office.

As he walked back to Holmes, Mr. Collins' warning about burning out nagged at him. Perhaps he was right. He should take the summer off, but besides trying to make up for a late start in history by taking two advanced courses during summer school, he had an even more compelling reason why he had to go. He simply could not bear the thought of being away from Dorothy for the entire summer. He had handled everything so well this entire academic year. Getting A's in all his courses and leading a rather full social life had not been at all easy. In fact, it had been extremely demanding but also exhilarating. He had succeeded in doing it. Why couldn't he continue on in the same way on through the summer?

May 2, 1972, Tuesday

Grant knocked on the door to Dennis and Renny's room, and he could hear Dennis' voice say, "Come in." As he stepped into the room, he smelled Ma's magnificently alluring perfume, White Shoulders. She had been wearing it since her youth, and it had become part of her identity among family and friends; and now the university students also regarded it as reflecting who she was. It had such a wonderful fragrance that corresponded perfectly to her nature. But besides the lovely scent of her White Shoulders, her voice filled the room, as she read something for Dennis. Renny was stretched out on his bed with headphones on, listening to one of his recorded textbooks. Dennis was sitting at his desk and using his braille writer occasionally to jot something down, and Dorothy was sitting at the foot of Dennis' bed reading to him.

Grant had shown up at his regular time to go with Dennis, Renny, and Bob to the dorm cafeteria for supper. But he had walked in on the very tail end of Dorothy's reading session with Dennis. Grant sat down on Dennis' bed about a foot and a half away from Dorothy and simply sat there while she and Dennis finished their work.

"Hey, guys," she cheerfully intoned, "how about we go grab something at Der Wienerschnitzel instead of you eating that dorm food you're always complaining about?" Her suggestion was met with an enthusiastic response from both Dennis and Renny. "Why don't we see if Bob is around," she continued, "and if he is, he can come along too."

As it turned out, Bob was not in his room; and so, just the four of them set off in Dorothy's car to Der Wienerschnitzel in northwest University City. It was a perfect spring day, sunny and comfortably warm. After Dorothy had parked the car, Dennis and Renny stepped out and confidently strode ahead with their canes from the car to the side of the building and then around to the entrance while Dorothy and Grant brought up the rear. Unlike the other two, Grant was walking with her, walking on her left side with his right hand on her left arm. For Grant, it was such a rare experience. With Nisa and Debbie no longer on campus, she seemed to be with Dennis and Renny much of the time, helping them both with so many things, but since that truly magical night of the afterglow and staying up past dawn together, Grant had been with her only during two organized events at the house or like now, when he had fortuitously come upon the three of them in Forester. How wonderful it was not only to be touching her arm, but also to be inhaling the lovely fragrance of her perfume. As they stood in line, placed their orders, and paid for their food, Grant realized that he had an erection. It was the very first time that Dorothy's presence had had this effect upon him. It rather took him by surprise, because hitherto he had always regarded his feelings toward her as romantic ones, but his erection was now telling him quite clearly that his strong affections could easily manifest themselves in a physical and sexual way.

They sat down in a booth, and luckily for Grant, Dennis and Renny chose to sit on one side, so that Dorothy and Grant sat down on the other. As they ate and conversed in their normally enjoyable way among themselves, the erection persisted; and even though it had come to him as a surprise, the sensation was quite pleasurable.

May 30, 1972, Tuesday

Grant had been spending the entire morning in reading through his daily quota of braille lecture notes for all his courses. Classes had ended the previous Friday, and they were now in the final exam period. Grant was determined to earn all A's again this semester. After putting away his notebook, he grabbed his cane, unfolded it, locked up his room, and walked over to Forester to see if Dennis and Renny were ready for lunch yet.

The scene he entered there was an all too typical one, chaos and disorder, accompanied by vociferous bantering between the two friends. Dorothy was amid this turmoil, patiently trying to make some order out of the mess. Dennis and Renny were going through all their things, and Dorothy was helping them pack. Grant simply sat down on Dennis' bed next to Dorothy and quietly observed.

"Hey, Ma, what's this?" Dennis asked, as he handed her a paperback book. "Looks like The *Death of a Salesman.*" "Ok, I guess we can put that in my pile of things to sell back to the bookstore." And so it went. As Grant sat there following it all, he became somewhat annoyed with Dennis and Renny, because so much of what they were doing did not require Ma sitting here and wasting her time. They could do most of this stuff on their own, leave some of it unfinished, and then have her come over to help them. But it seemed to Grant that they were very inconsiderate, having her sit amid all this chaos, sorting and packing. But what Grant did not realize was that Dorothy really enjoyed being here in a college dorm room and associating herself with college students. It was a situation so very different from her home life, and she really loved it.

"Ma," Grant finally remarked, "how can you put up with these two guys?" Dennis clapped his hands together and hooted with laughter, "Ah man, she's such a great sport." "No, that's not it. I think I've got holes in my head and just don't know any better," Dorothy said with that lovely smile in her voice." "She just can't resist our charming personalities," Renny said with mock bravado.

"Yeah, I guess you're right, Renny. That's what it must be," replied Dorothy in a tone of amused irony.

With Dorothy in the room, Grant's usual impatience with Dennis and Renny's lackadaisical dilatoriness took second place to his enjoyment of this wonderful woman's company. It was simply magnificent to be in her dazzling presence, no matter how mundane the circumstances.

Chapter 5

The Magical Summer

June 5, 1972, Monday

It was a beautiful spring morning, cool and sunny, and Dennis was in a very joyful mood as he walked along Maple Street back to Forester. He had just paid a visit to Kitty in her dorm room in Miller to tell her that he was breaking up with her as his girlfriend. He had left Kitty in tears and misery to await the arrival of her parents later that morning to take her back to Ohio for the summer, but that couldn't be helped. The demise of their relationship had slowly developed during the spring semester. Despite her wit, charm, and intelligence, Kitty could be manipulative and possessive; and these traits had been obvious to Dennis over the past few months, probably largely due to the fact that he and Renny had been rooming together. A kind of tug-of-war had been going on between Renny and Kitty, as each competed for the lion's share of Dennis' attention. It had even placed tremendous strain on the rock solid friendship between Dennis and Renny, so much so that they had been discussing whether they should continue as roommates next year. In any case, Dennis had freed himself from Kitty and felt greatly relieved.

Not long after he returned to his room in Forester, Dorothy and George arrived, and they were joined by Grant and Bob. The group of six then traveled by car to Uncle Joe's Pancake House at Lexington and Armstrong, just to the southwest of the university's campus. This would be their last formal gathering for this academic year, a celebratory brunch. The four young men were all in a happy mood. Their classes were over, and they had just one more day of exams to go before everything would be officially completed for this school year.

They were seated in a large wrap-around booth. Dennis sat at the bottom of the u with Renny and Bob to his left and George, Dorothy, and Grant to his right. While the others were engaged in non-stop conversation, Grant remained relatively quiet, something that they were all used to, but he was secretly savoring once again being so physically close to this wonderful woman, breathing in the fragrance of her perfume, just listening to her beautiful voice engaged in conversation with the others, feeling her leg against his, and enjoying the occasional brush of her forearm against his.

Because of all their talking, they spent a good long time over their meal, and of course, Dennis and Renny were rarely in a hurry to do anything except to go off and have more fun somewhere else. But when they did finally finish eating and talking, they all returned to Forester, where Dorothy and George were planning to spend the rest of the morning helping Dennis and Renny do their last bit of packing. While Bob returned to his own room, Grant hung around in Dennis and Renny's room. He had his last exam to take tomorrow morning, but he was already well prepared for it and was in no hurry to absent himself from Dorothy's presence. He therefore simply sat on the edge of Renny's bed and enjoyed being there amid the normal hubbub that always seemed to swirl around these two blind guys. While sitting in the booth at Uncle Joe's, Grant had succeeded in casually telling Dorothy about a record that Bob had recently purchased. It was an album of humor made by a couple of comedians called Cheech and Chong. Grant was currently borrowing it from Bob, so that he could record it on tape. It was extremely funny, and Grant suggested that when they returned to campus, Dorothy might want to come over to his room for a few minutes to listen to part of it. She had agreed. So, as the packing in Dennis and Renny's room was nearing its end, Dorothy announced to George that while he oversaw these last details, she would walk over to Grant's room to listen to a record that he wanted her to hear.

Dorothy had not visited Grant's dorm room in Holmes at all. There had been no need to, because Grant had always come to Dennis and Renny's room in Forester to go off with the group. This visit, therefore, was unique. After entering the room, Dorothy moved over to the right side and sat down on the bed, the one that had been Grant's roommate last semester, and which he never used. He then placed the record on the turn table of his stereo, started it up, and sat down at his desk. The humor of this record centered around aspects of contemporary college life and the popular culture of the young. Consequently, funny scenes involving blacks and whites, drugs, and sex were common; and Dorothy laughed at them, but soon their pleasant enjoyment of the record was interrupted by George's arrival. The packing was completed, and he had come to collect his wife to return home. "What are you two up to?" George asked, as he entered the room. "We're just listening to a funny record," Dorothy cheerfully replied. Grant had detected in George's tone a note of disapproval at seeing his wife sitting alone in a dorm room with another male. As the record continued to play, and as George realized what sort of record it was, he said, "Well, the packing's all done. So we can head back home now." It was obvious that he did not regard the content of the record as the least bit amusing or appropriate for his wife's ears, and he was not going to stay here listening to it. "Ok!" Dorothy responded. "We'll see you later, Grant," she said, as she stood up from the bed, and the two departed. Within less than a minute Dorothy had left her obvious enjoyment of her alternative life with her college kids, where she was always embraced unhesitatingly by their love and appreciation, and was swept back into her more conventional life as wife and mother.

June 7, 1972, Wednesday

It was the middle of the afternoon, and Holmes Hall was almost entirely deserted. At noon tomorrow it would be officially closed for the summer. Grant was one of the few still remaining. His parents would arrive tomorrow morning to return him and his things to Fairmont for just one week, and then they would bring him back again for summer school. He was relaxing on the big rust colored rug that occupied the space between the two beds, and the stereo was playing a newly purchased record, magnificent guitar playing by Chet Atkins and Jerry Reed.

There was a knock on his door. "Who in the world could that be," he thought to himself, as he shouted, "Yeah, come in." "Hi, Grant," Dorothy said, "I just stopped by to give you some bread pudding. I made up a big batch this morning and took some over to Dennis, Renny, and Bob. I thought you might like to have some too." Grant sat up from his prone position on the floor and held out his hand, into which Dorothy placed a bowl. As he took it from her, he observed, "This is just like some bowls my mother has." "They're Tupperware," Dorothy explained. "When are you coming back for summer school?" Dorothy asked. "Next Thursday, a week from tomorrow." "Well, when you get back, give me a call, and I'll be happy to help you with things. You know, Debbie's also going to be in summer school. So we should plan on doing all sorts of things together." "That really sounds great," Grant replied, as he took his first bite of the pudding. "Thanks so very much for thinking of me and bringing this by. It really tastes great!" "You're welcome, and I hope you enjoy it. I can't stay any longer. George's out in the car waiting. So give me a call when you get back in town next week." "Ok, I certainly will." She had been standing a foot away from him during this brief visit, and the closeness pleased Grant very much. She now turned and departed.

After she left, Grant consumed the rest of the bread pudding. Of course, it was delicious! After all, Ma had made it. She was such a marvelous cook and had introduced him to so many new foods or to variations on things, such as potato pancakes, Rice Krispie candy, snickerdoodles, Russian tea cookies, vanilla wafers instead of graham crackers in banana pudding, this very bread pudding, penuche fudge, pralines, cheesecake, fruit cocktail in jell-o, Mandarin oranges in jell-o, or Dream Whip in jell-o. He had never eaten lasagna until she had made it from scratch and had served it to the entire group at her house one evening. That too had been so delicious, like everything else she made in the kitchen. What an incredible woman she was! After making up this big batch of bread pudding, she had come over to campus to give about half of it away to Bob, Dennis, Renny, and himself.

June 15, 1972, Thursday

Grant had had a restful week at home and was now rarin' to go to summer school. Earlier that morning Grant's father had driven him back to University City and had helped him move all his things up to the fifth floor of Walker Dormitory. It was one of the few dorms open to accommodate students for the summer. Since it was located on the other side of the Quad from where he had been living in Forester and Holmes dormitories, Grant was not very familiar with where he was, and how he would have to travel to get to places. He was therefore going to have to call Ma and ask her to come over to give him some mobility instruction.

Grant finally made the call after he had everything in his new dorm room neatly put away. Dorothy suggested that he and Debbie have supper with her, George, and Carol at the house. They did; and when Dorothy brought them back to Walker, Grant returned to his room and waited while Dorothy acquainted Debbie with the dorm's layout. The building's eastern and western halves, each five stories tall and forming three sides of a rectangle, were mirror images of one another with the central north-south axis, which bisected the whole structure and separated the two halves, containing the front desk, lounge area, and cafeteria. The western side was for female students (Debbie was living on the third floor), and the eastern side was for the males. When Dorothy was finished with Debbie's orientation lesson, she came alone to Grant's room, and they set out on Dorothy's second session of mobility instruction for the evening.

Dorothy first showed him a few of the same things that she had just shown Debbie: the general plan of the building, its front desk area, elevators, lounge, and cafeteria. They then worked on Grant learning his way out of the building's main entrance on the south side, around the big circle driveway, out to the main sidewalk along the north side of Michigan Avenue, and then the block between Chestnut and Nathaniel to the east side of the Quad. None of it was difficult. It simply took some time to explain and to walk through.

It was a pleasant evening, sunny and warm, thankfully not hot. Grant, of course, was elated simply by the two of them being together. Their hour of mobility instruction seemed especially perfect to him as they covered the last segment of the route that Grant needed to learn: an east-west sidewalk that ran between Chestnut and Nathaniel between two large campus buildings. As they walked along, they were flanked on either side by well-maintained greenery, were sheltered from traffic noise by the imposing grandeur of the two buildings, and had both the warm sun and a gentle breeze in their faces as they walked west.

As soon as they arrived on the west side of Nathaniel on the eastern edge of the Quad, there was no need to proceed further, because Grant was now on familiar territory. They therefore ended the mobility lesson by turning around and having Grant walk back unassisted to his dorm room with Dorothy trailing a few feet behind. As always, Dorothy had enjoyed being with and helping two of her university kids and was in no hurry to return home. Consequently, when they arrived at Grant's room door on the fifth floor of Walker, she came into the room, and they began to tell one another what all they had done during the past week. Since Grant did not think that she would be staying very long, he did not bother to sit down; and since Dorothy also did not sit, they remained standing about a foot apart facing one another near the desk located in the right rear corner of the room. Grant imbibed the beautiful fragrance of her perfume and, as always, was charmed by her lovely and expressive voice. How truly delightful it was merely to be in her presence! Dorothy for her part was also thoroughly enjoying herself. It was slightly thrilling to be alone with his handsome young man, who obviously relished her company so much. Their physical closeness pleased them both. As she described their visit to George's mother in Newton this past weekend, Dorothy mentioned that George had begun to grow a mustache, but she didn't like how it brushed against her whenever he gave her a kiss. She recounted this latter detail as if it were a natural part of the story of her week of events, but Grant was struck by its intimacy and felt as if by hearing it and by sharing this with her, they had just engaged figuratively in a kiss. In fact, Grant wanted to reach out and touch her, perhaps even draw her to him and either kiss her or ask if he could kiss her. But Grant's innate shyness kept him from doing either. Dorothy's telling of this detail thickened the emotional atmosphere surrounding them, And Dorothy felt pleasure at disclosing this intimate secret to Grant.

June 16, 1972, Friday

Grant unlocked his dorm room door and ushered Debbie and Dorothy inside. The trio had just spent part of the morning over in the huge open interior of the Armory, where Dorothy had taken her two blind students around to the different tables set up for registration for summer school. They now settled in to listen to a cassette recording that Grant had made a few days ago of Nisa's appearance on the NBC *Today Show* along with a few other blind college students in recognition of their academic achievement and receiving a scholarship from Recording for the Blind, the single largest volunteer agency that recorded books onto tape for blind students.

Debbie sat down on the edge of the bed on the left side of the room, the bed in which Grant had decided to sleep during his stay here this summer. Dorothy sat down on the bed to the right, but it was a set of bunk beds. Grant went over to the desk at the left rear of the room, punched the play button on his cassette machine, and then he swung himself into the top bunk above Dorothy and lay there as they all three listened to the recording.

It did not last very long. Joe Garaggiola presided over this segment of the *Today Show*. After a brief laudatory introduction of the students, he conducted very brief interviews with them by posing different questions regarding their fields of study and career goals. It was all very pleasant. Of course, as soon as Nisa had learned that she would be appearing on national

TV, she had excitedly spread the word. Grant had not only recorded it, but had made several copies, one for himself, another for Dorothy, and a third to be given to Nisa, who in fact would be coming to University City tomorrow afternoon on the bus to spend much of the day with Sora and would then return to Chicago on Sunday after staying the night at Dorothy's house.

After the tape had ended, Dorothy and Debbie left, so that Dorothy could give her the same mobility lesson that she had given Grant last evening. They would then return to Grant's room, and all three would go to Dorothy's house for the weekend.

June 18, 1972, Sunday

It was just now 10:00 P.M., and everyone else (Dorothy, George, Carol, and Debbie) had gone off to bed a few minutes ago. Grant was the only one up. He switched on the portable TV in the family room and sat down in a large stuffed chair to listen to the fifteen minutes or so of local and national news before going off to bed.

It had been a really nice weekend. They had done nothing special except to relax and be here at the house. Debbie had gotten a start on one of her summer school courses by having Dorothy read to her for about two hours yesterday afternoon. Nisa had come and gone, but after everyone but she and Grant had gone to bed last evening, the two of them had sat up together in the front bedroom and had had a nice long friendly conversation about nothing in particular, while Nisa knitted away on a sweater that she was making. Of course, Ma had been the one who had taught her how to knit and was helping her execute this pattern. Then this afternoon Dorothy, Debbie, and Grant had taken the three dogs for a long walk across the open field to the highway and back. Indeed, it had been such a nice quiet weekend here, Grant mused to himself, as he listened to the news. Before the sports and weather segments began, the anchor man ended the news with a short curious little item: several men had been arrested in Washington D.C. very early that morning while they were apparently orchestrating a break-in into the headquarters of the Democratic National Committee located in the Watergate Hotel. "What the hell is that all about?" Grant wondered to himself, as he arose from the chair, switched off the TV, and proceeded into the living room, where he would sleep on the floor in a sleeping bag.

The first two weeks of summer school unfolded so grandly for Grant. The Rehab Center had succeeded in either obtaining or in having recorded all the textbooks for his two history courses on fascism between the two world wars and Alexander the Great and the Hellenistic world. He was therefore using his four volunteer readers to do supplemental reading. Two of these readers were people who had read to him throughout the previous academic year, and both were in electric wheelchairs. Terry Wilson, an undergraduate, who like Kitty Carpenter, came from Ohio, had read German to him and Dennis. He happened to be staying around for the summer and was happy to keep reading for Grant once a week for two hours. Larry Smithson was about six years older than Grant and was earning his Master's in education to teach mathematics in high school. Larry had begun as Grant's reader for his courses in calculus, but he had also been reading a good bit of Grant's ancient history, which Larry also much enjoyed, because he had studied Latin many years ago. He was therefore happy to read for Grant.

Larry had been stricken with polio as a child and now had only limited use of his hands. He could turn the pages of a book on the little table top of his wheelchair, but in order to type, Larry had to punch at the keys with a mouth stick. He was able to travel about in his battery driven wheelchair by using his hand to operate the control stick. Since he was not married and could not look after his personal needs by himself, he always lived with a roommate in graduate student housing, a building just a short walk from Walker. Larry's roommate had to be someone who was willing to do all the necessary shopping, prepare their meals, do the laundry, keep the apartment clean, and to bathe and dress Larry. As it turned out, Larry's roommate for the summer was a really nice young man named Phil, who was also enrolled in the history course on Alexander the Great. He therefore offered to serve as Grant's reader for this course as well.

Grant had no difficulty in filling his little bit of free time with other things. Of course, Dorothy wanted him and Debbie over at the house as much as they pleased; and in fact, they had both spent the next two weekends there, doing their reading and studying with Dorothy serving as one of Debbie's readers. But Grant had also been attending once a week a series of classes offered by the Rehab Center that taught disabled people the basics of cooking and sewing. These classes were both fun and useful. Everything therefore seemed to be going along nicely.

July 3, 1972, Monday

It was 8:15 in the evening, and Grant had just walked into his room from having had a two-hour reading session at Larry Smithson's apartment. He could relax somewhat, because there would be no classes tomorrow on the Fourth of July. He decided to call home just to see how things were going there.

"Hello, mom," Grant said, as his mother answered the phone. "How are you doing?" she asked. "Oh everything is just fine. My two classes are going well. I just got back from a session with a reader; and since I don't have classes tomorrow, I thought I'd give you a call to check in." There was then a slight pause before his mother began, "Well, I'm sorry to say that we had some real trouble here yesterday." "What happened?" Grant asked with some alarm evident in his voice. "Well," his mother replied with obvious weariness, "I'm afraid your dad and Neil [the husband of Grant's sister Patricia] got into a fight. Patricia and Neil were here for the afternoon with Troy [their very young son]. Your dad and Neil sat out on the porch drinking beer and arguing about baseball. You know how they are. It ended up in a fight, and Neil hit your dad in the mouth and busted his lip. They then left. When Patricia later called to see how her dad was, I said that we expect Neil to apologize. But she said that since dad had started the fight, they didn't need to apologize. This and that was said back and forth, and it looks like we won't be talking with one another or seeing each other anymore."

There was another pause, as Grant's mother finished her story. When Grant failed to fill the silence, she continued, "I didn't want to call to tell you all this, because I didn't want to get you upset and have it interfere with your studies." Grant was dumbstruck and really did not know what to say. "Wow, I just can't believe it," he finally managed to say with obvious shock and sadness in his voice. "Well, I guess there's not much you can say. Your dad and I are really angry and upset, but so are Patricia and Neil. So I don't know what else to tell you."

After a few more words, the conversation ended, and they hung up. As Grant sat in the chair at the desk, he was overwhelmed by powerful emotions, probably a combination of panic and grief. Thus far in his young life his family had never before been disturbed by anything like this. He and his sister Patricia, of course, had had fights as they were growing up; and they had sometimes overheard their parents engaged in heated arguments, but nothing like this! What did it mean, and what would it mean? He simply didn't know. It was all so very upsetting!

Grant reached for the telephone and dialed Dorothy's number. When her pleasant voice answered, he greeted her and quickly explained what he had just learned from his mother. Dorothy clearly heard strong emotions in Grant's voice. He sounded as if he were on the verge of tears. She therefore naturally offered to come over to talk with him if that would be any help. After all, during the past fall and winter she had served as Debbie's therapist, a role that she was now already resuming; and since the other university kids had never hesitated to talk over their problems and concerns with her, why shouldn't she do the same in this situation? Grant thanked her for her offer and gladly accepted. Just the thought of her presence made him feel better.

After briefly explaining the situation to George, Dorothy left the house, drove over to Walker, and went up to Grant's room. He was pacing back and forth so wildly that she suggested that they go out and walk as they talked. By now it was dark and cool outside, a pleasant early summer evening. They not only walked the route that Dorothy had taught him two weeks before, but they walked all the way over to Milton Hall, where Grant had his two history classes; and they even went inside the building, and Grant took her to the two classrooms. As they walked, the frenzy in Grant's voice slowly diminished. Being in Milton Hall, the place that he associated with the joy of learning history, seemed to relax him considerably. When they finally returned to Walker, Dorothy found a spot beneath a tree, and there they sat together for the remainder of her visit that lasted until midnight. By then Grant was back to his normal self, but during the course of the preceding three hours he had told her so much about himself and his family; and as he did, Dorothy provided similar information about her own relatives and experiences, so that by the end of their lengthy conversation they had developed a strong bond of mutual understanding.

Grant's sister Patricia, whom he usually called Pat, was his only sibling and was fifteen months older than Grant. Dorothy observed that Grant's sister was the same age as her Sally. Since Patricia and Grant were so close in age and both had the same bright red hair, for many years strangers often took them to be twins. They had been inseparable as they grew up; and since Pat had been a real tomboy up until she was in high school, they often played the same games with other boys in their neighborhood. It all reminded Dorothy so much of her relationship with Bethany, who had also been a rowdy tomboy and was about a year and a half younger than she.

Just like Sally, Pat had graduated from high school in June of 1969. Grant's parents had wanted her to go to college, because she was almost as good a student as Grant, but by then she had begun to date Neil and was not interested in college. Neil was a few years older than she. He had already graduated from high school and had served in the army. Grant's parents had thought that their daughter, just fresh out of high school, should not become so serious with someone several years older than her. But despite these parental misgivings, Pat and Neil had been married just as Grant was about to graduate from high school. Their son Troy was born toward the very end of Grant's first semester at the university. Pat had even chosen to give her son the name Troy, because she knew how fascinated her brother was with Troy and the myth of the Trojan War.

Their parents' concerns about Neil seemed to be proven when early on in the marriage Neil spent much of his free time running around and drinking with rather unsavory friends. Pat and Neil had quarreled over this, and she had even come back to stay in her parents' house for a short time, but then they patched things up, and everything seemed ok. But Grant's parents continued to feel uneasy about Neil. The recent fight between Neil and Grant's dad had simply been the explosive culmination of a long sequence of events and mutual distrust.

July 4, 1972, Tuesday

Although Grant's average sleep was about six and a half hours per night, he sometimes slept much less or much longer than that. Given his emotional distress of the night before, he fell asleep after Dorothy had left at midnight, and he slept very long and heavily until he was awakened by the ringing of the telephone. It was about 9:00, and Dorothy was calling to see if he would be interested in joining them later in the afternoon to attend a Fourth of July celebration and fireworks show. Grant thanked her for asking, but he really wasn't interested and just wanted to get some extra rest today before classes resumed tomorrow.

After hanging up, Grant fell back onto the bed and dozed off again. As he finally began to awaken for good, he realized that he had an erection, and it seemed to be caused by having a dream that somehow involved Dorothy. It felt so good to lie peacefully in bed while thinking of her; and the sensation of the erection was also very pleasant. He therefore began to masturbate to prolong and to intensify the pleasure; and as he did, he found himself fantasizing about how Dorothy would look naked. The thought came to him automatically, but when it did, it both shocked him and made him feel ashamed. He should not be thinking of her in this way. Nevertheless, despite his feelings of shame, the fantasy stubbornly persisted until he finally ejaculated.

July 6, 1972, Thursday

At 2:50 when the bells in Milton Hall rang, Grant stood up from the desk in his last class for the day, walked down the stairs to the first floor, came out of the front entrance to the building, and made his way along its curving entrance, down the wheelchair cut in the curb, across the broad bicycle path, and up onto the concrete barrier that marked the boundary between Wagoner Street and the parallel zone for bicyclists. During their long conversation two evenings ago Dorothy had offered to read for Grant any time that he wanted or needed her to during the summer, and they had agreed to have her read today for two hours between 3:00 and 5:00. It would be the very first time that she had read to him.

After he had been standing under the hot sun for about a minute, Dorothy drove up. Grant sat down in the passenger seat, and they went to Walker and up to his room on the fifth floor. They sat about a foot and a half apart, side by side on Grant's bed; and Dorothy began to read W. W. Tarn's description of Alexander's conquest of the Persian Empire from volume VI of *The Cambridge Ancient History*. To Grant, all this represented a perfect union of pleasures: Dorothy's presence, the alluring scent of her perfume, her beautiful voice, and the reading of ancient history, a subject that fascinated him to no end.

Within the space of a half an hour Grant had slowly eliminated the distance between them. Dorothy had her back up against the brick wall of the room, her legs across the width of the single bed, and her knees bent upward, so that she could easily hold this massive book on her thighs. Grant was now slumped over onto her with his head and shoulder pressing against her shoulder and upper arm, and his left thigh against her right leg. Dorothy's arms and legs were bare, because she was wearing a pair of summer shorts with a matching short-sleeved top. Grant's arms and legs were also bare, because he was wearing his usual summer garb of a t-shirt and shorts. It was not until he found himself in this intimate position with her that Grant actually realized what he had done. He was drawn to her so automatically and naturally that he had moved himself against her without giving it any conscious thought. But now that he was in this position, he hated to withdraw abruptly, because doing so would clearly bring attention to what he had done. So, he was able to rationalize to himself his decision to remain motionless in this position that was so very satisfying to him.

Dorothy was eventually aware that Grant was gently leaning and pressing against the right side of her body. But she made no effort to readjust her position or to indicate in any way that she disapproved of how they were sitting together. It actually felt nice. So why bother? She therefore allowed their two bodies to remain in intimate contact for the rest of the reading session. She simply concentrated on the printed words on the pages in front of her while also being vaguely aware of how soothing it was to be sitting here like this with Grant.

When he noticed from his braille pocket watch that it was 5:00, Grant interrupted Dorothy's reading to announce the time and that their reading session should probably now end. They now finally moved apart on the bed; and as Dorothy stood up and was preparing to leave, they agreed to meet tomorrow at the same time for another two-hour reading session. Neither of them said or did anything that drew attention to how they had been sitting. They both acted as if nothing out of the ordinary had occurred.

As soon as Dorothy had gone through the double doors between the dormitory hallway and elevator area, Grant walked down to the large men's room at the other end of the hall. He entered a stall, unfastened his pants, and pulled down his shorts and undershorts to sit on the toilet. As he did so, he noticed that the inside of the front of his underwear was a complete mess. Sitting so long and so intimately beside Dorothy had given him an erection that had been slowly secreting sperm. In fact, he still had quite a whopper down there. Golly, how wonderful it had been to be so close to her!

As Dorothy left Grant's room and returned home, she tried to work out in her own mind just what had transpired between them. At least one thing was quite obvious to her. Grant was genuinely attracted to her. Now that she realized it, several other things in the recent past made sense: his desire to have her come to his room in Holmes at the end of the spring semester a month ago, and many other times when he seemed so pleased to be walking with her or sitting beside her. Their time together Monday night might have contributed something to what had just happened in his room, but she was now fairly sure that Grant was genuinely attracted to her. The realization was both very surprising and flattering. Of course, she had enjoyed being with him Monday night to try to help him through a most difficult personal situation, and having him close to her this afternoon had also been pleasant. But how much of this resulted from her pleasure in helping him, and how much was her own delight in him being attracted to her? As she tried to sort these things out, most of her attention had to be given to driving home safely and worrying about what they were going to have for supper.

Ever since she had read *Gone with the Wind* a few years ago, she had been struck by Scarlet O'Hara's "I'll worry about that tomorrow," because it seemed so fitting for her own chaotic life in which she was forced to juggle so many things simultaneously, while knowing that she could only take care of one or two major things at a time. Since she had known her university kids over the past two years, she had said, "I'll worry about it tomorrow" so often that it had become a kind of personal motto for her. Although she did not consciously invoke Scarlet O'Hara now, circumstances obliged her to act as if she had. The situation with Grant had to be left unresolved in her mind until they met again tomorrow.

July 7, 1972, Friday

Just as the day before, Dorothy picked Grant up out in front of Milton Hall, and they went to his dorm room for another two-hour reading session. The only major difference was that rather than it taking a half an hour for Grant to slowly close the gap between them on the bed, he almost immediately snuggled up against Dorothy, who did nothing to disturb their physical contact, as if it were the most natural thing in the world. At one point Grant had stopped her and had excused himself to go down to the bathroom to urinate. As on the day before, he found the inside front of his undershorts covered in sperm from his slowly secreting erection. Then when he had returned to the room, he did not hesitate to sit down beside her and move over against her, and Dorothy did not mind having him do so. As on the day before, when the reading session ended, they arose from the bed, and neither said or did anything to suggest that they had been doing anything unusual.

Unknown to Grant, however, when he had arisen from the bed to go off to the men's room during the reading session, Dorothy noticed that he had a very obvious erection. Then when they arose from the bed at the end of the reading session, she noticed again that he still had an erection. It did not disturb her at all. No, indeed! In fact, it thrilled her! She was now convinced that he was very strongly attracted to her, and she wondered what all it meant, and how they should and would deal with it.

July 8, 1972, Saturday

When Grant awoke in the sleeping bag on the living room floor, he could already feel the sunlight coming in through the picture window. According to his braille pocket watch, it was 5:30 A.M. After their reading session in his dorm room yesterday afternoon, they had collected Debbie and had come back to the house for the weekend. He and Debbie had enjoyed a quiet evening doing some schoolwork and just relaxing along with Ma, George, and Carol.

Dorothy awoke and looked over at the bedside clock. It was 5:35. She carefully slid out of bed so as not to disturb George, put on her pink quilted robe, stepped into her slippers, and walked out into the hall and then into the main bathroom. After urinating, she came down the hall with the three dogs following her, led them to the door in the family room, and let them out through the garage into the fenced-in side yard. When she came into the dining room where she enjoyed sitting alone at her desk at this time on so many mornings, she saw Grant lying on the living room floor in a sleeping bag. His hair was so brilliantly red. As she gazed upon him, she saw him move slightly, indicating that he was also awake. The past two afternoons in his dorm room had been quite unusual. Not only had she come to understand that Grant was strongly attracted to her, but she had also derived some contentment from their physical closeness. Although she kept telling herself that her interaction with Grant stemmed from the same sort of concern that she had for Debbie and her emotional difficulties, she was slowly becoming vaguely aware that she was also somewhat attracted to him too. Rather than sitting alone at her desk this morning to do some letter writing, she walked around the end of the couch, knelt down beside the sleeping bag, and greeted him.

"Good morning," she said very quietly, as if to speak more loudly would arouse others and end their solitude together. "Good morning," Grant replied with an equally lowered voice. "We're the only ones up right now," Dorothy elaborated. "Did you sleep well?" she asked. "Oh yeah, fine." "Isn't the floor a little uncomfortable to sleep on for the whole night?" "Not at all. The carpet is so thick that it's like sleeping on a firm mattress. Sleeping on the dorm room floor, now that's uncomfortable."

As they were talking quietly about nothing in particular, Dorothy took Grant's right hand that lay alongside the sleeping bag just in front of her knees and held it between her own two hands. She pulled his hand toward her and propped their clasped hands just above her knees. She was wearing only her robe, nightgown, and slippers; and as she had knelt on the floor, she had placed her lower legs straight behind her, kept her knees together, and had sat back on her heels. She was now holding his hand between hers and was resting them just where her lower thighs and knees came together to form a cleft. Dorothy hoped that their hand-holding would serve to calm Grant and his obvious attraction to her, whereas Grant was elated by their hand-holding along with the position of their hands on her lower thighs. To him it was all wonderfully intimate.

They remained motionless in this position and talked for about a half an hour. Grant told her a bit about his course on Alexander the Great. It was much on his mind, because he had to be writing an essay for it over the next few days. What really mattered for him right then, however, was not the content of their conversation, but the mere fact of them having it in this way: alone together early in the morning and holding hands so tenderly. Grant was fully aware of the shape of her lower thighs beneath the fabric of the robe and nightgown, and this greatly added to his enjoyment of this beautiful experience.

When one of the dogs began to bark, Dorothy released Grant's hand, rose to her feet, and went to bring them back inside the house. When she began making dish sounds in the kitchen, as if she were preparing something, Grant decided that their intimate morning together was over. He therefore slid out of the sleeping bag and joined her. While she made a pot of coffee and took things out of the refrigerator to begin making breakfast for everyone, Grant opened up the dishwasher and began to remove the clean dishes and put them away. This allowed him to have a perfectly good reason to be near her and also help her with her chores. Whenever he did not know where an item was kept, Dorothy stopped to tell or show him.

They were eventually joined by the other three; and as they sat around the kitchen table leisurely conversing, they with equal leisure ate a breakfast of scrambled eggs, toast, and sausage. Carol would be heading off soon to spend most of the day baby-sitting, while the other four drove out to a small rural community called Parkfield, about a half an hour away, to go horseback riding. It was a special event organized by the Rehab Center for their visually impaired students.

It looked to be a perfect day for the outing, sunny and clear. Perhaps they would even be back before it became too hot in the afternoon. Dorothy was not sure what exactly to expect. Just in case they might be sitting outside on the ground, she decided to take a white blanket along. George drove, but rather than sitting in the front seat beside him, Dorothy told Debbie that she should sit there. It seemed to please Debbie; and everyone simply regarded it for what it actually was, another small gesture by which Ma was attempting to bestow a kindness and a bit of special distinction upon one of her beloved university kids. Grant and Dorothy sat in the back seat, and the blanket lay on the seat between them. But soon their hands had found one another beneath the blanket, and they secretly held hands all the way to Parkfield. Dorothy consciously told herself that she was merely attempting to provide comfort to Grant and to signal to him that she was well aware of his attraction to her, and that she was ready to hear his confession and to help him with his feelings. But to Grant the hand-holding was truly magnificent!

The only other visually impaired university student at this morning outing was Susan Williams. She was not attending summer school, but simply happened to live in University City. She had been Dorothy's mobility student this past September; and the two were happy to see one another again. Grant had met her recently during the cooking and sewing classes at the Rehab Center. The event lasted about two hours. Their horses plodded along a wilderness path in single file. For most of the ride Grant was behind Susan and in front of one of the guides. It was nice being outside in the cool morning stillness, passing in and out of shade as they moved along the well-trodden path.

As it turned out, they did not use the blanket, but as soon as their horseback riding had ended, they came back to University City. Dorothy, however, sat in the front passenger seat on the return trip, and Grant and Debbie sat in the back. Before returning to the house, they stopped off briefly at Der Wienerschnitzel to pick up hot dogs and fries to bring home for an easy lunch. By the time they had eaten while sitting around the kitchen table, it was early afternoon. Grant declared that he now needed to get some real work done on his Alexander paper and indicated that he would go sit on the couch in the living room to organize his ideas and write out a braille outline. Debbie decided that she would retire to the back bedroom and do some of her own reading by using her cassette machine. Ma announced that she needed to refresh herself with a nap. Since George was in the early stages of organizing a construction project in Newton, he would simply get some paper work done by working at a table in the family room.

After Grant had seated himself on the couch, he was, to his surprise, joined by Dorothy. She came into the living room, carrying a pillow. She explained that she would simply stretch out on the floor to take her nap. If she napped there rather than in one of the beds, she was more likely not to oversleep. Despite her explanation, she had chosen to be close to Grant once again and to signal to him that she was well aware of his attraction to her. Consequently, as Grant thought away on his paper, Dorothy lay nearby on the floor, near where he had spent the night in the sleeping bag. It was such a soothing thing to have her close by; and it reminded him so much of how the five of them had stayed up all night exactly three months ago following the afterglow.

By the late afternoon Carol had come home from her baby-sitting job and was in her room with her friend Betty. Grant was beginning to type out his paper, and Dorothy scrounged around in the kitchen to whip up an easy supper for everyone. After Grant finished typing up his essay, he played Wesley's guitar; and as usual, his music greatly pleased Dorothy, and their two voices joined together in singing many of the songs. When Grant finished playing, Debbie helped Dorothy clean up the kitchen for the night and then talked with her until bedtime.

July 9, 1972, Sunday

After yesterday's near perfection, today had turned out much the opposite. The morning had gone well enough. After attending early church and teaching Sunday school, Dorothy returned home and fixed a nice noontime dinner. The problem was that Debbie was sliding down into one of her low moods. Dorothy read to her for a while in the afternoon, after which the two of them talked for quite some time in hopes of lifting Debbie's spirits. But when this did not seem to help much, Debbie simply followed Dorothy around the house for the rest of the afternoon and evening, wanting to talk even more.

Grant had spent the morning and much of the afternoon in reading things for his two classes. History courses always involved a large amount of reading; and so, there was usually plenty of it to be done, especially for a blind student, whose reading on tape progressed much more slowly than that of a sighted student. But by the early evening Grant decided to call it quits for the day and was ready to relax. Dorothy fixed her usual Sunday supper of popcorn for everyone, but Debbie was still trying to enlist her full and constant attention throughout the evening.

The previous three days had been so gloriously wonderful for Grant: the two reading sessions in his dorm room followed by yesterday's hand holding. There had, however, been no such opportunities for Grant and Dorothy today. Grant yearned to be close to Dorothy for a time, and the lack thereof, caused by Debbie, had succeeded in plunging Grant into his own low mood as bedtime approached. He was beginning to wonder whether his overwhelming desire to be with Dorothy was causing him to become slightly mentally ill like Debbie. As Dorothy moved around the house trying to straighten things up and always with Debbie on her heels, she noticed that Grant seemed somewhat moody. She therefore tried to cheer him up by giving his arm or shoulder an affectionate pat or squeeze as she walked past, but she only did so when George and Carol were not around. The gestures did cheer him up, but they also made him realize that Dorothy was fully aware of his low mental state and its probable cause. Was she and had she simply been treating him over the past few days as she treated Debbie, as a somewhat mentally ill person who required her loving therapy? Probably so, and the conclusion led Grant further downward into depression and despair, because he was so powerfully attracted to her, and the idea of the hopelessness of his feelings for her was hard to endure.

As Dorothy slowly became aware of Grant's moodiness that evening, it saddened her greatly, and she had done what little she could to try to brighten him up with her furtive affectionate touches. Finally, at 10:30 Debbie had decided to go to bed. Dorothy now came to Grant, who was lying on one of the twin beds in the front bedroom reading some braille. She asked if he would like to go for a short walk before they all went to bed. He gladly agreed. Since it was becoming somewhat cool outside, Dorothy went into the master bedroom and put her pink quilted robe over her regular clothes, and then she and Grant went out the back door, around to the front of the house, and then down along Boardman with Grant holding onto her arm and enjoying the feel of her robe.

Dorothy was relieved to be rid of Debbie for the night and was pleased to be alone again with Grant. Maybe now he would tell her how he felt about her, and the confession would succeed in easing his inner misery. So, after they had walked a considerable distance along the street, Dorothy finally asked, "Grant, is there something you want to tell me?" "No," Grant replied. "Are you sure? There seems to be something that is really bothering you. Wouldn't you like to talk about it?" "No," Grant simply and stubbornly replied. Dorothy soon realized that he really wasn't going to talk with her right now. She therefore turned them around; and they retraced their steps, came back to the house, and then went off to bed for the night.

July 10, 1972, Monday

Grant returned to his dorm room at 8:15 P.M. after a two-hour reading session at Larry Smithson's apartment. All day long he had been trying to decide what to do. Dorothy had obviously wanted him to make a confession of his affection for her last night during their walk, but he simply could not bring himself to do it then. The situation just wasn't right. He did not want to disclose his feelings almost casually during the hurried walk of a mere few minutes. He had no way of knowing how making such a disclosure would affect him. If he happened to suffer a complete emotional meltdown, how could he return to the house and go to bed as if everything were normal? He could not afford to bring any more attention to his actions and feelings than he could help. What would happen to Dorothy's domestic situation if George were to learn of how he felt? All these things had caused him to remain silent last night when Dorothy questioned him so pointedly.

Exactly one week ago he had called home and had gone off the deep end, so to speak, when he learned about the irreparable division between his sister and parents. One week later he found himself in another highly emotional state. He knew that George had left this morning and would be gone all week in Newton. Now was probably the best time to do what Dorothy had wanted him to do last night. He therefore picked up the telephone and dialed her number.

After she had said "Hello" into the telephone with that wonderfully rich and lovely voice that captivated him so much, Grant said, "Hello, Ma. This is Grant. I was wondering if you could come over to my room. I need to talk with you about something." "Ok," she replied, "I'll be right there as soon as I can." No further exchange of words was necessary. They both already knew what the agenda would be.

As Grant ran over in his mind what he should do and say when she arrived in about fifteen or twenty minutes, he decided that he would do what he had done three months before with Nisa. He would simply try to tell her how strongly she appealed to him, and perhaps as had happened with Nisa, the confession would allow him to regain his inner peace, but he suspected that it might not work this time. He thought that he felt far more strongly for her than for Nisa, and that inner peace would not come easy. The whole situation made him utterly miserable, because it was so obviously hopeless.

Dorothy let the dogs outside for a few minutes and brought them back inside for the night before leaving the house. She also went to Carol's room to tell her that she needed to run over to campus for a while. She then checked all the doors and went out to the Falcon. As she drove, she felt some degree of excitement. But why? Was it simply because she was on one of her countless errands of mercy to succor one of her university kids? This is what she consciously told herself to be the case; and she remembered the letter that Nisa had written to her about Grant. Nisa had expressed the hope that Dorothy might someday be able to help him, and it looked as if the time had arrived.

When she knocked on the dorm room door, Grant opened it. "Thanks for coming," he said, "Why don't you sit down on the bed, and I'll try to tell you what this is all about." "Ok," was her only response. As she sat upright on the edge of Grant's bed, he paced restlessly back and forth in front of her. In fact, it was just like the scene with Nisa three months before.

"I don't really know how to say this. I guess there really isn't an easy way to, except just to say it." After a long pause, he continued, "I find you to be so attractive, and for several months now I have been feeling a really strong attraction to you. I have been trying to hide my feelings, but it isn't easy and seems to be harder all the time. I really don't know what to do about it, but I really feel the need to let you know."

When he finished speaking, Grant continued to pace back and forth; and after some silence Dorothy said, "Why don't you come lie down on the bed and rest instead of pacing back and forth like that," and she patted the area beside her to accompany her words. Grant obeyed. Within seconds he was lying flat on his back in the middle of his single bed, and Dorothy was still perched on its edge. They sat there in silence for some time. All the wonder that Grant had felt during their two reading sessions here last week now flooded back and intensified. He desired her so very much! Finally he could bear it no longer but had to ask, "Would you mind if I give you a kiss?" She sat there motionless and silent for what seemed like minutes, but it was no more than fifteen seconds. At first Grant feared that his question had offended her, but then without uttering a word Dorothy turned her upper body to face him, lowered herself down over him, and carefully placed her moist and slightly parted lips upon his. Her lips were so soft and wonderful, and they held the kiss for some time. It was not at all a chaste kiss. It was quite obvious that she had wanted and enjoyed the kiss as much as he. When their mouths finally parted, Grant said in a low and serious voice, "Thank you. That was really wonderful." Shortly thereafter Dorothy gave him her own response in the form of another tender kiss. Her attraction to Grant, hitherto concealed behind the facade of helping him, now swelled to a crescendo and fully dominated her thoughts, feelings, and actions.

Ever since her first association with this group of blind university students, Dorothy had been slowly attracted to Grant without her really being aware of it. First, of course, there was his wonderful guitar playing and singing that always pleased her so much. Then over the course of this past academic year she had participated in intellectually stimulating discussions with Dennis and Grant concerning major works of literature, such as *Crime and Punishment* and *The Source*, during which Dorothy had developed a real respect and admiration for Grant's knowledge and learning; and his study of German made him further appealing to Dorothy. And now his confession of being attracted to her somehow seemed to bring all these separate elements together to form her own strong attraction to him. Over the past few days she had, of course, become acutely aware of his attraction to her, and she had been considering the whole matter in her mind continually. Her thoughts, she believed, had been those of concern and sympathy, but it was now quite apparent that they were much more than that and had been intensifying to form her own attraction to Grant.

Their respective emotional dams had now burst, and they were being swept along by the powerful onrush of those pent-up emotions. For the next three and a half hours they did little more than kiss passionately. They explored one another's lips. They sometimes parted their mouths and had their tongues touch and engage in erotic play. They varied the length and pressure of their kisses and thus made the marathon into a lovely and magnificent game. After they had been kissing for a while, Grant suggested, "Why don't you lie down beside me on the bed? You'd be more comfortable." "No, I'm a married woman, and I really dare not do that," Dorothy replied. Other than this and a few additional exchanges, they spoke very little. Their whole attention was paid to their passionate kissing, and the words uttered were simply exclamations of wonder, as they both were completely thrilled and captivated by their continuous kissing. They remained in their same positions on the bed for the entire time: Grant lying on his back and Dorothy sitting beside him with her body turned and lowered to face him. Grant had both his arms around her back, and his hands explored her arms, shoulders, and back as they kissed and kissed.

When Dorothy realized that it was around midnight, she was so surprised. She had been so transported with pleasure and exhilaration that she had lost all track of time. When she set out to come to Grant's room tonight, she certainly had not intended to stay this long. "Oh my golly," she exclaimed, "it's midnight. I really must get back home. I left Carol there in the house." She stood up from her position on the bed, picked up her purse from the top bunk on the other side of the room, and prepared to leave. Grant sat up, got to his feet, and walked out with her, going down to the first floor on the elevator. The building was perfectly still. No other people were up and about; and since they would have to walk past the main desk to exit the building, Dorothy suggested that Grant not accompany her any further than the elevator. They should not be seen together by anyone at such an odd time. Grant agreed. Accordingly, when the elevator reached the first floor, Dorothy stepped out alone, and Grant returned to his room.

July 11, 1972, Tuesday

It was hard for Grant to believe what had just transpired. He had gone from the depths of despair to clouds of exhilaration. As he walked over to Milton Hall for his 9:00 class on Alexander the Great, he could not have felt any more elated. It was the first time in his life that he had engaged in passionate kissing. He never had a girlfriend before, and last night had been so spectacular! And despite his total inexperience, kissing Dorothy and enjoying her mouth and lips had come to him so naturally. After class he returned to Walker and began composing a poem in an attempt to express how he felt about her. After working it out in his head, he first wrote it down in braille and then used the braille text to produce a print copy on his portable typewriter. When he returned from his second trip to campus in the middle of the afternoon, he called Dorothy.

"Hello, Ma, how are you?" "Oh I'm fine," she replied smoothly and with her perfectly feminine voice that always enchanted Grant. "I've got something to give you. So I was wondering if and when you would like to come over, so that I could give it to you." "Well, I have Sweet Adelines practice tonight, and I could come by then if it wouldn't be too late. I wouldn't be there until sometime after 10:00." "No, that would be fine," "Ok, I'll see you then."

Grant had been concerned as to how she might receive his telephone call. Would she be cautious toward him and regard last night as a terrible mistake? The natural sweetness in her voice had clearly indicated that all was well with her. How could he possibly wait until 10:00 before seeing her again? He tried to busy himself with his history reading, but his mind refused to remain engaged except for short segments of time, and he had to keep listening to the same passages over and over again.

Dorothy's day in the aftermath of the kissing marathon had been the usual series of various activities: swimming in the morning, home to do things around the house and to have lunch with Carol, laundry and more things around the house in the afternoon, and then supper and getting herself ready for Sweet Adelines. But of course, it had not been her usual day because of what had happened last night. She could still hardly believe it. When Grant had first asked her if he could give her a kiss, her intention, she thought, had simply been to comfort him by bestowing upon him a tender affectionate kiss, but she was immediately caught up in a whirlwind of her own emotions and was carried along by them for the next several hours. How utterly wonderful it had all been! She had not felt or experienced anything like that for twenty years or more! Like Grant, she had been walking on air all day long in the afterglow of what they had experienced, but she was also deeply troubled. Of course, she had not loved George for a long time and had wanted some miracle to happen to extricate her from her unhappy situation. But how could this possibly be that miracle? It looked much more like a disaster. A married woman with three children, about to turn 44 in a few more days, involved with a nineteen-year old blind college student? What insanity! Dorothy had often toyed with the idea of leaving George once Carol was finally out of school and on her own, but she still had a few years to go. Dorothy therefore could not afford to jeopardize her stable domestic situation just yet. She and Grant had to keep their powerful attraction for one another in check.

Ever since she had become such an able swimmer and respected singer in Sweet Adelines, Tuesdays had become her favorite day of the week. Both activities made her feel really good, but neither could even come close to matching what she had experienced last night. Like Grant, she could hardly wait for them to be together again. She therefore did not join the other women in winding down their evening at the Jolly Roger. But instead, she drove over to Walker as soon as Sweet Adelines had ended. She was feeling her usual elation that resulted from the enjoyment of singing, but she was also remembering the spectacular joy of twenty-four hours ago. What was it that Grant had to give her? Probably some little gift or other.

When she entered his room, she placed her purse on the top bunk to the right and sat down on Grant's bed to the left. Grant walked over to his desk and picked up some papers. "I spent a good bit of today writing a poem. I really needed to write something that tried to express how I feel about you. Here it is, a copy in braille and another one that I have typed out. I've given it a Latin title, Semper Dulcis. It means "Forever Sweet," because despite our difference in age, you possess such wonderful sweetness of character, and I can't imagine that it will ever desert you, no matter what; and I also really think that I will always be attracted to you, no matter what." He handed her the two sheets, one of them regular typewriting paper with the print copy on it, and another much heavier sheet of braille paper. She received them from him in silence and read:

Semper Dulcis

When time has come so swiftly on
that thine own hair shall silver be,
then thou shalt think of old days gone,
yearning once more to catch the eyes
of them who once admired thee.
But nay, my love, they shall not glance
upon thine aged face, but me
alone shalt thou behold enhanced
by thy benign aspect, thy tones
of youth, thy beauty, pure and free,
inscribed with life's travail. Perchance
thou then in joyous wise shalt see
my fettered heart by thee entranced
and patient love for my dear one.

Dorothy had not at all expected a gift of this sort. She slowly read the words on the printed sheet and was moved and touched by them. Grant stood nearby in silent anticipation, awaiting her reaction. After reading the poem, she sat still and fought to control her emotions. When she finally thought that she could trust herself to speak, she said, "Thank you, Grant. It's so very beautiful." She arose from the bed and stepped over to her purse.

She folded up the printed sheet and carefully tucked it inside a small inner pouch. But she did not fold the braille sheet, because that would probably damage the writing. She therefore simply laid the unfolded braille sheet on top of her purse. Then she sat back down on the bed. Grant sat down beside her; and despite what she rationally knew to be the safe thing to do, and despite all her earlier inner resolve not to allow something like last night to repeat itself, they immediately and unhesitatingly resumed their kissing marathon of the evening before.

They assumed the same positions that they had had the night before: Grant lying on his back on the bed with Dorothy sitting beside him and with her upper body turned and lowered toward him. He also embraced her with his arms and caressed her lovingly with his hands, as they kissed and kissed and kissed. Grant's hands traveled all over her, exploring her clothing, a matching top and shorts that she had made herself out of a lovely double-knit polyester material. The outfit had a matching belt tied around her waist, and the top was worn outside the shorts and was slit up both sides a few inches from the bottom hem. It was really beautiful and made her look so very stunning to him. Grant examined the outfit amid their kissing and eventually asked, "What color is your outfit?" Kiss. "It's a blue and white pattern." Kiss. "Did you make it yourself?" "Yes," Kiss, Kiss. "It looks so lovely!" Kiss, kiss. "I have two other outfits just like this one, one that's yellow, and another that's pink." Kiss, kiss, kiss...

Grant's hands even traveled down her body to feel her bare legs. She made no effort to stop his exploration of her body. His hands felt so right on her, and he too thoroughly enjoyed what his hands discovered: a well-shaped and beautiful woman so lovely in this adorable outfit that she herself had made.

"Wunderbar!" Dorothy quietly exclaimed after one of their kisses. "It sure is!" Grant replied. Kiss, kiss, kiss. "That's the title of an old song," Dorothy explained. Kiss, kiss. "How does it go?" Grant asked. They halted their kissing long enough for Dorothy to sing part of the song. It was a song that expressed the wonder of love between a man and a woman, so perfectly fitting for what they were experiencing. Kiss, kiss, kiss...

Around midnight Dorothy announced in a cute little girl voice, "I've got to go potty." "Ok, but the ladies' room is down on the first floor," Grant reminded her. They both arose from the bed, walked out into the hall and to the elevator, took it down to the first floor, and then walked together through the perfectly still hallways all around to the other side of the building to the ladies' room. Dorothy pushed the door open and went inside. Grant stood near the door, as he waited for her. In the perfect stillness of the night he had no trouble in hearing her open the door to one of the stalls and shut it. He was now wondering how utterly beautiful she must look right now in taking down her shorts and panties. The thought made him feel somewhat ashamed of himself, but the thought had arisen in his mind quite naturally. He heard her flush, open up the stall door, and then she was beside him. They retraced their steps and reassumed their positions on the bed and resumed their kissing. Around 1:30 Dorothy announced again in her cute little girl voice, "I'm sorry, but I've got to go potty again." They repeated the process all over again, including Grant's imaginings of her sitting there with her shorts and panties down around her ankles and her knees spread apart. They then returned to Grant's room for another hour and a half of passionate kissing.

"This really is wunderbar," Dorothy said for about the twelfth time, "but you know, we really can't go on like this forever. I am married. We need to put temptation behind us. Like Jesus told the Devil, 'Get thee behind me, Satan'." She uttered this admonition in a very gentle voice, but their kissing continued for a while longer.

When Dorothy happened to glance at her watch and notice that it was now a few minutes after 3:00, she announced that she really needed to be getting back home. Like the night before, she now stood up and stepped over to collect her purse and braille sheet in preparation for her departure. Grant stood up and moved over to the door to open it and to accompany her down the elevator; but as Dorothy turned his way, her eyes automatically went down to the front of his shorts and beheld his very obvious erection for her. She then said, "You have a wet stain in the front of your shorts. I don't think you'd better go out into the hall with me like that."

Grant was taken by surprise and was only momentarily embarrassed by her observation. As he stood just a few feet directly in front of her, he unfastened his pants, slid them down his legs, stepped out of them, reached over to a drawer under his bed, pulled out a clean pair of shorts, and put them on. As he did so, Dorothy saw him for the first time in his undershorts, and his erection was now much more discernible, as was the copious amount of sperm that his erection had been secreting over the past four hours or so in response to their kissing and Grant's petting of her body. The front of his undershorts was saturated with moisture that clearly advertised his desire for her. Dorothy did not avert her eyes, but she kept her gaze fixed upon his erection and derived pleasure from the sight. She could easily see the large round head of his penis stretching the fabric of his undershorts, as if it were the rounded top of a tent pole. When Grant had his new pair of shorts properly in place, they took the elevator down to the first floor and parted company.

July 12, 1972, Wednesday

After about four hours of sleep Grant arose and prepared to go off to his 9:00 class. But unlike the morning before when he was floating happily way up in the stratosphere, today he was once again plunged down into the depths of despair, because Dorothy had indicated toward the end of their second kissing marathon that this extraordinary magnificence had to end. Grant found that idea to be devastating, so much so that he began to cry and could not stop, even as he walked from Walker to Milton Hall. Before he entered the building, he wiped off his face; and when he arrived in the classroom, he sat at the back in the hope that no one would notice that he had been crying.

July 14, 1972, Friday

They had not talked since their parting early Wednesday morning, and Dorothy was wondering what Grant had planned for the weekend. Thus far he and Debbie had stayed at the house every weekend since they arrived in town for summer school. She feared that her admonition that they had to control themselves had deeply hurt or angered Grant. They really needed to talk and to agree on how they should handle their difficult situation. She therefore lifted up the receiver and called his dorm room.

After he answered, she began, "Hi, Grant, I'm calling to find out what you want to do about coming over this weekend." "Well," Grant began with some hesitation, "I wasn't sure. I thought that perhaps I shouldn't come over at all." "That's not really necessary, is it?" Dorothy asked. "I don't know." "Why don't we get together and talk about it?" Dorothy suggested. "Ok." "How about we meet after your 2:00 class." "That would be fine. I'll see you then."

Dorothy picked him up in front of Milton Hall just as she had done last week for their two reading sessions, but when Grant sat himself down in the passenger seat, she said, "I'm going to drive a good distance from here to a park, and we can sit outside somewhere and talk." Grant was rather disappointed by this announcement, because they would not have an afternoon of kissing interspersed with their conversation. Dorothy had, of course, decided that she must avoid being alone in Grant's room. They really had to get control of themselves once again. She had also decided to go to a park on the eastern edge of University City, several miles away from her neighborhood, because she knew fewer people in that area; and she would rather not be seen alone with Grant by a friend or acquaintance.

After parking, they walked together across the grass and sat down underneath a tree. It was rather hot, but the shade afforded them some protection from the sun's heat. They sat cross-legged in front of one another with their knees almost touching.

"Grant," Dorothy began, "I would really like to have you at the house this weekend." "I really don't think that I can do that," he replied. "Why not!" "I don't think that I can act normal around you." "But, Grant, if you don't, we might have to stop seeing each other and being together." When Grant failed to respond, she went on to explain. "I like you very much, as you know by now; and I know that you really like me, but we really must control our feelings, and then we can be together and enjoy one another's company. We can be such special friends," she pleaded urgently.

By now they were holding hands, their forearms resting upon their knees and both their hands clasped together. After a long pause, Grant finally replied, "You might be able to do that, but I really don't think that I can. I'm simply not good at hiding what I feel if I feel something strongly. I just don't think I can do it. If I'm around you, I'll wind up doing or saying something that will let other people know."

Their conversation continued like that for over a half an hour with Dorothy pleading with Grant and him unwilling to try. As they talked, Grant lowered his face and rubbed his cheek along her forearm. Her White Shoulders perfume was so wonderfully fragrant and so entranced him. The shape of her forearm was lovely, and the smooth skin was delightful to the touch of his face. As Dorothy continued to state her case and sweetly plead with him, she still could not keep herself from giggling with pleasure whenever his cheek caressed her forearm. It was "wunderbar" and "Get thee behind me, Satan" all over again. Her rational side knew that they needed to keep firm control over themselves, but her emotions were in firm opposition to her rational resolve.

"I'm sorry," Grant replied with real sincerity, "I don't have your perfect diplomatic skills of dealing with things like this." Indeed, in addition to always seeming to know how to act and what to say in every situation (her surprise silver anniversary party being the one notable exception), Dorothy had had years and years of actual practice of keeping her feelings bottled up and hidden away, especially from George. Grant was so young, so full of passion, and so devoid of such experience. "Grant," Dorothy finally conceded, "I'm so sorry too, because I really want us to be together and to keep seeing one another."

They eventually arose from the ground, returned to the car, and Dorothy took him back to Walker, picked up Debbie, and returned home.

July 15, 1972, Saturday

When George and Debbie had asked about Grant's absence, Dorothy had explained that he had too much work to do with midterms coming up and had therefore decided to spend the weekend in his dorm room. She had spent much of the morning reading to and then talking with Debbie; and that had at least kept her mind occupied. But now it was lunchtime, and all that she could think about was Grant. How was he doing? She therefore finally surrendered to her concern and gave him a call.

"Hello, Grant. How are you doing?" "Ok, I guess." "Is there anything that I can help you with?" After a slight pause he said, "Well, it would be nice to have some things here in my room to snack on and eat." "All right, how about I take you to the grocery store?" "That would really be nice." "Ok, I'll be there soon. I'll call again just before I leave, and you can meet me downstairs out in front."

When she arrived, they went to a supermarket not too far away on Lexington. They then had a very enjoyable time walking together up and down the aisles of the store, pushing a cart in air conditioned comfort. They rounded up various things: several small cans of peas and corn, a box of vanilla wafers, etc. When they arrived back at Walker, Dorothy parked the car and came up to Grant's room. After she had helped him arranged his items in a desk drawer, so that he would know which cans were what, they sat down side by side on the bed and were soon locked in one another's arms and kissing passionately. Despite her rational resolve, Dorothy simply could not resist her powerful emotional urges. She so desired to have his kisses and to feel his arms around her and hands touching her. But she possessed enough reason to know that she could not be absent from the house too long without arousing questions. Therefore, after about forty minutes of exhilarating embracing and kissing, Dorothy politely excused herself. When Grant rose and stepped over to the door to walk out with her, her eyes went down to the front of his pants and beheld the bulge of his erection as well as a wet spot. she then said, "You've got a wet spot again at the front of your shorts." Today Grant simply smiled, opened up the door for her, and allowed her to depart on her own.

As Dorothy drove herself home, she chastised herself for her weakness. She was supposed to be the mature adult who should know better. She knew what was right, but she did not seem to possess the strength to do it. In being so hard on herself, she failed to take into account the fact that she had been emotionally starved for genuine loving affection for years and years. It was only normal and natural for her to respond so positively to Grant's passionate attraction to her. She was married to George, and she felt morally bound by that bond, but the marriage had not provided her with happiness for many years. Was she supposed to remain faithful to the bond alone and walk away from a relationship that might give her happiness and joy?

July 19, 1972, Wednesday

Grant met Dorothy out in front of Milton Hall, and they drove over to Walker to meet Debbie in her room, so that Dorothy could help her with various small things before the trio went off for some supper at Steak and Shake. Although Grant had not come to the house for the weekend, Dorothy and Grant, often joined by Debbie, were frequently together either running errands or simply being at the house during the week, because George was now usually spending the week in Newton and coming home for the weekend.

Since Grant wanted to get rid of his notebook and things, Debbie went off to her own dorm room, while Dorothy and Grant proceeded to go up to his room. But as they walked past the main desk on the first floor, Grant was unexpectedly accosted. "Hey, my man," said a young well-built black man behind the desk, "how ya doing? Hey man, this is your old buddy Dell!" he said with both pleasure and enthusiasm. Grant halted his forward progress toward the elevator and stepped over to the desk to greet his former wrestling coach. Grant stuck out his hand, and the two shook vigorously. "Hey man, what the hell are you doing there behind that desk?" "Ah man, I'm working here part time for the summer. How's it hanging?" "Oh everything is fine," Grant allowed placidly but smiling broadly in genuine delight of meeting this man again. "Oh don't give me that ok shit. I've seen you shacking up with your old lady!" Dell laughed. Grant laughed in return and said, "Well, gotta run, but hey! It's really great to see you here. Hope to run into you again soon." "Yeah man, take it easy!"

As soon as they had shut the door behind them in Grant's dorm room, Dorothy exclaimed in genuine panic, "He knows about us!" "Who?" Grant asked somewhat puzzled. "That guy down there at the desk!" she said excitedly. "Oh Dell, don't worry about him. He was the wrestling coach that Dennis and I had this spring. He's always talking a bunch of silly shit." "But he said he saw you shacking up with your old lady!" Dorothy insisted with her panic unabated. "That was just his crazy talking. He didn't mean anything by it." "Are you sure!" "Oh yea, I'm sure," Grant said calmly and assuredly, "Don't worry about it." "Ok," Dorothy replied with evident relief, "but it sure did scare me."

They now left his room and went over to the other side of Walker to Debbie's room. Debbie was, for once, in a cheerful mood. She was bubbling with laughter as Dorothy helped her go through mail and a few other things. As they did, Debbie sat at her desk and Dorothy nearby at the foot of her bed. Grant hovered about the room, but was usually not far from Dorothy. Since Debbie was blind like himself, he did not hesitate to touch this wonderful woman who infatuated him so. He ran his hands over her clothes to see what she was wearing today, a practice that Dorothy did not at all object to, as long as they were alone together, or as now, in the presence of another blind person. She was wearing one of those outfits that she had made, consisting of a top and shorts with a cloth belt tied around the waist and the top slit up the sides for a few inches from the bottom. As always, she was dazzling and adorable. But as Grant's hand felt her right shoulder, he noticed that the bra strap beneath her top had a twist in it. Without thinking he casually commented, "your strap has a twist in it." "Grant," Debbie asked in laughing surprise, "What are you doing? Are you getting too fresh with Ma?" They all laughed and soon departed to enjoy themselves at Steak and Shake.

July 22, 1972, Saturday

Once again Grant was staying in his dorm room for the entire weekend. It saddened Dorothy very much. She missed him and wanted him to be at the house. It also disappointed her that he did not trust himself in her presence, but perhaps he was right, because she too found it so hard not to reach out and touch him and to be pleased when he touched her. It was therefore probably unwise for the two to be together in George's presence.

They had finished supper not too long ago, and she was cleaning up the kitchen and loading up the dishwasher. George was already busy with paperwork for the construction project in Newton. When the telephone rang, she stepped over to it and picked up the receiver.

It was Grant on the other end, and he was so glad that Dorothy had been the one to answer. Otherwise, he had decided, he would hang up. "Hi, it's me," Grant said, "What are you doing?" "What or how?" she asked. "What," he replied. "Ummmm," she said in such a beautiful way that it thrilled Grant just to hear it. "Right now I'm loading up the dishwasher. What are you doing?" "I'm in my dorm room, and Terry Wilson, one of my readers, is here, and we're listening to some records." "That sounds nice." "Golly, I miss you!" Grant said with obvious emotion. "You shouldn't say that with him there in the room," Dorothy cautioned. "Oh don't worry. He's wearing my headphones right now as he's listening to a Merle Haggard album. The headphones are heavily padded, so that you can't hear anything else." "Are you sure?" "Yep, I'm sure. Dorothy Patterson, I love you!" Grant said with tremendous force and emphasis. "Don't say that," Dorothy replied in alarm. "Dorothy Patterson, I love you!" Grant repeated with equal vehemence. "I'm sorry," he said gently in response to her obvious alarm at Terry overhearing him, "But I really had to call and tell you that. I just had to; and I thought that now would be a good time." They then said goodbye and hung up.

Despite its brevity, Dorothy was truly thrilled by their conversation, especially by hearing Grant say those five words: "Dorothy Patterson, I love you!" Over the past two weeks, whenever they talked about their feelings for each other, they had deliberately avoided using the word "love." They both clearly understood that it was such a loaded word and should not be spoken out of respect of Dorothy's marital status. But he had now used it and had called her up on the phone to utter those words, because he apparently felt a compelling need and desire to do so. It was what? Surprising, somewhat stunning and unsettling, but also so very glorious, wonderful, enchanting, and thrilling!

July 27, 1972, Thursday

After her swimming in the morning, Dorothy had gone to Walker to pick Grant up. They had then returned to the park on the eastern edge of

University City where they had sat and talked almost two weeks ago. They had planned to spend the rest of the day together, and they would start it off by sitting again alone in this lovely little park. Dorothy had brought along the same white blanket that she had taken to Parkfield on the day of their horseback riding, and underneath which they had held hands. They found a nice shady place, spread out the blanket, and settled down on it. They both simply craved one another's company and physical presence acutely. Grant took her purse from her and held it in his lap. They both enjoyed that, because holding fondly an item so intimately identified with a woman, her purse, was itself a form of shared physical intimacy.

Within moments Grant was feeling inside and removing the contents, item by item. As long as he could not touch and caress her out here in a public place, he would do the next best thing: handling things that belonged to her, and which often came into direct contact with parts of her body. Dorothy as well realized this instinctively, so that his handling of the contents of her purse was a kind of erotic teasing between the two of them.

He removed a folded-up headscarf. He raised it to his nose and sniffed. "Oh my golly, it smells just like you, just like the hair spray that you use, I guess. What a wonderful fragrance! Have I ever told you how much I love your White Shoulders perfume? It is so beautiful and becomes you perfectly." Dorothy said nothing but was greatly pleased at his words. "What's this thing?" Grant asked. "It's for curling a woman's eye lashes," Dorothy replied. "See," she said, as she reached out to show him how it worked, "You open it up like this and hold this part right under your eye lashes. Then you carefully close it together, and it gives your eye lashes a nice shape." They both relished their hands touching as she demonstrated the device for him. And so it went, item after item. It was such a lovely intimate experience between them.

"You know," Grant said, "you are my first real girlfriend. I was too busy in high school to bother with girls. Besides, I was the only blind guy in my high school of about 3,400 kids and therefore a freak. I always figured that none of the girls would ever be interested in me." "You never should have thought that, Grant," Dorothy interjected in protest, but Grant continued on as if not hearing her. "So I never bothered. Anyway, I was there to get myself as well educated as possible before going to college. All that other stuff in high school seemed to me so stupid and such a waste of time. You know, I never bothered having my picture taken for a year book? Hells bells, I don't even own a high school year book! And I never even considered going to the senior prom. I was probably one of the very few kids in my class who didn't.

So, like I say, you are my first girlfriend. What do you think of that?" "I like it," Dorothy said quietly and in her low pitched tone of voice that, Grant had learned by now, meant her expression of very serious emotion. "Going through your purse like this is so very nice," Grant continued, "Thank you for letting me do it. You're teaching me so much about women, things that I never knew before, like that eye lash curler. It's so wonderful." "I'm glad to be your teacher," Dorothy said again in that low serious voice of hers. "Yep, and you know what?" Grant asked. "What," Dorothy replied, this time with a bit of laughter in her voice. "I couldn't ask for a better teacher, because you're the most wonderful and classiest woman I've ever met. I really mean that!"

They eventually arose and had fun in folding up the white blanket together. They walked to the car and went to the house, where they had planned to spend the rest of the day together. But since Carol was there, they had to conduct themselves as Ma and Grant the blind student. Nevertheless, as always, it was simply wonderful for them both to be together in sweet companionship around the house. When Grant later played the guitar, their enjoyment of the music and their singing together now took on a different quality. They now shared the experience as secret lovers.

Around 4:00 in the afternoon the doorbell rang; and when Dorothy answered the door, she was surprised to see a delivery man there. He had a large package for Dorothy Patterson. It was several days before her forty-fourth birthday, but she was not expecting a package from anyone. Usually she simply received cards from relatives, sometimes with a small check enclosed. Dorothy inspected the package for a return mailing address, but it simply bore that of the company from which the product came. Thus mystified and laughing with excitement, she put the package on the kitchen table, took a knife out of a drawer, and slit it open. Inside she found a large variety of cheese and dairy products. Up till then Grant had conducted himself as an uninvolved and dispassionate observer, but now he finally let the cat out of the bag. He had asked his mother to send this to her for a birthday present. Dorothy was truly surprised, overjoyed, and exclaimed as she examined each item.

July 28, 1972, Friday

Before attending his afternoon class, Grant walked over to Spruce Street and bought two dozen doughnuts from Dunkin' Donuts to have at the house tomorrow morning to feed all the people who would be there. It would relieve Dorothy of the necessity to fix breakfast for everyone. Dennis, Renny, and another blind friend were coming to University City on the bus tonight to stay until Sunday afternoon. It would be a little weekend vacation for them from their summer jobs at the Lighthouse for the Blind on the south side of Chicago.

After his class, Dorothy picked Grant up in front of Milton Hall, and they then went to his dorm room. There they sat snuggled together on the bed while Dorothy did some reading for him. When Dorothy had finished reading, she said that since it was bound to be a long evening with Dennis and Renny arriving so late, she would like to take a short nap right there on Grant's bed before they headed off to the house. Dorothy told him to wake her up in twenty minutes if she had not yet awakened on her own. Grant agreed and moved over to the lower bunk on the other side of the room. There he stretched himself out on the bed and stayed as still and quiet as he could. Dorothy now lay down on her side, bent her knees up, and tucked Grant's pillow under her head at the foot of the bed.

After twenty minutes had elapsed, Dorothy was still sound asleep. Grant quietly arose from the lower bunk and stepped across to the other bed. He stood there for several seconds, trying to decide exactly how to awaken this beautiful and wonderful woman who so thoroughly enchanted him. Should he lie down beside her? As much as he wanted to do that, he feared that it would alarm and offend her. He therefore decided upon a kind of halfway measure. He slowly bent down over her, carefully and tenderly enveloped her in his arms, and covered her with his upper body. His left arm went behind her upper legs and bottom; his right arm encircled her head; and his chest lightly rested upon the side of her body. "It's time to wake up," he said softly. Dorothy responded by moving her head, letting out a sigh, and then stretching out her legs. Grant held his gentle embrace for as long as he dared. He hated to break contact with her, but he also did not wish to cause her any unease by doing something that she would regard as out of bounds. In fact, this had become such an integral part of their interaction: their mutual pleasure and joy in being together, but Dorothy's concern about how they interacted physically, and Grant carefully moving forward like a soldier over a mine field, hoping against hope that his next cautious move would not result in an explosion.

They now left his dorm room and went to the house, where they set to work in the kitchen. George would be arriving home soon, something which neither of them looked forward to. Grant lent whatever assistance he could in preparing things, such as cutting up a tray of brownies. Sally stopped by briefly from her day of work at her job, and George showed up not long thereafter. Debbie, however, was not there, because earlier in the week she had been admitted into the Mental Health Ward of Mercy Hospital. Despite her efforts to continue her college education during summer school, she was gradually overcome by such depression that she required serious professional help. The tables had therefore been turned. Debbie had stayed at the house in Grant's absence for the past two weekends, and now he was going to be there for the weekend for the first time that summer in her absence, but also, of course, in George's presence, the first time since the nights of the two kissing marathons.

After a seemingly normal evening of quiet activities around the house, George, Dorothy, and Grant went by car to the bus station. There they sat, Dorothy with George to her right and Grant to her left, as they waited for the bus to arrive. It finally did shortly after 11:00. Dennis and Renny were their usual boisterous selves. Their friend was Jim Regan, whom, as it turned out, Grant had known years before as a fellow student in Jacksonville, Illinois at the Illinois Braille and Sight Saving School, a residential school for the blind and visually impaired.

When they returned to the house with their three weekend guests, they sat for a short time around the kitchen table while the three snacked on various things. Then everyone went off to bed. Carol had already been in bed in her middle bedroom (Wesley's old room) for quite some time. Dorothy and George, of course, retired to the master bedroom, and Grant went into the far bedroom just across the hall from them, while Renny and Jim slept in the twin beds in the front bedroom, and Dennis camped out in a sleeping bag on the living room floor.

July 29, 1972, Saturday

Grant awoke early and came into the living room, where he woke Dennis up. They had not seen or talked with one another for almost two months, during which so much had happened between him and Dorothy. Since Dennis had always been his confidante during the previous academic year, he wanted to talk with him, but he was not sure exactly how much he should tell him. While they talked quietly on the living room floor, largely about what Dennis had been doing during the summer, the others slowly made their way to the kitchen. There they spent a leisurely morning eating doughnuts and talking non-stop.

By late morning, Dennis and Renny, now well fortified with calories, were eager to do something. They decided to go out into the fenced-in side yard and take turns in hitting a large softball with a bat. They had engaged in this sport at the house several times before, but Grant had never been around when they had. He wasn't interested in the game anyway, and that didn't surprise anyone. While Jim, George, and Carol went outside to play with Dennis and Renny, Grant stayed inside with Dorothy. She had many things to do in the kitchen for tonight's supper, and he once again used the excuse of helping in the kitchen as his valid cover for remaining close to her.

When Dorothy and Grant had done everything that they could in the kitchen, everyone else was still outside playing. One person stood at one end of the yard with the bat and ball, tossed the ball up in the air, and swung at it with the bat. When contact was successfully made, everyone else who had been standing around near the other end of the yard served as fielders, retrieved the ball, and tossed it back to the batter. Of course, everyone had their turn at bat. They were all having such a good time, but since Grant and Dorothy were not the least bit interested in the game but wanted to be alone together for as long as possible but without drawing attention to the fact, they decided that they could walk over to Walgreen's. Dorothy therefore went to the back door and informed George that she was going to walk with Grant over to Walgreen's, so that he could buy some necessary items.

It was a walk of several blocks and thus allowed them to be alone together for about another hour. They first walked east down Boardman, turned north onto Center Street, walked until they came to Lexington and then east along Lexington until they came to Walgreen's on the southwest corner of Madison and Lexington. Luckily, it was not too hot a day, so that the walk was a rather pleasant one. As they walked over and back, they simply enjoyed being out of the house and alone together, but they also talked seriously about how they were doing, especially Grant. Dorothy was so happy to have him at the house during a weekend again when George and others were there. She regarded it as a hopeful sign that her plan for them might succeed after all, for them to be very special secret friends. If they did succeed, it would involve her in performing the most difficult balancing act of her life, to keep her marriage intact, unhappy though it was, while at the same time holding in check her powerful attraction to Grant.

"So," Dorothy asked, "How are you doing?" "Ok, I guess," he replied rather grudgingly, "But it's not much fun." "I know it isn't, and I know it isn't easy, but we don't have a whole lot of other choices, one being that we stop seeing one another altogether; and I know we both don't want that." "Yeah, I know," Grant reluctantly agreed, "But I really don't like it. I love you! I really do love you!" There was that word again. Despite her feelings, Dorothy dare not and could not reply in kind if she intended to respect her marital status. "Well," she said instead, "I'm proud of you. I know it isn't fun or easy, but please just keep going along like this for me. Please? It's so nice having you at the house with me when other people are there."

Supper that evening was wonderful. Dorothy had made lasagna and served it with garlic bread, and they had a delicious single layer sheet cake for dessert. Then they drove over to campus to one of the theaters near Wagoner and Foxwell Streets to see the movie *Nicholas and Alexandra.* Unfortunately, since Dorothy and Grant had already spent so much time together earlier in the day, they thought it best not to sit side by side during the movie.

July 31, 1972, Monday

It was 8:40 A.M., and Dorothy was driving Grant and Dennis over to Milton Hall for Grant's first class of the day. Renny and Jim had returned to Chicago yesterday afternoon on the bus, but Dennis had decided to hang around for another day. He and Grant could go to his classes together, have a chance to talk, and then he would catch the afternoon bus back to Chicago. After the 9:00 class, the two blind friends walked over to the library and sat in a reading room reserved for blind students and their readers. The room had the advantage of giving them complete privacy to talk.

Much of what they said simply brought them up to date on what the other had been doing during the summer. Grant's big news, of course, concerned him and Dorothy, but he was not sure how much to reveal. Although he was bursting to tell Dennis everything, he realized that doing so was a very bad idea. He therefore simply provided Dennis with a few basic facts and left it at that.

"Well, Dennis," Grant began, "I guess my biggest news involves Ma." "Oh yea?" Dennis replied. "Three weeks ago today I told her that I was really attracted to her." "You're kidding? What did she say?" "Well, she really didn't say anything right away, but she seems to be attracted to me too." "Ah man,

I don't believe this! So what are you doing about it?" "Well, that's the big question, isn't it? She obviously doesn't want to do anything to ruin her marriage. She would like to have us just be special friends." "You're still seeing each other and doing things together?" "Yeah." "I tell you, man. You take it real easy, and don't rock the boat!" Dennis warned rather sternly. "Ok, I will," Grant replied in a somewhat chastened tone.

August 1, 1972, Tuesday

After swimming this morning, Dorothy had picked Grant up at Walker; and now they were spending the rest of the day together at the house in their usual sweet companionship. George was away in Newton for the week; Sally was working the day shift at her job; and Carol was going to be occupied all afternoon with baby-sitting. They would therefore be alone in the house for the next few hours.

As Dorothy heated up some left-overs from the refrigerator for their lunch, Grant walked into the dining room and began to examine all the things on top of Dorothy's desk. Like the contents of her purse, the objects there were intimate extensions of this wondrous woman whom he so adored and loved. Dorothy's desk was her own personal island of serenity in the house. No one else ever sat down there. The area was hers alone, and she took great pride in it. The desk was a beautifully crafted piece of furniture and thus revealed Dorothy's consummate taste in such matters. In addition, the top surface of the desk was adorned with numerous objects, each of which Dorothy had carefully chosen both for function and aesthetics. The overall effect was one of elegance, a perfect reflection of Dorothy herself. Grant picked up a letter opener, solid metal and flat, but the handle was shaped like a lovely rose. It was so very tasteful and pretty, just like Dorothy herself, he thought to himself. The same was true for the brass-colored metal turtle whose shell was hinged on one side, so that it could be lifted up, and inside was a small storage tray where Dorothy kept paper clips. Both her writing pen and pen stand were very stylish but also possessed a simple grace.

As Dorothy stepped into the dining room from the kitchen to see what Grant was doing, she saw him standing at her desk and examining her pen stand. "What are you doing?" she asked with mild curiosity. "I'm just looking at these things on your desk. They're all so pretty and nice, just like you." "They are, huh?" Dorothy replied with delight and pleasure in her voice.

"They most certainly are, and so are you!" Grant stated emphatically. "Well, let's come and eat lunch."

After eating and putting their dishes in the dishwasher, Dorothy led Grant back into the dining room and had him sit with her on the floor. Instantly, their arms went around each other, and they began to kiss. They were in the perfect position in the house for avoiding detection. The couch, which divided the living room from the dining room with the former facing the picture window looking out onto the street and with the latter situated behind the living room, screened them from the view of anyone passing along the front of the house who might glance into the living room through the picture window. On the other hand, if someone happened to come unexpectedly into the family room through the back door, they could quickly stand up, and nothing unusual would be suspected.

They sat together on the floor for a very long time, locked together in one another's arms and kissing amid desultory talking. "There's something you could do for me as part of my birthday present that would please me very much," Dorothy stated. "What's that," Grant asked. "I would like to hear you recite Semper Dulcis for me as we sit here right now. Do you have the poem memorized?" "Of course I do," Grant replied tenderly. "I would like to hear those words from you in your own voice." After pausing to gather his thoughts, Grant laid his head between Dorothy's breasts and then recited the poem slowly with the proper cadence and emphasis. She was thrilled to hear his low voice speaking those words that he had composed just for her in attempting to express how fervently he loved her and would always love her despite their difference in age. Oh how she dearly cherished this boy-man who was about the age of her Sally and Wesley! They remained on the dining room floor for a long time and consumed part of the afternoon in conversation amid their passionate kissing and embracing.

August 5, 1972, Saturday

Following Grant's successful handling of being at the house over the previous weekend with George and others there, he had agreed to spend this weekend as well at 1801 Rachel Drive. His decision was also predicated on the fact that there was only one more week left of summer school, and then he would be leaving and gone for a month. Although he and Dorothy had been spending much time together during the week, he still wanted to be around her as much as he possibly could.

Last evening and today had been average and uneventful. Dorothy and Grant had succeeded in being alone by doing the grocery shopping and taking the dogs for a long walk. Dorothy had spent the rest of her time in ordinary around-the-house activities, such as laundry, meals, and dishes. Grant had occupied his remaining idle time in reading for his summer courses. Unfortunately, however, he had been obliged to withdraw from both courses, because as he had become increasingly involved with Dorothy, he found it harder and harder to concentrate on his work, and he fell farther and farther behind. Consequently, Evan Collins' cautionary advice about attending summer school appeared to be vindicated, but of course, he had had no inkling of Grant's emotional entanglement. Even though he had officially withdrawn from his two courses, he was still spending time in doing much of the reading for them, because he was nonetheless interested in the subjects but had simply not been able to muster sufficient mental strength to bring them fully to completion.

"We're going off to bed now," Dorothy announced to Grant as she walked from the kitchen into the living room. "Ok," Grant replied, "I will too, as soon as I finish this chapter." He was sitting on the couch listening to a tape of Moses Hadas' *Hellenistic Culture.*

Dorothy and George retired to the master bedroom, and Dorothy proceeded to go through her nightly ritual of brushing her teeth, placing her thumb plate in a jar of water to soak overnight, combing out her hair, and removing makeup. She did these things in part because she was such a well-organized and systematic person, but also in part because it often allowed her to employ a bedtime delaying strategy. By the time Dorothy had completed all these personal tasks, George had already undressed and was in bed. Dorothy came out of the adjoining bathroom, turned off the bedroom light, walked around to her side of the bed, and sat down in the dark. After first kicking off her shoes and removing her socks, she pulled the top off over her head, quickly unfastened and removed her bra, and with the same rapidity pulled her nightgown over her head. Not only was she undressing in the dark to avoid having George's eyes enjoying the sight of her female body, but she undressed so as to leave no part of herself unclothed for only the briefest time possible. She now stood up from the edge of the bed and was able to take off her shorts and panties while being shielded by the nightgown.

After carefully laying out her top and shorts so as not to become wrinkled, Dorothy lay down in bed and lay on her side with her back to

George. He then rolled over from his back onto his side, pressed his body up against hers, and placed an arm around her waist. "How about we have intercourse tonight?" he asked. "I guess we can," Dorothy replied, trying to keep the tone in her voice level as her heart sank with wretched dismay and loathing.

George arose from bed, stepped over to the bedroom door that went out into the hallway, and quietly pushed the door shut. He then went into the adjoining bathroom, found and unwrapped a rubber, removed his undershorts, and rolled the rubber onto his erection. He usually used a rubber for having intercourse, but sometimes if he were too lazy to get up to get one or was too eager, he simply enjoyed Dorothy's vagina without one. When he returned to bed, Dorothy obediently rolled over onto her back, pulled her nightgown up, bent her legs and parted her thighs. After petting her sex a few times, George lay down between her thighs, guided his penis inside her vagina, and began to thrust himself rhythmically into her.

Grant finished the chapter, turned off the tape recorder, and first stopped in the main bathroom in the hallway before proceeding to the far bedroom situated right across the hall from the master bedroom. As he came out of the bathroom and trailed his hand along the wall, he noticed that the door to the master bedroom was closed. That was very odd, because it was usually left open all the time, even during the night. Then Grant suddenly realized what the closed door meant. Dorothy and George must be having intercourse. By logic, of course, he knew that they did this on a regular basis, because they were husband and wife and slept in the same bed at night. Of course, he also hoped that they did so as infrequently as possible, but he had never before been confronted as now with the actual concrete fact of them engaging in intercourse. What exactly were they doing right now behind that door? His mind raced through so many possibilities, and every one of them sickened him and made him physically convulse inside. But if he were feeling this awful merely by thinking about it, how was Dorothy feeling in having to actually submit to it? Despite her obvious strong attraction to him and great pleasure in being with him, having him touch her, and their kissing, she had remained totally silent about how she really felt toward George, because she apparently did not wish to undermine their respect for her marital status in the abstract by denigrating her husband. But ever since their first night of passionate kissing, Grant had drawn the obvious conclusion that she must be very unhappy in her marriage. Consequently, with a truly nauseated heart Grant went into the far bedroom for the night and did his best not to think of what Dorothy must now be experiencing, but it was not at all easy. Perhaps he should have spent the weekend in his dorm room after all.

As Dorothy lay beneath George and the working of his penis inside her, she strove to numb herself to the ordeal. Although these bouts usually lasted for five minutes or less, any length of time at all, no matter how brief, was still far too long. As George arose to flush the spent rubber down the toilet, Dorothy pulled her nightgown back down into place and rolled over onto her side, so that her back would be to George. As she lay there with her mind slowly recovering from the ordeal, a few tears of sadness and hurt trickled from her eyes, and she truly wondered why the world was so constituted that she had to sleep in this bed with George and not in the one across the hall with Grant.

August 6, 1972, Sunday

Shortly after they had eaten popcorn for their usual Sunday supper, a nurse from the Mental Health Ward at Mercy Hospital had called to ask if Dorothy could bring some clean clothes for Debbie. George, Dorothy, and Grant had then gone over in the car to Debbie's room, and Dorothy had gone upstairs and rounded up a bag of things, after which they proceeded to Mercy Hospital; and while she and Grant waited in the car, George delivered the clothes. None of them had said much at all as they performed this errand, but while George was away from the car, Dorothy suddenly broke the silence by turning around in the front passenger seat to address Grant.

"I was here once," Dorothy began, "in the same Mental Health Ward where Debbie is now." "Really," Grant answered in astonishment. "Yes," Dorothy smoothly continued, "I was in there for a few days not long after we were living here in University City. George's construction partnership with John Thompson went bankrupt while we were living in Kimball, Nebraska; and we left there with all sorts of debts following us here. Then when we got here, Carol started having all her trouble with reading and things in school; and it all got to be too much for me to take. George was gone so much of the time, and I was the one who answered the telephone and was yelled at and threatened by angry people to whom we owed money. I finally felt so ill that I admitted myself, but after staying just a few days and seeing some truly nutty people in the ward, it scared me so much that I discharged myself and came back home; and resolved that I would never let myself sink down so low that I would ever have to go back."

Grant was truly amazed by this revelation and had nothing to say in reply. Her confession had been straightforward and matter of fact and spoken in that low-pitched voice that Grant knew to be the sign of deep emotion in her. Dorothy did not bother to tell him that now there were only three people who knew this fact about her life: herself, George, and now Grant. Not even her mother, sisters, or children knew it. But as she and Grant sat there in the car, she felt compelled to share this innermost secret with him and with him alone. George's knowledge in that sense did not count, because the necessity of the situation had required that he know. Dorothy's conscious decision to share this with Grant was, therefore, a telling token of how far their relationship had advanced over the past few weeks.

August 10, 1972, Thursday

The day had followed what had by now become a rather familiar pattern. After swimming in the morning, Dorothy picked Grant up at Walker, and they had lunch together at the house and then a very nice afternoon, part of which was taken up with Grant's guitar playing and their singing together. Although they were feeling strongly drawn to each other, Carol had been there and had thus prevented them from acting upon their emotions.

Dorothy fixed an easy but delicious supper of beans and weenies, a meal that Carol and Grant always liked. Then Dorothy and Grant had to go back to Walker to pack up all of Debbie's things and take them down into a storage area in the basement, where they would stay until Debbie could reclaim them. So, for about three hours that evening Dorothy and Grant filled boxes in Debbie's room, took them down the elevator, and then carried them into the basement storage room.

Clearing out Debbie's room took them far longer than it should have, because they spent a considerable amount of time engaged in hugging and kissing. As usual, it started off slowly and then accelerated, as Dorothy's reason gradually retreated under the onslaught of her emotions. Over the past several weeks Dorothy had been careful not to have them engage in full-length body embraces, either as they stood or were lying down. But tonight that all changed, and for the first time she felt the insistent passion of Grant's erection pressing hard into her.

Whenever they came up from the basement and entered Debbie's room for packing the next load, Grant shut the door and locked it, so that no one would walk in on them unexpectedly. He then took Dorothy into his arms.

She always came willingly and eagerly. They stood in the middle of the floor, firmly pressing their bodies together and holding the embrace longer and longer with each trip. The embraces were accompanied with passionate kissing, which, of course, kept Grant's penis fully and thoroughly aroused. The pleasure that Dorothy gave him through his erection was further enhanced by Grant pushing his hard manhood firmly into her abdomen, which he achieved by shifting his hands from Dorothy's back to her bottom and then holding her lower body tightly against himself. Dorothy did not object, because by the time they were doing this routinely, her reason had totally lost out to her emotions, and she was enjoying the erotic pleasure as much as Grant.

As they neared the end of their packing and moving of boxes, they lingered longer and longer in the middle of the floor, because they did not want to leave the isolation of this room and the pleasure that they were enjoying in it. After one such prolonged embrace and pressing together of their loins, accompanied with kisses, Grant withdrew his face from hers, breathed in the lovely fragrance of Dorothy's White Shoulders, and enjoyed the magnificent pleasure of his erection pressing into her. He then became aware of a shining brilliance. For a few years after his eye surgery when he was eleven, Grant could see light fairly well, and under certain conditions he could even make out shadows or reflections. But he now had only very poor light perception and could only detect the brightest of lights. But now he was sure that he was seeing the light overhead reflecting from the fair skin of Dorothy's face.

"My gosh," he whispered in amazement, "I think I can see your face, or at least the light reflecting from your face." Dorothy remained silent. "It's beautiful!" They stood motionless, as Grant continued to see what he took to be the pale white skin of this wonderful woman's face; and all the while his erection felt so magnificent up against her. He hated to move at all and thus disturb this perfect experience, but they eventually did.

They finally left Walker to return to the house around 10:30. Since by now it was quite dark outside, Grant did not sit in the passenger seat of the Falcon near the door, but instead, he moved to the center of the bench seat, so that he and Dorothy were sitting very close together. He desired her so very much! As they were traveling along Lexington, he finally summoned up his courage and asked, "In the movie *Camelot* King Arthur sings a song, 'How to Handle a Woman'. How would you say I am handling you?" "Very well," were her only words in reply. They both knew that the answer to the question posed by the song is "simply love her."

When they arrived at the house, Carol was already sound asleep in her bed in the middle bedroom. Grant and Dorothy quietly walked down the hall together; and rather than turning right and going into the master bedroom, she went left and followed Grant into the far bedroom where he would be sleeping. As they reluctantly whispered their good nights while standing at the foot of the bed, Grant reached for her and for one last time briefly held her tightly against his erection that was wild with desire for her. When he broke their embrace, Dorothy commented, "You just want me." She then walked across the hall into the master bedroom.

Grant was deeply hurt by Dorothy's parting remark. Of course, he desired her and desired her very greatly, but he was sure that what he felt for her was far more than youthful carnal desire. Moreover, when he had asked her a few minutes ago in the car how he was handling her, she had replied "very well." Grant therefore lay down in bed, both very hurt and confused, as well as feeling considerable shame for having displayed his desire for her so openly and for having offended her.

Just across the hall Dorothy was also lying down in bed with conflicting feelings and thoughts raging inside her. It was the same old story, her reason versus her emotions. She logically understood the need not to jeopardize her marriage and wreck her home, mostly for Carol's sake; but she was also powerfully attracted to Grant. Her body wanted him, just as his wanted hers. She had not uttered her parting remark to hurt him or shame him. Rather, it had been more directed against herself, partly out of fear of what she might allow herself to do, and partly to rebuke herself for also feeling such strong desire. As she lay there alone in her nightgown in the double bed, she seriously wondered what she would do if Grant now walked across the hall and approached the bed. She would probably throw back the covers and invite him in for at least part of the night. To do what, she wasn't sure, but they would most certainly enjoy themselves! But she was spared such a dilemma, because her parting words had shamed Grant into conforming to her rational resolve.

It had been just one month ago tonight that Dorothy had come over to Grant's dorm room to hear him confess his strong attraction to her, which was followed by their first kissing marathon. So very much had happened between them since then! During the past month they had both wanted to be in one another's presence as much as possible; and they had succeeded quite well in doing so. Their time together had spawned countless conversations on virtually everything and had therefore begun to forge a very strong bond of understanding and closeness between them, which went hand in hand with their powerful emotional and physical attraction to each other.

August 11, 1972, Friday

After arising and having breakfast together, Dorothy took Grant back over to campus to attend classes for one last time and to take care of a few other things, one of which was paying another visit to Dunkin' Donuts, because Grant wanted to relieve Dorothy of the need to make breakfast for everyone tomorrow morning. By the middle of the afternoon he had returned to his dorm room. He now called Dorothy to let her know that he was ready for her to come pick him back up and bring him to the house again. It would be their last weekend together for the summer. But it would be an abbreviated one, because Grant planned to return to his room sometime on Saturday. His father would be arriving at Walker around 11:00 A.M. on Sunday to take him and his things back to Fairmont. Consequently, although George would be returning from Newton around suppertime today, both Dorothy and Grant still wanted to be in one another's presence and to make the most of their remaining time together.

When Dorothy drove into the circle drive in front of Walker, Grant was standing there with a paper sack in his hand and a large book under his arm. As he settled himself into the passenger seat and shifted these objects into his lap, she asked, "What ya got there?" "I bought two dozen doughnuts from Dunkin' Donuts over on Spruce Street. I figure we can have them tomorrow morning for breakfast and save you some work." "That's nice. I appreciate that." They were both pleased: Dorothy for this small act of kindness and consideration for her, and Grant for her appreciation. "But what's that big book you got there?" "Oh, I just picked it up at the campus bookstore. I ordered it a long time ago last fall, but it took all this time to arrive, I guess. "It's *Ancient Near Eastern Texts Relating to the Old Testament*, edited by James B. Pritchard. From what I gather, it's supposed to be a large collection of texts in translation from the various ancient Near Eastern Civilizations of Egypt, Mesopotamia, the Phoenicians, and the Hittites that shed important light on the cultural background to the ancient Hebrews and the ideas and practices found in books of the Old Testament."

"That really sounds interesting," Dorothy truthfully replied. "Yeah, I think so at least," said Grant. "We can probably find time to read some of it at the house." "That's what I was hoping." "You know," Dorothy continued, "while we were living in Great Falls, Montana, we were really good friends of Roger and Olive Robinson. Roger was our church minister, and his wife Olive was the daughter of Roland Bainton, a very well-known professor of Church History; and we actually met him once when he was visiting. I have his book on Martin Luther, *Here I Stand*, and I really like it. He seemed like such a nice man, and it was exciting meeting someone who had actually written and published a book." "That's really neat," Grant replied.

Dorothy went on, "Both Roger and Olive were such nice people, the nicest minister couple I've ever known. They were both so friendly and kindhearted and always willing to help people. They were one reason why our time in Great Falls was so very special. I really missed them when we moved away to Kimball. Then after we got there and became involved in our new church in Kimball, I missed them even more and realized how truly special they were, because the church there, both the minister and the people, were not nearly as wonderful. But while we were in Kimball, I actually signed up for two courses offered through our church. One was on The Reformation. That was when I read Roland Bainton's *Here I stand*. The other course concerned the historical background to the writing of the various books of the Bible. For that we read a series of pamphlets, each one concerning some important aspect relating to several books of the Old or New Testament, perhaps something like that book you have there. You'd probably be interested in the collection. When we get home, I'll show it to you." "Ok, I would really like to check that out."

After parking the Falcon on the driveway in front of the closed garage door, they were greeted by three vigorously wagging tails attached to Frau, Gretchen, and Erica as they entered the family room. As they passed through the kitchen, Grant placed his two boxes of doughnuts on the counter and followed Dorothy down the hall and into the front bedroom. As he sat on the twin bed nearest the doorway with his new big book held on his lap, Dorothy stepped over to a set of shelves standing against the wall at the foot of the beds and next to her phonograph and sewing machine. "It's right here." She removed the book from its place and sat down beside Grant. "See," she said, "It's a big hardback binder with a collection of twelve pamphlets inside, and you can easily take out which one you want." As she spoke, she had Grant's hand and was showing him how the pamphlets were held in by a wire along their inside spine. "It's called *Know Your Bible* and was written by Roy L. Smith in consultation with a large number of scholarly experts. It's published by Abingdon Press." "I've heard of that," said Grant. "The series is designed to provide ordinary people who are not scholars, but who are interested in the Bible with solid information about the history and background of the Bible, both Old and New Testaments, based upon sound scholarship." "That really does sound interesting," Grant responded, "Maybe sometime I can borrow it from you and read it." "I'm sure you would enjoy it and probably learn a lot from it. It's really good." She then proceeded to read off the titles of the twelve pamphlets, each about sixty or seventy pages long for a grand total of nearly 800 pages, quite an impressive compendium of biblical scholarship. "You read all this?" Grant asked in amazement. "Yep!" Dorothy proudly answered. "Man! That's really something! I can see now why you enjoyed James Michener's *The Source* so much. Yeah," Grant confirmed, "I really must read this someday."

Later that evening after George had arrived from Newton, and after they had eaten supper, Dorothy and Grant settled down at the dining room table with *Ancient Near Eastern Texts Relating to the Old Testament*. Dorothy, of course, had been an avid reader for longer than Grant had been alive, and she knew the excitement of obtaining a new book and wanting to read it right away. She could therefore easily understand what frustration someone like Grant, so intelligent and such a fine student, could feel when he had a brand new book like this in his hands but could not do anything with it because of his blindness. It therefore pleased her greatly to be his eyes. She had, of course, been doing that off and on all summer as she read things to him, like *The Cambridge Ancient History*, but tonight this was something different. They would now begin exploring a brand new book together on a subject that interested them both.

When George observed them sitting at the dining room table with the big book opened before them, he casually asked, "What's that?" pointing to the book. "It's a new book that Grant just got. It concerns the historical background to the Old Testament," Dorothy answered. Since George was accustomed to his wife needing to spend substantial amounts of time regularly in preparing herself for Sunday school, her reply to his question made him content with the idea that Dorothy would be spending the rest of the evening looking through that book with Grant.

Since Grant knew nothing about the book, they began with the contents, which was very long and detailed. When Dorothy read "The Legend of

Sargon," Grant exclaimed "Yeah, let's look at that!" Dorothy turned to page 119 and read aloud, "My mother, the high priestess, conceived me, in secret she bore me. She set me in a basket of rushes, with bitumen she sealed my lid. She cast me into the river which rose not over me." "That sounds like Moses," Dorothy remarked in wonder. Then when they came across the heading in the contents "The War Against the Peoples of the Sea," Grant excitedly urged, "Turn to that!" Dorothy turned to page 262 and read the translation of the ancient Egyptian text from the reign of Ramesses III in the early twelfth century B.C. Grant sat in wonder as she read; and when she had finished, he proceeded to explain its historical significance in providing what little scholars now knew about the sudden collapse of the Bronze Age in the eastern Mediterranean. And so it went for the rest of the evening until bedtime. At one point they opened up one of the boxes of doughnuts and snacked on a few, as they continued this shared intellectual experience of browsing through this rich and fascinating collection of ancient texts.

Of course, Dorothy had been an avid reader for her entire adult life; and over the past few years she had been serving as a volunteer reader (usually two hours each week, but sometimes more) for different blind students; and those reading sessions had combined her love of reading with her natural enjoyment of assisting people, as well as her joy in associating herself with a college environment. But tonight's reading at the dining table was something rather different. As the result of her involvement in church activities, she had spent a considerable amount of her time in reading various books to prepare herself for church services and her teaching of Sunday school, almost always with devotional purposes in mind; and of course, as she had explained to Grant earlier in the day, she had really enjoyed the two courses that she had taken through her church in Kimball concerning the historical setting of the writings of The Bible and the history of The Reformation. But now she was seated before this large scholarly book, impressive enough in its mere size, but even more so by the lavish layout of annotations to accompany the translated texts. It was reading about the historical setting of biblical literature at a much higher level; and this novel intellectual experience greatly interested her, and it was made even more enjoyable by the fact that she was sharing it with her secret lover.

August 12, 1972, Saturday

While sitting around the kitchen table leisurely eating doughnuts for breakfast, Dorothy asked if Grant wanted her to read more from Pritchard. He gladly agreed. They therefore left Carol and George at the kitchen table and moved to the dining table, where they enjoyed sitting together for another hour and a half or so with the book. Dorothy was clad in her pink quilted robe over her nightgown and sipped at several cups of coffee as they resumed their browsing and reading. But since Grant had arranged to meet with Larry Smithson in the afternoon for one last reading session, he needed to be back to his dorm room by noon or shortly thereafter. They therefore somewhat reluctantly brought their communion at the dining table to an end. Dorothy went off to dress and to prepare herself to go out in public. Then after a quick and simple lunch, she drove Grant back to his dorm room at Walker for the last time. As Dorothy drove, they both felt some sadness at their parting and were acutely aware of how truly magical this summer had been, but they dared not give voice to these profound feelings and thoughts. Instead, they overlaid them with relatively casual talk.

"When will you be returning to campus?" Dorothy asked. "Probably Sunday September 10, four weeks from tomorrow." There were a few moments of silence as they each tried to absorb that fact. They would not see each other now for four whole weeks! "Well, as soon as you get moved into your room, give me a call, and we'll get together." "I will, and my room will be the same one in Holmes but with a new roommate, I suppose. Are you going to be involved with mobility instruction this year?" "I guess so," Dorothy replied. "Well then, when I get back, you can tell me who all the new blind students are." "What will you be doing over the next four weeks?" she asked. "Oh just all sorts of things, I guess. How about you?" "I suppose we'll go up to Homewood to visit my mom, two sisters, and their families; and maybe we'll drive down to Newton to spend some time with George's mom. But that's probably about it except for swimming and Sweet Adelines."

As Grant prepared to exit the vehicle at the main entrance into Walker, he said, "I love you, and I'm going to miss you." "I'm going to miss you too," Dorothy replied. They both knew and well understood why she could not use those other words in her reply. They now parted ways, but their minds were fully occupied with thoughts of each other for the rest of the day and all other days for the next four weeks.

August 13, 1972, Sunday

After meeting Larry at the cafeteria in the Student Union and spending two hours in reading part of C. Bradford Welle's *Alexander the Great and the Hellenistic World*, Grant had returned to his dorm room and had packed up all his things. He had been thinking of her constantly, of course, and kept wondering what she was doing right then, and wishing so much that they could still be together. Time now seemed to crawl along so slowly as he waited for his father to arrive. Since his stereo could be closed up in seconds, he had left it out and had been passing the time in playing records. This morning with his mind thinking of nothing but her, he only wanted to listen to the Camelot record. But after hearing the album all the way through, he began to play over and over again the one song sung by Sir Lancelot when he reveals his love to Queen Guinevere, "If Ever I Would Leave You." As the song played, Grant joined in and sang it again and again, fully identifying with the words, as he was physically aching inside and crying constantly as he sang.

Early that afternoon at about the time that Grant arrived home in Fairmont, Dorothy and George went to Lincoln Park to participate in an outing of their church. She was glad when George became engaged in conversation with a few other members about church affairs. Dorothy simply did not want to deal with anything serious or important right now. All that she could think of was Grant and the fact that they would not be together again for an entire month. How awful that would be! She therefore wandered off on her own, fully absorbed in her own thoughts and feelings of sadness. Eventually, however, she came upon another loner like herself, a boy probably about ten years old. She greeted him with her lovely voice and radiant smile; and of course, within one or two exchanges she had touched him with her sweetness and charm. She stayed with him as he did various boyish things, such as showing off by jumping over a ditch, hunting for rocks and other curiosities on the ground, etc. Dorothy saw in this young energetic child, so exuberant and eager to take on what the world had to offer, her image of Grant.

Chapter 6

The Tumultuous Autumn

Thus far, dear reader, you have read an account of how a most stupendous woman, trapped for many years in an unhappy marriage, struggled to find meaning to her life through learning how to swim, singing in Sweet Adelines, and then discovering an entirely new world through her association with a group of blind students at the university; and how her university kids quickly realized and acknowledged her extraordinary humanity, and how one student in particular fell in love with her. Having followed the events of the couple's magical summer of 1972, you now come to their tortured and tortuous autumn of 1972. Before proceeding further, you must be warned, dear reader, that what you will now encounter you may regard as too erotically explicit, too sexually graphic. Consider carefully, therefore, whether you wish to press on in this narrative: for if you do decide to read on and are offended by what you encounter, you have no one but yourself to blame, because you have been properly forewarned!

But know full well, dear reader, that although the following chapters contain numerous detailed descriptions of sexual activity, the narrative is not at all pornographic, because it does not describe activities of mere physicality. Rather, the narrative is beautifully erotic and merely records accurately numerous intense expressions of the physical pleasure of Grant's and Dorothy's all-encompassing love.

If you do read on, dear reader, you shall discover the following truths: that sex in the absence of love is vacuous and often hurtful and cruel, whereas when combined with true love, sex is heavenly and ethereal.

September 10, 1972, Sunday

It was around 4:00 in the afternoon when Grant finished putting everything away in his dorm room. Tomorrow would be the first official day of orientation week for the new incoming freshmen, and classes would not actually begin until Tuesday September 19, but Grant had returned as soon as Holmes Hall was opened to receive students, because he wanted to see and be with Dorothy as soon as possible and for as much as possible before classes began. He now picked up the telephone and dialed Dorothy's number. Luckily, she was the one who answered the phone, and he was so pleased once again to hear the sound of her beautifully feminine voice greet him with her most elegant and rich sounding "hello."

"Hello, Ma, this is Grant." "So you're back now?" "Yep." "When did you get here?" "About two hours ago." "Would you like to come over for the evening? Pam Stewart, the new blind student that I worked with last week, is here." This had been the first big question that Grant had been debating with himself all day long. Of course, he wanted to see her as soon as possible, but he also did not want to have that meeting encumbered by the presence of other people, especially George's. He really had no way of knowing how he would feel or react after being away from her for four weeks. He had therefore finally decided to err on the side of caution and not to go over to the house today, but in order to have a plausible cover story in case Dorothy needed to employ one on his behalf, he would say that he wanted to spend the evening in his dorm room, so that he could record on tape from his small portable TV the next hour program in a series describing the life of Leonardo da Vinci.

After a slight pause, he said, "I don't think so. I've decided to stay here to record the Leonardo da Vinci program later tonight. But I was hoping that we could get together tomorrow. How would that be?" Dorothy understood exactly what Grant was thinking. No explanation was necessary, and she really could not find fault with his decision. "Well ok then. We can plan on that." "When are Dennis and Renny returning?" Grant asked. "Not until Thursday," she replied and then concluded with, "I'll give you a call tomorrow morning. Have a nice evening, and I'll see you then."

September 11, 1972, Monday

It was 10:00 A.M., and Grant was standing outside of Holmes Hall on Walnut Street, waiting for Dorothy to come pick him up to take him back to the house. George had left early that morning to spend the week in Newton, and Carol had just left for her first day of school in ninth grade. Dorothy would have come earlier, but it looked as if the teachers at Carol's school might go out on strike, but at the last minute an agreement was reached, and the first school day was simply delayed by two hours. Since Dennis and Renny would not be arriving in town until Thursday, he and Dorothy would probably be able to spend the next three days more or less alone together. As he stood there waiting for Dorothy to show up, he wondered how she would greet him. He knew that he wanted to embrace and kiss her passionately, but is that what she would want? Probably not.

Dorothy had had four weeks in which to have her life, so convulsed by her relationship with Grant during their magical summer, settle back down into what it had been before this past July. She had also had plenty of time to think things through, and she had arrived at the same conclusions that she had reached during the summer, namely, that she and Grant must control their passionate attraction for each other and had to be content with being very special friends. Dorothy once again told herself these things as she drove the Falcon over to campus, and she hoped that the intervening four weeks had also strengthened her reasoned resolve sufficiently to withstand the powerful urges of her emotions. There he was, standing on the sidewalk waiting for her with his bright red hair. She was so very pleased and excited to see him again.

"So," Grant asked, as he sat down in the car, "What have you been doing with yourself other than mobility week last week?" "Oh, just the usual sorts of things. Visiting my family in Homewood, going down to Newton to visit George's mom, writing letters, swimming, going to Sweet Adelines, etc. About the only unusual thing is that I have been watching a lot of the summer Olympics. That's been so neat! I especially enjoyed the swimming events and watching Mark Spitz win his seven gold medals. Wow!" "Yep," Grant agreed, "That really was something. I also followed much of the Olympics. It's so awful that they had to be marred by the Black September terrorists killing the Israeli athletes a few days ago." "Boy! That's for sure! Wasn't that terrible? I'll never understand why there is so much hate and intolerance in the world!" Grant concluded, "If everyone in the world had just a tenth of your loving kindness and goodness, we'd be living in paradise." "You think so!" Dorothy replied, slightly embarrassed. "No," Grant said emphatically, "I don't think so. I know so!"

As soon as they entered the family room, Grant greeted all three dogs with many pets, pats, and hugs. When he turned to Dorothy and put his arms around her, she kept her own upper arms tight against her sides and her forearms linked together across her middle. Her message was clear but also polite: "You may want to hug me, but I don't have to hug you back, because we should just be very special friends." That was how she responded all morning and afternoon whenever Grant put his arms around her. Her sweet passive resistance did at least discourage Grant from trying to kiss her, but whenever he put his arms around her, he usually snuggled his head against her neck and sometimes kissed her there.

They filled the day with their talking, describing what all they had done and experienced over the past four weeks. They had written one another a few braille letters during that time period, but they were insufficiently detailed to satisfy their curiosity of what all the other had done. Now for the first time Dorothy explained who all her relatives were, because Grant wanted to know everything about her. In fact, there had been a major change in her family recently. Her sister Bethany, who had divorced her husband Richard of twenty-three years, had just married Buddy Morgan, whom she had known and had apparently been seeing for quite some time before the divorce. This was the time of the so-called sexual revolution that so greatly affected the behavior of young men and women, especially on college campuses. It was also a time when divorce was becoming more socially acceptable; and many marriages, which had been formed shortly after the end of World War II and by now had run their course of happiness, were breaking up.

After Dorothy had brought him up to date on all her activities, Grant responded in kind by describing his trip with his parents to Kentucky to visit relatives on both sides of his family. They had also driven down to Nashville to spend one day in touring the Country Music Hall of Fame and buying some records at an enormous record store, the Ernest Tubb Record Shop. He had bought two albums, one of Hank Williams and another of Jimmie Rodgers. In fact, he had made two cassette recordings that he now presented as gifts to Dorothy: one was a selection of songs from his numerous albums of Chet Atkins, and the other was a similar selection of Hank Williams' songs, many of which Grant sang with the guitar, and which Dorothy greatly enjoyed. She was very pleased with this gift. Their continuous talking was conducted while they did various things: taking the dogs for a long walk across the big open field to the highway and back, and doing all sorts of chores around the house, such as emptying the dishwasher and doing two loads of laundry. As usual, just being together and doing things, no matter how mundane, gave them both joy and pleasure.

Carol arrived home from her first day of school in the middle of the afternoon. By then Dorothy had decided that they would have tuna fish casserole for supper. As usual, Grant was eager to help her in the kitchen. In fact, since the preparation largely consisted of simply opening up cans and mixing ingredients together, Grant insisted that Dorothy simply sit at the kitchen table and order him about, telling him how to assemble the casserole. Grant had never eaten it before, but not to his surprise, he very much liked it. After all, if the wonderful Dorothy had it in her standard repertoire of meals, it must be good.

While they were in the kitchen preparing the casserole and then cleaning up the kitchen after supper, Dorothy had the Hank Williams cassette playing in the background. Grant therefore continued the musical theme by getting out Wesley's guitar and playing it for more than an hour. After Carol went to bed, they sat together on the couch in the family room; and by now Dorothy's reasoned resolve was slowly giving way to her emotions: for now when Grant put his arms around her, she put hers around him and also was happy to receive his lips with hers.

September 12, 1972, Tuesday

After Carol had left for school, they again had the house entirely to themselves. Dorothy had not bothered to dress. She simply put her pink quilted robe over her nightgown and tied the belt at her waist. They had a slow leisurely brunch of Canadian bacon, toast, and scrambled eggs. Once again, this simple meal epitomized how this wonderful woman introduced Grant to new things, because before meeting her he had never encountered Canadian bacon, nor had he ever eaten scrambled eggs enlivened with cheese, as she always made them. This breakfast also involved another Dorothean novelty for Grant, she being clad in nothing except her cotton nightgown and her pink quilted robe. As Dorothy moved about the kitchen and stood at the stove, Grant was always close by. They embraced and kissed several times, and Grant could now feel her shapely feminine body beneath the two layers of clothing that took the precise shape of her curvaceous form, because it was not distorted at all by any elastic in her clothing.

"I really like this robe," Grant commented. "You do huh," Dorothy replied with a satisfied smile in her voice. "I sure do. The material feels so smooth and lovely, just like you; and it also contains your sweet fragrance of White Shoulders. What color is it?" "Pink, and the material is called quilted. So it's my pink quilted robe." "Well, I really like it, and it looks wonderful on you!" Dorothy enjoyed feeling his hands move over her body.

"So," Grant asked, as his left hand fondled her bottom while she was standing at the stove overseeing the progress of the eggs, "How did your mobility instruction last week go?" "You wouldn't believe it," Dorothy said, as she laid the spoon down and turned around into an embrace. They were also enjoying the feel of Grant's erection pressing urgently into Dorothy's abdomen. To her, it felt like a huge hard iron railroad spike; and its presence down there filled that area below her navel with such sweet pleasure. After kissing, Grant asked, "What do you mean?"

"Well, Pam is a really nice sweet young lady; and from what I can tell, she seems to have been an excellent student in high school, but boy! She can't find her way anywhere! From what she told me, her mother has always been so protective that Pam has had little experience in traveling on her own. Anyway, I would explain things to her, and she would respond as if she understood what I was saying, but then she usually could not go where she needed to."

The affectionate touching, embracing, and kissing continued as a loving ballet performed to accompany their talking. Dorothy continued. "Doctor Potter one day noticed that I wasn't making much progress with Pam, and he came over and said that he would take charge of her for a while, as if he were going to show an amateur like me how to do it. But after working with her for about an hour and failing to teach her anything useful, he gave up and turned her back over to me. I just laughed to myself."

After eating brunch and cleaning up the kitchen, Dorothy went into the master bedroom and dressed. She and Grant then went grocery shopping at the nearby IGA, came home, and put all the groceries away. One item purchased had been kohlrabi. Once again, Grant had never encountered this vegetable before, but he sampled its taste as they sat at the kitchen table together while Dorothy cleaned them and cut off their tops. Once again, simply being together and doing ordinary things had given them both great pleasure.

The afternoon and evening proceeded as usual with Carol coming home from school, followed by supper, dishes, Carol doing her homework and listening to records in her room, and Grant and Dorothy talking as they moved around the house to straighten things up. But once Carol had gone to sleep, they settled down on the family room couch and began to enjoy a night of serious kissing, embracing, and petting amid their non-stop talking. Since the weather had turned chilly, they were both wearing full length slacks. Unlike the summer, their lower legs were covered. As their kissing escalated in its fervor, Grant became so sexually aroused that he used his embrace of Dorothy to carefully lift her off of the couch and lay her on her back on the floor. He then lay down on top of her. She obligingly parted her knees, so that he could lie on top of her. Then as they engaged in a very prolonged and passionate kiss, Grant pressed his erection with considerable force into Dorothy's crotch and held her pinned firmly to the floor until they terminated the kiss. He then picked her up and placed her back on the couch beside him. It was the first time that his erection came into contact with her love-zone, and it thrilled them both.

After more kissing, Grant took Dorothy's right hand, placed it on his erection, and asked, "Oh please! Rub me there and masturbate me!" Dorothy complied, gently rubbing his penis through his clothes until his body shuddered with an orgasm. They had both enjoyed this novel experience, and their kissing continued thereafter until they finally decided to go off to bed, Dorothy, of course, in the master bedroom, and Grant in the front bedroom in the twin bed closest to the doorway. It had been a truly exciting and amazing night.

September 13, 1972, Wednesday

It was supposed to be much warmer today. When Grant awoke, he put on a clean t-shirt and shorts. He and Dorothy would have the morning to themselves, but they had to be at the Armory at 1:00 for fall registration. Dorothy was planning to assist him and other visually impaired students in going to the various tables and standing in line to sign up for their classes. Since they would not be leaving the house until shortly before 1:00, Dorothy did not bother dressing, but as on the day before, she simply went around the house all morning in her pink quilted robe, which by now Grant so adored on her, worn over her cotton nightgown.

They easily filled the morning with their constant talking that accompanied Grant assisting Dorothy with various household chores, as well as touching, hugging, and kissing. By now they knew a great deal about one another. Grant had told her all about how he had lost his eyesight at the end of 1963 and had gone to St. Louis for eye surgery. President Kennedy's assassination was therefore the last big news event that he had actually seen on TV. Dorothy, of course, told Grant about her beloved father dying at about this same time. He had developed cancer in his throat from smoking. As the disease approached its culmination, Dorothy had left Kimball, Nebraska, by herself to come to Chicago to be with her parents. She was later joined by George and the kids just before her father died. Dorothy had not talked about these things with anyone for many years. She described so many things in detail, such as her father lying on the living room couch with so little energy to do anything, but at least enjoying the scenery depicted in a wall painting. Dorothy now owned that picture, took Grant to it, and described the landscape. Dorothy was obviously reliving much of the sorrow that she had experienced then, and Grant was greatly moved by her narrative and also felt so privileged and honored to be the one in whom she was confiding these innermost thoughts and feelings.

Their conversation and activities around the house were accompanied by their resumption of physical intimacy. Besides their usual kissing and embracing, Grant's hands were moving all over Dorothy's body, and she did nothing to check his caresses and exploration. Indeed, she welcomed them and allowed him to touch, squeeze, and fondle her as he wished. Grant, however, was careful to avoid her breasts and lower abdomen, concentrating on her back, shoulders, bottom, and hips that offered him plenty of delight. In addition, as they embraced and kissed with his hands enjoying the feel of her, they pressed their bodies together and felt tremendous physical pleasure as his very obvious erection pressed firmly into her abdomen just below her navel.

When Dorothy noticed that it was approaching noon, she announced: "If we're going to be on time for early registration, we've gotta get cuttin', because I need to stop and get dressed and put my makeup on, but if you want, you can stretch out on the bed and rest while I do." Grant had always been careful about going into the master bedroom, because he had not wanted to do something that would offend Dorothy and her sense of propriety. But now, in response to her invitation, he followed her into the bedroom and lay down on his back on the bed and lay there quietly as Dorothy moved about the room. Unlike the previous hours that had been filled with their talking, they were now both silent. Grant lay there motionless while listening to the faint sounds that Dorothy made: a drawer softly sliding open and then shut, the slight rustle of material, the sound of cloth sliding over bare flesh. He tried to imagine exactly what she was doing just a few feet away from him.

After walking around to the closet on the right side of the bed, Dorothy removed her robe and hung it up. As she stood there, she also stepped out of her slippers and left them on the floor inside the closet. She next stepped around to the foot of the bed to the dresser, slid open a drawer, and removed a pair of panties. After stepping into them and pulling them up into place under her nightgown, she pulled the latter garment off over her head, folded it, and walked back around to the side of the bed to place it beneath her pillow. She was now facing Grant and was clad in nothing except her panties. As she bent over to slide the nightgown beneath her pillow, she was aware of her bare breasts swaying and feeling so much alive with their nipples fully erect. Grant was simply lying there motionless, just a foot away and unable to see her, but she enjoyed the sight of him, as well as herself being unclothed in his presence. In essence, Dorothy was performing a silent striptease before her blind young man, and it thrilled them both. She went back to her lingerie drawer, took out a bra, and fitted it into place. It was also exciting to touch herself in Grant's presence.

Fifty hours earlier, as she was driving over to campus to pick Grant up, she had firmly resolved that they would not become physically intimate. But her rational resolution had almost entirely abandoned her as of yesterday morning. She was drawn so powerfully to this young handsome intelligent man! She now stepped back alongside the bed, gently lowered herself onto it, and lay herself against Grant's right side. He reflexively placed his right arm around her neck and upper back and drew her to him. She lay on her left side with her right leg thrown across Grant's legs. Her left hand had gone behind his neck, and her right hand was resting upon his chest. They simply lay there in total silence. Dorothy's nearly nude appearance beside him had taken Grant totally by surprise, but what a welcome one it was! His lovely woman was now lying beside him clad only in her panties and bra, inviting him to feel her all over her body. Everywhere he touched he encountered flawlessly smooth skin: her back, shoulders, belly, and thighs. They both thoroughly relished this closeness and dared not disturb its magic by saying anything. Dorothy had greatly enjoyed having him feel her body through her nightgown and robe all morning long. It had been so pleasurable that she wanted to feel those same two hands caressing her bare flesh; and she was happy to offer him this new erotic delight. Besides feeling her bare body from her knees to her shoulders, front and back, Grant was now even emboldened to caress her breasts and love-front through her bra and panties.

After several minutes of lying together in this magnificent manner, Grant was driven by wild desire to break the silence. By now his erection was frantic with excitement. He therefore whispered, "Would you mind masturbating me?" Without speaking a word in response Dorothy moved her right hand from his chest down to his waist and slowly and carefully unbuckled his belt, unfastened the snap of his shorts, unzipped them, tugged the pants aside, and pulled his undershorts down to reveal his erection. She had been feeling that wonderful love-spike pressing into her all morning. But now she had to see it with her own eyes and to hold it in her hand. She had been thrilled and aroused by his erection through his clothes ever since she first saw it two months earlier on July 6, their first reading day. What she now saw did not disappoint her in the least. It fully captivated her. His pale skin was covered with bright red hair, which, of course, also surrounded his erection, so hard and slightly pinkish with excitement. The whole area down there was quite messy with sperm, which Grant's erection had been slowly leaking all morning. She now held him in her hand, surrounding the shaft with her fingers and thumb and having the large head resting in her palm. She masturbated him by gently moving her envelope of fingers and thumb up and down along the length of his penis. The sperm served as a lovely lubricant for her manipulations, and it greatly heightened the pleasure that she was inflicting upon him. She enjoyed the feel of him in her hand, and her eyes never left the site of this sexual activity. Grant had never felt pleasure like this before! In fact, she had surprised him once again by unfastening his pants and taking his erection into her hand, because when he had asked her to masturbate him, he had expected her to do what she had done the night before, simply to rub his erection through his pants until he ejaculated. But what she had now done and was doing was magnificent beyond belief! The touch of her dainty hand and her delicate handling of him gave him such extraordinary pleasure!

It looked as if Grant had already ejaculated at least once this morning and perhaps even twice. As Dorothy worked away on his erection that seemed very uninterested in reaching a climax but was thoroughly content to receive her touch forever, Grant decided that Dorothy might wish to receive some erotic stimulation of her own. He therefore used his free left hand to try to lift up the cup of Dorothy's bra from her right breast with the intention of taking it into his mouth and sucking it, but as he fumbled with the close fitting bra with a single hand, Dorothy released his penis, brushed his hand away, and resumed masturbating him. Once again, Grant felt deep chagrin, because he was so afraid that he had done something that had gravely offended her. Neither spoke, but the pleasure of the masturbation continued for them both. All this time her eyes were fixed upon her hand working his penis and his beautiful bare body. The sight thrilled her exceedingly!

But then Dorothy glimpsed through the bedroom window Sally's car coming around the house on the driveway. For whatever reason, she had apparently decided to come to the house during her lunch hour from work. Dorothy instantly sprang up from the bed and exclaimed, "Sally is here!" While Dorothy ran into the adjoining bathroom and closed the door, Grant also jumped up from the bed and ran out into the hall and into the main bathroom. After shutting the door, he resumed the work that Dorothy had been performing so perfectly, because his erection was almost painfully excited and needed release. Finally, after a considerable time of manipulation, he ejaculated and slowly felt his acute sexual desire subside. He then put his clothes in order and emerged from the bathroom as if nothing unusual had happened.

Dorothy also soon emerged from the other bathroom, fully dressed and wearing her makeup; and after eating some lunch, they went by car over to campus for registration. Grant was among about a half dozen visually impaired students who required assistance to register. Dorothy took each in turn to the different tables set up for the various courses. While she was busy with one, the others sat together in a group and simply passed the time in talking, mostly about what they had done during the summer. Finally, after more than two hours, Dorothy had succeeded in getting everyone registered for all their classes. She and Grant then departed as they had come, together and alone. They walked back to Holmes; and before parting ways for the next several days, they sat down on a bench at the western end of the dorm that faced onto Walnut Street. No one else was around, but just to be completely on the safe side, Grant said in a low voice, "You know what I did after we jumped up from the bed?" "What?" "I ran into the hall bathroom and continued to do what you were doing so perfectly, but of course, it didn't feel quite as good as your work." "It didn't huh?" "Certainly not! I had to work at it for quite a while, but finally he came and then slowly settled down to normal size again. But I think he's getting big again. Do you think we could go in the car to some secluded place where you could put him out of his misery once again by inflicting such wonderful pleasure on him?" "I don't think it's a good idea to try that in the car in the daytime." "I guess you're right, but thanks. It was really fantastic!" "Well," Dorothy concluded, "I guess I'd better get going. I'll be picking Dennis and Renny up at the train station tomorrow afternoon, and I guess they may then want to come over to the house. So when will I see you again?" "I don't know," Grant replied, "I guess we'll have to keep in touch and see what happens."

September 14, 1972, Thursday

As Renny and Dennis sat together on the train, they talked about many things, but the only topic of any real importance was what was going on between Ma and Grant. Dennis had told Renny what Grant had told him earlier that summer. It wasn't much. About all he knew was that something was apparently happening between them. After discussing the matter, they had decided to speak with Ma about this later today.

Dorothy met them at the train station and then took them and their luggage to campus. Renny would be in the same room in Forester as last year, but he and Dennis had decided not to room together. Instead, Dennis had left the dorms altogether and would be living in a small apartment building, called Beaumont Manor, that housed other college students. It was situated on Spruce Street, one block west of the Quad and a few blocks north of the Men's Dormitory Area.

Since suppertime was approaching by the time they had all their stuff stashed away in their rooms, Dorothy brought them back to the house to have a simple meal of whatever she happened to have at hand and could quickly fix up. Luckily, Carol was spending the early evening at Pam Gibson's house, so that Dennis and Renny were able to engage Dorothy in serious conversation.

As they sat at the kitchen table eating, Dennis opened up the subject, "Hey, Ma, Renny and I would like to talk with you about something." "Oh yeah," she replied with a sweet amusing smile in her voice. "Yeah," Dennis said neutrally. He then continued, "When we were down here this summer around the time of your birthday, Grant said something to me then about you and him being somehow involved." Dorothy said nothing, and so Dennis continued, "We just wanted to tell you that we're a little concerned about that, because we don't want your home life messed up. We also just wanted you to know that if there is anything that we can do to help, just let us know."

Dorothy now chose her words carefully and replied in a level serious tone, "Yes, Grant did tell me this summer that he is really attracted to me, and we have spent a lot of time together. I like him very much, but I also don't want my home life ruined, especially for Carol's sake. I want the two of us simply to be very special friends, and I have been trying to get Grant to see and understand the necessity of that. I am just helping him through what is proving to be a very difficult time for him."

"How is that going?" Renny asked, speaking for the first time. "Well, it isn't easy, but I think that we have things under control." "You know," Renny said, "Just in practical terms you can't let anything serious get started between you two. You have way too much to lose. If George began to suspect something, he could pretend to go off to Newton and then return unexpectedly to catch you guys in a compromising situation. He might even go after Grant with a gun." "Do you really think so?" Dorothy asked with evident alarm. "Ah, don't listen to Renny, Ma. You know him. The boy grew up in a ghetto where all sorts of things are settled with a gun." Renny and Dennis now sensed that the conversation had become too serious. They therefore tried to lighten the mood with some humor. "Well," Renny said, "we didn't want to pry too much. We know you must like the boy very much," he added with a laugh. "Yeah," Dennis said, "He is a pretty neat guy." "Well," Renny concluded, "That's about all we had to say. We just wanted to let you know that we were concerned about you and are willing to help if you need us." "Thanks, Renny. I'll be sure to let you fellas know if there's anything you can do."

When shortly thereafter Dorothy returned them to campus, she dropped them both off at Forester, because Renny's roommate had not yet arrived on campus, and Dennis decided to spend the night with Renny. As soon as they were alone in the dorm room, Renny asked, "So, what do you think, man?" "I really don't know," Dennis seriously replied, "I don't have any clear idea about what's going on between them, and I'm also not sure that she really has things under control like she thinks." "Well," Renny added, "All I know is that if anything is going on between them, she needs to end it right now! Anything at all is likely to be too risky, but I also agree with you. I'm not so sure that she really does have things under control."

As she drove back home, Dorothy was very troubled by their conversation. If Dennis and Renny had their way, she would end everything between herself and Grant, and perhaps they were right. She seriously wondered whether they really did have things under control. Her reason kept telling her that she really wanted them simply to be very special friends, but whenever they were together by themselves for any length of time, it seemed that her resolve was always slowly eroded, and her emotions began to influence her behavior. She would just have to try harder. That's all.

September 18, 1972, Monday

Around 8:30 A.M. Dorothy drove over to Holmes to pick Grant up and to bring him back to the house to spend the day with her. Carol had gone off to school, and George had left for Newton for the week. What next transpired was largely a repeat of the week before. Dorothy began their day together with the firm resolve not to allow herself to be drawn into physical intimacy with Grant. So, when he put his arms around her, she kept her arms closed to him by holding them crossed in front of her body, but by lunchtime her resolve had once again retreated in face of her powerful emotions, and they were now beginning to embrace and kiss amid their talking and household chores.

By the middle of the afternoon they were both aflame for each other. Whenever they embraced, Grant took her shapely bottom into his hands and forced their two bodies tightly together, because feeling his erection pressing into her abdomen felt so wonderful, as if she were gently masturbating him with that part of her body; and for her part, Dorothy likewise received extraordinary pleasure from having his love-spike, big and hard, pressing so urgently into that area below her navel, and she wanted the pleasure to go on and on without interruption. Carol came home from school, but she left again shortly thereafter to be with her friends. Consequently, they were left alone again in the house, but since classes were beginning tomorrow, Grant had decided that he would return to his dorm room after they had eaten supper together, but neither one of them was looking forward to the separation. But Dorothy especially hated to see him go and wanted him to stay the night. When she suggested that he stay, he said that he really needed to get back to his room; and he was not even persuaded to stay when Dorothy proposed that he spend the night there, and she take him back to campus first thing in the morning.

After they had eaten a simple supper of hash browns and beans and weenies, Grant's appointed time for departure was now at hand, but both did not wish to leave the other's company. So, rather than going out the back door of the family room to the car, they instead halted at the large stuffed chair that was near the door. Dorothy sat down in the chair, and Grant perched himself on one of its wide upholstered arm. There they sat minute after minute, touching, petting, and kissing, and also talking about nothing in particular but simply delaying their departure and separation. The thought of Grant not staying the night with her was almost more than what she could bear, because their day together had set her afire for him. Like last week, they had talked about many things throughout the day, including Dorothy's conversation with Dennis and Renny and Grant's Japanese roommate, but there was one subject that Dorothy had wanted to mention but had thus far not found the courage to bring up. Her period should have begun about a week ago, and she had been wondering if she were pregnant. She probably was not, because this sort of thing had happened before, and it always turned out that her period had simply been late. But she had been wondering how having a baby would affect her relationship with both George and Grant. How would they each react? Would Grant become angry with her, or would it scare him off entirely? Wouldn't the latter be a good thing in the long run? She really didn't know and had been putting off the subject all day, largely because she was actually afraid to find out.

On the other hand, their hours together had become increasingly eroticized. She felt so very good down there below her navel and wanted Grant to spend the evening with her so as to continue stimulating that sweet delicious pleasure. Despite their obviously erotic activity since July, they had both been very reticent in putting their powerful desire for one another into actual words. But now, faced with the imminent departure of her young man, whose company she wanted to enjoy for several more hours, she used her need to mention the possibility of her being pregnant to eroticize further an already highly charged sexual situation between them. So, without any preamble she decided to take the plunge. Therefore, amid their casual remarks to one another Dorothy simply announced, "I think I might be pregnant, because my period is late."

Her surprising announcement did in fact provoke an immediate reaction from Grant, but one which she had honestly not even anticipated with all her commingled worrying and desire. As soon as the remark had been spoken, Grant's face was instantly transformed as if someone had driven a stake through his chest. His pain was so obvious and severe that Dorothy was genuinely surprised and felt really terrible for the anguish that she had caused him. She therefore responded immediately by saying in a low and tender voice, "Oh, I'm so sorry!"

Grant was so overcome with emotion and hurt that he was unable to say anything for some time. Despite all their intimate activity and serious conversations, they had never before openly mentioned sexual intercourse in any way. Like Grant discovering the master bedroom door shut, Dorothy's remark brought out into the open the fact that she and George engaged in sexual intercourse. It was a subject that Grant could not tolerate contemplating directly. Being forced to imagine Dorothy's vagina receiving George's penis caused Grant incredible mental anguish, which Dorothy could now easily see.

Eventually Grant regained his voice and asked, "How late is your period?" "About a week." "Is that unusual for you?" "I've always been very regular, but there have been exceptions now and then, and this sort of thing has happened before, and it turned out to be that my period was simply late."

There then followed another very long pause as Grant attempted to formulate what to him was a very important question, but he needed to ask it so as not to offend Dorothy. He eventually found the words that he wanted and asked, "How would you feel if it had been me who was responsible for getting you into that condition?" She answered with a sweet smile in her voice, "That would please me very greatly!" After another lengthy pause Grant again carefully and emphatically commented, "In my view, I am the only one who should be in the position to cause you to become pregnant. You do understand exactly what I mean?" "I do" was her only reply, but she thought of other things as well, none of which she could openly express in words without further encouraging him and spawning contempt for her marital status. It gratified her tremendously to know that her compulsory intercourse with George troubled and nauseated Grant as much as it did her. Although it was a subject that they should and could not discuss, it was nevertheless comforting to know how strongly this affected him. This was yet another thing that they could share, albeit tacitly. In addition, Grant's questions and obvious proprietary claim to her were thrilling and filled her with joy. She did in fact wish that her life could somehow be magically reconfigured, so that George was no longer a part of her life, but that Grant was in his place. Oh how gladly she would receive into her vagina that beautiful penis that she had held in her hand last Wednesday! And oh how she would love to become pregnant by him and to bear him a lovely little red-haired baby!

Dorothy's announcement had totally altered the situation between them. Grant was obviously stunned and felt profound anguish that was only slightly reduced by Dorothy's responses to his questions on the subject. They now arose from the chair and went out to the car, but Grant's entire demeanor had been transformed from a love-sick youth not wanting to leave his darling to a deeply wounded and hurt young man. Dorothy was saddened that her remark had hurt him so severely, and she wanted to somehow reduce his obvious emotional suffering. Before dropping him off at Holmes, they first needed to go past Beaumont Manor, so that Dorothy could return Dennis' braille writer that she had been borrowing all summer to use for writing occasional braille letters to her university kids, especially to Grant. By now her mastery of braille was excellent. Grant stayed in the car while she went inside to take the machine to Dennis. When she returned, she suggested that they simply drive around campus for a while, and that he lie down across the front seat and place his head in her lap. She wanted to comfort him and did not want him returning to his dorm room in the condition in which he currently was. Grant obeyed. By now darkness was falling, and no one could see Grant lying across the seat with his head in Dorothy's lap. She simply drove aimlessly around one block after another, occasionally touching Grant and trying to say something soothing. She eventually turned into the parking area at Forester. Grant sat up, but rather than opening the door and departing, he simply sat there, and they resumed talking, very slowly at first, because Grant was still not feeling at all well, but gradually their conversation picked up and became more or less normal again. Earlier in the day Grant had been firmly resolved to spend this night in his dorm room to be ready for the first day of classes tomorrow. This was the old Grant who was fully responsible about such things. But Dorothy's announcement had rendered him emotionally vulnerable, and he was now dreading leaving her comforting company. Since he had only one class tomorrow, a physics lab, in which they would doubtless do nothing really important, Grant decided that given his present state of mind, it made much better sense to return to the house and to try to restore his emotional balance with Dorothy's caring assistance.

When they returned home, Carol was back from an evening with her friends and soon went off to bed. Dorothy and Grant then sat down on the couch in the family room just to be together and to talk about whatever entered their heads. Dorothy's comforting and soothing touches and words slowly brought Grant out of his state of deep depression. After an hour or so

Grant was seeking reassurance in the form of their embraces, petting, and kisses; and as Dorothy freely gave him such loving attention, his spirits were gradually lifted until eventually both found themselves seeking comfort from one another by retreating into the delicious delights of the present moment. Tomorrow would come and would bring with it a reality that they did not enjoy facing.

Ever since last week's lovely intimacy on the bed in the master bedroom, Grant had been thinking of Dorothy's breasts. He now accompanied his attentions to her with something new. He inserted his fingers inside the front of her collar and gently touched and explored the tender smooth skin below her collarbone and above her breasts. Since she did nothing to halt his touching, he continued these exploratory caresses off and on as they kissed and hugged. Eventually, however, Grant was emboldened to ask what had been troubling him ever since their time on the bed together.

"Last Wednesday when I tried to take your breast into my mouth, why did you stop me? Did you not want that to be done to you?" "No, I just didn't want you to be doing it just because you thought that you had to please me." Grant was surprised by her answer. It had never occurred to him that she had stopped him out of some kind of consideration for him. He had simply assumed that his action had offended her or had caused her genuine alarm. "But," Grant went on to explain, "I did want to please you. Of course I did, but I wanted to do it for me, to please both you and me!" When Dorothy offered no other response, Grant finally asked after a considerable pause, "So, would you now mind letting me see your breasts?" Dorothy's answer was immediate, but it was a wordless one. She instantly unzipped the front of her top, reached behind her back and unfastened her bra, so that the cups fell away from her breasts. But rather than taking them through the zipper opening of her top, Grant reached for them from under the bottom of her top. He also pushed the garment up and ducked his head under it. He now filled both his hands and mouth with her two lovely breasts. Like all the rest of her body that he had thus far had the grand privilege of exploring, her flesh was perfectly smooth. Her breasts were both soft and firm, and their weight in his hands felt like a physical manifestation of absolute female beauty. While holding them in his hands, Grant began to kiss, lick, and suck them with his mouth and to explore their flesh with his lips and tongue. How wonderful and magnificent they were! For her part too, Dorothy thoroughly enjoyed having her breasts adored and loved by her infatuated boy-man lover. But after a few minutes of such perfect delight, she whispered, "Ok, that's enough for right now. We need to stop in case Carol might get up and walk in on us." Grant obediently withdrew his mouth and hands, and Dorothy readjusted her bra and top.

Grant's first experience of Dorothy's magnificent breasts had greatly increased his physical desire for her. So, after additional petting and kissing, he finally asked, "Would you mind masturbating me?" "No, not at all. Lie down on the couch," she commanded sweetly. Dorothy knelt on the floor in front of the couch while Grant stretched himself out on it. After he had unfastened his pants and had pulled down his undershorts to expose his erection, Dorothy proceeded to masturbate him for the third time and in a third way. She took his penis between the thumb and index finger of her right hand at its base and masturbated him by whipping his manhood quickly and almost violently back and forth, first toward Grant's head and then toward his feet. Ever since gazing upon his beautiful penis last Wednesday at noon, she had thought about it again and again and now rejoiced in handling his beautiful manhood once more. The rapid whipping action of her masturbation thrilled them both. She was truly whacking him off and enjoying it immensely! As she was thus employed in rendering him this most pleasurable service, Grant said, "Let me do something to please you." As he spoke, he reached out with his right hand, located her crotch, and began to gently rub her there through her slacks and panties. Dorothy did not withdraw from his touch, because that too pleased her mightily. When Grant finally achieved an orgasm, semen was slung onto his shirt, pants, and the couch, but neither of them minded in the least. Although Dorothy was a very tidy housekeeper, she was not at all bothered by his sperm being spattered on the couch. On the contrary, the thought of Grant's semen being present on her couch was quite gratifying. It was now marked with the signature of their love. When his penis began to shrink, Grant withdrew his hand from Dorothy's crotch, put his clothes back in order, and they both sat down on the couch to resume their night of talking and kissing for a while longer before finally heading off to bed.

September 19, 1972, Tuesday

As usual, Dorothy was up with the dawn and oversaw Carol as she arose and prepared herself to go off to school. She did not bother waking Grant up. There was no reason why he should not sleep and rest until Carol left. As she busied herself around the house letting the dogs out and back inside, fixing her coffee, and making breakfast for Carol, her mind kept going back to last evening, when they were about to part, and her announcement had turned everything upside down. It had inflicted such pain upon Grant, but then what followed had gone from her comforting him to their mutual enjoyment of such exquisite pleasure on the family room couch: all their passionate kisses, his hands and mouth on her breasts that he so obviously enjoyed, his erect penis once again in her hand, and the feel of his hand between her legs. It was all such a confusing muddle of conflicting emotions and loyalties. She had once again strayed across the line between comforting friend and therapist and a woman very much in love. She had been so emotionally starved for so long in an unhappy marriage, how could she be expected to keep herself on such a starvation diet, especially when Grant was so eager to provide her with a banquet of joy and pleasure. Wasn't she entitled to some brief happiness now and then? It was "Wunderbar" and "Get thee behind me, Satan" all over again. How could she ever do the right thing, right for her, right for George, and right for Grant?

As she sat on the toilet and then dabbed at her vulva, there were still no signs of her period. Could she really be pregnant? Probably not, but until her period started, the possibility was always there. The question had changed things so much last night. As she stood up from the toilet with her nightgown falling down to conceal her body, she remembered Grant's hand being there between her thighs last night. Last Wednesday she had lain down beside him in nothing but her bra and panties and had allowed him to caress all of her bare skin. Last night she had shown him what had been hidden beneath her bra. The only secret remaining unrevealed to him was what she had covered last Wednesday with her panties. Today, if he wanted, and if he asked, she would reveal that to him as well. Perhaps that would be the proper compensation for having hurt him so much by alluding to George's exclusive enjoyment of her womanhood. In addition, the thought of Grant caressing her down there thrilled her through and through. His words yesterday at the back door had given her great pleasure. She loved the idea of him being her one and only man and herself as his woman. How wonderful it would be to have his beautiful red cock inside her vagina!

After Carol had gone off to school, Dorothy returned to the master bedroom, stepped out of her slippers, removed her pink quilted robe, and hung it up in the closet. She then came quietly down the hall and into the front bedroom where Grant was sleeping in the twin bed nearest the door. She was now wearing only her cotton nightgown. She stepped up to the left side of the bed, carefully pulled back the covers, and slid herself into the bed beside Grant, but she did so in an upright sitting position with her back against the headboard and her legs straight out in front of her. As she moved herself in alongside Grant, he slowly awoke from sleep and took a few seconds to realize that she was sitting up in bed beside him with her legs under the covers. He moved over slightly to give her more room in the narrow confines of the twin bed and also rolled himself onto his left side to be facing her. He slid his left arm between Dorothy's lower back and the headboard, while he laid his right arm across her thighs and his head against her hip.

"Good morning," Dorothy said quietly, as Grant came awake and adjusted his position to accommodate her presence beside him. "Good morning," he replied. There they lay in such delicious intimate contact, the narrowness of the bed contributing to their closeness. It was so exquisitely wonderful that Grant had no intention of moving for as long as possible. What perfect joy he felt with her beside him like this! The same was entirely true for Dorothy. As the minutes slowly passed by, they simply reveled in one another's intimate company, their exchange of words being minimal and unimportant and even unnecessary. They were like two cats drunk on catnip and too groggy to do much of anything. They were both drunk with pleasurable delight, and their slight movements to readjust their positions simply added to their enjoyment as they touched and rubbed against one another. Grant's free right hand occasionally moved about to touch her leg, to brush across her lower belly, and to bump against her breasts that were so deliciously covered by a mere thin layer of cotton. Grant's left hand also sometimes moved slightly about on her left hip and waistline to relish her feminine shape.

"My gosh," Grant commented in a hushed and awestruck voice, "You are so shapely and feel so wonderful!" "I do, huh?" "You really do! Gosh! You're so beautiful! After feeling your waist and hips, I now understand what Homer meant when he used the epithet 'deep waisted' in referring to beautiful shapely women. You certainly are a deep-waisted woman!" As he spoke these last words, his left hand again played along her side, waist, and hip. "That's also known as an hour-glass figure," Dorothy added. "Well," Grant said, "You certainly have one. As I told you this summer, you are my very first girlfriend, and you are teaching me so many wonderful things about a woman."

One hour ended, and another began. Still they remained virtually motionless on the bed. Their mutual pleasure was simply too magnificent to disturb. The second hour ended and became the beginning of a third. It was now midmorning, and yet neither wished to move from the bed. Finally, however, Grant's passion for more of this perfectly wonderful woman was responsible for breaking them out of their love-induced lethargy. Grant increasingly began to desire to lift up Dorothy's nightgown to admire her most intimate womanhood. But of course, he was afraid of causing offense and alarming her. He therefore lay beside her and began giving thought to how he could properly ask her for such an extraordinary honor. He eventually came up with what he thought most appropriate and then said.

"You really are my first girlfriend, and I have never before seen a woman's vagina. I would really like to see yours. I promise that I will not do anything except look at you. But I really want to see your vagina. You could slide down into the bed, and then I could simply lift up your nightgown."

As had happened so many times when Grant had made such requests of her, Dorothy's answer was wordless but immediate, so perfectly eloquent and majestic. As soon as Grant had finished speaking, Dorothy totally surprised him by pushing herself out of bed and standing up beside it. As she did so and turned herself toward him, Grant sat up in bed facing her. Then in the perfect silence of the room, he heard the slight rustle of material as she pulled her nightgown off over her head and dropped it to the floor. She was now standing before him totally naked, and Grant was so dumbstruck with wonder and surprise that he did not know what to do or say. As soon as the nightgown fell to the floor, Dorothy bent forward slightly, placed her hands on his shoulders, and whispered, "What do you want me to do?" As she uttered her beautiful question, Grant responded to her touch by reaching his own hands forward. They encountered her lovely breasts. He briefly held them in his hands with loving tenderness, as he replied, "Lie down on the bed."

As he stood up out of her way, she lay down on the bed with her legs well parted to reveal fully all the female beauty between her thighs. Grant knelt beside the bed and reached out his hands. When he found her bare lower legs, he slowly followed them up along her thighs to her sex. Her thighs were so flawlessly smooth and lovely, a perfect mixture of feminine softness and firmness, no doubt resulting in part from her swimming. The area between her thighs was glorious beyond words: soft, tender, covered with the perfect amount of hair, not too much to obscure her flesh but just the right amount to embellish her sex to equal Aphrodite herself. This area of perfect female beauty was bisected by her magnificent vulva, the lips of her vagina. Above this lay the love-delta of her lower belly. Its skin too was flawlessly smooth and was similarly adorned with the perfect amount of hair forming a v of divine beauty. Grant carefully examined her with awestruck concentration, trying to commit to memory every single detail that his fingers encountered. He traced and retraced her womanhood again and again, admiring the hair of her delta and how her delta sloped so majestically down into an awesomely lovely triangle of more hair adorning each side of her vulva. He caressed her inner thighs and studied with amazement how beautifully they joined and framed her sex. Dorothy lay motionless and allowed Grant to study her all he wanted, and his loving and admiring inspection thrilled her beyond belief. Grant ended his awestruck examination of her sex by softly placing the tip of his middle finger against her vulva, and then by gently pressing he parted her lips and slid his finger inside her vagina. Although Grant did not know it at the time because of his basic ignorance of such things, his finger had entered her effortlessly, because her vagina was wet and dilated from pleasure and desire. Dorothy was surprised that Grant had entered her with his finger, but the surprise was a most pleasant one. After leaving his finger inside her for fifteen seconds or so while his other fingers caressed the beautiful outer flesh and hair of her vulva, Grant slowly removed his finger, and his erotic examination of her womanhood was over.

"I'm afraid you're going to have to masturbate me now," Grant said, as he stood up from beside the bed. He pulled off his t-shirt and stepped out of his undershorts that he left beside the bed with her nightgown. They now exchanged positions. Dorothy arose from the bed and knelt naked beside it, and Grant lay down on his back. She was now seeing him fully naked for the first time also. He had such a muscular body, especially his legs. His stomach was flat and also very muscular. His flesh was very pale and covered with reddish golden hair, but the hair surrounding his penis was as bright red as the hair on his head. She once again eagerly took his erection into her right hand; and as she had done last Wednesday, she formed her fingers and thumb into a dainty hollow and moved them up and down as if he were thrusting rhythmically inside her.

When she had finally succeeded in inflicting upon him a most exquisite orgasm, she said, "I think we should get dressed now, and maybe we should be thinking about getting something to eat. I don't know about you, but I'm getting hungry." "Ok," Grant replied as he lay on the bed, dazed and relaxed from the climax of Dorothy's handling of his penis. Dorothy stood up, reached down to pick up her nightgown, and, beautifully naked, walked down the hall and into the master bedroom, where she dressed herself and then went into the adjoining bathroom to put on makeup. Meanwhile, Grant went into the hall bathroom, washed away the semen from his penis and surrounding area, dressed himself, and then joined Dorothy in the other bathroom, where he sat on the toilet lid as a seat while she finished making up her face and fixing her hair. They went out to the car and drove to a restaurant called The Blue Bird. After being seated, they placed their orders, Grant asking for fried chicken, cottage fries, and coleslaw, while Dorothy ordered a Reuben sandwich with a salad and coffee.

They were still delirious and high with erotic excitement from what they had just experienced and shared; and it dominated their conversation as they waited for their meals and then ate. As they talked, they kept their voices low so as not to be overheard. Dorothy's lovely voice was so erotic and beautiful: low both in pitch and volume, earnest, urgent, playful, teasing, humorous, but also quite serious and very excited. Their banter was therefore simply a verbal continuation of the magnificent love-play that had occurred on the twin bed in the front bedroom.

"That was the most beautiful thing that I have ever seen!" Grant said urgently. "What was?" Dorothy teasingly asked. "What you let me look at this morning." "Oh yeah?" she again said with the most wonderful amusement and joy in her voice. "You bet it was!" Grant emphasized seriously, "I can't imagine encountering anything else nearly as beautiful!" "You think so, huh?" she said with real pleasure.

After they had eaten their meals, they discussed whether they should have dessert. When Grant asked what was available, Dorothy said that they could choose between apple or cherry pie. "Why don't we get one piece and share it?" he suggested. "Ok," she agreed. "Which do you prefer?" he asked. "Cherry is my favorite pie." "Is it really? How fitting." "What do you mean by that?" "Well, I think you just showed me the prettiest cherry pie in the world." "Oh yeah?" "You sure did!"

When the pie arrived, their banter continued as they shared the one piece. "Are you going to give me your cherry?" "What cherry? I don't have one." "Oh yes you do. I just saw it." ... "Can I have a bit more of cherry pie?" "Haven't you had enough?" "I don't think I could ever get enough of your cherry pie."

When they returned to the house, Dorothy wanted to take a nap. They therefore lay down together in the same single bed that had witnessed their love-play that morning, but they were now fully clothed. They both fell asleep and slept quite soundly, but after about an hour Grant awoke with a start from some kind of frightening nightmare. He was still half asleep, very confused mentally, and also emotionally troubled from fear that their relationship would end. Dorothy was upset by his strange state of mind, got him to stand up, and walked him up and down the hallway until he was wide awake and was rational once again. By now it was the middle of the afternoon. Carol would soon be home from school, and Dorothy needed to go to Sweet Adelines that evening. It therefore seemed to be the proper time for Grant to return finally to his dorm room, So ended their most spectacular and memorable night and morning.

September 22, 1972, Friday

It was the first major party at Dorothy's house for this academic year, and they were having it near Dennis' birthday. The party was attended by many of the usual suspects as well as a couple of newcomers. Debbie was there. Although she was not enrolled in classes, she was still living in town in an apartment that she shared. Bob Snider and Kitty Carpenter were there, a newly formed romantic couple; of course, Dennis and Renny were there, the former with his new girlfriend Lisa Harris; and Pam Stewart and another new blind student, Paul Lindquist, were also there. Dorothy was disappointed that Grant had decided not to come, because he thought that it would be very hard for him to behave merely as one of her university kids.

Dennis had just recently met Lisa in Beaumont Manor, where she was also living. Her father was a professor in the university's Department of Sociology. She was an extremely vivacious and charming young woman; and when Dennis asked if she would be interested in going to this party, she was truly astounded to learn that it would be held at the house of a middle-aged woman who had no direct connection with the university other than through mobility instruction and volunteer reading. She simply could not imagine anyone her parents' age doing anything like this. But when she actually came to Dorothy's house for this first time and observed how beautifully she interacted with everyone and exhibited such perfect charm and consummate grace, she was even more astounded and captivated by this wonderful woman, whom Dennis had tried to describe beforehand, but whose actual magnificent presence eclipsed and greatly exceeded his mere words. Henceforth Lisa became a regular member of Dorothy's group of university kids, and the two eventually became fondest friends.

September 24, 1972, Sunday

When Grant answered the telephone in his dorm room late that afternoon, he was very pleased to hear Dorothy's lovely voice greeting him. "Hello, Grant, I'm going to meet Pam Stewart in about an hour at 5:00. She still is having trouble finding her way into the Armory from Jordan Street, and she wants me to help her figure out what she is doing wrong. I thought that since I would be on campus, we could be together while I helped Pam." "Yeah, that would be really nice," Grant replied. "Ok, why don't you just walk over there around 5:00, and I'll act as if we just happened to cross paths." "Ok, fine. See you then."

Since their unbelievable experience five days earlier, Grant and Dorothy had simply kept in touch by telephone. He was busy getting his readers set up and beginning work on his courses, but since he greatly preferred being alone with Dorothy, chances for another meeting had been limited. Dorothy had just now called him surreptitiously to arrange this rendezvous. She was eager to see him again, and the circumstances of their meeting would keep them from becoming physically intimate in any way.

Once they had successfully orchestrated their "chance" encounter, Dorothy and Grant were able to walk and talk together quietly as Pam walked several paces ahead. They were occasionally interrupted by Dorothy's need to explain things again or in more detail, followed by further repetition of the route. Dorothy and Grant simply exchanged bits of information about what each had been doing since they last talked on the telephone, but they were also both very pleased to be in one another's physical presence once again. Grant was enjoying her company so much that he really did not want it to end with Pam's mobility lesson. "Hey," he suggested, "Since the dorm cafeterias are closed for Sunday suppertime, why don't we go get some Kentucky Fried Chicken and take it back to your house to eat for supper?" When both Dorothy and Pam agreed, they did just that; and they had a rather pleasant time sitting around Dorothy's kitchen table along with George. When Dorothy left to take Pam and Grant back to campus, she dropped Pam off first at Nash Hall and then took Grant to Holmes, so that they would have a few extra minutes of talking and being alone together in the car, during which they figured out that they could meet again this coming Wednesday afternoon.

September 27, 1972, Wednesday

It had now been eight days since Dorothy had gladly allowed Grant to admire her womanhood. Since then she had had plenty of time to think things over. In rational retrospect, what she had done that morning in bed with him had both shocked and frightened her. If Grant was not so inexperienced in such matters, it was likely that instead of being content with exploring and adoring her love-zone that morning, he might have asked her to receive his penis inside her, especially since she was late with her period and was likely to be infertile. If he had made such a request that morning, given her emotional state of mind, she would have gladly consented and would have eagerly taken his beautiful red cock inside her vagina, and they would have enjoyed marvelous sexual intercourse for the first time but in violation of her marriage bond.

All along, her rational side had been trying to develop their powerful feelings for one another into a very special friendship, but it was now becoming all too clear that her emotional involvement with Grant was becoming so serious that she could not trust herself to make rational judgments in his presence. Perhaps Dennis and Renny were right in thinking that they should simply end everything immediately. Such a harsh and abrupt solution, she knew, would hurt Grant greatly; and it ran counter to her own most caring and generous spirit. She therefore had to somehow persuade Grant to adopt and implement her idea that they simply be very special friends. Of course, if she had her druthers and could push a magic button to change everything, she would be thrilled to have Grant as her ardent lover and prospective new husband. But even when she allowed herself to think along those lines, things still did not make much rational sense. Given the large difference between their ages (44 vs. 19, about to be 20),how much of a chance did they really have to make their relationship succeed and flourish? Grant seemed to be so passionately in love with her, but he was also so young. Wasn't it likely that he would eventually tire of her and leave her for someone else, after Dorothy had made a ruin of her existing life to accommodate him? She had long hoped for a miracle to rescue her from her very unhappy marriage, but how likely was it that Grant could be this miracle?

Shortly after returning to the house with Grant, when he first tried to embrace her, she stepped back and said, "Grant, I'm sorry, but I really don't think that we should be doing that anymore. That's the real reason why I wanted to talk with you today. We really must get control of our feelings for one another and work very hard at simply being very special friends, because if we don't, I'm afraid that I'll have to quit seeing you altogether, and I really don't want to do that. There's just too much at stake. I know we both don't like it, but I have to keep my marriage together for Carol's sake. She needs and deserves a stable home situation until she is out on her own. If all this between us had happened a few years later, things would be entirely different, because I could do what I wanted without having to worry about Carol, but that's not how it is."

As Dorothy laid out her case, Grant was stricken with genuine fear and alarm, and his insides felt very nauseous. All his pleas for the status quo and his protestations of passionate love fell upon deaf ears. Dorothy was adamant and could not be moved from her position. They talked for well over an hour, but nothing that Grant said could change Dorothy's resolve and decision. When Grant finally realized that Dorothy was standing firm, he asked her to take him back to his dorm room. By now he felt very ill, both physically and mentally. Dorothy could see that what she had decided for them was causing him tremendous anguish; and although it pained her very much to see this, Dorothy was able to tell herself that it was the only sensible thing for them to do.

They rode back to Holmes in silence; and when Grant opened the car door to leave, he nearly fell out onto the pavement, because he was feeling so ill. He went into his room and stretched out on his bed and simply lay there in mental and emotional agony until he forced himself to eat supper in the dining hall. He then returned to his room and bed and simply lay there until late in the evening. Since he was sure that he would not sleep well that night, he left his room so as not to disturb his roommate and went over into the lounge, where he sat for several hours.

September 28, 1972, Thursday

By the early hours of the morning Grant had sunk into a state of very deep depression. What he had been worrying about since early July, and which had kept him precariously balanced between normality and an abyss of despair had now happened. Dorothy had decided to slam the door shut and tightly lock away forever their passionate love for one another. Thus far, the only thing that had kept the door slightly ajar with a slim chance for their love to escape and expand into something truly glorious was Dorothy's own troubled ambivalence resulting from the tremendous conflict between her rational resolve and her powerful emotional yearnings. Her precarious balance between the two had kept Grant teetering all summer long and had been the major reason why he had failed to successfully complete summer school. Dorothy's decision today had sent him headlong into that dreaded abyss of despair, where the utter darkness resulted from the total absence of Dorothy's love.

After their experience on the twin bed in the front bedroom more than a week ago, how could he possibly contemplate not having their passionate love as part of his life? Seeing her beautiful female sex on the bed had been a truly transforming experience for him, akin to a powerful religious experience. In fact, he was now beginning to term the event The Revelation, or to use its Greek equivalent, The Apocalypse, meaning "The Unveiling." To him, what he had then seen and admired with such awe was not simply a female sex, but the womanhood of the most spectacular human being whom he had thus far encountered in his life. The considerable physical beauty of her sex was to Grant amplified tenfold or more by the incomparable magnificence of her personality and character. Dorothy might have doubts about the longevity of Grant's passionate love for her, but he did not. He was now firmly convinced that she would be his one and only woman, and he should and would be her one and only man, if only their love were given a chance to survive. Right now he felt that she was deliberately strangling it in its crib.

By now Grant was in such a state of depression that he could not endure normal interaction with other people. He therefore did not bother going to class, and he secluded himself in the perfect stillness of the lounge, and especially its small TV room that was usually unoccupied. Whenever he became so tired that he needed sleep, he simply stretched out on a couch and dozed off.

Sept. 29-Oct. 1, 1972, Friday-Sunday

What now follows, dear reader, is a brief account of a most unusual series of events that transpired over the course of a weekend.

After a day and a half of suffering tremendous emotional anguish, Grant had finally formulated a plan in his mind that was now very confused with severe depression. If he could not escape his mental agony, he would at least escape physically from his unbearable situation by running away. He even left his wallet hidden away on the radiator behind the couch in the TV room of the lounge, because he intended to shed his identity and eventually assume a new one, possibly with the name of Julius Cook. Around 4:00 A.M. on Friday September 29 Grant set out with his cane to walk to the bus station, a very long walk from Holmes, and one which he had never attempted before.

After accomplishing the journey without much difficulty during the silent darkness of the early hours of morning, Grant bought a ticket for the first bus going to Chicago and arrived in the main bus station in downtown Chicago in midmorning. He then stood around in a real quandary as to what to do next. He first considered taking a bus to San Francisco, because it was about as far away from University City as he could travel by bus. Eventually, however, he decided to take one to De Kalb Illinois, because an old school friend from the state residential school for the blind in Jacksonville, Joe Burton, still might live there and would probably be willing to take him in. Grant therefore boarded the bus for De Kalb.

When the bus let him off at the student union at Northern Illinois University, he located a telephone and called directory assistance to obtain Joe's telephone number. The operator informed him that the number was unlisted, but when she heard the despair and panic in his voice in saying that he was the only person in town whom he knew, she relented and gave him the number. Grant therefore made the call. His wife answered and gave him directions on how to get to their apartment. It was a very long walk, part of it along a very busy highway with no sidewalk; and he was lucky not to have been hit by a car. When Grant finally arrived at the apartment in the middle of the afternoon, Joe was still at work in the university's cafeteria. Mike's wife Norma was very considerate in not asking him obvious questions as to what had brought him into their life. She decided to let Joe do this when he returned home, since Grant and Joe had been good friends years ago.

But after treating their guest with great hospitality, Joe did not get around to finding out what was really going on until Saturday evening when he invited Grant to go with him to a theater to watch a movie. As they walked there and back, they talked very seriously about what had brought him to De Kalb under such odd circumstances. After Grant had explained to him the hopeless relationship in which he was involved, what Dorothy had decreed, and how utterly miserable it made him, Joe's advice to Grant was quite simple, at least in its words. "If you really love her, go back and make her yours." That is what Grant decided to do.

Joe walked him back to the bus station the next morning, and Grant boarded a bus to take him back to University City. Although his desperate peregrinations had gradually brought him back to his senses by forcing upon him the realization that his initial crack-brained decision to slip off into oblivion was futile and impractical, Grant was still not entirely thinking straight: for at one point when the bus stopped to let people off and on, a woman came aboard and sat a seat or so away from him. She was wearing White Shoulders perfume. Since he had never encountered anyone except Dorothy who wore this rare and distinctive fragrance, Grant's strange state of mind convinced him that this woman must be Dorothy, who was deliberately taunting him by sitting there in silence but knowing that Grant knew that she was there. Eventually, however, he succeeded in convincing himself that he was being irrational.

· When Grant arrived back in University City in the late afternoon of Sunday October 1, he discovered that his absence had caused considerable alarm among Dorothy, Dennis, and Renny. When a student discovered his wallet and took it to the dorm advisor, inquiries were made, and it was soon determined that no one who knew Grant had any knowledge as to where he was. In the meantime, Dorothy had called his room several times and had learned from his roommate that Grant had not been in the room for quite some time. Given the nature of their last meeting and his emotionally vulnerable frame of mind, she began to suspect that Grant had somehow placed himself in a very unhealthy or dangerous situation. She therefore called Dennis early Friday afternoon and asked if they could meet and talk.

As soon as she picked Dennis up and was driving off, she said, "I'm so totally discombobulated that I'm finding it hard to concentrate on driving." "Ah man, Ma," Dennis replied in surprise, "Please try to relax. Let's not talk at all right now. Just take it slow and easy. We'll be back at your house soon, and then we'll be safe and off of the streets."

After coming into the house, they sat down at the kitchen table and began to talk. "So, Ma," Dennis asked, "What's this all about?" "I think that something serious has happened to Grant, because he hasn't been in his room or seen around by anyone for two days now." "Well," Dennis suggested plausibly, "He could be at the library in one of those reading rooms, or he could be staying in someone else's room for some reason or other." "I don't think so, Dennis. We had a really serious conversation two days ago, and it really upset him. I could tell. It just doesn't feel right, and I'm sick with worry!"

As soon as she said this, Dennis finally began to understand that something rather serious must be going on between the two of them, and that the current situation was likely to be quite unusual, if not dangerous. After several moments of silence, Dorothy asked, "Do you think we should call Grant's parents?" "Oh no," Dennis replied, "At least not right now, because it might not be anything serious, and we wouldn't want to alarm them unnecessarily. But even if it turns out to be something serious and a bit crazy, it might be better if they don't know what silly thing their son has done." After further discussion, Dennis assured her that he would go around to as many places as he could think of to see if Grant was or had been in any of them.

After racking his brain as to where Grant might be there on campus. Dennis talked with Terry Wilson, one of his German readers with whom Grant was quite friendly, as well as with Moses Truman, who had been one of the original seven blind students in their freshman group, but nothing was turned up by these and other inquiries. Before this crisis had arisen, Dorothy had made plans to have some of the group over to her house that Saturday evening, but she was not her normal self, mentally or emotionally. The burden of keeping things lively at this gathering thus fell upon Dennis and Renny. At one point during the evening Dennis and Dorothy succeeded in going off together briefly into the front bedroom to talk; and as they did so, Dorothy burst into tears. Dennis was truly amazed, because he had never before seen her seriously shaken by anything. They also succeeded in going outside for a brief walk, during which Dennis did his best to allay her worst fears.

When news of Grant's whereabouts had still not materialized on Sunday, Dennis and Renny decided that the police should be informed first thing Monday morning. But luckily, Grant finally showed up later that day. Dennis and Renny then telephoned Dorothy to let her know that Grant was back in his room safe and sound, and that he would contact her tomorrow.

October 2, 1972, Monday

At 9:00 Grant lifted up the receiver on the telephone and dialed Dorothy's number. His roommate had left not too long ago for his morning classes, and Grant was fairly sure that by now George had left for Newton. Dorothy had been anxiously waiting by the telephone when it rang. They were now speaking to each other for the first time since the previous Wednesday afternoon. Given what all had happened over the weekend, it was not surprising that their conversation was rather strained. They both wanted to see each other desperately, but with very different expectations. Now that he had emerged from his depression, Grant had reassumed his position that was based upon his emotions and passionate infatuation with Dorothy. Since he desperately wanted her to abandon her notion that they simply be very special friends, Grant asked her quite pointedly, "Who will you be when we meet?" Dorothy clearly understood the challenge in his question, and her reply was also a restatement of her long-standing rational position: "Dorothy Patterson, a mother, wife, and your friend. Who else would I be?" "How about a woman who loves me?" Grant pressed. "I'm not sure about that, depending upon what you mean." It was clear that their respective positions were at odds, but despite their differences, they wanted to see each other so badly that they were forced to overlook this divide for the time being.

Following their brief interchange, Dorothy left immediately to come pick Grant up and bring him back to the house, but when she arrived, she parked the car and came to his room. When she sat down on his bed, Grant knelt before her on the floor, and she hugged his head fiercely against her breasts and said with emotion choking her voice and tears in her eyes, "Oh Grant, I can't begin to tell you how worried I have been! I thought that you might be lying dead somewhere!" They then arose and went out to the car.

Grant now proceeded to tell her in detail what all he had done from the time that they had last seen one another last Wednesday until he arrived back in University City yesterday afternoon. Dorothy in turn described what she, Dennis, and Renny had done and talked about when they realized that he was probably no longer on campus. Once they entered the house, their physical contact was affectionate but restrained and subdued. Dorothy clearly wanted them to abide by her decision to be very special friends, as she had ordained last Wednesday afternoon; but the events during the previous weekend had somewhat muddied the waters once again.

As the semester unfolded, Dorothy and Grant experienced a seemingly endless and emotionally painful war both within themselves and between each other, as the two radically different possible outcomes to their relationship competed for dominance, either to keep it contained within reasonable bounds so as not to disturb the status quo, or to let it develop and to accept the consequences. Rational consideration clearly favored the former, but their emotional feelings strongly desired the latter. At this time, despite her obvious emotional involvement, Dorothy was definitely inclined toward the rational; whereas Grant was clearly being more powerfully driven by his strong feelings of attraction for this wonderful woman, without whom, he thought, his life would be empty and meaningless.

October 5, 1972, Thursday

It was 11:45 A.M., and Grant had no more classes for the day. He was standing out in front of Holmes waiting for Dorothy to come pick him up after her morning swim; and then they would be spending the next three hours or so together until Grant had to meet a reader in the late afternoon. As he sat down in the passenger seat, he asked, "What color are your eyes?" "Green," Dorothy replied, "Why?" "I was just wondering and thought that it might help me picture what you looked like. You know," he continued, "Green is my favorite color. Even though I can't see anymore, I still remember colors and can picture them. It's really neat that your eyes are my favorite color. I can now think of you as my precious emerald or my green-eyed goddess.

What color is your hair?" "Brown." "Oh yeah?" and then after a pause in which he took in that new piece of information, he asked, "And how about your other hair?" "What do you mean?" "You know. That hair that forms such a perfect Venus V!" "It's the same," Dorothy replied, now with a tone of sweet amusement in her voice. "Wow!" Grant added after another contemplative pause, "with your pale and perfectly smooth skin, what I can picture in my mind is really quite beautiful!"

"When I was a child," Dorothy began, "the other kids often teased me about my ears, because they stuck out so far from my head; and it made me feel like such a clown." Grant reached across the seat with his left hand and began to examine her ears. "They look perfectly ok to me," he concluded, "And even though you just got out of the pool, your hair also looks very nice, at least as far as I am concerned." "I've often also thought that my neck is a little too long." Grant's hand now moved down to her neck; and after further examination, he passed a completely favorable judgment on that part of her anatomy too.

When they parked on the driveway, Grant picked up her swimming bag from the middle of the seat, and they entered the house. They were now greeted not by three, but four dogs. Sally had once again acquired a dog and had again given it up to her mother, but this was in part due to the fact that she would soon be moving to Houston, Texas, because ever since the fiasco in March of her wedding with Bob What's-his-name falling through at the last minute, she had become increasingly unhappy and had finally decided that perhaps she needed to move away and make a new start. Dorothy's brother Tim and his wife Marilyn had agreed to let her stay with them until she found a job and had enough money to have her own apartment. Sally was therefore leaving her dog, a cute Miniature Dachshund named Schatzlein ("little Treasure" in German) or Schatzi for short, with her mother. Although the other three dogs were many times her size, she made up for it with her spunky personality and adorable vivacity.

After they had gone into the bathroom adjoining the master bedroom to empty out the swimming bag and to hang up Dorothy's wet suit, they came into the kitchen, where Dorothy began to fix them grilled ham and cheese sandwiches for lunch. Grant had now been asking Dorothy all sorts of questions about her early years, especially her growing up during The Great Depression; and Dorothy was narrating so many interesting things that she could remember or had been told by her parents.

Her first house, a small brick structure, was made available to them rent free for as long as her father did not have a regular job, on condition that they keep it well maintained. Before moving in, Babe and Gloria with their friends Lee and Jan Thomas had to first strip the floors and walls of a thick layer of chicken dung, because the building had not been a place of human habitation, but a place to house chickens. There was only one bedroom, and all three girls slept together in the same bed with Dorothy jammed in between Ginger and Bethany. Their parents slept in the living room on the couch that folded out into a bed. Their only running water was in the kitchen. Thus, every Saturday evening Gloria hung up a curtain near the coal-burning stove, heated up several pans of water, poured them into a large metal tub, and had the three girls take their baths. It was not until Dorothy was in seventh grade that they moved into their second house that had a regular bathroom with a bathtub, and oh what a luxury it was to be able to sit down in the tub and stretch out her legs! Dorothy then for the first time also had her very own bed.

When the three girls were still fairly young, they and their parents often spent their evenings visiting other relatives or friends in the neighborhood. They usually traveled to and from these places with the three girls riding in a kind of rickshaw pulled by their two parents. Dorothy enjoyed this so very much as they returned home, because she lay on her back and gazed up at the stars overhead.

She told Grant about how her family had heard about the bombing of Pearl Harbor while listening to the radio that Sunday afternoon. A year before, Ginger's boyfriend had gone to Canada to enlist in the RAF and was eventually shot down and killed. A son of one of her mother's friends had been killed by a sniper on Iwo Jima, because after the fighting had ceased, he had thought it safe to remove his helmet. She vividly remembered the jubilation in the streets on V-J Day. In fact, she had received a severe burn on her cheek when a man with a cigar in his mouth gave her an excited hug as they were all celebrating wildly.

Dorothy's stories continued on and on, as they sat down to eat and then put their dishes away, and even as Dorothy began to move around the house to do other small chores, accompanied and assisted by Grant. She was such a good storyteller, had so many interesting things to relate, and really enjoyed sharing them with him. He was also such a good listener and always asked excellent follow-up questions and offered his own insightful comments. Their interaction through such conversations had been going on since early July. This had been and continued to be a very important way in which the two of them were forging a bond of extraordinary closeness and trust that went hand-in-hand with their passionate attraction to one another. Since Jeanne Douglas had moved away a year ago, Dorothy had not had another really close friend with whom she felt fully comfortable in confiding her thoughts and feelings. Grant was now fulfilling this role for her, and he did this well and gladly, because he simply could not know enough about this remarkable woman.

They eventually sat down at the dining table across from one another. "So," Grant asked, "Tell me about your boyfriends. You're so magnificent. I'm sure that you had many of them in high school." "Well yeah," Dorothy allowed with pleasure and a laugh in her voice, "I did have several. There was one boy who lived on my block and was always giving me his balsa airplanes as tokens of his affection. Then there was the kid in my biology class. He always sat next to me and was always happy to be my partner in dissecting things; and of course, I was always happy to let him do all that messy stuff while I watched. During my last year in high school someone who had graduated the year before had gone off to college and was the member of a fraternity. Once, when he was home visiting, he came over to our house, and the two of us sat out on our screened-in porch eating popcorn. When we began tossing unpopped seeds at one another, he threw his fraternity pin into my bowl without telling me, because he was too shy to ask me to accept it and to become his girl. I picked it up from the bowl and threw it at him without realizing what it was; and since it fell to the floor and made such a different sound, he knew what had happened and then told me. We then turned on the porch light to find his pin."

It was approaching the time for them to end their lovely afternoon together, but by now an atmosphere of sweet intimacy had developed, and Grant had enough courage to ask her to tell him about the very first time that a man's penis had entered her vagina. Dorothy did not hesitate to do so, largely because they were now both fully wound up emotionally and desiring one another, although they sat across from each other at the table. It was the very first time that she ever related this story to anyone, another clear sign of their emotional closeness and trust in one another. Her telling of the story was not just the description of an event many years in the past but was an object of passion and desire that formed a bridge between them in the present.

To Grant's delight, her story did not involve George, but another young man whose name she no longer remembered. "It happened," she began, "during the summer after I had graduated from high school. So, that would have been 1946. My best friend was Paula Blackburn, who soon married Donald Parker, but while they were engaged in their pre-marital dating, we once formed a foursome with some friend of Donald's to be my date. The four of us decided to spend a weekend at a lakeside resort where we rented two small cabins. My mom, of course, was dead set against me going, because she was sure that it would result in some kind of hanky-panky, but I went anyway. We must have stayed there two days and one intervening night, probably Saturday afternoon to Sunday afternoon. I'm quite sure that Paula and Donald used the opportunity to have sex in their cabin. My date was, I suppose, also hoping for the same thing. Our cabin was equipped with one set of bunk beds. I slept on the bottom, and my date on top. During the morning after we awoke, we lay in our beds talking, and the guy eventually asked if I would allow him to lie with me and briefly insert his penis into my vagina. I agreed. He lay between my legs, entered me, and lay motionless inside me for a short time until I asked him to withdraw. He did so obediently, and that was the end of my first sexual encounter with a man's penis; and I didn't have any more until George and I were married."

Grant allowed her to tell this story without interruption. The house around them was perfectly still and silent. Apart from the ticking of the ornate clock in the shape of a horse-drawn carriage that sat on top of the piano several feet away in the living room, the only sound was the sound of Dorothy's voice, lovely, low, and serious, which heightened the sexual intensity between them. By now their minds, bodies, and souls were on the same wavelength, the shared wavelength of their love and passion for each other. Therefore, when Dorothy ended her story, they both knew instinctively that their time together today had reached its climactic point. Without either one of them uttering a single word, They stood up from the table simultaneously; and while she stood motionless, Grant came around the table toward her. They silently opened their arms to the other and entered a loving and passionate embrace, followed immediately by their lips and tongues engaging in a prolonged kiss. Grant then shifted his hands down to her bottom and pressed their bodies together, so that the intensity of their kiss was joined and commingled with the delicious pleasure of his love-spike and her love-delta enjoying and pleasing the other. After ending the kiss and parting their mouths briefly, they commenced a second one; and as they did, Grant shifted his hold once again on his lovely woman. His left hand and arm came up around her lower back at her waist, and his right hand came around to her front. Dorothy responded by shifting her own position to accommodate what they both desired. After using his right hand to pull open the elastic waistbands of her slacks and panties. Grant slid his hand down inside the two garments, caressed her perfectly smooth belly, and descended further to feel her lovely sex and hair. Since Dorothy had obligingly moved her feet apart to give him full access to her womanhood, Grant moved his hand down even further to feel and hold her entire sex in his hand. Before releasing her female perfection and withdrawing his hand, he slowly and carefully thrust his middle finger up inside her vagina. His finger entered her easily, because she was dilated from pleasure and desire and brimming full of love-honey. As they stood there enjoying their second prolonged kiss, her vagina was lovingly impaled upon his finger. Given her marital status, the latter was a perfectly acceptable surrogate for Grant's penis. By engaging in this wonderful act of sexual intimacy, they had relived and reinterpreted the event of many years ago that Dorothy had just described. They had now taken possession of that memory for themselves and had incorporated it into their own lives. Dorothy was pleased to be

Grant's first woman, and he was overjoyed in having such an extraordinary female as his first love.

When he finally withdrew his finger, it was moist with her love-honey. They then walked wordlessly from the dining room out to the car, and Dorothy took Grant back to Holmes. But since Grant still had ten or fifteen minutes before he needed to leave to walk over to the Undergraduate Library to meet his reader for the late afternoon, he first lay down on his bed and placed his hand over his face, so that his right middle finger was beneath his nostrils. He now simply breathe in the lovely scent of Dorothy's love-honey. How very wonderful and enchanting! This was his very first experience with the divine scent of her vagina. He could not imagine anything else in the entire world even coming close to the wonder and enchantment of this fragrance.

October 12, 1972, Thursday

Like last week, Dorothy was on her way after her swimming in the morning to pick Grant up and to bring him over to the house, so that they could have a few hours alone together before Carol came home from school, and before Grant had to meet a reader at the library. This past Sunday George, Carol, and she had spent about two hours in the evening with several of the university kids at the Student Union Bowling Alley. Renny and Paul Lindquist had organized a small bowling league of about two dozen people, about one-third blind students and the other sighted students, among whom she, George, and Carol were also included. Dorothy had wanted Grant to join, but he still did not feel very comfortable in trying to behave normally around her in a group of people. Whenever she tried to persuade him to try, he kept saying that he was a mere ordinary mortal and did not possess her saintly and extraordinary ability to compartmentalize her feelings and to present her dazzling self to the unsuspecting outside world. She was also still trying to talk him into coming to their party Saturday night following the autumn Sweet Adeline show. He had thus far agreed to attend the concert, but he was still reluctant to come back over to the house afterwards for a party with the other university kids. Consequently, their interaction consisted of these meetings at the house once or twice a week on weekdays, like this one today, as well as very lengthy telephone calls in the evenings with Grant calling her from a telephone booth to ensure privacy. If she was totally free to talk when he called, they talked for hours and were both always reluctant to hang up, just like a couple of love-struck teenagers. Grant had also recently stopped addressing her as Ma and now called her by her name, which he usually shortened to Dorth.

When Grant opened the car door in front of Holmes and sat down, he asked, "So what's going on with you?" "Well," Dorothy said with obvious pride in her voice, "I finally have my Sweet Adelines gown all done!" "That's really neat," he replied, "How did you become so expert at sewing?" "Well, it's a long story. I started learning some things as a kid from my mother. Back then in The Depression we had to economize in every way we could, and making your own clothes was one of them. But that was pretty basic stuff, nothing at all fancy. then as I got older, I simply made more and more things, learned stuff from other people here and there, but I guess I made a really big jump when I took a sewing class while we were living in Great Falls, Montana. I then learned all sorts of things, such as how to make button holes." "You know," Grant rejoined, "I'm not surprised, because everything you do, you do so exceptionally." "Flattery will git ya nowhere, buddy," she retorted in her funny little girl voice. "Oh I don't have to flatter you, sweetheart," he replied with equal silliness before changing back to being serious, "The truth itself is so wonderful that only those who know you would believe it. Not only are you beautiful and possess the most remarkable personality I've encountered, but you're an expert in the kitchen and know how to knit, crochet, and sew so many lovely things! I also should have added from personal experience, you're also a good reader, mobility instructor, and a really magnificent kisser." "Hey watch it there, buddy," she again said in her cute little girl voice, "I've shot men for less than that!"

While they were sharing a can of Campbell's tomato soup for their lunch, Dorothy stood up to retrieve her thyroid pills. When Grant asked about them, she began telling him another interesting story. Not long after they had moved to Baltimore (Carol had not yet been born), Dorothy began to feel very tired and depressed. She laid around so much with no motivation to do anything, and even some of her hair began to fall out. When she consulted a doctor, he simply gave her medication to treat these various symptoms, but when they returned to Homewood that summer to visit on vacation, she went to their old family doctor, Dr. Dawson. As soon as she had described what all she had been experiencing, Dr. Dawson used his fingernail to scratch the skin on her arm and instantly diagnosed her problem as an improperly working thyroid gland. As soon as she began taking the medication, all her problems disappeared, and she was back to normal.

The story led Grant to asking additional questions about their time in Baltimore, and Dorothy responded by filling this afternoon of theirs with so many wonderful memories of her four years there: how the locals call the city Balmer; Fort McHenry, where Francis Scott Key was inspired to write the Star Spangled Banner during the War of 1812; the monument in Washington D.C. of the raising of the American Flag on Iwo Jima, one of whose figures the kids always thought must be their Uncle Jim Lawson, because they knew that he had been there; how a German couple, who lived directly above them in their initial apartment, were so polite and considerate that whenever they came home, they removed their shoes so as not to make too much noise for those living directly under them.

Then when they moved into their house in a residential area, there were many other young families like themselves; and the wives helped each other in all sorts of ways, especially watching over someone's kid or kids while the mother went off to appointments or to run important errands. Dorothy had been especially fond of Linda Wyatt, who was highly artistic and spent much of her free time drawing and painting, in fact, so much so that she tended to neglect her housework, so that her house was always messier and more disorderly than those of the other wives. As a result, many neighbors did not ask Linda to watch their kids while they went off to do something, because they were afraid that the child might be hurt or get into something when Linda was not watching. Dorothy, however, learned very quickly that despite her somewhat messy house, Linda was a very nice person. They had become good friends, and Dorothy did not hesitate to leave any of her children with Linda, because she understood that the mess in her house was simply the result of Linda needing to devote her time to more important things than keeping the floor spotlessly clean. In fact, Dorothy still treasured a piece of paper on which Linda had drawn a picture of Carol when she was a small baby. Dorothy one day asked Linda to keep her for a short time for some reason or other; and when Carol became fussy and cried, Linda succeeded in settling her down by persuading her to sit really still, so that she could draw her picture and then show it to her. When they were preparing to move from Baltimore, Linda presented Dorothy with the gift of a painting that she had done, a very nice street scene. Dorothy now took Grant to this very picture hanging in the living room and described it to him.

After they admired the painting together, Grant said, "Well, before it gets to be too late, I would really like to see the gown that you just finished making." "Ok," Dorothy brightly replied, "Let's go look at it. It's hanging up on the back of the door in the front bedroom."

Within seconds they were at the very spot that twenty-three days earlier had been the site of The Great Apocalypse. After Dorothy eagerly guided Grant's hands to show him the design of the dress as it hung on its hanger, he then asked, "Would you mind putting it on, so I can see you in it?" "Of course," she pleasantly agreed. In exactly the same place where she had removed her nightgown and had dropped it to the floor, she now removed her clothes except for her bra and panties. Clad in only these two articles of clothing, she sat down on the edge of the bed with the gown on its hanger in her lap. Grant was sitting beside her and ran his hand down her bare back, feeling the strap of her bra, her smooth lovely skin, and the back of her panties. He wanted so much to unfasten her bra and to fondle and perhaps even suck her breasts, but his innate shyness kept him from doing so; and since it had still been such a short time since their reunion after the traumatic episode involving De Kalb, he was afraid that unfastening her bra would offend his beloved woman. Dorothy, on her part, enjoyed the feel of his hand on her back and would have welcomed much more; but since the two lovers remained silent and waited for the other to make the next move, the opportunity to become more intimate passed, and it well illustrated the uncertainty and precariousness of their relationship at this time.

When Dorothy had freed the gown from its hanger, she arose from the edge of the bed, turned to face Grant, and slid the gown over her head and down her body. When the gown was in place, Dorothy turned around and asked Grant to zip it up the back for her. She then turned back around to face him and proudly stood there while Grant ran his hands over both her and the gown, from her shoulders all the way down to her feet, where the gown ended. As Grant knelt on the floor before her, feeling the material and the musical notes sewn onto it, he remarked, "It's really beautiful, or to use your own lovely and cute rendition of that word, it's beauteous; and so are you! You are so very beauteous!" She turned back around and said, "Ok, you can unzip me now." But as Grant did so, the zipper became stuck about halfway down in the edge of the surrounding material; and despite Grant's effort to dislodge it, it would not budge. As he struggled with it, Dorothy patiently stood there with her back partially bare and the rest of her covered only in the single layer of the gown's fabric. When they finally agreed that the zipper could not be moved, they worked to remove the gown by having Dorothy wriggle out of it. As she did, and as Grant assisted her, of course, she was again clad only in her bra and panties and was a lovely sight for Grant's hands to assist, handle, and behold. Although she dressed herself right away, her lovely gown had given them both a sweet and delightful incident to cherish and remember.

October 14, 1972, Saturday

The annual autumn Sweet Adeline concert had gone off quite well, and in attendance had been Dorothy's university kids, including Grant. But he had not agreed to come back to the house for a party. While George and Lisa Harris drove the others back to the house in their two cars, Dorothy and Grant left alone in the Falcon, so that they could be alone together briefly as she returned him to his dorm. Everyone else readily accepted Grant's absence from the party on the grounds that he wanted to spend his time more profitably with his studies, because he had the reputation of being the most studious one of their group. But of course, the real reason for his absence was far otherwise. As Dorothy drove Grant back toward campus, she made one last appeal to him to come to the house to be with the others. She really wanted him to be there with her, but Grant remained steadfast in his refusal. So, they were again engaged in this tug-of-war involving the nature of their relationship, and how they should behave. As Grant saw it, Dorothy was wanting him to be there just as another one of her university kids, and that status both offended and hurt him deeply. Dorothy, of course, viewed the matter quite differently. They were in fact very special friends, but they had to keep their special relationship completely secret. Consequently, this divide, which had erupted in its worst form two weeks ago with Grant's hair-brain, but frightening flight to De Kalb, was still causing the two lovers to be at odds.

When Dorothy finally accepted failure in trying to persuade Grant, he asked her to drop him off at McDonald's near the corner of Foxwell and Wagoner Streets. They then parted company for the night. After purchasing a meal, Grant went outside and sat down to eat at one of the tables. Since it was now quite late in the evening and rather chilly outside, he was the only person in the outdoor sitting area, and this suited his gloomy and depressed state of mind perfectly and even reinforced it. Once again, the peculiar circumstances of their relationship tonight were making him feel utterly miserable, as if Dorothy's desire to have him as a member of the party at the house was her way of denying the existence of their relationship altogether. Their love meant so much to him that anything at all that stood in its way bothered him; and if Dorothy herself seemed to be the one who was diminishing the importance of their love, it totally unnerved him and frightened him to his very bones, because just two and a half weeks earlier she had threatened to have them break off all contact with one another.

When Grant finished eating, he dropped the food wrappers into a garbage bin and set off on his walk back to his room in Holmes. It was now approaching midnight, and it would soon be Sunday October 15; and as he realized this, he recalled that October 15 was the birthday of the great Roman poet Vergil. Thus, in his troubled state of mind he attempted to regain some degree of emotional stability by the following bizarre act of false bravado. Instead of walking directly to Holmes, he detoured and walked through the first floors of Garfield and Forester dormitories; and as he walked through their corridors with the usual Saturday night sounds of students and their music coming out of their dorm rooms, he proclaimed in a loud voice: "Praise be to Vergil on the Ides of October!" Since he was blind, he had no idea as to how his announcement was received, or even if anyone actually heard it. He entered his dorm room and did his best to quiet his jumble of mixed emotions before finally being able to fall asleep. But he certainly did not do any studying, which had been the supposed reason for his absence from the party. As had been happening since the beginning of this semester four weeks ago, Grant found himself too emotionally unsettled to concentrate on schoolwork. Meanwhile, Dorothy was playing her role as the charming and beloved Ma in hosting her other university kids at her house for the party and sleep-over.

October 16, 1972, Monday

Dorothy had just finished eating her lunch alone at the kitchen table. She arose and now began to gather all the things that she needed to make an apple pie for Grant's upcoming birthday. She would not be here then, because her mother and she would be on the road, their first day of driving to take Sally to Houston. Earlier in the morning she had run out to the Book Emporium and purchased a small book of love poetry to be her gift to Grant. He would be coming over this evening to spend the night, and she could then give him the pie and book; and if he wanted, she would read the book to him.

Ever since that horrible weekend two weeks ago when he left town and dashed off to De Kalb, she had finally realized that she truly loved this young man; and if he left her life, it would hurt her very much. She really had no idea as to where all this would lead. About all that she could do was to make sure that they conducted themselves in such a way as not to attract suspicion; and she also needed to make sure that they did not go too far in things, that is, not to have sexual intercourse or anything closely approaching it. Other than that, she could really only take it a day at a time and simply hope that things would eventually turn out ok for them. But still, it was so scary.

October 19, 1972, Thursday

When Dorothy answered the telephone at 7:30 A.M., she was somewhat surprised to hear Grant's voice greeting her. "Hello, Dorth, I'm calling to see if you could come get me right away." "Well, I can come in about a half an hour when Carol has left for school." "Yeah, that's what I mean. I happened to run into Dennis last night over at Renny's room, and we wound up staying up all night talking. I'm beginning to get tired and need to sleep, but if I go back to my dorm room, my roommate will probably disturb me. I thought that I could come over there and go to sleep, and then you could wake me up and bring me back at 3:00 to meet my reader at the library." "That would be fine. As you know, I won't be going swimming today. I've got too many things to do around the house between now and early Saturday morning when mom and I leave to drive Sally to Houston. So I'll pick you up in the usual spot around 8:00."

As she drove up alongside the curb and stopped, she noticed that Grant was holding her empty pie pan. "So," Dorothy asked, as Grant sat himself down in the car, "How did you like the pie?" "Ah man, of course, it was great!" he exclaimed. "Did you share any of it with your roommate?" "What?" he said in mock outrage and surprise, "Are you kidding? Hell no! I ate the whole damn thing myself! Do you think that I would let someone else eat any of that lovely apple pie that you made for me?" To Grant the pie had been a physical manifestation of Dorothy's love for him, and it therefore rightfully belonged entirely to him. "You mean you ate that whole big pie in what, two days?" "Fuckin' A right! You bet I did!" he boasted. "Boy!" she said with obvious amusement and delight in her voice, "You, Dennis, and Renny are such pigs! You guys eat everything in sight." "We certainly do when it's something you've made, because you're such an excellent cook. But thanks so much. I really enjoyed the pie, and coming from you, that meant very much. I really mean it."

"You're quite welcome," she replied and then said to change the subject, "Ok, so what did you fellas talk about all night?" "All kinds of stuff," Grant replied, but then in order to assure her that their relationship had not been any part of their discussion, he further elaborated, "You should know us college guys well enough by now, and how much we like to sit around and bullshit. Since the semester started, I really haven't seen Dennis much at all, because he's not around all the time in the Men's Dormitory Area like he used to be. So, we just had lots of things to get caught up on, mostly about our classes and what we've been learning, especially in German. We have the same German course but in two different sections, and the instructors are doing very different things. Plus, Dennis was interested in knowing what I've been reading and learning about ancient history and classical civilization; and you know how I am when someone gets me started on those subjects. Renny finally kicked us out of his room when he got tired of listening to us and was ready for bed. We then went over into the Holmes lounge and just kept on talking. Then of course, we got hungry. You know how we are about food. So, then we headed over to the Snack Bar and sat down there at a table and kept on talking while we ate; and before we knew it, it was dawn."

As soon as they reached the house, Grant announced, "I think I'll first take a shower before lying down, because if I sleep all day, I might not get up in time to take one before we go back again." He now went into the bathroom located between the master bedroom and the laundry room, the one with the shower stall. After he undressed and was moving about naked and looking for what he needed (soap, shampoo, wash cloth, and towel), Dorothy, always the perfectly helpful Ma, came in to make sure that he was finding everything, and that he knew how to operate the water controls. Dorothy's presence caused Grant to have an erection, which she could not help but notice. She loved the sight of his young muscular naked body and especially of his erect penis surrounded by his bright red hair. Since her first sight of the latter five weeks ago, it always thrilled her mightily to gaze upon what she was now thinking of as "his beautiful red cock," because his aroused state was entirely the result of Grant's desire for her. How very flattering! Grant, of course, was glad to show himself to her; and by the time that he was ready to take his shower, they both realized how much the two of them were both enjoying Grant's erection. He could tell from how Dorothy was standing near him and positioning her body that she was feasting her eyes upon his manhood and did not want to let his erection out of her sight. It created very pleasant stirrings down there below her navel. His penis was bright pink from all the blood swelling it, almost red, a beautiful red cock! Grant, of course, was exhilarated by Dorothy's fascination with his penis, and it felt so good to be big and hard and to know that she enjoyed the sight. It was almost as if she were masturbating him. Indeed, she was masturbating him with her eyes, and he wanted the pleasure never to end. It all therefore quickly became a perfect feedback cycle: Grant eager to display his manhood to her, she completely willing to consume his proffered product with her eyes, and her obvious enjoyment greatly pleasing Grant and ensuring that his manhood would remain standing at full attention for as long as she looked.

They both now began to contrive ways of delaying Grant's entry into the shower stall. They kept asking one another questions or making comments to prolong their conversation. Very soon, Grant no longer felt fatigue from being up all night, but he was so excited and aroused that he forgot all about his need to sleep and decided to enjoy their lovely erotic interaction through the medium of his erect penis for as long as possible. Although nothing was openly said by either of them as to what was really going on between them, Dorothy was tacitly in full agreement with Grant that the exhibition should just keep going on and on. Since she was already busy doing several loads of laundry and needed to tend the washer and dryer that were in the laundry room adjoining the bathroom, it was quite easy for them to prolong the erotic display. The result was a wonderful cock show that lasted for several hours.

Then, as they moved about from room to room, they conversed about the upcoming trip to Houston, and Dorothy also used the occasion to give Grant a full family history of her much younger brother Tim and his wife Marilyn, as well as numerous anecdotes about her magnificent trip to Hawaii with her mom and Bethany to visit Tim when he was on leave there. Their interaction accordingly resembled their other recent times together at the house, but with the important addition of Grant's erection being constantly on display for their mutual pleasure and enjoyment.

Grant finally did enter the shower, but as soon as he stepped out, she was there to watch him dry off, and they resumed the erotic exhibition of his beautiful red cock as they had done before. They found countless things to do and talk about as Grant was supposedly about ready to lie down for his snooze. When he finally did lie down on the bed in the front bedroom, the very site of The Great Apocalypse exactly one month ago, he did so fully naked without his usual t-shirt and undershorts that always served as his pajamas. Dorothy lay down beside him. She was wearing a double-knit top and slacks. When he rolled against her, she spread her thighs and thus invited him to mount her. If she were not married, she would undress and eagerly receive that beautiful red cock inside her. Grant humped her crotch with his erection and ejaculated into her clothes. As soon as his penis had finished convulsing against her, Dorothy wailed in a voice full of anguish, "I should just give myself to you for as much as you want, and you could then rid yourself of the infatuation that you have for me!" Her heart-wrenching lament seemed to mourn two things: the fact that she was married to another man; and her fear that his infatuation would eventually pass away, and she would then be abandoned. Grant was greatly moved by her pain and said in reply, "Dorth, what I feel for you is much more than crude youthful lust. I really love you. It is not some short-lived infatuation, believe me! Of course, I want you and desperately so. Why wouldn't and shouldn't I? You're so utterly wonderful as a person and also so very beautiful as a woman, I love you, and I'm young with the normal physiological responses of a young man."

Grant mounted her again and came a second time. She then arose from the bed to go do other things, while Grant lay down to sleep. But even though he had been awake now for over twenty-four hours, he soon realized that he was too stirred up to relax and go to sleep. He therefore arose, and they both gladly resumed their enjoyment of The Cock Show. As before, Dorothy went about the house doing various things to have everything in order before leaving for her trip to Houston; and Grant accompanied her everywhere and placed himself on continual display, and she was a most assiduous spectator. She was amazed at his incredible stamina, his ability to remain fully erect hour after hour, even after he had ejaculated twice into her crotch. At one point Dorothy called Houston to speak with Marilyn about their upcoming trip; and while she sat on the edge of the bed in the master bedroom and talked on the telephone, Grant sat at her feet on the floor, caressed her body, and discovered to his delight that her crotch now had the smell of his semen. Although he had covered her clothes there with a large amount of his semen, she had not bothered to change into other clothes, because she enjoyed having his mark down there, the signature of his love and passion for her.

After eating lunch, they lay down together again, and Grant mounted her a third time and came in her crotch as before. When it was time for them to leave to take him to the library, they went into the master bedroom to dress. Since her slacks and panties had been saturated with his semen, she was obliged not only to remove and change her slacks, but also her panties. As soon as Grant sensed that she was naked, he embraced her with his own naked body, so that his love-spike burrowed into her bare love-delta. "Why don't you let me enter you?" he urgently asked. In a very weak and sad voice she replied, "I really wish you wouldn't." They were both torn by conflicting thoughts and emotions. He desired her so greatly and also knew that what he was asking of her was improper and virtually impossible for her to grant. She really desired to have him inside her, but apart from her marital status, she also feared that his penis, whose stamina had been so evident throughout the day, might impregnate her. Nevertheless, she sat down on the side of the bed, lay back across it, and spread her thighs for him. Grant bent down over her but could not get his penis to enter her vagina. Unknown to him at the time, his failure was due to the fact that her legs were dangling over the edge of the bed and therefore kept her vagina tipped downward, not upward, so that penetration was virtually impossible from where he stood. After rubbing the head of his erection inside the lips of her lovely vulva, Grant gave up the attempt of actually entering her. He then straightened up and proceeded to dress himself. Dorothy sat back up with obvious relief and also proceeded to get herself dressed. Grant, on the other hand, was somewhat disappointed but also felt rather ashamed that he had attempted this without her full willingness and cooperation. They dressed in silence, and she then took him to the library. His desire and failure to enter her vagina and their mixed emotions about it all perfectly epitomized the wonderful but painful and turbulent nature of their relationship at this time.

October 25, 1972, Wednesday

During Dorothy's visit in Houston, Grant experienced major emotional tumult nearly as serious as what had resulted four weeks earlier in his bizarre absconding to De Kalb. For the past two years or so Grant had been keeping a dream diary, written in braille, and which by now had become quite voluminous. It not only recorded Grant's dreams, but his commentary upon and analysis of his dreams. Dorothy had therefore recently expressed her grave concern, bordering upon panic, that Dennis or Renny could come upon these writings in Grant's dorm room and read portions of the dream diary that might reveal details about their love affair. Although Grant had assured her that Dennis and Renny never visited his dorm room, Dorothy's worrying about their secret relationship becoming exposed through Grant's dream diary was not the least bit allayed by Grant's assurances. Consequently, as Grant sank into depression and despair over the apparent futility of their love, exacerbated by Dorothy's absence, Grant convinced himself that he could win credit with his darling by sacrificing his dream diary upon the altar of their love affair. When he finally arrived at this determination and summoned up the necessary resolve, around 10:00 that evening he carried the two large notebooks containing his dream diary from his dorm room and out into an open area near the front doors of the dorm, where a large trash barrel was located. He then proceeded to empty out the notebooks and then to tear all the braille pages into pieces as he dropped the destroyed material into the barrel. While doing so, Grant was crying and felt utterly miserable both for the loss of his dream diary and for what seemed to be the hopelessness of their love. As a result, this month began and ended with events that inflicted severe anguish and torment upon Grant, greatly interfered with his ability to concentrate on his schoolwork, and caused his academic performance to suffer significantly. Grant soon deeply regretted destroying this irreplaceable material, but its destruction epitomized the volatile and tumultuous nature of their relationship at this time.

November 6, 1972, Monday

It was nearly 11:00 P.M., and Grant was spending the night at the house. Since there was now an autumnal chill in the air, they were not sitting side by side on the couch in the family room, but instead, they were lying down on it, fully clothed and lovingly snuggled together and wrapped up in a wagon wheel afghan that Dorothy's mother had made. Dorothy had returned from Houston just a few days ago, and this was their first meeting since then. They had not been together since October 19, that marvelous day of The Cock Show. As they conversed, they punctuated their remarks with delightfully erotic kisses, and they also both enjoyed having Grant's perpetually hard manhood pressing amorously into her.

"You know," Dorothy said, "When George picked me up at the airport here in University City a few days ago, I noticed how old he looked." "Nothing like your young red-headed boyfriend?" Grant asked mischievously. "Well," she replied with some embarrassment, "I really didn't mean that, exactly!" "Oh yes you did, and it's ok. In fact, it's wonderful! Besides, you're not old at all! You're so damn beautiful! And my golly, what's even more important, you have such a young inner spirit and outlook on everything. In that way you're so much like us university guys."

"But I guess, you haven't heard," Dorothy continued, "While I was away in Houston, Carol got herself into a bit of trouble, mostly because she should have told an adult parent what was about to happen." "What did happen?" Grant asked. "One of Carol's friends, Pam Gibson, decided to run away from home to visit her boyfriend, because his family had moved away to Wisconsin. Carol decided to go along with Pam to keep her out of trouble. They first went to the bank and withdrew all the money in their savings accounts, took a taxi to the bus station, and boarded a bus to Chicago. But before they changed to a bus that was going to Wisconsin, Pam called another boyfriend in University City. He told his parents what Pam and Carol were doing, and the parents informed George and Vivian Gibson. They called the police; and a police car eventually caught up with the bus, pulled it over, and took Pam and Carol into custody. Then when a policeman asked them if they would stay in a hotel room if they were placed there, Carol answered honestly that her friend Pam would not, but she would run away again. So, they put the two girls in a jail cell until George and Pam's parents arrived to bring them back to University City. We're not punishing Carol over this, because she realized that Pam was doing a foolish thing, and she just went along with her to try to keep her out of some really serious trouble."

The incident naturally led them to talk at length about Carol. It was so obvious from the way in which she talked about her younger daughter that Dorothy loved her as dearly as a parent could love his or her child. She told how Carol as a small child kept insisting that she be taught how to tie her own shoes, but Dorothy kept telling her that she was too young. Eventually, however, Dorothy gave in and tried to teach her, and Carol did not give up until she finally learned. When they and another family were driving in two cars through Yellowstone Park, Carol, who was only about five, happened to be riding with the other family; and when they stopped and rolled down a window to give something to a bear, Carol read them the riot act about not feeding them. Then there was the time that Carol had a tear in her slip, but instead of telling her mother and asking her to fix it, she tried fixing it on her own. When Dorothy noticed that her dress was looking funny, she asked to look at it and discovered that Carol had used about fifty safety pins to try to mend the tear. She was only about seven at the time. Dorothy then said, "She has such determination when she wants to do something. She's been like that ever since I can remember; and she's the only one of the three kids who really likes to help around the house. She has such a sweet and wonderful disposition and really enjoys doing things for other people." "Just like her mom," Grant interjected. "Oh yeah?" Dorothy replied with obvious pleasure both for Carol and herself. "You bet ya!" Grant emphasized and then underscored with a loving kiss.

Then Dorothy poured out her heart to Grant about all the agony that Carol had gone through with school. Both Dorothy's words and voice carried such obvious pain and sadness for her beloved daughter. Grant was deeply touched and did his best to sympathize. Dorothy then began to talk about her other two kids, Sally and Wesley; and it was also evident that Dorothy severely blamed herself for their shortcomings. Sally was so self-centered, if not actually very selfish, stubborn, and often so hard to get along with. Wesley was an odd mixture of things: sweet and often willing to help like Carol, but also too much like George in not sticking to anything very long, although he clearly was very gifted mentally. During his years in grade school he had driven her nutty, trying to get him to do his homework. She virtually had to stand over him to motivate him to get it done.

These feelings, especially the ones of self-blame, had been locked up inside of Dorothy for a very long time; and it felt so good to unburden herself to Grant. He responded by trying to prove to her that she had little to blame herself for. "Now look here, Lady," he began somewhat sternly, "I really don't want you blaming yourself for how your kids are turning out. I don't know them well, but well enough, I think; but I also know you extremely well. Let me first tell you that any kid in his right mind would absolutely love having you as their mother. I've never encountered anyone who has done so much in supporting their kids in all their activities and schooling as you. From what I can tell, you have always been so energetic and fully involved in your kids' lives; and you are also so totally open hearted and loving, like no one else I've ever met. I don't want to find fault with my mother, who has actually been a very good mother as far as I am concerned, but she can't even come close to you. Now just think about it. You have three kids, all of them growing up in the same household, and they have turned out so very different. But did you raise them differently?" "No, but I had to treat them a little different because of who they are and how they behave," Dorothy answered. "Exactly," Grant stressed. "And that's because they are different in some very basic ways that your childrearing has nothing to do with. There's that old idea that when we are born, we are like a completely blank slate upon which our upbringing and experiences write out what we become, but that theory just doesn't hold up well to reality. Let me give you an example. When I was about seven years old, I was already using my weekly allowance to buy books to learn about science. Now where did that come from? Neither one of my parents encouraged that. Just the opposite. I remember when I asked my mother for a chemistry set for my eighth birthday or something, she was really bothered by my request. She wanted me to be like the other boys in the neighborhood in wanting a toy gun or something like that. She really gave me the impression that she thought that I was a freak of some sort. I did get the chemistry set, but my parents both came from simple farm backgrounds with very rudimentary educations. So, I guess what I'm trying to point out to you is that of course how we are raised does influence us, but there are also so many things already built into us that even the best or the worst child rearing cannot change or only modify. Just think about it. If we are born with a certain eye color, hair color, blood type, or shape of our nose or something, we can't change those things, and many of them are determined by what we inherit from our parents. Why shouldn't there be other things about our personalities and characters that are also greatly influenced by what we have inherited from them? So, Dorth, I really mean this. Do not blame yourself for your kids' shortcomings, because I can see very clearly that you have been about the best parent that anyone could ever hope to be, and whom any child would really love to have."

What Grant had just said made such good sense. For years and years Dorothy had been investing so much of her time and energy into her three kids, and she had become so discouraged so many times, because it did seem as if none of her effort much mattered, and she had often blamed herself for it. Grant had given her an entirely new perspective, one that seemed so obvious and also lifted from her an enormous burden of guilt.

"You know what?" she asked. "No. What?" "You're mature beyond your years." "Oh yeah?" he replied with amusement and pleasure. "Yeah, you really are!" she answered seriously and with genuine admiration. This conversation therefore became important in bringing the two lovers much closer together.

November 16, 1972, Thursday

Shortly after supper, Carol had gone off for a while to do something with a friend; and while they were left alone in the house, Grant asked her to get out her encyclopedia to find a section on the female sexual anatomy, because he wanted to learn all the terms for the different parts. Dorothy gladly agreed, but when Grant wanted her to correlate the book's diagram to her own female anatomy for him, she had politely declined with a lovely and affectionate smile in her voice. Nevertheless, the lesson had been fun and informative for them both. Later, when Carol had returned home, they had busied themselves more primly by sitting on the living room couch and going through a book catalogue from Blackwell Publishers of London to find and order books on ancient history that Grant wanted.

"So," Dorothy asked, "why are you wanting to buy all these books on ancient history? I know that you enjoy learning this stuff, but these books are going to cost you quite a bit of money." "Yeah well," Grant replied, "I've been reassessing my career goals." "Oh yeah?" "Yep! As you know, I came here to the university, intending to become some kind of engineer or specialist in physics, hoping that I would someday be employed by NASA, because I enjoy astrophysics so very much. But, you know, the Apollo space program seems to be winding down, and I'm not sure that my original goals along those lines will pan out. So, I've been wondering if I should switch my interests over to ancient Greek and Roman history and plan to become a college professor teaching those subjects. I've therefore decided to start spending part of my scholarship money in buying books like this to start forming my own personal professional library that I would need if I do in fact become a college professor." "That sounds reasonable," Dorothy responded, "You talk about the Greeks and Romans all the time and do so with such obvious passion and interest that it gets other people interested too. Just based on what I've seen so far, I'm sure that you'd be a really good teacher of those subjects." "I'm glad you think so. Ever since my senior year in high school when we read Vergil's *Aeneid* in my Latin class, I've been becoming more and more interested and really fascinated with ancient Greece and Rome. During my freshman year here and the following summer break I found myself spending most of my free time in reading Latin texts and classical literature in translation." "Wow!" Dorothy exclaimed, "I don't think that I know anyone whose idea of having fun is reading Latin in their spare time." "Yeah well," Grant laughed, "That's me, I guess. So it made sense for me last year to take the ancient history survey course and courses on classical civilization to fulfill some of my basic curriculum requirements; but to me, they're just like you." "What do you mean?" Dorothy asked in genuine puzzlement. "Well," Grant said smiling broadly, "I just can't get enough of them or you!" "Ok," she replied laughingly as she punched him on the shoulder, "That's enough of that! Time to get back to work."

They then turned their attention back to the book catalogue; and by the time that they had made their way completely through it and had filled out the order form with a check, Carol had gone off to bed. They had moved from the living room couch to the one in the family room, because the latter was somewhat more secluded and thus afforded them a greater sense of security in not being seen if Carol were to arise from bed and to come looking for her mother.

As midnight approached, they were again wrapped up together in the wagon wheel afghan, lying on the family room couch, fully clothed but amorously pressed together and trading wonderful kisses. Dorothy had been thinking recently about her father, because he had died nine years ago around this time of the year, and she still missed him very much. Consequently, after she and Grant had talked even more at length about him becoming a college professor of ancient Greek and Roman history, she began telling him once again about her father. It still pained her to remember how the cancer had turned the skin of his neck so hard and dry that it had the appearance of alligator skin. But most of what she shared with Grant were things that showed what a truly wonderful man he had been. He fed the squirrels in their yard; and they became so accustomed to him that they would come up and take nuts out of his hand. She remembered him getting her down out of a tree, because Bethany had taunted her into climbing up, but then she was too afraid to climb down; and Bethany was the one who got in trouble for it. When she and Bethany were still small, Gloria would entrust them to Babe as they shopped in a store, so that she could go off to look at things, but Babe would eventually release the girls' hands and let them run off; and when Gloria went racing after them, he simply stood there and laughed. After several more anecdotes of this sort, Grant finally said, "Your father sounds like he was like you in being so young at heart. I really wish that I could have known him." "I do too," Dorothy replied, "I'm sure you would have liked him."

When they finally arose and went off to their different beds, Dorothy continued to mull over in her mind what they had discussed that evening. It felt so good to confide in Grant her thoughts and feelings about her dear father. Sharing them with him had felt so good and was emblematic of the growing emotional bond between her and Grant. It was the first time in a long time that she had talked with anyone about her beloved father. In fact, ever since their magical summer, she always felt so very contented from being with Grant and talking with him about whatever happened to be on her mind. One other result of their talking tonight had been Grant sharing with her his newly formulated dream of becoming a college professor of ancient Greek and Roman history. She had been genuinely intrigued and excited by their conversation on this subject. He became so animated when he spoke of this dream. His enthusiasm was infectious. It was a truly beautiful dream. It captivated her. She had long recognized that of her university kids Grant was by far the most studious and academically gifted. If anyone could achieve that beautiful dream, she thought, Grant was the one. It was still far from clear as to how and in what way their relationship would work itself out, but she now began to wonder if she could join him in his beautiful dream. How lovely that would be! She therefore resolved that henceforth she would do all that she could in helping him realize that dream; and her resolution became another important element in drawing the two lovers closer together.

November 22, 1972, Wednesday

The university was rapidly closing down for the Thanksgiving holiday, but Grant had decided not to return to Fairmont. Rather than going home and being with his family, he much preferred being alone with his schoolwork and his thoughts about his darling Dorothy. She and Carol would be leaving later that afternoon to drive down to Newton to spend the holiday with George and his mother, but right now Grant and Dorothy were moving some of his things out of Holmes into Watson, a nearby dormitory. The latter was the only dorm that was being kept open during the holiday for students who could not or chose not to leave. Grant therefore needed to move whatever he was going to need over the next few days into a room in Watson. To do this, they used a large cart somewhat similar to a child's wagon, although its bed was much wider and longer, it was very low to the ground, and it had to be pulled by a large upright rectangular frame welded to one end. They had to make three trips between Holmes and Watson with this cart; and when they unloaded it and were ready to return with it empty, Grant insisted that Dorothy sit down on the bed, so that he could give her a ride. By doing so, they transformed the work of moving into a lovely little game, as if they were children playing outside with a wagon. It was delightful! Grant thought to himself, "How many 44-year-old women would regard this as fun? What a perfect illustration of my darling's joyful love of life and of the eternally young spirit within her!"

November 23-25, 1972, Thanksgiving Holiday

Although Grant had planned to use these three days to do nothing but study in order to regain much of the ground that he had lost over the past two months in his academic work, his attempt failed. Since classes had begun that fall, his relationship with Dorothy had been so all-consuming that it had almost entirely dominated his mind with either exhilarating highs or plunges downward into the lowest despair. As the result of such emotional instability, he had not been able to concentrate upon his schoolwork as he should. Indeed, during these three days of the Thanksgiving break Grant did spend all of his time in reading for his courses, but his total isolation from all human contact in the dorm room of Watson Hall had the effect of causing his mind to be so absorbed with thoughts of his darling and what she was doing in Newton that he found it all but impossible to absorb what he was reading. So, like October, this month too wound up being an academic disaster for Grant, caused by the standoff between keeping their physical involvement within reasonable bounds and allowing it to develop further. They had, as usual, been spending as much time together as they could manage; and on week nights, when they were not together, they usually engaged in lengthy telephone conversations. They therefore continued to become closer emotionally and spiritually, while their physical interaction was limited to embracing, petting, and prolonged passionate kissing, which strayed considerably beyond Dorothy's reasoned resolve to have them simply be very special friends, but it had not progressed further into the direction that Grant's passionate ardor for his woman desired. Consequently, by the time that these three days had expired, Grant found himself to be no better off academically, and his mind had been so fully occupied with Dorothy and his passion for her that he was simply interested in being reunited with his wonderful woman.

November 26, 1972, Sunday

"Your hair's looking a bit long and ragged there, buddy," Dorothy said jokingly. "Oh yeah?" Grant replied. They were sitting at the kitchen table eating popcorn, Dorothy's traditional easy Sunday night supper. Carol and she had driven back by themselves from Newton after Sunday dinner at noon; and shortly thereafter Dorothy had called Grant and asked him if he wanted to come over for the night. Of course, he did, but first they had to move his things from Watson back to Holmes. After that the three of them (Carol, Dorothy, and Grant) had just been enjoying a quiet Sunday evening in the house. Carol was watching TV just a few feet away in the family room.

"How would you like me to cut your hair for you?" Dorothy offered. "That would be really neat!" So, as soon as they had finished their popcorn, Dorothy sat one of the kitchen chairs a few feet away on the edge of the carpet of the family room. "Ok," she said, "Sit down here in this chair, and hold this towel tight around your neck." Grant did as commanded and then sat still as Dorothy moved around him, combing his hair and clipping it with a pair of scissors. Grant wore his hair long and parted straight back along the left side. It was such an enjoyable experience, having this wonderful woman touching his hair and being so close. Dorothy likewise enjoyed handling and shaping the bright red hair of this boy-man of whom she was so very fond. It was one way in which they could be somewhat intimate while Carol was still up.

As Dorothy worked away on his hair, Grant asked her what all they had done while in Newton; and Dorothy chattered away telling him, but when she happened to mention quite innocently that Ellen Patterson had called late Thursday night from South Carolina and had gotten them up out of bed, Grant's overly sensitive mind conjured up the image of Dorothy and George lying together in bed, and the picture greatly disturbed him. He hoped that he had not betrayed his anguish at hearing those words. Dorothy did not seem to notice, because her narrative did not lose a beat.

Dorothy finally stopped clipping and used the comb to touch up his hair. She then carefully rolled up the towel and asked, "How does that feel?" Grant raised his hands to his head and looked it over. "It looks fine, I think. Thanks. That was really nice." "Here," she said, as she handed him the towel, "Step out on the back porch and shake it off, while I get the vacuum cleaner and sweep up the carpet." Grant again happily obeyed. He had just received his first haircut at the dainty hands of this dazzling and adorable woman. In fact, for the next thirty years Grant never went to a barbershop to have his hair cut. Instead, that task would be henceforth performed carefully and lovingly by his darling Dorothy, and he always regarded her cutting his hair as an expression of their closeness and true love, as it certainly was!

Chapter 7

The Erotic Winter

During the autumn of 1972 Dorothy lived not simply a double life, but a triple one. First, there was her conventional life as wife and mother. Then there was her second life, continued from the previous year, being the ever solicitous Ma to her beloved university kids, who now included not only Dennis, Renny, Bob, and Kitty, but also Pam Stewart and Lisa Harris. As before, this second life took the form of occasional parties at the house and helping the kids with shopping and other errands, but it also now included bowling at the Student Union for about two hours every Sunday evening. She also met with Debbie regularly to help her shop for things and simply to talk, because Debbie still often suffered from depression.

Dorothy's third life was, of course, what had now become her secret love-life with Grant. Carol was the only outsider who was somewhat aware of their times at the house together, but since she was accustomed to her mother being so heavily involved in the lives of her blind students, and since Carol was fully occupied with her own friends and teenage concerns, she did not give the matter any serious thought. In fact, one night in November as Dorothy and Grant were lying wrapped up together in the wagon wheel afghan on the couch in the family room, Carol had awakened; and when she did not find her mother in bed in the master bedroom, she walked through the house to find her and happened to see them on the couch together. Dorothy was obviously greatly concerned by what Carol had seen and might think. When she explained to her the next day that she had simply been comforting Grant, because he was having serious problems, Carol accepted her mother's explanation and never gave the matter further thought.

Central to Dorothy's third life were her lengthy conversations with Grant on the telephone and in person. These were very important in gradually drawing them even more closely together emotionally and spiritually; and this closeness finally began to have its powerful physical counterpart during the last month of the year.

December 5, 1972, Tuesday

It was 10:20 P.M., and Dorothy was on her way home from Sweet Adelines practice. She had no interest in accompanying the others to the Jolly Roger Restaurant for a late night snack. What she had waiting at home for her interested her far more. She had picked Grant up from campus in the late afternoon; and he, Carol, and she had had supper together, before Dorothy went off to her Tuesday singing. Carol by now would be in bed asleep, but Grant would still be up waiting for her, after he had spent the evening studying.

She entered the house, went into the master bedroom to hang up her coat, stopped in the adjoining bathroom, and then joined Grant on the living room couch, where he had been reading during her absence. He now stopped his work, and they sat side by side and began to tell one another quietly how their respective evenings had gone. Touching and embracing eventually led them to lie down together fully clothed on the couch, where they continued to talk, but it was now accompanied by kissing and the shared pleasure of Grant's erection pressing urgently into her.

Usually, when they lay down together on the couch in the family room or living room, Grant lay along the back of the couch, and Dorothy lay on its outer edge with Grant's arms around her to keep her from falling off. Dorothy always preferred this position, because if Carol happened to arise from bed and walk in upon them, she could quickly sit up as if nothing unusual were happening between them. Tonight, however, for some reason or other, their positions were reversed. Dorothy lay along the back of the couch, and Grant along its outer edge. The reversal had an important difference that they had not previously experienced. Since Dorothy's body was sandwiched between Grant and the back of the couch, he could press his erection into her abdomen much more forcefully, and the contact between his love-spike and her love-delta gave them both tremendous pleasure.

Their positions also led to another hitherto unexperienced delight. Since Dorothy was about eight inches shorter than Grant, whenever they were standing on their feet and embracing, his erection pressed into her abdomen not far below her navel. But when they were lying on the couch as now, with their upper bodies in alignment, rather than their feet, his erection was pressing into her abdomen much lower, actually into the very apex of her love-delta and her vulva. Despite the layers of clothing that separated their flesh, the persistent pressure of Grant's penis into the apex of her love-delta soon began to inflict sweet pleasure upon her clitoris, so that Dorothy became increasingly sexually aroused. Their lips and tongues were acting out the passion that they were feeling even more intensely by their loins locked together. It felt so very good that neither of them wanted to move to disrupt the magnificent pleasure. Soon they were enveloped in a cocoon of pleasure and desire in perfect harmony: their desire spawning the sweet delicious pleasure, and the latter sustaining their desire for each other. Consequently, they wound up lying there in this manner for more than two hours.

"I think it's about time that we should be going off to bed," Dorothy said reluctantly, "I'm beginning to get tired and sleepy, and I shouldn't take the chance of falling asleep here on the couch." After a languorous pause punctuated with several kisses, Grant replied, "yeah, it is getting late, but I really don't want to move." "Neither do I, but we do need to be going to bed soon." After an even longer pause, Grant plucked up his courage and uttered as a question what he was now desiring passionately, the direct result of their prolonged sexual intimacy there on the couch. "Would you mind if I came into the bedroom and helped you undress?" "I guess that would be all right," she answered mildly," as if there were nothing unusual about this request. Then she continued, "But first let me check on Carol and make sure that she's in her own bed, because sometimes she comes and gets in bed with me."

Despite the apparent casualness of Grant's request and Dorothy's assent, they were both in fact entirely unprecedented. Grant had never before asked to undress her, and she had never allowed him to do so. In addition, throughout the month of November, apart from a few quick feels of her sex as he reached his hand down inside her slacks and panties, Dorothy had been very successful in resisting Grant's most intimate advances and her own desire to exhibit her womanhood to him. But tonight's loving on the couch had joined them into such a wonderful atmosphere of erotic pleasure and desire that they were both willing and eager to carry their love-pleasure beyond the customary and into a new realm of delicious experience.

As Dorothy stood and went down the hall to look into Carol's room, Grant sat anxiously on the couch. She soon returned and whispered, "Ok, let's go." They now walked quietly through the kitchen, laundry room, and bathroom to enter the master bedroom. They walked straight ahead until Dorothy came alongside the bed and stopped. She then turned around to face him. What followed was done in perfect silence in the darkness of the room.

After allowing him to unzip the front of her top, she pulled it off over her head and then carefully laid it down on the bed beside her. She next held her arms out to the side, so that Grant could reach his hands behind her and unfasten her bra. He then removed it by sliding the shoulder straps down along her arms. As he did, he could feel the cups coming away from her breasts; and after handing her the bra, he filled his hands with those twin beauties, soft, firm, heavy, warm, and so alluringly fragrant with her White Shoulders perfume. After tenderly kissing each one and reluctantly releasing her breasts, he knelt on the floor before her, untied her shoes, and slipped them off her feet. Their hands now met at her waist, as they both began to pull down her slacks. Grant moved the garment down to her feet and helped her step out of it. When he handed the slacks to her, Dorothy folded them up and laid them down on the bed. As she was thus employed, Grant was moving her panties down off of her shapely hips. It was the very first time that he had had the honor of doing this, and it was a truly wonderful experience: first working the elastic over her wide feminine hips, then pulling the panties down from her bottom, and finally freeing them from the apex of her sex and sliding them down her legs to her feet. As he slipped the panties off one foot at a time, she was standing totally undressed in front of him with her naked womanhood just inches from his face. He wanted to kiss her there, but he was afraid that it might offend her. Instead, his hands traveled over her warm smooth body, caressing her beautiful female flesh, but there was one place that he hesitated to touch, her lovely sex. While he hesitated, Dorothy, sensing his caution, stood naked before him and occupied herself by picking up her cotton nightgown from the edge of the bed and fiddling with it, while waiting for her young man to muster up the sufficient courage to claim his grand prize for the night, as they both greatly desired him to do. When his hands ceased roaming about on her body, she knew that the moment had arrived. She was aware of him shifting his position; and as he did, she finally opened up the nightgown and prepared to drop it down over her head. Grant placed his left arm around her lower back to offer her support, and at the same time he slid his right hand up between her legs. She parted her thighs in response to the upward movement of his hand and thus spread herself open for him. As her cotton nightgown was cascading down over her body, Grant filled his right hand with her female perfection and even inserted his middle finger into her vagina. As on earlier such occasions, his finger entered her easily, because she was wet and dilated with desire from their kissing and lying together. But most thrilling of all, his finger's entry into her sex caused her such intense pleasure that her already heightened state of sexual arousal instantly brought her to the edge of an orgasm, and her body shuddered as she uttered a small gasp of surprise and ecstasy. In fact, the pleasure struck her with such force and suddenness that she nearly crumpled to the floor in delight, but she kept herself from doing so by reaching out with her right hand and taking hold of Grant's left shoulder for support. After withdrawing his arm from her lower back and from underneath the nightgown, he also reluctantly removed his hand from between her thighs, arose from the floor, and went off to his own bed. He had wanted to linger, but he was afraid that he had already taken things as far as she wanted them to go. But when he settled down in bed, he enjoyed the heavenly scent of her love-honey on his finger.

The climax of their night together beside her bed had not lasted very long, but it had been absolutely marvelous for them both!

December 6, 1972, Wednesday

By 7:00 A.M. they all three were up and about. Dorothy was in the kitchen making breakfast for everyone, while Carol washed and dressed herself for school. Grant went back into the living room and busied himself with his schoolwork so as to be out of the way and to allow mother and daughter to have as normal a morning as possible without him intruding upon them. When Dorothy announced, "Breakfast is ready," the other two eventually drifted in to have a bowl of cornmeal mush. Grant then returned to his work in the living room until Carol left for school, at which time he rejoined Dorothy in the kitchen, where she was cleaning things up and setting out the left-over cornmeal mush to cool and harden. She was clad in only her house slippers, cotton nightgown, and pink quilted robe.

"I've never eaten cornmeal mush before," said Grant, as he came back into the kitchen. "Haven't you?" Dorothy asked. "No. my mother used to fix me and my sister oatmeal on cold days like today, but we never ate cornmeal mush. In fact, I still associate oatmeal with cold winter mornings before going off to school, and I can remember how my sister sat across the kitchen table from me and irritated me by making a kind of clicking sound as she struck the spoon against her front teeth. You know, it's really funny what little things like that a person remembers." "Yes it is," agreed Dorothy, "Bethany every now and then reminds me of some incident about a bicycle in which she, according to her, got the raw end of the deal from our parents. I don't even remember it, but it sure stuck in her craw and seems to form the basis of her view that our parents often treated her unfairly."

As they were talking, Grant walked up behind her and put his arms around her. When she finished what little task she was doing at the counter, she turned around and hugged him back. They then kissed, and Dorothy could feel his erection pressing into her. Their bodily contact instantly revived the extraordinary pleasure that they had enjoyed not too many hours earlier on the couch and beside her bed. When they finally broke their embrace, she returned to her work. "So," she asked, "how did you like the mush." "It was ok," Grant replied. "Just ok?" she asked with amusement in her voice. "Yeah, I must admit it's about the first thing that I've eaten of yours that I really don't love." "You mean I'm not the perfect cook you keep saying I am?" she asked in mock outrage. They embraced and kissed again.

"Well," Dorothy continued, "I guess it's not the greatest thing in the world, but my family likes it. My sisters and I grew up on it during The Depression, because it was so inexpensive. Many families who had never eaten it before wound up eating it a lot, because they couldn't afford much else. I guess, since we girls ate it so much from an early age, we came to like it; and even after The Depression ended, it just became another possible meal."

As Dorothy resumed her work at the counter, she stopped briefly, lowered her hands to her wait, and untied her robe, allowing it to fall open. So, when Grant returned for another embrace and kiss and discovered that the belt of her robe was untied, and her robe was open to him, he slid his hands and arms around her inside the robe and enjoyed the feel of her body beneath the thin single layer of cotton fabric.

"Right now," Dorothy explained, "I'm putting the left-over mush in a big container to set out and harden; and then when Carol comes home from school today, I'll slice it up into thin pieces, fry them in a skillet, and we'll eat fried mush with syrup and butter, sort of like pancakes." "Oh yeah?" Grant asked, "That's a new one on me too." "Well, that's another reason why so many people ate mush during The Depression. They not only ate it for breakfast as a cereal, but then they fried it up and ate it for supper."

This time when Grant came to embrace and kiss her amid her work, he did not take her shapely bottom into his hands and press her tightly against him. Instead, he held his body slightly to the side and slid his left arm inside her robe and around her waist, while his right hand held and fondled her sex through the nightgown. His fingers could easily feel everything, her lovely Venus V, her smooth soft but firm skin, her hair, and the cleft of her vulva. As they stood in the kitchen kissing with his hand enjoying the feel of her sex, Dorothy remained motionless and did nothing to indicate her disapproval of the fondling. In fact, her motionless receptivity signaled to Grant that she did not mind any of it in the least. She was once again in a state of sexual arousal that had easily been revived from their time on the couch and beside her bed hours earlier.

By now their erotic activity was taking on its all too common aspect. Grant would cautiously and slowly up the ante until Dorothy politely said or did something to check his advances, at which point he would halt and go no further. But in this case this morning in the kitchen Dorothy's state of sexual arousal down there in her love-zone ensured that she would not be halting the attentions of her young man. In addition, as their love-game continued, nothing was overtly said by either of them to draw attention to their erotic play, but their conversation went on as usual and served as a mask of normality over what they were doing and enjoying. Consequently, Dorothy's narration continued as if they were simply having an ordinary friendly talk, but the embracing, kissing, and fondling through the nightgown continued as lovely punctuation marks between all the small things that Dorothy was doing to tidy up the kitchen.

"I fix cornmeal mush every now and then, and all my kids like it. I'll make up a big batch in the morning like today; and we'll eat it for breakfast. Then we eat it later on or the next day as fried mush."

Since she had not done anything to prevent his fondling of her sex through the nightgown, Grant went the next step farther. As they kissed with her arms around him and his left arm around her, he slowly and cautiously lifted up her nightgown and fondled her bare womanhood. Dorothy again did or said nothing to indicate disapproval. Rather, since she stood motionless and greeted his lips eagerly with her own as his fingers loved and adored her sex, it became clear to Grant that his caresses down there were totally welcome to her this morning. For them both, it was the natural resumption of his finger entering her vagina and his hand clasping her sex beside the bed last night. That had felt so marvelously good to Dorothy, and so did his hand and fingers now. To Grant, of course, her female sex was the loveliest thing in the entire universe, and he could not fondle and admire her beauty enough!

"Anyway," she continued amid their mutual enjoyment of these delicious caresses, "Lee Thomas, the husband of my mom's best friend Jan, never would eat mush again after The Depression. I guess he never really liked it and probably also associated it with those bad times and didn't want to be reminded of them."

As she spoke, Dorothy interrupted her kitchen work to turn into another loving embrace; and once again, Grant encircled her waist inside her robe with his left arm while using his right hand to lift the curtain on what was now becoming Dorothy's Beautiful Pussy Show. Seven weeks earlier, just before she went off to Houston, Grant had given her a magnificent Cock Show that had lasted all morning long and into the afternoon. Although Dorothy had been quite protective of her sex during the month of November, last night on the couch and beside her bed had succeeded in opening a new door in their erotic activity, and she was quite willing to have her pussy pleasure them both. Thus, as she worked at the counter, she kept stopping and allowing her young man to put his left arm around her and to lift up her nightgown, thus raising the curtain on another act of her Beautiful Pussy Show. She was glad to have his one arm around her, because the pleasure of his finger-loving was so exquisite that she could hardly stay on her feet by herself. His fingers traveled over her sex again and again, exploring, examining, admiring, adoring every aspect of her: her lovely hair, her flawless skin, and the beautiful lips of her vulva. When his finger slipped inside her pussy lips and touched her most sensitive spot, her clitoris, it was all that she could do to maintain her steady flow of conversation in order to keep up the illusion that nothing the least bit unusual was transpiring between them. Since Grant simply could not get enough looking, their love-play there in the kitchen dragged on and on. As a result, what should have taken Dorothy less than ten minutes to complete at the counter stretched out to nearly an hour; and by the time that "Dorothy's Beautiful Pussy Show" finally ended, she had given her young man more access to her sex than she had given him over the past three months put together.

"Well, it looks like I'm done here." As she turned once again into Grant's embrace and allowed him to lift up her nightgown for a few more minutes of admiring her female sex, she finally ended her Beautiful Pussy Show by simply saying barely above a whisper, "Let's go lie down for a while."

Grant said nothing in reply. He simply followed. She was the one setting the agenda.

After walking through the laundry room and into the adjoining bathroom, they establish another new erotic precedent that henceforth became a standard aspect of their love-life. As she stopped at the toilet and sat down to urinate, for the first time Grant was standing next to her, and she said or did nothing to indicate her disapproval of his presence beside her. They both remained silent, the only sound being her urine pouring from her vulva into the toilet bowl. To Grant, it was a lovely sound; and even though he could not see her sitting there with her nightgown hiked up and her thighs parted, he could imagine it; and like his blind silent presence on the bed on September 13, when Dorothy undressed as he lay there, they now both relished their sharing of this experience.

After flushing and standing up, Dorothy led him into the master bedroom, where she stood at the foot of the bed, removed her robe, and laid it across the bottom of the bed. She then moved alongside the bed where they had undressed her last night. "Ok," she said, again barely above a whisper and after lying down, "come join me."

Grant wordlessly bent down and removed his shoes and socks, and then he took off his pants, all of which he simply left lying there on the floor. He was now wearing only a t-shirt and undershorts. Before lying down, he used his hands to see where she was, and how she was situated. To his amazement and great delight, he found her lying on her back on the bed's edge nearest him. Her nightgown was gathered up around her waist. Her knees were bent and tilted slightly upward, so that her thighs were spread beautifully open, as they had been on the Day of the Apocalypse. For the first time in their love-life she assumed the pussy-fuck pose, the position that a woman assumed when beckoning her man to mount her and enter her. She was clearly inviting her young man to lie down in her beautiful brunette love-nest. After caressing her spread sex in genuine awe, he lowered his body on top of her and between her legs. Not long after Grant's penis began nuzzling into her love-spread, he felt her hands down at his waist, tugging at the elastic band of his undershorts. Her message, though wordless, was loud and clear: "No, Silly Boy, I want to feel the real thing!" As soon as Grant realized what she wanted and was doing, he quickly came to her assistance, pushed down his shorts, and kicked them off.

They lay there together with their sexes enjoying the feel of the other. Dorothy reached down with her right hand between their bodies, took Grant's erection into her hand, and carefully guided it into her vulva, so that the underside of its large swollen head was touching her clitoris. As Grant moved his body slightly, the motion caused them both such sweet pleasure, as his penis masturbated her, and her vulva masturbated him. Because of his relative lack of experience in such things, Grant, of course, did not fully understand that his penis was gently masturbating her and giving his woman such deliciously sweet pleasure. All that he knew was that it felt magnificent, and for the first time his penis and her female sex were delighting one another: her pussy kissing his magnificent cock, and his cock caressing her pussy with such loving erotic tenderness.

Dorothy would have loved taking him fully inside her, but in addition to her marital status, the past few months had demonstrated to her what extraordinary stamina her young man's beautiful red cock possessed. He seemed to be able to stay erect for hours, could reach a climax several times in succession, and seemed to have an endless supply of sperm. Thus, what really made her reluctant to feel him inside her was not her marital status, but her fear of becoming pregnant. Her sex was affording her so much pleasure this morning that her marital status was actually quite far from her mind. She was so fully aroused and near the peak of an orgasm that she just wanted the pleasure to continue and continue; and having his beautiful red cock inside her vulva and caressing that most sensitive spot was the only thing that she could think about right now.

Whenever his penis slid out of her vulva, Dorothy instantly took him into her hand and positioned him again inside her lips for the continuation of this exquisite pleasure. For a very long time neither of them uttered a word, partly because doing so might break the beautiful spell of their love-pleasure and prompt Dorothy to reconsider what they were actually doing, and partly because they were both fully absorbed in the ecstasy. Dorothy was now completely sexually aroused and wanted to keep the gentle masturbation of her clitoris going without interruption. It was not vigorous enough to have her achieve an orgasm, but as long as his penis was moving in exactly the right place, it kept her in a continual heightened state of smoldering pleasure and desire. Their loving kept Grant's penis near or at the pinnacle of an orgasm, sometimes raising him to the very peak, but mostly sustaining him just below that point. Since Dorothy's pleasure required the stimulation of her clitoris, she kept using her hands, sometimes the right and other times the left, to reach between their bodies and move his penis slightly so as to keep her pleasure at its peak. She was therefore totally focused on managing the precise placement of his penis inside the lips of her sex. Grant was perfectly happy to do his job, to keep his erection moving slightly and gently to please them both, and oh how he also loved to feel her hand touching his penis and making the necessary minor adjustments!

They eventually began to utter occasional words or phrases, all of them associated with this extraordinary erotic entertainment. "Oops," one would say usually with a little laugh, as Grant's penis slipped out of her vulva once again. Or "There we go," as his penis was properly repositioned. Unfortunately, since Grant had to meet a reader at 11:00, their pleasure had to be terminated after a mere hour and a half, but they had never before so enjoyed themselves for such a long period of time. It was their first time to lie in bed together in the master bedroom and also their first real sexual activity involving the direct physical interplay between his penis and her sex. Dorothy had given her young man his first real taste of pussy pleasure, and oh my! how wonderful it had been! The experience also suggested that Dorothy's sexual appetite, dormant for so many years, had now finally been fully reawakened and was probably on a par with Grant's.

As she arose from the bed to dress for their departure, she was pleased to discover that her vulva and love-delta were richly adorned with his man cream. She did nothing to wipe it away. She would wear it throughout the day as a mark of their love and passion for one another. Their enjoyment of such intense love-pleasure during the night and this morning now formed an important landmark in their love-life. Henceforth, whenever Grant reached for her love-delta, either inside or outside her slacks and panties, she did not draw back or rebuff him. Instead, she always stood, sat, or lay still, allowing her young man to take his pleasure of her, because the pleasure that his touching of her sex gave him was always equaled by the pleasure that it gave her; and if he were too hesitant or shy to give her all the attention that she desired down there, she would invite him to look and look and to play and play.

In addition, from this day forward, whenever Grant happened to be in the house at bedtime, Dorothy allowed him to undress her before she put on her nightgown. similarly, whenever they were alone in the house, and Dorothy needed to go potty, Grant accompanied her into the bathroom, stood nearby as she urinated, and then clasped his hands to her bare sex and bottom when she stood up from the toilet. Only when he released her female beauty, would she pull her panties and slacks up and into place. Consequently, their night on the couch and beside her bed, Dorothy's Beautiful Pussy Show in the kitchen, and their love-play in bed henceforth totally redefined their sexual relationship, so that from now on, in a real sense, Dorothy was Grant's Pussy Woman, just as he was most definitely her Cock Man.

December 13, 1972, Wednesday

It was 11:00 A.M., and Grant should have already arrived at the Education Building to meet Larry Smithson in his office for their weekly reading session, but here he was still shambling along on Jordan Street with two whole blocks to go; and this damn ice and snow weren't helping the matter either. Unlike a sighted person, who can vary his pace and care on such a sidewalk by looking ahead to see where the surface is clear, and where it is not, a blind person, in order to travel safely, has to proceed slowly with the assumption that the very next step could spell disaster.

When Grant crossed Spruce Street and turned south to walk along its east side, he discovered that the sidewalk had been fully cleared of snow. So, in order to make up for lost time, he began moving along the sidewalk in a slow jog. Unfortunately, as he neared the end of the block just across the street from the Education Building, he hit the only small patch of ice on the sidewalk. His feet instantly flew straight out in front of him, his body went horizontal, and he fell very hard flat down on his back onto the concrete. The impact was so hard and sudden that it knocked the breath completely out of him, and all that he could do for several seconds was to utter animal-like sounds of pain. After recovering his breath, he slowly regained his feet and limped the rest of the way to Larry's office with his back hurting him severely.

When Larry saw Grant hunched over in obvious pain, he suggested that he call the student health center immediately, but Grant refused and insisted that they go ahead with their reading. They did, but after about fifteen minutes, Grant realized that he was feeling extremely nauseous inside and had better make it to the restroom as soon as possible. Since he had never been there before in this building, Larry guided the way in his electric wheelchair with Grant holding onto the back. He entered a stall; and as soon as he sat down, he instantly expelled an enormous amount from his large intestine. Apparently, the fall had literally knocked the shit right out of him. When they returned to Larry's office, Grant finally realized that he really needed to lie down to rest his back. He automatically called Dorothy, his angel of mercy, to have her come pick him up and return him to his dorm room, where he could spend the rest of the day recuperating in bed.

Luckily, she was at home and came immediately. After parking the car at Holmes, she walked him to his room and helped him undress and lie down. Even though he was experiencing discomfort from his back, he nevertheless derived much satisfaction from Dorothy's attention. "You look so lovely in your polar bear coat," he commented, as he ran his hand along the coat while she stood next to his bed. It was her heavy winter coat, whose outer surface had a slightly shaggy texture. Although Dorothy had told him that it was brown in color, he always pictured it in his mind as white whenever he touched it. He had therefore called it her polar bear coat; and whenever she was wearing it, he thought of her as his cuddly teddy bear.

"Is there anything else I can do for you before I leave?" she asked. "Actually there is," he replied, "How about masturbating me?" "What?" she exclaimed in genuine surprise, "You're hurt! You shouldn't be thinking about that right now!" "Yeah, I am hurt," he agreed, "but I still have an erection for you. Ah come on, you don't want me lying here all worked up, do you? I need to relax and rest." "But what if your roommate happens to walk in?" "Oh don't worry about that. He won't be coming back for quite a while yet." "Well ok," she agreed with a laugh, "but boy! I tell you!..."

Grant threw back the covers and pushed his shorts down. Dorothy bent over him and took his erect penis into her right hand; and after enclosing it in a delicate envelope of her fingers and thumb, she carefully moved her hand up and down rhythmically until he ejaculated. "I hope you're feeling better now," she teased. "That was wonderful," Grant said sincerely, "Thanks. I'm already feeling better." "Ok, you rest now, and call me if you need me to help you with anything else." "I will." She walked out and shut the door behind her, and Grant rested peacefully in bed for the entire afternoon.

December 19, 1972, Tuesday

Like two weeks before, Dorothy had brought Grant over to the house late in the afternoon, so that he could have supper with her and Carol and then study while she went off for the evening to Sweet Adelines. Afterwards, when they had been enjoying one another's company on the living room couch for a while, Dorothy said that she wanted to get out of her clothes and into her nightgown. When Grant asked, "Do you mind if I come along?" she replied, "No, that would be fine." What then followed was an undressing similar to what they had done two weeks before, except they did it more slowly with much more caressing to satisfy them both. After removing her bra, Grant knelt down before her; and in addition to holding those beauties in his hands, he stretched his body upward, so that he could take each breast in turn into his mouth to suck and lick. Dorothy enjoyed nursing her young lover. Next, they had the mutual pleasure of removing her slacks and panties. As Dorothy stood before him naked and was taking her time in finding her nightgown under the pillow on the bed, Grant caressed her whole body and finally stopped to fill his hands with her shapely ass. As he fondled this lovely part of her female anatomy, he moved his face forward, nuzzled his lips into her pubic hair, and gently planted a kiss on her love-delta at the beginning of her vulva. Dorothy instantly but gently placed her hands on Grant's head and pushed him away as she whispered, "Please! Don't do that. Ok?" "Why not?" Grant whispered back. "I probably don't smell very good," she apologized. "I doubt that," Grant answered in all honesty, but he obediently kept his face away from her sex as she preferred.

After putting on her nightgown and pink quilted robe, she stepped into her house slippers, and they returned to the living room couch, where they sat together with an afghan wrapped around them. The activity in the master bedroom had so aroused Grant that he placed her hand on top of his erection and asked her to masturbate him through his pants; and she did so by gently rubbing his penis. By now they were both thoroughly worked up, and their conversation took a backseat to their physical activity. As they chitchatted about the upcoming Christmas vacation, Grant's hands were inside her robe and underneath her nightgown, caressing and touching her body. They dared not, however, lie down on the couch for fear of Carol seeing them again. But after an hour or so of delicious petting, Grant had Dorothy masturbate him a second time.

The petting and chitchat continued until about 2:00 A.M. Dorothy now indicated that she was becoming sleepy and suggested that they be going off to bed soon, But even after she had pleasured his erection twice by rubbing him into an orgasm, Grant's penis was still craving her relentlessly. Accordingly, in order to bring their night to a perfect end, Grant said, "I really want to enter you." After a pause she replied, "I don't think we should." She certainly had the sexual desire to have him inside her. "But I really want to have my penis inside you!" Grant repeated urgently. After another pause, she asked, "But what about me getting pregnant?" When he said nothing, there was another long pause, and then she suggested, "Ok, I guess we can use one of George's rubbers."

Dorothy stood up from the couch and walked into the bathroom off of the kitchen between the laundry room and master bedroom. She opened up the medicine cabinet, removed one of the small flat packages, and returned to the living room. As he sat waiting on the couch, Grant began to have serious second thoughts about his suggestion to gratify his urgent desire for her. It was obvious from her behavior that Dorothy was both willing and reluctant. Perhaps this really was a bad idea. If they were going to have intercourse, they should do so without either one of them being hesitant. When Dorothy returned, she found Grant sitting on the floor at the end of the couch in an open area between the living and dining rooms. He had removed his outer shirt and trousers and was clad in only his t-shirt and undershorts, as if he were ready for bed or for what they were contemplating. She handed him the flat little package, but Grant had never even seen a rubber before and was therefore slightly embarrassed and even somewhat fearful that George might know exactly how many were supposed to be there, and he would realize that one was missing. Accordingly, as the result of his own doubts as to the wisdom of him entering her vagina, he fumbled with the little wrapping half-heartedly without successfully opening it. He certainly could have done so rather easily if he had used his teeth to break the tough plastic wrapping, and if he had really been convinced that they were doing the right thing. When Dorothy realized that he was not succeeding in opening the package, she took it from him and began to fiddle with it herself, but Grant intervened before she had a chance to rupture the plastic. "Hey, stop," Grant said, "I've got a different idea. Instead of me entering you, why don't I just rub the head of my penis inside your lips?" "All right. That would be fine."

Dorothy was also relieved and was happier with this alternative. She now simply lay back on the floor, opened up her robe, hiked her nightgown up to her waist, bent her legs, and spread her thighs. There she lay patiently, waiting for Grant to enjoy her as he wished. He first felt her carefully and lovingly from her bare lower belly to her shapely thighs and then back to the central area of her sex. She was so breath-takingly beautiful and inviting. She was revealing everything in full view for him to touch and enjoy: her love-delta, her hair, the lips of her vulva slightly parted. What a beautiful love-smile! Aphrodite herself, he thought, could never look more magnificent! She was his golden goddess, spreading her dazzling sex for him on this lovely gold carpet. Grant thought that he could caress her reverently forever, but Dorothy whispered, "Better not take too long. We don't want Carol walking in here." He therefore somewhat reluctantly ceased admiring her, removed his undershorts, crouched over her and used his hand to rub the head of his erection up and down inside the lips of her vulva. He became excited so quickly that he reached an orgasm after only two or three full traversings of her labia. As soon as he felt the orgasm coming, he withdrew his penis from her sex and allowed his erection to convulse with pleasure just inches away. But Grant had ejaculated so much semen during the previous hours that there was nothing left to come out, and so his penis simply shuddered without staining Dorothy's lovely gold carpet. They then arose from the floor and went off to bed.

December 21, 1972, Thursday

Tomorrow would be the last day of classes for the university and the schools in University City, after which would begin the Christmas holiday. Today would therefore be the last day for her and Grant to be together until he returned at the beginning of January. Since she still had some Christmas shopping to do, they had decided to do it together this morning, and then they could spend the early afternoon here at the house alone together before Carol came back from school.

Dorothy stood before the mirror in the bathroom adjoining the master bedroom, carefully looking at herself as she applied eye shadow and just a bit of rouge. Then after combing her hair, she used hair spray to hold it all in place. She really felt elated, like a young woman about to embark upon a long awaited date with her favorite heartthrob: for the latter is exactly what Grant now represented to her. He was her college boyfriend, and she was his college sweetheart, a status that pleased her greatly.

After putting on her heavy winter coat, she bade the dogs goodbye, went out to the car, and drove over to campus to pick Grant up in front of Holmes. As he sat down in the passenger seat, he said, "Boy! You smell good enough to eat!" "I do, huh?" she replied with obvious pleasure. "You sure do!" Grant's left hand reached across the seat and caressed her coat. "Man! You look adorable in your polar bear coat!" His hand traveled farther up to her neck and the back of her head. "You're even wearing a necklace and have hair spray on. No wonder you smell so good! Are you going out on a date?"

"Yep, I sure am!" she answered with smug satisfaction. They were both excited to be together and were sure that this morning of rather ordinary Christmas shopping would actually be quite extraordinary. Last year at this time Grant had been secretly harboring his affections for both her and Nisa while they were Christmas caroling. A year later he found himself so wonderfully entangled in love with this exciting and dazzling woman. Neither still knew what would come of all this; and although the uncertainty was the source of melancholy and fear when they were apart, it also caused them to greatly treasure times like this when they could coordinate their two schedules to be alone together.

Their first stop was the post office, where Dorothy mailed off a Christmas package of assorted goodies to Wesley, who was now stationed on Adak, a small, cold and remote island in the Aleutian chain between Alaska and Siberia in the Bering Sea. Then after running past the Lincoln Bank to make various deposits and withdrawals, they spent the rest of their morning shopping at Sears and Penney's for Dorothy to buy a few more things for Carol and other relatives. Grant bought nothing. He was simply here to be with her. His parents and sister had still not communicated at all with one another since the fight between his father and Neil in early July. Christmas would therefore simply involve himself and his parents; and since he had no idea what to buy them, he had decided not to trouble at all with Christmas shopping this year. Dorothy and Grant were also not giving one another anything, in part so as not to arouse any suspicion, and in part to avoid further complicating their already too complex situation with gifts that might be misinterpreted or over-interpreted. They were perfectly content to have this day together serve as their Christmas present to each other.

After having a cozy lunch at Dorothy's favorite Steak and Shake, they arrived at the house shortly after noon. They now had about three hours before Carol would be home. Grant followed Dorothy into the master bedroom; and after she took off her coat and hung it up in the closet, he said, "All right now, you lovely woman, let me see what you've been wearing all morning." "Ok!" Dorothy brightly replied. As she stood still, Grant explored her clothing. She had on a dress made out of a heavy fabric, just right for the cold winter weather. He playfully squeezed her breasts as he examined the upper part of the garment. "Hey! Watch it there, fella," she humorously warned, "or you'll pull away a bloody stump!" As Grant's hands traveled further down and discovered that it was a dress, he remarked, "Wow! You're wearing a dress. I don't think I've ever seen you in one before. My golly! It's really pretty, but you make anything you wear look lovely. But man! You're a real doll in a dress! You look so damn feminine and beautiful!" His hands now went under her dress. "Oh man!" he exclaimed in joyous surprise, "You're even wearing pantyhose! I've never seen you in them before either!" As he spoke, his hands traveled up her legs and caressed her bottom and lingered in front to trace her Venus V. "My God!" he said in amazement, "They make you look so sexy!" "What's this?" he asked, as he felt and tugged on her slip. "It's a slip." "Why do you wear that?" "It's to make sure that someone can't see through the fabric of the dress to see the woman's shape." "My golly! I really love it on you! Its fabric is so fine and perfectly smooth. My God! I can't get over how lovely you look in all this! You are all woman!"

Dorothy now walked back into the adjoining bathroom, took down her hose and panties, and sat down on the toilet to urinate. Ever since Grant witnessed this act about two weeks ago for the first time, his presence beside her as she used the bathroom had become routine, a custom that they both enjoyed as a lovely act of intimacy. Once, as they were together in the bathroom, Grant interrupted the sound of her urinating by remarking in a hushed and reverential tone, "I really love that sound! It's beautiful!" "You do, huh?" Dorothy replied with obvious satisfaction in her voice. It was truly wonderful that even this biological function, which many would regard as unappealing, was so very erotic for them both. Another aspect of Grant's witnessing her urinating came when she was finished. He could hear her tear off a piece of toilet paper and sometimes also the slight rustle of her clothes as she spread herself wider to dab at her vulva. Then when she stood up, they embraced to enjoy a passionate kiss while Grant's left hand clasped her bare ass, and his right hand held her love-front. When they finally completed their kissing, Grant released his beautiful woman and allowed her to pull her clothes back into place.

Now, as Dorothy sat there and finished urinating, she said, "You can take off my hose and panties if you like." Grant immediately knelt on the floor, removed her shoes that also possessed a simple feminine elegance and were so dainty. "Just be careful as you take off the hose, so that you don't snag or make a run in them. But first you need to take off my peds." "What are those?" Grant asked. "They are those small sock-like things on my feet. Women wear them when they have hose on, because they just cover the foot inside the shoe." "Gee whiz!" Grant commented in true wonderment, "I've never heard of them before. You're teaching me all kinds of things today."

After wiping herself and standing up, Dorothy put down the toilet lid, flushed the toilet, and said, "Here, I'll take those from you." Grant held out his hands and gave her her shoes, peds, hose, and panties. His hands then traveled under her dress, clasped her female beauty front and back, and they enjoyed a delicious kiss. He really enjoyed feeling her naked beauty underneath her dress. To Grant, she was all female sex! They now returned into the master bedroom. "I'm now going to put the peds and hose in a lingerie laundry bag. See. It's a bag perforated with holes, so that delicate things like hose can be washed in the machine without being damaged." As she spoke, she showed the bag to Grant, who had never before seen such a thing. "Ok, why don't we lie down on the bed to rest and take a nap; and since the bed is made, we'll cover up with this white blanket." As Dorothy was talking, she returned to the closet, unzipped her dress, stepped out of it, and hung it up. Meanwhile, on the other side of the bed, Grant was removing everything except his t-shirt and undershorts. After Dorothy unfolded the blanket and spread it out on top of the bed, they each slid under it from opposite sides. As he felt the blanket, Grant asked, "Is this the same blanket that you took last summer to Parkfield when we went horseback riding?" "It certainly is," Dorothy proudly affirmed. Nothing more needed to be said. The blanket that had served them so well that day in covering their held hands was now covering them for a lovely afternoon together on the bed.

Dorothy had already given her college boyfriend a lovely lesson in feminine apparel, but she was about to show him even more wonders. After moving about on the bed a bit, they finally settled into a position that both regarded as perfect. Grant lay flat on his back with Dorothy lying to his right. She had her body turned onto her left side, so that she could lie up against him. It was basically the same position that they had enjoyed while lying on this bed for the very first time three months ago on September 13 when Dorothy took down his pants and held his erection in her hand, also for the first time. Grant had his right arm under her neck, and her head was on his shoulder. But what really made their snuggling so special was the fact that Dorothy was wearing only a bra and her slip.

They had often engaged in erotic play with Dorothy wearing her cotton nightgown, but this slip was a garment of extraordinary eroticism. First of all, it was thinner and finer than the cotton. It was almost as if Dorothy were naked. The fabric glided across her skin and moved so lightly as Grant caressed her body, and its feel to his touch was so exciting. Secondly, it simply had shoulder straps and therefore exposed her shoulders and upper chest much more so than the nightgown; and he could easily explore her smooth shoulders and the upper parts of her breasts, and cleavage either with his free left hand or to a lesser extent with his right one. Moreover, as they lay together, Grant breathed in the beautiful fragrance of her White Shoulders, which he now so strongly associated with her that it alone was sufficient to give him an erection. Thirdly, the slip was much shorter than the nightgown. It came down only to her middle or lower thigh. As Dorothy lay up against him, she kept her left leg straight along his right leg, but she bent her right leg and placed it on top of him, so that her lower thigh was resting on his erection. Given the slip's shortness and ease of movement, the garment could be made to glide effortlessly upward to fully expose Dorothy's sex and bottom.

As Dorothy placed her leg over onto Grant, she used her free right hand to lift up her slip both to free the movement of her leg and to offer her spread womanhood to him. He was immediately aware of what she was placing on display for him, and he began to use his left hand to examine and caress her sex. Dorothy soon withdrew her leg and used her own free hand to pull down his undershorts. She then moved her leg back into position, so that now her bare lower thigh was enjoying being in direct contact with his beautiful red cock. It also seemed as if Dorothy were attempting to ride his manhood. The erotic illusion greatly pleased them both. She slipped her right hand under his t-shirt and enjoyed feeling his hard muscular body and the thick hair on his chest. "Oh my!" she said in obvious delight and wonder, "You are so beauteous and also so totally male!"

Grant resumed his fondling of her womanhood, tracing her lovely hair and feeling the delicate skin of her love-delta, hip, upper thigh, and shapely bottom. "She has such a perfect ass," he thought to himself in amazement. Since her slip was now bunched around her waist, he could enjoy that entire perfect female mound; and given how she was lying, he could, for the first time, follow her lovely ass down between her thighs and up to her pussy, and down the front of her pussy and back up to that gorgeous ass. He would later term this juncture of perfect womanhood her pussy tail, and oh how extraordinary it was! But what especially captivated him was her vulva, whose lips were slightly parted, as if her pussy were smiling at him and inviting him to play and play, which was in fact what Dorothy was inviting him to do. Their time together shopping had gradually aroused them both, and now they were giving one another the most exquisite Christmas present imaginable. She could feel his beautiful cock underneath her lower right thigh, and his fingers were inflicting magnificent love-pleasure upon her down there, while she was giving her young man sweet sweet beautiful pussy. His left hand was constantly moving about, fully enchanted by her pussy tail. His fingers also studiously traced the outline of her pussy smile, carefully probed inside those rosy-pink lips, and traversed the full length of her moist inner velvet. Dorothy nearly reached an orgasm whenever his finger caressed her clitoris. As always, Grant was totally enchanted by the beauty of her sex and simply could not get enough looking; and that was perfectly fine with Dorothy. She wanted her young man to look and look and look and look, because it all felt so wonderful!

There they lay motionless and wordless, only Grant's hand and fingers in motion, loving and adoring her beautiful sex, and giving them both such tremendous pleasure that their complete absorption in it rendered them speechless. They had supposedly lain down to rest and to take a nap, but although they rested and did so enveloped in a cloud of soothing and smoldering pleasure, they did not fall asleep but devoted their time together to this newly discovered form of erotic entertainment, which did not end until they had to arise just before Carol returned home from school.

January 1, 1973, Monday

It was about 6:25 P.M. when Grant picked up the telephone in his dorm room and dialed Dorothy's number. When her lovely voice greeted him, he said, "Hello, Dorth. I'm back. Got back here just about fifteen minutes ago and have nothing really to do here." "Carol and I are the only ones here. Would you like me to come get you to stay for the night?" "I sure would." "Ok, I'll be there in about fifteen minutes." Classes did not resume until Wednesday, Jan. 3, and most students would be returning tomorrow, but since the dorms opened today at 5:00 P.M., Grant had wanted to be here as soon as he could, so that he and Dorothy could spend as much time together as possible before classes started up.

Soon after Grant got into the car, Dorothy began, "I've got some really sad news to report." Grant's insides suddenly felt nauseous, as he anticipated that it would be a death sentence that she was about to deliver on their relationship, like the one last late September. Perhaps she had been totally reevaluating their situation over the past ten days and had decided that it was all a very bad mistake that had to be ended immediately. "Aemilia Dickerson," Dorothy continued, "the twenty-year old daughter of my friend and neighbor Evelyn, died yesterday morning." Grant was instantly relieved, but he also felt greatly ashamed for feeling thus at the announcement of the death of someone who was exactly his age.

"Evelyn found her dead in her bedroom early yesterday morning. She had bled to death during the night after giving birth to a still-born infant, born prematurely." "Oh my God!" Grant said in genuine shock and horror, "Oh my God!" "Yes," Dorothy replied in a low sad voiced, "It's such a terribly sad and tragic thing. As a parent, I can't even begin to imagine how I would feel if this had happened to me with Sally or Carol. I've known Evelyn ever since we've been living here in University City. We've been neighbors and members of the same church; and although Aemilia was never a good friend of either Sally or Carol, I've known her as Evelyn's daughter. Evelyn and her husband didn't even know that Aemilia was pregnant. She'd been seeing a young man named George for quite some time, and they seemed very serious. They must have been having sex, and she got pregnant, but apparently she did not think that she could let her parents know. I just can't imagine how much that must hurt Evelyn, and what tremendous guilt she will feel for so many years!" After a pause, Grant said, "That's just incredible! Man! How terrible! I'm so sorry, Dorth. It's such a horrible thing to happen to someone you know. I really am sorry."

Aemilia's sudden and shocking death had cast a real pall over their reunion. When they arrived at the house, Grant happily greeted all four dogs, but then he and Dorothy settled down on the living room couch to talk. Carol was sitting in the family room watching TV. After informing each other of what all they had done during the intervening ten days or so, their conversation turned back to Aemilia Dickerson. Grant observed that the big news item right now was the death of Roberto Clemente, the famous baseball player for the Pittsburgh Pirates. He had lost his life yesterday in an airplane crash as he was flying from his native Puerto Rico to bring supplies to earthquake victims in Nicaragua. Like most people his age in the United States, Grant had rarely been touched closely by death, usually just that of an elderly grandparent or other distant relative. It was rather uncommon for someone his age to know death up close and personal. Even though he had never met Aemilia or her parents, Grant was genuinely saddened by Dorothy's news, because he knew that it affected her deeply, and that in turn affected him. Plus, the situation itself was very sobering and sad by any standard.

"You know," Grant said, "When I was about fourteen, my best friend Keith Watts had a younger brother named David who died by drowning. That was so very awful. Keith and I were always together doing things, and David was constantly hanging around wanting and trying to be part of what we were doing. Of course, we teased him relentlessly and were always giving him a hard time; but he was such a spunky kid, so full of energy. And so his death was such a terrible shock and such a tremendous source of sadness. You're right. It's just impossible to imagine having to be Aemilia's parent in this situation."

Even after Carol had gone off to bed, Dorothy and Grant continued to sit on the living room couch and talk. But eventually they came into the kitchen, so that Dorothy could make herself a pot of coffee, because they both knew that it would be a very long night for them. She was wearing her pink quilted robe over her regular clothes, a top and matching pair of slacks. As Dorothy tidied up the kitchen, she and Grant encountered one another and embraced, with his hands and arms going around her inside her robe, but their physical interaction was somewhat subdued. Rather than having its usual passionate and erotic character, it had the quality of sweet tenderness, because Grant sensed that Dorothy was in need of emotional comfort for the sorrow of her friend's unspeakable tragedy.

Aemilia's successful concealment of her pregnancy prompted Grant to ask, "How did she keep her condition hidden from her parents?" "Well," Dorothy replied, "many women, especially when it is their first pregnancy and they are still young and very slender, often do not swell up all that much and look pregnant. When I was carrying Sally, I was just twenty-two and still weighed about 98 pounds." "Really?" Grant replied in astonishment. "It's very hard for me to imagine you that small." "Well, I was. In fact when we moved here from Kimball in early 1965, I still only weighed 105 pounds, but then over the next year I began gaining weight and finally lost my youthful slenderness." "Wow," Grant remarked, "Don't get me wrong. I really like you the way you are now with such a voluptuous figure, but it's too bad I didn't get to know you a few years earlier. I could have seen what you looked like then." Dorothy laughed and continued, "Yeah well anyway, I didn't show much at all with Sally, even right up to the time that I gave birth. I was working as a bookkeeper for Perfection Gear and did so just a week or so before she was born. I remember going into a place where a girlfriend of mine was working; and when I told her that I was pregnant, she looked me over and asked, 'What are you having? A peanut'?"

This then led them to talking about Dorothy's experiences with her three pregnancies in general. Grant remembered that his sister had been in labor for nearly 24 hours before finally giving birth to Troy, and that the whole experience had been such a miserable one. "Yeah," Dorothy observed, "pregnancy and giving birth are such funny things. Some women have all sorts of problems, and others don't. I was lucky, I guess, because I didn't have any trouble with any of mine. When I went into labor, I never had any problems. They just came right out. I remember when I went into the hospital in Baltimore with Carol, the nurse wanted to give me a hypo to relax and drug me, but I refused and insisted on being wide awake during the whole thing.

Sometimes," Dorothy went on, "a woman can be pregnant for a long time before she realizes it. For example, my mom was about four months pregnant with Tim before she found out. She had been going through menopause. So, when her periods stopped, she didn't think about it, but then she went to the doctor with various complaints about her insides and not feeling well. The doctor examined her and then told her that her problem was that she was pregnant. Boy! Was she surprised. Then Ginger, Bethany, and I kept kidding her. We'd say, 'Hey mom, if you have a girl, you can name it Take, and then we can call her Miss Take'. Get it! Mistake?" "Only after you explained it," Grant commented, "I guess my sense of humor is the normal sophomoric male variety with grossness and obscenity being the key features."

January 2, 1973, Tuesday

By 1:00 A.M. they were both going strong with their talking and just enjoying being together in sweet tender companionship. "How soon do you want to be going to bed?" Dorothy asked. "I'm ok," Grant replied, "I'm well rested up from my vacation. I guess I could stay up the rest of the night." "Well," Dorothy said, "I'm not getting tired at all. Maybe we'll just go ahead and stay up, but I may lie down and get some sleep, so that I'm up and fairly fresh when Carol is getting ready for school." "Ok, that sounds fine. Let's do that." "And as long as we're going to be up a while yet," Dorothy added, "I might as well fix up something that we can have for lunch and/or supper tonight; and then I won't have it to worry about later in the day."

As she started pulling out pots and pans and things from the refrigerator, Grant asked, "So, what are you going to make?" "Well, I don't know what it's called, but I just call it sausage noodles. Have we ever eaten it together here at the house?" "I don't think so," Grant answered, "What is it?" "Well, I learned it from my mom, and she got it from the grade school cafeteria that she worked in for many years. They fixed it a lot there, because it was so easy to make, and the kids liked it. I've been making it quite a bit over the past few months with just me and Carol here during the week. All it is is sausage mixed up with egg noodles and tomato sauce. It's very simple and tastes really good."

As they continued to talk, the kitchen gradually began to smell so nicely of frying sausage, and Dorothy periodically left Grant's embrace to step over to the stove to check on the boiling noodles and sausage. Once, as they were lovingly standing against the sink with their arms wrapped around one another, she gently broke their embrace with the apologetic words, "Excuse me. I need to go check the sausage to make sure that it doesn't get Elfie Brown." "What the hell does that mean?" Grant asked in genuine mystification. "You mean you've not heard me say that before?" "I don't think so." "It's something my mom always said. When we three girls were growing up, she would sometimes let something get too done; and when we complained about it being black and burned, she always agreed by saying 'Yeah, it's a little Elfie Brown', because she knew a black woman named Elfie or Elfie Brown. I don't remember which. But that has always been her way of apologizing for letting something get too done."

When Dorothy had mixed everything up, she said, "Come here, and have a taste." Grant came to her at the counter and soon felt a tablespoon gently touching his lips. He opened up, and Dorothy placed the spoonful of sausage noodles in his mouth. After he had chewed and swallowed, she asked, "So, how do you like it?" "I like it," he replied honestly. "That's good," she playfully retorted, "because if you hang around here today and tomorrow, that's what you'll have to eat. Does it need any more salt?" "I don't think so. It tastes fine to me."

When they had finished washing up the big pots and pans from the cooking, Dorothy announced, "Well, it's about 3:00, and I think I'll go off to bed now and get a few hours of sleep before getting up with Carol." "Ok," Grant replied, "I think I'll just stretch out on the couch in the living room and do some reading with my cassette machine, and I might doze off for a bit. But I'd rather just stay awake, I think, because if I let myself go to sleep, I'll sleep a big chunk of the day away; and I want to be awake to spend as much time as possible with my darling." "You do, huh?" Dorothy asked with a satisfied laugh. "I sure do," Grant replied seriously but with a tender smile.

All three were up by 6:30, and Dorothy simply moved about the house doing numerous small things while being available if Carol needed her for anything. Grant stayed in the living room to be out of their way. Then when Carol went off to school, Grant and Dorothy first took the dogs out for a nice long walk. It felt good to be out in the cold. It helped to refresh them both. Then when they returned to the house, they spent the rest of the morning in quiet contentment of simply being together and doing chores around the house. Dorothy really appreciated Grant's willingness and eagerness to help her with anything that he could. His participation converted the chore from work into a nice shared experience. Their affectionate hugs and kisses accompanied all that they did, but they were both rather tired and thus found real ardent passion hard to generate. Besides, it still seemed so out of place in view of Aemilia Dickerson's tragic death. The one exception, however, which had also applied to the late night and early morning before, was when Dorothy used the toilet. Grant always accompanied her; and as she stood up, he embraced her with one hand clasping her bare love-delta and his other hand going around to her beautiful bare bottom. He held her lovely front and back while they engaged in a long delicious kiss. Then he often sat down and urinated himself. Quite often, as Dorothy sat down on the toilet with Grant standing beside her, he would say, "Don't bother flushing. I've got to go also." It pleased Dorothy that he sat down like a woman to urinate and always put the seat and lid down, unlike some men who make a mess by standing up as they urinate, miss the toilet, and are stupidly inconsiderate in leaving the seat up.

Shortly after they ate sausage noodles for their lunch, Bob Snider arrived at the house. His brother Jeff had driven him back to campus, but they stopped off to visit for a while before Bob had his brother take him to his dorm room. Then right after they left, a delivery man showed up with a package from Blackwell of London. The books that Dorothy and Grant had ordered about six weeks ago had finally arrived. Since they were afraid that the books might come during Christmas break, Dorothy had suggested that they be sent to her house. Grant was really excited, and they now sat down on the living room couch and opened up the box to see what was there. Dorothy was herself such a book lover that she relished this experience about as much as Grant, and once again she was so happy to be his eyes in telling him what the books were. She began reading off the titles as he pulled them out of the box and handed them to her. "*Central and Southern Italy before Rome*, by David Trump," she intoned seriously. "*Samnium and the*

Samnites, by Edward Togo Salmon; *Roman Colonization under the Republic*, also by Edward Togo Salmon." "What's this God damn big thing?" Grant asked excitedly. "*The Oxford Classical Dictionary*, Second Edition, edited by N. G. L. Hammond and H. H. Scullard," she explained. "Oh really?" Grant nearly shouted, "Hey that's really neat! How is it organized?" Dorothy began to turn the pages. "Well, it's just like the title says. There's printing in two columns on each page, and it has entries on all sorts of things in alphabetical order, just like a dictionary or encyclopedia." "Really? Hey, look up Marsi." She turned more pages until she located the entry and then said, "It's on page 651 and is just one paragraph, about a fourth of a column." Then she began to read, "Inhabited mountains and strategic passes in central Italy near the Fucine Lake. Their chief town was Marruvium...."

Grant had now begun to spend serious money on buying important books for his dream to become a college professor of ancient history. This was a baby-step along that long path, and his beloved Dorothy was taking it with him.

Carol soon arrived home from school but was gone again to be with friends. They therefore again had the house to themselves, but by now Grant was becoming extremely tired and needed to lie down and sleep. Since Dorothy would be soon going off to Sweet Adelines for the evening, Grant decided to go to bed early. So, after they sat down at the kitchen table and ate more sausage noodles for their supper, they arose, and they bade one another a very affectionate and fond farewell to their respective goals: bed for Grant and Sweet Adelines for Dorothy. Grant walked her toward the master bedroom, where she would change clothes and get herself all prettied up to go, but as they stepped from the kitchen into the laundry room, he embraced her, and they gave one another a last long magnificent kiss. As they stood there with their bodies pressed together, the bright afternoon sun that was setting in the west streamed through the window and enveloped them in its warmth. Grant also slid both his hands inside Dorothy's slacks and panties, moved them down around her bottom, gripped her gently but firmly, and pressed her hard one last time into his erection. He then went into the front bedroom and was immediately sound asleep on the bed nearest the door, the site of The Great Apocalypse. Dorothy changed clothes, fixed up her hair and face, and then went off to Sweet Adelines.

When she arrived back home around 10:30, both Carol and Grant were sound asleep. After hanging up her coat, she undressed and then slipped into a new pair of pajamas that George had just given her for Christmas.

The bottoms were made like trousers, and the top like a shirt with buttons down the front. They were made of a very sheer material. Although George had intended the gift to be a source of pleasure in bed with his beautiful wife, Dorothy, of course, was not the least bit thrilled in having to wear them in bed with him. But she was eager to show herself off in them to her boy-man lover. Clad in these pajamas, Dorothy now came into the front bedroom and knelt beside the bed.

"Hey, Grant, Grant," she said softly as she touched his shoulder. When he finally awoke, she said, "I've got something to show you." "What's that?" he asked very sleepily. "I'm wearing a new pair of pajamas. I wanted to show them to you." Grant was now lying on his left side facing her. He reached out his right hand and encountered her chest. He proceeded to feel the thin fine fabric and her beautiful breasts that it did little to conceal. "Really nice!" he said softly with his voice heavy with desire. His touch felt so good to Dorothy, and her nipples became erect with pleasure. As Grant continued to caress her, she raised her hands and began to unbutton the top. She pulled it open and moved her upper body even closer to Grant. He responded by moving himself to the edge of the bed, so that he could kiss her breasts and take them into his mouth. She was fragrant with White Shoulders, and her skin was so beautiful. His hands caressed and held her breasts as his lips and tongue kissed, licked, and sucked. After a minute or so, Dorothy said, "Ok, that's probably enough. I don't want you waking all the way up and then being awake all night. You need to go back to sleep and rest." Grant obediently withdrew his hands and mouth. Dorothy then refastened the buttons and went off to bed.

January 3, 1973, Wednesday

Today was the day of Aemilia's funeral. Grant would have liked to attend it with his darling, but of course, that would have raised all sorts of questions. So, he did the next best thing. He decided to skip his classes and simply stay there at the house until Dorothy returned. He wanted to be there when she came home, so that they could talk about it, and he would be there to offer her additional comfort. Thus, when Dorothy returned in the afternoon, she described everything that had transpired and did so without exhibiting much anguish. Dorothy then took Grant back to his dorm room for him to resume his classes.

Not long afterwards, as Grant one day was playing the guitar, he happened to compose a little tune of his own. It was played finger-style with 3-4 timing in the key of A minor. Since the tune sounded rather somber, he called it Aemilia's Song in honor of this unfortunate young woman. Aemilia's tragic death was something that Dorothy and Grant had shared, and they both were reminded of it whenever he played the song.

January 4, 1973, Thursday

After eating supper in the dorm cafeteria and spending another two hours studying in his room, Grant walked down to the opposite end of Holmes and used the one pay phone there to call his darling. It was about 8:30 in the evening. The telephone was simply housed inside a cubbyhole attached to the wall, a horizontal shelf with two upright sides. A person had to stand while using the telephone. Although it did not afford complete privacy as did a regular booth, it was private enough, because it was placed in a large open entryway into the dorm where people never stood any length of time but were always on their way in or out of the building. Besides, Grant had no trouble in keeping his head inside the cubbyhole and speaking softly if he needed to say something very personal. This phone had been the means by which they had been conducting their very long telephone conversations over the past few months. If they needed to talk briefly to set up a meeting or the like, he could use his dorm room phone, but for serious talking Grant always used this public phone. Luckily, since calling Dorothy was a local call, he could talk with her indefinitely for just a quarter.

Dorothy answered the phone. By now her day was basically at an end. Carol would soon be asleep in her room. She therefore settled herself down on the bed in the master bedroom to have a nice long enjoyable talk with her boyfriend. As usual, they had nothing really serious or important to talk about, just sharing the events of their day, going off on all sorts of tangents, but mostly simply enjoying the sound of the other's voice, the next best thing to being together in person. After about two hours of such love-struck chitchat, Dorothy suggested that they be hanging up soon, because she was becoming sleepy. Since by now Carol was in bed asleep, Grant proposed, "As long as you'll be undressing soon, why don't you do so now and describe it all to me as you do?" "I don't think I should do that. It would certainly look odd if Carol happened to come into the bedroom." "Ok," Grant accepted, "but it would have been nice! All right then, I guess we'd better be hanging up. I love you." "I think," Dorothy replied, "you just want me." They then said goodbye and hung up.

Dorothy's parting words, "I think you just want me," were an echo of last August 10 when she had ended a very passionate night of erotic embracing in Debbie's dorm room with similar words. As then, they stung and hurt Grant very deeply. Of course, he wanted her! Hells bells! He was crazy about her! But he was sure that what he felt was not mere physical infatuation and lust. He truly loved this wonderful woman. He loved her soul and entire being; and since he did, it was natural that he also desire her physically. What was so damn hard to understand about that? By now he was in a fury of hurt, outrage, and anger. Damn it! This all made him so mad! She had come so close to letting him fuck her, and she was complaining that he just wanted her? This little monster that kept cropping up from time to time had to be killed once and for all and not allowed to undermine their relationship. It made Grant so angry that he wisely decided that talking with her directly was not a good idea, because he would probably not be able to conduct a cool and reasoned conversation with her about this topic. He therefore decided that he needed to take his time in organizing his thoughts and writing them down in a letter. Then she could read it on her own and also be able to think about these things without the two of them being caught up in an emotional argument.

January 6, 1973, Saturday

It was about 2:00 in the afternoon, and Grant rolled out the sheet of braille paper from the braille writer as he finished writing this document for the third and last time. He was now ready to give it to her to read. Since their conversation Thursday evening, they had not talked or seen one another, but that was not at all unusual. He now picked up the telephone in his dorm room and dialed Dorothy's number, but when George answered with his usual silly sounding and nasal "Nyellow," he hung up. He neither wished to talked with him, nor to let him know that he (Grant) was calling to speak with his wife. Consequently, after occupying himself with things in his room for about a half an hour, he tried calling again. This time her lovely sweet voice greeted him. "Hello, Dorth, Grant here. I'm calling to let you know that I have a braille letter for you. If you happen to go out today or tomorrow and want to come by to pick it up, let me know." "OK, Debbie wants me to take her grocery shopping, and I can stop by before I pick her up. I'll call you just before I leave." "All right, I'll wait to hear from you."

An hour or so later Dorothy called to say that she was on her way. Grant met her outside on Walnut Street in front of Holmes and handed her the manila envelope of braille pages through the car window.

January 8, 1973, Monday

George had left very early that morning to return to Newton, and Carol had gone off to school not long ago. Dorothy was now alone in the house. It was now the perfect time for her to read Grant's braille letter. She had looked it over a bit yesterday as she sat at her desk writing letters to Moms Patterson and Klingner, but she wanted to read it again now word for word, so that she could absorb it all and think about what it said. She therefore poured herself a fresh cup of coffee, went into the living room, and sat on the couch where she could be comfortable and could use the bright morning sunlight to read the braille letter with her eyes.

Beware of what you read! It may simply be propaganda designed to seduce you out of or me into your panties! I am writing in order to respond to your remark made to me as we ended our telephone conversation Thursday evening. You indicated that you do not believe that I really love you but only want you. Having you say and think this upsets me very much. I therefore decided to write you this letter to address this matter, so that I can put my thoughts down clearly and have you read them and think about them yourself without us having an emotional argument.

I can certainly understand how you might think that I just want you and really do not love you, but I do not believe it to be at all true. Of course, I desire you and desire you wildly, but that does not mean that I simply want you with animal desire. I am a young male with normal bodily functions, and you are a very beautiful woman. If I am totally in love with you, as I believe, why wouldn't I desire you passionately? What you take to be nothing more than animal lust is to me simply the normal physical manifestation of my genuine and overpowering love for you.

I know that I am young and have had little experience with members of the opposite sex, but my feelings for you have been so very strong and consistent for nearly a year now, and I cannot see them changing. You are right to be extremely cautious about how we feel for one another, because you have so very much to lose if we are mistaken, but I think that these feelings are real and abiding. I have never encountered anyone as magnificent as you, and the real proof of this is that our difference in age does not matter at all to me. You are so very young at heart that I find it difficult to think of you as being 44 years old. You are so like us young energetic college students with such a zest for life. I have known you plenty long enough to know how truly special and extraordinary you are as a human being, in fact the most remarkable one whom I have thus far encountered in my life. Our long conversations over the past months have simply reinforced and confirmed my conclusions on this matter, and I have come to love you so very deeply and fully as a most wonderful person. I truly love your character, your personality, and your soul. I have never met anyone as charming, gracious, poised, elegant, and refined as you. Falling in love with you seems so perfectly logical and understandable. How could I not fall in love with such a fantastic person? That is the real question.

Besides possessing such a dazzling personality and being capable and talented in so many ways, you are so very beautiful as a female. It is therefore so very normal that I should desire you as I do. Let me try to convince you of what I am saying. Sometime when you are all alone in the house, take off all your clothes, and stand naked before the mirror at the end of the hallway. Look carefully at yourself, and try to see what I see: a marvelously beautiful woman. Your hands and feet are so dainty and feminine. The skin of your entire body is so flawlessly smooth and lovely. I just wish that I could see you with my eyes and enjoy your skin so fair and its contrast to your lovely brunette hair, especially in your love-front. Your legs may be short, but they are so very shapely and beautiful. You have such a classic hourglass figure and breasts that are neither too big nor too small, and how soft, smooth, and firm they are!

Words cannot even begin to describe the splendor of your love-front. Please pardon me, but I am now going to use the term "pussy" to describe this part of your anatomy. To me this word is the loveliest five-letter noun in the English language, because I will use it to refer not to just any female body part, but to yours and yours alone. When you removed your nightgown and showed your pussy to me for the first time this past September 19, I could not believe and still cannot believe that you are so beautiful. I have never encountered anything in my life so lovely as your pussy! Your hair is so very lovely there, not a thick forest or jungle but a fabulously beautiful love-meadow that must be tended regularly by the three Graces of Aphrodite in order to be so lovely. What truly divine beauty there is in that place where your lower belly and upper thighs come together! Your skin, your hair, your pussy lips are all so flawless! Should there be any surprise that I am so desirous to touch you there as often as I can?

Obviously, I am well aware of you being married, although unhappily so for many years now. Perhaps I am just being young and foolish, but our love seems so very right to me. So very right indeed! How can we ignore or deny it? I love you so powerfully that it pains me awfully to know that you must submit to having sex with someone whom you do not love, someone other than me, even though he is your lawful husband. From my own subjective perspective of being so madly in love with you, I regard myself as the only person entitled to make love to you, and you are the only woman whom I wish to love in that way. I see nothing at all wrong with how I feel about you. I am just so sorry that things are so complicated by the fact that you are already married, but I am not going to be able to change how I feel toward you. Despite what you said to me last Thursday night on the telephone, I declare most emphatically that I both love you ferociously and also desire you passionately. Henceforth I will continue to insist on the veracity of the former and will not apologize at all for the latter!

As Dorothy read these lovely and eloquent sentiments, she cried from her own strong emotions. She now sat on the couch pondering what she had just read. Her remark last Thursday night had not been a serious one. She had intended it to be something of a joke, but they had immediately hung up, and Grant had apparently misinterpreted what she had said and had been very hurt by it. She could understand that, because their relationship had been so very turbulent and tortuous. It was very easy for him to misunderstand what she had said. Dorothy had come to realize that she also desired him so very much, and this often frightened her terribly, given the situation of her marriage and Carol still being in school. What were they to do? She really wished that she knew. At first she had indeed wondered seriously whether they really did love one another or simply were experiencing some form of wild physical infatuation, but as the months had gone by, the evidence of them really being in love seemed to be there. Grant was right. Their passionate desire for one another was likely to be the physical manifestation of their genuine, all-encompassing love for each other.

Since she was still dressed in nothing but her slippers, nightgown, and robe and needed to undress anyway to put on her clothes for the day, she decided to take Grant up on his challenge. She went into the main bathroom near the end of the hall; and as she stood at the two sinks, she stepped out of her slippers, took off her robe, and pulled the nightgown off over her head. After placing them on the counter, she stepped out into the hallway and stood before the tall mirror. A pair of beautiful emerald green eyes looked back at her, and the smile on her face was enchanting. Grant could always hear this beautiful smile in her voice when she talked, and it utterly captivated him. Her smile was a normal and natural manifestation of her inner sweetness and radiant charm, poise, and grace that he saw in her, and for which he had praised her over the past months. Her hands indeed were dainty and fine. She lowered her gaze to her feet and saw how dainty they were too, and how fine were her toes. They were only slightly marred by a corn on each of her baby toes, but they simply added some distinctive character to them. She did in fact have a very nice hourglass figure, and her breasts did look quite nice, perfectly proportioned for her size. No wonder he enjoyed them. There were two small moles near the nipple of her right breast, but again, they were not unseemly but simply added some individuality to that feminine part of her body. As she examined them in the mirror, her thoughts of how Grant enjoyed feeling and sucking them caused her nipples to become erect. She wanted him here now to take them into his mouth, as he had done the other night when she came home from Sweet Adelines.

That had felt so very good! She now finally focused her attention on her love-front. In his letter Grant had used the P word for this part of her body, and it thrilled her to have him see her as a truly desirable woman, and she liked the idea of calling this part of her body her pussy. Henceforth she would not at all mind having Grant use this word to refer to this most intimate part of her anatomy.

Since she had gained a bit of weight about five years ago, she was no longer the extremely slender girl that she had been for twenty years beyond her high school graduation, but the added weight had simply made her figure full and voluptuous. True, she did have a slight belly, but even that was attractive in its own way. It gave her the look of a full-figured, fecund female, willing and able to have energetic and delicious sex and to become pregnant. In fact, over the past few months she had occasionally fantasized about her having Grant's child, a lovely little red-haired girl or boy with her own beautiful emerald green eyes. She was always thrilled at the sight of his erection surrounded with his bright red hair. She wished so much that circumstances were different, so that she could enjoy having him inside her.

How wonderful it would be to have them make love again and again to get her pregnant. What rapture that would be, and how wonderful it would be to have his child! She would truly love to give him that gift.

Grant was right again. Her pubic hair was quite stunning and enhanced the beauty of her sex. With her right hand she caressed her hair and watched herself do this in the mirror. She wanted his hand to be there again, as it had been many times over the past several months. His letter and her own thoughts had given her that funny feeling way down inside her. She was probably now full and wet with honey for him, something that never happened to her for George. She had hated sex for so many years, but now she wished so much that her bed partner and husband could somehow miraculously not be George but Grant.

Caressing her hair felt nice. The skin around her vulva was a lovely rosy pink. She spread her feet apart and slid her hand between her thighs. Grant had inserted his finger inside her this past September 19 and on a few other occasions since then. Although it always troubled her when he did this because of her marital status, she still loved the physical sensation of his finger inside her. She now placed her own index finger inside her vagina and confirmed the fact that she was wet with yearning for him. After being sexually dead for so many years, she had gradually been coming back to life as part of her love for Grant.

About twelve hours later, around 9:00 P.M., Dorothy answered the telephone in the master bedroom and was pleased to hear Grant's voice on the other end. After their exchange of greetings, Grant asked, "What are you doing?" "Oh nothing much, just getting ready to sit down on the bed and roll my hair and then call it a night, I guess." After a slight pause, she continued, "I read your letter today, and I'm sorry that what I said the other night on the telephone hurt you so much. I didn't intend to at all. I meant it to be a joke." Grant was greatly relieved to hear those words and replied, "I'm sorry too. I guess I shouldn't have been so overly sensitive, but I guess that too is all part of our complicated situation." "Yes, it is," she agreed, and then she asked, "How would you like to come over tomorrow night? I could pick you up for supper here, and you could study while I'm away at Sweet Adelines." "I would really like that." They were both so very relieved and pleased that the misunderstanding between them was now cleared up, and they were already looking forward to one another's company tomorrow night. After a lengthy and animated conversation of an hour and a half, they reluctantly decided to wrap it up for the night. "I love you," Grant said seriously. "I love you too," Dorothy replied.

January 9, 1973, Tuesday

As they sat down at the kitchen table to have Dorothy's delicious chili mac for supper, Grant asked, "Where's Carol?" "She's spending the night with her friend Donna Hopkins," Dorothy replied. As soon as she spoke the words, Grant realized what an incredible windfall of luck this was for them. They could be in the house all night together without having to worry about Carol finding them in a compromising situation. He had no idea what they might actually do, but the potential alone was very exciting. Dorothy, of course, had been aware of the situation for about two hours, as soon as Carol came home from school and asked to spend the night with her friend. Like Grant, she had no clear idea as to what they would do with their night alone, but it was really wonderful to look forward to.

The mood for the night began to take shape after they had eaten and had retired to the master bedroom for Dorothy to get dressed for Sweet Adelines. Grant stretched out on the bed, and they talked casually about various things as Dorothy moved around the room. She had been wearing a simple house dress all day and now pulled it off over her head and carefully hung it up in the closet. She was now clad in only peds, shoes, panties, and a bra. She picked up her bottle of White Shoulders perfume from the dresser and sat down on the side of the bed to apply it to her arms, shoulders, and between her breasts. Grant reached out his hand and discovered to his delight that she was now wearing just her panties and bra, and she was happy to have him running his hand along her bare back and slipping his fingers inside the waistband at the back of her panties to feel part of her bottom. After anointing herself, she arose, went to the closet, and picked out a pair of slacks and a nice blouse to wear for the evening. She came back to the bed and stood beside it facing Grant as she removed the clothes from their hangers. As she did this, Grant reached out and touched her bare left thigh, moved his hand up to her bare belly, and then began to touch her love-front that was concealed only by the fabric of her panties. Once again, Dorothy stood there patiently and welcomed his caresses and fondling, as well as him slipping his fingers inside the elastic band of her panties around her upper thigh so as to touch her hair and even the top part of her vulva. But the delight had to end, because she now had the clothes removed from their hangers and proceeded to dress. But she again sat down on the edge of the bed and allowed Grant to stroke her as he wished while she was pulling on her clothes.

She was now beautiful in her evening attire and smelling so sweet and fragrant. Grant arose from the bed, and they went into the adjoining bathroom, so that Dorothy could fix her hair and apply some makeup. As she stood at the sink looking into the mirror, Grant stood behind her with his arms around her waist and his hands tenderly holding her abdomen. He lowered his mouth to the left side of her neck and kissed her several times. "I'm going to give you a hickey," he said in a humorous monster's voice. "You are, huh?" "I sure am, and then what will you tell the other ladies?" "I guess I'll have to tell them about my boyfriend." Dorothy enjoyed the mirror's image of their heads together, his bright red hair and her own brunette.

"I'd better go potty before I leave," she said in her cute little girl voice. She took down her slacks and panties and sat on the toilet. As was usual by now, Grant stood beside her; and when she arose, his hands enveloped her bare bottom and love-front. They stood there together and kissed long and passionately several times, as they both enjoyed Grant touching her female beauty. "Well," Dorothy finally said between kisses, "I hate to tell ya, fella, but I've got to get cuttin'." "Yeah, I guess you do," he agreed as he released her and allowed her to put her clothes back in order.

Grant had brought schoolwork along, but unlike other Tuesday evenings, tonight Grant simply could not concentrate on his studies, because although he did not know what was going to happen, he did know that for the very first time they would undress and spend the entire night between the sheets of the double bed in the master bedroom. The notion was so exciting and gave him such an erection that he could think only of her. He therefore went into the front bedroom and removed all his clothes, which he folded up and left there on the other twin bed. He took from his pants pocket his watch, so that he could keep track of the time. As he stood there naked, he reveled in his erection. His penis felt so hard, just like a billy club. He thought to himself with satisfaction as he examined its hardness and rigidity that it might even be strong enough to hammer in nails. He then walked down the hall and into the master bedroom, where he began to look around for that white blanket that they now regarded as their own special coverlet. When he finally located it on a shelf in the closet, he went into the family room, lay down on the couch on his back, and covered himself with the blanket to await Dorothy's return. Soon all four dogs had come in to join him and had settled down in various places. Grant simply lay there enjoying both the smoldering pleasure and the acute desire pent up in his erection and remembering how lovely Dorothy's sex was. Occasionally, when his penis became less than rock hard, he caressed himself to remedy the situation. There he lay for the next four hours in a kind of stupor of erotic anticipation, the only sounds in the room being one of the dogs occasionally sighing, scratching, or shifting about.

The singing at Sweet Adelines always put Dorothy into such a happy frame of mind, but she was already flying high when she arrived at practice due to her amorous interaction with Grant. The singing that evening simply served to heighten her already existing mood of euphoria. By the time that their session had ended, she was so eager to return home, but unfortunately, Dorothy had promised to stop at Debbie's apartment before coming home, and she wound up staying there for quite some time. Debbie was somewhat upset and in one of her moods to talk it all out. Dorothy patiently tried to settle her down, but eventually, after more than an hour of talking, Debbie asked if she could come spend the night at her house. Dorothy had been hoping to avoid such a complication, but how could she refuse without arousing Debbie's suspicion? She therefore agreed. Therefore, rather than arriving home shortly after 10:30 as she had hoped, it was instead a quarter before midnight.

As they came through the back door into the family room, Dorothy and Debbie were engaged in a lively conversation, but Dorothy interjected, "There he is, lying covered up on the couch." "Hi, Grant," Debbie said in response. "Hi there Deb," Grant replied. "Have you been asleep?" Dorothy asked. "No, I've just been laying here a while resting." "Ok, Debs," Dorothy said, "let me get my coat off, and I'll get you settled down in your room for the night." The two walked off, leaving Grant on the couch, but within a few seconds Dorothy had raced back from the master bedroom and came over to the couch, where she whispered, "Just give me some time to make sure that Debbie is settled in bed for the night, and then I'll be back." "Ok," Grant agreed.

Dorothy now went to join Debbie in the far bedroom just across the hall from the master bedroom. "Are you going to need anything before I go off to bed, Deb?" "No, Ma, I have everything here in my bag. Thanks so much for talking with me again. I'm feeling better and can probably get to sleep now. It's always so relaxing to be here in the house with you." "That's good. I'm glad." They continued to chitchat for nearly twenty more minutes about nothing in particular. Debbie was a real expert in dragging things out. Dorothy was so anxious to rejoin Grant, but she also needed to make sure that Debbie was definitely down for the night. Accordingly, as she was finally leaving the room, she said, "Since Carol is staying all night with a friend, I don't need to get up with her tomorrow morning; and since this situation almost never arises, I've decided that I'll take the opportunity to sleep in late. So I won't be up at the crack of dawn as I usually am. I just wanted you to know. So go right ahead and sleep as late as you want, because I won't be getting up all that early." "Ok, I would like to get a good sleep too," Debbie replied. Dorothy walked across the hall into the master bedroom and stood there momentarily to make sure that Debbie was actually going to bed. The last thing they needed was to have her get up and come across into her room during the night to wake her up to talk more, but when all was silent and still, Dorothy went back to the family room.

January 10, 1973, Wednesday

It was 12:05 when Dorothy rejoined Grant. For the past twenty minutes or so he had been patiently impatient. To use one of Dorothy's expressions, he knew what a pill Debbie could be. "Sorry," Dorothy apologized, "but I had to make sure that Debbie was really settled in for the night." "That's ok. I know you did. We both know what she's like." "Yeah, we sure do!" Dorothy laughed. "So," she asked, "what did you do all evening while I was gone? Did you get lots of studying done?" "No, I didn't do any studying tonight. I just didn't feel very well." "Oh no?" she asked with a bit of alarm in her voice, "How don't you feel well?" "I'll show you," and as he spoke these words, he threw back the white blanket and revealed himself fully naked with his erection standing at attention for her. "That's what's been ailing me all evening," he explained.

Dorothy said nothing in reply. She was totally surprised and entirely spellbound by what she saw. As always, she was truly enchanted with the sight of his erection, his smooth beautiful shaft and very large head, standing upright from Grant's flat muscular stomach and surrounded by that lovely bright red hair. Like Grant, she had been excited all evening long with the prospect of them being able to spend the entire night together in bed, although she had not really given any definite thought to what they would actually do, but as she feasted her eyes upon this lovely sight, she knew instantly what she wanted to do. She wanted him in her bed just like that, lying fully naked on his back with his erection standing upright and hard, all because he desired her so powerfully. She would then mount her beautiful young red stallion and ride him passionately. After ten or fifteen seconds of silence, during which she arrived at this decision while adoring his beautiful red cock, Dorothy finally said, "Ok, just let me check on Deb one more time, and then I'll come and get you."

After walking down the hall to the far bedroom to check once again on Debbie and finding everything there perfectly still and quiet, Dorothy came back to the couch in the family room. "Ok, let's go," was all that she whispered to Grant as she took him by the hand. He sat up on the couch and with the white blanket still wrapped around his nakedness, he allowed himself to be led wordlessly to whatever wonders Dorothy had in store for them both. She guided him silently through the kitchen, laundry room, and bathroom into the master bedroom.

As they stood beside the bed, where Grant had undressed her several times before, she removed the blanket and whispered, "Lie down in bed on your back." Grant obeyed and lay there motionless, straining his ears to hear whatever tell-tale slight sounds she might make and wondering with joy what would be coming next. Dorothy first folded up the blanket, walked over to the closet on the other side of the room, and laid it back up on the shelf. She then turned around to face Grant from the other side of the bed and began to remove all her clothes until she was entirely naked. She reached back into the closet, took out her pink quilted robe that they both now loved so much and put it on. Then after hanging up her slacks and top and going into the bathroom to drop her panties into the hamper, she came over to the side of the bed on which Grant was lying. It just so happened to be the one on which they had lain together in early December when they had their first serious sexual play in which she used his erect penis to masturbate herself, and her vulva to masturbate him.

She now pulled back the covers and sat astride Grant's middle. Their positions were now reversed from what they had been a month ago. Her lower legs were bent behind her, and her body positioned, so that her spread open vulva was perfectly aligned with the shaft of his penis. Dorothy now took his hard manhood into her right hand and carefully laid him in her vulva, so that the underside of his length lay in the length of her lips. She now began to move herself slightly forward and back, so that her sex and Grant's penis were masturbating one another. He felt so marvelously good inside her like that! His young manhood felt so firm and hard and so eager to please her as much and for as long as she wanted, and she wanted him so very much! She could not honestly remember when her womanhood had ever felt more pleasure, and she wanted it to continue for as long as she had the energy to ride him like this.

As she rode him in such sheer delight, her robe was open and presented to Grant her entire naked front. Her beautiful breasts were there for the taking, and take them he did, with his hands and with his mouth. As Dorothy moved her vulva up and down along the length of his penis, her breasts jiggled and danced so seductively. Her White Shoulders perfume added to Grant's pleasure in kissing, sucking, and licking her breasts. While she was busy pleasuring them both through mutual masturbation, Grant did the same by playing with her breasts.

Dorothy had mounted Grant's penis and had begun to ride his manhood shortly after midnight, and incredible as it sounds, she rode him like this for a little more than five hours. She did not dismount from riding her beautiful red stallion until about 5:20 that morning. She did not even dismount a single time to use the bathroom, but she stayed astride and rode Grant with insatiability for those five hours without a single break. She maintained the same rhythm of her riding for this entire period, moving her sex slightly up and down along the length of his penis as steadily as a metronome. There were only two things that interrupted the perfect rhythm of her riding. Many times she became too exuberant in her pleasurable riding and lifted her womanhood up too far, and Grant's erection slipped out of her lips. She then immediately used her hand to place him once again inside her vulva and then resumed her riding. At other times Grant interrupted her rhythm by taking her hips into his two hands and holding her down on top of his erection, and she responded by inflicting pleasure upon them both by rapidly wriggling herself sideways on him. This variation in pressure and motion further enhanced their enjoyment of this exquisite pleasure.

Her rhythmic riding was also accompanied by Grant's own erotic activity. In addition to his enjoyment of her beautifully swaying breasts, his hands were wandering over her naked body, enjoying the feel of her perfect complexion, feeling her hour-glass figure, her thighs, her back, her curvaceous hips and beautiful bottom. He even caressed her love-delta, feeling her lovely hair and watching her vulva moving along his penis. The latter sight was truly awesome and captivating. His caressing and fondling added additional fuel to both their erotic fires and thus acted as a constant stimulus to her riding him, as well as making sure that his manhood remained huge and hard and well worth her riding. They did not utter a single word during the entire five hours. They were fully absorbed in a silent nocturnal realm of utter ecstasy. The only sound to be heard in the bedroom was the slight rustling of the bed covers as Dorothy rode her man. Finally, at 5:20, after riding for five hours and a few minutes, she brought to an end this remarkable erotic performance. Without any slackening of her rhythm she abruptly halted, dismounted from her beautiful red stud, took off her robe, lay down fully naked beside Grant, and they both instantly fell asleep.

They were not allowed to sleep too long, because around 9:00 Debbie walked across the hall and came into the bedroom. "Ma," she asked in a soft voice, "are you awake yet?" As soon as she spoke these words, both Dorothy and Grant were jolted awake, and Grant kept himself perfectly still so as not to let Debbie know that he was in bed with Ma. "Yeah, Deb," Dorothy replied. "but stay right where you are. You've got a dog in front of you on the floor," she quickly fabricated, because she did not want Debbie walking up to the bed and sitting down on it. "Ok, just wait a second," she continued, as she sat up naked, grabbed her robe at the foot of the bed, put it on, and stepped into her slippers. She then arose, took Debbie by the hand, and carefully steered Debbie around the bed and through the adjoining bathroom and laundry room and then into the kitchen. Shortly thereafter Grant also arose and joined them. They sat at the table and talked leisurely while they all ate either Special K and Frosted Mini-Wheats for breakfast. After clearing their dishes away, Dorothy said, "Ok, Guys. I suppose that we can now settle down somewhere nice and comfy to talk for a while. How's about we sit down on the living room floor and have a little pow-wow?" When the other two agreed, the three stood up from the table and moved into the living room. When they came before the couch, rather than sitting on it, Dorothy used her two hands to steer her two blind guests to the places where she wanted them to sit on the carpet, forming a triangle, but Dorothy and Grant sat directly in front of one another and Debbie was off to their side, to Grant's right and Dorothy's left.

As they chatted about a wide range of things in a perfectly normal manner, a far more serious drama, totally unknown to Debbie, was being played out between Grant and Dorothy. The latter were both sitting cross-legged with their knees nearly touching; and shortly after they began talking, Grant cautiously moved his left hand forward, encountered Dorothy's crossed legs covered by her pink quilted robe, and then went inside. What his hand now discovered was truly magnificent. Her sex was spread open about as wide as she could be. Grant therefore proceeded to caress and fondle her with loving awe and admiration. Dorothy made no attempt to move his hand away, but allowed him to enjoy her in this way as long as he wanted, which, of course, was a very long time. Meanwhile, the trio conversed as if nothing unusual were taking place.

During her early morning riding of Grant's penis, Dorothy had been highly aroused, as her clitoris was masturbated by the shaft of his erection. She had not actually achieved an orgasm, but for much of that five-hour period she was very close to reaching that ultimate peak of pleasure. It had been so exquisite that her sex still felt a sweet smoldering afterglow of pleasure and desire. She had therefore deliberately orchestrated their positions on the floor with the intention of Grant giving her even more pleasure. His touch felt wonderful, as his fingers gently and carefully examined her Venus V, her hair, her upper thighs, and especially her vulva. Her lips were slightly parted, and Grant explored their outer edges and her moist inner velvet with genuine fascination. He was now beginning to think of this sight as Dorothy's love-smile or pussy smile. He could hear the smile in her beautiful voice so often. He knew the lips of her mouth so well from their kissing, but he could not imagine how lovely her smile must be. But he had no trouble seeing her love-smile, and to him nothing at all in the entire world could possibly come close to its beauty.

January 16, 1973, Tuesday

They were now in the final exam period of the semester. The previous Friday (Jan. 12) had been the last day of regular classes, and the preceding day (Monday, Jan. 15) had been the first day of final exams. Earlier that morning Grant had taken a second exam at the Rehab Center. Then Dorothy had picked him up at Holmes shortly before noon after her swimming, and they had gone off to grab a quick lunch and to run a few errands together. They were now returning to the house to be alone during the early afternoon until Carol came home from school.

"Ok," Dorothy said, "let's lie down on the bed and rest and maybe even doze off for a while." She was over at the closet in the master bedroom, hanging up her polar bear coat and then removing all of her clothes except for her bra and slip. Kin keeping with being Grant's pussy woman, she had been beautifully attired in pantyhose and a very nice dress. Grant was on the other side of the bed and stripping down to his t-shirt and shorts. They then lay down and assumed the very same position that they had enjoyed so thoroughly a few days before Christmas. Dorothy's slip was pushed up to reveal her bottom and sex as she spread herself in placing her right lower thigh on Grant's manhood. His left hand was providing them both with sweet pleasure by admiring her vulva and love-delta. They were also, of course, covered up with their white blanket.

"I've been thinking of Henry Wadsworth Longfellow lately," Grant remarked. "Oh yeah," Dorothy responded, "I really like his poetry. He wrote some really nice poems for children. I still have my high school literature book that has several of his nicest poems in it, including 'The Wreck of the Hesperus'. Maybe when we get up, I'll get out the book, and we can enjoy the poems together. But anyway, why have you been thinking about him? You're always talking about all those ancient guys, like Homer and Herodotus. You're not being tested on Longfellow are you?" "No, not at all. I've been thinking about his famous poem about the midnight ride of Paul Revere." "Why is that?" Dorothy innocently asked. "Weeellll," Grant said in an exaggerated manner, "because I recently witnessed and thoroughly enjoyed a spectacular midnight ride of a different sort." "You did?" Dorothy said with obvious pleasure and a bit of naughtiness in her voice. "I sure did! Since Longfellow immortalized Paul Revere with a poem for his midnight ride, I've been thinking that I should try to write a poem to commemorate that most heroic exploit of yours." "Heroic, huh?" Dorothy queried with pleasure and amusement. "You bet ya! Five hours without a single break, not to mention all the cheer and joy that it generated. Maybe I should start calling you Mrs. Mountjoy." "You think so, huh?" "Why not? And here's the first couplet of my poem. 'Come listen, my children, and you shall hear of the midnight ride of my Dorothy dear'." "Something tells me that the poem wouldn't be very suitable for children to listen to."

January 17, 1973, Wednesday

It was around 11:00 in the morning, and Dorothy and Grant were sitting side by side on a couch in the Holmes lounge with one of Grant's heavy plastic braille relief maps spread across their laps. Grant was giving her a geography lesson, because as he talked about his ancient history to her, they both began to realize that she did not know where many of these places were. Dorothy had learned quite a bit of modern geography many years ago in school; and in fact, when she was in the seventh grade, she won a contest in her school by correctly answering the question, "What does U.S.S.R. stand for?" But she knew very little about ancient geography, a situation that Grant was now beginning to remedy by teaching his darling things that were important to him, and which he therefore wished to share with her.

As Grant picked up the map and slid it back into the large cardboard carton with the other maps of the world's continents, he said, "I have something important to tell you." "Oh yeah, What's that?" Dorothy asked with genuine curiosity. "I've decided to take next semester off." "What?" she exclaimed in surprise, "Why?" "I didn't do too bad this semester. It looks like I'll get B's and C's, but that's really not what I should be doing. I should be making all A's or maybe A's with a B. It's just too hard for me to do my best work with all this turmoil going on between us. I really think that I shouldn't take any classes at all next semester. I'm hoping that by the fall I will be able to get back to doing my best."

"So," Dorothy asked, "if you don't take classes next semester, what will you do?" "I'll go back home to Fairmont and just stay there, rest up, and even do lots of studying to get myself well prepared for next fall." "You mean you wouldn't stay here in town?" "No, how could I? But I could plan to come visit here every few weeks or so. I've already found out that there's going to be four public lectures sponsored by the local chapter of the American Institute of Archaeology, and I could tell my parents that I really should attend these lectures and then plan on staying the whole week." That answer of Grant's allayed some of Dorothy's alarm caused by the notion that they might not see one another for several months. But another matter also caused her to feel real anguish at what he was telling her. "Grant, it really hurts me to think that our relationship has caused all this." "Oh Dorth, please don't look at it like that! I don't want you blaming yourself for any of this, because it really isn't your fault. It's the fault of the situation in which we are both trapped. So please," Grant stressed with real tenderness, "don't blame yourself at all."

They sat and discussed the matter for fifteen minutes more. Dorothy had been totally surprised by it all, and she kept trying to find valid reasons why Grant's decision did not make sense. But as they continued to discuss things, Grant answered her objections with well-reasoned counter-arguments. He had obviously been giving this much thought, and he eventually succeeded in convincing Dorothy that he was making the right decision. He also succeeded in convincing her that she was in no way to blame; and finally, the idea of him coming to University City for a week at four different times throughout the semester made his decision at least bearable for them emotionally, because neither could have endured the idea of not seeing one another for seven whole months. Their relationship had come to mean too much to both of them.

After Grant returned his set of maps to his dorm room, they had an early lunch at Uncle Joe's Pancake House. Grant then eagerly tagged along as Dorothy ran several necessary errands to the post office, the Lincoln Bank, and the grocery store. Then they came to the culmination of their day together: returning to the house, undressing, and lying down on the bed together almost naked under their white blanket until it was time for Carol to come home from school.

As on similar previous occasions, Dorothy had fixed herself up in a lovely dress with a slip and pantyhose; and when they came into the bedroom, she took off everything except her bra and slip and lay beside Grant with her slip pushed up above her sex and her right leg thrown over him, so that her womanhood was fully available for his loving admiration. Today, however, they were both very tired and in need of a nap. Yet, when they lay down, Dorothy hiked up her slip to expose her sex, pulled down Grant's undershorts to reveal his penis, and threw her bare right leg on top of his beautiful red cock. She was intent on taking a nap, but she wanted to do so in full erotic style.

Although Grant was also rather tired from spending long hours in studying for his exams over the past few days, Dorothy's alluring White Shoulders and especially her spread and fully available sex perked him up in a jiffy. He was therefore instantly caressing and fondling her love-delta and vulva with his usual enraptured attention as if he were in an erotic trance. "What are you doing?" Dorothy protested, "We're supposed to be lying down to take a nap!" "How in hell can I possibly take a nap with you spreading yourself like that on me? If you're going to do that, then you have to expect that I'm going to feel you." Dorothy's reply was simply a very satisfied laugh. They soon forgot all about their weariness and need for a nap. They instead spent their remaining time together in delicious erotic play and pleasure.

January 19, 1973, Friday

As soon as Carol left the house to go off to school, Dorothy went back into the master bedroom, took off her pink quilted robe, hung it up, pulled off her cotton nightgown, placed it under her pillow, and slipped into the new sexy pajamas that George had given her for Christmas. She then came into the front bedroom where Grant was still sleeping, and she slid into bed beside him.

He had come over yesterday afternoon to have supper with her and Carol and then to spend the night. Of course, after Carol had gone to bed, they had stayed up very late, sitting together on the couch in the living room, wrapped up in an afghan and engaged in serious kissing and fondling. After letting Grant undress her, Dorothy had put on her nightgown and robe that offered suitable cover if they happened to be seen by Carol, but also allowed Grant to please them both tremendously with his caresses.

As soon as Dorothy slid into bed beside him, Grant awoke and began to explore her lovely feminine form that was so well outlined through the thin sheer fabric. Her whole body was on display for him: her smooth skin, her breasts, and especially her female sex, whose hair and vulva he could feel perfectly through the material. "Let's go into the other bedroom," Dorothy whispered.

Not long after they had lain down together in the master bedroom, Dorothy was totally naked. They had cooperated in unbuttoning her top and pulling it off to fully reveal her breasts, but she had given Grant the full honor of removing her bottoms, and oh how he was enchanted by the sight of her bare ass and beautiful pussy emerging as he pulled off the garment. Dorothy lay on her back, spread her thighs, and wordlessly beckoned Grant to come lie there. As he moved himself between her legs, there were four hands frantically pulling down his undershorts, so that his penis could begin worshipping her vulva. As on the previous December 6 for the first time, as well as on other occasions since then, they now lay in bed for a very long time, fully occupied in their mutual masturbation, and Dorothy used her hands between their bodies to carefully manage the precise positioning of his penis so as to give her the maximum amount of pleasure through the stimulation of her clitoris.

By midmorning the worst of their hunger for one another had been somewhat satisfied, to be replaced by a steady and strong flame of desire. But the latter was also now accompanied by a growing hunger in their stomachs. Finally, Dorothy said, "I hate to tell ya, but maybe we should be thinking about getting up and having something to eat." "I suppose," Grant grudgingly agreed, "but this sure is really nice!" "We can't be doing this all morning, can we?" "We can sure try!" They both laughed. "Doesn't that guy down there ever get enough?" Dorothy asked teasingly. "Look who's talking," Grant protested, "Who was the one who went on all night for five hours?

And besides, who came into my bed this morning with nothing on except those sexy pajamas, and then after I began feeling her, she invited me back into her bed?" "I guess you're right. I'm just getting what I deserve." "You sure are, and I hope you like it." "Well, I wouldn't be lying here for two hours if I didn't, would I?"

When Grant finally moved from between her legs, Dorothy began to move herself to the edge of the bed; and as she did, Grant's hands followed various parts of her body. "Tell ya what, fella," she said playfully, "I'll go fix us some breakfast and serve it to you in bed." "That sounds nice," he replied. Dorothy then dressed herself in her clothes for the day. Then she went into the kitchen and began preparing toast and scrambled eggs. Meanwhile, Grant simply lay naked in bed, listening to her sounds in the kitchen and enjoying the tingling sensation of sexual pleasure and desire in his penis that was still fully erect. He then decided to give his darling a very pleasant surprise. He found the bottoms of her pajamas and put them on. He liked how they felt on his skin, especially that of his penis.

When Dorothy entered the room fully clothed and carrying a tray of food, Grant was lying in bed covered up to his neck. He then suddenly threw back the covers and revealed himself with his lower body clad in her feminine garment. "Oh wow!" Dorothy exclaimed in surprise and pleasure. She loved the sight, especially of the large bulge in his crotch where the thin material carefully outlined his testicles and erection. She instantly sat the tray down, came over to the side of the bed, reached down to take Grant's manhood into her hand through the material, and with him still lovingly in hand lay down on top of him. Their mouths met in a passionate kiss that they held for a long time; and while they were still kissing, Grant moved his right hand between their bodies; and as he began to insert his fingers inside the waistbands of her slacks and panties, Dorothy assisted him by lifting up her body and spreading her thighs. Grant's hand slowly descended down her love-front and traced the length of her vulva. As his hand clasped her sex between her thighs, he also inserted his middle finger up inside her vagina and kept it there, impaling her sex on his finger as they continued to kiss.

When they finally broke apart, Grant sat with Dorothy on the edge of the bed to eat breakfast, and he did so wearing her pajama bottoms, which Dorothy found to be so sexy on him. "Ok, Guy," she seriously intoned, "time to get cuttin'. The day's a-wastin'. You promised me that you'd play the guitar for me to record, so that I would have it to listen to while you're gone this coming semester." "Ok," he replied in mock exasperation. "I know," she said,

"I'm a real slave driver and no fun at all." "Well," Grant said with a laugh in his voice, "I wouldn't go that far. You're actually quite a bit of fun." "I am, huh?" she said with obvious pleasure. "Boy! You sure are!"

Grant now arose and dressed and joined Dorothy in doing various things around the house, but he eventually settled down in the living room with a small reel-to-reel tape recorder that Dennis had left at the house, and with this machine he made a music tape for Dorothy. He played various songs, both finger style instrumentals and songs that he sang along with the guitar. Dorothy moved around the living room, dining room, and kitchen as he played and often joined him in the singing. Moreover, Their verbal interchange continued the mood of playful pleasure that their activity and words in bed had so sweetly established between them. They were both well aware that they would soon not be seeing one another at all, and they were eager to enjoy their remaining time together as fully as possible.

January 20, 1973, Saturday

Yesterday afternoon's mood of sweet playful euphoria had finally been disturbed by a telephone call from Bob Snider. He was coming down with the flu or some kind of terrible cold, and he was feeling very miserable. He had therefore called to ask Dorothy to please come over and take him to the student health center. Dorothy therefore had to step out of her secret love-life and into her role as Ma. After dropping Grant off at Holmes, she went to Bob's room in Forester and walked him out to her car. She sat and waited as he was examined by a doctor at the student health center; and since it was so obvious to her that Bob was really in bad shape, she suggested that rather than returning him to his room, where he would have to fend for himself, she should bring him to her house, where she could look after him. Bob thankfully agreed. Thus it was that Bob spent the entire weekend at Dorothy's house, bedridden the entire time in the far bedroom. While Richard Nixon was taking his second oath of office and delivering his second inaugural address, Bob was sleeping soundly and was oblivious to everything. Dorothy quietly looked in on him several times and brought him food, liquids, and medicine whenever he was awake and was in need of them.

January 24, 1973, Wednesday

As soon as Carol left for school, Dorothy began dressing. She had already taken a shower while Carol was getting herself ready to leave. She had even shaved her legs. Since then Dorothy had just been wearing her robe around the house; and since today would be her last full day with Grant, she had been especially conscious of her nakedness beneath one of his favorite garments. She gave thoughtful care to every item of clothing that she put on, because she wanted to be as beautiful as possible for him. After removing her robe and hanging it up in the closet, she took out a pair of panties, stepped into them, and pulled them up into place. As she did so, she glanced down at herself and was very pleased with what she saw. Later this morning Grant's hands would be removing this garment. She next sprayed her arms, shoulders, and breasts with White Shoulders, placed her bra around her waist, fastened it at the back, and then moved it up into position by slipping her arms through the shoulder straps and fitting the cups around her breasts that Grant enjoyed so much. She now returned to the closet and looked through her dresses. She finally selected one made of heavy but very soft material. Its heaviness would protect her from the winter cold, and its fabric would be to Grant's liking. But first she chose a very delicate slip and put it on before stepping into the dress and zipping it up. Then, after donning her pantyhose and peds, both of which Grant found so irresistible on her, she gave further thought to what shoes to wear. She finally decided upon a pair of medium-height heels. In addition to being feminine and elegant in a very simple but attractive way, they were quite comfortable. Not only would they make her feel sexy, but the sound that they made as she walked would doubtless please Grant. Last of all, she went into the adjoining bathroom and stood before the mirror to apply makeup and hair spray. Although Grant would not be able to see the former, he would probably notice the latter, and that also would heighten her sex appeal for him.

While Dorothy was thus employed in preparing herself for this very important date with her college boyfriend, Grant had arisen from his dorm bed and was now over at Forester in Renny's room. He had taken his last final exam yesterday and had spent the evening in packing up all his things, so that he could spend all his remaining time on campus with his beloved Dorothy right up until his father arrived Thursday morning to return him to Fairmont. Since Renny had called yesterday to ask Ma to come over to help him find some things for his packing, Dorothy and Grant had agreed to meet this morning at his room. In addition, since Renny's roommate had already gone home for the semester break, Dennis had spent the night there and was in Renny's room when Grant arrived. The two friends were just chitchatting. But then Dennis, followed by Grant, went into the bathroom to brush his teeth and to do a few other things, because he had to be leaving soon to take his own last final exam at the Rehab Center. When Dorothy arrived twenty minutes later, she found Renny and Dennis resting on the two beds and Grant just leaning against the wall. She walked over to the desk on the left side of the room and sat down in the chair. "So, Renny," Dorothy asked, "what do you need me for?" "Ah just to find a few particular boxes way up in the top storage area of my closet." "What?" Dorothy exclaimed in mock outrage, "You expect little ole me with my short legs to get those boxes down for you?" "Hey, Ma," Renny said with laughter in his voice, "you might be short, but we all know how great you are. I know you can do it." "You do, huh? We'll see about that, Renny," Dorothy replied with sweet irony.

As they were engaged in their gentle verbal combat, Grant had drifted over to the radiator beneath the window and perched himself on it. He was now within arm's reach of his darling. He therefore proceeded to touch and caress her, placing his hands on her shoulders and back to feel her dress and hair. The fabric felt lovely, and her hair was all done up so carefully. "My golly!" he thought to himself, "she looked like a woman all dressed up for some fancy event!" In fact, she was. She wanted her boy-man to escort her through their last lovely day together. As he lightly ran his left hand along the side of her neck, Dorothy shuddered inside with pleasure, and her toes even curled up inside her shoes.

"Tell ya what, Ma," Grant interjected, "We can pull that chair you're sitting in over to the closet. I'll help you stand up on it and hold it steady while you look up in that storage space." "Ok, that sounds like a good idea. I'm glad someone here has good ideas," she said with heavy sweet irony directed again against Renny. "Hey!" Renny said in his rasping tone of protest, "now what's that supposed to mean?" "I still like ya, Renny," Dorothy replied sweetly.

Dorothy now stood up, and Grant pulled the chair over to the closet. After he opened up the door and put the chair in place, he used one hand to hold the chair steady while giving the other to Dorothy for support as she stepped up onto the seat. After standing up, she began to rummage around in the storage area and to tell Renny what boxes were up there. As he indicated which ones he needed, Dorothy dropped them onto the floor.

While she did this, Grant had his body braced against the chair to keep it from sliding, and he also had his hands on Dorothy to make sure that she would not fall, but rather than holding her in a chaste way with his hands lightly resting on her outer clothing, he kept his hands under her dress and held her by her bottom and love-front that were so perfectly outlined in her pantyhose. Then when she was finished, Grant simply lifted her down to the floor slowly and gently with his hands still under her dress and with her hands and arms around his neck and shoulders.

By now both of them were already drunk with desire for one another. They therefore enjoyed touching hands as they stacked the boxes on Renny's desk. Then while the four of them talked about nothing in particular, Dorothy and Grant remained on their feet, slowly moving around the room and constantly touching each other, Dorothy's hand squeezing Grant's forearm, his hand caressing her bottom or cupping her breast. At one point as Dennis and Renny were fully occupied in talking, they halted in the very middle of the floor to embrace; and as Dorothy placed her arms around Grant, he slipped his hands once again under her dress and caressed her bottom and love-delta. Shortly thereafter they excused themselves on grounds that they had to be off to run various errands.

As soon as they left the room and shut the door behind them, Dennis said, "Hey man, did you hear what I heard?" "Yeah, I did," replied Renny. "Dennis then continued in genuine surprise and awe, "It sounded like they were hugging. I could hear their clothes rustling." "She sure did smell good," Renny observed, She must be all dressed up real pretty." "Yeah," added Dennis, "While Grant and I were talking a while ago in the bathroom as I was brushing my teeth, he said that he and Ma would be spending the day together." "Boy!" Renny exclaimed in joyous wonder, "I wonder what they have planned." Then Renny cackled in genuine glee, "That boy just might be getting himself some of Ma's pussy. But he'd better watch it, because if George finds out, he might come after him and shoot his pecker off." "Hey!" Dennis protested, "Look who's talking? You've been chasing after John Daniels' wife Cindy. You'd better watch out yourself!" "Ah shit man! I'm not worried about that blind mother fucker. If he came after me, he wouldn't be able to shoot straight."

When Dorothy turned to go out to her car, Grant gently checked her by tugging on her arm. "Dorth," he said, "let's go this way," indicating the other exit to that part of Forester. "I want to run past my room and grab my set of maps in case we want to do some more geography today." "Ok," she simply replied. After coming into his dorm room that was luckily devoid of a roommate, Grant quickly located the box of maps, dropped them on his bed, and turned to Dorothy, "Let me kiss and feel you again," he said in a low voice full of desire. "But what if your roommate walks in?" Dorothy asked. "We can fix that," Grant replied. He then walked over to his closet, swung open its door, so that it rested against the room door. "Ok, that should do it. Now if he shows up, he won't be able to come in until we let him, and I can pretend that I was just standing there in my closet doing something with my stuff." Dorothy now came to him; and as they stood together at the closet, they again embraced with Grant's hands going under her dress. After caressing her love-delta, he took her bottom into his hands and pressed her hard into his erection, and they kissed. As their lips met, Grant was aware of her carefully applied lip stick, one more indication of how carefully Dorothy had made herself up for this day.

Their only errand was to go to a music store to buy some guitar strings and sheet music for Wesley. Dorothy would then have to package it all up and mail it off to him in Adak. As Dorothy was parking the car, Grant asked, "Where exactly are we?" "At the music store," she replied. "Yeah, I know that, but where?" "Just a small parking area." "Are there any other people around?" "No, it's early enough that it is deserted." As Grant came around the car to take her arm, she finally realized why he had been asking such odd questions when she felt his hand pass across her rear. He had been aching to have another feel. Even through the thickness of her polar bear coat, they both enjoyed the intimate touch.

As soon as they entered the house, they removed their coats and dropped them into the chair near the door, and then they again embraced and kissed with Grant's hands wandering about under her dress. While they continued to stand pressed together in the family room with Grant's hands cupping her bottom and pressing his erection firmly into her, Dorothy asked, "Are you hungry?" "Actually," Grant replied "I am." "Ok, I'll fix us some breakfast right away." She then stepped into the kitchen, pulled out a pot and a pan, and proceeded to fill one with strips of bacon and the other with eggs and cheese to be scrambled together.

"You know," Grant began, "I heard something really interesting on the news last night in my room as I was packing." "What's that?" Dorothy asked. "There was a Supreme Court decision yesterday about the legality of abortions. If I understood what they were saying, there's been some case in the courts for some time, and now the Supreme Court has decided that women have a legal right to an abortion. I guess it's going to overturn a number of state laws that either place certain restrictions on abortions or outlaw them altogether." "Huh," Dorothy responded, "That is interesting." "Yeah," Grant continued, "as soon as I heard it, I first thought about Aemilia Dickerson. I wonder if it could have somehow made a difference with her." "I don't know," replied Dorothy, "It's such a terrible thing!" "Yep," Grant agreed, "It certainly is!"

Now that Dorothy had everything assembled and cooking on the stove and was standing there overseeing things, Grant drifted over, stood behind her, and felt under her dress, her hips, her bottom, her thighs, her love-delta. "God!" he exclaimed in a low voice full of desire, "You look so damn beautiful! And man! Are you ever beautifully dressed up!" "I'm glad you noticed," she said with genuine satisfaction and pleasure in her voice. "My God!" Grant replied, "How could I not? Even a blind man could see how lovely you are!" They both laughed. Grant continued, "You look like you're going out on a really hot date with your boyfriend." "I am," Dorothy replied in a low serious tone. "Am I your boyfriend?" he asked with equal seriousness. "Of course you are," she replied with tender sweetness.

After a pause that seemed to become charged with their passionate desire for each other, Grant broke the silence by saying in a very low voice that was almost an animal growl of pure emotion, "You're my woman!" He said these words slowly and with heavy emphasis. Dorothy said nothing. She could not, in view of her marital status. They both understood and accepted that, but Grant's declaration had pleased her so very much. "Oh God!" he now said more loudly and with obvious passion, "I'm sorry, but I've got to see the real thing!" As his hands moved up to the elastic waistbands of her hose and panties, Dorothy let go of the spoon in her right hand and let it rest against the rim of the pot. She now spread her feet slightly to give herself added stability and held onto the front edge of the stove with one hand and the adjoining counter with the other. She stood motionless as Grant slowly and carefully worked her hose and panties downward from her hips, off of her bottom, and down her love-delta and away from her sex. He did not stop until he had them down to just above her knees. His hands returned again under her dress and began to fondle her bare skin everywhere. After making one careful tour of her front and back, his hands repeated his amorous inspection, and then again for a third time. He then withdrew his hands to begin the next phase of his entranced admiration. Dorothy felt his body press up against her back. His left arm came gently around her belly and held her firmly against him, so that she now felt his erection pressing into the upper part of her bottom. His right hand went under her slip and dress, and his fingers began to worship and adore her sex, tenderly feeling her perfect V, her hair, the smooth skin of her delta, and her vulva.

They stood there wordlessly with their whole concentration centered on Dorothy's sex. Grant's fingers continued their awestruck examination. Eventually, however, the situation suddenly changed when he carefully inserted the tip of his middle finger inside her lips to touched her moist inner velvet. As soon as he lightly brushed her clitoris, Dorothy felt an instant pang of extraordinary pleasure pass through her body. She had been growing increasingly aroused all morning from the time of wearing her robe over her nakedness until now, and she was on the verge of an orgasm. Her legs felt as if they would not support her, but luckily, Grant had his arm around her. "Oh my golly!" she exclaimed breathlessly in response to him touching her clitoris, "Let me lie down." When Grant removed his arm and hand, Dorothy first turned off the two burners, carefully eased her body to the floor, and then stretched herself out on it right in front of the stove. She was totally indifferent to the floor's cool hardness. All that concerned her right then was having Grant inflict exquisite sexual pleasure upon her sex.

"Come here," she urgently commanded. Grant knelt beside her on the floor. She was lying on her back with her hose and panties around her knees and her dress and slip pulled up to reveal her womanhood. "I need you to give me a climax. Here. Give me your hand." Grant obeyed. "Now keep your finger right there and move it back and forth gently but quickly." Grant first adjusted his body into a more comfortable position. After he was lying down beside her, Dorothy used her hand to guide Grant's hand and finger into the proper place. He then began to masturbate her for the very first time with his finger. "That's it," Dorothy urged, "Just like that!" Then her breaths came in rhythmic gasps, as the orgasm began to come. Her thighs tensed together in response to the intense pleasure, and Grant felt her vulva correspondingly contract around the tip of his finger that was giving her such wondrous pleasure. Then her entire body went rigid for several seconds and then slowly relaxed. "Oooohhhh!" was Dorothy's only but perfectly eloquent response to Grant's first success in giving her an orgasm. Finally, she said in a voice groggy with pleasure, "Oh my! I'm not sure I can even get up. I feel like an old worn-out dishrag!" Grant said nothing. He was simply pleased with having given her such ecstasy, but he did keep his hand cupped over her sex. It was so magnificent to have his hand full of her beautiful womanhood. "Oh my golly!" she repeated in amazed pleasure, "Help me up, will you?" After getting her to her feet, Dorothy pulled her hose and panties back into place, and Grant allowed her to finish cooking their breakfast without further sexual molestation. He figured that they would have plenty of time for that as soon as they had eaten.

Since September the kitchen had been almost as important a stage for their passion as had been the front bedroom, master bedroom, or the two couches. So often, as Dorothy prepared things for them to eat, Grant could not keep his hands off of her, and this morning it had culminated so beautifully in Dorothy having her first orgasm inspired by her love and desire for Grant. She could not remember how long it had been since she had enjoyed such extraordinary sexual pleasure. Her five-hour riding of his manhood two weeks ago had been such a lovely forerunner to this climax on the kitchen floor.

As soon as the food was ready, they ate and then moved into the bathroom. As Dorothy sat on the toilet to urinate, Grant knelt at her feet and had the great honor of removing her shoes, peds, nylons, and panties. As she stood up and walked into the master bedroom, Grant followed behind with one hand full of her articles of clothing and the other one under her dress to watch her bottom move beautifully as she walked ahead of him. Then in less than a minute they were naked in bed with Grant lying between her legs, and Dorothy was carefully guiding his erect manhood inside her vulva to begin another deliciously long session of mutual masturbation.

They remained naked in bed together for the next three hours and more, and they had no difficulty in filling the time with glorious erotic happiness. Their lengthy initial session of mutual masturbation was followed by a bewildering variety of delights. Dorothy took him into her hand and forced him to come and ejaculate. She allowed Grant to fondle and caress her body as he pleased. Whenever Dorothy arose to use the bathroom, Grant walked behind her with his hands on her hips and bottom to see how she moved. He was obviously fascinated with every aspect of her nakedness, and it thrilled Dorothy to be the object of such rapt attention. As she sat on the toilet, he stood naked beside her and took advantage of her upright sitting position to fondle her breasts. As he did, Dorothy feasted her eyes on his erect penis and the rest of his beautiful youthful body.

As they came back to the bed from a second trip to the bathroom, Grant commented, "My golly! You have such a beautiful bottom!" "I think you're prejudiced," she replied humorously. "I sure am!" he rejoined. "Lie down on your stomach," he commanded; and as she sat down and positioned herself on the bed with her legs together, her forearms tucked under her, and her head turned to the side to face him, his hands never left her body, but studied how she moved. "God! You're beautiful!" he exclaimed in a hushed tone filled with awe. His hands began to travel the full length of her body, from the back of her neck down to her feet. "Your complexion is so flawless!" he said again in hushed awe. "That's what called a peaches and cream complexion," Dorothy explained in a soft voice that conveyed her genuine pleasure at his admiration of her. "Boy! I tell you. If you could somehow take the most perfectly formed peach and cross that with the loveliest female flesh, what we'd get would be this." As he ended the sentence, his hands moved to her bottom. After carefully and gently feeling her flawlessly smooth buttocks and hips, he filled his hands with her ample flesh and kneaded it lovingly. It was the very first time that someone was making love to her bottom, and it felt so wonderful. The pleasure was recharging her sex with such stimulation that she might have to ask Grant for a second orgasm.

"One day," Dorothy began, "as my two sisters and I were shopping, I was walking ahead of them, and they both made fun of how my bottom looked as I walked." "Well," Grant said somewhat scoffingly, "what do you expect of your two sisters? They are women and wouldn't look at that part of you as a man does. Besides, I bet you anything that what they really felt was jealousy and covered it up by making fun of you. Don't you worry about what your sisters think of your bottom. There's nothing at all wrong with it. In fact, she's about as perfect as can be." What he had just said greatly pleased her, because since her sisters had ridiculed her bottom, she had always been somewhat self-conscious about it, but now her young blind college boyfriend was telling her how much he loved her there.

"Stay still," Grant said, "Don't move at all. I want to lie down on top of you like that." As he carefully lowered his body over hers, he spread his legs to either side of hers that were together, and he used his right hand to guide the head of his penis gently into the cleft of her bottom. He now began to hump her. As he did, his mouth kissed the left side of her neck, and it sent pleasure throughout her body. Dorothy finally felt his penis enlarge, shudder, and then relax. He had just used the beauty of her bottom to masturbate his manhood and had also left on her there the signature of his love and desire for her.

When Grant arose, Dorothy rolled over onto her back and spread her thighs to place her sex once again on full display for him. Grant sat down on the bed between her feet and began to fondle her womanhood with one hand and with the other to caress her thighs. Dorothy gazed at his face. It was serene, content, but also serious as if he were studying or contemplating something very profound, as in fact he was. The object of his study was her female sex. Like the morning after her five-hour ride when she wanted him to caress her there endlessly, the orgasm on the kitchen floor had so awakened her womanhood that she simply wanted him to keep touching and caressing her there, either with his hands and fingers or with his penis, and he certainly did not disappoint her. She lowered her gaze and looked down the length of her body and was thrilled by the sight of his hand playing in her love-garden, and beyond that she could sometimes catch a glimpse of his erection and his bright red hair.

Dorothy now decided to give him another lovely variation of her female anatomy to study. She closed her knees together, lifted up her feet, also held them together, and pressed them against Grant's chest. The movement caused her thighs to be bent upward toward her body and also presented much more of her bottom to Grant. He instantly caught on to her new erotic pose and began admiring her bottom. Then Dorothy suddenly opened her knees to display her spread sex, but as Grant was starting to caress her there, she teasingly shut the door on him. But she had not closed up quite quickly enough, because his fingers were now pleasurably trapped between her closed thighs and against her sex. "Open up," he demanded. "Why?" she teased. "Well, ok, if you insist," she allowed, as she spread herself open for him. She still had her feet on his chest, but now Grant could see both her spread sex and much of her bare bottom in the same lovely pose, and he was genuinely awestruck at her beauty. Her love-smile was so majestically enhanced by the beauty of her shapely bottom.

Once, as they were lying side by side, Dorothy had her right leg bent up at the knee and propped up against Grant's left leg. Her own left leg was stretched straight out. As always, Grant's hand was fondling her sex. He had never seen her before quite like this either. She was spread open on the right side but not so on the left, and the asymmetry fascinated him just as did every newly encountered love pose that their interaction offered him. The way in which her leg rested against him was wonderful. It conveyed to him that she was relaxed and fully comfortable in her nakedness with him. Her pose also seemed to embody her perfect trust in him.

As they lay there together with Grant's fingers causing them both pleasure by touching her sex, he said, "I would like to tell you something, but I don't want you saying anything in reply. Ok?" "Ok," she answered. "Dorth,

I love you. I truly love you in every way that I can possibly love you. I have never encountered anyone with as marvelous a personality and character as you. I truly mean that. I love you so fully as a person and as a woman who has the most beautiful spirit that I have ever known. Please believe me. But I also know that I could never be satisfied as your platonic friend, because I also love you so completely, and that includes loving you as a man loves a woman. I know you have often thought that I simply desire you and am infatuated with your female beauty. Well, I certainly am. Oh golly today has been so wonderful! But Dorth, I truly do love you, and my desire for you is not just carnal lust. It is part of my complete and total love for you. Well, that's about what all I wanted to say." He then fell silent, and as promised, Dorothy said nothing in reply. But his words had moved her deeply; and although Grant could not see, she silently shed a few tears of her own strong emotions.

What Grant had just said summed up very well the turbulent and tormenting nature of their relationship ever since it began. They had both been and continued to be tortured by it. The chronic instability had kept Grant teetering precariously between emotional highs and lows, and that in turn had kept him from doing his very best academically. Dorothy had been and was tortured in her own ways. Their love and her marital status had forced her to live a secret life. Because she had always been a person of outstanding decency, that in itself caused her much anguish and shame. She knew with what horrible words she would be labeled if her friends, family, and church acquaintances knew what she had been and was doing with Grant. But it had been about sixteen years since she first realized that she no longer loved George. Was that not a long enough sentence to serve in a loveless marriage, which had not only been so terribly tormenting but also very unhappy? Over the years she had tried to sort out her feelings and had often blamed herself for the failure of the marriage, but whenever she tried talking to George about serious things, they never succeeded in getting anywhere. Her university kids had been the one real source of happiness in her life for such a long time, and then Grant had come along and had brought her back to life as a complete woman. How could anyone, exercising reason and mercy, find her guilty and condemn her to a life sentence in her unhappy marriage?

Eventually, as they continued to enjoy their nakedness together in bed, Dorothy looked at her watch and said, "I really do hate to tell you, but it's about 2:00. We're going to have to be getting up soon." They both did not want these hours of paradise to end, because when they did, they would have to face so many days bereft of such joy. After a short period of silence, Grant asked, "How about we go take a shower together?" "Gee, I don't know. I'm really afraid that George might come home and find us there." Grant took her reply as a negative answer to his question, and it greatly disappointed him. But as they lay there, Dorothy continued to consider the matter. She looked out the window. Despite the cold, the sky was blue, and the sun shining brightly, excellent working conditions for the construction project in Newton. Consequently, there was very little chance of George coming home today. Besides, they had been in bed together for more than three hours and had not given his possible return a single thought. So, why not! "I guess we can," she then said.

They arose from bed and walked naked together into the bathroom. The shower was just barely big enough to accommodate them. It seemed that no matter how she stood or where she turned, Grant's erect penis was always brushing or banging against her, but how wonderful that was! "Can't you keep that thing somewhere else where it isn't always in the way?" she teasingly asked. They both laughed. Then she suggested, "Let's first shampoo our hair and wash our faces, and then we can wash one another." And that is what they did.

Dorothy first washed Grant, spreading the soap over his body from his shoulders to his thighs, both front and back. Her hands loved the feel of his masculine hardness. When she lathered up his penis and testicles with her hand, it was as if she were giving him a special form of masturbation. He became even larger and harder under the touch of her dainty hands. Then it was Grant's turn. Other than using a washcloth to scrub her back, he relied entirely upon his hands to soap her up and wash her beautiful body. The soap simply served as a kind of lubricant in his enjoyment of handling her anatomy. He began with her back and went down to her bottom that he had so loved earlier. She then turned around, and he began doing her front from her shoulders on down to her feet. It was, of course, especially marvelous to wash her breasts, belly, love-delta, and female sex between her spread-open thighs. As he knelt down on the floor to wash her legs and feet, he reached up with his mouth and closed it over each of her breasts in turn. He then lowered his mouth to her sex and took it in as well. Although Dorothy had previously discouraged him from taking her sex into his mouth on grounds that she would not smell or taste good, he figured that she could not object now. He had just washed her there. Dorothy stood still as he took each side of her vulva into his mouth to feel her with his tongue, and then he inserted his tongue inside her vulva itself and gently licked her several times. It caused her very sweet pleasure.

When they emerged from the shower stall, they enjoyed the additional pleasure of drying one another off. They then dressed and went into the living room to have themselves engaged in normal around-the-house things when Carol arrived home from school. The rest of the afternoon and evening was spent quietly and sweetly in the afterglow of what they had enjoyed earlier in the day. After supper they sat together on the living room couch, so that Grant could give his darling another geography lesson with his maps. They did not stay up very late. Their hours earlier in the day had to be their last time of delirious pleasure together.

January 25, 1973, Thursday

When Dorothy arose from bed this morning, she went ahead and dressed herself. She would be taking Grant back to his dorm room shortly after 9:00, and there would be no real time for amorous activity. Indeed, they had both begun to settle into a mild state of depression as the time for Grant to leave approached.

As soon as Carol went off to school, they sat down on the family room couch to spend their last moments together and to exchange last-minute bits of vital information.

"I called the Classics Department on Monday," Grant said, "and they told me that the first AIA lecture is on February 26. That's 32 days from today." In fact, all four AIA lectures this coming semester will be on a Monday night. You can give them a call and ask them to send you a schedule of the lectures, and then you'll have all that information for your own calendar." "Ok," Dorothy quietly replied. Grant continued, "I figure that I can come down on the bus on Monday and stay until Friday. Can you check the bus schedule for buses between here and Peoria?" "Sure, and then I'll let you know in a braille letter." "Well," Grant went on, "my dad is supposed to be here around 10:00. So I suppose that we can stay here until about 9:20, and I'll be at my room a half an hour in advance just in case he gets here early." Ok."

Grant now reached into his pants pocket and pulled something out. As he held it enclosed in his hand, he said, "I have something to give you." "Oh?" Dorothy said in real surprise, "What's that?" Grant opened up his hand and said, "It's my initial ring. It's nothing fancy, just a plain ordinary kid's initial ring. I had a really nice one made of sterling silver just before I went into the hospital for my two eye operations, but when I left it on my finger before going into surgery, someone saw it and took it off, because you're not supposed to have anything like that on, and I never got it back. So, I replaced it with this cheaper ring. But I want you to have it as a token of my love for you." He held it out, and Dorothy took it from him, genuinely moved by the gesture. "Thank you so much, Grant. I will treasure it. I obviously can't wear it on my finger, but I think I've got a long chain that I can put it on and then wear it around my neck and under my clothes, so no one can see it, but we will know that I am wearing it." "I would like that very much," Grant replied.

By now they were both on the verge of tears and simply sat quietly together holding hands, touching one another, and occasionally making small talk. When it was 9:15, Grant stood up from the couch and said, "I would like to say goodbye to all the dogs." "Ok," Dorothy answered, "It looks like the three big ones are already here with us. Just Schatzi is missing. She's probably in her little bed in the bedroom. I'll go get her." Grant waited until she returned with Schatzi in her arms, and they all three embraced; and after Grant talked to the dog, Dorothy put her down on the floor. Grant now knelt and called the dogs to him; and as he hugged each one, he told them goodbye with his voice choking with emotion. He was now softly crying. He stood up and said, "Well, I guess it's time to go."

They went out to the car on the driveway and covered the journey to Holmes in relative silence. There was really nothing more to be said anyway. When Dorothy stopped at the sidewalk leading up to Holmes, Grant reached out his hand across the seat and said, "I love you." "I love you too," Dorothy replied, as they lovingly clasped hands. Grant stepped out of the car and started down the sidewalk. Dorothy did not drive away until he disappeared from her view as he turned to go inside the building. Till then she had succeeded in holding back her own tears, but she could no longer.

Chapter 8

Their Springtime Weeks
of Delirious Love

Over the next month Dorothy's life was somewhat less complicated than it had been in recent months, because her secret love-life was now reduced to writing braille letters to Grant and receiving his replies along with other letters recorded on cassette tapes. Her other two lives went on as they had been: her conventional life as wife and mother and her second life as beloved Ma to her university kids, including bowling every Sunday night in their league.

Just days after Grant left, Bethany came down to be with Dorothy to celebrate the former's forty-third birthday. When her deceased father's birthday followed not long thereafter, Dorothy thought tenderly of him. She wrote her letters on Sundays to Wesley, Mom Klingner, and Mom Patterson, and other friends and relatives; and she sent a special letter and birthday card to Uncle Les.

When Grant left to go back home, only Dorothy and he knew that he would not be returning for the spring semester. When his grades for the fall semester arrived in the mail, his parents, accustomed to his stellar academic performance year after year, were disappointed and then went through a whole range of emotions when he announced that he was taking the semester off to rest: anger, outrage, dismay, confusion, and eventually just serious concern for their son. He and his sister had largely been model children and had rarely given them any major headaches as they were growing up, but things had changed. They were still not on speaking terms with their daughter and had not seen their one and only grandson for seven months. Now something disturbing might also be going on with their son.

Ever since he had lost his eyesight, Grant's mother had worried especially about him. She was constantly wondering whether he would grow up and be able to enjoy a more or less normal life. Accordingly, one day when Grant happened to be spending time in the living room as she was house cleaning, she finally summoned up the courage to ask him several questions. "I've been worrying about you, Grant," she began in a voice that she hoped conveyed loving concern and not disapproval, "I just want to be sure that nothing really serious is going on. You haven't gotten some young girl pregnant, have you?" "Oh no," Grant answered in genuine surprise. "Well, that's good." You haven't been involved in drugs, have you?" "Mom, I would never do that," he answered perfectly truthfully, "That is such a stupid thing! Mom, don't worry about me. Ok? I'm all right. I just need to rest up, and things will be ok." "Well, all right then."

Grant lived a very isolated and austere life in Fairmont. His few high school friends had by now gone their own ways. Since he could not drive a car and had no other siblings around, he spent all his time in the house, and primarily in his own room. But the isolation did not bother him all that much. In fact, he rather liked it, because he had always lived largely in his own mind; and since he had also always been a self-starter, he quickly organized all his free time into a regimen of reading all sorts of things and studying calculus, physics, Latin, and beginning-level Classical Greek. He even devoted some of the space on his cassette letters to Dorothy with small lessons on ancient history and Latin pronunciation and basic grammar. Dorothy enjoyed these lessons, because she regarded them as important steps in their joint goal of preparing Grant to be a college professor of ancient Greek and Roman history. Moreover, just as Grant's mother had greatly assisted him with his reading and homework during his last three years in high school, so now she regularly read to him from books on ancient history that he wanted to read.

The two lovers had initially communicated by writing a few braille letters, but they were soon keeping in touch almost exclusively through the exchange of cassette tapes. They proved to be superior to braille letters, because it pleased them both to hear the other's voice, and the recordings were usually quite long and contained far more information than what was usually written in a braille letter. Not only did Grant inform his darling of all his studious doings, but he commented on events in the news, as well as telling her about the books that he was reading. Dorothy, for her part, described all of her own activities and kept Grant informed of everything going on there in University City involving the other blind university students. One other adorable aspect of her recordings was that she often carried the cassette machine with her around the house as she talked and worked, and Grant thereby became a distant participant in her ordinary daily chores around the house, all of which they had shared numerous times, and which had long been an integral part of their loving closeness. In addition, Dorothy greatly pleased Grant on one of her recordings by informing him that she was now wearing his ring on a chain underneath her clothes and hung in such a way that the ring lay in the cleavage of her breasts. But more than anything else, they both missed one another mightily, and they both simply looked forward to their first reunion and wanted it to arrive speedily.

February 26, 1973, Monday

As soon as Carol left the house to go off to school, Dorothy ran out to the car and drove over to the bus station. She did not want to be late. Grant's bus from Peoria would be arriving around 8:15, and it was now just 8:00. She was so excited to see him again, but over the past month as she had settled back down in her life, she had decided once again that she had too much to lose right now in allowing their relationship to go too far. She had therefore resolved that they could not become too physically intimate.

She parked the car, got out, and walked over to the area where the bus would be pulling in. She wanted to be able to greet Grant as soon as he stepped off. Luckily, the bus was right on time, and she had to wait only a few minutes. As the bus turned off from the street and into the parking zone, she caught a glimpse of his bright red hair through one of the windows, and the sight made her pulse quicken slightly. As soon as the bus came to a standstill, she walked up to the vehicle and stood just to the side of the open door. Thus, when Grant was the third person to step down onto the pavement, she reached out her hand and caught him by his right arm and said merrily, "Hey there, fella, over this way," as she guided him along the side of the bus. "It's so nice to see you," "It's so nice to see you too," Grant replied. They then embraced; and as Grant's hands went around her, he said, "How very nice! You look so lovely in your polar bear coat." The remark so pleased her. No one had called her coat that since he had been away, of course, because it was one of their own intimate secrets. "Well, let's go," Dorothy said, as they broke their embrace, and she turned to offer her arm for Grant to take to be guided to the parked car.

As soon as they arrived at the house, Grant carried his only item of luggage, a duffel bag, into the front bedroom and placed it on the floor between the two twin beds. Then after hanging up his coat on a hanger on the back of the bedroom door, he removed three items from his bag, placed them under his arm, and joined Dorothy in the kitchen. She had just returned from hanging up her own coat in the master bedroom. As Grant walked in, she asked, "Are you hungry?" "No, not really, I ate some breakfast very early before getting on the bus."

"What's that you got tucked under your arm?" she asked. "One small present for you and two other things that you might not consider presents." "Uh-oh!" she intoned humorously in mock dread. "Well," Grant replied, "let's begin with the good stuff." Having said so, he removed from under his arm and placed on the kitchen table a large flat package wrapped in plastic. "What is it?" Dorothy asked. "It's a wall map of the world. Last Thursday my mom and I went shopping on her day off; and after we looked at music albums, I had us go into a bookstore, so that I could buy this map for you. It cost a grand total of one dollar, but I figure that since I'm not here all the time now to give you geography lessons with my braille maps, you can pin this up on a wall somewhere; and when you're listening to the world news on the radio here in the kitchen in the morning and hear some place mentioned whose location you don't know, you can go over to the map and find it."

As Grant was talking, he was removing the plastic wrapping and unfolding the large paper map. As he held it up in front of him to display it for her, Dorothy said, "Thanks. That's really nice. It's a wonderful gift, and I think I know the perfect place for it." "Where's that?" "On the wall in the front bedroom near my sewing machine. Let's go see." As Grant proceeded down the hall and into the front bedroom, Dorothy followed, after having first rounded up some thumb tacks from her desk. Grant then positioned the map on the wall as Dorothy instructed; and as she stood some distance back, she told Grant exactly where to pin down the corners in order to have it properly aligned. "That really does add something to the room," she concluded, "The map and my shelves of books complement one another nicely; and I'll be sure to do as you say. Whenever I encounter some country or city whose location I don't know, I'll come in here to find it on the map."

When they returned to the kitchen, Grant said, "Ok, now the bad news." He now picked up from the table the two other objects. "Here's my paperback of Herodotus' *Persian Wars* translated by George Rawlinson. I'll start giving you reading assignments along with my own little lectures on our cassette tapes." "Well," Dorothy responded, "as my mother always says, there's no rest for the wicked. So, I guess I must be pretty wicked from all the work that you give me to keep me busy." As they were smiling at one another, Grant resumed, "Well, I'm afraid that's only the half of it." "Uh-oh! What else do you have planned for little ole me?" Grant's demeanor now changed as he cautiously asked, "I was wondering if you'd mind recording this other book on cassette for me. It's a survey history of Carthage and the Carthaginians. I got it through the campus bookstore just before I went home a month ago; and since I'm now reading Livy's account of the Hannibalic War in translation, thanks to Educational Tape recording for the Blind in Chicago, I would really like to be reading this book as background to reading Livy." "Grant," Dorothy replied softly and sweetly, "Of course I'll record the book for you. I'm happy to do it, and we can be learning about Carthage together." "Thanks, Dorth. I really appreciate it." "I know you do."

Having disposed of these matters involving their joint education in ancient history, they took the four dogs out for a long walk in the refreshingly chilly outdoors. Then they turned their attention to cleaning up the kitchen and tidying up around the house. They were both so pleased to be together once again in the house and doing ordinary chores together that gave them so much joy and satisfaction. But when Grant now approached Dorothy and put his arms around her, she kept her own arms against her sides and folded across her middle. Grant's heart sank. How could she possibly think that they could roll back the clock in their emotions and forget what all they felt and had experienced together, he thought. But as lunchtime approached, Dorothy began to open her arms to Grant and to eagerly receive his embraces, as her reserved manner slowly melted in consequence of their working around the house together while conversing non-stop. Her rational resolve might have been rallying its forces over the past month, but it took a very short time to expose how feeble its forces were in the face of a much more powerful army that now showed up on the battlefield of their relationship. Rational resolve had been put to flight and decisively defeated once and for all by the vastly superior forces of their love and powerful attraction for each other. By the early afternoon their embraces were frequently accompanied by kisses, both of which, of course, they had to put on hold when Carol arrived home from school.

Grant sat at the kitchen table talking with his darling while she spent the late afternoon fixing a large batch of chili mac. He was now giving her a minor lesson in the Bronze Age and Minoan civilization on the island of Crete, because the latter would be the subject of the AIA lecture that night. Then after the three of them had eaten a supper of Dorothy's delicious chili mac, Grant went into the living room and sat on the couch to be out of the way while Dorothy dressed and made herself up for their evening date. When she finally emerged as beautifully dressed up as she had been on their last full day together nearly five weeks ago, they went out to the car and drove over to campus to attend the lecture.

It began at 8:00 and was over shortly after 9:00. The lecturer was British, who had served as director of the British School in Athens and had recently published a book on Minoan Crete. As a result of his scholarly prominence, the local chapter of the AIA had really gone out of its way for the event and had succeeded in making sure that the lecture was well attended. It was held in a large elegant auditorium. Dorothy and Grant thoroughly enjoyed sitting together as a loving couple, and the ambiance added a real air of romance to their experience that evening. But as far as Grant could tell, the lecture had nothing really all that exciting or new to say about Minoan civilization. Nevertheless, for Dorothy and Grant the event itself was what was important. They were attending a formal public event as a romantic and loving couple. Since they had long had to keep their relationship a secret from everyone, their open appearance in this public setting greatly thrilled them both.

Not long after they returned home, Carol went to bed, and the couple then settled down on the couch in the family room, still dressed as they had been for the lecture. Their talking now became secondary to their embraces and kisses, and soon they were lying on the couch with Dorothy's back pressed against the back of the couch and Grant pressing himself full length against her, including, of course, his erection. There they lay for about two hours, simply chitchatting to have something to go along with their passionate kissing and the feel of Grant's ardent manhood so very prominent between them.

"Well," Dorothy said between kisses, "It's about midnight, and perhaps we should be going off to bed soon." After a long pause Grant replied with a carefully formulated request, "Can I come into your bedroom and undress you?" After another long pause during which Dorothy pondered his request, she answered, "Why don't I go get my nightgown and bring it into the front bedroom, and we will shut the door and undress together. It might be a little safer that way." "Ok," Grant agreed. They then arose, and Grant followed her into the master bedroom. They then came down the hall and into the front bedroom. After they entered, Dorothy quietly pushed the door shut, and the two now faced each other at opposite ends of the twin bed in which Grant would soon be sleeping. It was, of course, the bed that had witnessed The Great Apocalypse of Dorothy's love-zone and was therefore the bed in Which Grant preferred to sleep. She was at the head nearest the door, and he was at its foot. They now began to remove their clothes, but while Dorothy enjoyed watching him become fully naked with his beautiful red cock facing her, he, of course, could not see her undressing. So, as soon as he estimated that she was probably fully naked and about to put on her nightgown, he stepped forward. He reached for her and found her naked and holding her nightgown. His arms went around her bare back and bottom as he pressed her lovely naked front against his own. He pushed his erection downward, so that it nuzzled into her love-meadow of pussy hair.

"Lie down, and let me hump you," Grant whispered passionately. Unknown to him, he had inadvertently chosen to use the wrong word in the passion of the moment. "When Dorothy heard him ask her to lie down to be humped, she instantly concluded that Grant wanted to enter her vagina for actual intercourse, but he simply was wanting her to allow him to climax all over her love-delta and to have her go off to her bed with his love signature down there on her. But as soon as he had spoken, she recoiled in genuine alarm, pulled her body away from him, and exclaimed, "Oh no, Grant! Please! Don't!" Grant was himself genuinely confused and hurt by her reaction. He stepped back. As they stood apart, Dorothy slipped the nightgown over her head. Grant now urgently repeated, "Please lie down on the bed, and let me hump you through your nightgown." Dorothy was still rather shaken by what she had thought Grant to be requesting with his first words, but she was now eager to lie down on the bed that had been the site of The Great Apocalypse, and was happy to have Grant lie down between her legs to hump her crotch until he ejaculated on the front of her nightgown. As soon as he arose from her, she stood up and left the room without uttering another word.

Grant stood beside the bed totally confused. After lying with her on the couch for two hours with his erection pressing so obviously into her, she had seemed so alarmed by having him come on her naked love-front. In addition, the one ejaculation was not nearly enough to relieve the overwhelming desire that he felt for her and had been feeling for her all day long. He walked into the main bathroom and sat down on the toilet to urinate. As he pushed his erection down between his legs, he noticed that the swollen head of his manhood had a single hair stuck to it by a bit of his semen. He carefully removed it and examined it with his lips and tongue that were far more sensitive than his fingers. Given the hair's position on the head of his penis, he concluded that it must have come from Dorothy's love-delta and had become attached to his manhood when he pressed his naked erection into the apex of her own bare sex. Thus, as he sat there on the toilet, he carefully nibbled at the hair, slowly consuming it one minuscule bit at a time as an act of worshipping her sex.

February 27, 1973, Tuesday

All three were up at 6:30. Dorothy did various things in the kitchen and around the house while Carol prepared for school. Grant sat on the couch in the family room and listened to a morning news program. When Carol left, Grant and Dorothy simply spent the day with him helping her in all sorts of housework, but unlike yesterday, Grant conducted himself in a somewhat reserved manner. Neither of them understood that they had been victims of a terrible verbal misunderstanding in the front bedroom last night. Grant had concluded that Dorothy still felt deeply divided inside over their relationship, and that she actually preferred that they simply be very special friends. The thought hurt him profoundly and had caused him to withdraw into himself and feel somewhat depressed. It took Dorothy some time to realize that Grant was behaving somewhat oddly, but it was hard for either of them to verbalize what they were feeling and thinking, because they were still trying to find their footing with one another after being apart for an entire month.

Finally, in the early afternoon Dorothy tried to break the ice between them. Twice, as they were together in the hallway, she suddenly threw her arms around him, hung her weight on his neck, pulled him down on top of her and between her legs on the carpeted floor, and exclaimed, "Oh My!" as she gave him a kiss. She wanted to feel his erection pressing into her love-zone through their clothes, but Grant's only reaction to both these displays of her passion was his continued withdrawn behavior. He did not even lower his body between her thighs to give her the erotic contact that she was desiring. The two displays had in fact further confused Grant. They had taken him completely by surprise, because he had concluded that Dorothy did not want them to do such things. He therefore could not understand what she really wanted, and how he should behave toward her. He therefore simply remained in his existing state of mild depression and aloofness over their relationship.

After supper Dorothy dressed herself for her usual Tuesday evening of Sweet Adeline practice. Rather than spending the evening in the house, Grant had decided to go visit old friends in Holmes. Dorothy therefore dropped him off, and he enjoyed himself in the dorm while Dorothy did so with her lady singers. When she came back to Holmes around 10:00 to pick him up, he was in a better frame of mind, and Dorothy herself was somewhat euphoric from the pleasure that singing always gave her. The disturbed situation between them was finally banished when they returned to the house. After going into the master bedroom to hang up her coat, Dorothy came out clad in only her slippers, nightgown, and pink quilted robe. She then had Grant join her on the family room couch beneath the wagon wheel afghan; and soon they were back to embracing, petting, and kissing passionately. Dorothy also allowed Grant to have his hands inside her robe to feel, caress, and fondle her as much as and however he liked. The misunderstanding of the night before and the confusion throughout the day that it had caused was now behind them.

February 28, 1973, Wednesday

Like yesterday morning, they were all up by 6:30 with each engaged in their own activities. Grant was again sitting in the family room listening to the morning news on the TV, while Carol was getting ready for School, and Dorothy was doing various things around the house. But as soon as Carol was gone, Grant joined Dorothy in the kitchen; and as she continued to do small chores to clean things up from breakfast, they resumed their amorous activity of the night before: embracing, kissing, and fondling. Dorothy was clad as she was last night on the couch; and soon Grant was lifting up her nightgown and enjoying her bare female sex in true wonderment. When Dorothy finally had the kitchen tidied up, she said, "Let's go lie down for a while."

Grant followed her into the master bedroom; and as they stood beside the bed, Dorothy removed her robe, laid it aside, lay down on the bed on her back, hiked up her nightgown to her waist, and spread her thighs invitingly. All this was done wordlessly. Grant therefore used his hands to see how

Dorothy was positioned in bed; and as soon as he saw her lying with her sex spread fully open for him, he knew instantly what she wanted. He therefore removed everything except his t-shirt, keeping his body facing her as he undressed, so that she could watch him and see his erection. He then lay down between her legs, and she took his manhood into her right hand and carefully guided it into her vulva, so that they could begin a long lovely session of mutual masturbation.

It had now been exactly five weeks almost to the hour when they had last lain in this bed, enjoying their naked bodies for more than three hours, followed by their first shower together. They were now picking up from where they had been forced to leave off on that last glorious day of erotic pleasure. As usual, Dorothy used her two hands to carefully manage the precise position of Grant's penis, so that he was constantly stimulating her clitoris and thus keeping her in a state of heightened arousal. When she arose to go to the bathroom, she removed her nightgown and Grant did the same with his t-shirt. They were now totally naked for one another. As she walked beautifully nude into the bathroom, he followed along with his hands never leaving her body. He caressed her breasts as she sat on the toilet, and her eyes were filled with the sight of his beautiful red cock. They were now reestablishing that lovely intimate custom of Grant witnessing her urinating with him sometimes doing so after her.

Their long initial bout of mutual masturbation was followed by other forms of playing and frolicking in bed. As always, Grant was so truly fascinated with the beauty of her sex that he was constantly caressing and feeling her, and Dorothy was by now so aroused that she welcomed all his attentions. She simply lay on her back with her thighs fully spread and offering her love-zone to Grant. Eventually, however, their erotic activity became more than just a mere reenactment of what they had enjoyed five weeks before. For months Grant had been desiring to enjoy her sex with his mouth and tongue. He now decided to do so, but since he knew that Dorothy might not want him to, he proceeded slowly and cautiously.

While they were lying side by side on the bed with Grant's hand caressing her love-spread, he pulled back the covers and began to kiss and suck her breasts. He then began to move his mouth down her body and was soon kneeling between her spread thighs, kissing her love-delta and gently nuzzling his lips in her hair, tracing her Venus V along one side down to the apex of her sex and then along the other side. He then began to plant soft little kisses at the front and to either side of her vulva.

"God!" he exclaimed in a low voice, "I can't get over how beautiful you are. I just can't imagine anything else in the world being as lovely as your pussy. I don't think anything else could ever even come close." This was the very first time that he uttered that magical term to her, "your pussy;" and it thrilled her mightily! He now lowered his nose to the slit of her vulva for several seconds and resumed, "You also smell so sweet and wonderful! With all our play you must be full of love-honey." He then told her how months ago he had lain on his dorm bed with his finger beneath his nose to breathe in her heavenly scent. He continued, "Your vagina must have been full of sweet honey all last fall whenever we were together." "Even before that," Dorothy replied, now speaking for the first time while Grant's face was near her sex. She was watching him and thoroughly enjoyed the sight of his face and red hair hovering around her sex. "I must have been wet for you all last summer, and I can even remember sometimes feeling funny way down inside while you were playing the guitar when the other kids were here. I suppose even then I was wanting you and not even knowing it." Grant now carefully inserted his index finger inside her vagina, withdrew it, and sniffed at is finger. "Ahh!" He breathed with delight, "You must have a honey bee in there, a pussy bee to make your pussy honey."

He now lowered his face between her thighs and moved his mouth to survey her hair and lovely vulva with his sensitive lips. He opened up his mouth and took one side of her vulva between his lips and gently tugged on her. He did the same on the other side and then slipped his tongue inside her and began to explore slowly the whole length and all the contours of her inner sex, finding her labia minora, her clitoris, and going down to find the entry into her vagina. The exploration caused Dorothy extraordinary pleasure, and she lay motionless and allowed Grant to do as he wished. After several tours up and down of her entire inner sex, he finally halted when he came to the opening into her vagina, inserted his tongue, and moved it all around inside her. As he did, his nose was pressing gently into her spread open labia, and they both enjoyed the lovely sensation of Grant's face being filled with her sex.

Grant withdrew his face, and Dorothy could see that his lips and nose were moist with her honey. He resumed kissing and nuzzling her sex and love-delta. "You smell and taste so good," he remarked seriously. "George has never liked doing that," Dorothy replied. "Whenever in the past he has done that to give me pleasure, he has then gone off to wash out his mouth, as if I don't taste good." "Well then," Grant answered with obvious scorn and annoyance, "He's a damn fool! The fragrance of your sex is truly wonderful." "I guess I've never produced honey for him down there like I do for you."

When Grant moved his mouth again to her vulva and began to lick and kiss her inner sex again, Dorothy commented, "Oh My! Don't stop! Your tongue feels so good!" she was now so aroused that she reached down with both hands to Grant's head and gently guided his tongue to her clitoris. "Oh please! Lick me right there, and don't stop until you give me a climax." Grant eagerly obeyed, moving the tip of his tongue rapidly side to side. As he did, her breathing began to come in violent and rhythmic gasps in time to the onset of the orgasm. Her thighs tightened around his shoulders and face like a vice. He slid both his hands beneath her bottom and took her two lovely buttocks into them and held her, as his face was also full of her sex. How glorious it was! Then, her rhythmic breaths began to be accompanied with shouts of "Oh! oh! oh!" as she came to the pinnacle of pleasure. It all came to an end with her sighing mightily and relaxing her thighs that had been pressing so tightly around him. "Ooooohhhh, I think that I just died and went to heaven! Wow! I don't think that I'll be able to move for the rest of the day!"

Grant remained where he was, lying between her spread thighs with her lovely sex before his face. When he resumed kissing and licking her, she said with an apologetic laugh, "Oh don't. I don't think that I could stand any more of that just yet!" He therefore contented himself with kissing and nuzzling her sex everywhere outside her lips.

As Grant continued to admire in awe her female sex with his lips, tongue, and nose, he said, "How about we combine our love-play with a Latin lesson?" "How do we do that?" she asked. "Well, let me explain. The Latin word for queen is regina, properly pronounced in Latin with a hard G and a long I, like regeena, but of course, in normal English it is usually pronounced with a soft G like a J, and the I is like the I in high. So in normal English it's pronounced like rejyna. Since that way it rhymes with vagina, how would you like me to call you Regina Vagina?" "I would like that," she replied sweetly.

"Now if we continue our little lesson," Grant resumed, "We need to think about translating that phrase into English. Regina Vagina has a really nice sound to it, because the words rhyme. I can't think of a nice rhyming English translation, but I can come up with one with alliteration." "What would that be?" Dorothy asked. "Well, I hope that I don't offend you, but it's Queen Cunt." "Would you mind very much if I also called you that?" Grant cautiously asked. "No, not at all. I would like that too." "How about I also call you Princess Pussy?" "That would be fine too," she replied with the same satisfied sweetness in her voice.

After Grant gave her countless more tender kisses all over her love-delta and sex while murmuring "You're my Regina Vagina," "You're my Queen Cunt," "You're my Princess Pussy," he finally lay down beside her. Dorothy rolled over onto her side, threw her leg across him so that his penis lay beneath her thigh, and spread her sex open for him to hold lovingly in his hand. With her head lying on his shoulder, she soon dozed off in perfect bliss. Grant simply lay there, enjoying this beautiful woman and what they had just experienced. He truly enjoyed kissing, smelling, and licking her sex. He also dozed off for a while; and when Dorothy finally awoke and looked at her watch, she announced in surprise, "Oh My Golly! It's already two o'clock! We've been here in bed for five and a half hours!" "Yeah!" Grant interjected, "and hasn't it been paradise!" "We'll have to be getting up soon," Dorothy continued, "because Carol will be coming home!"

March 1, 1973, Thursday

Dorothy awoke around 6:30 and arose with Carol. When Grant did not arise, she did not bother to wake him up. Since the two of them would be here at the house again all day, there was no need to. For the next hour and a half mother and daughter went through their usual morning routine of Carol getting herself ready for school and Dorothy doing some straightening-up around the house while fixing them breakfast. Every time Dorothy walked down the hall, she glanced into the front bedroom and saw him lying asleep in bed, and the sight thrilled her and stirred her deep down inside. The latter sensation must be what he was talking about yesterday in speaking of her love-honey. What he had called her Pussy Bee must already be busy making honey in response to him. Since Grant was not in the family room with the TV on, Dorothy had the kitchen radio turned on to catch the news and weather, as she usually did at this time of the day when she was the only one up and working in the kitchen. It was a bright cold sunny day; and according to the radio's weather report, that's how it would be all day long. Good, that meant that George would be staying in Newton, and they would not have to worry about him coming home today to end the work week early. That was the only way in which George intruded upon her thoughts this morning, only as a possible obstacle to her being alone again in the house with Grant.

His kissing and licking of her sex yesterday had been so utterly exquisite. His tongue had not only spread opened the lips of her vulva, but it had opened up an entirely new world to her. The orgasm had been so all-consuming and powerful, not merely a physiological phenomenon, but an experience that had united her mind, soul, and body into a perfect completeness. After nearly eight months of protecting her vagina from penetration by his penis, she now felt with all sincerity that the time had finally come. It seemed so very right, the culmination of a long step-by-step evolution in their complex relationship. Her mind was perfectly content with this decision. There was no inner conflict anymore between her reason and emotions. Yesterday's orgasm had somehow strangely resolved that conflict, and it had not been simply a matter of sex. What she had experienced had been so transforming and revolutionary. She now finally understood with full clarity exactly how rare and sublime their love for each other was, something that came along very infrequently in one's life, if ever. It was truly wunderbar, and "Get thee behind me, Satan" was totally inappropriate. It was in fact that miracle for which she had been hoping for so many years in her barren marriage. Their love was so rare and fine, like a precious flower. It had to be carefully tended and cherished for its beauty and rarity. She had come so close to crushing it. Only Grant's single-minded persistence and perseverance had protected it from destruction by the adverse circumstances in which they found themselves. Henceforth, however, she would fully embrace their love and not fight against it.

Since her period was about to begin, she was probably not fertile. They could therefore engage in real sexual intercourse without fear of her becoming pregnant. She wanted and needed to feel him big and hard inside her vagina, not just inside the lips of her vulva to masturbate her, and not shielded or hampered by a rubber, but fully inside her vagina, her flesh enveloping his flesh, her vagina feeling his every move and quiver and receiving all his sperm to be mingled with her love-honey for him. In a figurative sense, for the past few months they had been besporting themselves along the bank of the Rubicon River that separated her marriage with George from her love for Grant. Today they would finally cross that river, and the die would be cast. How it would all end up, she really did not know, but she felt deep down in her bones that what they were about to do was so totally right!

Throughout her life she had avoided using vulgar and obscene words and expressions, but his love-talk yesterday had truly thrilled her. For the very first time Grant had used the terms pussy and cunt to refer to her love-zone, and those words uttered by him had filled her whole being with wonderful pleasure. He had bestowed upon her with her permission three lovely royal titles. His use of the words pussy and cunt had seemed so perfectly appropriate in the context of their love-play. He had not used them in a degrading fashion, but they had been directed to her and her sex alone and had been used to emphasize how he desired her so passionately, and how beautiful she was to him. It had all made her feel so loved and so lovely and desired as a woman. She could not remember the last time when she had felt so alive. Today she would in fact become his Regina Vagina, his Queen Cunt, his Princess Pussy.

When Carol went off to school at 8:00, Dorothy let the dogs outside one more time and went around the house to check the locks on the doors. She wanted to make sure that they would not be interrupted or intruded upon in any way. She then came into the front bedroom, sat down on the edge of the bed, and allowed him to awaken in response to her physical presence. He did within seconds, and he pulled her into the bed, so that she was sitting upright beside him as she had on the morning of The Great Apocalypse.

"Good morning," she greeted him softly. "Good morning. What time is it?" "It's already about 8:15, and Carol has gone off to school." As his hands moved lightly over her body outlined by her pink quilted robe, Grant said, "As usual, you feel so damn nice! But boy! I've got to pee pretty bad. I'll be right back." He slid out of bed and went into the hall bathroom, but when he emerged, Dorothy met him in the hallway and simply said, "Let's go lie down." He then obediently followed her into the master bedroom; and like yesterday morning, Dorothy wordlessly removed and laid aside her robe, lay down on the bed, pulled her nightgown up to her waist, and spread her thighs for him. Grant removed his undershorts and lay down between her legs, expecting them to begin another long session of mutual masturbation. She did in fact take his erection into her right hand, but rather than placing his manhood inside her lips at the front of her vulva to stimulate her clitoris, she instead carefully guided him to the base of her labia, placed his large head at the mouth of her vagina, and gently pushed him inside her. His penis slid into her effortlessly, because she was wet with honey and dilated with desire. The pleasure that they both now felt was incredible.

Grant now began to move his body, so that his penis was thrusting inside her slowly but rhythmically. For the very first time they were enjoying actual sexual intercourse. Like their first time to engage in mutual masturbation, neither of them spoke for a while, as if to do so would somehow make the magic of what they were experiencing suddenly disappear. But in order to confirm what he could hardly believe to be true after months of desiring her and having her rebuff him, Grant soon asked her in a very low and tentative voice, "Are we having intercourse?" She replied in a whisper, "Yessss!" Her pronunciation of this single syllable was exaggerated and lengthened, so that it clearly conveyed the message, "Oh yes indeed! We are, and isn't it the most magnificent thing?"

The last two pieces of their love-puzzle were now finally in place: his penis inside her vagina. It was no longer a puzzle but a picture of perfected love. Over the past eight months they had come to know one another so well through their conversations and shared experiences. They had come to love and respect one another through a harmonious meeting of their minds and souls. Their bodies had gradually come to know and enjoy one another, but despite all the erotic pleasure that they had thus far enjoyed, it had never been complete until now. Through the medium of his penis and her vagina they were now for the first time enjoying complete love due to the perfectly harmonious union of their entire spiritual and physical beings, the most perfect and complete love that a man and woman can ever experience and enjoy.

They began this first bout of intercourse around 8:15 that morning and did not end it and get out of bed until 12:30 in the early afternoon. They thus enjoyed themselves in this way for a little more than four hours, and the sexual marathon was interrupted only a few times by necessary brief trips to the bathroom. As soon as they had done so, they returned immediately to bed and resumed their enjoyment of their perfect love. When they began, she still had on her nightgown, and he was wearing his t-shirt, but after their first trip to the bathroom, they removed these articles of clothing and enjoyed their intercourse completely nude. Also, during this entire four hours Dorothy lay on her back with her legs spread open to him, and Grant lay on top of her and between her legs. She never once complained about him becoming too heavy or her legs or back being tired. She was floating on a cloud of sexual pleasure and desire, and physical discomfort of this sort simply did not matter or exist for her. Similarly, Grant enjoyed every moment of those four hours of having his manhood inside her.

Throughout their morning he varied both the rhythm and vigor of his thrusts. There were periods when he simply kept his penis inside her motionless and just savored being enveloped by the moist warm velvet of her vagina, just as she enjoyed the feel of him inside her. At other times he moved his penis slowly and gently. At other times he increased the rate and power of his thrusts, so that he was ramming his erection into her with considerable force. Since it was his very first time to be inside a woman's vagina, Grant was utterly fascinated with how they fit together, how he could move his penis inside her, and how every action or inaction yielded such magnificent pleasure. Dorothy's response to the varied action of Grant's penis was twofold. On the one hand, she really did not care how or what he was doing inside her vagina, because it all felt so perfectly wonderful. On the other hand, since she knew and understood that this was his very first time, she simply allowed him to move his penis however he wished. She sensed his awe and wonder of being inside her and reveled in it for both his sake and hers. As he had told her before, she was his first girlfriend and was teaching him so many things about Woman, of which in his opinion she was the perfect embodiment. But she was now both pupil and teacher, allowing her intelligent and gifted student to experiment and learn, but she was also learning how truly wonderful it was to engage in sexual intercourse when combined with their complete and total love. They quickly lost track of how many times Grant reached an orgasm inside her. Although he eventually succeeded in ejaculating all his sperm, his penis nevertheless remained big and hard and continued to move to and fro inside her tirelessly, and her vagina received him with equal wonder and inexhaustible joy.

During the first hour or so they said very little to one another. The pleasure was so awesome. Their bodies were doing the real talking, and their words were mere extensions of this heavenly pleasure. They often laughed and exclaimed with delight as his penis and her vagina engaged themselves in the most intimate conversation of sexual joy. Months of teasing and tortured sex play had now given way to the real thing. He was twenty years old with a very fit body and a penis to match. He had never before been seriously involved with a female. But now, after so many times of serious and exciting love-play with his beloved woman, his penis was eager and perfectly primed for his very first vaginal intercourse, and there was nothing at all lacking in his performance. She was forty-four years old, a woman at the pinnacle of her female adulthood and voluptuous beauty. Her female sex had come to love and enjoy his young energetic virility. As these four hours demonstrated, they were perfectly matched for one another.

By midmorning they had become so delirious and drunk with sexual pleasure that they began to act a bit silly. Once, after Grant had gone to the bathroom, he returned to the bed and found his darling with the top sheet wrapped firmly around her body. She was lying on her stomach with her legs held tightly together. "What are you doing," he bellowed in mock outrage. "You're not going to get any more," she answered. "Anymore what?" he asked, "Come on, let me hear you say it." "You're not going to get anymore pussy." They were both enchanted and excited by hearing her speak that lovely word of sexual intimacy. "Say it again," Grant commanded. "You're not going to get anymore pussy. You're not going to get anymore pussy." He tugged roughly on the sheet until he had it pulled off of her, and by then she was lying on her back, but she still held her knees tightly together in supposed modesty and in a playful attempt to keep him from reentering her vagina. "You're not going to get anymore pussy!" she kept saying. He forced her knees apart with one of his own. As soon as he did so, she relaxed, spread her thighs wide apart, and eagerly surrendered her vagina once again to the ministrations of his erection. He rode her and rode her and rode her and rode her until it was 12:30 in the early afternoon, by which time they had both been thoroughly satisfied.

After they finally arose from their bed of extraordinary physical pleasure of their perfect love, they dressed and went off shopping. They first stopped at Steak and Shake on Foxwell Street on campus for lunch; and while they sat in the privacy of the car eating their burgers and drinking their milk shakes topped off with a maraschino cherry, they engaged in erotic verbal banter in which they teased one another about Dorothy's cherry and cherry pie. Among their stops was one at a campus record store, where Grant purchased a double album of Chet Atkins commemorating his silver anniversary of guitar playing. When they returned to the house, Grant sat in the dining room playing the records for the first time, while Dorothy worked in the kitchen preparing their supper and joyfully sang along with many of the songs. They were both totally euphoric from their first experience of sexual intercourse.

Late in the afternoon they returned to campus to pick Dennis up to be their guest for the evening and to stay the night. They had arranged this event at the beginning of the week, before Dorothy and Grant had any idea that their meeting would come on the heels of the love-pair's first marathon of sexual intercourse. The three of them spent the evening after supper in enjoyable conversation, but Dorothy eventually excused herself and went off to bed, leaving Dennis and Grant to stay up until about midnight talking.

March 2, 1973, Friday

Shortly after Carol left for school, Dennis arose and decided to take a shower before he returned to campus; and as soon as he was occupied in the bathroom, Dorothy came into the front bedroom, awoke Grant, and led him into the master bedroom. No words needed to be spoken as to what they were about to do. Yesterday morning's enjoyment of perfect physical love was to be resumed with full gusto. But even so, there was something that Dorothy first needed to clarify.

As she stood beside the bed with Grant nearby, she adjusted the bed covers and said, "I'm afraid I've started my period. I'm not flowing very hard right now. I just started this morning. If it's ok with you, I don't see why we still can't enjoy ourselves and have fun. It will be just a little bit messy. That's all." "That's ok with me," Grant replied, eager to be back inside her as soon as possible. "George never has liked the mess, and so he leaves me alone whenever I'm having a period. But we can go ahead and do it anyway." The idea greatly pleased Grant. How wonderful it was that Dorothy used her period to avoid intercourse with George, but she was very happy to enjoy it with him. "All I need to do is to lay a towel down on the bed underneath me to catch any blood that might drip out." As she said this, she was spreading a towel out where her bottom would soon be lying.

"I've got something else I want to show you." As she spoke, she removed her pink quilted robe. "I'm just wearing this girdle to hold my pad in place." Grant reached out his hands and felt her body. She was completely bare from her waist up, and his hands automatically moved up to envelope her beautiful breasts. Then when he moved his hands down to her midsection, he encountered a garment that had the appearance of a large pair of panties, but made out of a heavier material. Dorothy moved one of his hands down to her crotch and said, "Feel that. That's my Modess pad for my period. Now let me show you this girdle. If you look at the seams, near the sides at the front and back and feel the material, you'll see that it's made of four pieces or panels." As she said this, she placed Grant's hands on her hips to feel the seams. "The two side panels are translucent and are made of nylon. The front and back panels are cloth woven with elastic and have a leopard skin pattern to them. George got it for me one year for Christmas. He always wants me to wear sexy looking things like this. But the only time that I get this girdle out and wear it is when I'm having my period, and he doesn't want to bother me about sex." How magnificently mischievous she was, and she thoroughly enjoyed sharing her intimate little secret with her college boyfriend. It was Grant's first real encounter with her menstruation, and she was explaining everything and teaching her blind lover-boy all about it. Her lesson in the wonders of Woman was beautifully intimate and exciting. The girdle's feline pattern was very sexually explicit and suggestive: pussy, pussy cat, large meat-eating jungle cat, a woman with a man-eating pussy, a pussy that hunted for men and was voracious for their virility. While George certainly bought it for her with these erotic fantasies in mind, Dorothy subverted them by wearing this object whenever she was having her period and not giving him any pussy.

She now pulled off the girdle, placed it aside on the dresser, lay down naked in the middle of the bed on top of the towel, spread her legs, and simply said, "Ok, I'm all ready." Grant had by now removed his undershorts and moved into position as soon as she was down and beckoning him. He lowered himself between her thighs and guided his erect penis back inside her vagina. After yesterday's experience of having to withdraw and reenter her several times as they had to arise to use the bathroom, Grant by now knew how to insert his penis inside her. They now began to enjoy intercourse for the second time. "Luckily," Dorothy said, as Grant was thrusting rhythmically inside her, "We can hear Dennis in the adjoining bathroom. As soon as he gets out of the shower, we should probably stop." "Ok," Grant agreed. As it turned out, Dennis wound up taking a nice long shower and thus gave them an entire half hour to enjoy themselves.

Apart from two times when he quickened his pace to achieve orgasms, Grant's rhythm was steady and tireless, giving them both exquisite pleasure just like yesterday. "What's your astrological sign?" Grant asked. "I'm a Leo." "That's what I thought. That's lion in Latin." "Yes, I know," she replied. "So, in my estimation, you're the Leo Lioness, the Queen Cunt of the jungle. How do you like that?" "I like it," she said with obvious delight in her voice. "How do you like that?" Grant asked, as he thrust his penis with additional force inside her. "I like that too very much!"

"I really like that girdle," Grant said. "You do?" she teased. "I sure do. I want you always to wear it for me." "Ok, from now on it will be our girdle." "That's really neat," Grant replied with obvious pleasure in having appropriated the sexy garment into their own love-life. "You're my lovely Pussy Cat," he said with ardent desire in his voice. "I am, huh?" "You're my Pussy Woman," he now said very seriously. "I sure am," Dorothy said with equal seriousness, "I'm your Pussy Woman, and you're my Cock Man." Grant was somewhat surprised by her words, especially her use of the word cock. She had never said anything much directly about his penis because of her wish to keep their physical interaction within some bounds of decency, although it had always been obvious to Grant that the sight of his erect manhood never ceased to thrill and excite her. "I'm your Cock Man," he confirmed, as he continued to demonstrate with his pleasure-filled plunges and churning inside her. "I love your beautiful red cock!" she said with wonder and desire in her voice. "You're my Queen Cunt," Grant declared to her in awe and reverence. "You're my King Cock," she replied with equal joy and loving fervor. Their ecstatic enjoyment of sexual intercourse was prompting them to create a new vocabulary and language with which to express their mutual passion and pleasure. These words, phrases, and concepts, such as Leo Lioness, would be henceforth shared between them as a sacred and holy language of their intimate love.

"When we get up from bed," Grant asked, "Would you do me a favor?" "What's that?" "How about you wear nothing at all under your robe except your girdle and pad? Then as you move around the kitchen fixing our breakfast, I can sometime reach inside and feel you." "Ok." Shortly thereafter they heard Dennis turn off the water and step out of the shower stall and shut its door. Grant withdrew his penis; and they arose from bed, quickly dressed, and were soon in the kitchen as if they had been doing nothing at all unusual. Grant's penis had been covered with her menstrual blood for the first time. How thrilling that was; and as promised, Dorothy moved around the kitchen clad only in her pink quilted robe and girdle and allowed Grant to caress her breasts and girdle whenever the situation allowed.

After eating breakfast, Dorothy and Grant returned Dennis to Beaumont Manor and came straight back to the house with only one thing in mind, to enjoy as much intercourse as they could before Grant's bus back to Peoria departed in the early afternoon. As soon as they entered the house, they walked into the master bedroom, and undressed except for Dorothy's girdle and pad and Grant's t-shirt and undershorts. As they sat side by side on the edge of the bed touching and caressing one another tenderly, Grant used the bedside phone to call his mother at work at the Supermarket to let her know when he would be arriving later in the afternoon. As soon as he hung up, Dorothy removed her girdle and pad, lay back down on the towel, and Grant mounted her and resumed their perfect physical love for the next ninety minutes. This third bout for Grant took on a somewhat frantic character, because he dreaded going back home and being away from his lady-love for the next thirty-one days.

Grant's life for the next month was more or less what it had been before his first trip to University City. It was filled with reading and studying of various kinds and writing and recording letters to his darling. Grant now coined two more names that immediately entered the growing vocabulary in their love language. He began to address Dorothy in all his letters as Dove, a contraction of Dorothy Love; and the new name greatly pleased and thrilled her. He also began to sign his braille letters at the end, not with Grant, but with Rufus Magnus, a Latin phrase meaning "Big Red" and alluding to his manhood that Dorothy lovingly termed "your beautiful red cock."

On the other hand, the month of March was quite a busy and exciting one for Dorothy. Of course, her weekly routine largely revolved around Sweet Adelines, her swimming, and Sunday evening bowling; but there were other activities added to her life during this time. Her mother, George, Carol, and she drove down to Houston to visit Sally, who was still living with Tim and Marilyn. They stayed about a week during Carol's spring break. Wesley came home on leave from the navy toward the end of the month and did not return until April 5. He was therefore in and out of the house constantly; and given the close bond between mother and son, they conversed frequently with Wesley recounting many of his experiences on Adak.

March 30, 1973, Friday

At 3:50 in the afternoon, as Grant and his mother sat in the living room, the door opened, and Grant's father and Dennis stepped in. "Hey man!" Dennis nearly shouted in his boisterous manner, "How ya doing, Grant?" "Hello, Dennis," Grant's mother said with obvious amusement in her voice. "Oh hi there, Mrs. Duncan." He cautiously stepped forward in the unfamiliar living room and stuck out his hand to shake. Grant's mother instantly rose to her feet and came to him to shake his hand. "I'm really glad to meet you," Dennis said. "I'm glad to meet you too."

Dennis had come to spend the weekend with Grant, and then they would take the 6:00 A.M. bus back to University City Monday morning for Grant to spend his second week there with Dorothy.

Grant's mother Nina soon excused herself to go tend to supper in the kitchen and thus allowed the two friends to sit in the living room and chat.

Then the four sat down around the kitchen table to enjoy a meal of pork chops, mashed potatoes, peas, and corn, all of which Dennis thoroughly relished and praised to the skies. By then he had won over Grant's mother entirely, who was so charmed by his extroverted nature, so very different from that of her son. After cleaning up the kitchen, Grant's parents left the house to go spend the evening visiting with some old friends, so that Grant and Dennis would have the house to themselves for several hours. It was very considerate of them.

Dorothy had been the architect of this visit. She often detected in Grant's cassette letters to her a rather melancholy tone, and she feared that his isolation in Fairmont was not proving to be entirely healthy for him. She therefore thought that he might benefit from having Dennis come visit, so that they could talk about anything and everything. That is exactly what they did all weekend, and they did indeed have a grand old time!.

March 31, 1973, Saturday

The two friends spent the day almost entirely shut up in Grant's room, engaged in conversation. By now they had run through the usual topics of what they had been reading and learning. That had been important in reestablishing the wonderful rapport between them. By the middle of the afternoon they had graduated to much more personal matters. Grant cautiously began to inform Dennis of what had been transpiring between him and Dorothy over the past months, including their last two days together of magnificent sexual intercourse. Dennis was utterly dumbfounded, but also very pleased for them, because he knew them both to be truly fine people; and as he and Renny had figured out a year ago, he knew that Dorothy no longer loved George and probably hadn't for a very long time. He repaid Grant's confidences in him by telling him about his own blossoming love affair with Lisa Harris.

Once again, Dennis charmed Grant's mother at the supper table and engaged her in a very lively conversation. When she served her coconut pie, which was the favorite of both Grant and his father, Dennis again went into ecstasies in praising it. The two young men then retired again to Grant's bedroom for more hours of non-stop talking.

Around 11:30, long after Grant's parents had gone to bed, the two friends were still wide awake and talking furiously. "Hey, Dennis," Grant interjected, "I'm getting hungry again. How about you?" "Ah yeah, you know me, man.

I'm always ready to eat something." "Ok," Grant suggested, "How about some more of that coconut pie?" "Hey!" Dennis enthused, "Fuckin' A! Do you think there's any left?" "I don't know. But we can sneak into the kitchen and look around to find out."

After quietly opening up the bedroom door, Grant carefully guided Dennis down the hall, through the living room, and into the kitchen. After sitting his friend down at the table, he conducted a search of the counters and discovered what remained of the pie. He then divided it between them on two plates, and they quietly crept back into the bedroom.

Once safely inside with the door shut again behind them, they sat down and fell to eating. But within seconds, Dennis asked, "Hey man, do you know what this coconut pie reminds me of?" They instantly burst into laughter, because the soft tender meringue and coconut on top was obviously reminiscent of the tender flesh and lovely hair of the female sex.

April 2, 1973, Monday

It was 1:30 A.M., and they would be on the bus to University City in just a few hours, but they were still up and talking as furiously as ever. Since Grant had only a single bed in his room, the friends had been taking turns sleeping on the floor. Dennis was in Grant's bed, and Grant was bedded down on the floor, but still they could not relax enough to go to sleep. Grant, however, was especially keyed up, because their explicit talking about the pleasures of intercourse over the weekend had succeeded in working him up into quite a sexual frenzy. He could not wait to see his darling again, after their thirty-one days of being apart. Dennis was growing tired and sensed that Grant was almost crazy with desire for her. He did his best to calm him down by advising him to relax and to reserve all his passion for her later in the day, but his words were unavailing: for after Dennis finally dozed off around 2:00, Grant could not rest and relax until he had quietly masturbated and ejaculated. Only then did his erect penis subside somewhat and gave him enough peace to drift off to sleep.

Grant's father took them to the bus station on his way to work. As they sat together on the bus, Grant was very quiet. Two things were troubling him very much. One was the weather. It was drizzling rain, and he was afraid that George would postpone his departure to Newton and would thus prevent him and Dorothy from being able to be alone as soon as he arrived. The other matter was doubts about what was going to happen when they were alone. Would they pick up from exactly where they left off thirty-one days before? He was honestly not sure. Dorothy had sounded so excited on her cassette recordings to him about his return, but since they had not yet become sufficiently comfortable to talk openly on their cassette tapes about their mutual enjoyment of intercourse, he really was not sure how she regarded their last twenty-eight hours together during which they had both thoroughly enjoyed six full hours of perfect physical love. In fact, she had said something on one of her tapes that Grant had construed or possibly misconstrued to mean that she wanted them simply to be very special friends. Was it possible that she was still trying to resurrect that old illusion, which, he thought, they had fucked to death a month ago?

When they arrived, it was drizzling, and Dorothy said nothing at all about George, one way or the other, and therefore kept Grant on pins and needles. Of course, she did not know yet that he had told Dennis about their love relationship; and so she behaved toward both of them as if they were just two of her university blind students. After dropping Dennis off at Beaumont Manor, the two rode in almost total silence. Dorothy apparently saw no reason to explain the obvious, whereas Grant was too apprehensive to ask any questions that might have dispelled his fears as to George's whereabouts and Dorothy's plans for them. Their entire conversation in the car concerned their need to first stop off at the Lincoln Bank to handle some business for George. After doing so, they proceeded on to the house, again in silence, and arrived there around 9:30.

When they entered the house, Dorothy finally began to dispel both of Grant's fears, not by any words, but by her actions. She led him over into the end of the family room near the door going out into the garage, where they could not be seen by anyone who might be outside in the yard. She then embraced him and placed her lips on his. They began to kiss long and passionately with their bodies pressed together. Her message was clear: "George is gone, and I'm your woman." As they kissed, Grant slid his hands down inside her slacks and panties to grip her lovely bottom and to push her abdomen hard into his erection. When they finally broke the kiss, he pulled her slacks and panties down and descended to his knees along with them. He took her female sex into his mouth and enjoyed kissing and licking her there. Since Dorothy had taken a bath that morning for this very reason, her sex was wonderful to enjoy in this way. When Grant removed his mouth and tongue from her vulva, she pulled her clothes back into place and walked immediately into the bathroom adjoining the master bedroom. Grant followed along, and she sat down on the toilet to urinate.

While she was walking to the bathroom and then sitting on the toilet, they conversed normally about his trip on the bus. Once again, as had happened so often in the past, their exchange of words was perfectly natural and served to conceal what was really happening. But since Grant was blind and still in some doubt, he continued to remain in a state of uncertainty. Unknown to him, as Dorothy sat there, she removed her shoes and socks and slid off her slacks and panties. As they walked into the master bedroom with their normal conversation accompanying their movements, she sat down on the edge of the bed, wearing nothing below her waist, and proceeded to remove her top and bra. She had just assumed that they were going to undress and begin their intercourse right away, and that none of this required any explanation to her blind lover-boy. Grant finally began to catch on slowly when she sat down on the bed, but in order to confirm his rapidly rising hopes, he reached down with his hand to see what she was doing. It just so happened that his hand landed between her upper thighs. As soon as he touched her beautiful bare flesh there, he knew where he was on her body and instantly moved his hand further up toward her sex. There her womanhood was! All naked, but the truly awesome thing was that she was wearing one of her tops that came down below her waistline. Thus, her sex, though bare, was teasingly peeking out at Grant from beneath the bottom edge of her top. It was as if her vagina was saying to him, "peek-a-boo, peek-a-boo, I want you, peek-a-boo, peek-a-boo, I'll fuck you!" The sight of her sitting there on the edge of the bed, beautifully bare from her sex on down, but with her perfect womanhood so fetchingly veiled from full view, was for Grant the sexual equivalent of being struck by a thunderbolt. He felt as if something powerful had hit him, and he had to have her that very moment. He tore off his clothes as quickly as he could, mounted her, entered her vagina, and began their long morning of the perfect physical pleasure of their complete and total love.

They did not emerge from the bed until 1:00 that afternoon. Since they had been apart for one full month, their bodies were so very hungry for one another. They simply fucked and fucked and fucked and fucked and fucked even more. By noon their intercourse had lost its frantic frenzy and was becoming sweet and sedate. They now became at least as interested in serious talking as in continuing with their wonderful love-pleasure. Accordingly, their final hour was filled with both talking and love-making in a more relaxed and desultory fashion. It was now that Grant finally broke the news to Dorothy that Dennis knew about them. At first she was somewhat alarmed that anyone at all would know, but she then became comfortable with the news, because it was a relief to know that such a good friend, with whom she could talk when Grant was not there, knew what was really going on.

When they eventually arose from bed with their bodies temporarily sated with one another, they glided through the afternoon and evening on a magic carpet of euphoria. After supper, Dorothy retreated into the master bedroom and adjoining bathroom and finally emerged all dressed up beautifully to accompany her boyfriend on their hot date to the second of the AIA lectures. As in the case of the first lecture, they both gloried in being together at this formal public event as a romantic and loving couple; and after they returned home and Carol was safely away in bed, Grant undressed his woman, and she put on nothing except her pink quilted robe. They then settled down on the couch in the family room and engaged themselves for the next several hours in the most delicious fondling and play. They would have only a few days together, and they both wanted to fill that time with as much love-pleasure as possible. If necessary, serious conversation could be temporarily put on hold and could be resumed through their exchange of cassette letters during their next period of separation.

April 3, 1973, Tuesday

As soon as Carol left for school, Dorothy came into the front bedroom, removed her robe, and slid into bed with Grant. She was still wearing a short nightgown made of a stretchy synthetic material. It was a garment that her mother had given her. Grant moved over to the edge of the bed to accommodate her, and she lay on her back, hiked up her nightgown, spread her thighs, and invited Grant to mount and enter her vagina. After years of being totally dead sexually, she was now entirely alive as a beautiful sexy woman, and her vagina wanted to have Grant's erect penis inside her as much as their schedule would allow. She was already wet and dilated and received Grant's erection smoothly. For his part, Grant's manhood was big and ready to begin a new day of loving, enjoying, and pleasing her. He maintained his size and hardness as he plunged rhythmically inside her, churning up pleasure for them both. His rhythm was steady and tireless, and he seemed to be in no hurry to come, but was content to remain erect inside her indefinitely, riding and riding, plunging and plunging, thrusting and thrusting. Her vagina and his penis were operating so well together, running smoothly like a one-cylinder love machine.

Unfortunately, their pleasure was rudely interrupted after about forty minutes when Dorothy's son Wesley came home. He was still on leave from the navy, but was spending almost all his time staying with friends. Just in case Wesley might come home like this, Dorothy had taken the precaution of locking the back door, thereby obliging Wesley to use his key to enter the house and to give the two lovers a few more seconds' notice of his approach. As soon as Dorothy heard Wesley at the back door, she leapt out from underneath Grant. The violent motion unceremoniously yanked his penis from her vagina. She then tried to get to her feet as fast as she could, but Grant's right knee had the bottom edge of her nightgown pinned to the mattress, and she lost a second or two in freeing herself. She threw on her robe and went into the kitchen to greet Wesley. Since Grant had not yet reached an orgasm inside her, he was somewhat frustrated sexually. His erection was big and hard from their forty minute of pleasure, but clearly needed much more. Grant therefore lay in bed hoping that Wesley would soon leave, so that they could resume, but unfortunately, Wesley stayed in the kitchen talking at length with his mother. Grant therefore eventually gave up hope and emerged from the bedroom to join them.

Wesley did eventually leave, and thus the lovers were able to return to bed for a while, but he returned, this time with his new girlfriend Mary Beth with him. It was Dorothy's first time to meet her. She was a very pleasant person, a student at the university whom Wesley had just met during this period of leave. They all four sat around the kitchen table and spent the afternoon talking. Wesley had rented a twelve-string guitar from a music store, and Grant had fun playing it as they talked. Since Wesley and Mary Beth had become sexually active, she had gone to the student health center to have an intrauterine device fitted inside her. Wesley and Mary Beth mentioned this during their conversation and seemed to revel in parading this sexually explicit knowledge before Wesley's mother. Unknown to them, of course, was what was going on between Wesley's mother and her blind student friend.

April 4, 1973, Wednesday

Luckily, today Wesley was busy making the rounds to see his friends for the last time. He would be leaving early tomorrow morning. Consequently, Dorothy and Grant were able to spend the morning and early afternoon in bed together enjoying abundant vaginal intercourse and other related delights. It lasted for hours, like their very first morning in bed on March 1. It was unrestrained sex, but it was not simply sex. It was both a physiological manifestation of their complete love for one another and was also the means by which their minds, as well as their bodies, were joined in perfect union. Their erotic enjoyment was therefore always accompanied by serious talking that served to establish an even closer spiritual bond between them.

Although they had already mentioned many important details of their past to one another on previous occasions, they now repeated them and went into further detail. Grant described how he had lost his eyesight in his one good eye from a detached retina, how the surgery had ultimately been unsuccessful, and how he had learned to adapt to his new situation and had completed his education from the sixth to the twelfth grade. He had lost his vision on December 31 of 1963 during the Christmas break, had entered the hospital on New Year's Day of 1964, and had returned home on January 31 of the same year. Then following a period of convalescence in which he slowly regained his strength, he had succeeded in finishing the sixth grade largely due to the heroic efforts of the principal of his elementary school, Mrs. Dearborn. She had been his first grade teacher, but by now she had become the school's principal and had taken a direct interest in him and his misfortune. She had Grant's mother bring him to her office several times every week for two hours, 9:30 to 11:30, during which Mrs. Dearborn read to Grant in her office from his textbooks and gave him his tests. Meanwhile, an instructor employed by the state of Illinois, Mrs. Thelma Becker, came to their house once a week to give Grant lessons to learn braille. So, by the end of the summer of 1964, Grant had both completed the sixth grade and had a basic mastery of braille. But rather than continuing his schooling in his local community, which was not often done in those days by blind children, his parents decided to enroll him in the state residential school for the blind, known at the time as the Illinois Braille and Sight Saving School in Jacksonville, about ninety miles from Fairmont. There he completed his seventh, eighth, and ninth grades with other blind and visually impaired students. The experience had taught him much about dealing with his blindness; and although he had greatly enjoyed learning how to wrestle and being on the school's wrestling team, as well as being a member of the school band and having regular shop classes to learn how to make things with his hands, the school was rather weak academically, because the entire student body from kindergarten to twelfth grade numbered only 210. Classes were therefore quite small, and the range of courses offered was very limited. By the eighth grade Grant had come to realize that if he wanted to go on to college, he really needed to return to his much larger local high school. So, after learning how to type and to travel with a cane, he had succeeded in persuading the chief administrators of his community's high school to allow him to enroll as a sophomore. He was the only blind student in a student body of 3400, had taken a very demanding curriculum, and had graduated ranked eleventh in a class of about 700 students.

At the very time that Grant was learning to adapt to his blindness and struggling to achieve a very good education in preparation for college, Dorothy had undergone her own misfortunes and had overcome major hardships. Her father had died at about the time that George had quit his job with Boeing and had formed his business partnership with a fellow Boeing employee named John Thompson. They built a few houses, including those in which both the Thompsons and the Pattersons moved into from their Boeing trailer court, built a car wash, and did small subcontracting jobs in the area around Kimball, Nebraska, including the construction of a swimming pool. The latter, however, developed faults in the concrete; and when John and George could not come up with the necessary funds to fix it, they had eventually gone bankrupt. This awful disaster had gradually unfolded over the course of 1964. They had moved out of their Boeing trailer and into their brand new house at the very beginning of April, and Dorothy had had to devote considerable energy to getting the new house into order, but then by the end of the following February, not quite eleven months later, they had had to pack up everything, abandon their new house, and move to University City, where George began his new job with CCC. Throughout their entire marriage George had always thought that the grass was greener on the other side and had subjected the family to constant uncertainty and instability, as he changed from one job to the next. The disaster in Kimball had merely been the worst in a long series of changes. All this had been especially hard on the three children; and of course, the chief responsibility of raising them and seeing to all their needs had fallen upon her, forming an endless cycle of washing and ironing everyone's clothes, fixing meals, keeping their house looking nice, overseeing the children's homework and education, and getting them to and from all their various activities. Despite the radiant charm and easy grace that she succeeded in projecting to the outside world, she had been so utterly frustrated and unhappy inside since about the time that Carol was born fifteen years ago. Dorothy found it to be so cathartic to be able to share all these thoughts, feelings, and experiences with Grant. She had never before enjoyed such happiness as that which resulted from the perfect union of their bodies, minds, and spirits.

After floating again through the later afternoon and evening on their magic carpet of euphoria, they were just getting ready to settle down together for a night of more erotic activity when the telephone rang. It was about 10:30. Carol was in bed, and Dorothy and Grant were tidying up the kitchen for the night. Dorothy answered the phone and was pleased to hear Dennis' voice.

"Hey, Ma," Dennis said, "How are you two guys doing?" "Oh we're doing really well." "I just thought I'd call to check up on you guys. I guess Grant's probably told you by now that I know all about you two?" "Oh yes, he told me that Monday morning." "So how do you feel about that?" "Well, at first I was shocked and a bit afraid, but I'm used to the idea. I'm glad to know that I can now talk with you if I need to." "I'm glad you're ok with it, and I'll always be happy to help you if I can in any way. So," Dennis continued, changing the subject, "Have you been enjoying yourselves?" "Boy!" Dorothy said with a lovely little laugh, "Have we ever!" "That's great!" Dennis almost shouted into the phone. "In fact," Dorothy continued, "We've been enjoying ourselves so much that my back is rather tired from all the riding. I'm not sure how much more I can take." They both laughed. "Wow!" Dennis exclaimed, "it sounds like you two really have been having a lot of fun!" "We sure have! And we still have a day and a half more to go."

Grant had been standing next to her as she conversed, and he smiled and laughed along with them. But even though they had spent the entire morning and the early afternoon in bed, they still wanted more. They went into the master bedroom, and Grant undressed her lovingly. She put on only her pink quilted robe, and they went into the living room. During the previous two evenings they had contented themselves with playing on the family room couch wrapped up in an afghan to serve as extra cover in case Carol walked in on them, but tonight they both wanted the real thing, so much so that Dorothy for once was not concerned about Carol arising from bed and discovering them engaged in their love-pleasure. Despite their previous hours and hours of intercourse, Dorothy's vagina was voracious for more of Grant's magnificent manhood.

Since Dorothy's back had become rather tired from Grant's constant riding of her, they hit upon another way of having intercourse. She sat down in the middle of the couch, scooted her bottom to the very front edge, opened up her robe to reveal all the female beauty of her naked front, spread her thighs wide apart, and offered her sex to Grant. As he knelt before her and eagerly began to kiss and lick her love-pie, he said slowly and emphatically, "Fee! Fie! Foe! Funt! How I love to smell your cunt!" She really enjoyed his naughty talk to her amid their love-making. It thrilled and excited her and heightened the pleasure. His hands were full of her breasts, as he continued to kiss and lick her spread womanhood that was so lovely and so beautifully fragrant. After giving her an orgasm that they both thoroughly enjoyed, he entered her vagina with his penis, and her orgasm then merged with his. Fortunately, it was a very low couch. So, when Grant positioned himself on his knees between her thighs, her vagina and his erection were perfectly in alignment, and they could engage in intercourse without placing the weight of his body on her. They gave and received pleasure in this new position for a very long time until her back became tired from being in a slumped position instead of sitting up straight. But since they both wanted even more sweet love-joy, they turned to another means of pleasuring themselves.

Dorothy was still clad in nothing except her lovely robe, and Grant was wearing only his t-shirt. He lay down on his back on the couch, and she lay on top of his penis, so that her breasts were positioned to receive his loving attention. He was wet with her love-honey and his own semen, which served as a lubricant for his penis' head, as Grant rubbed and rubbed it all over her two breasts, nipples, cleavage, and even under her arms. Dorothy loved having her breasts caressed in this way, and so did Grant. It was truly awesome and delicious. They continued this form of ecstasy for a very long time and did not halt until about 2:00. At that time Dorothy announced that her back felt better, and she could withstand being mounted and ridden one last time before they went off to bed. She therefore simply slid down from the couch onto the gold living room carpet beside the couch and parted her thighs for Grant. He mounted her and entered her vagina, and they had a delicious final bit of love-joy to end their more than three hours of extraordinary pleasure. It had been a night that they would never forget: pussy fucking on the front edge of the couch, followed by prolonged titty fucking, and ending in a final session of pussy fucking on the floor.

April 5, 1973, Thursday

Since Dorothy had to take Wesley to the airport in University City for his flight departing at 6:45 A.M., Grant and Dorothy arose at 5:30, after sleeping for only about three hours. Since Carol usually slept like the proverbial log and would not be getting up for another hour, Dorothy and Grant went into the main bathroom in the hallway, so that they could perform their necessary morning preparations together. They shut the door, took off their clothes, and stood naked side by side at the two sinks. Grant fondled and caressed her lovely naked body as she stood there washing her breasts and between her legs. As Grant washed his own groin, she returned the favor by offering his penis some sweet comfort. Since its head was slightly irritated from two hours of pleasuring her breasts earlier that morning, she rubbed some Vaseline on it, and the loving touch of her dainty feminine hand was fantastic, akin to masturbation. They dressed, collected Wesley from a friend's house where he had spent the night, and proceeded to the airport. When they came back to the house, Carolyn was still getting herself ready for school. Grant therefore turned on the TV in the family room and sat down on the couch to catch a bit of the morning news. But as soon as Carolyn left, Dorothy went into the master bedroom, took off all her clothes, put on her robe, came into the family room, and sat down beside Grant. When he reached over to touch his pussy goddess, he found that her robe was open, and what he found was nothing but fully bare female perfection. He therefore instantly arose, turned off the TV, and the two lovers headed for the bedroom. Although they had spent the entire morning yesterday in bed engaged in hours of love pleasure and then even more hours during the night on the living room couch, they both still wanted even more. They simply could not get enough. They now proceeded to have another two hours of magnificent pleasure, during which they enjoyed vaginal intercourse in a new position, what might be termed the sidesaddle position.

Dorothy lay on her back, bent her legs, and spread her knees apart as usual, but instead of Grant mounting her by lying on top of her and between her legs, he entered her in a different way. He lay beside her to her right and moved his upper body obliquely away from her. She then lifted her right leg, so that he could slide his two legs under, but then he rolled onto his left side and placed his thighs around her left thigh. Grant was now turned onto his left side and had his penis positioned between her thighs and directed toward her sex. He could now enter her easily and ride her without having the weight of his entire body on top of her. But this method of intercourse was especially delightful for Grant, because her entire womanhood and body were available for him to feel with his hands, as his penis and her sex engaged in intercourse.

"My golly!" Grant enthused, as his penis plunged rhythmically inside her, and as his right hand caressed and fondled her love-delta and sex, "It is so fantastic to enjoy your pussy like this! I can feel all of you as we're fucking! And I can actually watch and enjoy the sight of us fucking!" As his right hand was engaged in feeling the action between her spread thighs, his left hand began to fondle her right breast. He now halted in his thrusting, and the fingers of his right hand continued to explore carefully how his penis was inside her. "Man alive!" he exclaimed again, "I can see my penis going inside you, your pussy lips closing around the shaft of my cock! My goodness! I can't imagine anything more beautiful than seeing your pussy mouth swallowing and taking in my pecker!"

As Grant talked and enjoyed her naked body with his penis and hands, she gazed upon his face. It was the perfect mirror of the rest of him, suffused with such joy and obvious pleasure. She then shifted her eyes downward along her body and was herself captivated by watching his right hand caressing and fondling her love-delta, female sex, and her thighs while his penis was fully inside her. It was so nice to feel him, to see him feeling her, and to see how it all pleased him so greatly. It also tremendously enhanced her own pleasure. "I like this way too," Dorothy said, "because you can ride me about as much as you want without bothering my back. I can also feel your legs." As she spoke, her left hand was gripping and squeezing his right thigh that lay over her own left thigh. "You have such muscular and well-shaped legs! They feel so nice! How did you ever get such nice legs?" "From lots and lots of running," Grant replied, as he continued to admire the union of their sexes. "Before I lost my eyesight, I used to run constantly, all the way to school, back from school, and simply doing lap after lap around our back yard. I had the strongest and most muscular legs of any kid my age. I guess that it was an early example of my self-motivation and perseverance." "I'll say," Dorothy agreed as she squeezed his leg again.

When Grant finally withdrew his penis, Dorothy rolled over onto her side, placed her head on his shoulder, threw her leg on top of his penis to place her love-spread on full display, and fell right to sleep, and so did Grant. They were both very tired from three consecutive nights of little sleep. When they finally awoke around 1:00 in the afternoon, they arose, dressed, and went off to do some shopping. As they drove up to the house again around 4:00, Dorothy saw George's car parked on the driveway and said, "Uh-oh! George's home." "Oh no!" Grant simply replied.

They entered the house and discovered that both George and his mother were there. George had decided to return home a day early to take care of some business in town, and his mother had also come to spend the weekend. As a result, Grant and Dorothy had to spend their last twenty-one hours together in ways contrary to their desires. Dorothy was obliged to revert to being George's wife, and Grant had to be just a university student who was a friend of the family. They therefore spent that evening quite conventionally there at the house. Since Grant had with him a braille book for learning Classical Greek, he occupied himself with studying.

April 6, 1973, Friday

By the next morning at the breakfast table Dorothy had come up with a plausible reason why the two of them had to be absent from the house. She explained that Grant needed to go to the campus bookstore and then needed to take care of other things at the administration building.

As they drove over to campus to pick Dennis up at Beaumont Manor, Grant said, "I've been studying my Greek grammar book, and I'm beginning to learn quite a bit. I now know what your name means." "Oh yeah?" Dorothy replied. "Yep! It comes from two different Greek words: *doron* meaning 'gift', and *thea* meaning 'goddess', although the second part of your name could be taken from an adjective meaning 'divine', rather than from the noun meaning 'goddess'. In any case, your names translates from Greek as 'Divine gift'." "That's real nice," Dorothy answered, "My name is somewhat old fashioned." "What do you mean?" Grant asked. "Well, it's not a very common or popular name these days." "Yeah well, so what? It's a beautiful name, just like you." "Oh yeah?" "Damn right!" Grant said emphatically. "In fact," he continued, "it's nice that it isn't very common, because you are so very uncommonly wonderful. A rare and wonderful name for a person with the rarest goodness and sweetness that I know. You truly are the divine gift to my life!"

After picking Dennis up, they proceeded to the eastern edge of the city, to the park, which Dorothy and Grant had visited during the previous summer. There the three of them sat in the car and enjoyed talking and just being together. Dorothy and Grant also engaged in petting. Then after getting some lunch, they stayed at Dennis' dorm room until it was time for Grant to catch the early afternoon bus back to Peoria.

April 11, 1973, Wednesday

It was well past midnight, and Grant was up and about in his room in Fairmont, busily occupied in making a lovely cassette recording for his darling Dove. He first used patch cords between his stereo and his cassette machine to record the double album of Chet Atkins' Silver Anniversary that he and Dorothy had purchased shortly after their first marvelous morning of intercourse on March 1; and then after returning to the house from their afternoon shopping, they had listened to the music for the first time as Dorothy worked in the kitchen to prepare supper. She had enjoyed it so very much, and her singing along with the songs with her lovely voice had pleased Grant immensely. He therefore made this recording for his darling to serve as a constant reminder of that most wonderful day that had finally brought them together in a perfect union of total love.

He recorded the music on a ninety minute cassette; and since the tape still had some room available on it, Grant decided to fill up the space with another musical delight. Among a few record albums that he possessed of contemporary German music there was one particular love song that was so haunting and beautiful. The orchestrated music was really lovely, and the man who sang the song did so enchantingly, which fitted the words of the song perfectly. Dorothy's grandparents had been immigrants from Germany, and she grew up hearing them speaking German to each other; and even though she only understood a few of the words and phrases that they spoke to one another, their German conversations always pleased her. Accordingly, when Grant and Dennis later came into her life and often conversed in German during their gatherings at her house, it pleased her very much, and she often commented how wonderful their German sounded to her. Grant therefore knew how much his darling would appreciate this lovely song sung in German.

After recording the haunting song on the cassette tape, he then proceeded to talk to his wonderful woman in order to translate the song for her into English, accompanied by his pronunciation of the German itself. Grant's translation was as follows.

Is it true when you say "I'm in love with you?" Or do you only say this for appearance? Is it true when you say that there is no other man? A lie can be of no value.

My love for thee is as deep as the sea, and it belongs to thee alone! Without you my life is lonely, gray, and empty, because I need you to be happy.

Is it true when you say "I'll always remain with you?" Or will you leave me tomorrow all alone? Is it true when you say "my heart belongs to you?" A lie can be of no value.

My love for thee is as deep as the sea, and it belongs to thee alone! Without you my life is lonely, gray, and empty, because I need you to be happy.

Since their two weeks of reunion had firmly cemented and perfected their true love through the complete and fulfilling enjoyment of physical love-pleasure, the theme of the song was no longer apt for their relationship, but their newly completed and perfected love was so recent that the previous uncertainties were still an all too vivid memory, so that the two lovers had no difficulty in relating to the words of the song. When Dorothy received the cassette recording in the mail a few days later, she was greatly pleased and deeply touched by Grant's gift. She played the tape repeatedly and kept it among her treasured musical recordings as a shining reminder of their magnificent true love.

April 23, 1973, Monday

It was a gorgeous spring morning, warm and sunny. As Grant sat on the bus that was returning him to University City for a third week, he was filled with thoughts of how he and Dorothy would soon be together again. Luckily, the third AIA lecture was tonight, so that this last separation had been just a bit more than two weeks. It was hard to believe all that had happened in their relationship since they first had intercourse about seven weeks ago on March 1. They were about to begin their third week as complete lovers and were becoming settled comfortably into this new role in their relationship. Their appetite for each other was insatiable, and the glory of intercourse was as phenomenal as their very first time together, but they were now beginning to expect this powerful and extraordinary phenomenon as an integral part of their lives, and it served to not only enhance their relationship, but to bind them together spiritually in a truly profound way and to grace them with a serenity and happiness that neither had ever known before. They were not, nor had they ever been, a young college student and a middle-aged woman merely intent on mere carnal gratification. The physicality had always been there and was real enough, but it was simply the manifestation of a truly deep, genuine spiritual love that they had for one another. Their past ten months together had been exhilarating and magnificent, as well as extremely stressful because of Dorothy's marital status. In addition, Grant's inner turmoil had prevented him from doing his academic work in a satisfactory manner and had also caused him considerable mental distress. But as Dorothy gave herself to him fully through sexual intercourse, he was now firmly convinced that she was and would be his woman. The realization was proving to be extremely curative in banishing his emotional instability that bordered upon mental illness. He was now quickly regaining his old confidence and inner strength. His regimen of study at home had him back on track academically, so that he was now sure that he would be successful in his work this coming fall semester. But, of course, the single most important thing of all was the way in which their loving relationship had now become complete and perfect. Although it was still far from clear how things would actually unfold in practical terms, they were now both thoroughly confident and secure in their love for one another, and that was a steadfast foundation, they knew, upon which they could build something truly permanent and beautiful.

After stepping down from the bus, he eagerly embraced his lady-love and was so pleased to discover that she was wearing one of her adorable summer suits that she had worn all last summer, short and a matching top. As the two set off to the house, Dorothy said, "I'm afraid that when we get to the house, we won't be alone right away." "Oh yeah?" Grant asked. "Yeah. Last week was semester and Easter Break, and a few of the university kids [Bob, Kitty, and Dennis] came over yesterday to spend the night before returning to the dorms. So we won't be able to do much until after they all get up, and we take them back to campus. They were all still sleeping when I left a little bit ago. But I've got an idea of how we can have a little fun as soon as we get there." "Do you?" Grant asked hopefully. "I do!" She said with a smug smile in her voice, "Just be quiet, and follow me when we get there." "Ok."

They entered the house quietly and were greeted by the four dogs. Dorothy left Grant in the family room and walked down the hall to see if everyone was still in bed and sound asleep. They were. She returned to

Grant and led him into the bathroom situated between the master bedroom and the laundry room. "Ok," she whispered, "take down your pants and undershorts, and sit down there on the toilet lid." Grant obeyed. His penis was already huge and ready for her. It was now standing upright like a flag pole, impatiently waiting. After sliding shut the two doors on opposite ends of the bathroom, she stood in front of him, took down her own shorts and panties, stepped out of them, and stood facing Grant. He held out his hands and found her bare lower body. Just like three weeks before, when he was galvanized by the sight of her sex peeking adorably out at him from underneath the edge of a top just like this one, he encountered her bottom, hips, and sex alluringly concealed partially by her top. After reaching around her to fondle and caress her beautiful bare bottom, his hands slowly came around to her love-front, first enjoying her hips and then giving full attention to her love-delta of pussy hair and the cleft of her vulva. "Oh my golly!" he exclaimed, "You're so damn beautiful, as beautiful as Venus herself!" As Grant's fingers continued to admire her female beauty in genuine awe, She moved forward, straddled him, and slowly descended onto his lap, thus offering her spread womanhood to his penis. Although he could not actually enter her vagina from this position, he could and did rub the head of his erection inside her vulva to masturbate them both. When he quickly reached an orgasm, he ejaculated onto her love-front. She then arose, pulled her clothes back into place, and said, "Ok, why don't we take the dogs out for a walk?"

They did; and as they walked together over the open field, their talk was fast and furious, as two weeks of pent-up thoughts and feelings began to pour out of them. Once, as they descended into a deep gully, they took advantage of their cover and embraced and kissed passionately. When they reached the highway marking the farthest point of their walk from the house, they sat down on the edge of the ravine that sloped down to the road and allowed the dogs to browse around as they continued to talk. They then retraced their steps.

When they returned to the house and discovered that everyone was still asleep, they went back into the bathroom and enjoyed themselves once again in the same way as before: Grant sat down on the toilet lid and erected his penis for her to descend upon with her female sex. He masturbated inside her vulva and came again on her love-front. Shortly after they emerged from the bathroom, everyone arose from bed and gathered in the kitchen, where they sat around the table and talked, while Dorothy stood at the stove frying bacon and scrambling eggs for their breakfast.

It was not until 11:00 that Dorothy and Grant returned from campus to an empty house and were then able to undress and to give themselves entirely over to the enjoyment of the wonderful physical pleasure of their perfect love for the next three hours in the master bedroom.

The rest of the day followed its established pattern: Grant assisting Dorothy around the house as they continued to talk, Carol coming home from school, the three of them having supper, Dorothy dressing herself up beautifully for her hot date that evening with her lover, their attendance at the AIA lecture, coming home and sitting together on the family room couch wrapped up in the wagon wheel afghan, and engaging in embracing, kissing, and fondling, as they talked and talked. As usual, Grant had been spending much of his time since their last meeting in reading several very interesting books. His brain was brimming with thoughts and ideas that he now shared with his lady-love, who listened carefully and made her own contributions. This in turn took them off onto numerous interesting tangents.

April 24, 1973, Tuesday

As soon as Carol had left for school, Dorothy walked into the master bedroom, stepped out of her slippers, took off her robe, hung it up, pulled off her nightgown, placed it under her pillow on the bed, and walked naked down the hall and into the front bedroom. Oh how she loved being naked in Grant's presence! And she wanted them to take the fullest advantage of their limited time together over these next few days. She gently pulled back the covers and slid into bed beside him. He awoke instantly and said, "Wow! What a way to be awakened in the morning!" They both laughed. Grant stood up from the bed, removed his T-shirt and undershorts, lay back down beside Dorothy, entered her vagina in the sidesaddle manner, and began his morning riding of her sex.

As his penis plunged rhythmically inside her, his two hands were wandering all over her body: her breasts, her love-delta, her sex receiving his manhood, and her lovely thighs. "My golly!" he exclaimed, "You're as lovely as Venus herself! I can't imagine anything coming close to being as beautiful as your pussy! Nothing can even come close!" "You sound like a broken record," Dorothy replied with obvious pleasure, "I think you said that yesterday several times too." "It bears repeating," Grant said, "And my gosh!

Nothing can ever come close to the physical pleasure that your pussy gives my pecker!" Dorothy had never felt more alive, content, and happy than as when they were enjoying this ethereal physical pleasure of their complete and total love. Her body was experiencing such joy and delight, and she relished feeling Grant's hands enjoying her nakedness, his penis being so fully excited and pleased, and his face reflecting all the wonder and pleasure that he was experiencing.

"It's a good thing that I'm not a sculptor," Grant suddenly remarked. "Why is that?" Dorothy asked. "Because if I were, your naked female body would be my one and only model. You'd have to pose for me naked every day, hour after hour." "I'm not sure we'd get much work done that way," Dorothy commented. "We'd have to have a bed in the workshop. You would model for me for about an hour, and then we'd have to lie down for about a half an hour before continuing on. I would love to be able to sculpt your feminine form, but if I did, I'm not sure that I could ever bring myself to part with the statue. In fact, I'd probably make statue after statue of you naked and could not sell any of them." "That wouldn't be very good for business." "Well, maybe I could make statues of your naked body and then make the heads and faces those of other women."

After about forty minutes of enjoying continuous intercourse, Dorothy said, "I'm afraid you're going to have to make Rufus Magnus stop for a little while. I need to make a pit stop." "Ah shucks!" Grant replied in mock disappointment, as he withdrew his penis. They arose from the bed and walked a few steps down the hall and into the bathroom with Grant following behind her with his hands on her bottom and hips. "Man! How I love to see your nakedness move as you walk!" "I'm a girl, not a man," Dorothy retorted playfully. "You certainly are, the very loveliest!"

As Dorothy stood up from the toilet with Grant beside her, she suggested, "Let's go into my bedroom where we'll have more room in bed." "Ok," Grant agreed. As they stepped out into the hall and turned in the direction of the master bedroom, Dorothy saw their naked forms in the full-length mirror at the end of the hallway. "Just stay right here beside me for a minute," she said, "We look so nice in the mirror." Grant stood alongside her, and their arms were around each other's backs with their hands resting on their hips. Dorothy was utterly enchanted by their full frontal nudity side by side. It was such a shame that they could not have a photograph of this image. They could never look more beautiful together: Grant's tall muscular form, pale skin covered in his golden reddish hair, Rufus Magnus, her own full voluptuous figure, her breasts, hour-glass figure, her love-delta and sex, her shapely thighs, and their faces aglow with joy and pleasure. As she stood beside Grant drinking in this beautiful image with her eyes, she suddenly exclaimed, "Venus and Adonis!" In their own minds, they certainly were!

April 25, 1973, Wednesday

It was approaching noon, and the two lovers were simply lying side by side in bed in the master bedroom. They were lying on their backs, and Dorothy had her right leg bent up at the knee and leaning on Grant's left leg. It was such a trusting and wonderful feeling for them both. Dorothy's sex was almost fully spread, and Grant's left hand was caressing her adoringly. They were slowing down from three hours or so of passionate pleasure and would be getting up soon.

"How about we take a little snooze before we get up to have lunch?" Dorothy asked. "That's fine with me," Grant replied, as his hand continued to admire her. Dorothy now rolled over onto her side, placed her head on Grant's shoulder, threw her left thigh onto his penis, and invited his hand to hold her womanhood. "Ok," she said, "I'm ready to doze off, but how about telling me a bedtime story?" "Ok," Grant replied, and then after a pause, he asked, "How about Romulus and Remus? Do you know that one?" "No, I don't." "That's good, and it fits with the calendar, because last Saturday (April 21) was what the ancient Romans regarded as the day on which Rome was founded." "Oh yeah?" "Yep! That's right!

Ok," Grant began, "Here's the story. Once upon a time in central Italy there were two brothers who inherited the royal throne of Alba Longa from their father. But rather than sharing things, the evil brother pushed aside his good brother and took over everything. Since the good brother had a daughter, the evil brother made her a Vestal Virgin, a priestess of the goddess Vesta, so that she could not have any children to dispute the throne with the evil brother. Her name was Rhea Silvia. But one day as she went to a well to draw water, the god Mars saw her and instantly fell in love with her. He had to have her, came down to earth, enveloped her in a cloud, and had his way with her. He really fucked her." "Hey now!" Dorothy interjected, "I don't think that's how the story is probably told. Is it?" "Well," Grant allowed, "not really, but what do you expect? Here I'm lying in bed with this beautiful woman with one arm and hand around and down her bare back and just above her lovely ass, and with my other hand I'm holding her perfect pussy. How else do you think I'd tell the story? But just think about it. Mars was a god. He must have had quite some pecker!" "Poor Rhea Silvia," Dorothy observed, "She must have gotten quite a workout." "She sure did," Grant explained, "He fucked her so much that she became pregnant, not with one child, but with twins. So you know he really must have fucked her, and the fact that she had twins was clear proof that she had been well fucked by a god." "Is that how you're going to teach Roman history when you become a professor?" "If you're sitting in the classroom, ya damn right!" "I'd better stay away from your classes. The parents and university administration wouldn't like your teaching style very much." "But I bet it would make my courses popular."

Grant continued his story, but when he reached the part where Romulus and Remus overthrew the evil king, he heard Dorothy snoring gently. He stopped talking, relaxed, and dozed off with this lovely and wonderful woman in his embrace.

April 26, 1973, Thursday

After a few hours of glorious pleasure in bed that morning, they had arisen and gone off to run various errands and to have lunch at Arby's. When they returned to the house around 1:00 in the afternoon, they still had about two hours in which they could fully enjoy themselves in bed again before having to worry about Carol arriving home from school.

As they walked into the master bedroom to undress and lie down, Dorothy said, "Let me first give Debbie a quick call." "Ok," Grant agreed. Dorothy sat down on the edge of the bed and made the call, but unfortunately, as might have been expected, Debbie wanted to talk and talk. Equally unfortunately, Dorothy and Grant had not thought to undress before the call was made. Consequently, as the conversation dragged on and on, Grant became increasingly frustrated. He therefore knelt on the floor in front of Dorothy, whose feet were dangling off the side of the bed. After removing her shoes and socks, Grant began to use his mouth and tongue to love and adore her feet that were so petite and dainty. While the two women talked on the phone, Grant held Dorothy's foot lovingly in his hands and kissed and licked it all over. He even placed different parts of her foot in his mouth: her toes and the sides of her foot that were perfectly wonderful to love. When Dorothy finally succeeded in ending the conversation and put down the telephone receiver, she immediately exclaimed, "My golly, Grant, that felt so wonderful! While you were doing that, I didn't think that I could think straight and talk with Deb." They then undressed and thoroughly enjoyed themselves until it was nearly time for Carol to come home.

After supper Carol's friend Betty Washington was at the house, but when the two girls went off to visit a friend in the neighborhood, both Dorothy and Grant, who were still on fire for one another, decided to enjoy more pleasure during their absence. Since the girls were not likely to be gone more than a half an hour, intercourse in bed was not a viable option. They therefore came up with an imaginative alternative. Dorothy was wearing one of her adorable summer outfits. They went into the master bedroom and left the lights off, so that no one outdoors could see what was happening inside, but from her position on the bed Dorothy could look out the window and would be able to see Carol and Betty walking up to the back door on their return. This would give them adequate warning to cease and desist. Dorothy lay on her back on the bed, slid her short-pants and panties down to her ankles, and spread her knees wide apart to offer her sex fully to Grant. As he stood above her and lovingly caressed her womanhood over and over again, he said with genuine awe filling his deep voice, "My oh my! would you look at that pussy smile!" Both his touch and his words gave her tremendous pleasure. Dorothy was always greatly thrilled by hearing Grant use such lovely utterances in expressing how marvelously beautiful she was to him. He bent down over her and took her sex into his mouth and licked and kissed her with complete ardor and delight. "How I love to eat your honey pie!" he enthused amid his loving, which continued magnificently for the next half hour or so until finally Dorothy saw the two girls going past the window. "Ok," Dorothy whispered, "We need to stop." Grant then stood up from his Venus and walked out of the room, while she pulled her clothes back into place and was ready to meet Carol and Betty in the kitchen as if nothing unusual had transpired in their absence.

April 27, 1973, Friday

As they walked from the bathroom back to the bed in the master bedroom to resume their last morning of pleasure that week, Grant walked behind her with his hands, as usual, on her hips and bottom, thoroughly enjoying her feminine motions. When they arrived at the side of the bed, Grant said in a somewhat commanding tone, "Lie down and spread." Dorothy gladly obeyed, but instead of lying back down and resuming their intercourse, Grant stood over her and began to caress her sex lovingly and admiringly.

"My golly! Please pardon me for saying so, but I really love your pussy so much!" he said in a hushed voice filled with emotion and awe. "I don't want you to think that that's all I'm interested in, because you really are the most magnificent person I have known, and it just so happens that you are also so beautiful as a woman. I love you fully and totally, and you are my Venus. I love your V." He now traced her Venus V from one hip bone down along one side of her love-delta and down between her thighs to her bottom, and then he did the same for the other side. "Ok, now I want you to put your knees together and stretch your legs straight out." Dorothy obeyed. "Now I'll trace out your lovely Y." After tracing her V along both sides of her love-delta to the apex of her sex, his finger then went down between her thighs toward her knees. "I love your V, and I love your Y so very much!" he continued in the same hushed and awestruck tone. "After I leave today, I want you always to remember that, especially when you're here alone and are undressing or dressing. Whenever you're naked by yourself, think of how I love your V and your Y." "I will," she simply replied.

"Ok, how about spreading again," he requested, "Your Adonis wants to worship his Venus!" After she did, he knelt down between her thighs and began to kiss and lick her sex. He continued to talk while worshipping his goddess. "As you know by now, I'm really interested in the ancient Roman calendar. Well, as it turns out, the last few days of April and the beginning of May were devoted to a major festival in honor of the goddess Flora, the goddess of blooming plants and flowers. April also takes its name from the Latin word 'to open', because it is the month of budding and blossoming plants. Oh Dorth, you are my lovely flower! My Flora! My pink pussy rose!" By now she was reaching her orgasm; and when she was at its peak, Grant came up from between her thighs, mounted her, entered her vagina, and had his own orgasm merge with hers.

May 14, 1973, Monday

Once again, like last time, their separation lasted for only seventeen days, because the last AIA lecture for the spring semester would be that night, just three weeks after the previous one. In fact, their separation was so brief that it hardly gave them time to exchange braille letters or cassette recordings. Dorothy met Grant at the bus station at the usual time, but today he was lugging a Sony TC105 reel-to-reel tape recorder.

"What are you doing with that thing?" Dorothy asked. "NASA will be launching Sky Lab today, and I wanted to record the TV coverage, so that I could listen to it later," Grant replied. As usual, they returned to the house, but even before they could undress and go to bed, the telephone rang. Someone from Carol's school was calling to say that she was not feeling well, and that Dorothy should come pick her up. After Dorothy and Grant went over to the school and brought her home, they were unable to spend the morning and early afternoon in bed as they had planned.

After inspecting the two TV sets in the house, Grant determined that neither one had an earphone or headphone socket that would allow him to make a direct recording from it. But he had come prepared for such a contingency. He had brought along a cable fitted with alligator clips on each end to serve as his patch cord into one of the TV's. After looking at them, he decided that the smaller set in the family room would probably be easier to use. Thus, after Dorothy had located a suitable screw driver, Grant removed the back from the set, and Dorothy assisted him in clipping the cord onto the terminals of the speaker. As they began this procedure, Dorothy asked, "Isn't it dangerous to be poking around inside a TV set like this?" "It can be," Grant replied, "but chances are that nothing will happen." Dorothy was not fully convinced or reassured by this answer. As Grant removed the back from the TV and began carefully looking around with his fingers, Dorothy stood behind him with her hands on his shoulders. She figured that if he happened to be electrocuted, she could either be there to pull him away to safety, or she could be electrocuted along with him. Grant was genuinely touched by her sweet concern, but they attached the cord and put the back onto the TV again without mishap.

They spent the rest of the day simply enjoying being together and doing chores around the house, as they talked and brought one another fully up to date on what they had been doing over the past two weeks. After supper, Dorothy once again dressed herself up so elegantly for her evening date with her college boyfriend, and they enjoyed being a loving couple at the lecture.

The speaker for the evening gave a very impressive presentation on the possible Phoenician origin of the so-called Carmona ivories from southern Spain. She carried it off in real style, so that following the lecture Grant commented, "Hey that woman is quite a babe!" "You think so, huh?" Dorothy asked suspiciously. "Well, I guess, but she can't come close to you." "That's good," she replied with satisfaction. Even when trying to tease her, Grant simply could not go very far, but had to relent and let her know how much he really loved her.

As had become their custom, when Carol was safely in bed, Grant had the great honor of undressing his lady-love. Then after having intercourse to relieve themselves of their worst pent-up desires from being together all day long, they sat on the couch in the family room late into the night wrapped up in an afghan with Dorothy clad in only her pink quilted robe that Grant loved on her so very much. As they embraced, kissed, and played on the couch, they continued to talk. Their conversation mostly centered around Grant's plans for the fall semester, which included his resumption of studying Latin, a key element in becoming a historian of ancient Greece and Rome. But since he would need to take a placement test, and since there would be no more AIA lectures to bring him to University City before the fall semester began in late August, they were now dreading the onset of summer and a possible three-month separation. They therefore decided that they could plan to have Grant return for another week to take his Latin placement test; and they finally agreed that perhaps a good time would be the second week in July. Not only would it be around the midpoint of their summer separation, but it would also coincide with the first anniversary of the beginning of their relationship.

May 15, 1973, Tuesday

As Dorothy sat naked on the toilet, Grant, also naked, stood beside her with his hands fondling her breasts. "I really like your titties," he commented with awe in his voice. "I'm glad you do," Dorothy replied sweetly. "I'm sorry that I don't give them more attention," Grant continued, "Your pussy always seems to get the lion's share, my lovely Leo Lioness." "Oh," Dorothy interjected, "You shouldn't worry too much. You don't neglect my tits at all, and my pussy really appreciates all your attention." "That's good to hear," Grant said, "But maybe I can give these beautiful breasts some consolation by giving them their own special love names." "That would be nice," said Dorothy, "Have you come up with names for them?" "I sure have." "Boy! You think of everything, don't you, especially when it involves sex." "Are you implying that I'm just a horny young guy?" "Well, you are, aren't you?" "I guess, but it sure helps to have a beautiful woman like you. You're so damn inspiring!" "I am, huh?" "You sure are! But anyway, getting back to names for these lovely titties of yours, I wish to name your right breast Kalliste and your left one Pulcherrima." "Ok, so what do those names mean?" "Glad you asked. Kalliste means 'most beautiful' in Greek, and Pulcherrima means the same thing in Latin. How's that?" "That figures." "What?" "That you'd name my breasts in Greek and Latin." "You mean you don't like the names?" "No, I really do. I was just joshing you a bit." "Well, how many other women do you know who have a lover that has given such lovely names to their breasts?" "Probably not very many," Dorothy replied with a satisfied smile in her voice.

When they returned to the bed, Grant asked, "Why don't you lie on your side, and I'll show Kalliste and Pulcherrima how much I love them." When she did, Grant proceeded to kiss, lick, and suck them each in turn while fondling them both with his hands. Then after they had enjoyed more intercourse and were simply lying side by side with Grant caressing her sex and love-delta, he said, "I would like to tell you a story." "Oh yeah," Dorothy answered somewhat suspiciously, "Is it an obscene one?" "Oh no," he replied, "It is a very serious story. Believe me." "Ok," Dorothy replied in a serious tone, "Let's hear it."

"This story is a Greek myth that occurs in a long Latin poem entitled The *Metamorphoses* by the Roman poet Ovid. It is a really long book-length poem that is an anthology of many Greek and Roman myths. The poem takes its name from the fact that many of the stories involve people being changed into various things, such as a woman being pursued by Apollo being changed into a tree. Most of the stories involve sex and/or violence with some god raping some lovely nymph or mortal virgin, but the story that I'm going to tell is nothing at all like that.

I first read this long poem in translation during my last year in high school and enjoyed it very much, but even though I liked reading the slightly obscene episodes involving a god having sex with a mortal woman, one story stood out from them all and really touched me profoundly. It is the story of Baucis and Philemon. The story goes like this.

"Once the god Jupiter decided to see how well people were treating one another. Since he presided over hospitality, he took on a regular human form along with his son Mercury, and they came down to earth. They went about as traveling strangers from house to house in a town to see how well people would treat them, but they were disappointed to have people shutting their doors in their faces. But eventually they came to the house of Baucis and Philemon, an aged couple who had been happily married for many years. They lived in a small simple cottage; but when the gods in disguise showed up, they welcomed them inside and did everything within their simple means to make them feel at home and to serve them a nice meal. After the two gods had eaten, they finally revealed themselves and said how pleased they were with them for having treated them so well. They now granted the aged couple one wish. After conferring, they announced that what they wished was to die at exactly the same time, so that one would never be without the other. The gods gave their word and departed. Time passed, and one day the aged couple were miraculously transformed into two beautiful trees."

As Grant neared the end of the story, his voice began to crack with emotion. When he finished, Dorothy commented, "That really is a beautiful story." "It really is, and it has always stuck in my mind ever since I first read it. But here's my moral, my darling Dove. I love you very much, and I want us to have a life together. Our difference in age doesn't matter to me. I wish that we could live and die together like Baucis and Philemon. But in any case, if you live to be in your mid-seventies, which is quite likely, that would still give us about thirty years together, and to me that would be so wonderful."

Dorothy was deeply moved by what amounted to a proposal. "Grant, I would love to spend the rest of my life with you, and we are already working toward that goal." "Yes, we certainly are. Oh Dorth, I want you to be my woman!" "I am." "And I am your man!" "You certainly are!"

May 16, 1973, Wednesday

As they lay together with Dorothy cuddled up against Grant, following another long and glorious morning of loving in bed, Grant said, "Tomorrow morning the U.S. Senate Select Committee on the Watergate break-in begins its first public session. It's going to be televised, and I would like to listen to it. So, if it's all right with you, we can roll the portable TV set from the family room into the bedroom, and I can listen to it as we have our morning time in bed." "That would be ok with me," Dorothy replied.

"Did I ever tell you about our experience during the Cuban Missile Crisis?" she asked. "No, you didn't, but please do," Grant responded. "Well, we were living in Great Falls, Montana at the time." "That was mid-October of 1962," Grant interjected. "Ok, if you say so, Professor Duncan," she replied with mock sarcasm. "Well, anyway," she resumed, "as soon as the crisis developed, all military bases were put on their highest level of alert. Since we were living in an area where there were Minute Man Missile silos, we were considered prime targets in the event of an actual nuclear attack from the Soviet Union or even from Cuba. Missiles were programmed for specific targets to respond to such an attack, and everyone was really rather frightened until the crisis finally passed. One of our best friends there was a major in the air force, and he was away from home and on base during that whole time."

"Wow!" Grant said, "That's really some story! I can vaguely remember the crisis. I was just a few days short of being ten years old, and all that I remember about it is seeing President Kennedy on the TV screen addressing the nation. I guess it must have been right after the crisis had been resolved. Man! It's so hard to think that I was just ten then, and you were thirty-four years old with three children living in Montana. But I tell ya. You never cease to amaze me. If you aren't amazing me with your dazzling personality and charm or with your beautiful female bod, then you amaze me with what you can do or have done and experienced. You really are amazing!" "I am, huh?" Dorothy replied with obvious pleasure. "You certainly are!"

"You know," Dorothy continued, "I've never been much interested in current affairs and following everything in the news like you do." "Well," Grant answered, "I've only been doing it for a few years, ever since the second half of my senior year in high school when my teacher for American history got me interested in such things. But I'm sure that as the mother of three kids, you didn't have much time to even worry about such things, because you were always so busy fixing meals, doing load after load of laundry, all the ironing, and running here and there to get the kids to and from places." "You sure are right about that!" Dorothy agreed, "but it goes even further than that." "What do you mean?" Grant asked. "Well, not long after we moved here to University City, there was a big uproar over school bussing to achieve racial balance in the schools. I went to several school meetings about it and was very much against the whole idea, because I did not want my kids wasting their time every day in having to go a long distance by bus to some school not in our area. I wanted them to have a normal kid's experience of walking to and from their local school, and that is how so many of us parents felt. I'm sure that there were some who were opposed to bussing, because they simply did not like or feared black people, but most of the people felt the way that I did, and we voiced our feelings at these meetings, but when these things were reported in the news, we were always portrayed as racists, and I really resented that deeply." "I can understand that you would have," Grant interjected. "Ever since then," Dorothy continued, "I have never felt much confidence in what I hear reported in the news, because I always wonder how much of it is the truth, and how much is simply the product of the reporter's own prejudice or laziness or whatever." "That's really interesting," Grant said quite seriously, "Like I said a minute ago, you never cease to amaze me."

May 17, 1973, Thursday

It was already 1:00 in the afternoon, and Dorothy and Grant were just now getting up from bed, following about four hours or so of lovely pleasure. Since the portable TV in the family room sat on a small folding metal stand on wheels, they easily rolled it into the master bedroom, so that Grant could listen to the televised senate hearings concerning Watergate. Consequently, the physical pleasure of their bodies uniting and playing for the first half of their morning in bed together was not accompanied by their usual love talk. Instead, they had enjoyed themselves in relative silence, so that Grant could listen to the TV. But when the committee adjourned for lunch and for a closed-door session in the afternoon, their pleasure in bed resumed its normal pattern of loving, love talk, and serious conversation as their passions slowly cooled down.

After dressing together, they went into the kitchen, where Dorothy heated up some left-over goulash for their lunch. "It looks really nice outside," Dorothy observed. "How would you like to help me give all the dogs a bath?" "Sure," Grant said, "that would be fun. How do we do that? In the bathtub here in the house?" "No, we'll do it outside in a big metal tub that we keep in the garage."

Thus, as soon as they put their dishes in the dishwasher, they went outside to set things up. Dorothy placed the metal tub on the ground near the back porch just outside the family room and used a hose attached to the outside faucet to fill the tub with water. Meanwhile, Grant was carrying load after load of hot water from inside the house to mix with the cold water. Then they began bathing the dogs, one after the other. Schatzi, because of her small size, came first. After shampooing her, they rinsed her off, dried her with a towel, and let her go back into the house; and the process was repeated for the three big dogs: Frau, Gretchen, and Erica.

It was a lovely warm sunny spring day, and they enjoyed doing this work together, in part because they were still euphoric and relaxed from their previous hours of being in bed, and in part because they always enjoyed just being together and doing whatever needed to be done. Indeed, ever since the beginning of their relationship ten months ago in July, their companionship of being alone together had always afforded them such satisfaction and joy. It was perhaps the most important aspect of their loving relationship and made everything else about it so very grand.

"I know pretty much what there is to know about all of the dogs except Frau," Grant said, "Because I have known them more or less since they've been small, but how old is Frau now?" "Let's see," Dorothy said, "We got her as a pup when we were in Kimball. That was in August of 1964. She was about three months old at the time and must have been born about the time of Carol's birthday. Gee! I guess that means that she's now just turning nine years! Boy! That's really something! It's hard to believe that she's that old."

"All the other critters," Grant commented, "are always happy to see us students and like us to pet them, but Frau is reserved. She seems to be entirely your dog." "She certainly is," Dorothy said with pride. "You know, I really like it when you call them critters and varmints." "That's good. That's from my hillbilly family, I guess, but I also like it when you call them animules in your adorable habit of humorously distorting words." "Well, anyway," Dorothy replied with a sweet laugh, "when we first got Frau as a pup, she was supposed to be the family dog, but you know how that goes. I was soon the one doing most everything for her and with her, because George was never around that much, and the three kids were usually too busy doing other things. We had just moved into our new house, and so I was, of course, really fussy about the floors, and Frau could not figure out why she couldn't go everywhere through the house when she came in from outside after being in the rain. Then, she was so cute when she saw her first snow that winter, jumping around and trying to catch the snowflakes in her mouth as they fell. Whenever I took her outside, we played fetch with a rubber ball, but she never liked to let it go from her mouth. But then someone told me that if I squeezed her front paw, she would release it, and that worked. "Really?" Grant asked in surprise. "Yeah, it really did. I also took her on walks, and a neighbor eventually saw us together and was really impressed with her. He was a policeman and asked if he could have her to train to be his police dog, but I wasn't at all interested in giving her up by then, but it was so nice to know that she had made such a good impression on the policeman."

"When Bethany was still married to her first husband Richard," Dorothy continued, "we often took her up to Chicago with us on our visits. They were living in an area where the houses were situated on the inside of a circular road, so that all the yards were shaped like the pieces of a pie; and even though the yards were not divided by fences, Frau somehow knew exactly where Bethany' yard ended, and she never would go off into a neighbor's yard. It was really interesting, and Bethany was so amazed."

"I used to be afraid of dogs," Grant now began, "until I talked my parents into letting me have one. After that I have always loved dogs. My dog was just an alley dog from a place where a family that my parents had known from Kentucky were living at the time. She looked like a cross between a German Shepherd and a Collie. She was real pretty and smart, and I named her Pal; and she really did become my pal. When she died of a heart attack while having a second litter of pups during my junior year in high school, I was really devastated. Her death bothered me so much, and I had dreams and nightmares about her for a long time and would wake up and feel so terrible."

"When we were living in Great Falls," Dorothy said, as she began another story, "Wesley learned in his school of a dog named Shep. He or she was a Collie that had been some boy's childhood pet. Then when World War II came along and the young man went off to the army or whatever, the dog came with him to the railroad station to see him off. The young man never came back from the war, but from the day of his departure for the next five years until the dog also died, it came every day to the train station and waited for its master to come home. When the dog died, they buried it at the train station and erected a monument in its honor. We drove out there one day and found it." "That's really amazing!" Grant exclaimed excitedly, "I heard about that several years ago, probably from some little news item on the radio. If you'd asked me about it, all that I could have told you was that it happened somewhere in one of the western states. That's really neat that you lived near that train station and saw the dog's grave and monument."

As they were still outside putting things away, Carol came home from school, and the three of them had supper together and spent a nice quiet evening in the house.

May 18, 1973, Friday

Today would be their last day together until Grant returned in about seven weeks or so. That seemed like such a long time for them to endure. In addition, since Grant's bus departed at 1:00 P.M., their last morning in bed would have to be a somewhat abbreviated session.

When Dorothy lay down naked in the bed and spread her sex for Grant, he began their loving by kneeling between her thighs and enjoying her with his mouth and tongue. "Oh my!" he exclaimed, "How I love to have a face full of your cunt! I think that I enjoy licking and kissing your pussy pie as much as I like fucking you with my dick." As soon as Dorothy reached her climax, Grant mounted her and joined his orgasm with hers, and their two bodies quivered and shuddered together, almost as if they were in pain instead of the most intense pleasure. He then withdrew his penis and lay down beside her. When Dorothy had slowly returned to the normal world again, she said quite seriously, "You really know how to please a woman!" "It's easy," Grant replied, "Since I have a woman with the most inspiring beauty."

He now reentered her vagina in the sidesaddle way and began to ride her again; and as he did, his hands were enjoying her naked body and the sight of their sexes interacting so magnificently. His steady rhythm soon quickened, and Dorothy felt his penis enlarge again inside her, then quiver, and ejaculate a second time. While Grant rested with his manhood still inside her, he fondled her sex and said, "I really cannot get enough looking at your pussy. She is so beautiful! And how wonderful it is to see my cock going inside you! There can't be anything more lovely than that!" "Like I keep telling you," Dorothy remarked with obvious pleasure, "You sound like a broken record."

Grant resumed his steady rhythm inside her again. After about ten minutes he began to thrust himself inside her more quickly and with more force. Dorothy felt his penis enlarge, then shudder, and ejaculate again. "Did you just come again?" she asked. "Sure did," Grant said with pride. In addition to the pleasure of his manhood inside her, Dorothy derived immense satisfaction from shifting her gaze between Grant's face and his hand as it caressed her womanhood. After a few minutes of fondling her, he began to thrust inside her again; and as before, he eventually began to quicken his rhythm, but this time he had to ram his penis with considerable force inside her in order to achieve the necessary excitement for a fourth orgasm. When he had ejaculated and was resting from the exertion, his body lightly covered in sweat, he asked, "Am I getting too rough with you?" "No, it's fine," Dorothy sweetly replied, "You're just getting a bit wild. That's all, but Rufus Magnus really feels good." "Golly!" he said emphatically, "I'm going to miss you so much!" "I'll miss you terribly too."

Grant was again moving inside her steadily and did so for nearly twenty minutes until once again his rate increased, and he was now banging his penis into her quite forcefully. He eventually came again and then slumped to the mattress in exhaustion. "Did you come again?" Dorothy asked. "Yeah." "So how many times has that been?" "Five, I think." "My golly, Grant, how many more times are you going to come?" "I think that's probably it, but let's lay here a while and see if Rufus Magnus wants any more." They did. Grant's manhood, however, did not revive for another go-around. Yet, he had given her vagina five of his own orgasms in the space of seventy minutes. His passionate riding of his Princess Pussy was a most appropriate farewell.

When they arose from bed, Dorothy asked, "why don't we strip the bed and put new sheets on, as long as you are here to help?" "Ok," Grant agreed. They did the work while still naked, and this too was a most fitting way in which to bring their beautiful week together to an end.

Chapter 9

Amor Omnia Vincit

May 19, 1973, Saturday

It was 9:10 A.M., and George had just gone off to run various errands in connection with the construction project in Newton. He would therefore be out of the house for a few hours. Dorothy came into the master bedroom, picked up the telephone, and dialed Dennis' number. When he answered on the third ring, his voice sounded sleepy. After greeting him, Dorothy said, "Did I wake you up?" "Yeah, you did, but that's all right. I needed to be getting up soon anyway. So," Dennis asked, "What's up?" "Well," Dorothy explained, "I would really like to get together with you to talk." "Sure. When would you like to do it?" "As soon as we can." "Ok, I can throw my clothes on and be ready right away." "That's really good. How about I leave right now and be there in about ten or fifteen minutes?" "That would be fine. I'll be waiting out on the porch here at Beaumont Manor." "Ok. See ya soon."

When Dorothy picked Dennis up, they first ran past the McDonald's on Foxwell Street, so that Dennis could run inside and grab something to eat. As Dennis sat back down in the passenger seat, he asked, "So, Ma, what would you like to talk about?" "Well," she replied, "It's kind of complicated, and I would like to wait until we find some place to park, and then I won't have to divide my attention between driving and talking." Dennis then turned his attention to his food. They rode in silence until they came to the park on the eastern edge of University City where she and Grant had been twice last summer, and where the three of them (Dorothy, Grant, and Dennis) had spent the morning of this past April 6 when the pair of lovers were wanting to get out of the house to be away from George and his mother.

"Ok," Dorothy began, "thanks for coming out to see me right away like this. I really need to talk to someone right now." "Sure, Ma," Dennis said, "It's no problem." "Well, what I need to talk to you about is what happened last night." Dennis simply waited to have her explain. "George came home in the early evening from Newton as usual; and when we finally were in bed for the night, he put his arm around me and said that he wanted us to have sex. I told him that I really wasn't at all interested, but he persisted and insisted that we have intercourse. When I still refused, he started pulling up my nightgown; and so that Carol wouldn't hear us across the hall, I finally agreed. Then when he took off his shorts and started to get on top of me, I objected, because he wasn't wearing a rubber. But by now he was so angry with me for refusing in the first place that he said he was just going to have me without one. But I was very dry inside. I'm always real wet for Grant. But anyway, because I was so dry, and he didn't have a lubricated rubber on, he couldn't get himself in me very easily. He actually hurt me a little bit, but of course, he really didn't care. But he finally did get inside me; and even though it didn't last all that long, it upset me terribly."

As Dorothy recounted her story, her voice clearly betrayed her emotions. Dennis could tell that she was crying, and it reminded him so much of how she had been last fall when Grant had run off to De Kalb that horrible weekend. He was genuinely moved by the pain and anguish that she obviously felt, but he also did not know what to say or do. He finally simply said, "Ah man! Ma, I'm so sorry. That really sounds terrible." "I know that there isn't much you can really say, Dennis, but I really need to talk to someone about this. It bothers me so much. I can't call Grant, because we don't use the telephone. We don't want anyone, like his parents or George, to find out about us by seeing from the phone bill that we have been talking with one another. Plus, this is something that I would rather not burden him with, or at least not completely, because he feels so strongly that I am his woman, and that despite my marriage, George should not have any right to intercourse with me, because I do not love him. I know that it would really bother Grant very much if he knew all the details. He would be so angry and upset and would worry about me and still not be able to do anything about it. But I really need to get these things off my mind."

"What would happen," Dennis asked, "If you just quit having sex altogether with George?" "Nothing good. That's for sure," Dorothy replied with real bitterness in her voice, "I suppose he'd consider it grounds for divorce." "Would he get violent with you?" "I really don't know. He's gotten pretty rough with the kids over the years. We've gone through times when I simply refused to have sex with him, and then we had some pretty heated arguments, but of course, I eventually had to go back to letting him have intercourse with me. I really don't know what he would do if I finally told him that was it once and for all. But I wouldn't put violence of some sort past him if he got angry and frustrated enough. I haven't enjoyed intercourse at all with him for many years now, and it's been so hard to have to put up with it. But now that Grant and I have been enjoying such wonderful sex, and I now know what sex between people who really love each other can and should be, it makes putting up with intercourse with George so much harder; and I really don't know how much more of it I can take."

After talking for another forty minutes or so along these lines with no obvious solution in sight, Dorothy started up the car and returned Dennis to Beaumont Manor. She did feel somewhat better from having unburdened herself, but she truly did not know what to do. She would simply have to take it one day at a time, or actually, one weekend at a time, and hope for the best, but the prospects were not very good. There could not have been a greater contrast between what she had experienced at the beginning and then at the end of yesterday. In the morning she and Grant had enjoyed more than an hour of the most perfect physical pleasure in their love for each other. Then that night she had experienced what really amounted to a form of sexual abuse, which she had had to endure simply because of her marital status. What she had now revealed to Dennis formed the tip of a very big, ugly iceberg in her marriage, year after year of loveless sexual intercourse that was both nauseating to her and hard on her nerves.

May 30, 1973, Wednesday

As soon as Carol left for school, Dorothy drove over to Beaumont Manor and picked Dennis up. They were on a quick trip to Chicago and back for Dennis to collect some papers that he needed. Since the university was now in the final exam period for the semester, Dennis was able to spend most of the day in traveling to and from Chicago without missing any classes.

"Hey, Ma," Dennis said, as he sat down in the passenger seat, "how are things going with you?" "Oh, not too bad," she replied cheerfully. "How are things going between you and George?" Dennis asked more pointedly. "About the same. But at least we didn't have intercourse this past weekend, because I was having my period, and George stays away from me then." Dennis laughed. "Well," he said, "That never stops me and Lisa." "It doesn't stop me and Grant either." Dennis clapped his hands in delight, as they both laughed. "But luckily for me," Dorothy continued, "It's always stopped George." "Have you told Grant about it yet?" Dennis asked. "Yeah, I did that on a cassette tape first thing a week ago Monday morning right after George left, and Carol was away at school. He's probably received the tape and has listened to it by now." "What did you tell him?" "Just the basic outline, and that I came over and talked with you about it right away. I know he'll be about as hurt by it as I was, so I didn't get too graphic. I should be getting a tape from him soon, maybe even today, and he'll be telling me what he thinks, and how he feels about it all.

So," Dorothy asked, changing the subject, "When will you be going home for the summer?" "A week from today, I think." "How are you getting home?" "Well, I really haven't decided that just yet." "Maybe I can take you home. I'll have to see what's going on, but it should work out ok, and we might even be able to take Renny back with us too." "That would be really great!"

"I'm really going to miss you this summer," Dorothy said, "to have around in case I need to talk to someone." "Well," Dennis replied, "Lisa and Kitty both know about you two now, and Lisa will be here in town, of course, because she lives here, and I might come down a few times on weekends to be with her. But did you know that Kitty is going to summer school?" "No, I didn't know that." "Yeah, she has just two more courses to take, and then she'll get her degree. So, both of them will be here all the time; and I'm sure they'll both be happy to help you out if they can; and of course, Lisa can drive and come over to your house and things. She really admires you so much. I know that she'd be happy to help you in whatever way she can." "Well, that really sounds good, and I feel much better knowing that."

Once they made their way through town and were heading north on the interstate to Chicago, Dorothy said, "Hey, Dennis, look there on the seat between us. There's my cassette machine. I brought it along, so we could make a tape to Grant." "Hey cool," Dennis replied, as he picked up the machine. "You press down the two buttons on the far left for play and record," Dorothy explained. "Ok," replied Dennis, as he depressed the two buttons. After waiting several seconds for the lead tape to play, Dennis began, "Hey, Grant, how are you doing, you crazy bastard?" "Hi, Darling," Dorothy said in the form of a voice over. "Yeah man!" Dennis went on, "We're here together in the car on our way to Chicago. Ma's taking me there and back today, because I need to run home to pick up my birth certificate and a few other things. Guess what, man? It looks like I'm going to spend this coming school year studying in Austria. I learned about a student exchange program this semester through my German course, and it sounded so neat that I looked into it, and it looks like I can probably do it financially. But I need all the paperwork done right away for a passport and all that sort of shit. We'll be flying out of Chicago sometime around the middle of August, even before you guys start classes." "Dennis," Dorothy said, "That really is so neat!" "Yeah man!" Dennis resumed, "I'll be studying at a small college in a town called Baden, just outside Vienna. I'm really excited about it, as you can tell." "Dennis, you get excited about everything." Dennis hooted with laughter.

The two continued on in this way for almost their entire trip to Chicago, talking and making a tape recording for Grant, letting him know what all they had been doing and were thinking. But then about a half an hour south of the city limits, the car began to sputter; and when Dorothy looked down at the dashboard, she realized that the gas gauge was sitting on empty. She therefore pulled off onto the shoulder of the road; and after about thirty minutes, someone stopped and gave them a lift to and back from a gas station for a can of gasoline. They were on their way again. Then they turned the cassette machine back on and explained, as they laughed, how they had been so absorbed in having fun on the trip and making the tape that Dorothy had not even thought about gas.

June 4, 1973, Monday

As soon as Dorothy was alone in the house that morning shortly after 8:00, she called Dennis. When he answered, and they exchanged greetings, she asked, "Are you free this morning? I would like to talk with you again." "Well," Dennis responded, "I have to be at the Rehab Center at 10:00 for my last test, but we could go ahead and meet right now, and then you could drop me off there." Ok. I'll be right there." "You can come to my room today, because my roommate finished his exams Saturday and has already gone home for the summer." "Ok, I'll see you soon there in your room."

When Dorothy came into his room and sat down in his rocking chair, Dennis said, "I hope this isn't about what I think it is." "I'm afraid it is," Dorothy confirmed. "George insisted on having sex with me early this morning before he got up to leave for Newton. I made it very clear that I wasn't the least bit interested and was not happy about it, but he wanted me, and so as not to cause too bad a scene, I went ahead and endured it as best I could, which isn't very good at all. I really don't know how much more of this I can take!" As Dennis listened, he noticed that Dorothy's voice today seemed to convey as much anger and outrage as emotional hurt. "Are you going to tell Grant about it?" "I don't think so. It will just make him angry and upset, and since he's not here, he can't do anything about it anyway. But I wanted to talk with you about it, because it really did help me the last time." After talking for about 45 minutes, Dorothy seemed to have regained her composure, and they spent the next half an hour in Dorothy looking up some last minute things for Dennis in connection with his final exam. Dorothy then dropped him off at the Rehab Center, as she returned home.

As soon as she was in the house, she gave Bob Snider a call. "Hey there fella, I wanted to call and wish you a happy birthday. I wasn't sure if you'd still be here in town next week." "Well," Bob replied, "I won't. My brother Jeff will be coming down to get me tomorrow, but thanks for calling. That was really nice of you." "Bob, I'm also calling you for Grant. He wanted me to remind you about you guys deciding to room together this coming year in Forester." "Yeah, I know. I think that it's all taken care of." "That will really be nice for you two. I know Grant is looking forward to it." "I am too." Dorothy and Grant had discussed this matter when he was last in town in mid-May. They figured that their situation could be made much less complicated if Grant roomed with Bob, because Dorothy could be in their room and be able to act naturally around Grant if Bob were his roommate. "Hey, Ma?" Bob asked. "Yeah, what?" "I know Kitty's going to summer school, and I was wondering if I could stay there at your house this summer if I decide to come down and visit." "Of course, you can, Bob. You should know that by now." "Well, yeah, but I wanted to ask just to be sure."

June 15, 1973, Friday

Dorothy was once again driving the little blue Falcon south on the interstate, heading back to University City after another trip north to visit her relatives. Carol had just finished her last day of school a week ago; and to begin her summer vacation, Dorothy had arranged for the two of them to spend this past week at Bethany' and Buddy's summer house in southwestern Michigan on the eastern shore of Lake Michigan. They had stopped off on Monday, on their way up, to spend the day with Dorothy's mother, before heading off the next morning to be with Bethany and Buddy. There they had enjoyed three days of relaxation, taking dips in the water, and going for rides in the motor boat.

But now as she and Carol sat in the car talking about various ordinary things, Dorothy finally decided to mention a very serious subject to her daughter. She had been debating for some time whether or not she should bring it up with her right out of the blue, but the more she thought about it, the more it seemed better to have it out in the open sooner rather than later. Thus, after their conversation had lagged for several minutes, during which Dorothy was able to carefully formulate her thoughts and words, she began.

"Carol, I have something very important to tell you now. I know that it will surprise you and will also probably upset you, but I'm mentioning it to you now, because I want you not to be surprised or upset even more if it happens without you knowing anything in advance." After pausing several seconds, she continued, "I want you to know that I may sometime in the near future leave your father. I really haven't loved him in a very long time, and I've often thought that as soon as you kids were all up and out of the house, I would leave him. I want you to know this, because if it happens, I do not want you to think that you were somehow to blame. Kids often get goofy ideas like that. I have thought about this for a long time, and it is something that I have decided all on my own, and it has nothing at all to do with you kids. Do you understand what I am saying?" "Yeah," Carol replied, "I think so, mom." "Ok, then that's really all that I need to say right now, and that's all you need to know. If it comes to that, it will be upsetting enough for you. But it might not be quite so bad if you're not taken totally by surprise, and I certainly do not want you to think that you are to blame in any way, because you aren't."

June 25, 1973, Monday

It was about 8:30 when the telephone rang. Grant was the only one in the house. Both his parents were away at their jobs. He therefore raced from his room into the kitchen, where the only telephone in the house was located on the wall.

"Hello," he said, as he placed the handset to his mouth. "Hello, darling," Dorothy replied on the other end, "How are you doing?" "I'm doing just fine, especially since I'm talking to you." "That's good," she chuckled. After a pause, she continued, "I'm calling to tell you something very important. Otherwise, of course, I wouldn't be calling. I wanted to call to let you know as soon as I could that I told George over the weekend that I would never again have sex with him or sleep in the same bed with him." "Really!" Grant responded in dumbfounded astonishment. "Yep, that's right." "Dorth, I'm so glad and relieved for you and for me, but especially for you, of course." "I am so glad and relieved too. These past few weeks have really been hell. When George wanted sex from me Friday night, I refused and told him that it was all over in that regard; and since I know you worry so much about me and would be so happy to learn about this, I wanted to tell you right away, so that you wouldn't worry anymore. So I waited to call as soon as both George and Carol were out of the house." "Thanks for calling and telling me. That is such great news." "Yes, it really is!" Then after another pause, Dorothy said, "Well, we probably shouldn't be talking too long. We'll have to talk about this more to each other on our tapes." "Ok, darling." "Ok then. That's all I had to say except, of course, I love you." "I love you too, and thanks so much for calling." "You're welcome."

As soon as they had hung up, Grant went back into his room and began recording more onto a cassette tape that he had already begun to Dorothy in order to place on record his immediate thoughts and feelings about Dorothy's wonderful news. Since they had last been together on May 18, they had been keeping in touch almost exclusively by sending one another cassette letters instead of braille ones. In fact, during this longest separation that they were having to endure, they received cassette recordings from one another at least twice, and sometimes, even three times each week. They had therefore been devoting a portion of almost every day to talking to the other into their cassette machines, and they talked about virtually everything, but especially about how they missed one another so terribly, how much their love relationship meant to them both, and what they wanted to do when they were together again. Their recordings had kept their love fresh and vibrant and had even deepened it, if that were possible, because they spoke to each other in complete honesty, confided their innermost thoughts to the other, and often recounted events and experiences from their past that they had not talked or thought about with anyone else for years. Their recordings had therefore become vital in their ability to cope with this longest separation. Grant thoroughly loved listening to Dorothy's beautifully feminine and expressive voice. No written letter could capture that magic!

When Dorothy was alone in the house these days, she usually carried her cassette machine around with her, either to record a tape to Grant or to listen to one from him. He loved hearing her talking amid the sounds of her daily household chores, such as fixing things in the kitchen accompanied by the whistling of steam through the spout of the tea kettle on the stove, doing loads of laundry, letting the dogs out and back in again, and especially the distinctive and beautiful sound of her going potty. One day, as Dorothy was moving around the house to do various odd jobs while talking to Grant into her cassette machine, she mentioned to him that she had set aside a drawer in the front bedroom where he usually slept, and in this drawer she kept items of his clothes that he had happened to leave during his visits that spring. She usually washed these articles and kept them there for him to use when he returned, but occasionally she would keep one of his shirts unwashed, because it retained his scent, and she would often come into the bedroom, open up the drawer, remove the shirt, hold it to her face, and simply breathe in his distinctive scent. She now told Grant on the cassette tape how much this pleased her. Dorothy in turn loved listening to Grant's voice. Their exchange of cassette tapes had therefore come to be substitutes for their late night conversations cuddled up on the couch together wrapped up in an afghan. These recorded letters allowed them to continue to be of one mind and to be so close spiritually and emotionally, despite the geographical distance between them.

Dorothy especially enjoyed hearing Grant talk to her about sex, and how much he wanted her. In fact, over the past few weeks Grant had developed the habit of masturbating on his tapes. He often became so sexually aroused as he talked to her that he began playing with his penis and talking their beautiful love language to her until he finally reached a climax and ejaculated. Dorothy absolutely loved these parts of his tape and sometimes listened to them with an earphone at night in bed; and when she did, she usually pulled up her nightgown and masturbated herself as she listened. Dorothy so greatly valued some of these recordings that she located a small briefcase that they had long had, and which had been stashed away in a closet and neglected for some years. She now retrieved it, located the key for locking it, and began storing these highly prized cassette recordings in it for permanent keeping.

According to their plans, exactly two weeks from right now on July 9 Dorothy would be picking Grant up from the bus station, and they would be spending the entire week together. That in itself was so exciting, but it was even more so now that Dorothy had made the decision not to sleep with George anymore. What this meant, of course, was that when they were reunited in two weeks, they would be coming together for the very first time totally and completely as one another's man and woman. As Grant now resumed his recording to her, he expressed how joyful he was about what she had just told him on the telephone. He supported her in her decision by reiterating that since she had not loved George for such a long time, what she had been enduring for so long was simply a form of sexual abuse, and how their own complete and total love for each other fully justified her refusing to have sexual intercourse with George. Grant eventually became so excited and aroused that he masturbated again for his darling, while engaging in sexually explicit love talk that they both greatly enjoyed.

But even after he had ejaculated, he was still so worked up that he continued to talk to her about sexual matters in reference to their upcoming reunion. First of all, he did not wish to embarrass or offend her in any way, but he would really like it, he said, if she wouldn't mind coming to the bus station without any panties under her slacks or shorts. It would be their own lovely little secret. Secondly, he was hoping that they could arrange for Carol to spend the night with someone on July 10, the anniversary of their first kissing marathon when he had finally confessed his strong attraction to her. If so, Grant proposed that they have intercourse in every bed in the house, on the two couches, and even on the two tables. By doing so, he said, they would sanctify the entire house with their love. Thirdly, he wanted them to try enjoying intercourse in a new position by having her on her hands and knees and him entering her vagina from behind.

From these proposals he went on to introduce her to a new word for their sacred language of sex. According to Grant, she did not have a butt, which ordinary women had. Instead, like all really lovely women, according to the sexual vocabulary of real, red-blooded heterosexual men, she possessed an ass; and as these same men would say in describing a woman who was beautiful and sexy from head to toe, "you are all ass!" So, "ass" in the context of sex did not mean either "dummy," "jerk," or "rump" as in ordinary speech. On the contrary, it was a word of exalted beauty, majesty, and magnificence. To a real man who appreciated female beauty, "ass" and "all ass" were not only sexually wonderful but even mystical. It therefore seemed so very appropriate that Dorothy's middle name was Alice. Consequently, in Grant's view even her very name indicated that she was a genuine all-ass pussy goddess.

June 28, 1973, Thursday

When the mailman arrived shortly after lunchtime, Dorothy was pleased to discover that the mail contained a mailer with two more cassettes from Grant. Since Carol was in the house, she decided to lie down to rest while using an earphone to listen to the tapes. She eventually came to the part recorded this past Monday morning and enjoyed to hear his reaction to her telephone call about her decision to no longer sleep with George.

She was also very pleased to hear Grant masturbate for her once again while giving her plenty of his naughty talk. The masturbation lasted a very long time and therefore resulted in a long period of very naughty love-talk. It was wonderful! She really loved his naughty talk and loved his explanation of the word "ass" and the idea that she was an all-ass woman to him. It thrilled her greatly and reinforced her growing self-identity as a lovely, sexually desirable woman. This was a way in which she had never viewed herself before, but her love relationship with Grant had obviously changed all that. She now regarded her love-zone in a very positive and wonderful way. Indeed, she was now quite proud of her pussy. It all made her feel quite differently about herself in most positive terms. So now, the term "ass" joined their lovely naughty vocabulary and ranked right up there in her mind with two other most magnificent terms, "pussy" and "beautiful red cock."

She also found to be utterly enchanting his proposal for her not to wear panties when she picked him up at the bus station, as well as his proposal to sanctify the entire house by them fucking in every bed, on both couches, and even on the kitchen and dining room tables. What a most glorious way in which to celebrate her sexual independence from George and her new life as Grant's all-ass pussy woman! After years of feeling self-conscious about her bottom, it was so thrilling to have this young lover-boy so infatuated with her, with every part of her female anatomy, including her ass. She loved the notion of her being to him an all-ass woman and her name Alice simply reflecting her extraordinary beauty in this regard.

Around 11:00 that evening, after Carol was in bed for the night, Dorothy went into the master bedroom and shut the door that led out into the hallway. She now placed her cassette machine on record and began to make her first masturbation recording for Grant. Thus far, she had not reciprocated Grant's wonderful sexual favor in this regard, but now that she was no longer troubled by the conflict with George and truly considered herself entirely Grant's woman, she felt perfectly comfortable in giving him this lovely gift on the tape. She described for him her undressing, garment by garment, and felt for him her breasts, bottom, and sex. As she told him very graphically in their sacred language of sex how much she wanted him, and what she wanted him to do to her with his mouth, tongue, and beautiful red cock, she lay down on the bed naked and proceeded to masturbate, allowing him to hear her rhythmic gaspings with the onset of the orgasm, as she continued to tell him how much she desired and wanted him inside her. It was a masterful performance! There was no acting at all involved. It was simply her expressing in perfect candor exactly how she desired him so passionately.

July 2, 1973, Monday

When Grant walked out to the street at 1:00 in the afternoon to collect the mail, he found a mailer from Dorothy. He therefore spent his afternoon in listening to her cassettes. When he finally came to her masturbating for them both, he could hardly believe how utterly enchanting and erotic it was. Of course, as he listened, he masturbated along with her. How could he possibly resist? It was so utterly captivating and magnificent! So, despite their physical separation, these sexually explicit portions on their tapes allowed them to express and enjoy together their erotic passion for one another.

July 7, 1973, Saturday

It was 8:00 A.M., and the bus traveling between Peoria and University City was turning off the interstate and entering the city. Soon Grant and Dorothy would be reunited. But their original plans had called for Dennis to leave Chicago late in the afternoon on the preceding day, to come to Peoria by bus to spend the weekend with Grant, and then for the two to come to University City together this coming Monday morning, as they had done in early April. But Dennis had not made it to the bus station in time to catch the bus to Peoria. Instead, he took another one that brought him to University City. After arriving, he called Grant to apologize and to let him know what had happened, and Grant had changed his own plans accordingly by deciding to come to University City two days early on this Saturday morning.

Since George was at home for the weekend, Dorothy decided that it was best for Grant to stay out of sight until George left for Newton Monday morning. This was easily done, because Kitty made her dorm room in Neville Dormitory available as needed. In addition, in order to explain her absence from the house at different times over the weekend, Dorothy said that Dennis needed to go various places to take care of things for his upcoming year in Austria. But just before leaving the house to go get Dennis and then go pick up Grant, Dorothy went into the main bathroom; and after urinating, she removed her panties and pulled her shorts back up into place. She was now in compliance with Grant's request. The absence of her undergarment was in fact a nice touch, because it made her fully aware of her sex. She then left the house, drove over to Beaumont Manor to pick up Dennis and then to the bus station to collect Grant. From there they proceeded to Kitty's room, which was presently empty, because she had spent the night at Dorothy's house.

As they traveled along in the car with Grant sitting in the passenger seat, he reached over to his darling and put his fingers down inside the waistband of her shorts. To his great delight he discovered that she in fact was not wearing any panties. When they arrived at kitty's room, Dennis stretched out on one bed, and Dorothy and Grant on the other. Since Dennis was very tired from having spent a long night with Lisa, he soon dozed off and was sound asleep. Dorothy then very quietly slid down her shorts and took them off. She was now beautifully bottomless. They now configured themselves into the "sidesaddle" posture, Grant entered her vagina, and they began to enjoy intercourse very gently so as not to let Dennis know what they were doing. Since their last sexual union had been fifty days ago, Grant came very quickly and filled her vagina with a copious amount of sperm. They lay there together for a while, simply enjoying the presence of his penis inside her; and Grant caressed and admired her love-delta, thighs, and the thrilling sight of his penis being inside her sex. He eventually withdrew Rufus Magnus, and Dorothy sat up, put her shorts back on, and went down the hallway in order to clean herself in the ladies room. Later, after Dennis had awakened from his nap, Grant told him how they had enjoyed a nice bit of pleasure while he was sleeping in the bed right beside them, and he was really surprised that they had succeeded in doing this without him being aware of it.

Dorothy and Dennis now left Grant alone in Kitty's room, went back to the house for lunch, and found other reasons why Dorothy had to be out of the house for the entire afternoon. When she had dropped Kitty and Dennis off at Beaumont Manor to spend the afternoon with Lisa, she came alone to Kitty's room, where Grant was waiting for her. They now had the entire afternoon to themselves, and they could not have made better sexual use of it. This turned out to be the most pleasure-filled Saturday that they had thus far experienced in their lives. They were alone together in this dorm room. The door was locked, and no one would be disturbing them for hours. The room was nicely air conditioned and perfectly silent except for any noise that they themselves made. What a perfect love-nest!

They removed all their clothes and remained completely naked for the afternoon. Because of their fifty-day separation from one another, their sexual hunger for each other was gargantuan, and their thoughts were on nothing at all except giving and receiving all the sexual pleasure that they could. For the first time they would be enjoying the perfect physical pleasure of their love monogamously. She was now without question his woman and no one else's; and Grant was her man. They could not get enough of each other, and their loving was further enhanced by its celebratory nature: for Dorothy was no longer and never would be again George's partner in bed.

They began their intercourse on one of the beds by using the frontal method. They then decided to try intercourse on their knees on the floor. They had talked about this on their cassette tapes to each other, but this was their first time to try it. Dorothy knelt on her hands and knees, but she soon lowered herself down onto her elbows so as to tip her pussy slightly upward in order to be at a better angle for receiving Grant's cock. . What a magnificent sight she was in that position! Her ass was perfect and on full display! Between her parted thighs and just under her gorgeous bare ass was her incomparably beautiful pussy! What lovely cunt hair! The lips of her vulva were slightly parted as if she were smiling at her lover and inviting him to enjoy her as much as he wanted. What a perfect pussy smile! The flawlessly smooth skin of her back from her shoulders down to her waist was stunning! Her breasts hung down with the nipples nearly touching the surface of the floor, and those twin beauties were full and perfectly shaped! She was a perfect pussy goddess!

Grant knelt between her lower legs behind her beautiful bare ass. It took a little bit of adjusting to get his penis to enter her, because in this position the opening of her vagina was slightly constricted, and Grant had to work carefully in order to insert the large head of his penis inside her without injuring her delicate skin. But as soon as he did, the rest of him entered her smoothly. "Wow!" Grant exclaimed in pleasure, "This feels so good! Your pussy feels so nice and tight around my cock!" "Boy! Doesn't it!" Dorothy responded, "You feel even bigger and harder inside me like this! I am completely full of you!" It really was extraordinary. This position gave their intercourse a slightly different feel that they both greatly welcomed and enjoyed.

Since the opening to Dorothy's vagina was somewhat constricted in this position, the mouth of her vagina was rather tight around the base of Grant's penis, and this forced more blood into his manhood and thus enlarged him inside her. The consequence was that Dorothy felt as if her entire vagina was occupied by his enormous loving cock, and it felt so very marvelous! In addition, from this position Grant could fondle her entire body. As they enjoyed this novel form of pleasure, he caressed her beautiful bare bottom and hips, perfectly smooth and shapely, a beautifully proportioned woman with a lovely hour-glass shape, what the poet Homer, as Grant had once told her before and told her again now, would have called "a deep-waisted woman." Grant also reached under her and felt her belly and love-front as his penis plunged rhythmically inside her. She had a slight paunch that now hung down. "Oh my golly!" Grant enthused, "That little belly of yours looks so cute and adorable! I think you're pregnant," he teased. "You think so, huh?" she replied. "And how I love knocking you up, you beautiful woman! You're pregnant all right! Pregnant with twins, in fact. And do you know their names?" Grant asked. "No, what?" "Pleasure and Desire! To me you will always be pregnant with twins of those names!"

He also reached underneath her and played with her lovely breasts. They were absolutely magnificent in this position and were so wonderful to take into his hands. In addition, as Grant thrust his penis into her and banged against her bare bottom, she swayed on her elbows and knees, and this made her breasts sway as well, and the motion was so captivatingly beautiful to behold. Grant could even grasp her hips with both hands and really drive his penis into her or simply press her tightly up against him, so that his manhood was fully inside her, feeling so enormous and hard to them both. It therefore took them no time to realize that this position was truly remarkable in giving them a wide variety of different possible pleasurable activities.

But when Dorothy's knees began to bother her because of the hard tile floor, they simply moved up onto one of the beds and continued to enjoy this "equestrian style" of intercourse. Grant was her strong red stallion, and she was his beautiful brood mare whom Grant was stud-fucking to impregnate.

And fucking and fucking and fucking her he certainly did! When they moved from the floor onto one of the beds, Dorothy positioned herself, so that she could lay her head down on the pillow at the head of the bed. She closed her eyes and simply enjoyed the pleasure created by the interaction of her vagina and Grant's penis. It was as if virtually all her being centered around her vagina. To call it pleasure was a considerable understatement. It was more like heavenly ecstasy!

They spent several hours that afternoon in delirious sexual pleasure. They had intercourse on both beds and in all three of their standard positions in each. His young, physically fit body was simply a penis-delivery system, whose sole purpose for existence today was to deliver as much hard woman-pleasing virility to her vagina as he possibly could. Dorothy's naked body was absolutely gorgeous, smoother and more lovely than the most highly polished marble. Grant simply could not get enough of feeling everything: her thighs, her bottom, her hips, her breasts, and especially her female sex. His penis was both insatiable for her vagina and indefatigable in riding her. She in turn enjoyed and pleasured him in equal frenzied excess. Her vagina responded to Rufus Magnus by flowing with love-honey all afternoon, like a maple tree running heavy with sweet sap in the springtime. After Grant had come in her several times and was drained of his semen, his penis did not lose its hardness but kept on riding her tirelessly. Exactly one year ago this afternoon they had been sitting on his dorm bed together with Dorothy reading to him; they were pressed together; and his penis was very erect and slowly secreting sperm in clandestine desire for her. Today they were together on a bed in another dorm room, but naked; Grant had given her sex all his semen; and she was giving him pussy, pussy, pussy, pussy, pussy!

After several hours of non-stop magnificent intercourse, they had finally succeeded in gratifying their seven-week store of pent-up love, passion, and desire. After returning home for supper, Dorothy came back to Kitty's dorm room with Lisa, Kitty, and Dennis to be with Grant for a short spell that evening. The atmosphere was that of a very sweet party. Dorothy and Grant were still floating on a euphoric cloud of their earlier erotic ecstasy. They eventually all left except for Grant and Dennis, who had decided to stay in Kitty's room, so that they could spend the night talking and getting completely caught up on things.

July 8, 1973, Sunday

Dorothy came past the dorm room around noon the next day to take Dennis to the bus station to return to Chicago. She then returned to Grant for a very brief visit. This was going to be their only time together that day. George would be leaving for Newton tomorrow morning, and then they would have the whole week to themselves.

They were the only two in the room, but when she had taken her temperature that morning before getting out of bed, she had decided that she might be fertile. Consequently, she preferred not to receive Grant's sperm into her vagina. But they were both nevertheless intent on sexual pleasure before she went home for the day. She therefore removed her shorts and panties, lay down on one of the beds, and spread herself open to receive him. Grant lay with her in the sidesaddle position and then used his hand to masturbate them both by rubbing the head of his penis inside her vulva.

As they were both thoroughly absorbed in giving and receiving this pleasure, Grant said, "I made a very interesting discovery last night after you left." "You did? What?" "When I went into the bathroom to take a shower, I scratched myself around my penis; and when I happened to bring my hand up toward my face, I noticed that my fingers smelled very strongly of your love-honey." "Really?" Dorothy exclaimed and asked in real delight. "They sure did," Grant affirmed, "You must have been flowing really heavy yesterday and put out more honey onto me than I shot sperm into you. You really are my Pussy Goddess, my Queen Cunt, my Regina Vagina!" Grant eventually reached an orgasm and shot his man cream onto her love-delta. After using his undershorts to wipe her off carefully, he withdrew his penis, knelt between her thighs, and used his mouth and tongue to enjoy and love her sex until she also had the exquisite pleasure of an orgasm. That was all that they could do for the day, because Dorothy needed to get back home before George became suspicious of her absence.

July 9, 1973, Monday

Shortly after George left for Newton around 7:30, Dorothy left the house, drove over to Beaumont Manor to pick up Lisa, and then went to Neville to get Kitty and Grant, so that the four of them could have a nice breakfast at Uncle Joe's Pancake House. When Dorothy and Lisa arrived at Kitty's dorm, Dorothy called her room from the telephone in the lounge.

"Hello," Kitty said sleepily after answering the phone. "Hello, Kitty," Dorothy replied, "Sorry to have awakened you, but Lisa and I are here now in the lounge. Is Grant up yet?" "No. He seems to be still sleeping soundly. It looks like the phone's ringing didn't even wake him up. We stayed up late last night talking." "Yeah, he must be very tired," Dorothy replied, "He probably hasn't had a good night's sleep for a few days now. Why don't you just leave him be; and after you meet us here in the lounge, I'll come back to your room and get him up." "Ok," Kitty agreed.

After they said goodbye and hung up, Kitty dressed herself and went out into the lounge. Dorothy then left Lisa and Kitty there and proceeded to the dorm room. She quietly opened the door, stepped inside, and shut the door again. She then walked over to Kitty's bed, removed all her clothes, and laid them carefully down on the bed. Now totally naked, she stepped over to the other bed in which Grant was still sleeping quite soundly. After slowly pulling down the blanket and sheet, she slid herself into the single bed and succeeded in positioning herself beneath his sleeping form. Grant was clad in his usual bedclothes, his t-shirt and undershorts. When he finally began to awaken in response to all the commotion in the bed, he was aware that Dorothy was completely naked beneath him. She was on her back with him lying between her open thighs, and she was using her hands to pull down his shorts. By now Grant was finally wide awake and racing with sexual excitement from this good-morning surprise. He helped her push his shorts down and then kicked them off his feet. He instantly entered her vagina, and they enjoyed a brief but powerfully intense round of intercourse. As his penis was plunging energetically inside her, he commented, "Man oh man, Dorth! This has to be the very best way I have ever been awakened in the morning! Thanks so very much!" "You're quite welcome," she replied with obvious pleasure both for him and for herself. They then arose from the bed, quickly dressed, and joined Lisa and Kitty in the lounge.

After breakfast at Uncle Joe's, Kitty went off to her classes, while Dorothy and Grant returned to her dorm room to be alone. They undressed, lay back down in bed, and enjoyed enthusiastic intercourse for a long time. They then fell asleep nicely crowded together in one of the single beds. They were still naked, lovingly entwined around each other, and wrapped together in a warm blanket of sexual euphoria and erotic afterglow. When they awoke, Dorothy had to urinate, but since she wished to stay there naked with him in the room, she located a large metal coffee can and used it. This was such a sweet act of intimacy. While Grant was there with her, she parted her thighs, placed the can beneath her spread sex, and tinkled her golden urine into the can. What a sweet sight and sound! They then lay back down together and listened to part of *The Autobiography of Malcolm X* on talking book. But they eventually had to get up and back into their clothes, because Kitty was due to return to her room at noon.

After going to Dorothy's house for lunch, the two lovers spent much of their afternoon together at the Rehab Center, where Dorothy served as Grant's reader to help him take a Latin placement test in order to be placed in the appropriate Latin class that coming fall semester. This was an important event in their relationship, because Grant's resumption of studying Latin was crucial for him in achieving his goal to become a professor of ancient Greek and Roman history, and Dorothy's role as his reader for the test marked her own formal entry into their joint realization of this dream. They then returned to the house for the rest of the day. After a quiet supper with Carol they just lounged around the house, because they were both quite tired, and they fell asleep around 8:30 P.M, Grant on the living room couch, and Dorothy on the one in the family room.

July 10, 1973, Tuesday

When Grant finally awoke and checked his pocket watch, he was surprised to discover that it was now nearly 2:00 A.M. Since he heard no noise coming from anywhere in the house, he assumed that Dorothy must be sleeping. He arose, walked down the hall, entered the main bathroom, and urinated. When he emerged, he made a slow quiet tour of the dining room, kitchen, and family room; and he was happy to find Dorothy sleeping on the couch beneath an afghan.

"Hey, sweetheart," he said quietly, "Would you like to wake up?" Since Dorothy had always been a light sleeper, she awoke immediately; and after she paid her own visit to the bathroom, she suggested that they take the dogs outside in the side yard. As the dogs browsed around the yard, Dorothy and Grant stretched out side by side on two lawn chairs. He was wearing his usual summer attire of t-shirt, shorts, shoes, and socks. Dorothy was clad in her usual morning clothes: her slippers, nightgown, and pink quilted robe. It was perfectly quiet outside. The only sounds to be heard were their low voices and an occasional noise made by one of the dogs. For the time being they were not interested in more sexual pleasure. Rather, they were both totally content to enjoy one another's sweet company in the perfect silence of the nocturnal darkness. It was so serene and peaceful.

"It's really so nice out here like this, us together in the quiet darkness," Dorothy commented. "Yes, it certainly is. It's wonderful," Grant agreed. "I remember," Dorothy continued, "when I was a small girl, Bethany and I sometimes would get up really early in the morning, just at dawn or maybe even before it was light. We'd go outside and walk together along the quiet deserted streets, and it was usually foggy outside, and the fog seemed to envelope us like a lovely blanket. I really enjoyed that." "Yeah," Grant offered, "I know exactly what you mean. I had the same experience a bunch of times with my sister and some of my cousins. When we'd go on vacation to visit our relatives in Western Kentucky and were staying at my Duncan Grandparents' house, some of us kids always had to sleep out in the wash-house. It was a small building about thirty feet or so from the main house and had a bed in it. We'd sometimes wake up really early like you and Bethany, and we'd go walking along the gravel access road that ran from the main highway in front of our grandparents' farm back a long ways through their farmland and to other farms. I could still see then, and I remember the same thing. It was often very foggy, and it seemed so serene."

After sitting together and talking quietly about nothing in particular, but simply enjoying this lovely time together, they finally decided reluctantly to go back inside, because they thought that they were probably being bitten by mosquitos. They then settled down on the family room couch and spent the next few hours engaged in serious conversation.

"So," Grant began, "What do you think is going to happen now between you and George?" "Gosh," Dorothy answered, "I really wish I knew. But I know one thing. I'll never again sleep in the same bed with him or let him have intercourse with me. I suppose that that means that we'll eventually get divorced, but it may take quite a while." "Does that bother you?" "Not at all. I'm more relieved than anything. You know, we've talked about this before. I've always thought that I'd leave George as soon as Carol was out on her own. This just speeds things up a bit. That's about all." "I'm really sorry that I don't have a job and won't for some time, so that I could support you." "Well, that's life. I've worked before in the early years of our marriage, and I guess I can do it again, although I've never liked the idea of me working as long as there's been kids in the house for me to look after. I worked before Sally was born and enjoyed it very much. I was working as a bookkeeper for Perfection Gear. That's where I met Gladys Hartman, one of my best friends in Homewood. I worked there to help support us while George was going to school to earn his architecture degree. But then after Sally and Wesley came along, I decided that I should stay at home and look after my two kids, and then things became even more busy when Carol was born."

"Well," Grant said, "There's another thing that I would like for you to consider." "What's that?" "I don't want you feeling guilty in thinking that you are exploiting George and taking him for a ride, as you continue to live in this house. Some people not familiar with your situation might think that, but you have invested so much of yourself in raising the three kids and in doing your best over the years to be a good wife that you should not feel the least bit guilty in living here and benefiting from George's income."

"Thanks for telling me that," Dorothy replied, "And you'll probably have to keep reminding me of that as things go along, because I know that I will sometimes feel guilty, but I do in fact know way down inside me that what you're saying is true. I've carried much more than my share of the load in raising the kids. I've done my best to support him, even when I thought he was doing the wrong thing, like quitting at Martin Aircraft in Baltimore or quitting Boeing to go into business on his own with John Thompson. But of course, to hear him tell the story, I never supported him in anything, and he always forgets how much help we had over the years from his parents and mine. When he was unemployed in Kimball as the construction partnership was going bankrupt, my mother gave us a lot of money to keep us afloat. She paid off our loans on our cars and furniture, so that we could move here to University City with all our stuff. But George seems to forget how his decisions have put us all through so much turmoil, and how many times our parents have helped us out. To hear him talk, he's a self-made man who's never received any help from anyone throughout his life."

"Well, darling," Grant said, "I really am sorry and wish that your situation looked much better. But I love you completely and want us to have the rest of our lives together as one; and I hope that whatever difficulties you are going to have to face in the near future, you'll consider it all worthwhile." "Grant," Dorothy answered, "I have no doubts about that; and since you've been trying to console me, let me console you too. I know how you must feel about not having a job right now to help me out, but please don't let that get you down. I want you to work hard on your studies to become the very best historian of ancient Greece and Rome that you can be. Things will work out." "Yeah, I know," Grant replied with humorous sarcasm in his voice, "That has to be one of your favorite expressions: things will work out. Yeah, they do, and sometimes the result is horrible." Dorothy laughed. "Oh you, my young pessimistic idealist. Like so many young people, you are so impatient; and if it looks as if things are not going to turn out exactly the way you want them, then you get down in the dumps. But listen here, my dear love, I've been around a lot longer than you, and I've learned a thing or two here and there. Things really do work out most of the time; and I don't mean that in terms of chance. People have so much to do with how those things work out; and I know you pretty well by now. Between me and you, I think we've got a pretty good chance of things working out really well, because we're both pretty fantastic." "You're certainly right about you being so fantastic. I hope you're also right about things working out for us," Grant replied seriously, "I know that we love each other as much as two people ever can." "I think that I am right to be a practical optimist in this matter, as I am in about everything," Dorothy said emphatically, but ever so sweetly. They sealed their agreement with a series of long passionate kisses and Grant feeling her female beauty inside her robe. Besides being a beauty with such remarkable grace and charm, she also possessed such sweet inner strength and wisdom.

They spent the morning and afternoon in enjoying being together while doing normal around-the-house activities. Dorothy had already made arrangements for Carol to spend that evening on campus with Lisa and Kitty, having supper with them, taking in a movie, and then staying the night in Kitty's dorm room. The lovers would therefore have the entire house to themselves that evening and night to celebrate the first anniversary of their love relationship. Around 6:00 P.M. they drove Carol over to campus; and as they returned home, they stopped to buy some Kentucky Fried Chicken for supper. They certainly did not want to waste any time that evening with preparing food or having to clean up the kitchen. They had much grander goals in mind. As they sat at the kitchen table, Grant first explained to his darling the background to Plato's philosophical dialogue called *The Symposium*, a discussion about the nature of love. Grant then played part of a cassette recording of a beautiful PBS reenactment of this dialogue. He wished to place their coming activities into the larger framework of love.

When they were finished eating, they retired to the master bedroom. But before they began their evening and night of unrestrained, abundant, and exuberant celebratory love-play, Dorothy wished to call Lisa to talk with her briefly to make sure that everything would go as planned. She therefore sat down on the edge of the bed to use the telephone.

When Lisa answered, Dorothy said, "Hello, Lisa, I'm just calling to make sure that everything is set for tonight." "Yeah," she replied, "I'll be taking us to the campus theater in a bit in my parents' car." By now Dorothy was lying down on the bed, wearing nothing but a nice simple dress over her bra and panties. Grant, sitting beside her on the edge of the bed, reached under her dress with both hands and pulled her panties down off of her lovely bottom, away from her sex, down her legs, and off her feet, something which never failed to thrill him so entirely! "And then, of course," Lisa continued, "after the movie is over, I'll take Kitty and Carol back to Neville." "Ok," Dorothy replied, "That sounds good." Grant now spread her thighs with his hands, ducked under her dress, and began enjoying a face full of perfect female sex. "I'll bring Carol back to your house sometime tomorrow morning," Lisa said, "but I'll give you a call before I even leave to go pick her up. That should give you plenty of time to stop whatever you guys are doing." She then giggled wickedly. "By the way, Big D," she asked, "what exactly do you guys have planned?" "Oh," Dorothy said in a teasing way, "we've got a pretty big agenda lined up. I'm sure that we'll be busy almost all night long." "I'm sure you will," Lisa laughed. Grant now removed himself from underneath Dorothy's dress, quickly undressed as he stood beside the bed, knelt over her, lifted up her dress, and plunged his ardent manhood into her vagina. As he began riding her rhythmically, Dorothy said, "In fact, I think that Mr. Duncan has already begun our party. I guess I should be hanging up now." "Ok," Lisa laughed again, "Eager boy, huh? Well, I won't keep you two lovers any longer. Have fun!" "We certainly will!"

Since Grant now had her pinned down to the bed with his penis, Dorothy had to make quite a stretch in order to hang up the telephone, after which they fully enjoyed their first sweet round of intercourse of the evening in her dress. In fact, this was the very first time that Grant had both devoured and ridden her sex under a dress; and since the sight of her wearing a dress never failed to inflame his desire for her, the experience was truly awesome and began their evening so nicely.

It was now about 7:00 when they embarked upon their ambitious program of having intercourse on all five beds, the two couches, and even the two tables in the house, an agenda that when Grant had outlined it on one of his recorded letters, Dorothy had eagerly embraced. They had just taken care of the bed in the master bedroom and had eight more rounds to go. Like ancient Greek athletes preparing themselves for a major context, they removed all their clothes and performed their other eight bouts of love-pleasure completely naked, finally ending their sexual contest around midnight, but even then they remained naked until they arose from bed the next morning. They now simply started making the rounds: intercourse in the bed in the far bedroom, intercourse in the bed in the middle bedroom (Carol's bed), then intercourse in each of the twin beds in the front bedroom. This was no whirlwind tour; they enjoyed themselves as much as they wanted at each site. While they were having their pleasure party in the front bedroom, where Dorothy kept her sewing machine, phonograph, books, and wall map, they listened to music. They then proceeded to employ the two couches in the living room and family room as platforms for their enjoyment.

Finally they faced their most formidable challenge of the evening: to engage in intercourse on the kitchen and dining room tables. Rather than both of them being upon the tables, Grant suggested that they could please and enjoy each other by having Dorothy lying on the table and him standing at the edge and entering her between her spread-open thighs. But since she was naked and did not want to lay her back on the cool surface of the tables, they opened up a sleeping bag and spread it out to serve both as a soft cushion and bedding for her. After Grant assisted her onto the dining table, she lay down and positioned herself, so that her bottom was at the edge of the table. He then stood between her legs and supported each of them with his hands as he entered her vagina. Given the somewhat awkward positions that they had to adopt, they did not prolong this bout of intercourse, but they had at least performed it successfully and were gratified. They attempted to enjoy intercourse in the same manner on the kitchen table, but it offered an additional problem. The height of the dining table had been perfect for his penis to enter her, but the kitchen table stood somewhat higher. Thus, in order to consummate this aspect of their program of pleasure, Grant stood upon a thick catalogue in order to raise himself up just enough to enjoy plunging Rufus Magnus into Aphrodite. They performed these acts on the tables with great joy, as if they were the most marvelous adventures, which in fact they were. They now completed their circuit of intercourse by returning to the master bedroom, where they enjoyed themselves more until they finally fell asleep. Their successful completion of their arduous but entirely pleasurable agenda bestowed upon them both a very deep and relaxing slumber.

Exactly one year ago this evening, Grant had first disclosed his attraction to Dorothy, and this had resulted in their first kissing marathon, which had initiated their love relationship with so many doubts and uncertainties.

Now, one year later, their evening had been devoted to a most extraordinary sexual marathon that decisively confirmed their relationship of unshakable love for each other. What an extraordinary year it had been!

July 11, 1973, Wednesday

When Grant awoke early the next morning, Dorothy was still sleeping soundly. They were in bed together naked, and his penis was still firmly lodged inside her. They had slept so soundly and peacefully that they had not moved at all during the night. They were both lying on their sides, and his manhood was entering her from behind. Her thighs were closed together, and this had the effect of holding his penis firmly inside her. Since he needed to urinate, he carefully withdrew Rufus Magnus from inside his beloved woman, where he had lain in perfect contentment the entire night. The withdrawal produced a small sound and sensation of suction, clearly indicating the fullness of their sexual fusion. This wonderful all-night union of their sexes seemed to Grant to have a profound symbolic significance: "Oh Grant, you are my one and only man, and I will keep and love you forever!" "Oh my darling Dorothy, you are my one and only woman, and you have utterly captivated me for life!" Grant's interruption of the love-link of their sexes awoke his darling, and they arose from bed and slowly began their new day together, luxuriating in a profundity of spiritual and emotional union produced by the preceding night's celebration of physical pleasure.

Later in the morning, as they were doing chores around the house, Dorothy began to sing joyfully, "I love you a bushel and a peck, a bushel and a peck, and a hug around the neck, a hug around the neck and a barrel and a heap, a barrel and a heap, and I'm talking in my sleep." The song was obviously directed toward her lover-boy, who said in surprise, "Hey wow! That's a neat song. I've never heard it before." "Yeah," Dorothy responded, "It's an old song from my youth." She then began singing it again; and when she had finished, Grant sang in response, "I love you a bushel and a peck, a bushel and a peck, and a hug around the neck, a hug around the neck and a barrel and a squeeze and a cock between your knees." "Hey," Dorothy nearly shouted in mock protest, "That's not how the song goes!" "It is when I sing it," Grant replied, laughing. "Hey!" he said, "How do you like this one. Pussy in the morning, pussy in the evening, pussy at supper time. Be my pussy woman, and love me all the time." "Wellll," she said with an exaggerated grin in her voice, "It's not how I learned the song." "But wouldn't you say it fits us pretty well!" "Yeah ok, you do have a point there, fella, and you do have a way with redoing the words of a song."

As a lovely epilogue to their night of magnificent pleasure, they decided to have a very special lunch. Dorothy suggested that they try The Great Steak House, a new restaurant located just off the northwestern corner of the university's campus. They were seated at a small table for two, which made their meal seem so perfectly intimate. What really pleased Grant was that they were immediately given two wicker baskets, one filled with peanuts in the shell, and the other filled with popcorn. They could eat these while they decided what to order, and as they waited for their food to arrive. In addition, the peanut shells were to be tossed upon the floor, which also gave the restaurant an interesting and unique ambiance.

Dorothy read through the menu for Grant's benefit; and when she was finished, he asked, "So, darling, what are you going to get?" "I think I'll order the ribeye steak. What are you going to ask for?" "I'm not sure. I'm not much of a steak eater." "Oh really? Why not?" "I just don't like it all that much, I guess; and my family never has had it much, because it's expensive." "When you've eaten steak, how have you had it prepared?" "What do you mean?" "Well, you can have it prepared rare, medium rare, medium, or well done." "I guess well done." "That's probably why you don't like steak very much, because having it well done cooks all the tenderness and flavor out of it." "Oh yeah?" Grant asked in real astonishment. "Yeah, that's right." "Ok, I'll try the ribeye too and have it like yours. How do you have yours done?" "Medium rare."

After they placed their orders, they continued to munch on popcorn and peanuts and simply chat congenially. Then after their food arrived, they were both absorbed in eating, but finally Dorothy asked, "So, how do you like that steak?" "I really love it." "See, darling, you just didn't know how to have it fixed for you," Dorothy said sweetly. "Like I keep saying, sweetheart, you just keep teaching me all sorts of things."

July 12, 1973, Thursday

Their night together in the house to celebrate their love anniversary had been so extraordinary and wonderful that Dorothy arranged to have Carol absent again from the house for that evening and night. The lovers spent the entire evening once again engaged in various types of erotic enjoyment, both of the regular and novel sort.

"Let's take a bath together," Dorothy suggested. "We've used the shower stall in the bathroom adjoining my bedroom to take a shower, but we've never used the bathtub in the main bathroom." "Sure," Grant gladly agreed, "that sounds like real fun." The main bathroom, it should be explained, was actually two separate rooms. One first stepped from the hall into one room that simply contained on the left a large vanity cabinet that stretched from wall to wall, fitted with two side-by-side sinks with a storage area underneath and a wall-to-wall mirror above it. To the right was another door that led into the other small room. It was simply fitted out with a toilet and a bathtub. The bathroom was configured so that one person could take a bath in privacy, while someone else could use the sinks and mirror in the other part of the bathroom.

"You know," Dorothy explained, "I use both the tub and the shower. When George's not here, I usually use the shower, because I can then shut my bedroom door and have the convenience of walking around naked or partially dressed between the bedroom and adjoining bathroom to get myself ready to go somewhere, and George isn't here to see me. But when he's around, I usually take a bath in the hall bathroom, because I can go in and be by myself without worrying about him. When I take a bath, I even lock the inside door, so that he can't come in there at all, and I have the excuse that the children (at least Carol these days) are in the house." "That's really neat," Grant replied, as they both chuckled and enjoyed this little bit of wifely trickery to keep her lovely nakedness concealed from her husband. "I would also like," Dorothy went on, "for us to take our bath together with the light off. I want to pretend that I'm also blind like you, and I figure that it will make it even more fun for me to have to feel around for everything, especially you, of course." "Hey," Grant enthused, "Now that sounds like a really good idea!"

The naked lovers came into the main bathroom and first rounded up everything that they would need: soap, wash cloths, and towels. Then after running a fair amount of water into the tub, they both climbed in. The two of them barely fit, but this simply made the bath an even more enjoyable experience. They sat at opposite ends with their feet and legs interlocking in parallel and with a foot occasionally playfully caressing the sex of the other. Dorothy did in fact enjoy having to grope around in the dark to feel for things. After washing their own faces, they proceeded to wash the rest of the other person, leaving their backs for last, because in order to accomplish this part of the enterprise they had to kneel upright in the tub. They then closed out this wonderful little experience by toweling one another off.

They now went on to other interesting experiences in the nude. Since Grant had never seen his darling in her swimming suit, he asked her to put it on for him, which she did, as well as modeling a lovely Hawaiian muumuu that she had purchased in 1966 when she, Bethany, and their mother had visited Tim in Hawaii. They then settled down in bed in the master bedroom and thoroughly enjoyed the physical pleasure of their perfect love for a very long time, after which they fell asleep together.

July 13, 1973, Friday

After awakening and beginning their final half-day together with more leisurely intercourse and bed play, they arose, and Dorothy went about the house clad only in her pink quilted robe and slippers, so that Grant could continue enjoying her female beauty all morning by simply slipping his hands inside her robe. They had fun stripping the bed and changing the sheets and doing other small things around the house until it was time for them to leave to meet Lisa for lunch, after which Dorothy would take Grant to the bus station to return to Fairmont.

Around 11:00 they went into the master bedroom, so that Dorothy could finally get herself dressed. As she was moving about to collect her articles of clothing, Grant was lounging on the bed; and since he wanted one last lovely encounter with her sex before she put on her panties, he asked, "Hey, sweetheart, how about coming over here and letting me have one last taste of your delicious pussy pie?" "I guess I can do that," she happily replied. Since he was lying on his back, he simply moved his body, so that his head was hanging upside down over the side edge of the mattress. Dorothy then walked up to his face, opened up her robe, and presented her sex to his mouth for one last time. She then dressed, they left for lunch and the bus station, and Grant returned home.

George soon learned from something that Carol had said casually that Dorothy had spent the night alone in the house with Grant. When he complained to Dorothy about this and said that he did not want her to be alone again overnight in his house with another man, she replied that it was her house just as much as his, and she would do what she wanted. George might have already begun to be suspicious about something serious going on between Dorothy and Grant, because the latter had not been part of the regular group of blind students for quite some time, but George now thought that something was definitely going on between the two of them, especially since Dorothy was no longer sleeping with him and refused to gratify him sexually.

When Grant returned to Fairmont, their final period of separation for the summer began and lasted for thirty-seven days, ending on Sunday August 19. Luckily for them, the university had changed its entire academic calendar, which had the effect of shortening this last separation by about three weeks. Rather than beginning classes in mid-September, having a Christmas break, followed by two more weeks of classes and a final exam period ending in late January with the spring semester beginning in early February and ending in early June, the fall semester henceforth began in late August and ended just before Christmas, and the spring semester began in early January and ended in mid-May. Nevertheless, the two lovers very impatiently awaited the arrival of the fall semester when Grant would be back on campus permanently. In the meantime, of course, they kept in very close touch through their steady stream of long letters recorded on cassettes, including several sessions of masturbation. They both eagerly looked forward to their reunion when they would no longer have to use masturbation as a barely adequate substitute for the real thing. Their glorious week of love in July had completely cemented their relationship, and they were both tremendously empowered by their love for each other. Grant's life in Fairmont returned to what it had been, consisting of much reading and studying, largely in connection with his upcoming courses for the fall. In addition, his sister had reestablished contact with him, had come to take him to her house to spend some time with her, including a weekend when Neil happened to be out of town; and eventually, Patricia sought a reconciliation with her parents, which was brought about when she and Neil came to the house one day when they were bringing Grant back home after a visit; and everyone sat in the living room and talked things out.

Dorothy's life largely returned to what it had been. She oversaw Carol's daily activities, attended her Tuesday evenings of Sweet Adelines, enjoyed her swimming at the YMCA, and spent considerable time with both Kitty and Lisa, going out with them for lunch or supper, going bowling in the evening, or simply having them over to the house. The two young women were very important in providing Dorothy with much needed moral support because of her on-going battle with George. Sally returned to University City from Houston for a week at the very end of July and the beginning of

August. She now learned for the first time that things were not going at all well between her parents.

But of course, the really big issue facing Dorothy for the rest of the summer was her situation with George. Despite her absolute refusal, George made several attempts to have Dorothy give him sexual pleasure. One time that summer, as they were on their way back home from Newton, George was driving the car on the interstate, Dorothy was sitting next to him in the passenger seat, and Carol and her friend Betty Washington were in the back seat. As he was driving, George unzipped his pants, pulled out his erect penis, and tried to get Dorothy to take it into her hand to masturbate. When she refused, George began to masturbate himself, and Dorothy became quite alarmed that he would lose control of the car, as well as having the teenagers in the back seat discover what was going on. Luckily, neither of her fears were realized.

On several occasions during the summer, while Kitty was staying at the house, George approached Kitty when they happened to be the only ones there. When he asked her to gratify him sexually, she always succeeded in declining to do so in a kindly fashion, but since Kitty was rather small and confined to a wheelchair and thus clearly not able to defend herself adequately, these unwanted approaches frightened her very much. Her only solace was confiding in Bob Snider when he came down to University City to visit her.

George's attempt to revive a sexual relationship with Dorothy culminated in the middle of the night during this same time period. When George was away in Newton, Dorothy slept either alone or with Carol in the double bed of the master bedroom, but when George came home, he slept alone in the master bedroom while Dorothy and Carol slept in the twin beds in the front bedroom. This was their sleeping arrangement on the night in question. It was quite late, and Dorothy and Carol were already asleep, but Bob Snider and Kitty Carpenter were still awake together in the far bedroom, across the hall from George and the master bedroom. Bob just happened to be in University City for a short time to visit Kitty, and they were about to listen to the music of Judy Collins on Dorothy's phonograph when things began to happen.

George arose, came down the hall, and went into the front bedroom to force himself, if need be, upon Dorothy. Carol was sleeping in the bed closest to the windows and away from the door, and Dorothy was sleeping in the one nearest the doorway, the bed in which Grant always slept, in which

Dorothy and Grant had often had magnificent sexual intercourse, and which had witnessed The Great Apocalypse. George sat down on the bed beside Dorothy and began to grab at her, but when she resisted and kept saying "no," Frau began to growl menacingly, so that George became alarmed and turned his attention to mollifying Frau. At this point Carol awoke, realized what was going on, fled out of the room in panic and distress, and came down the hallway to the far bedroom, where Kitty and Bob were. At this point Dorothy succeeded in getting out of bed and onto her feet, but George was still grabbing at her and pulling on her roughly. In order to keep from having to give into him, Dorothy held tightly on to one of the upright bedposts at the foot of the bed. It was about six feet high, because the bed was designed to hold a canopy. But George's wrenching on Dorothy was so violent that their struggle broke off the bedpost near its base. It made such a loud cracking sound that Kitty and Bob became quite alarmed. At Kitty's insistent urging that she go back down the hallway to intervene and end this horrible scene, Carol returned to the front bedroom, stood in the doorway, and simply screamed. By now George had Dorothy back down on the bed and was sitting beside her, but Carol's scream finally brought him to his senses. He released Dorothy, embraced Carol, and tearfully apologized to her. George then left the room and returned to the master bedroom. Bob then went in on the living room couch to sleep for the night; and when Kitty began to play the Judy Collins music in the far bedroom, Dorothy called out from the front bedroom, asking her to stop, because she had gone through too much, and the noise was hard on her terribly overwrought nerves. This event finally convinced George that Dorothy really meant what she said, and would probably never again sleep with or submit to him sexually. As a result, he began to spend even more time away from home in Newton.

August 11, 1973, Saturday

Dorothy, George, and Carol spent the day traveling by car to Chicago to attend Nisa's wedding with Sora. It was a large formal wedding with many relatives and friends in attendance. When the festivities finally ended, the Patterson trio returned to University City. This was the second-to-last important public event in which Dorothy and George participated as a married couple.

The very next week (Monday-Friday, Aug. 13-17) was freshman orientation and mobility instruction week for the incoming blind students, and Dorothy was happily busy serving for her fourth and final time as a volunteer. Her student for the week was a young man from Malaysia. He already had his B.A. degree in economics and had been employed in the Malaysian government. He was now going to attend the university to earn his M.A. He was a very pleasant young man, and of course, he and Dorothy got along famously. On her last recorded letter to Grant for the summer Dorothy described her activities during this week and her interaction with her mobility student, as well as another new blind student, an older man who had lost his vision in Vietnam. He was married and a very outspoken defender of the American involvement in Vietnam at a time when such a view was extremely unpopular on a college campus, but Dorothy was very impressed with how he set forth his ideas, vigorously and persuasively.

August 19, 1973, Sunday

Grant's father brought him back to University City in the early afternoon. He was now assigned to a dorm room in Forester. It was just a few doors down and on the opposite side of the hall from where Dennis and Renny had roomed the year before, and where Grant had also lived during his first semester as a college student. Unfortunately, however, something had gone wrong in the room assignment, and rather than Grant and Bob Snider being assigned to the same room, Grant wound up having a roommate whom he did not know; and Bob was assigned to a triple room with two other fellows on the fourth floor of Watson.

As soon as Grant had put away all of his things on his side of the dorm room, he called his darling, and she soon came over to be with him, but they were both extremely disappointed about the dorm room situation. Bob had also returned that same afternoon and was getting himself settled into his room; and since Dorothy and Grant could not be guaranteed any privacy in his room, they walked over to Watson to visit with Bob and to talk with him about trying to have their room assignments changed. They agreed to do so, but in the end, it proved to be too complicated, and they had to wait until the spring semester to be assigned the same room. Consequently, very much contrary to their desires, during that fall semester Dorothy and Grant had to work around the obstacle of not being able to have Dorothy in his room.

There were, of course, other changes in the situations involving Dorothy's other university kids. Dennis had already left the country just a few days before, traveling with a group of other American students to spend the entire academic year in Baden, Austria. Renny was no longer in Forester, but he and another young man named Tom Hamilton were sharing an apartment on the fourth floor of a building situated to the northwest of the Quad and several blocks away from where Bob and Grant were. Lisa was still living in Beaumont Manor. Kitty Carpenter, although she had just graduated at the conclusion of summer school, was not interested in returning right away to her home in Ohio; and Dorothy had obligingly agreed to let her stay as a guest in her house for the semester.

While Dorothy and Grant were still lounging together on one of the beds in Bob's room in Watson, Grant asked, "Hey, Bob, can I borrow a cassette machine from you for a bit?" "Sure," Bob replied and then located the device and handed it over to Grant. "Ok, Sweetheart," Grant said to Dorothy, "I have something here for your birthday present. I'm sorry that it's a bit late, but it took me quite some time to make; and besides, I wanted to present it to you personally." As both Dorothy and Bob waited to hear what it was, Grant removed from his pocket a cassette tape, inserted it into the machine, and pressed the play button. Within seconds the machine began to play instrumental guitar music. "Wow!" Dorothy exclaimed, "That's you playing, but it sounds like there are two guitars." "There are," Grant said, "I used my stereo reel-to-reel tape recorder to record me playing the lead for a song on one track, sometimes using my acoustical guitar and other times using my electric guitar. Then after recording my chording accompaniment with the acoustical guitar on the parallel track of the reel as I listened to the lead through headphones, I used patch cords to blend the two tracks into one and recorded the merged music onto this cassette." "Boy!" Dorothy exclaimed again, "That's really neat!" "And guess what?" Grant asked. "What?" "There's even a new song on this tape that you've never heard me play before. I made it up myself, and I've called it Dorothy's Song." "Ah Grant," Dorothy said with obvious pleasure, pride, and love, "Thank you so very much! It's a beautiful birthday present."

After staying in Bob's room for a while longer as they listened to much of Grant's music tape, including Dorothy's Song, the lovers finally left and went in the car to The Great Steak House to have a nice supper and simply to be together. Then shortly before 8:00 they went past Beaumont Manor and Nash Hall to pick up Lisa and Pam Stewart respectively, and they all four returned to Dorothy's house to spend the evening together. George was not there, because he was occupied the whole evening until quite late with a business meeting. Kitty was spending the night on campus with friends, and Carol was off enjoying herself with her own friends too. Thus, the four of them had the house all to themselves for quite some time.

After entering the house, they all sat down at the kitchen table and talked, but after a while, when Lisa had Pam fully engaged in conversation, Dorothy quietly arose from her chair, took Grant's hand, and led him into the adjoining dining room, where they sat down on the gold carpet and began to kiss, embrace, and pet passionately. This was the first real physical intimacy that they had been able to enjoy all day, and after being together for the past five hours or so, they were both ready to indulge themselves. Lisa, of course, knew all about the two lovers, but Pam Stewart did not. The former therefore kept the latter, who was, of course, blind and unaware of exactly what Dorothy and Grant were doing, fully occupied in talking at the kitchen table, so that the lovers could have some time to themselves.

After several minutes, Dorothy silently arose to her feet, again took Grant by the hand, and led him down the hall and into the middle bedroom. In equal silence she led him across the floor to the single bed that was in the room. When she came to its side, she turned herself around, so that she was now both facing Grant and had the backs of her legs against the side of the bed. She then began to take down her shorts and panties, slid them all the way down to her ankles, lay back across the bed, spread her knees wide apart, and thus offered her sex to Grant. As soon as he was aware of her taking down her shorts and panties, he knew instantly what she had in mind for them. He therefore quickly unfastened his own shorts, pulled his pants and undershorts also down to his ankles, and simply fell upon her and entered her receptive vagina with his very erect penis. As soon as he entered her, they both began to convulse and shudder with pleasure. Grant ejaculated immediately, but then enjoyed plunging rhythmically inside her briefly until Dorothy finally whispered, "Ok, that's probably all we should do right now." Grant then withdrew himself, they both put their clothes back in order, and they rejoined Lisa and Pam at the kitchen table as if nothing unusual had taken place.

After they had conversed more in the kitchen, Dorothy and Grant took Lisa and Pam back to their dorm rooms, and they returned to the house. By now Carol was home and going to bed in the middle bedroom, but George was still not there. Dorothy went off to bed in the far bedroom, and Grant assumed his usual sleeping post in the bed nearest the door in the front bedroom.

August 22, 1973, Wednesday

Since classes at the university did not begin until next Monday August 27, Grant intended to spend the entire week (except for the upcoming weekend when George would be back from Newton) with Dorothy at the house. George had left very early Monday morning and was already gone when Grant and Dorothy arose. They had thus been enjoying the past two and a half days in their usual pattern of sweet harmonious companionship: doing things together around the house, taking the dogs for walks, going grocery shopping, running errands, and enjoying intercourse and love-play whenever Carol happened to be away from the house.

When the telephone rang in the early afternoon, Dorothy answered it and was pleasantly surprised to find Mary Beth, Wesley's girlfriend, on the other end of the line. She had just returned to campus for the new academic year and wanted to say hello. As they talked, Dorothy invited her over to have supper and to spend the night, and Mary Beth gladly accepted the offer. As a result, the three of them spent the evening sitting around the kitchen table and bringing one another fully up to date on what all had been going on in their lives, except, of course, Dorothy and Grant's torrid love affair. They stayed up until nearly midnight; and when they finally went off to bed, Carol was already asleep in the middle bedroom, and Dorothy had Mary Beth sleep in the far bedroom, which, although usually occupied by Kitty, was not, because the latter was still on campus visiting various friends. Grant, of course, settled down in his usual place in the front bedroom.

August 23, 1973, Thursday

Not long after midnight, while Grant was still fully awake, Dorothy came gliding silently into the room. "Are you still awake?" she asked in a whisper. "Yeah," he responded. After quietly closing the bedroom door behind her, she explained, "I didn't want to sleep alone in the master bedroom tonight. I figure that since there are twin beds in here, we can sleep side by side, and it still wouldn't seem to odd if Mary Beth were to see us in here." "That's really nice," Grant said, "I love having you in here with me." "I do too."

By now Dorothy was under the covers in the other twin bed. "How about I come over to visit you, and we have a little fun there in your bed?" Grant asked suggestively. "I don't think we should risk it," Dorothy replied, "I'm afraid that Mary Beth might get up for some reason and wander around the house and find us here in bed together. It just isn't a good idea." "Ok," Grant reluctantly agreed. they then simply lay in their two beds, talking pleasantly about many things, wondering how Dennis was making out in his new environment in Austria, discussing how nice it would be if they could be on the same bowling team that semester. After about forty-five minutes of such conversing, Grant finally announced, "You know, Rufus Magnus isn't the least bit interested in going to sleep." "He isn't, is he?" Dorothy replied teasingly. "Nope, he sure ain't!" Grant replied emphatically, "Are you sure we can't have at least a little quickie, so that he'll be able to settle down for the night? Otherwise, he's probably going to keep me up all night." After a long pause, during which Dorothy gave the matter serious consideration, she finally answered, "Ok, I think I know where we can do it without Mary Beth coming upon us. Just follow me and keep quiet."

They arose from their beds, opened the door, and went silently down the hall and into the living room. Dorothy then led Grant over to the front of the room near the picture window. After pushing a rocking chair forward a little to give them more space between the wall and the furniture, she lay down on her back on the carpeted floor, hiked up her nightgown, spread her knees, and offered her sex to Grant. He removed his undershorts, enjoyed caressing her magnificent love-smile, lay down between her thighs, entered her, and gave them both several minutes of exquisite pleasure with his ejaculation and steady riding. "Ok," Dorothy finally whispered, "I hate to tell ya, but we should probably not make this a long drawn-out affair." "He's long, all right," Grant humorously replied, "But he's not interested in drawing himself out. He wants to stay in there." "Ok, wise guy," Dorothy said with obvious delight in her voice, "You know what I mean." Grant obediently, but reluctantly withdrew. They arose from the floor, returned to the bedroom, and eventually fell asleep in their separate beds.

Much later in the day, as Dorothy was assisting Grant and other blind students at the Armory in registering for their classes, she happened to realize that it would soon be George's birthday. Throughout their marriage George had always expected as part of his birthday present his enjoyment of her pussy, a wifely duty that she had found increasingly nauseating over the years. This year, of course, was different. She would never again have to carry out this most distasteful duty as his wife. She was so glad to be liberated from that shackle. At the same time she remembered what a nice bit of pleasure she and Grant had enjoyed very early this morning on the living room floor. There was nothing at all distasteful about that for either of them, and she was looking forward to giving him and receiving from him much more of the same later this evening, if all went well. She was now totally his woman, and he her man. When their bodies merged together again tonight, his beautiful red cock would find a most welcoming and loving pussy-mate between her thighs.

August 28, 1973, Tuesday

When Dorothy awoke early that morning around 6:15, she reached over to the table beside the bed in the master bedroom to get the thermometer for taking her temperature. It looked as if she might be fertile today. So, unfortunately, she and Grant would have to avoid actual intercourse with his sperm ejaculated inside her. Ever since they began enjoying intercourse, checking her temperature first thing in the morning was the only means that they had been using to guard against pregnancy. It was not by any means foolproof, but they both enjoyed their intercourse together so thoroughly that neither wanted anything but the complete real thing, Grant's actual penis inside her, uninhibited by any rubber. She loved the feel of him, how his penis quivered and shuddered, and how his sperm felt as he ejaculated inside her.

She arose, stepped into her slippers and put her robe over her nightgown. Then after paying a visit to the bathroom, she wandered into the kitchen, turned on the radio to hear the news and weather, and made herself a pot of coffee. She needed to get her daily quota of caffeine in her right away with time enough for all the liquid to run through her system before they set out for Chicago. Renny needed some papers for his DVR financial support or something, and she had agreed to run him up to his mother's house and back today. Grant had spent the night, and he would be going along with them, but since he had his class on Greek history at 1:30 this afternoon, they had little time to spare.

Grant and Carol soon joined her in the kitchen, but Carol then went off to get herself ready for school. As soon as she left, Dorothy broke the sad news to Grant: "I'm sorry that Dickie Boy won't be able to have too much fun today, because it looks like I might be fertile." "Ah shucks!" Grant responded. "But we can still have some fun," Dorothy teased. After returning to the master bedroom, Dorothy took off her robe and nightgown and came into the adjoining bathroom fully nude. They now proceeded to perform the pleasurable procedure that they had devised and executed twice earlier that year on the morning of April 23. Grant sat on the toilet lid and exhibited his erection, while his beautifully bare darling descended upon him with her magnificent love-spread. He then rubbed the large head of Rufus Magnus inside her vulva and thus masturbated them both. When he came, he ejaculated his semen onto her love-delta. But since they had no time to spare, that was all that they could afford right then by way of physical pleasure. Dorothy hastily dressed herself, they left the house, picked up Renny, sped off to Chicago, collected the necessary papers, and returned to University City.

They arrived back in town shortly before 1:00. They therefore first dropped Renny off at his place and returned briefly to the house. They entered the bathroom; and after Dorothy urinated, they exchanged places, so that they could repeat their pleasurable procedure once again before Grant had to go off to his class. So, just as on the morning of April 23, they enjoyed this novel form of sexual gratification twice; and Grant went to his first class on ancient Greek history in the afterglow of this wonderful pleasure.

September 1, 1973, Saturday

Like last year, Renny and Paul Lindquist, another blind student who had arrived on campus last fall, organized many of the blind students together with sighted students into a bowling league for the new academic year. The only non-student members of this league last year had been Dorothy, George, and Carol, a perfect testimony to how fully Dorothy had woven her life into that of her beloved university kids. Because of the great turmoil in their relationship, Grant had not been a member of the league last fall, but he was very much interested in being one now, so that he could be with Dorothy Sunday evenings.

Since Dennis was now far away in Austria, he could no longer serve as the lovers' immediate confidant, advisor, and helper. These roles were now taken over by Lisa and Renny. When Grant and Dorothy talked to Renny about trying to arrange having the two of them on the same bowling team, Renny was able to have Grant made one of the six team captains; and when they met that afternoon in Paul Lindquist's dorm room to organize things, Grant succeeded in choosing Dorothy to be one of the four members on his team. George wound up being on another team, so that even in this matter of the bowling league the two lovers succeeded in being together and having Dorothy detached from her lawful husband. Grant and Dorothy were so very pleased that they had been able to engineer this configuration, because now every Sunday night when the teams met in the Student Union and bowled, they would always be sitting together quite justifiably as members of the same team.

It was this weekly bowling schedule that largely determined George's visits to University City that fall. The bowling was always scheduled to begin at 8:00 Sunday night. Thus, unless he needed to be in town to take care of business matters, George often returned to University City from Newton on Sunday late in the afternoon, had supper at the house, went bowling, slept alone in the master bedroom that night, and arose the next morning to return to Newton. Consequently, at least in terms of his physical presence, George was now a mere peripheral character and would have been non-existent altogether if he had not been a member of the bowling league during that fall semester. But when he dropped out at the end of the autumn term, he had few reasons to come to University City regularly; and therefore, by the beginning of 1974, apart from a few sporadic visits, he existed merely as Dorothy's legal husband, whom she was in the process of divorcing.

For the very first time in the history of their relationship, Grant's and Dorothy's life together now began to have a definite and lovely routine of activities, because they were now able to be together almost constantly. Indeed, for almost the next two years (from August 19 of 1973 to May 31 of 1975) the house at 1801 Rachel Drive in University City was not only Dorothy's house, but in a sense, their house. During the fall semester of 1973 Grant spent about half of each week with his lady-love there. Unless George had to spend the entire weekend in University City, Grant came over to the house Friday afternoon and stayed there until the early afternoon on Sunday. He also spent at least one week-night at the house as well. As usual, Dorothy swam on Tuesday and Thursday mornings and was always finished by 11:00 or so. Since Grant had his Greek history class beginning at 1:30 on those afternoons, she usually came to campus from swimming and took him home with her, so that they could enjoy lunch together. They then lay down to rest and relax and quite often had deliciously sweet sex before she returned him to campus for his afternoon class. On such occasions they left one another's company in the euphoric afterglow of their love-pleasure, as Grant ascended to the third floor of Milton Hall to attend class. They did, however, on a few occasions decide to have a picnic on campus. Dorothy came with Kitty to the university's library and met Grant, Bob Snider, and Lisa Harris; and they sat on the stone benches there and enjoyed themselves until time for Grant's class. In addition, when he stayed overnight with her during the week, they normally had sweet wonderful intercourse in the morning after Carol had gone to school, and then Dorothy took Grant over to the university and dropped him off on campus for his Latin class. On these occasions too, it was so magnificent for them to leave one another's company after enjoying the wonderful physical manifestation of their complete and total love for each other. How totally different this was from a year ago when their unstable relationship had created so much uncertainty and turmoil that it tormented Grant to the point that he found it difficult to concentrate on his studies!

Their solid love relationship that fall also brought about a major change involving Dorothy's relationship with the other university blind students. Now that she and Grant were a fully committed loving couple, Dorothy reduced her activities and assistance to these other students. During the past three years she had opened her home to her university kids on numerous occasions, and their gatherings had served as an important emotional outlet for Dorothy. Her university kids had filled a void in her life caused by her unhappy marriage and the constant challenges posed by her three, somewhat problematic children. Her complete and total loving relationship with Grant had now made such previous involvement with her university kids quite superfluous. There was no longer any void in her life or happiness. In fact, her life now seemed to be bursting with love and joy, and she could hardly believe that she felt so happy with her Grant! Consequently, she now devoted herself almost exclusively to assisting her blind love-mate. As a result, her house was henceforth only rarely the scene of sizable parties. Instead, Dorothy much preferred having the house become the tranquil home for her younger daughter, and herself and her darling Grant. She truly loved this new arrangement that excluded George and incorporated her beloved Grant into George's place. Having Grant in the house always filled her with wonderful peace, satisfaction, and contentment. In addition, as part of this new configuration, Dorothy was no longer serving as a reader to any other student except her darling Grant, and that was exactly how she wanted it. Since they were now a couple bound together by their complete and total love for each other, Dorothy was fully committed to assisting her man in every way possible to achieve his beautiful dream of becoming a professor of ancient Greek and Roman history. That dream therefore united them into an unshakable team to realize their common goal. Accordingly, Dorothy was always ready and eager to read to him, especially when the material involved ancient history; and whenever she did, Grant usually made a permanent record of her reading by preserving it on a cassette tape. He thereby began to compile his own personal library of recorded material to be used and used again in future years as Grant needed; and it was so wonderful to have these readings performed with Dorothy's lovely voice.

Dorothy also began to serve as his assistant in studying Latin. Grant had succeeded in placing into fifth semester Latin. Although he had the textbook in braille and had a braille Latin dictionary (consisting of twenty bulky volumes), Dorothy absolutely insisted on her becoming his eyes in reading the explanatory notes to the Latin texts and in looking up any Latin words as Grant needed them. Part of Dorothy's insistence to help Grant in these ways was based upon the simple fact that Dorothy could look up words in a print dictionary and read the textbook's explanatory notes on the text much more quickly than Grant could do so in braille. She therefore persuaded Grant to have her assist him in these ways, because it saved him valuable time. But, on the other hand, her insistence to help Grant with his Latin also stemmed from Dorothy's desire to become an integral part of Grant's education and their joint endeavor to realize their long-term academic dream. In fact, Dorothy was so committed to helping him with his daily Latin work that whenever Grant happened to be working on his Latin in his dorm room, he always called Dorothy, and she provided him with her assistance over the telephone. And oh how they both loved having a perfectly valid excuse to hear one another's voice! Given Dorothy's considerable intelligence, it took her no time at all to learn the rules of Latin pronunciation, so that Grant never had to spell out any words to be looked up in the dictionary, because she knew their spelling from Grant's pronunciation. Likewise, whenever she read out any explanatory notes or other material containing any Latin, her own pronunciation was flawless, and Grant knew exactly what it was that she had read.

Despite these positive developments in their relationship, there were other external factors that encroached upon the edges of their happiness. Dorothy was determined to divorce George, but doing so would create major practical problems of how she and Grant would survive financially. Would they be able to keep the house? Would she have to go to work full time? What kind of employment would she be able to find after not working full time since the very beginning of her marriage? How would all these changes affect Carol? In addition, by now her family (her mother, sisters, and brothers-in-law) knew that she and George were not sleeping together, and Gloria and Ginger in particular disapproved of what Dorothy was doing and sided with George, whereas Bethany, who had gone through her own divorce and remarriage not too long ago, was much more sympathetic. Not having the full support of her immediate family in opposition to George, whom she had not loved in many years, hurt her very deeply; and even though she was absolutely sure that she had done the right thing, their disapproval still bothered her very much. All these worries sometimes made her somewhat depressed. As a result, on a few rare occasions during this fall when she and Grant were lying in bed together, he was very desirous of her and wanted to have them engage in love-play, but she had so many things on her mind that she was somewhat depressed and was not interested in either giving or receiving love-pleasure. Instead, she was in need of understanding, caring, comfort, and sweet affection; and on such occasions she would say, "I really am not interested in sex right now, because I have too many worries on my mind. I just need you to hold me and comfort me." Grant, of course, always obliged by holding his beloved darling in his arms tenderly and offered her the solace that she needed so much.

September 7, 1973, Friday

It was 5:15 in the afternoon, and Dorothy and Grant were sitting in the living room. Grant had been at the house all afternoon, but since they expected George to be arriving home sometime soon, they had decided to configure themselves into a reading session, so that when George showed up, nothing would appear out of the ordinary. Thus, Dorothy was sitting on the couch reading from Grant's paperback copy of J. B. Bury's *The Ancient Greek Historians*, while Grant sat on the other side of the room in a rocking chair intently listening to her.

When George arrived five minutes later, he walked from the family room and into the living room, obviously attracted by the sound of his wife's voice. As he entered the room and took in the scene of Dorothy engaged in reading, he simply said "Hello" in a low voice, and Dorothy responded by raising her hand in greeting but not stopping or in any way interrupting her reading of the text. George walked off down the hall and into the master bedroom, and Dorothy continued to read for another ten minutes. She then stopped and went off to tell George that she was done reading to Grant for the afternoon and would now leave to take him back to his dorm room.

As they traveled in the car back to campus, they first talked about what they would each be doing from now until Sunday evening when they would again be together bowling at the Student Union. They then began to discuss George. "I really don't like him being around you at all," Grant said, "It gives me the creeps." "It's ok," Dorothy replied, "He hasn't tried anything violent with me since that horrible night a few weeks ago." "Yeah well," Grant grumbled, "That doesn't mean anything. He could become annoyed or frustrated over the weekend and try something like that again." "I don't think he will," Dorothy responded reasonably, "I think he's decided that force isn't going to work with me. He now realizes, I think, that if there's any chance of him salvaging our marriage, he has to be nice and considerate to me, and that makes it real easy for me, because I just have to be polite in return without giving into him in any important way." "I hope you're right," Grant grudgingly answered, "But I still really don't like him being around you." Grant had great difficulty in not always thinking of George as the one who had been sexually abusing Grant's beloved darling year after year under the legal guise of marriage. "Don't worry, sweetie," Dorothy said lovingly, as she reached across the seat and playfully patted his arm, "I'll be ok."

September 9, 1973, Sunday

Grant and Lisa stood together in front of Beaumont Manor. It was 7:15 in the evening, and Grant had walked over to meet her, so that they could go to bowling together, but he had also left in plenty of time, so that they would have extra time to talk and just be together. Lisa was already greatly missing Dennis; and like Dorothy and Grant, they would use cassette recordings to keep in touch throughout the year while Dennis was in Austria, but given the turn-around time in sending tapes back and forth over such a distance, it was going to be more difficult for them to maintain a close relationship. Consequently, just as Dennis and Lisa in recent months had done much to help and support Grant and Dorothy, the latter were now doing the same for the former, as best they could. By now Dorothy and Lisa had a very close friendship, but the same was just now being created between Grant and Lisa, because up until the beginning of this fall semester the former had been absent from University City for about seven months in Fairmont; and when he did come to University City to visit, he spent virtually all his time with his beloved Dorothy. The two had therefore not spent much time with each other, but as the new academic year unfolded, that would change, and they too would become very close friends. But besides Grant serving as a sounding board for Lisa's loneliness caused by Dennis' absence, with which he could easily relate, Lisa also allowed Grant to express his own mixture of love and longing for his darling, who had been spending the weekend with George. As they talked, they began to walk very slowly toward the Student Union, where they would meet the others. This walking and talking at this time became an important weekly experience for them both.

September 18, 1973, Tuesday

As soon as her Sweet Adeline practice was over around 10:00, Dorothy came over to the university and picked up both Grant and Renny, and then she found a nice secluded spot to park, where the three of them could simply sit in the car and talk for a while. Since the semester had begun, apart from their Sunday evening bowling, Dorothy and Grant had seen rather little of Renny, and they both wanted to spend some time with him to see what he had been doing, and what thoughts he might have about their relationship.

"So, Renny," Dorothy began, "How are things going with you?" "Ah, they're fine." "How do you like living in an apartment as opposed to a dorm room?" "Well, it has its advantages and disadvantages. We don't have to eat the dorm food, but of course, we have to go out and shop for our own food and then make things and clean up after ourselves. Hey Ma, you wouldn't be interested in moving in and becoming our cook and cleaning lady, would you?" Renny asked with a laugh. "Are you kidding?" Dorothy replied. "But seriously, Renny, if there are things that I can help you with, please don't hesitate to call." "Ok, I certainly will, and you know me, I'm not shy about asking for help. You might get more than you've bargained for with that open-ended offer." "Don't worry about that, Renny. I can handle you. You should know that by now," Dorothy teased.

Eventually the three of them got around to talking about George and the relationship between Dorothy and Grant, on which Renny actually had two important bits of information. "Well, you know," Renny began, "George does actually suspect that something is going on between you two." "He does?" the other two asked in some surprise and alarm simultaneously. "Yeah, he does. Ma, do you remember, about two weeks ago I came over to the house one Saturday to help George look over the cars and to tune them up?" "Yeah," Dorothy allowed. "Well, as we were out there on the driveway messing with the cars, George asked me if I knew whether anything was going on between you two. Of course, I played dumb and said that that was news to me." "I guess he's slowly been putting two and two together to figure things out," Dorothy said, "He just happened to learn from something that Carol said to him that Grant stayed all night with me in the house this past July, and it really made him angry." "Well," Renny said, "He does suspect. So, you two really need to be careful. The other thing," Renny continued to explain, "is that he then went on to ask my advice on what he might be able to do to win you back." "What did you tell him?" Dorothy asked. "Well, again, you know, I certainly didn't or couldn't really tell him the truth, that there was nothing he could do to have you back as his loving wife, but once again, I just played kind of dumb and really had nothing much to offer him." George had apparently considered Renny a very good source of possible information and advice on these two matters, because of his position as an insider in the group of Dorothy's university kids, and also because his constant joking about women and sex easily gave one the impression that Renny possessed some expertise in such matters.

Since Renny almost exactly a year ago had mentioned to Dorothy the possibility of George coming after Grant with a gun, the three now discussed the likelihood of George using some form of violence against Grant. He had certainly shown himself capable of some physical violence toward Dorothy, a much smaller female and his lawful wife, but none of them had any clear ideas what this might mean for George's attitude toward Grant, who was much bigger and stronger. Following further futile speculation on this point, the three decided to end their little pow-wow and call it a night.

After Dorothy dropped Renny off at his apartment and was driving over to Forester to return Grant to his dorm room, Grant asked, "Do you know what today and tomorrow are?" After a pause during which she gave the matter some thought, Dorothy finally replied, "No, I guess I don't. What are they?" "Well," Grant proceeded to explain, "It was about this very time a year ago tonight that you loosened your bra on the family room couch and showed me your titties for the first time." "What?" Dorothy cried out in mock modesty, "I did that?" "Yes," Grant eagerly continued with evident glee in his voice, "And that's not even the worst of it. The following morning you took off your nightgown and showed me your pussy for the very first time." "I did?"

Dorothy said, again but this time with obvious growing pleasure. "You sure did! And I tell you, it's the loveliest thing in the whole universe, and ever since then I haven't been able to feel and look at her enough." "I can tell," Dorothy observed, "that I'll never have to worry about you forgetting an anniversary or birthday." "You sure won't," Grant confirmed, "just the opposite. But truly," he went on, now quite seriously, "that time a year ago on the bed in the front bedroom when you took off your nightgown for me and showed me the beauty between your thighs for the first time, Oh gosh! I can't even begin to tell you what that still means to me! From that time on I have known that I wanted you as my one and only woman! My Golly, it's so wonderful what has happened to us over this past year!" "It certainly is," Dorothy now seriously and lovingly mused, "It's been like a dream come true!"

September 20, 1973, Thursday

It was 10:50 in the evening. Carol had been in bed asleep for some time, and Grant and Dorothy were still up, sitting on the living room couch, but the former was deeply engrossed in looking over his Latin reading assignment for the next morning's class. He and Dorothy had just finished going over the notes in the textbook together, and Dorothy had also been looking up Latin words in Grant's little pocket Latin dictionary that he had had since his sophomore year in high school.

"How much longer do you think you'll be up?" Dorothy asked. "Oh," Grant replied, "a while yet. After looking over this Latin one more time, I thought that I'd also do some reading for Greek history." "Ok," Dorothy said, "In that case, I think I'll go off and take a bath; and when I'm done, I'll come back here and lie down on the couch to doze off until you're done. Then you can wake me up. Ok?" "Yeah, that sounds perfect."

Dorothy went into the master bedroom, removed her clothes, and then came into the main bathroom, where she went into the inner room to take a bath. As she ran the hot water, she not only rounded up her soap, wash cloth, and towel, but she also poured Avon Skin So Soft Bath Oil into the tub. Her constant swimming in chlorinated water dried out her skin; and consequently, she every so often took a bath like this in order to moisturize her body. After washing herself all over, she simply lay in the tub to allow her skin to benefit fully from the bath oil. While she was still soaking, she heard the outer bathroom door open, and then Grant was stepping through the inner door. "I have to pee," Grant explained. But when he was finished, he knelt beside the tub and began to feel her naked body. "My golly!" he exclaimed, "You feel so damn nice, and oh man! How wonderful you smell!" "That's because I'm soaking in Avon Skin So Soft." "Man! I love it! It's about as wonderful and exciting as your White Shoulders! Man! I really do love it!" "Ok, fella," Dorothy replied, "You'd better get back to your studying. We can play a little later when you're all done."

Dorothy finally emerged from the tub, dried herself off, and put on nothing except her pink quilted robe that Grant adored so much on her. Since Kitty was again staying with a friend on campus, Dorothy retrieved from the far bedroom a sleeping bag, came back into the living room, and unrolled it on the floor. She then lay down on the couch. In order to accommodate her, Grant moved himself to the very end, so that she could lie full-length on her back with her feet barely touching him. In order to keep her lower legs and feet from becoming cold, she threw an afghan over herself as a blanket. How wonderful this was for them both! Dorothy now softly drifted off into sleep near the one whom she loved and adored, but occasionally she was aware of his hand under the afghan and inside her robe, fondling and caressing her womanhood, and once or twice Grant even pulled back the afghan and opened up her robe and placed his mouth on her sex to kiss her and nuzzle her hair.

"Ok," she heard Grant saying, as his hand was gently petting her female sex, "I'm all done now." As Dorothy awoke, Grant was already spreading her thighs and had a face full of her female sex, kissing, licking, and actually devouring her with such tender zest that always gave her the most exquisite pleasure that she had ever experienced. Oh how she loved having his lips and tongue loving her there! "Don't be such an eager beaver," Grant said amid his loving, "Take your good sweet time. I could lick you like this all night long!" But despite his urging, the pleasure was so magnificent that her orgasm came within minutes; and as soon as she reached its pinnacle of perfection, she slid herself off of the couch and moved her body over to the sleeping bag that now served as their make-shift bed of love and gave her back more cushioning. Grant instantly lowered himself between her thighs, entered her, and added his orgasm to hers, after which he simply rode her steadily for quite some time until he reached a second orgasm. Only then did he finally withdraw himself from her. They then moved back up to the couch; and as Grant sat at her feet, his hand stayed under the afghan and inside her robe to caress and fondle her continuously. "My golly!" he whispered in awe, "Your pussy is always so wonderful, but with that Skin So Soft it's even somehow more magnificent!" Dorothy was thoroughly pleased with his pleasure in her. "You know," he went on, "if we could somehow cross-breed female pussy and cotton candy, what we'd have is what you just gave me, cotton candy pussy or cotton candy cunt."

Henceforth Avon Skin So Soft became a standard feature of their enjoyment of the physical pleasure of their perfect love.

October 5, 1973, Friday

Dorothy had received her first cassette tape from Dennis yesterday, and she was so excited that she immediately called Grant and Bob and arranged for them to come over to the house tomorrow night, so that they could hear it along with her and Kitty. Renny was unable to make it, because he and his roommate had already planned something else, and Lisa wished to borrow the tape to hear by herself at another time. Accordingly, in the late afternoon Dorothy drove over to the university and picked up the two fellows and brought them to the house. Following supper, which also included Carol, who soon left to spend the evening at a baby-sitting job, the four moved into the living room to listen to the cassette machine. The tape began with Dennis sitting on the airplane with other American students awaiting take-off from O'Hare Airport in Chicago. It then took them through a general survey of things that now formed Dennis' daily environment: his dorm room, his Austrian roommate Andreus, his fellow American students, his classes, etc. It was so interesting and exciting. When the two hour recording finally ended, the four all agreed that they would now proceed to make a reply to Dennis' recorded letter. Using Dorothy's cassette machine, they simply sat in a group there in the living room and took turns talking, holding a long-distance conversation with their absent friend. Once their excitement and most important messages had been recorded, things began to settle down, at which point Grant got out the guitar and began to play and sing, so that the recording was now a combination of on-going talk interspersed with their singing that they all knew he would thoroughly enjoy. Bob had also brought along his accordion; and although he was usually too shy to play, he now followed Grant's guitar playing with his own accordion music and singing. It turned out to be a wonderful evening!

October 6, 1973, Saturday

As soon as all five of them were up that morning, they congregated in the kitchen for breakfast. At this point Dorothy asked, "Ok, guys, I guess I'm the cook around here. So, let's see what I can rustle up for our breakfast." "Hey, Ma," Kitty challenged, "How about you try fixing breakfast blind-folded, pretending that you're blind?" "Yeah," seconded Bob enthusiastically, "That sounds like it would be fun." "Fun for who?" Grant pointedly asked in defense of his darling. "You don't think I could do that?" Dorothy asked. "Sure you can," Grant confidently responded, while at the same time Bob said in a humorously sneering way, "Naah, I bet she can't." "Oh yeah?" Dorothy replied, "We'll just see about that!"

"You can't just shut your eyes, Ma," Kitty suggested, "Because you'll probably open them sometimes without thinking about it. You'll need to cover them up somehow." "I know," Dorothy said, "I can use my swimming goggles and put tape over them." She then went into the bathroom, collected the goggles, and returned to the kitchen. Then after finding a roll of masking tape in a drawer, she carefully taped over the transparent parts of the goggles and put them on. "Ok, you guys, I'm ready to start."

As Dorothy now moved cautiously between the stove and refrigerator and began to fix a pan of eggs to be scrambled, she provided everyone with a running commentary of exactly what she was doing, and how she was managing to do it. Meanwhile, Kitty and Bob good-naturedly teased her, and Grant was always quick to interject comments favorable to his darling. Carol mostly laughed but added her own comments now and then too. The simple task of fixing breakfast had now been converted into an amusing enterprise in which Dorothy was perfectly happy to play along as the possible butt of the joke. Grant was so pleased to see that fun-loving child inside her eager to enjoy this novel experience and to do so with the full confidence of a mature and well-adjusted woman. After about twenty minutes of work, Dorothy had succeeded without mishap in setting the table, fixing toast for everyone, setting out margarine and jars of jam, and preparing the scrambled eggs. When she had carefully spooned portions of the eggs onto everyone's plates, she then said in an obvious note of triumph, "All right you guys, now tell me how you like your breakfast." Within moments of tasting the eggs they all agreed that Dorothy had passed the test with flying colors. "It really wasn't that hard," she commented. "All I had to do was to use just a bit more ingenuity, care, and concentration than I normally do." To Grant, who shared her pride in her success, this single episode typified so much of what made his darling such an extraordinary person: her willingness and ability to view things from other people's perspectives, her eagerness to take on new challenges, her consummate skill in doing virtually everything, and her childlike joy in embracing every single aspect of life.

October 20, 1973, Saturday

George had returned home from Newton yesterday afternoon, and then the three of them (George, Dorothy, and Carol) drove up to the Chicago area to attend the wedding of Patti Decker and John Crawford, the former being Bethany' one and only daughter and Sally's age. By now, of course, everyone in the family knew that Dorothy and George were not sleeping together, and Dorothy was accommodated in this regard when they all settled down to sleep Friday and Saturday evenings. But amid all the hubbub surrounding the big wedding George spoke with Dorothy's mother, her sister Ginger, and her husband Jim and received their commiserating support. Despite his hopes, however, their opposition to Dorothy's conduct had no effect upon her, other than to make her feel deeply hurt and rejected by those whom she loved very much, and whose support in this difficult time she wished so much to have.

Meanwhile, as Grant was to turn twenty-one, Kitty, Bob, and Lisa had a birthday party for him at the house. Around suppertime Lisa borrowed her parents' car, came over to Forester and Watson, picked Grant and Bob up, and they all joined Kitty at the house. Since Grant liked bananas so much, Kitty and Lisa made up a simple banana nut sheet cake that they all ate as the birthday cake. In fact, the banana theme to Grant's birthday had begun the day before when he returned to his dorm room and had his face assaulted with bananas suspended by strings from the ceiling that Lisa had fixed up. Their phallic symbolism was obvious and clearly alluded to how thoroughly and with what stamina Grant and Dorothy enjoyed sexual intercourse. The birthday celebration culminated with the three friends presenting Grant with a t-shirt, on back of which was written Marcus Unrealius Britannicus, a name that Kitty and Dennis had devised for him two years ago. The front of the t-shirt bore the title Peter the Great.

October 21, 1973, Sunday

Around 11:30 A.M. Grant's parents, his sister Patricia, and her son Troy (about to be three years old) arrived at Grant's room to take him out for Sunday dinner for his twenty-first birthday. When they showed up, they told him about what came to be known as the Saturday Night Massacre in which President Richard Nixon fired several high-ranking investigators of the Watergate scandal. It dominated the news all day long.

After sitting and chatting in his room for a while, Grant finally suggested that they have dinner at The Great Steak House, which was now becoming his and Dorothy's favorite restaurant as part of their beautifully unfolding life together.

After a very enjoyable and leisurely meal there, Grant conducted from the car a tour of the university campus that by now he knew extremely well from having walked it from end to end. They even parked the car in the library parking lot, so that he could take them on a walking tour of the Library with its reading rooms set aside for blind students, a place where he spent quite a bit of his time with his volunteer student readers. His parents and sister were very impressed by how well he traveled about on his own with his cane and seemed to know where everything was. This in part, of course, was due to his darling Dorothy, about whom and whose relationship with Grant they knew nothing at all at the time. Grant's relatives left shortly thereafter, but the event symbolized the reintegration of their family life, as well as Grant's successful return to his studies at the university.

Meanwhile, while Grant was occupied with his immediate family, the Patterson trio were on their way back down on the interstate, returning to University City from the wedding in Homewood. It turned out to be the very last formal occasion that George and Dorothy attended as husband and wife. Shortly after returning from this event, George seemed to give up any hope of a reconciliation with Dorothy, emptied the master bedroom of his clothes, and took them to Newton. A mere three years ago Grant had answered his dorm room door to find Dorothy and Carol there to greet him with a simple birthday present, and their appearance had so amazed him, because he then hardly knew this wonderful woman. Three years later, as he was turning twenty-one, her marriage with George was slowly but surely coming to an end, and their own life together was coming into being.

October 23, 1973, Tuesday

Since Grant's Monday schedule was filled with classes and an afternoon reader, they were not able to get together again until Tuesday, as they often did after Dorothy's swimming. But today was such a special day that Dorothy had decided to skip swimming, so that they could have virtually the entire morning together before Grant had to return to campus at 1:30 for his class on Greek history.

As Dorothy stopped at the side entrance to Forester on Walnut Street, Grant sat down in the car with a large box on his lap. "What's that?" Dorothy asked. "It's my birthday cake that my mother brought with them on Sunday. She had it made at a bakery. It looks really wonderful." "You mean you haven't eaten any of it yet?" "No." "Why not? I can't believe that, you pig!" Grant laughed, "Yeah, it is hard to believe. Isn't it? But I wanted to keep it whole until we got together to celebrate my birthday, so that we could then share it." Dorothy was genuinely touched.

"That's really nice," Dorothy responded, "And I appreciate you feeling that way, but you know, I've got my own birthday present for you when we get back to the house." "You do?" Grant asked. "I sure do," Dorothy sang sweetly. "I bet I can guess what it is." "Do you think so?" Dorothy replied teasingly.

After entering the house and being greeted by the four dogs, Grant placed the cake carefully on the kitchen table, and then he and Dorothy went through the laundry room and bathroom into the master bedroom. Kitty was again not in the house but somewhere on campus, but the two lovers were not alone, because a school friend of Carol's, Dan Livingston, who had been having serious trouble with his parents, had spent the night and was sleeping across the hall in the far bedroom. His bedroom door was still shut, and there was no sound coming from there. They therefore assumed that he was still sleeping soundly, but just in case, they moved about very quietly and shut the door between the master bedroom and the hall and also slid shut the door between the bedroom and the adjoining bathroom. Then to make absolutely sure that they could not be intruded upon, they moved the dresser slightly, so that its front edge was against the door going out into the hall, so that someone on the other side would not be able to open it. Having thus barricaded themselves safely inside the room, Dorothy proceeded to give Grant his birthday present for his twenty-first birthday.

She had chosen her attire for this morning carefully in consideration of Dan Livingston's presence and what she wanted to bestow upon Grant. She kicked off her shoes and was now wearing only her panties and bra underneath a simple dress. After reaching under the dress and sliding her panties down, she stepped out of them, lay down on the floor on her back, spread her knees wide apart, and said, "Ok, come get your birthday present."

After removing his own shoes, pants, and undershorts, Grant knelt down between her feet, ducked his head under her dress, took her lovely ass into his two hands, and filled his face full of her magnificent female sex. "We're going to have some birthday cake in a little while," Grant said, as he was fully engrossed in kissing and licking her Venus. "But what I love best is your pussy pie." After a few minutes of delicious eating, he arose and entered her vagina. They did not prolong their pleasure too much beyond his ejaculation, because they were still afraid that Dan might be waking up any moment. They then arose from the floor, moved the dresser back into place, and returned to the kitchen.

Now in the sweet afterglow of sex they had the rest of their birthday celebration. Dorothy opened the cake box and cut several pieces from it. "Cut a piece into smaller ones," Grant requested, "And we'll give them to the dogs, so that they can be part of the party we're having." Dorothy was delighted with the suggestion, cut one piece into four smaller ones, and placed them in the dog bowls. Needless to say, those parts of the cake vanished immediately to the sound of canine licking and the rattling of bowls as they were jostled about on the floor.

As the lovers sat in sweet companionship at the kitchen table enjoying their pieces of cake, Grant commented, "Well, today, at least in the eyes of the law, I am now a man, but you've made me a man in another way." "I have, huh?" Dorothy asked with sweet mischief in her voice. "You certainly have! I am your man, and what a woman you are!" Two months ago had been George's birthday, on which Dorothy had been so thankful not to have to give him her pussy as part of his birthday present. Today she had willingly and gladly bestowed that honor and privilege upon her young blind lover-boy as his very first birthday pussy for his twenty-first birthday.

Chapter 10

Forging the Beginning of their Love-Life

By the midpoint of the fall semester of 1973 Dorothy and Grant had been elevated by their love to a high plateau of happiness, where the sun shone on them almost ceaselessly. After being so unhappy in her marriage for so many years, Dorothy could not believe how happy she was, and that anyone could ever be so happy. The two spent as much time together as they possibly could, with Grant staying overnight at the house as frequently as his school schedule allowed. He was now beginning to make important strides toward becoming a college professor of ancient Greek and Roman history, and his darling Dorothy played an increasingly integral role in that process by assisting him in countless ways. Grant also increasingly became her man around the house, upon whom she could depend to assist her in many ways as well. Their life and loving now took on a regular routine of activities that began to weave their two lives seamlessly into one. As always, the one true barometer of their complete and total love for each other was its manifestation in the form of physical love-pleasure, which they enjoyed passionately and as frequently as they could.

As noted in the introduction, our human memories are such that we easily and almost entirely forget the routine activities and events in our lives, even ones that have occurred within the past few days, but what really stays firmly fixed in our minds are extraordinary activities and unusual events. Consequently, the reader may assume that the time covered in this chapter, a space of about nine months, was indeed fully occupied by countless routine activities and events shared by the loving couple in their usual sweet companionship that Grant, many years later, with few exceptions, could remember, but which, like the countless threads of a garment, were tightly woven together to form a strong and beautiful fabric of their love-life; whereas the extraordinary ones that he does remember are chronicled here to further trace the love history of Dorothy and Grant leading up to their marriage. So, if we extend the metaphor of weaving threads into fabric, their countless routine interactions and activities constituted the sound basic fabric, and the unusual events recounted here formed striking and beautiful patterns and images woven into that fabric to create a most magnificent tapestry.

October 30, 1973, Tuesday

As Dorothy drove home from Sweet Adeline practice, University City was just beginning to receive its first snow that fall. Carol and Kitty were still up along with Grant; and since Dorothy was excited to tell her lover-boy something in private, she came to him as he sat alone studying on the living room couch, and suggested that they take a little walk together. After Grant put on his coat, they went outside and started to walk across the open field where they always took the dogs. The snow was coming down gently, and it was a very delightful scene for them to enjoy together. As they walked arm in arm, Dorothy asked excitedly, "Guess what I just did?" "Gee," Grant replied in perplexity, "How would I know that." "Before coming home, I stopped off at a drug store and bought us some rubbers, so we can enjoy ourselves whenever we want and not have to do without intercourse on days when I think I'm fertile. Isn't that neat?" "Yeah, it sure is," Grant replied with both excitement and glee in his voice.

There had only been a few occasions, lasting a couple of days each month, when her temperature reading had kept them from having sexual intercourse, but they were always so desirous of one another that even an interruption of their sexual pleasure for only a day or two was hard for them to withstand. Even when they engaged in other forms of love-play, they were never fully satisfied, because it was good, but never as exquisite as having his penis and her vagina enjoying fully interactive intercourse.

October 31, 1973, Wednesday

After Carol had left for school, the lovers had some time to enjoy themselves before Grant had to be on campus for his morning classes; and

Since Dorothy was now at the midpoint of her menstrual cycle, they decided to try out one of the rubbers. They were in the double bed in the master bedroom. Dorothy was lying on her back with her nightgown hiked up, and Grant was kneeling between her legs with his mouth and face filled with her sex, kissing and licking her for his own enjoyment, as well as to give her an orgasm. As soon as she came, he sat up, unwrapped the rubber, rolled it onto his erection, and entered her vagina, which was very impatiently waiting to have her orgasm joined with his. The rubber was lubricated on the outside in order to assist penetration of the vagina, a thing which they certainly did not need, but since the room was somewhat cool because of the weather, the rubber's moisture felt rather chilly to her. In addition, once Grant ejaculated, his semen inside the rubber acted as an internal lubricant, so that when he attempted to continue his rhythmic thrusting, the rubber remained immovable inside her vagina, and his penis was simply having intercourse with the immovable rubber. Consequently, in order to continue their pleasure, Grant had to use another rubber. They therefore soon realized that using a rubber might be better than total abstinence, but it certainly could not replace the real thing that they had come to know and enjoy so much: Grant's unshielded penis plunging inside her vagina for as long as they wanted. Henceforth, they therefore employed rubbers only when they thought it absolutely necessary to avoid pregnancy.

November 9, 1973, Friday

It was 6:35 in the evening, and Dorothy was bringing Grant from campus back to the house to spend the weekend with her. As she steered the little blue Falcon from Lexington Avenue onto Center Street, just a few blocks from the house, Grant asked, "So, where is Carol right now?" "She's going to be gone all evening baby-sitting." "So, is Kitty the only one in the house right now?" "Yep!" Dorothy answered with mischievous cheer, knowing exactly what Grant was getting at. "Good!" he replied in a low earnest voice, "I really want to fuck your pussy!" "You do, huh?" she asked in pleased amusement. "I sure do!" "So what else is new?"

As they were parking the car in the garage and lowering its outer door, Grant remarked, "I've got an idea." "What's that?" "How about we begin our fucking right now in the back seat of the car. We've never done that before. Since Kitty's in her wheelchair, she won't come out here to see why we haven't come in yet." "Ok, that sounds like fun."

Grant opened the back door, and Dorothy knelt down on her elbows and knees across much of the back seat. After using his hands to pull her slacks and panties down to her ankles, Grant knelt behind her between her lower legs, felt her entire bare bottom and female sex, and exclaimed, "How can you be so damn beautiful!" "Just lucky, I guess," she replied, fully enjoying the compliment. "But boy!" Grant further exclaimed, "Ain't I the lucky one!" He then took his own pants and undershorts down and entered her vagina in their beloved equestrian manner. His hands gripped her hips as he thrust himself inside her vigorously for several minutes until he finally ejaculated. After he withdrew his penis, they restored their clothes to their proper positions and entered the house as if nothing at all had happened. It had been a truly nice bit of novel intercourse to begin their weekend together!

November 20, 1973, Tuesday

It was the middle of the afternoon, and the two lovers were sitting side by side on a couch in the otherwise deserted lounge of Forester Dormitory. Thanksgiving was two days away. The university had therefore all but shut down. As usual, Grant was one of the last students to leave, because he and Dorothy wanted to be together for as long as possible. Grant's father would be showing up in a couple of hours to bring him home and thereby to subject Dorothy and Grant to a brief separation of about five days. But no matter how brief the separation, the two lovers always dreaded being apart. Besides squeezing in their last bit of time together, Dorothy was reading to Grant from J. A. O. Larsen's book, *The Greek Federal States*. This was one of several books that had arrived recently from Blackwell Publishers of London, resulting from Dorothy assisting Grant in going through another Blackwell's book catalogue and placing an order for more books on ancient history, just as they had done for the first time one year ago. Dorothy's reading was important for Grant's research paper for his ancient Greek history class; and he intended to be busy all during the Thanksgiving break in working on the paper; and then when he returned on Sunday, Dorothy would again be available to assist him in the last stages of completing the assignment. When Dorothy now completed her reading of the book's treatment of the Arcadian League, Grant had her stop, and they simply sat together and talked quietly until it was getting close to the time when Grant's father might be arriving. The two lovers then arose, and Grant accompanied his darling out to her car in the parking lot, and their brief separation now began.

December 20, 1973, Thursday

Final exam week would be ending in two more days, and then the university would be shutting down for an entire month for the Christmas and semester break. As usual, Grant wished to stay on campus for as long as possible, so that he and his darling could spend as much time together as they could. In contrast, Grant's roommate had been eager to leave as soon as he could and had just left for home that afternoon, while Grant was taking an exam at the Rehab Center. Consequently, when he returned, he did so to a dorm room that would no longer be visited by his roommate. Since he had known this in advance, he had asked Dorothy to come visit him in his room for the sole purpose of enjoying sexual intercourse, because throughout the entire semester Dorothy had deemed it best to stay away from Grant's room so as to avoid any suspicions as to their possible relationship with one another. Furthermore, having such an erotic assignation now in his room was additionally safe, because only a few students were still residing in the building.

During this entire week Dorothy was working full time at the House of Flowers, a florist where she was called in to work during heavy business seasons, such as Christmas and Easter. So, after leaving work at 5:00, she went home and had supper with Carol. She then excused herself for a while on grounds of needing to help Grant with things in his dorm room. After arriving around 6:30, she and Grant wasted no time. Dorothy carefully removed all her clothes and laid them out neatly on the other bed, while he also undressed. They then lay down in his single bed and began enjoying themselves. As Grant caressed and kissed her sex in his usual manner of awe and admiration, he said, "I can now honestly say that you have the cutest cunt on campus, and I have the most extraordinary honor of kissing and fucking her."

But while fully engaged in sexual intercourse, they were rudely interrupted by the ringing of the telephone. When Grant withdrew himself from Dorothy's vagina and answered, he discovered Bob Snider on the other end of the line. "Hey, Grant," Bob said, "Is Ma there with you?" "Yeah, she is." "Can I talk with her?" "Yeah, just wait a second." As he turned to hand the phone to Dorothy, he explained, "It's Bob. He needs to talk with you." "Hello, Bob," Dorothy said, as she positioned herself on the foot of the bed near the telephone on the desk, sitting fully naked, "What's up?" "I'm sorry to bother you. But I called you at your house, and Carol answered and said that you'd be at Grant's room for a while. So, I thought I'd try to catch you there to see if I could leave some of my things at your house during the break, because my brother Jeff's car is not all that big." As Bob was talking, Dorothy tugged the blanket on the bed loose from the foot of the bed and wrapped it around her body to keep herself warm against the room's coolness. "Well, Bob," Dorothy replied teasingly, "It all depends. If you want me to come over right now to pick your things up, well, I'm kind of occupied right now. You see, Grant invited his girlfriend over to his room for a little fun in bed, and here I am right now, sitting on the bed, talking to you on the telephone with nothing on; and on top of everything, he doesn't even have enough heat in the place to keep a poor necked girl like me warm."

She deliberately mispronounced naked as necked in her delightful way of playing with words and expressions. It was a verbal manifestation of her entire youthful and childlike joy in everything. In addition, she clearly enjoyed advertising the fact to Bob that the two of them were having real fun in the nude as girlfriend and boyfriend in a dorm room like other college students, and she knew that what she said and how she said it greatly pleased Grant as well. She was his lovely college girlfriend, and how wonderful it was to enjoy her naked female beauty in his dorm room! She was also equally thrilled by the experience. Although she had missed her opportunity to attend college many years ago, now in her second life with Grant she was enjoying sexual pleasure that would have been the envy of many young college women half her age, and she had as her love partner a young college boyfriend who thought the world of her.

After hanging up the phone, the two lovers went back to their enjoyment of pleasure for quite some time until their bodies were finally sated with one another. They then arose, dressed, went out to the car, and drove over to Lisa's parents' house. Lisa would soon be flying to Austria to spend the Christmas break with Dennis. But before her departure to Austria, Lisa and Dorothy had things to exchange in connection with this upcoming trip. When they arrived, it was rather late in the evening, and Lisa's parents and her younger brother had already gone off to bed. Only Lisa was still up waiting for them. They sat down in the living room and chatted briefly in hushed voices so as not to disturb anyone.

"I bet you're really excited about your trip and seeing Dennis again," Dorothy commented. "Lisa beamed and giggled as she replied, "Oh man! Am I ever! I can hardly wait!" "That's really great! Just be sure to set aside a little bit of your time to make a tape to us," Grant said. "We can probably squeeze that in among other things," Lisa replied suggestively. "Ok, Lisa," said Dorothy, as she withdrew a small package from her purse, "Here's our Christmas present for Dennis." "What is it?" Lisa asked, as she received it in her hand. "It's a peter heater," Dorothy said, smiling broadly. "It's what?" Lisa asked laughingly. "A peter heater," Dorothy repeated, "Grant gave me the idea. It's just a tube-like thing that I knitted, about the length of a guy's dick. We thought that Dennis would really get a kick out of it." "Oh man!" Lisa answered, "Will he ever! And I won't tell him what it is until he's opened it and tries to figure out what it is. It should be real fun!" They all chuckled together mischievously. "Ok, Big D, here's the check that Dennis needs to have deposited in his account." After placing it carefully in her purse, she and Grant arose, said their goodbyes, wished her a safe and wonderful trip, and left.

Dorothy now drove to the Lincoln Bank to drop the check into an overnight deposit box, so that it would be processed first thing tomorrow morning. But as they drove into the parking lot, Dorothy exclaimed, "Wow! You wouldn't believe the size of the mounds of snow here in the parking lot!" Let me show you." After they had dropped the envelope containing Dennis' check into the box, Dorothy led Grant to the bottom of a mound of snow that a snow plow had scooped up to clear out the area. "It must be ten feet high or so," Dorothy commented. Grant now began to scramble his way to the top. "Man!" he exclaimed, "You're right. These things really are big!" As he reached the top, Dorothy also made her way halfway up the mound, and then the two enjoyed shrieking like children as they slid back down to the pavement. After repeating this amusing activity several more times, they returned to the car; and as Dorothy drove them back to the house, Grant commented, "You know, you're really something." "I am, huh?" she asked with pleasure. "You really are. No wonder I can never think of you as being in your forties. You have the spirit of a child or teenager in how you view and enjoy everything." "I do, huh?" "You sure do!" Grant emphasized as he reached across the seat and patted and squeezed her right thigh.

December 22, 1973, Saturday

As Grant sat anxiously on the edge of his bed, a gentle knocking that he had been awaiting finally sounded upon his dorm room door. "Come in," he said in response. The door opened, and Dorothy stepped in, clad in her polar bear coat. It was 6:45 A.M., and Dorothy was on her way to work all day long at The House of Flowers, and by 8:00 or so Grant's father would be here to take him and all his things back to Fairmont for the Christmas break. After dropping him off at Forester yesterday morning on her way to the florist shop, Grant had spent the entire morning studying for his last final exam before taking it at the Rehab Center in the afternoon. He had then chosen to spend his last night here in his dorm room, because he needed to pack up everything. But even so, they had agreed to have this last rendezvous at his dorm room.

As soon as she entered the room, Dorothy stepped to the right to Grant's roommate's bed, took off her coat, and began to quickly undress. When she was totally naked, she turned to face him as he sat also naked on his bed, and said, "Ok, fella, let's get this show on the road!" "That's fine with me," he replied, "I'm all ready," as he used his hand to waggle his erection at her. Dorothy lay down on her back in Grant's bed; and after he had caressed her spread sex and had kissed and licked her there several times, he lay down between her thighs, entered her vagina, and began their last round of intercourse for the year 1973. "Thanks for the Christmas present," Grant said. "What Christmas present?" Dorothy asked in mock innocence. "This wonderful pussy," he replied, "I can't imagine ever having a better Christmas present than this." "You're quite welcome, but you know, your cock ain't so bad either. You're really not too bad for a young whipper-snapper. I think I'll keep you around a while." "Gee, I hope so." Unfortunately, their intercourse could not last too long, because Dorothy had to be at work very soon. Consequently, after about ten minutes, he withdrew himself from her vagina; they both quickly dressed, and he walked her out to her car, where they bade each other a fond farewell. The fall semester was ending along with the calendrical year, and how utterly marvelous they had been for the lovers; and they had concluded it with two very special sessions of intercourse in Grant's dorm room, the only two that they would ever be fortunate enough to enjoy in Forester.

January 6, 1974, Sunday

It was around 11:30 in the morning, and Grant's parents had just left to return to Fairmont after bringing him back to University City and leaving him here at Renny's apartment. Classes would not begin again for another two weeks, and the dorms would not be open until the beginning of next week. Consequently, since Dorothy and Grant wanted to be reunited again as soon as possible, they had asked Renny before the Christmas break to give Grant his apartment key, so that he could return early and stash all his things in the apartment while spending all his free time at the house with Dorothy. Grant, of course, had told his parents that he wanted to return early in order to get lots of reading done before classes actually began (which was true enough), and that he would be staying with a friend in this apartment for a few days before the dorms were actually open. But as soon as he and his parents had succeeded in lugging all his things four floors up to Renny's apartment and had said their goodbyes, Grant located the telephone and gave his darling a ring.

When her lovely feminine voice answered the telephone with that rich and wonderful "Hello" that always thrilled him, he said, "Hello, Dorth. I'm here safe and sound in Renny's apartment." "Oh, very good," she replied cheerfully, "I'll come over and get you as soon as I can, but right now I'm standing at the stove with the kitchen phone, and I'm watching our pork chops finish cooking for Carol and my Sunday dinner. Do you mind waiting a little until we've eaten?" "No, not at all. That would be fine. I can start listening to a tape or something until you get here, but I do have one important request to make." "You do, huh?" Dorothy asked with amusement in her voice and obviously expecting something sexual. "Yeah, when you come here, would you mind not wearing anything under your dress? I want to be able to feel you as soon as you step through the door." "I can probably swing that," she replied with smug satisfaction, as if his request was not all that unusual.

After they hung up, Grant opened up his reel-to-reel tape recorder, located his tapes of J. B. Bury's *A History of Ancient Greece*, and stretched out on the living room couch to listen to his narrative of Greek history for the fourth century B.C., because he would be studying that specific period in a history colloquium this spring semester. As he was relaxing and awaiting the arrival of his sweetheart, Dorothy was setting the kitchen table for two, using her mixer to whip up a batch of mashed potatoes (or smashed potatoes, as Dorothy called them in her cute way of distorting words), and getting the other dishes of food on the table for their Sunday meal. Then after mother and daughter had eaten, they cleared the table, and Dorothy went into the master bedroom to dress herself for their reunion.

As soon as Dorothy stepped through the apartment door from the outside cold, Grant was there to take her into his arms, but after embracing her in her polar bear coat, his hands went under it and her dress, and he was delighted to discover that she was wearing thigh-high hose but nothing else. As they embraced and kissed, his hands caressed and admired her bare bottom and love-front, but since they were both ravenous for one another from their two weeks of separation, they quickly broke their embrace, walked down the hall to Renny's room, threw off all their clothes as quickly as they could, dove into the bed, and began enjoying intercourse immediately. As soon as Grant's penis entered Dorothy's vagina, they both began to moan and convulse as if they were experiencing pain instead of the most exquisite love-pleasure. It was so incredibly intense! What a glorious way for them to begin the new year together! But since Dorothy was supposed to have been coming over simply to pick Grant up to bring him back to the house, they ended their enjoyment after about a half an hour, so that Carol would not regard her mother's absence as anything unusual.

The two lovers then spent the afternoon in tranquil companionship in the house, telling one another of all that they had done over the past fifteen days. "But you know," Dorothy said, as she changed the subject, "What has really been on my mind since you've been gone is the thought that I really must go to work full time, so that Carol and I have enough money to cover our expenses. George hasn't been sending us all that much, and our savings are quickly being used up." "I really hate to hear that," Grant replied, "And I wish that there was something that I could do to help you, but there isn't." "I know, and I understand all that. We've talked about it before. I worked full time before Sally was born and supported George as he was getting his architecture degree, but I've always hated the idea of having to work, at least full time, as long as any of the kids need me at home." "I agree with you about that, but if it's any consolation, my mother was always at home with my sister and me until we were both in school; and then she began to work full time, because we needed the income; and it really wasn't bad at all for my sister and me. We both turned out fine. Besides, it's not as if Carol is in the second grade or anything. She's almost out of high school and should be able to do just fine if you're not here as soon as she's out of school in the afternoon." "Yeah, you're right, but I also just feel so creepy about having to go back to work after so many years of not working. Will anyone want to employ someone like me?" "Well, if they have any brains and can see how charming and efficient you are, they will." "Oh, you! Flattery will get you nowhere." "No, I mean it! If you're applying for some job for which you are qualified, you have such excellent skills in working with people that someone is going to notice and offer you a job." "Well, I just wish you were the person about to interview me. Then I wouldn't be nervous." Grant reached out and touched her. He did not embrace her for fear of Carol seeing them. "Sweetheart, please try not to get yourself all worked up about this. I know that's easy for me to say, but really all you need to do is simply be yourself, and that is so magnificent. Someone will see that and will want to hire you. That's all you had to do to make me fall in love with you!" "What's that?" "Simply being yourself! You are so dazzling and wonderful!"

After enjoying their usual Sunday supper of popcorn, Grant asked Dorothy to read to him from Donald Kagan's *The Outbreak of the Peloponnesian War*, which she gladly did. This was one of the books that Grant had purchased from Blackwell's about two months ago. By the time that they had completed their reading session, Carol had gone to bed and was sound asleep, the lovers therefore settled down on the family room couch and closed out their quiet, enjoyable evening by listening to the premiere broadcast of *The CBS Radio Mystery Theater*. It began at 11:06, following the news on the hour and ended at midnight. As Dorothy had been listening to the radio in the kitchen during the past few mornings to catch the news and weather, this new radio show had been much touted, and she thought that they would both enjoy hearing this together, which, of course, they did. Dorothy had grown up during the era of entertainment shows on the radio, such as *The Green Hornet*, *The Lone Ranger*, *The Shadow*, and *Inner Sanctum*. She therefore had been looking forward to this broadcast; whereas ever since losing his eyesight, Grant, like so many blind people, preferred radio to television. Henceforth, whenever they happened to be together at this time of the night, they usually turned on the radio and listened to this program.

January 8, 1974, Tuesday

It was the early afternoon, and Grant was standing beside his darling as she was looking through a rack of winter coats in University City's largest department store. As much as they both liked her polar bear coat, it was beginning to show signs of age. Dorothy had therefore decided that the after Christmas sale was the best time to replace it. Carol would return to school tomorrow, but since it was cold and icy outside, she had stayed in the house all day yesterday and the same so far today. Therefore, in order for the two lovers to have some time alone, they had gone off shopping yesterday afternoon to buy groceries, just as they were shopping for coats today, but before they actually did the shopping on both these days, they had first gone over to Renny's apartment, quickly undressed, and had enjoyed themselves for quite some time before dressing and doing the shopping that they were supposed to be doing. So, they were standing there together in the department store in the sweet afterglow of magnificent intercourse.

As Dorothy tried on each coat, she not only looked at herself in a mirror, but she also had Grant give his opinion, which he did after running his hands all over the coat and seeing how it felt and looked on her. Dorothy eventually found two coats that she and Grant both really liked. One was a blue cashmere coat, and the other was a brown camel-hair coat. Both fit her very well; and even though Grant preferred the cashmere to the camel-hair because of its smoother texture, Dorothy finally decided that since both were on sale and could go well with different clothes, she would simply buy them both. Not only did Dorothy return home triumphantly from this shopping expedition because of what she had purchased, but the lovers were elated by sharing this ordinary experience that was rendered extraordinary by their love for one another. Grant had relished being alone with his woman and serving as her one and only man; and Dorothy had enjoyed having him with her and seeking his admiration and approval in what she chose to buy.

January 11, 1974, Friday

It was 9:30 in the morning; and as Dorothy moved around the house from room to room, putting things in order, she kept glancing out the windows to watch Grant. Since they had received a few inches of snow during the night, the long, curving driveway was covered over in snow once again and was likely to develop into a hard-packed icy surface if not removed right away. As soon as he had arisen this morning, Grant had dressed and had begun work on the driveway with the snow shovel. He had already been out there about two hours and was fairly close to done. Dorothy's heart swelled with pride as she beheld her blind love-mate working so efficiently. She truly loved having this man around the house. She was still wearing her nightgown, pink quilted robe, and slippers and would be sure to show him how very much she appreciated his labor when he came back inside and was fully rested. Since Carol was back in school, they could finally take their time in enjoying their love-play.

When Grant finally came into the family room after nearly another hour of shoveling, Dorothy stepped out of the laundry room where she was folding clothes, and asked, "Are you tired?" "Yeah, a little, but not too bad. I'll probably have lots of sore muscles tomorrow. I've always enjoyed working like that out in the cold and in the snow. There's something really satisfying about it, but since I haven't done that sort of thing in a while, I'll have quite a few muscles that haven't been worked so much in that way, and they'll be telling me about it tomorrow morning."

By now Grant had his outer gear removed and was ready to leave the doorway area of the family room. "I've got an idea," Dorothy said. "What's that?" Grant asked. "Since you're probably tired now and could use a rest, how about we settle down on the living room couch and make a tape to Dennis and Lisa?" "That sounds great!" A few days earlier they had received a cassette from Dennis and Lisa in Austria, describing how much fun they were having during their Christmas break there. But thus far Dorothy and Grant had not yet begun making a reply.

They now snuggled together on the living room couch, and Dorothy wrapped an afghan around them to give them additional warmth and intimacy. She then placed her cassette machine on record, and the two lovers began talking to their friends. They both enjoyed the fact that the two of them were sitting together so lovingly as they made this tape, and they wanted their two friends to receive the message, loud and clear, that Dorothy and Grant were a genuine couple, bound together into one by their complete and total love. After talking for more than an hour, they arose to have lunch, and then they went off to the master bedroom to spend the first half of the afternoon in enjoying the physical pleasure that their love gave them in such abundance.

January 12, 1974, Saturday

It was nearly midnight, and Carol was by now sound asleep in the middle bedroom. Dorothy and Grant were cozily snuggled in bed together in his twin bed in the front bedroom. Since it was quite cold outside, and the thermostat was set at 67 degrees to conserve energy, the bedroom was on the chilly side. The narrowness of the twin bed kept the two lovers close to one another. Only their heads were not well covered by the bedding, and their faces felt the cool air of the room, while their bodies under the sheet, blanket, and heavy bedspread felt so nice and toasty warm. It was such a nice contrast, further heightened by the fact that the heat of their two bodies was fused into one, just as their love was merging their two lives into one.

They were engaged in what was now becoming their usual bedtime custom of spending some time in bed talking and loving before parting company for the night. They were lucky that Carol was not only a heavy sleeper, but she also seemed to need more sleep than either one of them, so that they could usually stay up at least an hour or so after she had gone to bed to have their secret tender loving time like this and still be able to be up in the morning at the same time that Carol arose.

While they were still talking, Grant lifted up Dorothy's nightgown and began to caress and fondle her sex. The heat of their bodies had Dorothy so warm, and the heat made her flesh seem so flawlessly smooth, even more so than its usual lovely complexion. In fact, her flesh seemed to glow under his touch. Grant therefore took his time in admiring the feel of her thighs and love-delta, before he removed his undershorts and moved his body, so that they could configure themselves into their sidesaddle position. Dorothy responded automatically in moving her own legs as this position required. Grant then caressed her fully spread sex that also seemed to have an extra aura of beauty caused by the heat of their bodies. As usual, his penis entered her vagina smoothly, because she was wet and dilated with desire for him, just as he was big and hard with desire for her. But the truly awesome thing about this particular sexual encounter tonight was how the heat of Dorothy's vagina and love-honey that now greeted his manhood gave pleasure even more exquisite than what they always enjoyed. The cocoon of heat from their two bodies that stood in such sharp contrast to the chilly air of the room enhanced the pleasure of their two merged sexes and their delight in their usual bedtime intercourse. It was such a shame that they could not yet spend the entire night in bed together, enjoying the loving comfort of one another's touch and warmth as they slept.

January 14, 1974, Monday

It was 10:20 in the morning, and Grant was sitting on the toilet lid in the bathroom adjoining the master bedroom, while Dorothy was standing at the sink and looking into the mirror to apply makeup and to fix her hair. She had noticed an ad in yesterday's newspaper for a bank teller at the Lincoln Bank, and she was scheduled for an interview at 11:00. Grant was doing his best to keep her from being nervous and insecure by pointing out all her relevant job experience, as well as what he regarded as her incomparable ability to put people at ease and to dazzle them with her charm and grace. "I really wish that I could come along," he finally said, "but that certainly wouldn't do." "No, darling it wouldn't, but I'll be ok."

After arriving at the bank ten minutes ahead of her interview, she sat in a customer area until a man came out to conduct her into his office, "Hi, you're Dorothy Patterson, I take it?" he asked. "Yes, I am," Dorothy replied cheerfully with her lovely smile. "I'm John Dickson, one of the bank's vice presidents. I'm pleased to meet you." She returned his greeting, as they shook hands. "Well, let's come into my office, and we'll talk there."

The interview covered the predictable subjects. Why was she applying for this job? What relevant work experience did she have? As Dorothy answered these and related follow-up questions, John Dickson observed her closely and was very impressed with what he saw. There was no doubt that she was well qualified for the position, and she would likely be a reliable employee, given the fact that she needed to work full time to support herself and her daughter, but what really impressed him was how she conducted herself. In addition to being a strikingly beautiful woman who knew how to make herself look very appealing, she had a most charming smile and seemed to have a very easy manner. He was sure that she would be excellent in dealing with customers. At the end of the interview he finally remarked, "I'll be getting back to you in a few days to let you know what we've decided. We'll probably have several more people applying for the position."

January 18, 1974, Friday

Dorothy and Grant spent the morning moving all his things from Renny's apartment to his new dorm room in Watson Hall. Bob would be arriving on Sunday, the day before classes began; and the two would be roommates for the spring semester. They had finally succeeded in getting their housing preferences acknowledged and implemented by the university housing bureaucracy. After they had everything put away on Grant's side of the room, they drove over to The Great Steak House for a nice lunch, and then they returned home and enjoyed themselves in bed until it was time for Carol to come home from school.

Around 3:45 in the afternoon the telephone rang; and when Dorothy answered it, she found herself talking again to John Dickson from the Lincoln Bank, who was telling her that they were pleased to offer her a job as teller at the bank if she were still interested. She was surprised and very pleased, and those feelings were evident in her voice when she replied, "Of course I'm interested. When do you want me to start?" "Well, you can start first thing next week, 8:00 Monday morning." Then after repeating the conditions of the position in terms of hours and salary, he congratulated her and expressed his belief that she would turn out to be a most valuable employee.

"Hey! I got the job!" she exclaimed excitedly as she hung up the telephone. "See," Grant said as he smiled at his darling, "I told you that you didn't have anything to worry about." "Oh I'm so pleased and relieved!" "I am too," Grant responded, "But I'm also very proud of you and know that you'll be the most beautiful and well-liked teller in the whole damn bank!" "You're prejudiced!" she answered with obvious pleasure. "Maybe I am, but whatever it is, I know you extremely well, and that's why I feel the way I do about you and how things will work out for you there at the bank." "It's really neat that my first day there will also be your first day of classes, and I can drop you off at your dorm room on my way to work." "That will work out just swell."

January 26, 1974, Saturday

Grant had spent the entire morning and afternoon studying, while Dorothy had done all sorts of chores around the house. Then after supper, Carol had left to spend the entire evening baby-sitting, so that the two lovers now had the house to themselves for the next several hours, which they intended to spend entirely in bed. Dorothy had just completed her first week at the bank. When she left work yesterday at the end of the work day, she had driven directly over to Watson and picked Grant up, so that he could spend the entire weekend with her at the house. Then, as they had done this past Monday, she would take him back to his room on her way to work, and this would now be part of their weekly schedule for the semester.

After letting the dogs outside for a while and then checking all the locks on the doors, they walked into the bathroom adjoining the master bedroom, so that Dorothy could use the toilet. As she sat there, Grant knelt at her feet, removed her shoes, socks, slacks, and panties, while Dorothy pulled off her top. Grant then unfastened her bra and was thrilled, as always, to see her breasts emerge beautifully bare. After carefully wiping her vulva, she stood up, but Grant did not move. Instead, his hands went around her bottom, and he turned his face up toward her. She responded by bending over; and as she did, her breasts swayed downward and forward, and Grant took her right one into his mouth to suck. "Uummmm!" was his only response. He eventually released her right breast and took her other one into his mouth; and after giving them equal attention, his mouth trailed downward and finally stopped at her love-delta, where he nuzzled his lips in the V of her lovely hair, kissed her sex, and inserted his tongue inside her vulva to lick her. "Oh my! You smell like sweet pussy!" he nearly growled with delight. "All for you!" she responded with such teasing sweetness in her voice. Only then did he arise and allow her to walk beautifully naked into the bedroom, where she pulled back the covers of the bed and slid under them. Grant was still wearing his undershorts. He walked around to the other side of the bed, ducked head-first under the covers, and was soon crouched between her spread thighs. "How about I enjoy some delicious honey pie, and you have a climax?" he asked before taking her sex into his mouth and enjoying her vulva and vagina thoroughly with his lips, tongue, and even his nose. "My golly!" Dorothy said with awe and pleasure, "That always feels so wonderful! It's like heaven!" "It certainly is!" Grant agreed, as he continued adoring her womanhood with his mouth, "And don't you ever worry about me. I enjoy it as much as you do, believe me! You can have as much of this as you want, but you always come too fast, and I don't get to lick you as much as I would like."

After she had fully enjoyed an orgasm, Grant asked, as he still lay lovingly with her sex in his face, "Where's the vaginal foam?" "It's on the left corner of the dresser." After using rubbers for the past few months during the few days of the midpoint of Dorothy's menstrual cycle, she had decided to have them try using vaginal cream as a contraceptive. They had tried it for the first time last night, and they had both enjoyed it much more than rubbers, because it allowed them to have fully natural intercourse. Dorothy had shown Grant how to fill the plastic syringe from the bottle of foam, and of course, he had asked to have the honor of inserting it inside her vagina and injecting her with the foam. Tonight he would perform the entire procedure unassisted.

After sliding out from under the covers, he went over to the dresser and filled the syringe. He then came over to her side of the bed, pulled the covers down to expose her nakedness, and used his left hand to guide into the proper position the syringe that he was holding in his right hand. "My goodness! Your cunt is so beautiful! I never can get enough looking!" "You can't, huh?" "No, I sure can't." Then after slowly and gently inserting the syringe inside her vagina, he depressed the plunger, and Dorothy could feel the coolness of the foam deep inside her, but it would soon be warmed by her body and their intercourse. Grant withdrew the syringe, pulled the covers back over his naked woman to keep her warm, and walked into the adjoining bathroom, where he took apart the syringe, washed the two pieces off carefully, and laid them out on a towel on the top of the clothes hamper to dry. When he stepped back into the bedroom, he was naked; and as he approached, Dorothy eyes never left the sight of what she called his beautiful red cock. He again pulled back the covers, lay himself between her thighs, and entered her vagina.

After several gentle trusts, he kept his penis motionless inside her and asked, "How about squeezing me?" Dorothy gladly obliged by contracting her vagina's muscles around his penis three times. This was something that they had recently discovered. "Man oh Man!" Grant said urgently, "That feels so good!" In response to the pleasure that she had just inflicted upon him, he resumed his thrusts, but then he stopped and made the same request. When Dorothy caressed his manhood again three times by contracting her vagina's muscles, Grant began to increase the vigor of his plunging. "I swear," he said, "It feels like you have a feather inside your pussy and you're using it to tickle the tip of my pecker while you're caressing his length." "Oh yeah?" Dorothy asked in real pleasure at the compliment. "It sure does. I think I'll start calling that your pussy feather. Would you mind that?" "Not at all! That would be very nice!" she replied in evident joy.

As they enjoyed intercourse, Grant lowered his mouth to hers, and they began to kiss passionately. Soon they had opened their mouths, and their tongues were engaged in their own form of intercourse in tandem with their sexes. It was now as if their physical pleasure was flowing in a completed circuit from their sexes through their bodies, up to their mouths, back down through their bodies, and to their sexes again. Over the past eleven months they had both been engaged in the thrilling adventure of discovering new ways in which they could enhance the fine art of giving and receiving exquisite physical pleasure that resulted from their perfect love.

Eventually the intense ardor of their physical loving and their accompanying love talk subsided and gave way to a more leisurely pace of erotic love-play; and as their passions cooled down even more, their talk, as it usually did, became serious conversation in which the perfectly harmonious union of their bodies helped to bring about a similar perfect union of their minds and sharing of their innermost thoughts. "You know," Dorothy said, "when I was having to endure sex with George, I used to ask myself why God had created sex between men and women, because it seemed like such a horrible and cruel thing; and it really is when the sex is not accompanied with love, but since we've been having intercourse like this, I can't imagine anything else more wonderful between a man and a woman. Isn't that something!" "It sure is," Grant replied, "And what we have and enjoy can't be improved upon!" "Boy! That's for sure!"

As they talked, they were configured into the sidesaddle position, and Grant was causing his penis to twitch inside her. That was his counterpart to Dorothy contracting her vagina around him. "That feels good too!" Dorothy commented. His right hand was also caressing her hair and sex and feeling her vagina enveloping his penis. "I'm taking this anthropology course now to fulfill part of my biology requirement," Grant began, "It's a rather advanced Anthropology class full of pre-med and veterinarian students. I might be in a bit over my head, but I figure that I'll learn a lot of things, and it's much better than taking some stupid Biology 101 course. Anyway, it's mostly about human and population genetics, and it really is interesting stuff. Today I was reading about what biologists call imprinting. It's known to occur mostly among birds. When one of these baby birds is born, it is genetically programmed to recognize as its parents the first creatures that it sees when it comes out of the shell. So, if a human happens to be there when a chicken or goose comes out of its shell, the animal will have that person's image imprinted upon its brain to recognize him or her as its parent, and the animal will follow that person around as if he's the parent." "Huh," Dorothy commented, "That really is interesting." "Yeah, it really is, but I wanted to tell you about it, because it seems to me to encapsulate how I feel toward you." "How's that?" "Well, please don't be offended, because I really mean this in the most positive sense, but when you took off your nightgown and showed me your pussy for the very first time a year ago on September 19, it's was as if I was somehow imprinted by the image of your lovely cunt, so that I would want you and only you as my one and only woman. I really mean it! Obviously, I'm not like a bird, or at least I don't think so." "You aren't, huh?" They both laughed. "But you're so wonderful as a person. I already knew that; and somehow when I beheld the beauty of your pussy, it was as if everything just fell perfectly into place for me in terms of me wanting you and only you. I probably haven't said it very well, and I hope that what I've said about imprinting doesn't bother you." "Grant, of course not. What you've said is really quite beautiful."

January 30, 1974, Wednesday

As Grant and Dorothy were clearing away the supper dishes, he asked, "I've got a project that I would like you to think about doing." "Uh-oh!" Dorothy replied ominously but humorously, "That's sounds like something I should avoid." Then after several seconds she said cheerfully, "Ok, let's hear it." Grant proceeded. "Well, you remember how last semester you used onion-skin paper and my tracing wheel to draw a few maps for me, so that I could learn some basic geography in studying Greek history?" "Yeah," Dorothy replied in a funny exaggerated way. "Well, I was wondering if you could do the same thing, only this time in making a much more detailed map of Greece, because I need to have something much more detailed than what you drew last fall." "Ok, we probably could do that."

By now they were finished loading the dishwasher, and Dorothy had started up the machine. "That would really be great," Grant enthused, "Let me show you what you'd be drawing." They went into the living room and sat side by side on the couch. Grant reached for his backpack that he always brought over to the house. He now pulled out a large flat book. "This is a book that came in my most recent order from Blackwell's. It's an atlas of the ancient world; and if you look at the contents," he now handed the book to Dorothy, "You'll find a map of Greece." After looking it over, Dorothy finally located the right map that showed mainland Greece and the surrounding islands.

"My golly!" she exclaimed, "Is this thing ever detailed! Do you want all of these places drawn in?" "Well, probably not all, but many of them, but we could start off with some and then add things as we go." "Boy! This would be a lot of work!" "Yeah, I know it would be, and I was even afraid to even ask you about it, because I know that it would be." "Well, you know me. I don't mind a challenge, but we're going to need some bigger onion-skin paper. These pages must be legal size, and then we can give it a try." "Ok, I'll go over to the bookstore and buy some legal size onion-skin paper. I'm sure they have it." "We're also going to need some kind of big tablet to draw your braille map on, something like an artist's tablet, because this map is as big as two legal size sheets placed side by side." "Ok, I'll see if I can buy a tablet like that too at the bookstore."

After coming to an agreement on undertaking this ambitious project, Grant spent the rest of the evening studying, and Dorothy occupied herself with various things. Since she had begun her full-time job at the bank, she had been forced to discontinue her beloved swimming, but she was still attending Sweet Adelines every Tuesday evening. Although she missed swimming, she regarded herself as more than compensated by her love with Grant. He was not only spending the entire weekend with her now, but he had his readers schedule so arranged that he could come over and spend Wednesday night at the house as well, and she dropped him off at his room on her way to work Thursday morning. Since Kitty Carpenter had returned to her home in Ohio, Bob Snider was no longer coming over all the time. The only people who now regularly occupied the house were herself, Carol, and Grant; and Dorothy truly loved the way in which they were developing a sweet domestic home life.

February 2, 1974, Saturday

Once again, Grant had spent the entire day studying, while taking occasional breaks for lunch, joining Dorothy in taking the dogs for a walk, and then supper. Since Carol was at home all day long, even after supper, Grant simply made a virtue out of necessity by continuing his schoolwork even after she had gone off to bed. Dorothy was dozing and stretched out on the living room couch, and Grant was sitting at her feet. When he finally finished looking over his Latin one more time, he awoke his lady-love. "Hey, darling," he said as he gently touched her between her thighs, "I'm finally done studying for the night." "Ok," she responded, and then announced, "I think I'd like to take a bath tonight before going to bed." "Would you like me to help you with that?" Grant asked. "Of course! I love it when you pamper me like that! Go into the bathroom in the hallway and wait for me. I'll be there right away."

As Grant was standing beside the two sinks, the door opened quietly, and Dorothy stepped inside. When he reached his hands out to her, he encountered her naked body. She had gone into the master bedroom and undressed. As she lay her pink quilted robe and cotton nightgown on top of the vanity cabinet to put on later, Grant's hands ran over her nakedness, and they continued to do so as she moved about to collect her soap, wash cloth, and towel. "Ok," she whispered, "Why don't you start the water for me." He obeyed. He went into the other little room, knelt down on the floor, and began to run the water, using his hand to test the temperature. While he was thus engaged, Dorothy stepped through the door, stood beside him, bent over, and poured Avon Skin So Soft into the running water. As she was bent over the tub, Grant used his right hand to admire her bottom and sex that were so perfectly revealed by her posture. She then placed her left hand on his shoulder to help ease herself down into the tub.

"Why don't you let me wash all of you," Grant asked, "except for your face?" "Ok." As she sat up in the tub, Dorothy soaped up her wash cloth and proceeded to wash and rinse her face. "Ok, I'm done, and you can now do the rest of me." Grant did, with tremendous pleasure, washing her back and then her breasts and belly. Dorothy then moved herself up onto her knees, so that he could wash her bottom, hips, love-front, and sex. He did not bother using the washcloth. Instead, he used his hands, so that he gave them both the pleasure of him handling and fondling her nakedness. She then lay down full-length in the tub and let him wash her legs and feet.

"Now I'll just lay here for a while and soak in the Skin So Soft, but if you want, you can use that tumbler in the corner at my feet to keep pouring water over me to keep me warm." "Sure. I'd love to do that." Grant now began to scoop up water in the tumbler and then pour the water gently over her body, and his free hand was touching her gently everywhere as well. As he poured the water onto her, he did so by first pouring it upon her breasts, followed by a second tumbler of water on her love-delta. It not only kept her warm, but the water served to arouse her sexually.

"You know," he began, "when you bent over to pour the Skin So Soft into the tub, you looked so beautiful." "I did, huh?" Dorothy replied with genuine satisfaction of having pleased her man. "You sure did!" he answered with awe and desire in his voice. "I always love the way you look when you're on your hands and knees when we fuck in our equestrian manner, and you looked a lot like that just then, but it was somehow a bit different and oh so magnificent! Whenever you bend over like that, would you mind taking your time, so that I can get a good long look at you?" "Ok. That's no problem, because, you know, I like it too." "Golly, Dorth!" he said again with such earnest desire in his voice, "You look so lovely like that! You'd even give a eunuch an erection for a week if he saw you like that!" "I would, huh?" "You sure would. Just make sure you don't let anyone else see you like that. It's all for me, just for me! She's all mine! Ok?" "of course, darling. She's all for you," Dorothy agreed with a smile in her voice. It truly delighted her when Grant made such complete and exclusive claims upon her, because she certainly considered herself entirely his woman. "That's your pussy tail," he said, "and I can hold both your lovely ass and your cunt in my hand when you're bent over like that, and ah man! it's just so wonderful!"

"You're really pampering me," Dorothy commented, as Grant continued to pour water onto her breasts and then her love-front. "I certainly am. Do you like it?" "I love it." "Well, you can be pampered like this anytime you want, because I love it too. It's the most wonderful foreplay there is!" Gone were the days when Dorothy came into this room to take a bath and locked the door to keep George from coming in to see her nakedness. Henceforth, the door would always be open to Grant, and he would be welcome to admire her and to assist her in her bathing however he wanted. "How would you like to shave my legs?" "Sure." After she told him where her razor was, Grant knelt back down beside the tub and began. Dorothy lifted one leg up out of the water and propped her foot on the faucet. After using the bar of soap to lather up her leg to serve as shaving cream, he began shaving her from her ankle up to her knee, using his left hand to see where he was, and the right hand to shave. When he reached her knee, she lowered her leg back down into the water but now bent her leg to offer him the upper part of the limb. As he slowly moved up from her knee, his hands eventually began to bump gently into her sex, which they both enjoyed. After repeating the process for the other leg, Grant dipped both hands down into the water and used them to spread the Skin So Soft all over her. "You know," he said, "for some reason the Skin So Soft clings to the underside of your body really well, but not to the upper part, so I'm moving it around better for you." Of course, he was careful to make sure that her sex, love-front, and breasts were amply treated with his oily hands.

When Dorothy finally sat up and stepped out of the tub, she used the towel to dry off her face and then handed it to Grant for him to dry off her body. As he did so, he planted numerous kisses on her lovely bare body, finishing by drying off her legs and feet and kissing her sex. "Let's enjoy your cotton candy pussy now," he suggested, "Right here in the bathroom." They stepped through the door into the other part of the bathroom, and Grant lifted his love goddess up onto the counter between the two sinks. She leaned back against the mirror and spread her thighs. Grant bent down between her legs, and she threw them over his back and used her heels to press him forward into her sex. As his hands went back around her, he began licking her with great desire and pleasure. Even though Carol was just a few feet down the hall from the bathroom, the orgasm was so powerfully magnificent that Dorothy could not keep herself from exclaiming "Oh! Oh! Oh!" quite loudly in rhythm to the rising pinnacle of pleasure. Grant was afraid that she was going to wake Carol up, but he also did not want to stop and deprive his darling of her exquisite pleasure. He therefore continued to masturbate her with his tongue until she finally started to come down from her pinnacle of perfect erotic enjoyment. After giving herself some time to recuperate from the ecstasy, she allowed Grant to lift her back down onto the floor. Then after slipping the nightgown over her head, she walked on very shaky legs into the front bedroom, lay down on Grant's bed, and they enjoyed vigorous intercourse for quite some time.

February 16, 1974, Saturday

Following supper that evening and another hour or so of Grant studying on the living room couch, Dorothy came into the room, stood beside him, and formally announced, "Ok, fella, I've got something to show you." "Ok," he replied, as he turned off his cassette machine and arose from the couch. "It's here on the kitchen table," Dorothy explained, as she led the way into the kitchen. Grant sat down in one of the chairs with Dorothy opposite him, and his fingers began to explore the large map of Greece that Dorothy had been working on for the past ten days or so. "My golly!" Grant exclaimed, "This really is magnificent! It is so detailed, just what I need to learn the geography of ancient Greece." As he spoke, Dorothy beamed with joy and pride at her handiwork and her man's obvious satisfaction in what she had done.

The technique employed in making this and other maps for Grant was simple in theory, but in execution required great care and attention to detail. Dorothy first secured a sheet of onion-skin paper to the print map that they wanted to reproduce. Then she used a pen to trace out the map and all necessary details. Onion-skin paper had to be used, because they needed a mirror image of the map to produce the braille map, and having the image on such thin paper allowed it to be viewed from both sides of the paper. Having produced this replica of the map on the onion-skin paper, she now turned it over and secured it to a sheet of braille paper, or in this case, the heavy paper of an artist's drawing tablet. She now had a mirror image of the map on top of the sheet that would bear the tracing of the braille map. She then produced the latter by carefully tracing out with a tracing wheel (a small sprocket of metal teeth fitted into a handle) the image that she had drawn out with the pen on the onion-skin paper. The tracing had to be done on a soft surface, such as a piece of cardboard, to allow the tracing wheel to cut gently into the heavy braille paper or drawing tablet. When this elaborate process was completed, a braille drawing of the map was now reproduced on the underside of the heavy paper. The mirror image of the onion-skin paper had now come out as a normal image on the other side of the heavy paper. Dorothy had approached this complicated and tedious project with the same meticulous skill that she used in her more challenging sewing projects. She was accustomed to using thin paper to trace out the pattern on material and then to cut out the pieces carefully. She was also accustomed to spending hour after hour in slow painstaking work to bring such a project to fruition. She had been devoting time to this map project off and on over the past ten days during the evenings, just as she would have done in making a dress or the like; and she had now completed it successfully. Besides exhibiting her considerable manual skill and dexterity, her investment of time was a natural outgrowth of her fundamental loving character and willingness to help others, and in this case, of course, she was fully willing to devote her time and attention to this project so as to assist her beloved blind love-mate. Her completion of this project also represented a very important milestone in their collaboration in providing Grant with the necessary tools for him to become a college professor of ancient Greek and Roman history.

This map had been far more challenging than the others that Dorothy had drawn for Grant last semester, because it was as big as two legal-size sheets of paper. She therefore had to draw out the image on two separate sheets and then to keep the two sheets in proper alignment as she traced them out. The map was beautifully detailed, showing the entire coastline of mainland Greece with all its peninsulas, gulfs, bays, and small offshore islands. As she had worked in tracing things out, she had consulted Grant as to which rivers should be included, and what towns and cities should be marked. All these were also drawn in carefully.

"This is so neat!" Grant exclaimed, "Thank you so very much, Dorth! Thank you so very much! I know that this was a lot of work and must have been really tedious, but I really do appreciate it so very much! I really do! It's going to allow me to learn Greek geography really well. This is so wonderful!" "You're quite welcome. You're right. It was a lot of work and was very tedious, but I enjoyed doing it, and I know how much it means to you, and that makes it all worthwhile." Since there was no way in which to label the map in braille, Dorothy had to use the print map to show Grant the location of various places. As they sat at the table with her giving him his first geography lesson with the aid of this magnificent map, they decided that in order to make the dots marking towns and cities more prominent, Dorothy would use her fingernail polish to help stiffen the small points. Therefore, when they had finished looking at the map together, Dorothy went over it carefully, dabbing fingernail polish on all the appropriate places; and they left the map out to dry overnight.

This large and beautifully detailed map henceforth became one of Grant's prized possessions and was used repeatedly over the coming years as he needed to refer to it in his study of ancient Greek history; and of course, it had all been made possible by his Dorothy, whose love for Grant and commitment to their long-term academic goal had inspired to execute so magnificently.

February 20, 1974, Wednesday

As they were finishing supper at the kitchen table, Grant asked, "Hey, Dorth, would you mind helping me with a few things as soon as we're done eating and cleaning up?" "Of course not," she answered. When they were finished in the kitchen, Carol retired to the family room to watch TV, while the two lovers went into the living room and sat down together on the couch. "First," Grant began, "I have some mail for you to look through to see what the things are." As he spoke, he withdrew from his backpack a small bundle of letters and campus junk mail. "Then when we're done with that, could you sit here with me and help me get through my Latin?" "Yeah, sure." As Grant was getting out his braille Latin textbook and finding where the class had left off, Dorothy was glancing through the items of mail. "Hey, What's your home address?" she asked in some puzzlement. "403 Elm Street, Fairmont." "Well, that's really funny, because you have a letter here from your mother, and it's addressed as coming from an apartment on Davis Street." "Really?" Grant said in surprise, "Open it up, and see what it is." After tearing open the envelope, Dorothy said, "All there is here is a check for twenty dollars signed by your mother. No note or letter or anything." "Yeah," Grant explained, "My parents usually send me about twenty dollars every two weeks or so." "But what about the address? Are your parents separated?" "It sure looks like it. Doesn't it?" "You mean, you haven't heard from them or anything to let you know?" "No, not at all." "Well," Dorothy added, "Isn't that interesting!" "Yeah, it really is." "Have your parents been having any problems?" "Well, about all that I can say is that sometimes I've noticed that my father was sleeping on the living room couch, and the only reason why I knew that was because he was snoring, and I could tell that he was sleeping there. I just figured that he was there because his snoring disturbed my mother, but I guess they have been having some major problems, and they must not have been sleeping together; and it looks like my mother has now moved out."

March 1, 1974, Friday

When Dorothy left the bank at the end of her work day, she drove over to campus to pick Grant up to bring him to the house to spend the entire weekend. As soon as she turned off of Jordan Street and onto Archimedes, the small alley-like street that formed the eastern boundary of the Men's Dormitory Area, she could see Grant standing in his usual place, where the sidewalk leading out of the end of Watson Hall ended at the curb of Archimedes. He had his bright orange backpack, full of everything that he would need for studying while spending the whole weekend with her. Oh Wow!, she thought to herself, their life had been developing into such a perfect dream; and tonight they would be celebrating the first anniversary for having real intercourse, that spectacular four-hour extravaganza of exactly one year ago. When Grant was seated, she drove over to The Great Steak House, where they sat together at a small table and enjoyed their anniversary meal together, talking in hushed voices as they remembered what magnificent pleasure they had first enjoyed at this time last year, including the glorious sex on their second morning. "Do you remember," Grant asked, as they munched on the peanuts and popcorn while waiting for their steaks to arrive, "how you showed me your lovely leopard patterned girdle that morning?" "I sure do," Dorothy answered with amorous mischief in her voice. "And do you remember what you told me about wearing it when you were having your period and not having sex with George?" "I sure do!" Dorothy replied with equal glee. "My golly!" Grant exclaimed in an undertone and while smiling at his darling, "We really did fuck up a storm those two morning! Didn't we?" "We sure did!" Dorothy confirmed.

Since Carol would be gone for the entire evening baby-sitting, the two lovers lost no time when they returned to the house. They walked immediately into the master bedroom and began to undress. Dorothy was so eager to begin their evening of commemorative festivities that she simply sat her purse on the floor and began to take off her clothes, but by the time that she was fully naked and about to lie down in bed, she noticed that Gretchen was standing at her purse with her nose sniffing around it. "Hey there, dog," she commanded sternly, "Stop that!" "What are you talking about?" Grant asked, as he was almost down to his undershorts on the other side of the bed. "I forgot all about my left-over steak in my purse, and Gretchen's going to get it if I don't stop her." They both laughed, and Dorothy, beautifully nude, removed from her purse the steak that she had wrapped up in a napkin, and carried it into the kitchen, where she placed it in the refrigerator. She then returned to the bedroom, and the two lovers began their evening of commemorative pleasure in bed.

March 13, 1974, Wednesday

As Dorothy drove home from the bank shortly after 4:00 in the afternoon, she was so eager to get home, because Grant would be there again, and oh how that made her heart sing with joy and happiness! Their love still seemed like such a miracle to her. Since they had surmised that Grant's parents were separated, and since Grant had never been all that close to his father, who was apparently the one still living in their house in Fairmont, he had not even bothered to call either parent about coming home for spring break, but instead, he had decided simply to stay there at the house with her all week long, for ten whole glorious days, from this past Friday until this coming Monday. They were therefore both so glad not to have to endure another separation caused by the university's spring break. Rather, instead of Grant simply spending the weekend with her as usual, the weekend was extended to cover the entire following week! How very wonderful! Accordingly, while Dorothy was working at the bank during this time period, Grant was in the house all day long, keeping the dogs company and letting them out periodically, as he did work for his various courses. Then he was always there to greet her when she arrived home from the bank, and they had the entire evening together, usually ending with their final secret session of talking and loving in bed before parting company for the night.

This spring semester was therefore turning out to be such a wonderful blessing for the two lovers. In contrast to a year ago when they had to endure two long separations and two shorter ones and were forced to cram so much loving activity into their shortened weeks together, they were now virtually living together and were able to enjoy their sweet companionship far more sedately, but just as pleasurably. Although the fall semester had begun this new wonderful pattern in their love-life, it had been somewhat hampered by the fact that Dorothy had not been able to visit Grant in his dorm room. That situation had now changed, since Grant and Bob Snider were roommates in Watson.

These two blind guys got along very well and really enjoyed rooming together. On the few week nights that Grant spent on campus they went through a very comfortable routine. After finishing their afternoon of classes, they went into the dining hall and ate supper together, and then they both settled down in their rooms for the next several hours to study. Then at 11:00 their studying ceased, and they made a batch of popcorn, taking turns with each of their popcorn machines on alternate evenings; and then they turned on the radio and settled down to eat their popcorn as they listened to *The CBS Radio Mystery Theater* to finish off the night.

This routine was very conducive to their schoolwork, because it ensured that they were both putting in several hours of serious study on a regular basis. But their rooming together was certainly not all work and no play. Quite the contrary. Their youthful energy and humor blended harmoniously and often resulted in the two engaging in all sorts of goofy gags that inevitably ended in them laughing themselves silly. Their rooming together also enabled Dorothy to drop by or drop in at any time before going to work at the bank or stopping briefly at the end of her work day before heading home to spend the evening with Carol. In addition, Dorothy could call their dorm room at any time and talk to Grant for as long as they wished without having to worry about arousing suspicions.

All these factors contributed to Grant and Dorothy developing a much more closely knit love-life together during this semester. Once they had endured a two-week separation caused by the Christmas break, Grant had returned to campus, and they had enjoyed two glorious weeks living together in the house before classes resumed, and Dorothy began her first day of work at the bank. And now they were spending the spring break together as well! Grant's absences from his dorm room this semester were so pronounced and regular that they soon attracted the attention and curiosity of another student who roomed on the same end of the first floor of Watson near Bob and Grant. He noticed Grant's comings and goings and long absences from his dorm room and began to suspect that this blind guy must be paying regular visits and longer weekend stays to some honey-love; and himself being a young male with the normal heterosexual urges of his age, he wondered who this honey-love could be, and what she looked like. Needless to say, his prurient curiosity was also accompanied by a fair amount of envy. But since he was too shy to question Grant directly, he occasionally asked Bob about his roommate whenever the two happened to encounter one another in the large men's room on their floor. But whenever Bob was asked about this roommate and the cause for his frequent absences, Bob always played dumb and said that he had no idea what his roommate was up to.

Bob reported these inquiries to Grant, and they both always had a good chuckle about them.

When Dorothy now arrived home from her work day at the bank, she was greeted at the back door both by Grant and the four dogs. It was so nice to be appreciated. But because Carol was in the house, Grant had to let her go alone into the master bedroom to change out of her good clothes and into something for around the house. When she came back out into the kitchen, Grant asked, "How about I make salmon patties for our supper tonight?" They had been talking about this all week, because it was one thing that Grant knew how to fix. He liked them very much; and since his mother had taught him how to make them, he was eager to use his limited kitchen knowledge to help her make one of their meals, especially on a day like this when she was coming home from having worked eight hours at the bank. "That would be really nice," Dorothy replied, "but what else should we have to go with them?" "Well, something like corn and fried potatoes, I guess." "Ok, while you're making the salmon patties, I'll take care of the other two things." The two of them therefore worked together in the kitchen in their usual sweet companionship as they prepared their supper, which turned out quite well. Carol had never eaten salmon patties before, but she liked them, and the lovers were so pleased with how they had cooperated in producing this delicious meal. Even the dogs made out well, because Grant shared out among them the bones and skin that he removed from the salmon meat.

March 16, 1974, Saturday

They were all spending a lovely quiet Saturday night together in the house. Carol's friend Betty Washington was staying overnight, and the two girls were sitting in the family room watching a scary horror movie on TV. Dorothy was playing her expected maternal part of watching the movie with her daughter, partly because Carol had always enjoyed sharing such things with her mother, and partly because having her mother there kept her from getting as scared as she otherwise would have become. Grant was sitting at the kitchen table doing schoolwork. He usually studied on the living room couch, but he had adopted this place as his work station so as to be closer to his darling as she viewed the movie with the two girls.

When the next commercial break occurred, Dorothy announced in her cute little girl voice, "I've gotta go potty!" She then arose from her chair, walked through the kitchen and laundry room, and into the bathroom that adjoined the master bedroom. Before sitting down on the toilet, she slid shut the one door between the laundry room and bathroom, but she left the other sliding door between the bathroom and the master bedroom open, because both girls were still sitting together in the family room. Grant had been desiring his darling all evening long and now decided to see if anything could be done about it. After waiting a minute or so after Dorothy had gone into the bathroom, he arose from the kitchen table and walked off, hoping that the two girls would assume that he had gone off into the living room to fetch something from his backpack. But instead, he turned down the hall, walked through the master bedroom and then into the bathroom. As soon as he entered, he quietly slid the other door shut behind him.

"What are you doing here?" Dorothy asked in a whisper. "What do you think," Grant replied with a knowing smile, "I've been wanting you all evening. How about we have a little quickie right here?" After wiping her vulva, Dorothy simply knelt down on the floor with her slacks and panties still around her ankles and offered her pussy tail to Grant. She was now facing the door leading into the laundry room. Grant quickly took down his own pants and undershorts, knelt behind her, entered her vagina, took her hips into his hands, and began thrusting himself rhythmically inside her. As always when they enjoyed intercourse in this manner, his thrusts made Dorothy sway slightly on her elbows and knees; and she was so close to the door that the motion made the top of her head bump rhythmically against the door, but even though the sound might have attracted the attention of the two girls, the two lovers were enjoying themselves so much that they did not stop their pleasure until Grant had reached an orgasm and left his sperm inside her as a token of their love. They then stood up, straightened their clothes, and returned to the kitchen and family room by different routes and at slightly different times, so that the girls would not notice or suspect anything. Fortunately, the girls had not left their seats during the commercial break and had hardly noticed Dorothy's absence, but the two lovers reveled in the wonderful bit of pleasure that they had secretly enjoyed.

April 2, 1974, Tuesday

It was 6:40 in the evening, and Dorothy was sitting on the edge of Grant's bed in his dorm room, while he was stretched out on the bed behind her, and Bob was sitting on the other side of the room at his desk. Shortly after she arrived home from work that day, Grant had called to ask if she could drop by before Sweet Adelines to help Bob with some paperwork. She had, of course, agreed, and so here she was. Grant and Bob had returned not too long ago from the dining hall, and Dorothy had helped Bob with what he needed. The three were now simply passing the time by chatting amiably, because it was still too early for Dorothy to leave for Sweet Adelines.

It was so very nice for Dorothy to be able to come into Grant's dorm room and be herself and not worry about someone regarding her presence there as odd. Moreover, since she had been working full time, Dorothy had seen rather little of Bob so far this semester, and the two enjoyed talking and getting caught up on what the other had been doing. As they talked, Dorothy and Grant held hands, and Grant breathed in the lovely fragrance of her White Shoulders perfume, because his lady-love was dressed up so beautifully for her evening out. When they had talked earlier on the telephone, he had reminded her that one year ago was when they had begun their second week of sweet reunion last spring; and while the three of them conversed, Grant became increasingly desirous of his darling, as he remembered that lovely week a year ago, especially how they had so frantically enjoyed intercourse on that first day.

"So, Bob," Dorothy asked, "Have you heard anything from Kitty lately?" "Yeah, I talked with her about two weeks ago." "How and what's she doing?" As Bob began to launch into a detailed recounting of their most recent conversation, Grant quietly unzipped his pants, pulled his pants and undershorts down, and placed Dorothy's hand on his erection. As she and Bob continued to chat away in a perfectly normal fashion, Dorothy obliged Grant by gently masturbating him until he reached an orgasm and ejaculated. He then put his undershorts and pants back into their proper position. They could have the real thing again tomorrow night when he spent the night with her at the house, but for the time being the wonderful feel of her dainty hand around his penis felt pretty damn good!

April 14, 1974, Sunday

It was Easter Sunday, but Dorothy had been spending the holiday weekend in a way she had never done before. She had not attended any service today at her church. In fact, since she and Grant had been spending their weekends together since this past fall, she had ceased going to church on Sunday mornings. It was far more pleasant to be in the house with her beloved Grant. Anyway, by then some of their church acquaintances knew that Dorothy and George were probably heading toward a divorce, and most of them sided with George.

Since Carol had traveled by bus Thursday evening to Newton to spend the weekend with George and his mother, Dorothy and Grant had, of course, been spending the weekend together, sleeping together all night long in the same bed for the past three delicious nights, doing chores around the house together in sweet companionship, Grant studying, Dorothy reading to him, and of course, enjoying intercourse and love-play in great abundance. In fact, here it was the middle of the afternoon, and she was just now getting herself properly dressed for the first time all day. Till then she had either been naked, clad in only her pink quilted robe, or wearing her nightgown under her robe. But now their weekend of work and play around the house was coming to an end, because they needed to go pick Carol up from the bus station and then go off later to their Sunday night bowling league.

Their glorious Easter was perfectly epitomized by a brief incident of sweet love early that morning. After sleeping together fully naked and arising from bed, Grant had dressed, but Dorothy had gone about the house for much of the morning clad only in her pink quilted robe and slippers. Oh what a delight that had been for them both! They had had breakfast in the kitchen with her in this lovely state of dress (or of undress!), and then she had gone about the house to tend to various things while still only wearing her robe. At one point she happened to come into the living room to do something; and as she did, she found Grant kneeling on the floor in front of the couch to retrieve something out of his backpack. As his darling came near, he reached out for her, encircled her waist with his left arm and used his right hand to open up the front of her robe; and then after slowly moving his hand appreciatively from her breasts down to her love-delta, he took her sweet pussy into his mouth and enjoyed the taste, scent, and wonderful texture of her love-pie. Oh how wonderful! The whole weekend had been like that!

April 26, 1974, Friday

When Dorothy picked Grant up at Watson at the usual time early in the evening after her work day, they would be going directly to The Great Steak House to celebrate. Dorothy had just been promoted from being a teller to a position in new accounts and customer services. She was really excited and so very pleased, and justifiably so. As Grant dropped his backpack over into the back seat and sat down in the passenger seat beside her, he said,

"Congratulations once again! See? I told you that you'd not have any trouble going back to work and being a success. You're just too damn talented to do otherwise." "You're prejudiced," Dorothy replied, nearly laughing with pleasure. "I'm not prejudiced. I just know you really well and how magnificent you are. That's really something. Just working there three months, and you get a major promotion. Obviously your incomparable way of interacting with people and your great efficiency and attention to detail made you a cinch for new accounts and customer services, where all those things must be needed to do a good job. I see all those qualities in you all the time. So I'm not surprised that other people at the bank have noticed them too and have decided that you were being wasted as a mere teller." "Yeah, well, there's another teller named Helen, a black lady about my age, who's been working there quite some time; and I'm sure she's really disappointed that she didn't get the position. I wouldn't be surprised that she's angry with me and probably blames it all on her skin color, but the truth is she's not a very pleasant person to work with; and I don't think she'd be the best in handling new customers. I know I'm going to like this job a whole lot better than being a teller. I didn't mind that job, but now, besides earning a bit more money, I'll be sitting comfortably at a desk for most of the day, and I'll enjoy talking with people coming into the bank for the first time."

May 4, 1974, Saturday

As usual, Grant was spending the entire weekend with his lady-love at the house, but since classes were about to end and give way to final exam week, he was beginning to review much of his course material. Thus it happened that by 8:00 that evening he decided that he would like to have a notebook that he had not bothered to bring with him in his backpack last evening. When he asked Dorothy if she minded running him over to his room to pick up the notebook, she gladly agreed as always.

As they were driving over to campus, Grant remarked, "You know, Bob isn't going to be in the room tonight when we get there." "He won't?" Dorothy asked, "Why not?" "He's going to some kind of party." "That's nice." "And it's especially nice for us. Don't you think?" "What are you suggesting, young man?" Dorothy asked mockingly, as if she were genuinely scandalized. "Well, we get to fuck in your bed all the time. How about you sanctify my bed for once with your divine pussy, my beautiful love goddess?" "I guess we could do that!" Dorothy replied enthusiastically. Thus, instead of sitting out in the car and waiting while Grant ran inside to grab the necessary notebook, Dorothy parked the car in the Watson parking lot, and they both entered the dorm and his dorm room. After undressing, they lay down in Grant's bed and enjoyed intercourse for as long as they dared, hoping that Bob would not suddenly return with a friend, or that Carol might wonder why they had been gone so long. As they drove back home in the afterglow of their shared pleasure, Grant said, "Thank you so very much for that. It really meant a lot to me to have you like that in my bed." "You're quite welcome. I enjoyed it too."

May 18, 1974, Saturday

It was around 11:30 in the morning, and the two lovers were bringing to an end a long session of intercourse in the bed that had witnessed The Great Apocalypse and so many of their late night bouts of talking and loving. The spring semester was over, and they were about to embark upon another period of separation, which neither of them wanted. This would therefore be their last enjoyment of lovely pleasure for at least a month or more. Fortunately, Carol had arisen rather early for a Saturday, and Dorothy had taken her and Betty to spend the rest of the morning and part of the afternoon bumming around in the Prairie Shopping Center, thus allowing the two lovers to have this last bit of tender loving time together before they had to part.

They were configured into the sidesaddle position, and Grant was now thrusting inside her gently and slowly, as he used his right hand to caress and admire her female beauty and the awesome sight of his penis enveloped by the lips of her vulva and vagina. "Do you remember what we were doing one year ago?" Grant asked. After thinking for a while, Dorothy finally confessed, "No, I really don't remember. I don't have your memory for things like that. So, tell me, what were we doing one year ago. I suppose we must have been having fun in bed. Otherwise, you wouldn't be asking me," she said mischievously. "Well, you got that right. That was the last day of our fourth week together that spring. It was a Friday, and before taking me to the bus station, I rode you furiously for about seventy minutes and came inside you five times. I did so because we were about to begin a fifty-day separation, and I thought that we needed to enjoy our last love moments in a remarkable way." "Oh yeah, I do remember that. That's hard to forget, and it was remarkable!" "Yeah, that really was something, but like today, one year later, we had to begin that long separation until we saw one another again in July. But another horrible thing happened that day too. If you remember, it was that same evening that George had intercourse with you, and it upset you so badly that you talked with Dennis about it the next day." "Yeah, that really was a terrible time, but thank goodness, it was the beginning of the end for me and George, and I'm so glad that it's all over now except for the divorce." "Yeah, just think of what all has happened with us since then. Isn't it amazing?" "It sure is, and it's like a miracle or dream come true.

Darling," Dorothy said very seriously, "I'm going to miss you so terribly. I wish you could stay here." As she spoke those last words, she was on the verge of tears. "Yes, I know," Grant tenderly replied, "I'm going to miss you too, but we'll be back together soon, and in the meantime we both know without any doubt that I'm your one and only man, and you're my one and only woman. I love you so utterly!" "I love you the same," replied Dorothy, again nearly crying. "Well, sweetheart," Grant again said as tenderly as he could, "I hate to say it, but we need to be getting up, so that you can get me over to Watson to be there when my father shows up around noon." "Ok," she agreed. Grant slowly withdrew his penis from her vagina and caressed her sex one last time before they arose from bed to dress quickly and leave.

When Dorothy dropped Grant off at the sidewalk on Archimedes that led into Watson, she did not leave, but simply pulled the car into the adjoining parking lot and parked. It was almost noon, and she wanted to stay there until Grant and his father had actually left. She therefore sat in the car and watched, as Grant's father arrived, and the two of them loaded up the car with all his things to go home for the summer. She did not start up the car and leave until Grant and his father were driving out of sight down along Archimedes. She then drove over to the Prairie Shopping Center, located the two girls, had lunch with them there, and returned home. She would now be sharing the house for the next few weeks with Carol alone, and it would seem so very empty until Grant returned to fill her life once again with their happiness and love.

Meanwhile, Grant's day, once he arrived in Fairmont, was extremely busy, because tomorrow afternoon he would be flying out of O'Hare in Chicago to go visit Dennis in Austria for the next twenty-four days. During the preceding Christmas break Grant had asked his parents if they would fund such a trip as his college graduation present, and they had agreed, thinking it to be a really wonderful idea; and even though he would not be graduating until the next spring, now was the time for him to visit Dennis, and for the two friends to enjoy being together in Austria. Dorothy, of course, in her perfectly efficient manner had assisted him in getting everything organized, so that he could be issued a passport in time; and she had also taken care of obtaining traveler's checks for him from the Lincoln Bank. But when Grant and his father arrived home that day, he had to pack all of his things in a single large new suitcase that his father had purchased, and they had to drive over to Peoria to a Western Union station in order to send a telegram to Dennis to let him know on which flight he would be arriving, and at what time.

June 22, 1974, Saturday

Grant and his father returned to the house in Fairmont around 2:20 A.M. After leaving Austria, Grant had stopped off for another eight days to visit his uncle Richard Berry and his family in a ritzy area of Westchester County just north of New York City. He had flown into O'Hare late last night, where his father had met him, and then they rode home together, as Grant entertained his father with stories of his time in Austria.

When he came into his bedroom, he discovered a large pile of boxes containing braille books that he had purchased, and which were now finally arriving in the mail. Most of the volumes were important Latin literary texts that he wanted to have to increase his knowledge of the Latin language and Roman literature, but he also had a few boxes containing volumes of the textbook that he would need to have this fall for his course on beginning Classical Greek, another very important step in his progress toward becoming a college professor of ancient Greek and Roman history.

As Grant rummaged around through all the accumulated boxes and other items that had arrived for him in the mail over the past month, he came upon a cassette letter from his darling, which he instantly opened and began to play. Apart from telling him what all she had been doing, and how much she missed him, her recording contained one important bit of news. Both Dorothy and George now had lawyers who were beginning negotiations for a divorce settlement. Interestingly, Grant's parents were engaged in the same process right now too. But in any case, since their divorce was now in the works, Dorothy had decided to tell Carol that she and Grant were in love with one another and were planning to have a life together. Dorothy felt so tremendously liberated by doing this, because they would not have to hide their feelings all the time when Carol was around. They still would not allow her to notice them in bed together, but they could be together and touch one another in her presence without being apprehensive. In addition, when she was not at work at the bank, Dorothy was now wearing Grant's ring on its chain not secretly under her clothes and out of view between her breasts, as she had been doing for over a year, but outside her top in full view; and this simple gesture was of great significance to her. She felt so good in having the ring, the token of their love, out for anyone to see. No longer would they be keeping their love hidden, but they were prepared to broadcast it to the entire world, and they were so very proud and pleased to do so. The ring was therefore now serving as their engagement ring. The cassette also contained an exquisite recording of Dorothy masturbating for Grant, which also pleased him greatly.

June 26, 1974, Wednesday

Dorothy had just left work at the bank and was now at the bus station, eagerly awaiting Grant's arrival. Luckily, she did not have to wait very long. The bus pulled into the parking area, and the passengers began stepping off the bus. As soon as Grant emerged from the door and was on the pavement, Dorothy said, "Hey, Grant," as she took him by the right forearm and guided him off to the side. It was so wonderful to see him again, and he was beaming at her with equal joy. Their separation of thirty-nine days was now finally over. "Oh gosh!" Dorothy said, her voice choking with emotion, "It's so good to see you again! "Oh my!" he replied, "It sure is!" After hugging each other fiercely, they walked over to the little blue Falcon and left the bus station.

"We won't go home just yet," Dorothy explained, "let's find a secluded place where we can park and be alone in the car together for a few minutes. Carol and my mom are at the house, and I want to hug you and kiss you right away without them being around." So, after driving about, Dorothy located a deserted parking area next to a large business building. She parked under the shade of some trees, and they simply sat side by side in the front seat, embracing, touching one another, and kissing again and again, as they both uttered small exclamations of joy in being together once more. After about five minutes of such activity, Dorothy started the car up again, and they drove on to the house at 1801 Rachel Drive.

When they arrived, they were eagerly greeted by the four dogs. Then as they stepped from the kitchen into the edge of the living room and hallway, Dorothy greeted her mother, who was knitting while sitting in a rocking chair in the living room. After Grant had also greeted her, Dorothy went on, "Ok mom, there's goulash in the refrigerator for you and Carol to have supper when you get hungry. I'm going to change out of my good clothes, and then Grant and I are going to head off to have supper together." "Ok, we'll be fine," Gloria replied. The two lovers then continued on down the hall. Grant turned off into the front bedroom, where he deposited his duffel bag and backpack. While he returned to the living room and sat down on the couch to try to engage Dorothy's mother in conversation, Dorothy went into the master bedroom to change her clothes. She had prepared herself for their reunion earlier that morning by taking a bath in Avon Skin So Soft and shaving her legs. She now removed her good shoes, peds, panty hose, slacks, and matching top and slipped on a simple but nice-looking dress. She put on a pair of comfortable casual shoes, went into the adjoining bathroom and looked into the mirror to check her hair and makeup. She was now ready for a lovely evening with her man.

"Ok," she announced, as she stepped back into the living room, "I'm all ready to go." Grant arose from the couch, and they went back out to the car. "How long is your mother going to be staying?" Grant asked. "She'll be here until Monday morning. I'll take her to the train station on my way to work Monday morning, but she knows about us now, and I don't see any reason why we can't be ourselves around her." "That's nice. So," Grant asked, changing the subject, "where are you taking us to eat?" "We'll be going to a new place called Top of the Town. It's within a block of the bank. It hasn't been open too long, and I've eaten lunch there several times with a few of the girls from the bank during our lunch hour, and it's a nice place. There's one thing that I know you'll like." "What's that?" "They serve you a loaf of freshly baked bread as an appetizer while you're waiting for your food to arrive." "Yeah!" Grant said with real enthusiasm, "now that's what I like, having something good to eat while we're waiting for our food to show up!"

Since it was early on a Wednesday evening, the restaurant had few customers and was quiet. While eating the fresh bread and waiting for their food to arrive, they were both so giddy with excitement, constantly smiling at each other and touching hands across the table between them. "What are you wearing now?" Grant asked. "Oh just a dress." As Grant reached under the table to feel the fabric that covered her right knee and then her bare skin just below, Dorothy said in mock admonition, "Watch it there, fella! I've shot men for less than that!" "I certainly hope so. You'd better shoot them all for much less than that, but you'd better let me do anything

I want." As they both chuckled, Grant concluded, "You're all mine!" "I sure am," Dorothy agreed, smiling sweetly. "It also looks like you shaved your legs." "I sure did, just this morning," she said with pride, "And just for you. So, tell me all about your trip to Austria and to your uncle's in New York." Dennis and Grant had succeeded in making one cassette letter to her, and Grant had also sent her a typed letter from his Uncle's, so that she already knew a good bit about what he had done, but there were so many details that he wanted to share with her, and he now began to do so, as they began eating their meal. Since they were engaged in eating, he began his debriefing (which actually continued off and on throughout their summer together) by telling his darling about many of the new things that he had eaten in Austria: the wonders of Wienerschnitzel, the heavenly delight of hazelnut flavored Mannerschnitten (a wafer-like cookie), Schwarzbrot (black bread), the Austrian standard roll called a Simmel for making small sandwiches with different cheeses and meats, the luscious desserts that they had eaten at a small pastry shop, the little produce store owned by a very nice man named Herr Schmidt where they bought fruit and vegetables, how they had made several large batches of vegetable soup in the dorm kitchen, and how one meal involving pork chops had turned out to be such a disaster, because the meat was almost all fat and must have been already spoiled.

As their meal was winding down, Dorothy suddenly said, "Guess what?" "What?" "I'm now in charge of issuing people automatic teller machine cards." "Well now! You really are getting to be important at the bank, aren't you? Congratulations! That's really nice and shows how much the people there value you." "Yeah, it really is nice, and I enjoy it. In fact, when we're done here, I'll walk you over to one of our automatic teller machines at our drive-through next to the bank. I need to get some more cash." And when they arose shortly thereafter to leave, they walked over to the facility, and Dorothy showed Grant the machine and how it worked, as she made her cash withdrawal. But while they were standing at the machine, Grant asked, "Is there anyone around right now?" After carefully looking all around, Dorothy replied, "No, not right now." At which Grant quickly reached under her dress and caressed her bottom clad only in her panties. It greatly pleased them both.

When they were back inside the Falcon and moving along again, Dorothy said, "Before we go back home, how about we try to find a nice isolated spot where we can park and have some fun?" "That sounds like a great idea." After several minutes of driving, Grant asked, "Where are we?"

"We're leaving the city and traveling along a two-lane highway, and we'll soon have just cornfields on either side of us. I want to find a totally secluded area, because I want you so much! I want to feel you inside me again!" "I want you too!" As they continued to ride in silence, their passion for one another grew. Eventually, Dorothy spotted a dirt road leading off of the highway, turned onto it, and drove down it a distance. "This looks good," she said, as she pulled the car onto the edge of the road.

As soon as the car was parked, she said, "Let's push back the front seat to give us more room." They both released the levers beneath the front edge of their seat and pushed back simultaneously. When the seat had gone as far back as it could, Dorothy kicked off her shoes, pivoted in her seat, so that she was now facing Grant and was leaning against the driver's door. "Ok," she simply said, as she reached under her dress and pulled her panties down and off of her feet. As she positioned herself with her right leg bent up and against the back of the seat and her left leg bent with her foot resting upon the floor board, Grant quickly took his shorts and undershorts down to his ankles and moved across the seat to his darling. His right hand went under her dress and touched her female love-nest for the first time since they were together in over thirty-nine days. He then lifted up her dress and knelt over her. Because she was wet and dilated with desire for him, his penis entered her easily. Just like their sexual reunion nearly six months ago in Renny's apartment, as soon as their sexes merged into one, Grant came instantly, and their bodies shuddered and convulsed with pleasure so intense that it was almost painful. After only a minute or so of further intercourse, Dorothy said, "We probably better not go too long. Someone may drive up along this road." Grant therefore withdrew, and they restored their clothes into their proper places and went on home.

June 28, 1974, Friday

Since Carol had a day-long baby-sitting job for this part of the summer, she was also away from the house. Consequently, apart from the four dogs, only Grant and Dorothy's mother had been there throughout the day yesterday and today while Dorothy was at work. On both days Gloria had arisen and had come into the living room, where she sat in silence virtually the entire day working on her knitting. So as not to appear unsociable or reclusive, Grant had asked her if it was ok for him to bring the phonograph into the living room, where he could keep her company as he listened to a talking book, a survey history of the Arabs from ancient to modern times. Dorothy's mother had consented. Grant had therefore spent yesterday and was spending today listening to the talking book in her presence, as he either sat on the couch or was stretched out on the carpeted floor. He hoped that Gloria was enjoying the book too, but she only spoke whenever Grant asked her a question; and when she did so, it was always a minimal answer, and she never once made a comment about the book itself. Grant was therefore unsure as to how she viewed his presence there in the room with her, but he honestly did not know what else to do.

June 29, 1974, Saturday

After breakfast Dorothy and Grant had taken the four dogs for a nice long walk, which had given them an opportunity to be alone together and to talk about whatever was on their minds. They had then spent the rest of the morning and part of the early afternoon in doing various things around the house together in their usual sweet companionship. After lunch Dorothy had taken Carol to the Prairie Shopping Center in northern University City to shop and to hang out with her friends until suppertime. As they were engaged in their housework, Dorothy had entered the living and dining rooms periodically; and while doing things there, she had engaged her mother in conversation about numerous mundane things. Shortly after lunch, when Carol was no longer in the house, Grant and Dorothy had sat down together on the couch that faced the rocking chair in which Dorothy's mother was sitting. While the two women were talking, Dorothy drew Grant toward her and had them lie down together on the couch to rest and be physically close together. As they did this, Dorothy did not interrupt her conversation with her mother, but she continued to talk as normally as before. After nearly two years of exercising strict vigilance over their relationship and keeping it a secret from virtually everyone, Dorothy was now reveling in a kind of joyous liberation. She was now separated from George, was engaged in divorce proceedings, and was so happy and excited about her new love and life with Grant that she had a kind of innocent wonder about it and was eager to show her mother this wonder and to share it with her.

Later in the afternoon, when it was evident that her mother had no real interest in getting out of the house to go shopping or to do anything else, but seemed to be ready to doze off in her chair, Dorothy led Grant into the master bedroom, where they shut the doors leading out into the hallway and into the adjoining bathroom. They then fully undressed and gave themselves entirely over to the enjoyment of erotic pleasure for a considerable time. Since Dorothy's mother was not interested in doing anything with her daughter, why should she pass up the opportunity to enjoy herself with Grant?

June 30, 1974, Sunday

Following their noontime Sunday dinner, Carol had gone off to enjoy herself with her friends; and while Dorothy and Grant were clearing off the table and loading the dishwasher, Dorothy's mother had retreated to her usual station in the living room. Dorothy had then gone into the bathroom adjoining the master bedroom; and while standing in front of the mirror to inspect her hair, Grant sat quietly on the toilet lid beside her. As she glanced over at him and beheld his pensive expression, she asked, "What are you thinking about?" He totally surprised her by replying that he had been thinking about the events of the Corinthian War of the early fourth century B.C. in Greek history. It had been the topic of his research paper that spring semester for his history colloquium. "What?" Dorothy said in astonishment and obvious pleasure. Rather than thinking of some contemporary mundane matter, her lover-boy, who was aspiring to be a college professor of ancient history, was simply sitting there thinking about some serious historical subject. It delighted her so much that as soon as she had finished with her hair, she walked into the living room and addressed her mother, "Hey, mom, you're not going to believe this. When I asked Grant just now what he was thinking about, he said 'the Corinthian war'. Isn't that something?"

Grant stayed with his darling love until Friday July 19, which, of course, suited the two lovers just fine. Almost an entire month of glorious cohabitation! Since his parents were now separated and getting divorced, his father was living alone in the house in Fairmont, and his mother had a small one-bedroom apartment. His mother clearly did not have room for him, and he really did not feel all that comfortable staying with his father. In truth, he felt as if his presence was something of an embarrassment or inconvenience to his parents. But of course, both he and Dorothy found this situation to be perfectly congenial, because they wanted to be together for as long as possible. Their time together became a long on-going summer dream, unlike last summer when they had enjoyed only a few fully passionate days in July.

During the week Dorothy went off to work during the day and returned home to spend the evenings and the weekends with her darling love. When she was working at the bank, Grant usually stayed at the house to be with the dogs, while he read and also spent quite a bit of time in following all the news surrounding the impeachment proceedings of Richard Nixon that dominated the news. This routine was interrupted by a few special events. He once accompanied Lisa on an afternoon of shopping; and one day, when Lisa took Carol and the two boys whom she was baby-sitting out to a nearby small lake to enjoy the water in the summer heat, Grant went along, and they all had such a swell time, especially going down a big water slide, but of course, Grant with his fair complexion wound up staying out in the sun too long and came back to the house with a painful sunburn.

As always, whenever they found themselves alone in the house during the evening or on the weekends, they filled these times with the most glorious love-play and intercourse. The week that they had enjoyed in July one year ago to commemorate the first anniversary of their love had been truly extraordinary, but it was now eclipsed by these three weeks that marked the second anniversary of their first magical summer together. Their bodies were as insatiable for each other as ever. The double bed in the master bedroom became their regular platform for giving and receiving magnificent pleasure. Since Dorothy was Grant's first girlfriend, and Dorothy had never been so totally in love, they both approached their love-pleasure with a kind of childlike wonder. Consequently, they were still so utterly thrilled and fascinated by the novelty of their extraordinary love-joy that they continued to experiment with new ways in which Grant's penis and Dorothy's vagina could be employed in expressing their complete and total love for each other, and they eventually discovered two new methods of exquisite intercourse.

One of them was a variation of their equestrian manner and could be enjoyed in a more relaxing posture. Dorothy lay on her left side with her legs together and bent at the knees, so that her thighs were perpendicular to her body. While in a sitting position near her bottom, Grant moved himself, so that his penis approached her sex that was presently concealed by her thighs being together. He stretched his left leg straight out and placed it along her back; and when she raised her right thigh to spread herself for him, he placed his right leg up between her spread open legs, so that it went along the front of her body; and at the same time his penis now came up against her sex. After working his penis inside her vagina, Dorothy closed her legs around Grant's manhood and upper right leg. He then moved his penis to plunge inside her rhythmically. They therefore enjoyed intercourse with him in a sitting position while she lay comfortably on her side. As their merged sexes loved one another, he ran his hands over her to enjoy and admire all her naked beauty. Like the equestrian position, this mode of intercourse gave them the pleasure of a very tight fit.

Their other new method of intercourse involved Grant lying on his back while Dorothy sat on top and rode Rufus Magnus. But getting themselves into this wonderful position was somewhat complicated. They began by lying on their backs with their feet toward one another and their heads in opposite directions. After bending their legs and spreading their knees apart, Grant moved his body toward Dorothy's and slid his legs under hers and past her body until his penis came to rest against her sex. After he inserted his penis inside her vagina, he took her two hands into his; and as Dorothy kept her upper body rigid, he slowly and carefully pulled her into an upright position, so that she was now positioned over his penis that was thrusting straight up inside her. She could now ride him by moving herself up and down, but he could also grasp her hips with his hands and either help or hinder her movement. He usually wanted to hinder her, because her movement felt so utterly wonderful that it caused him to reach a climax and ejaculate quickly. Accordingly, while Dorothy was eager to ride him vigorously, he wanted to proceed more slowly to prolong the pleasure. He could also hold her firmly down on himself and have her wriggle side to side, which felt magnificent. Another wonderful thing about intercourse in this position was that they could reverse roles, as it were. Once again, by joining their two hands Grant could slowly lower Dorothy as he raised himself up. When this movement was successfully completed (and it had to be done carefully, or else his penis would slip out), she wound up on her back with him on top, but she now had her legs bent together and between them in such a way that it constricted her vagina and made their love linkage feel so very nice. He then moved his penis carefully and slowly inside her, and it produced really wonderful sexual pleasure. This formed such a tight fit of penis and vagina that his inward thrusts pushed a small amount of air into her vagina, but the withdrawing motion did not allow the air to escape. Consequently, whenever they finished having intercourse in this way, Dorothy's vagina expelled the air that Grant had pumped into her, and it sounded like farting. But these "pussy farts" were truly lovely sounds. As the two lovers lay together naked on the bed, these sounds resulting from their intercourse made them laugh with wonder, joy, and pleasure. In addition to these marvelous and enchanting pussy farts, enjoying love-pleasure in this peculiar position produced another magnificent consequence. When they finally ended their glorious love-fucking, and Grant withdrew his penis from his darling, the opening to her vagina was enlarged and perfectly circular from having been so tightly constricted around the shaft of Grant's thrusting manhood; and the unusual shape of her vagina's opening, as Dorothy lay on the bed with her thighs fully parted, was a wonder to behold and further heightened the ecstasy of their love-joy.

The only sour note that entered their life at this time arrived in the form of a letter from Dorothy's mother. Gloria had been quite taciturn during her stay with her daughter, and in fact during her entire stay she and Dorothy had not had a single meaningful conversation about anything; but now Dorothy's mother expressed herself in no uncertain terms in condemning Dorothy, whose attempts to show her mother how happy she was with Grant had completely failed and had even backfired. Gloria stated her total disapproval of how her daughter was currently conducting her life. She regarded her divorcing George as a very foolish mistake, and she even called her daughter a whore for carrying on as she was with her young blind lover. She predicted that their relationship would not last, so that behaving as she was was totally misguided. Of course, she thought that their difference in age made their relationship most inappropriate, and that Grant's blindness would ensure that he could never be a good provider for her, but instead, Dorothy would always have to work to support them both. The letter hurt Dorothy very deeply. When her mother had been there visiting while Grant was there, Dorothy had hoped to show how truly they were in love with one another, and how their love made Dorothy so very happy. She had wanted to share this wonder in her life with her mother. She had also hoped that her mother would understand that the divorce was setting her free from a marriage that had been so unhappy for many years. But none of this had apparently sunk in. On the contrary, her mother had apparently been disgusted by their behavior. Although Dorothy loved her mother dearly, she had been on the receiving end of her very sharp-tongued criticism for all sorts of things over the years, almost always unjustifiably so. Nevertheless, whenever they came her way, they always hurt, and this letter in particular hurt her very much. Although she summarized the letter's content for Grant, it was so vicious and hurtful that she did not actually read it word for word to him, because she did not want him to be so angry with her mother that they could never be friendly toward one another. But they did discuss the letter at great length and rightly decided to dismiss it. Although they knew exactly how they felt toward one another, they could understand how odd their relationship might appear to an outsider. Dorothy kept the letter for quite some time as a clear reminder of how her mother had roundly condemned her. It might help her in the future to maintain a better perspective on how her mother judged her.

July 22, 1974, Monday

John Stevenson was a black man who was the parking lot attendant for the Lincoln Bank. His job was to make sure that the only people coming into the parking lot were either bank employees or customers visiting the bank. For the past few weeks he had been paying rather close attention to one particular woman who had been employed at the bank for only the past few months. He knew that her first name was Dorothy, because she had told him that; and whenever she drove into the lot in the morning in her little blue Falcon and drove out again in the late afternoon, she always addressed him by his first name, usually waved, and always gave him a pleasant smile. Her voice, facial expression, and entire manner conveyed such charm and grace that he had slowly become quite interested in her. She was very good looking, always well dressed, and on a few occasions he had even smelled her perfume, which was very alluring, just like all the rest of her. He had noticed that she did not wear a wedding ring; and after making subtle and not so subtle inquiries about her from other bank employees, he had learned that she was separated from her husband and currently in the process of getting a divorce. He had therefore finally concluded that she was likely to be free and available.

For several days now he had been waiting for the right moment to ask her out on a date. He needed to catch her either entering or exiting the parking lot when there were no other cars behind her, so that they could do more than simply exchange quick greetings or goodbyes. It looked as if his opportunity had finally arrived this afternoon. She must have been held up by something in the bank, because by the time she walked out into the parking lot to leave, most other employees had already left, and the stream of departing vehicles had slowed down to a trickle. Thus, as Dorothy drove up to his station to leave, he first casually commented, "It's a hot one today." "It sure is," she replied with her usual lovely smile, "and of course, I don't have air conditioning in this car." Then before she could drive on past, he hastily asked, "I've been wondering if you'd be interested in going out with me on a date." There again was that beautiful smile of hers, "I'm really sorry, John, but I'm already taken." With those devastating words that made his heart sink, she drove out of the lot. "Damn!" he thought to himself, "Just my luck. She was already seeing someone steady, maybe the one responsible for the break-up of her marriage, and what a lucky son of a bitch he must be! She was a really foxy lady!"

July 23, 1974, Tuesday

It was late in the morning, and Grant was listening to the radio while straightening up his room. He had come back to Fairmont this past Friday afternoon, and he was already missing his darling so very much. His father had started his annual vacation this past Saturday, so that rather than being at work right now, he was out on the car port doing all sorts of basic maintenance work on the car.

One of the items in the news for the day was the baseball All Star game to be played between the American and National Leagues that evening. Grant was not the least bit interested in the game itself, but as the sports announcers on the radio kept touting the event, he kept thinking to himself how his lady-love had the world's All Star pussy, and how much he was already missing having intercourse with her. They had agreed that he would return to University City again this coming Thursday, just two days hence, to stay with her for another long stretch, before returning home one more time before the beginning of the fall semester. But as Grant kept being distracted by thoughts of his woman's body and the pleasure that her beautiful sex always gave him, he desired her so desperately that he began to wonder why they should bother waiting two more days. Damn! He wanted her right now, and why should he just be sitting around the house here for two days doing little or nothing when he could just as easily be back in University City? Since the decision for him to return this Thursday had been quite arbitrary, he began to think how nice it would be to spring a surprise upon her by arriving two days early. Yeah! That really would be neat!

The more he thought about it, the better the idea seemed. He therefore stood up from the floor, where he had been arranging things on his book shelves, and walked into the kitchen. After calling Directory Assistance and obtaining the telephone number for the bus station in Peoria, he called to ask about possible buses going to University City later today, and was really pleased to learn that one would be departing at 4:00. Then after walking out of the kitchen, onto the back porch, and then around to the carport, he asked, "Hey, dad, would you mind taking me back to the bus station later this afternoon, so that I can return to University City?" "No," he replied, "I don't mind. What time does the bus leave?" "4:00." "Ok then, we can leave here about 3:15." "All right, thanks. I appreciate it."

Thus it was that Grant returned to University City and arrived around 6:30. Since he wanted this to be a total surprise, he decided to take a taxi from the bus station to Dorothy's house, so that he could arrive unexpectedly at her back door. By the time he succeeded in getting a cab and directing it to Dorothy's house, it was just a few minutes before 7:00. As the cab came down Boardman, Grant informed the driver, "It's the house that we first come to on the right as Boardman turns into Rachel Drive. There's a driveway that leads around to the back of the house. Go ahead and pull around onto the driveway and let me off there." "Ok," the driver agreed.

After coming home from the bank, Dorothy had gotten out of her good work clothes and had slipped into one of those lovely summer suits of a matching top and shorts with a tie belt around the waist that Grant adored so much. Then after she and Carol had had a simple supper of macaroni and cheese, Carol had gone off with her friends, thus leaving her alone in the house. As Dorothy sat at her desk in the dining room going through mail and writing out checks for bills, the air conditioning had made her bare arms and legs chilly. She had therefore gone back into the master bedroom to put on her pink quilted robe. While she was still working at her desk, she noticed through the picture window a Yellow Cab turning from Boardman onto Rachel Drive, and within seconds the dogs were running to the back door and barking. She therefore arose from the desk and walked through the kitchen to the back door in the family room to see if someone was coming up to the house. When she reached the door, she could hardly believe her eyes; and what she saw jolted her with such pleasure. Grant was standing beside the taxi cab and was paying the driver. He then grabbed his backpack and duffel bag and came up onto the porch.

"Hey there, stranger," Dorothy said so pleasantly, as she stepped out to greet him, "What a wonderful surprise!" "Yeah," Grant replied with a big smile, "I just couldn't stay away until Thursday, and I decided to surprise you." "Well, you certainly did, and how wonderful it is to have you back like this!" As soon as Grant stepped inside with her and dropped his things into the large chair next to the door, their arms went around each other, and they embraced fervently. "Oh my!" Dorothy exclaimed, nearly in tears, "It's so good to have you back!" "Ah! It's so good to feel you in your pink quilted robe again! Oh darling, I love you so!" "I love you too!" By now Grant's hands had gone inside her robe. "You're even wearing one of my favorite outfits. How very nice!"

As they finally broke their embrace, Dorothy simply said, "Come on," as she turned and took Grant by the arm to lead him. They walked through the kitchen and into the dining room, which Dorothy for some time now had arranged with the couch serving as a divider between the larger living room looking out toward the picture window and the slightly smaller dining room to the rear. As they stood at the back of the couch, Dorothy removed her robe and laid it across the back of the couch. She then knelt down on the dining room floor, so that the couch was now concealing her from the view of anyone who might look through the picture window. Grant caught on immediately to what she had in mind, and was now doing what she was: taking his shorts and undershorts down to his ankles. He then knelt behind her between her lower legs, caressed her offered bare beauty, and then carefully guided his ardent penis inside her vagina. After reaching a climax and ejaculating inside her, Grant withdrew himself, and they put their clothes back in order.

As they sat down on the couch and held hands and kissed, Grant explained, "I just had to come today, because all morning long as I was listening to the radio, the only sports event in the news was tonight's All Star game between the American and National Leagues; and the more I heard them talking about it, all that I could think of was your All Star pussy. Darling, you are my All Star woman, and I decided that we really had to enjoy your All Star Pussy today." Dorothy was extremely pleased by this lovely compliment and responded, "Well, I'm glad you think that way. It's a lovely thought, and I'm happy to give you my All Star Pussy. In fact, you didn't enjoy me nearly enough just now. So there's plenty more for you to have later."

July 27, 1974, Saturday

It was just 6:00 A.M., but they were already on the road, on their way to St. Louis to take Carol to the airport to spend two weeks with Sally in Houston. It was about a three-hour drive to St. Louis itself, but they figured on another hour to get them to the airport, to park the car, and then to go inside to find the right terminal. Carol's flight would be departing around

11:00. Besides Dorothy, Carol, and Grant, the little blue Falcon had a fourth passenger: Schatzi, the Miniature Dachshund that had been originally Sally's dog, but then had become Dorothy's fourth canine critter until now when Sally was reclaiming her and had asked that Carol bring her with her to Houston. About halfway along on their trip Carol fed Schatzi a tranquilizer that Dorothy had obtained from the vet, because they did not want Schatzi to be too upset and restless during the trip. Given her small size, she was going to ride under Carol's seat in a small cardboard box, but when they finally arrived at the airport and were ready to leave the car, Schatzi, although sluggish from the medicine, still put up quite a struggle when Dorothy and Carol started to put her in the box. They might want her to ride in that thing, but she sure had other ideas. Once they had her pushed down far enough, however, they were able to close the box and then proceeded to comfort and reassure her by talking sweetly and putting their fingers inside the container through the large air holes. Once secured inside the box and resigned to her fate, they locked the car and proceeded into the airport to get Carol checked through and to the right departure gate.

When Carol's plane finally took off, Dorothy and Grant made their way back out to the car. But rather than simply driving back to University City, the two lovers now began their own day of activities. One of the AIA lectures during the previous academic year at the university had concerned the large Indian settlement at Cahokia, a site on the Illinois side of the Mississippi River not far from St. Louis. Consequently, when Grant learned that Dorothy would be taking Carol to St. Louis to fly to Houston, he had suggested that they take advantage of the trip by stopping off to visit Cahokia before returning to University City. So, after leaving the airport, they made their way back across the river into Illinois and to the Cahokia site. When they happened to go past a Kentucky Fried Chicken, they stopped to buy a nice meal to serve as their lunch. Then before actually entering the Cahokia site itself, they sat down at a picnic table in a visitor's area to eat.

It was a typical hot July day, but Dorothy was able to spot a picnic table beneath the shade of several trees. As they sat across from each other and began eating, Dorothy remarked, "I really like Kentucky Fried Chicken's coleslaw. It's about the best." "Yeah, it really is, but I like about everything they make. You know," Grant said, changing the subject, "today is my parents' wedding anniversary, and in a few weeks they'll be finally divorced; and then a few days from now will be your birthday." "Yep, it sure will; and I'll be forty-six." "And you'll be the loveliest forty-six year old woman on the planet." "I will, huh?" "You sure will. If someone had told you four years ago just before we blind guys arrived on campus that in four years you'd be enjoying this new life with your young lover-boy, what would you have said?" "I would have thought the person was crazy; and although I might have wanted to believe them, it would have seemed too good ever to become true." "Gosh, Dorth, I love you so much, and I'm glad that we found one another." "Oh Grant, I am too. It still seems so unbelievable."

As they were finishing their meal, Grant asked, "Are there other people around?" After glancing about, Dorothy replied, "No, we're the only ones here." "Good!" Grant said emphatically as he arose from the picnic bench and came around to her side of the table. He now stood behind her, placed his arms around her, bent down, and began to kiss the left side of her neck. "Oh my golly! That always feels so good and even makes my toes curl up." "I'm going to give you a hickey. That way, when we are walking around the park today, everyone will know that you're mine and will leave you alone." "They will, huh?" "They sure as hell better!" Dorothy was wearing one of her summer suits that was both comfortable and looked so very nice on her. As Grant stood there behind her, his hands explored her body, and he breathed in the alluring fragrance of her White Shoulders perfume. "Well," Dorothy said, as she gathered up the debris on the table, "you'd better stop molesting me, and we'd better get going if we're going to look over this place."

Their first stop was the small museum, where Dorothy described all the items in the glass cabinets and read their descriptive labels to Grant. The place was nearly deserted, but before leaving the museum, they found an employee, and he gave them a brief oral history of the site and pointed out on their brochure map how they could tour the site and see the most important things. They then left the air conditioned comfort of the museum and went back out into the summer heat and humidity.

They soon came upon a group of college students engaged in excavating an area where they had found traces of post holes of dwellings. After chatting with them, they proceeded on to walk the site, which gave Grant a very nice feel for its size and contours. The area had once been a very large Indian community that had supported itself by agriculture; and over time the inhabitants had constructed several large earthen mounds on the site.

After they had been walking about for quite some time, Dorothy finally announced, "I need to make a pit stop." They then halted, so that she could consult her map and figure out where the facilities were located. When they found them, and as Dorothy was about to go through the door, Grant checked her by tugging gently on her arm and said, "I want to come inside with you." After looking about and seeing that no one was anywhere in sight, Dorothy said, "Ok," and the lovers stepped inside the ladies' room together. After Dorothy had urinated, she stood up and allowed him to caress and fondle her sex before pulling her shorts and panties back into place. Much later in the day, as they were walking on Monk's Mound, so called because there had once been a monastery on its summit, Grant said, "I need to take a leak. How about I just pull out my pecker and pee right here?" Once again, Dorothy looked around and reported that it would be ok, because there was no one else around. He therefore unzipped his pants, pulled out his penis, and proceeded to urinate on the world's largest man-made earthen structure. As he did, Dorothy kept glancing around, but she also happily watched Rufus Magnus do his business. Then when Grant zipped up again, he said, "Let me reach inside your shorts. I want to feel you again." "You've seen it before," Dorothy exclaimed in mock surprise and bewilderment. "Yeah, I know. I see it all the time, and I still can't get over how beautiful you are there." Then after looking around once again, she said "Ok, go ahead," and he certainly did.

As the sun was beginning its descent in the western sky, they completed their tour of this most interesting site. It had been very informative with Dorothy serving as Grant's eyes, but it had also simply been so very enjoyable for them to share this experience, which they had even succeeded in making so nicely erotic. But when they returned to the car, Dorothy discovered that she had locked her keys inside the vehicle. Luckily, they soon found a man who was able to use a wire to reach inside the car to release the lock on one of the doors. Then after stopping for a quick bite for supper, they were on their way back home on the interstate highway. Since the car was not equipped with air conditioning, they rolled down the two front windows and had to put up with the constant roaring of the air in order to stay comfortable. "Who says you can't combine business and pleasure," Grant remarked, "I think we did a pretty good job." "We sure did," Dorothy answered sweetly and with a knowing smile in her voice. "Thanks so very much for agreeing to go there with me. It was really interesting." "You're quite welcome, darling. I enjoyed it too."

As soon as it began to become dark outside, Grant began to fondle Dorothy's breasts. At first he simply inserted his fingers down inside the front of her top and caressed the tops of her breasts. After some time, during which both were warming up to this form of pleasure, Dorothy unzipped her top and thus gave Grant much fuller access to Kalliste and Pulcherrima. But even this was not enough. Grant eventually reached behind Dorothy as she obligingly leaned forward in her seat to have him unfasten her bra. He now lay across the front seat with his head and shoulders in her lap, so that he could lean up and take her lovely breasts into his mouth to kiss, suck, and lick in turn, as his hands continued to fondle and caress them. As they sped along the interstate with the cool nocturnal air rushing in through the windows, Grant gave them both wonderful pleasure, as Dorothy steered the car. It was so enjoyable that they did not stop a single time along their return journey, nor did Dorothy ever once ask Grant to stop. It simply felt too good. In the past Dorothy had often become drowsy while driving and had used singing to help keep her alert. No such stratagem was needed tonight. Instead of singing, Grant's titty play kept her so aroused that she had no difficulty at all in staying fully awake.

By the time they pulled into the driveway, they were both so sexually worked up that they dashed out of the car and into the house with one thing in mind, to engage in immediate and frantic intercourse. So, as soon as Dorothy had the door unlocked, they rushed past the three dogs who were eager to greet them, raced through the kitchen and into the living room, where the dogs were not allowed to go. As the dogs stood expectantly near the living room, Dorothy and Grant pulled down their shorts and undergarments, fell on the floor together, and began to enjoy very passionate intercourse. When their bodies had been sufficiently sated for the time being, they arose, put their clothes back into order, and then greeted the dogs and let them outside. The dogs had been in the house for nearly eighteen hours and needed to go outside quite badly. The lovers then settled down in bed for the night, fully naked and enjoying intercourse more leisurely. With Carol away in Houston, they would be sleeping all night together all night long for the next twelve days.

July 28, 1974, Sunday

After their long day of traveling and sightseeing at Cahokia, the two lovers were content to sleep late, after which they enjoyed intercourse and the rare pleasure of having spent the entire night in bed together. When they eventually did arise, Grant slipped on his t-shirt, undershorts, and shorts, while Dorothy stepped into her slippers and covered her nakedness with only her pink quilted robe.

Then after taking turns on the toilet and letting the dogs out and back in, Dorothy asked, "So my dear, what would you like to have for breakfast?" "How about a southern breakfast of sausage, biscuits, and gravy?" "Well, let's see," Dorothy replied, as she opened up the refrigerator to look inside, "We do have sausage and even a can of biscuits, but I've never made gravy from sausage. I've always just made it from pork chops or turkey to go on our smashed potatoes, but not to eat for breakfast. How do you make it? Do you know?" "Gee, I don't know. I've just eaten what my mother or grandmothers have made over the years. I guess you must make it like the other gravies but with drippings from the sausage. I know you add some milk and maybe a little flower along with salt and pepper." "All right," Dorothy concluded, after carefully listening to Grant, "I think that I probably know how to fix it from what you've just said. We'll give it a whirl and see how it turns out." As Dorothy put the sausage on to cook, they worked together in unloading the clean dishes from the dishwasher and putting them away. After turning on the oven to pre-heat, she showed Grant how to unwrap and open the biscuit canister. Grant then prepared a cookie sheet by smearing it with a bit of Crisco before placing the biscuits on it.

Now that they had things well underway, Grant finally asked, "So, what's going on at the bank these days?" "Oh, more or less the usual. I really enjoy working in new accounts and customer services." "And I'm sure that no one does a better job at those things than you." "You're always so prejudiced," Dorothy said with evident delight, and then she continued, "But besides doing my job every day, I have lunch with some of the other girls, either downstairs in the basement, where we have a lunch room, or we sometimes go out to one of the nearby restaurants like Top of the Town. There's also a nice South Korean restaurant that makes the most heavenly egg rolls! We'll have to go there some time." "So, who are some of the women there who lunch with you?" As Dorothy proceeded to tell Grant about three friends in particular, a much older woman named Sibyl and two others her own age named Judy and Shirley, she removed the sausage from the skillet and began preparing the gravy. It came as no surprise to Grant that his wonderful woman was fitting so well into her job at the bank and was already establishing nice friendships with some of the other women. It was simply the way that she was!

"Oh! You know, there was something really kind of funny that happened just this past week." "What's that?" "The black man who is the parking lot attendant asked me out on a date." "He did?" Grant exclaimed rather forcefully in surprise. "Yep, he sure did!" Dorothy replied with mischief. "And what did you tell the guy?" "I simply told him that I was already taken." "Good! I don't want anyone else ever sniffing around my Pussy Woman! I'll cut his pecker off!" "You will, huh?" Dorothy said with a chuckle in her voice. "I sure will!" Grant said in mock bravado, "It sounds like you might be making too good an impression with people at the bank if you've got guys chasing after you." "Oh don't worry, sweetheart. I am already taken, and I love it just the way it is." During this interchange Grant came over to Dorothy at the stove, gently turned her around, opened up her robe, and took her love-delta fully into his right hand. "You're all mine," he said as he caressed her lovely hair and skin." "I certainly am, and that's all yours and no one else's."

As Dorothy stood still, allowing them both to enjoy Grant's fondling of her love-front, she continued, "Did I ever tell you about the dentist who made advances to me?" Dorothy now asked. "No, I don't think so." "Yeah, it happened just as we were about to move from Great Falls. I had several cavities that needed to be filled and went to see our dentist several times over the course of a few weeks. He first commented on how nice my White Shoulders perfume smelled, and how he could always tell when I had arrived in the office because of its fragrance. Then another time when I was sitting in the chair and he was getting ready to drill my tooth or fill it or something, he said something like 'I could really go for you. How about we get something going'?" "What did you say?" "Oh something like 'sorry, but I'm not interested'." "I'm very interested in this," Grant said, as his fingers traced the lips of her vulva. "I can tell, and I'm glad you are." "But seriously," Grant said, "I'm not the least bit surprised about all that. You really are such a beautiful woman, but your physical beauty is so greatly enhanced by all your magnificent charms and virtues as a human being. I love you so very much, and it was so easy to fall in love with you. In fact, it would make better sense to ask how could I not fall in love with you?"

As they had been talking, Dorothy had one arm around Grant and was using her other hand to gently stir the gravy to keep it from becoming lumpy. Grant, for his part, continued to lovingly admire her beautiful womanhood. His gentle kneading of her delta and vulva were now accompanied by several tender kisses. Grant finally said, "You're my woman, and all this is mine, every single lovely hair. You're all mine!" "I am your woman and am all yours," she repeated solemnly in total agreement. "And I'm your man in the same way as you're my woman." "You certainly are," she said nearly in tears of joy as she hugged him fiercely.

When the gravy was done, they sat down to eat; and when Grant began to tear two biscuits into pieces and spread them out on his plate, Dorothy asked, "What are you doing?" "I'm getting ready to eat. What do you think I'm doing?" As he spoke, he lifted up his plate and held it toward her across the table, "Would you mind covering the biscuits with gravy?" he asked. "So that's how you eat them, huh?" "Yep, I guess you never ate a meal like this before?" After taking two bites, Grant pronounced judgment, "Well, you made the gravy just right." Dorothy beamed with satisfaction. "That's pretty damn good," he continued, "first time making it and you did it perfectly without even using a recipe. You really are remarkable." "Well, I had you to tell me how," she said in obvious pleasure, "We really do make a great team."

As they continued to eat, Grant asked, "So, do I get some dessert after this main meal?" "Oh I don't know," she replied coyly, "what did you have in mind exactly?" "How about some delicious pussy pie filled with love-honey?" "Well, my dear, you've filled me so full of your cream that I probably smell like a dead fish. So if you want that kind of dessert, maybe I should first take a bath." "That sounds like a great idea to me!" So, after they had cleared the table, they retired to the bathroom in the hall, where Grant assisted his darling in taking a bath in Avon Skin So Soft.

As he poured water over her recumbent body and caressed her nakedness, he said, "While I was in Austria, I learned some really neat vocabulary." "You did?" "I sure did. For example, I learned that the Austrian word for cunt is *fut*, spelled f-u-t, but pronounced as if it rhymes with flute. I suppose it must derive from the Latin word *futuo*, meaning 'I fuck'. Now in German there are two different verbs used for eating. *Essen* is used to refer to people eating, but *fressen* is used to describe the eating of animals. So I now regard myself as your *futfresser*, the one who eats your pussy; and when we get you out of the tub, I'll please us both by devouring your delicious pink cotton candy pussy."

They did not emerge from bed again until early afternoon, at which time Dorothy finally dressed herself for the first time, so that they could take the dogs for a nice long walk. They then spent the rest of the day quietly and lovingly in the house. While Dorothy sat at her desk writing a few letters and putting other things in order, Grant sat nearby at the dining table reading Latin and studying Greek. After having popcorn for their Sunday evening supper, they retired to bed early to enjoy sweet physical intimacy and serious talking, including more stories about Austria, before eventually falling asleep.

The next eleven days unfolded as if the two lovers were enjoying a blissful honeymoon, interrupted only by Dorothy's absence at the bank. Apart from running various errands and going grocery shopping, they were perfectly happy to be alone together in the house. As soon as Dorothy came home from work, she took off her clothes and went about the house clad in nothing except her bra, panties, slippers, and robe; and Grant, of course, was always eager to relieve her of the bra and panties. For the first time in the history of their relationship they were able to sleep all night in the same bed for twelve consecutive nights. One evening Dorothy attempted to make Wienerschnitzel by following Grant's description, and it actually turned out fairly well. Another evening Grant made a large pot of vegetable soup of the sort that he and Dennis had made several times in Austria; and all these experiments in the kitchen were accompanied by Grant telling her more about what he and Dennis had done together there.

The two lovers ventured from their domestic bliss out into public on two different occasions. One day when she returned home from the bank, Dorothy announced that she had tickets for them to attend an event at the University City County Fair. She refused to tell Grant exactly what it would be, because she wanted it to be a surprise. All that she would say was that it involved music and would probably be very much to his liking. They drove out to the fairgrounds; and as they sat in the outdoor stands in the evening coolness, Grant soon discovered that the star of the show was going to be none other than Jerry Reed, who apart from his funny songs, was about as great a virtuoso on the guitar as Chet Atkins himself. They both enjoyed their evening of music immensely.

Their other venture out into the public involved their good friend Lisa Harris treating them to a movie for Dorothy's birthday. It was not just any movie, but one which Lisa regarded as so perfectly appropriate for these two lovers and for Dorothy in particular. It was called *Alice Doesn't Live Here Anymore*. The story involved a young woman ending an unhappy marriage in divorce and then going off to try to begin a new life with her small son. While working in a restaurant, she meets a man who falls head over heels in love with her, and eventually the two become lovers and begin a new glorious life together. The story of unhappiness in love followed by struggle and redemption through new happiness in true love paralleled Dorothy's life so neatly and served to validate what she and Grant were planning to do with the rest of their lives.

As Dorothy celebrated her forty-sixth birthday, she was looking to the future with such joyful anticipation and back to the past recent years with real pride in herself. After years of unhappy marriage with George and a very busy and hectic life as mother of three problematic children, who so tried her patience and ingenuity that she had often had to take tranquilizers, she had begun to blaze her own path through that wilderness of constant toil and sadness by finding self-fulfillment and realizing her own considerable worth first through swimming and singing in Sweet Adelines, then even more so by involving herself in the lives of her university kids. The latter had then resulted in one of her blind students falling madly in love with her and she with him. Although at first their love seemed to be a colossal problem for them both, it had been so overpowering and had so dominated their lives that it had liberated her from her marriage and was now sweeping them along into a new and exciting life together. In addition, over the course of the past year, as word of Dorothy and George's separation and impending divorce had slowly spread among their neighborhood friends and church acquaintances, George had succeeded in eliciting much sympathy as the victimized husband, and Dorothy experienced having people turning their backs on her as the wrongful party. This hurt her very much and caused her to walk away from her church without ever once looking back, because she knew deep down inside herself that over the years she had done her best to be a good wife to George, and that her newfound love with Grant was so perfectly right; and how could anyone in their right mind possibly condemn that? In contrast, Dorothy had by now become fully integrated into a college environment, so totally different from her previous life, in which her young college friends admired all of her fine qualities and respected her new life with Grant. Moreover, although she had dreaded going back to work full time, that too was turning out to be an unexpected blessing, because she was finding new avenues in which to express and utilize her incomparable charm and grace in dealing with people, as well as her intelligence and ability to carry things out down to the minutest detail. Working at the bank was also bringing her into contact with other people who never once thought of her as George's wife, but simply appreciated and enjoyed her for who and what she was, a truly captivating woman, a single mom struggling to support herself and her youngest child, a middle-aged woman going through a divorce, but also one whose life was being totally transformed and revolutionized by the thrilling and passionate love that she shared with her blind Grant.

Epilogue

Love and Marriage

After leaving University City on Friday August 9, Grant returned again nine days later on Sunday August 18 as soon as the dorms were open for freshman orientation week, so that he could spend an entire week at the house with Dorothy before classes began on Monday August 26. Their life settled into the same lovely routine of him staying all weekend from Friday night when Dorothy picked him up at Watson to Monday morning when she dropped him off at his room on her way to work. In addition, he spent one night during the week at the house as well. As always, Dorothy assisted Grant substantially with his courses and especially with an advanced Latin course on the writings of Cicero and a history course on the Roman Republic. She read various important ancient texts in translation, including the first book of Polybius, Sallust's *Catilinarian conspiracy*, some of the writings of Cicero, and several of Plutarch's Roman Lives. Many of these reading sessions occurred on Sunday afternoons, as the two lovers sat side by side on the living room couch, and as Grant recorded Dorothy's lovely voice doing the reading, so that Grant would have a permanent record of the material to join his growing collection of important sources for his study of ancient Greek and Roman history.

To complement her domestic bliss and enjoyable work with Grant, Dorothy received another major promotion at the Lincoln Bank. She was chosen by John Dickson, who had originally interviewed her for her first position as teller, to become his personal secretary, as well as being in charge of the bank's safe deposit boxes. In the latter capacity she was responsible for renting out the boxes, making sure that their rental fees were kept current, signing people in and out to visit their boxes, and even supervising the occasional drilling open of a box. She really loved her new position. It involved an interesting variety of duties and responsibilities, and her supervision of the safe deposit boxes gave her the opportunity to meet interesting customers. She once met a man whose name on his safe deposit registration card was Stanley S. Stanley. When she asked him what his middle initial stood for, he said "Stanley." Thus, the man's full name was Stanley Stanley Stanley. Dorothy also made the acquaintance of an elderly and rather wealthy lady named Bernice. She came into the bank quite often to put things in or to take them out of her box. She and Dorothy became quite friendly; and eventually Bernice learned that Dorothy's lover-boy was blind. Her response to this was "he can't possibly know how beautiful you are!" Dorothy simply replied, "oh no, Bernice, believe me, he knows!" When Bernice persisted and said "he really can't know how beautiful you are," Dorothy ended the discussion by repeating firmly and emphatically, "Bernice, believe me, he knows!"

Dorothy's divorce from George became official as of Thursday September 19, exactly two years after what Grant called The Great Apocalypse. Even before the legal papers were finally registered, however, George had remarried. His new wife was a woman whom he had been seeing in Newton for quite some time. Although Dorothy was now single, she and Grant decided not to rush into marriage. They were both firmly convinced that their love for one another was the real thing and would stand the test of time, but they saw no reason why they should not err on the side of extreme caution by giving their relationship more time just in case there might arise unforeseen problems resulting from their difference in age. But there were other, much more important reasons as well. To Grant, in particular, marriage was still too strongly associated with George and what Grant considered the oppression of his darling. Moreover, since he regarded their perfect love as vastly superior to the mere legal convention of marriage, the latter was to him totally unnecessary. Besides, they were living in a rather libertine and libertarian college environment in which fully committed relationships without the legal sanction of marriage had become increasingly common in recent years.

It was also at about this time that Dorothy introduced an important innovation into their vocabulary of love by calling Grant by the endearment of Babe. This name, of course, had been her father's nickname; and her application of her beloved father's nickname to Grant was a lovely expression of how Grant had come to totally dominate her life in the most wonderful way. Grant returned the lovely compliment of this appellation by calling her Babes. As he was growing up, Grant's parents had often called one another honey, which always struck him as a particularly silly form of endearment, but he greatly enjoyed having Dorothy call him Babe.

The two lovers spent their first Thanksgiving together. They enjoyed a lovely meal at the dining table along with Carol and a friend named Sam. Then when the fall semester ended, Grant went back to Fairmont for just a few days and for the last time as a single, college student in order to spend Christmas with his parents and sister, after which his father brought him back to Dorothy's house (not to one of the dorms), where he stayed for the next three weeks until the spring semester began. What a glorious time that was! He and Dorothy spent midnight of New Year's Eve in bed, having magnificent intercourse, as they welcomed the arrival of the new year.

As Dorothy continued to work happily at the bank while assisting Grant with his studies for the spring semester of 1975, the two lovers faced a major dilemma. George's financial assistance in making house payments would be ending that spring when Carol was scheduled to graduate from high school; and since Dorothy's salary was insufficient to cover the house payment and all other necessary expenses, they had to sell the house and move into a two-bedroom apartment on the eastern side of town, which they did on June 1 of 1975. Although they had much less space than they had had in the house, the apartment was located in a very scenic area; and Dorothy served as Grant's mobility instructor in teaching him how to walk from their apartment to the university's campus. Within a few days of moving into their new place Dorothy traded in the little blue Falcon and used the profits from the sale of the house to buy a brand new copper-colored Ford Granada. The two also began to visit the new Physical Education Building on campus, where they swam in the outdoor pool two or three times a week. Dorothy was so very pleased to return to swimming and to now share it with Grant.

In late July and early August Dorothy flew out to California to spend a week with Sally and Wesley. In March of the previous year, while still living in Houston, Sally had married Edward Lowenstein, but they were now living in California near Los Angeles and not far from Wesley, who was now out of the navy. Shortly after returning and enjoying a very passionate reunion with Grant, the two lovers drove up to Chicago one weekend to tour the Museum of Science and Industry, to see Dennis and Renny, and to spend an afternoon with Dorothy's beloved Uncle Les. The two lovers never once considered including visits to Dorothy's mother or two sisters in their weekend trip, because they assumed that as an unmarried couple, they would not be well received. On the other hand, when they visited Uncle Les, he never once asked who this young blind guy was who was accompanying his niece. The three of them simply had a very nice visit that lasted most of the afternoon; and Grant came away with a deep respect and affection for Uncle Les. When they were ready to depart, Uncle Les insisted that they take with them the only heirloom-like object of sentimental value that he owned: a secretary, a lovely piece of wooden furniture, measuring about six feet tall and no wider than about fifteen inches. It stood on four shapely legs; and about three feet up there was a small chest that could be locked with a key, hence the furniture's name, secretary for secreting valuable objects or papers; and above the chest were smaller open bins for holding things. When the secretary proved to be too long to lay across the backseat of the car, Grant used a screwdriver to take it apart into two pieces. Henceforth this lovely old object became a valued piece of furniture for Dorothy and Grant and always made them think lovingly of Uncle Les.

When the latter died about one month after their visit, Dorothy took two days off from her job at the bank, drove up to Chicago, and settled all of Uncle Les' affairs; and she returned to University City with only a few of his effects worth keeping, one of them being a suitcase full of tools, of which Grant took possession. They included a hammer, screwdrivers, a wood plane, a whetstone, a set of Allen wrenches, an iron file, and other things, all of which Grant henceforth used, valued, and cherished as mementos of the dear old man. Dorothy divided the small amount of money in Uncle Les' bank account equally among herself and her three children and did not share any of it with her sisters or their families, because no one but she had had any kind of contact or relationship with Uncle Les during his later years, and the families of her sisters at the time were much better off financially than herself and her children.

Grant began his first year of graduate school that fall semester, and his studies included his third semester of ancient Greek. During the previous academic year he had used a braille textbook to learn ancient Greek grammar and to begin reading a selection of texts. But his Greek class in the fall of 1975 required him to read two major ancient texts, one of Plato and another of the Greek historian Xenophon. Since he did not have a Greek dictionary in braille, Dorothy now became his Greek dictionary by looking up the words that he needed to find. After mastering the Greek alphabet and learning how the letters were pronounced, Dorothy was soon able to understand Grant's pronunciation of a Greek word in order to locate it in the print dictionary, and then she in turn read the English meanings along with the various Greek forms. Not only did this demonstrate Dorothy's great intelligence, it also marked a very important step in Grant's ability to become proficient in ancient Greek and in their collaboration in his goal to become a college professor of ancient Greek and Roman history.

Since the lovers were now fully living together, Grant did not bother at all to go back to Fairmont for Christmas when the fall semester ended, but he and Dorothy spent their first Christmas together, and like the year before, they welcomed the new year by enjoying wonderful intercourse as the waning minutes of 1975 became the first moments of 1976. When the spring semester began, Grant continued his graduate work, but Dennis and Renny were no longer on campus but had moved back to Chicago.

June 8, 1976, Tuesday

The spring semester had ended about three weeks ago, and once again Dorothy had been invaluable to Grant with his studies, especially with his Greek course in reading large portions of Homer's *Odyssey*. As always, over the course of the entire semester she had served as his Greek dictionary in looking up words and had also read all the editor's explanatory notes accompanying the Greek text, so that by now Grant had acquired a very good mastery of ancient Greek. Then just a week ago they had driven up to Chicago to spend a very enjoyable Memorial Day weekend at Renny's apartment on the north side not far from Lake Shore Drive.

It was now just a few minutes after 4:00 in the afternoon, and Grant was stretched out on their king size bed in their bedroom. The bed was actually the two twin beds from the front bedroom of the house on Rachel Drive simply pushed together to form a single bed. One of them, of course, had been the scene of The Great Apocalypse, that truly momentous event in their love-life. As Grant lay there enjoying a cool breeze coming in through the window, he was again thinking over an important topic that he had been wanting to bring up with Dorothy; and as soon as she came home from the bank, he hoped to have them talk about it.

When Dorothy parked the Granada in the apartment's parking area at the back of the building, she entered through the rear door, climbed up the two flights of stairs to the building's second and top floor, and walked to their apartment door. After using her key, she stepped inside the apartment, walked straight ahead between the living room and kitchen to her right and left respectively, came down the short hallway, and continued straight ahead into their bedroom. When she saw Grant on the bed, she asked, "So, Babe, what have you been doing today?" "Oh just lots of reading and putting things away that I didn't have the time for during the spring semester. And how did your day go?" "Oh just the usual." While they were talking, Dorothy was standing at the closet and was pulling off her good work clothes to hang them up. Following a slight pause, Grant resumed, "I've been thinking about something and want to talk with you about it." "Uh-oh!" Dorothy responded in a mockingly ominous tone. "Yeah, well, I've been thinking that we should get married." "What! Get married? After we've been living in sin for two years or more, you finally want to make a decent woman of me?" she asked in pretended outrage. "Yeah," Grant answered, now smiling, "Let's get married!" "So, you really do want to make me a decent woman?" Dorothy said with a laugh. "Yep, I guess so." "So why all of a sudden do you want us to get married?" "It just seems like the right thing to do. I know we decided not to rush things and to give our relationship some time, and we also didn't think that marriage was really all that important, and that it could add anything to our perfect bliss; but since our love is as strong as it has ever been, and I don't see that ever changing, it seems so natural now that we should go ahead and get married. So, what do you think?" "I guess I feel the same way and fully agree with you."

By now Dorothy had removed everything except her panties and bra and was busy hanging up her clothes. Grant now arose from the bed and came to her, as she stood in front of the closet. They embraced each other. Grant could smell her lovely White Shoulders perfume that was so alluring and always aroused him; and her skin was so soft, smooth, and perfect to his touch. Dorothy could feel his erection pressing into her. "Gosh, Babes," Grant said in a low serious voice, "I love you so very much, and I always will. Maybe I've matured or something, but I really want us to be husband and wife." "I love you too, and I think you're right. The time has come for us to get married."

Grant had now drawn back slightly from their embrace, so that he could reach his right hand down inside her panties and hold and fondle her sex. "As far as I am concerned," he continued, "We were married more than three years ago on March 1, 1973, when you guided my dick inside your pussy, and we fucked for the first time. We were then married in love and have been ever since; and that to me has always been much more important and all-encompassing than having us stand before some judge to become legally married. But it just seems so right that we do that now too." "I agree," Dorothy replied simply.

She made no objection when Grant unfastened her bra and began to pull her panties down. After she stepped out of them, Grant knelt before her, filled his two hands with her lovely ass, and took her vulva into his mouth. When he finally released her, she stepped around to the side of the bed, lay down on her back, and fully opened her thighs to her love-mate. the two lovers then sealed their agreement most appropriately by giving and receiving the physical pleasure of their perfect love.

July 6, 1976, Tuesday

Today would be the day on which they would legally become husband and wife. Neither of them wanted any kind of big ceremony. They both knew and understood that what really mattered was that they love one another completely and totally; and since they did, just standing before a civil judge to be married was all that they needed. When Grant suggested that they get married on July 10, the fourth anniversary of their first kissing marathon following his confession of being strongly attracted to her, Dorothy observed that the day would be a Saturday, and the courthouse was likely to be closed. They then settled upon July 6, in part because Dorothy said that their wedding day would then be in numerical terms 7, 6, 76. Afterwards, Grant realized that this day too was perfectly appropriate, because four years earlier, that day had been the first of the days when Dorothy had come to read to him in his dorm room, where they had sat together so intimately for the first time.

Two days earlier Dorothy and Grant had joined their fellow citizens in celebrating the nation's bicentennial. Early in the morning they had watched the parade line up near their apartment on the eastern side of town. Then later in the day they had gone over to the western side of University City and had stood on Foxwell Street to watch the parade pass by. They would therefore always think of this special national celebration in connection with their wedding anniversary.

Dorothy had gone into work today at 8:00 as usual, but when her lunch hour arrived, she left the bank and drove back to the apartment. Her boss,

John Dickson, who was always so obliging, had agreed to let her have an extended lunchtime today, so that she and Grant could appear before a judge at the Courthouse at 1:00.

After coming into the apartment, she and Grant first had a quick and easy lunch in their small kitchen. Then they retired to their bedroom, where they put on nice clothes for the event. Dorothy slipped out of her top and slacks and put on the lovely golden dress that she had made for herself for Sally's big fancy wedding seven years before. Grant wore a nice shirt to go with a new pair of pants that they had bought for the occasion. They were green with a pattern of other colors running through the material. They then walked from their apartment over to the courthouse, where they met Carol, their only witness to the ceremony. Although the other bedroom in the apartment was hers, she was often not there, but frequently stayed with a friend named Paula. The ceremony before the judge lasted only a few minutes, and the two lovers were then legally married. Carol left to return to Paula's, and Dorothy and Grant walked back to their apartment.

As soon as they came inside, Dorothy announced in her little girl voice, "I've gotta go potty," and Grant added, "Don't flush. I've got to go too." They both entered the bathroom; and as Grant stood at the sink, Dorothy took down her panties and pantyhose and sat down on the toilet. As always, Grant loved to hear the sound of his beloved darling as she urinated. In fact, they both always enjoyed sharing the sweet intimacy of this simple act; and to Grant, the sound she made was so sweet and gentle, a perfect encapsulation of her entire being. Then after parting her thighs and carefully wiping her vulva, she said, as she stood up, "Ok, it's all yours." As Grant took down his pants and undershorts and sat down on the toilet, Dorothy walked out of the bathroom and into their bedroom. While Grant was still sitting, Dorothy called out from the bedroom, "When you're done there, come on into the bedroom. I've got something to show you." "Ok, I'll be right there," he replied, as he stood up, flushed the toilet, and pulled his clothes back into place.

When he stepped into the bedroom, he innocently asked, "Ok, what's up?" "Look here on the bed," said Dorothy. When Grant stood beside the bed and reached out his hands, he encountered his darling kneeling on her knees and elbows. Her body was positioned diagonally with her feet near the bottom of the bed closest to him. As soon as he felt her feet with her panties and hose gathered around her ankles, he knew instantly what it was that she wanted to show and give him and in turn to receive from him. His right hand moved quickly up along her lower legs and under her lovely golden dress to find her bottom and sex, all beautifully unclothed just for him. There she was, his golden Aphrodite.

"Oh my golly!" Grant exclaimed, "You're so damn beautiful!" "I thought you could have your first legal pussy before I went back to work," Dorothy said sweetly. "We won't be living and fucking in sin anymore," she added in such a coy and sexy way. "That's right!" Grant confirmed emphatically, "But I'm sure that your legal pussy will be just as fantastic as the sinful sort." "You think so, huh?" Dorothy asked mischievously. "I'm sure of it. She sure does look as perfect as she always does." "That's good. I'm glad to hear it, darling. At least I know that standing before the judge for those few minutes has not dampened her appetite for Rufus Magnus." "That's quite obvious. Even a blind man can see that." As he lovingly fondled her, he continued, "My oh my, Dorth, what a beautiful honey pie! I'm sure she's as sweet and delicious as she looks!"

Grant took down his pants and undershorts again, knelt on the bed between her lower legs, and threw the golden dress up over her back to expose her female beauty. They had both been tremendously thrilled and excited by the way in which Dorothy had concealed her womanhood beneath the sexy gold dress and by Grant's discovery of her perfect feminine treasure under it, but equally or even more thrilling and exciting was Grant's dramatic tossing of her dress onto her back. Dorothy reveled in her lover-boy, now her lawful husband, ardently exposing her naked beauty. She well knew from more than three years of experience of their magnificent love-making that this pose could not be more captivating. She gloried in placing her womanhood on such stunning display for them both, for them alone, here on their bed in their bedroom on this special day. She would soon be 48 years old, but she neither looked nor felt her age. She was quite beautiful and sexy; and the way in which Grant totally loved and made love to her made her feel so young and beautiful. Although he constantly raved about how much pleasure her female beauty gave him, his love and loving had always given her the same amount of extraordinary pleasure and euphoria. She was thrilled and excited once again to have her bare bottom and sex be the central focus of the perfect physical pleasure of their true love. They were about to consummate their marriage, but the truly remarkable thing was that this magnificence was typical of their love-making.

As he caressed and admired her bottom, hips, and sex, whose beauty always utterly enraptured him, he exclaimed in a hushed but vehement awe-struck tone, "My oh my, you really are so damn beautiful, and I can never get enough of you, Dorothy Alice Duncan, but boy! It sure is fun trying!" "It sure is," she agreed with obvious pleasure and desire in her voice. He then lowered his body to her feet and lower legs, placed his head upturned between her thighs, and took her sex into his mouth. As he kissed and licked her inside her vulva and even thrust his tongue inside her vagina to begin their intercourse, Dorothy began to experience the most exquisite pleasure. "Oh my," she said in a passionate whisper, "it feels so wonderful to have your tongue inside me! It's heavenly!" "Oh darling, believe me, I love it as much as you do!" While he worshipped and adored her womanhood with his mouth, his hands continued to caress and admire her perfectly shaped bottom and hips, and his exclamations of wonder also continued: "You are my Dorothy Alice, my Dorothy All-Ass woman, my Regina Vagina, my Princess Pussy, my Queen Cunt, and now you are my most beautiful and beloved wife, and I am your most monogamous man! Oh Babes, you look like Pussy Personified in this lovely golden dress! You are my Golden Aphrodite! And as always, your cunt smell sand tastes so wonderful! I could lick and kiss you all day long, but Rufus Magnus is demanding to have his turn." "That's good," Dorothy replied, obviously greatly pleased herself, "I'm glad you like and love my pussy so much, and I really like all the love-names you give me, but I especially like the sound of that new one, Dorothy Alice Duncan; but getting back to business, or should I say pleasure, I do need to be going back to the bank soon. Let Rufus Magnus have his turn, and there'll be plenty more for you when I come home from work."

Following their interchange of words, Grant withdrew his face from her sex, knelt behind his adorable woman, and carefully guided his penis into her vagina, after which he grasped her hips and began plunging his manhood rhythmically inside her, but they still took their time in enjoying their first intercourse in marriage. Grant stopped his thrusts several times, so that his hands could fondle her nakedness, especially the flawless skin and beautiful hair and cleft of her love-delta. Also, while he held her bottom firmly up against himself, so that his penis was thrust fully and tightly inside her, she wriggled magnificently from side to side. Thus, after they had been enjoying their equestrian manner of intercourse in all the ways in which it gave them pleasure, Dorothy felt him become even larger, and then his penis quivered and shuddered as his man cream joined and mingled with her love-honey. She felt the sperm shoot into her and then to spread inside her. Rather than returning to the bathroom to have his sperm drip out of her vagina, she intended to hold this wonderful love potion inside her all afternoon at work to serve as the perfect token of their two lives harmoniously blended into one. "Thank you so much, my loving husband!" "You're quite welcome, my dearest wife, and I thank you too! You really are my Dorothea, the divine gift to my life!"

Semper Dulcis

When time has come so swiftly on
that thine own hair shall silver be,
then thou shalt think of old days gone,
yearning once more to catch the eyes
of them who once admired thee.
But nay, my love, they shall not glance
upon thine aged face, but me
alone shalt thou behold enhanced
by thy benign aspect, thy tones
of youth, thy beauty, pure and free,
inscribed with life's travail. Perchance
thou then in joyous wise shalt see
my fettered heart by thee entranced
and patient love for my dear one.